Families in Context

An Introduction

Marilyn Ihinger-Tallman
Washington State University

Teresa M. Cooney
University of Missouri–Columbia

An Instructor's Manual/Testing Program and
interactive Student Study Guide are available.

Roxbury Publishing Company
Los Angeles, California

A comprehensive **Instructor's Manual/Testing Program**, a dedicated **Website**, and an **Interactive Student Study Guide** are available.

Library of Congress Cataloging-in-Publication Data

Ihinger-Tallman, Marilyn.
Families in context: An introduction / Marilyn Ihinger-Tallman, Teresa M. Cooney.
   p. cm.
Includes bibliographical references and index.
ISBN 1-931719-07-1
   1. Family. I. Cooney, Teresa M., 1959– II. Title.

HQ503.I355 2005
306.85—dc21

2004014062
CIP

FAMILIES IN CONTEXT: AN INTRODUCTION

Publisher: Claude Teweles
Managing Editor: Dawn VanDercreek
Production Editor: Jim Ballinger
Copy Editor: Jackie Estrada
Proofreaders: Eileen Delaney and Renee Ergazos
Cover Design: Marnie Kenney
Typography: Pegasus Type, Inc.

Printed on acid-free paper in the United States of America. This book meets the standards of recycling of the Environmental Protection Agency.

ISBN 1-931719-07-1

ROXBURY PUBLISHING COMPANY
P.O. Box 491044
Los Angeles, California 90049-9044
Voice: (310) 473-3312 • Fax: (310) 473-4490
Email: roxbury@roxbury.net
Website: www.roxbury.net

Dedication

To the children who joined the family during the past eight years:
Patrick and Liam, Michael and Will, Delia, Charlotte,
Gheslaine, and Marilyn Alexandra.
Oh, and the one on the way!

To Adam, Eddy, and Jacob—for their love and support.

Contents

About the Authors . . . . **xii**

Preface . . . . **xiii**

Acknowledgments . . . . **xvii**

Chapter 1: Studying Families: Micro and Macro Perspectives **1**

   Families, Communities, Society: Interconnections 2
      Guiding Frameworks. 4
   What Is a System?. 4
      Interrelatedness and Interdependence 5
      Wholeness 6
      Organization. 7
      Structure 9
      Boundaries 9
      Stability 11
      Equilibrium 11
      Adaptability 12
      Open Versus Closed 12
      Feedback 13
   Families as Small Groups 13
      Commitment. 14
      Consensus and Conflict 14
      Communication 15
   The Family as an Institution. 15
      Societal Differences 16
      Changes in the Family Institution 16
      The Interrelatedness of Institutions. 17
   Ecological Systems Perspective 17
      Ecological Systems Concepts. 18
      Integrating Family and Ecological Systems 20
   Diversity Among Families 20
      Race and Ethnicity. 21

       Social Class 21
       Family Structure. 30
       Sex and Gender Differences 31
    Methods for Studying Families 32
       Research and the Scientific Method 32
       A Sampling of Research Methods 34
    Summary 39
    Endnote. 40
    Chapter Concepts 40
    Suggested Activities 43
    Suggested Readings 43

Chapter 2: Commitment: To Self, Family, Community **45**
    The Importance of Commitment. 46
    Commitment to Self. 47
       Identities 49
       The Development of Identities, the Self, and Self-Meanings . . . 50
    Socialization: The Creation of Identities and the Self. 54
       Gender Socialization 55
    Commitment to Family 57
       The Commitment of Children 58
       Family Behaviors That Forge Commitment 59
       Types of Commitment 61
    The Big Picture: Commitment to Community 62
       Community 62
       Neighborhood 63
       Why Are Neighborhood and Community Important? 64
       How Do Neighborhoods Benefit?. 66
    Summary 68
    Endnotes 68
    Chapter Concepts 69
    Suggested Activities 71
    Suggested Readings 72

Chapter 3: Developing Close Relationships: Making Lifestyle Choices **73**
    Building Intimate Relationships 74
       Experiences and Emotions That Promote Intimacy 74
       What Is This Thing Called 'Love'? 76
       The Romantic Ideal 79
    Social and Behavioral Processes That Bring Couples Together 80
       The Wheel Theory of Love 80
       The Filter Theory of Mate Selection 81
       Dating. 84
       Breaking Up Is Hard to Do (For Some). 85
       Network Influences on Relationship Formation. 85

Lifestyle Choices 88
    Sexual Orientation 88
    Nonmarital Cohabitation 90
The Big Picture: The Influence of Macrolevel Forces on the Formation of
    Intimate Relationships 92
    Social Change in Views and Behaviors Regarding Sex, Sexuality, and
        Gender Roles 92
Summary 96
Endnote 97
Chapter Concepts 97
Suggested Activities 98
Suggested Readings 98

Chapter 4: Maintaining Intimacy: Marriage and Enduring Unions 99
Marriage Patterns: Historical Trends and Racial and Social Class Differences . . . 101
    How Economic Factors Contribute to Marriage Behavior 101
    Social Class and Marriage Patterns 103
Transition to Marriage 103
    Levels of Commitment Symbolized by Marriage 103
    Psychological and Relational Changes Accompanying Marriage 104
    His and Hers: Are the Costs and Benefits of Marriage Different for
        Men and Women? 106
The Internal Dynamics of Marriage 108
    Marital Satisfaction and Marital Stability 109
    Power in Interpersonal Relationships 111
    Sexual Relations 114
    Communication 117
    Conflict Resolution 118
    Maintaining Relationships Over Time 121
The Big Picture 124
    Women's Employment and Marriage 124
    Changes in Views of Marriage: The Rise of Individualism and the
        Culture of Divorce 125
Summary 126
Chapter Concepts 126
Suggested Activities 127
Suggested Readings 128

**Chapter 5: Moving Through the Life Cycle: Family Experiences in Early to
Middle Adulthood 129**
The Transition to Parenthood 130
    Contemplating Parenthood 131
    Changes in Self With Entry to Parenthood 134
    Changes in Couple Roles and Relations With Entry to Parenthood 136
    Pressure on the Father to Be the 'Good Provider' 137

Changes in Couple Relations 139
Factors Influencing Positive Adjustment to Parenthood 140
Parenting 146
Parenting Stages 147
Parenting Functions and Styles. 148
Predictors of Parenting Behavior 149
Parenting Changes From Childhood Through Adolescence 156
Infancy 156
The Toddler Years 157
Early Childhood 157
Middle Childhood 159
Adolescence 160
Sibling Relationships in Childhood 161
The Firstborn's Adjustment to a New Sibling 162
Sibling Influences and Relationships 162
Interactions Among Sibling, Parent-Child, and Couple Subsystems 164
The Big Picture: Historical Change Affecting Young Families 165
Shifts in Parenting Values 166
Media Influences on Family Life 167
Summary 170
Chapter Concepts 171
Suggested Activities 173
Suggested Readings 173

Chapter 6: Moving Through the Life Cycle: Family Experiences in Middle to Late Adulthood. **175**
Renegotiating Parent-Child Relationships in Late Adolescence and
Early Adulthood 176
Acting on One's Own 177
Adjusting Family Boundaries. 178
Adjusting to the Empty Nest Period 179
Parents and Children in Middle to Late Adulthood 181
Types of Parent-Adult Child Relationships 181
Conflicting Needs and Views of Parents and Adult Children. 184
Aged Parents and Adult Children 185
Caregiving for Older Adult Family Members 186
The 'Uplifts' of Caregiving 190
Marital Relations in Middle to Late Adulthood. 191
Marital Satisfaction 192
Marital Roles and Issues 193
Adult Sibling Relations 194
Variations in Sibling Ties in Adulthood 194
Adult Sibling Types 195
Race Differences in Sibling Relationships. 195
Family Structure Influences on Sibling Relationships 195

Grandparenting 196
    Styles of Grandparenting. 196
    Grandparents as Surrogate Parents 197
Experiencing the Death of Family Members 198
    Parental Death 198
    Widowhood 199
    Death of an Adult Child 200
    Death of a Sibling 201
The Big Picture: Societal Influences on Family Relationships
   Across Adulthood 201
    Societal Context and Parent-Child Relationships in Adulthood 201
    Societal Context and Aging Families 202
Summary 203
Chapter Concepts 204
Suggested Activities 205
Suggested Readings 205

Chapter 7: Balancing Work and Family **207**
Labor Force Participation 208
    How Employment Affects Adults' Lives 208
    Workplace Versus Home-Work 210
    Part-Time Workers 211
    Childcare Arrangements 211
    Work Schedules: How Shift Work Affects the Family 214
    Commuter Marriages 216
Work-Family Spillover 216
    The Interdependence of Work and Family 217
    The Effects of Stress 218
    Telecommuting and Work-Family Balance 219
    Workplace Appeal for Women 221
Household Division of Labor 222
    Housework in Different Types of Families 224
    Cohabitation, Marriage, Remarriage, and Housework Contributions . . . 225
    The Fairness Issue 226
    Changing Norms: What Has Changed? 229
Children's Work 230
    Children's Contributions to Housework 230
    Adolescent Employment 232
Effects of Unemployment on the Family 233
    Work as a Source of Status and Self-Esteem 233
    Coping With Unemployment 234
    Behavioral Reactions to Unemployment 235
Retirement 237
    Patterns of Retirement 237
    Reasons for Retiring 238

Retirement and the Quality of Marriage 238
Retired but Still Working. 239
The Big Picture: Family and Work in the Larger Society 240
Exosystem Factors 240
Social Class Differences 243
Poverty as a Result of Structural Factors in the Macrosystem 245
Summary 247
Endnotes 248
Chapter Concepts 248
Suggested Activities 249
Suggested Readings 250

Chapter 8: Family Transitions: Divorce, Single Parenting, Remarriage **251**
Divorce 253
Who Ends the Marriage? 253
Separation and Reconciliation 254
Sociodemographic and Psychological Characteristics Associated
With the Probability of Divorce 255
Perceived Reasons for Divorce 257
Postdivorce Adjustment 260
Parenting After Divorce 262
Does It Matter Which Parent Has Residential Custody? 263
Children in Single-Parent Households 271
Negative Impacts of Divorce on Children 272
Parental Socialization Practices 273
The Effects of Stress 274
Remarriage and Stepparenting. 275
Types of Remarriages 277
Effects of Remarriage on Children 281
Kin and Extended Family 283
Death as the Cause of Marital Dissolution 284
Why Do the Widowed Remarry? 285
Labor Force Participation 285
Kin Support 286
Children Living in Widowed Single-Parent Households 286
The Big Picture: Family Transitions in a Social Context 287
Exosystem Effects: Does Neighborhood Matter? 288
Effects of the Exosystem on Family Behavior. 288
Macrosystem Effects on Family Behavior. 292
Summary 293
Endnotes 294
Chapter Concepts 295
Suggested Activities 295
Suggested Readings 296

Chapter 9: Distressed Families: The Darker Side of Family Life 297

Partner Violence. 300
    Prevalence of Partner Abuse 300

The Demographics of Partner Violence. 305
    Race and Ethnicity. 305
    Social Class 306
    Couple Status Incongruence 307
    Age 307
    Marital Status 308
    Sex 308

Marital Rape 309

Violence Among Same-Sex Couples 310
    Bridging a Micro and Macro Explanation 311

Child Maltreatment 312
    Child Neglect 313
    Physical Abuse. 313
    Sexual Abuse 314
    Causes of Child Maltreatment 316

Abuse of Siblings and Parents 316

Elder Abuse and Neglect. 317

Alcoholism and Substance Addiction. 320

Children Who Run Away 322

If They Are Family, Why Are They Mistreated? 325
    Psychiatric Approach to the Study of Family Violence 326
    Social-Psychological Approach to the Study of Violence. 326
    Sociocultural Approach to the Study of Violence 327

The Big Picture: The Social and Cultural Context of Violence. 327

Summary 330

Endnote. 331

Chapter Concepts 331

Suggested Activities 332

Suggested Readings 333

Chapter 10: Families in a Social Context: The Big Picture 335

Beyond the Family Microsystem. 337
    Community Businesses and Workplaces 337
    Childcare in the Community 338
    Schools in the Community 340
    Community-Based Services. 343

Governmental Exosystem and Macro-Level Influences 346
    Family Policy 347
    Family Policy Examples 350

Summary 358

Chapter Concepts 358

Suggested Activities 359
Suggested Readings 360

Photo Credits **361**

References **363**

Author Index **401**

Subject Index **409**

About the Authors

Marilyn Ihinger-Tallman received her Ph.D. in Sociology from the University of Minnesota in 1977. She is Professor Emeritus in Sociology at Washington State University where she also served as Departmental Chair. Ihinger-Tallman received the Faculty of the Year Award for excellence in teaching. Her research and writing have centered on remarriage, stepparenting, and sibling socialization. In collaboration with Kay Pasley, she co-authored numerous research articles, a textbook, *Remarriage,* and two edited volumes, *Remarriage and Stepparenting: Current Research and Theory* and *Stepparenting: Issues in Theory, Research, and Practice.* Dr. Ihinger-Tallman and her husband are remarried partners and have a total of seven children and 14 grandchildren.

Teresa M. Cooney received her doctorate in Human Development and Family Studies from The Pennsylvania State University where she was a pre-doctoral fellow funded by the National Institute on Aging. Upon graduation she was awarded a post-doctoral fellowship at the Carolina Population Center, University of North Carolina–Chapel Hill. After eight years on the faculty at the University of Delaware she assumed a faculty position in Human Development and Family Studies at the University of Missouri–Columbia. For the past three years she has served as Department Chair. Dr. Cooney focuses her research on adult child-parent relationships and has studied such issues as the impact of later life parental divorce on adult offspring, the adjustment of adults to divorce after long-term marriages, the effects of reduced family size on relationships between aging parents and their offspring, and the adjustment of grandmothers to providing custodial care for grandchildren. She has taught introductory family studies courses for over 20 years and has received faculty teaching awards at both the University of Delaware and the University of Missouri. Dr. Cooney and her husband have two sons. ✦

Preface

You bring to your reading of this text a lifetime of knowledge about family life (your own, those of friends and relatives) as well as years of exposure to family life in books, motion pictures, television, and many other media sources. Information about the family is ubiquitous in the American culture. Marriage and family are two of our most revered and protected institutions. So, you can consider yourself an expert of sorts.

However, what you probably don't have is an understanding of family life that falls outside your circle of exposure. Few of us can comprehend the family dynamics of that small child who lived in a crack house, found a loaded gun under the bed blankets, brought it to his first-grade class, and shot and killed a 6-year-old classmate (*San Francisco Chronicle*, 2000). Few of us have insights into how the very rich raise their children (is it different from the middle class?), or the family experiences of the young women who are hired as nannies to raise them. More than a few children have had the experience of sitting down with their siblings to hear a parent announce a pending divorce. What factors contribute to child neglect? Why does a couple divorce? Why would a divorce affect children in the same family differently? This text will provide you with information and insights into situations such as these as well as a diverse array of other family behaviors.

We felt the best way to tackle this information was to make choices. First, we chose for this textbook what we believe are the core concepts in the field, and illustrated them with examples and selected research findings from sociology and family studies literature. Second, we chose to emphasize two theoretical frameworks that incorporate these concepts to guide your study. From this informational foundation suggestions are offered for further reading, and we suggest ways that the ideas you learn about might be discussed, analyzed, and applied to help you broaden your understanding of families. Your job will not end after reading these chapters. Rather, we hope you will use this material in order to apply what you know, use it to help clarify misunderstandings, and gain insights into others' behaviors—family-related or otherwise.

There are many ways to study the family. We have chosen to focus on what we believe are the most utilitarian and interesting. We emphasize two approaches to studying the family: a micro approach that emphasizes family processes and the dynamics of family interaction, and a macro approach that views the family as an institution embedded within a social and cultural context. The theoretical thread we use to tie together these approaches is systems theory: Two systems theories, to be exact. *Family systems theory* is a heuristic tool that utilizes a set of concepts to help you understand the micro aspects of the family. The *ecological systems perspective* focuses on the social and cultural settings in which families are embedded: It provides the macro focus. These system theories are highly compatible and serve to bridge micro and macro family phenomenon.

In Chapter 1 we discuss these two theories in detail, defining concepts and illustrating them with family examples. We address the diversity of families living in the United States, including race, ethnicity, social class and gender. You will also find comparisons of race, ethnicity, social class and gender in chapters throughout the text. We conclude this chapter with a review of how family research is conducted. Much of the material you will be reading stems directly from scientific studies of the family, and this material will help you to have a clearer idea about the research process and how family scholars conduct scientific studies.

Commitment is the focus of Chapter 2. We begin with a discussion of commitment to one's "self," stressing why and how the self is formed and why it is the foundation for family relationships, and interpersonal relationships in general. An individual's self and associated identities are not created in a vacuum. Rather, they develop within a social context—including family, neighborhood, community, and the larger social system. These are all necessary for individuals to develop, maintain, or change their identities. After the discussion of the self and identity formation we continue with a discussion of socialization. Socialization behavior illustrates the interplay between human development and family development. Socialization is discussed in terms of the changes that occur in an individual over the life course, emphasizing the transitions from childhood, adolescence and young adulthood to midlife and old age. The reciprocal influence of an individual on the family (as well as the family on individual members), and the normal changes in relationships between family members over time are examined using systems terminology. We conclude this section using the ecological systems perspective to analyze aspects of the social order within which children and adults grow. This is the context from which many different agents of socialization emerge to influence individual growth and change.

Chapter 3 continues the examination of commitment by studying the choices people make regarding close relationships. Who are they attracted to? Who do they date? Do they date people they would never consider marrying? When and why do they cohabit? When do they feel ready for marriage (if they ever do)? What happens when they cannot marry the person they love (i.e., gay and lesbian couples)? To what extent is there continuity in love and commitment norms over time (e.g., did your great grandmother cohabit before her marriage? Did your mother?). In this chapter we examine how relationship choices are redefined over time and how the culture adapts when behaviors are reevaluated.

In Chapter 4 we explore how intimate relations are maintained. How do relationships evolve as power struggles are resolved and control is negotiated between partners? Do spouses who are good at problem solving and conflict management resolve their differences any more successfully than those who lack these skills? What types of communication patterns develop in families? We conclude the chapter by examining the changing view of marriage over time within the larger society and the increasing cultural emphasis on individualism. Is this change associated with a de-emphasis on child and family well-being?

Chapter 5 focuses on family experiences and expansion as families go through various life stages. Parenting is the key concept in this chapter. We examine couples' planning before children are conceived and their behavior after children are born. Changes in parent-child relationships are discussed, as is the reciprocal nature of the parent-child relationship. In what ways do developing children affect parents, and vice versa? How does parenting change over the life course of children? How important are siblings in the socialization process? How are sibling relationships affected by other subsystems in the family, and how do these change as children become adults? We conclude with a consideration of macro-level issues affecting parent-child relations, such as historical changes in parenting values and the growing influence of media and technology on families.

In Chapter 6 we examine midlife and aging experiences. The focus is intergenerational connection and commitment. In midlife, attention is focused on raising adolescents, and for some, caring for elderly parents. Family boundaries must be adjusted during this life stage. Adult child-aging parent relationships are the focus here, and we look at the role of caregiving in depth. We also discuss the variety of ways older adults play out grandparent roles, how siblings negotiate their relationships in adulthood after their own child-rearing roles are completed, and the ways adult children respond to the death of parents.

Chapter 7 examines work and the family in order to understand the interconnections between them. We look at the division of household labor and childcare concerns. The work experiences of wives, husbands, and children are compared. What happens within the family when the primary wage earner loses his or her job and becomes unemployed? What are the relevant factors that affect retirement, when paid work ends? Do these factors differ for men and women? The chapter concludes with a discussion of how events within the larger society (read: good economy/bad economy, social welfare, health, retirement policies) affect the nation's families.

In Chapter 8 the focus is on family transitions. What happens to couples when they marry after cohabiting, divorce after marriage, remarry after some time as a single parent, or marry for the first time bringing the children of a former partner to a new union? The unique problems and solutions associated with these changes at both the family and societal level are analyzed.

Chapter 9 explores some of the saddest of family situations (domestic violence, alcohol and drug abuse, child abuse and neglect, child runaways). The prevalence and causes of partner aggression (heterosexual and gay/lesbian) are discussed. We report on sibling violence, the abuse of parents by their children, and discuss elderly abuse. Addiction problems and the role they play in creating family distress are discussed. Children who run away from home often do so because of a family that suffers from one or more of the problems mentioned above or because they feel they are misunderstood or mistreated by their parents. Many children are short-term runaways, gone for only a night or two, and soon become reconciled with their parents. The children we write about are more distressed and vulnerable to more severe consequences. The chapter incorporates a discussion of the exo-, meso-, and macrosystem contributors to family distress. We close with a review of some of the solutions to problems such as substance use and domestic violence that are proposed by agencies or institutions in the exosystem.

Lastly, in Chapter 10 we look at families in the context of the larger social system, focusing on maintaining connections to nonfamily members and the broader community. How might services and supports outside the family help or interfere with parenting behavior and other family processes? What are the consequences of government social policy aimed at families? What part do families play in maintaining good schools and neighborhoods, and healthy communities? For example, what did the members of a one-industry community, Thomaston, Georgia, do to regroup and move forward when Thomaston Mills, the industry that paid for schools, streets, and many of the town's cultural events, declared bankruptcy and closed in 2001? (For the answer, go to: <http://www.edtv.gatech.edu/AnnualReport01/Teamwkthomas.pdf>.)

An important goal of your authors is to bring you to a new level of knowledge so that you have the ability to use that knowledge. Are you familiar with the adage: **If you hear it, you forget it; if you see it, you remember it; if you do it, you *know* it?** We want you to complete this text with enough expertise to analyze and interpret the situations you may face outside the classroom. To sharpen your thinking and put you in the mood for the material in each new chapter, we begin each one with information that directs your thoughts toward the particular topics to be covered in the chapter. We end every chapter with a selection of exercises that will give you practice applying the information you learn. Your instructor will likely come up with other assignments. You will find a list of suggested readings at the end of each chapter providing additional information on the topics covered in that chapter. We hope this text gives you a head start toward expanding the knowledge base you have already gained as a result of your own family life. ◆

Acknowledgments

Our indebtedness to many others became increasingly obvious as we neared completion of this writing task. Our conversations with colleagues, graduate students, and undergraduate students over many years helped inspire the development of this text.

Special thanks are due to Irving Tallman, Debra Henderson, and Erika Bonds who read and reread drafts of the manuscript. Adam Bickford kept things going at the Cooney-Bickford household when deadlines were pressing Terri for time, which was greatly appreciated. He, Eddy and Jacob always showed unfailing support for this project. Our Project Editor, Jim Ballinger, offered expertise and encouragement in seeing the project through to completion.

Valuable assistance came from other people as well. Thanks to Amy Enderle for her excellent photographic contributions, and Carolyn Shaw and Ryan Williams for the professional graphics work they provided. The helpful comments and insights offered by reviewers around the country made the book more complete: Judy Aulette (University of North Carolina), Mary Bold (Texas Woman's College), Charles Calahan (Purdue University), J. Kenneth Davidson, Sr. (University of Wisconsin–Eau Claire), Patricia Dyk (University of Kentucky), April Few (Virginia Polytechnic Institute & State University), Roma Hanks (University of South Alabama), Jennifer Hardesty (University of Illinois Urbana-Champaign), Charles B. Hennon (Miami University–Ohio), Dave Klein (University of Notre Dame), Shelley MacDermid (Purdue University), Gail Mosby (The University of Tennessee, Knoxville), Susan Murray (Andrews University), Scott Sernau (Indiana University South Bend), Bahira Sherif (University of Denver), and Sonia Solari (University of Utah). ✦

Chapter 1

Studying Families

Micro and Macro Perspectives

Did You Know?

- The average family size in 2000 was 3.17 persons (Wright, 2003b).
- The so-called "typical" American family, a married couple with their own children under the age of 18, made up only 23.5 percent of households in the United States in the year 2000 (Wright, 2003c).
- The estimated median family income in the United States was approximately $56,500 in 2003 (U.S. Department of Housing and Urban Development, 2003).
- There were 34.6 million Americans (12.1 percent) living below the poverty line in 2002. This figure included 7.5 percent of married couples with children under the age of 18 (U.S. Bureau of the Census, 2004b).

Things to Think About

- Is a married couple a family? Or does it take a child to make a family? Is a same-sex couple with a child a family?
- How would you define "family"? Would you include something about shared residence? Would you specify relationships, such as marriage and adoption? What about the rights, duties, privileges of family members? How would you convey the idea of the totality of families within the larger society? Write out your definition before you start to read this chapter.
- As a way to direct your thoughts to the material in this chapter, think about the families of your friends and the members of your own family (include married siblings, grandparents, aunts, uncles). List the people in each separate family and then label each one according to these categories: widowed, step, single parent, child-free, gay, lesbian, communal family. Keep this list for use later in the chapter.

Families, Communities, Society: Interconnections

Families, their interpersonal relationships, and their connections to organizations and institutions in the community and the larger society are the focus of this text. Stories about these interconnections are in the news every day. Here is an example of one family and its interconnection with religion and the law:

> An unmarried father of a 9-year-old daughter argued a case before the Supreme Court of the United States in March 2004. He was arguing that the words "under God" be removed from the Pledge of Allegiance on the grounds that it is an unconstitutional endorsement of religion. An atheist, he reaffirmed that the First Amendment calls for the separation of Church and State. He believes that each time the Pledge is recited in his daughter's fourth-grade class the First Amendment principle is violated and her classmates, teacher and the school are telling his daughter that her father's beliefs are wrong. (*USA Today,* 2004)

This story illustrates the action of an individual father on behalf of his child; if the Court decides to judge the case, it will make a ruling pertaining to all fathers, mothers, and children. The lives of this particular family will no doubt be changed in one way or another by the father's actions, especially since the mother, a born-again Christian, supports the "under God" language.

Two distinct perspectives related to your study of families are evident in this example. One is a "micro" perspective that depicts the family as a *small group.* This approach emphasizes the *processes* that occur within a family. It focuses on the interpersonal interactions among family members. Processes that are studied from this perspective include (a) communication patterns (to what extent do you think the parents in this example talked about their religious differences?); (b) conflict resolution (the father in this example is fighting for custody of the couple's child; evidently they were unable to resolve their differences without going to court); (c) negotiations for fair treatment (what was "fair" in terms of child custody and visitation was not successfully negotiated between the couple); and (d) power relations (when cou-

This 'typical' family makes up less than 25 percent of U.S. families today. But could you tell by looking if the couple was cohabiting, or remarried?

ple negotiations break down, who "wins" is usually determined by who has more resources and power). Issues of intimacy, love and affection, child rearing, family roles and responsibilities, and the development and expression of personal identities are included when studying families as small groups.

A second way to look at families is from a "macro" perspective that emphasizes the purposes families serve for society, their interactions within the environment, and the social contexts in which they are embedded. This approach treats the family as a **social institution** within society. When examining the family institution the focus is on families in the aggregate: how families affect, and are affected by, the physical and social settings in which they live their lives. This approach might analyze, for example, how American families began to change in the 1950s when a growing economy encouraged the rise of the service industry and was faced with the need for an accommodating workforce. An increasing number of white, middle-class married women willing to enter the labor force solved the problem. Another issue for this approach is the increasing number of children whose parents do not marry each other, a changing pattern of behavior that is altering the definition of family in our society. Other topics of investigation might be the degree to which community services assist families in dealing with the typical (e.g., childcare) and less common (e.g., domestic violence) problems they encounter. The ways that family-related behaviors change over time (age at first marriage, average family size, number of unmarried parents) in response to changes in the economy or changes in social values are also topics pertaining to the family as an institution.

Clearly both approaches are valuable. Accordingly, our definition of family incorporates both viewpoints. Compare the definition you wrote with ours. We define **family** as a group of two or more persons related by blood, adoption, marriage, or marriage-promise[1] who live together, or have lived together at one point in time, and who share the expectation and obligation to care and provide for one another. When aggregated, family group expectations and obligations fulfill specific purposes that serve the needs of the larger society. What does a society need from families? Families are expected to bear, rear, and socialize children who will become the next generation of society's citizens. Certainly not all families meet the normative expectations of the larger society, and expectations and accepted standards within society change over time as the needs of individual families change. Nevertheless, it is expected that there is sufficient agreement within a society, at any single point in time, about the composition of family positions, roles, rules, and standards that serve to guide individual families' behaviors so that a "family" institution can be clearly differentiated from other social institutions.

In the sections that follow, you will be introduced to vocabulary terms and concepts with which you may be unfamiliar. We have attempted to keep the text as jargon-free as possible; however, we cannot overlook many of the concepts scholars use when they write about families. If you are unfamiliar with these terms, you will find most of them in the Chapter Concepts at the end of each chapter. Many social science concepts have become part of our common language (e.g., norms, roles), but their scholarly definition is emphasized in the glossary. Because the study of families depends on scientific data (as discussed in the final section of this chapter), it needs a clear and unambiguous vocabulary so that scholars can communicate using similar language and shared meanings.

Guiding Frameworks

Two distinct but compatible system theories, *family systems* and *ecological systems*, are the frameworks applied throughout this textbook. They are integrated in this chapter to assist your understanding and interpretation of families at the small-group and broader societal level. Other key frameworks from which family behaviors are studied include exchange, symbolic interaction, structure-functionalism, and the life course. We believe that many of the interpersonal processes and macrodynamics that are studied using these frameworks can be incorporated within a systems perspective. Many of the frameworks share similar concepts. The versatility and comprehensiveness of family systems and ecological theories made it the basis for our selection.

We take a moment here to discuss the importance of theory and tell you why this text adopts a systems perspective. In the social sciences, a *theory* is an idea or set of ideas that explain some phenomenon. As was stated by some unknown scholar, theory is like a net thrown out to catch the world—to rationalize, explain, and dominate it. Rather than just describe, a theory is designed to provide (a) logical explanations, (b) predictions, (c) a sense of understanding, and (d) some measure of control. The elements of a theory that were devised to meet these goals include *concepts*, which embody ideas that have labels and definitions (e.g., husband, wife); *variables*, which are concepts that take on two or more values (e.g., number of years married); and *propositions*, which state the relationship between two or more concepts (e.g., the larger the family size, the more complex the family division of labor). A proposition frequently states that if one variable changes in a regular fashion, predictable change will occur in another variable (e.g., as industrialization increases, extended kin ties decrease). Finally, *hypotheses* are untested propositions that have clear implications for measurement and testing.

In this chapter we provide a set of concepts from family systems theory and ecological systems theory that will help you understand and interpret the material presented in subsequent chapters. Think of these concepts as a set of building blocks you can use as a foundation for your new knowledge. You will be expected to use these concepts as you think about and critically analyze the most current information we could assemble about families.

In the remainder of this chapter we introduce the concepts of the family system framework then go on to discuss the family first as a small group and then as a social institution. Ecological systems theory is introduced next, followed by a section on the diversity of American families. The chapter ends with a review of the various ways families are studied.

What Is a System?

Generally defined, a **system** is "a set of interacting units with relationships among them" (Miller, 1978, 16). From a micro perspective, the "units" in a family are the people who are included within a specific group. Traditionally, two types of family groupings have been identified. A **nuclear family** is composed of two interacting units (two partners) and their biological or adopted children. An **extended family** is composed of the people included in the nuclear family plus related kin who may or may not share the same household (parents, in-laws, adult siblings, and so on). Scholars have differentiated two types of nuclear families. One is a **family of orientation,** which is the family a person is born into (his or her parents and siblings). The other is a **family of procreation,** which is the family a person establishes through marriage or marriage promise as a wife, husband, or partner with biological or adopted children.

The definition of a nuclear family listed in the paragraph above excludes a large number of family groups. Cohabiting couples with children, stepfamilies, and gay and lesbian families would not be considered a "family" using this definition. We have attempted to take into account the complexity of American families by expanding our definition of family (on page 3) to include the phrase "marriage promise" in order to permit gay, lesbian, and cohabiting couples to be studied as family systems. Divorced and separated adults, and adult children who have moved from the nuclear family residence, can be studied as part of a family system as well. However, our definition views an absent parent who is not in contact with and no longer cares for or provides for children as excluded from the family system.

A systems perspective assumes that specific behaviors and relationships *cluster in meaningful ways* and affect one another. Behaviors associated with a family, such as sexual intimacy, sharing a daily life together, and child rearing, for example, cluster together in ways that are different from behaviors associated with, say, elementary education (teaching, attending meetings, grading schoolwork, conferences with parents). The range of behaviors associated with every social institution—legal, religious, educational, political—cluster into predictable, specialized systems of their own. These clusters of behavior are the essence of social institutions, and when all institutions are taken as a whole they make up a **social system.** From a macro perspective, the "units" of a social system are social institutions: family, religion, education, the economy, the law, and politics.

We will discuss the interactions within and between social institutions in more detail later in the chapter. First, we turn our attention to understanding the salient concepts associated with systems analysis and the family system in particular. Learning about these characteristics will help you interpret and understand the behaviors that take place within family and social systems.

Interrelatedness and Interdependence

Interrelatedness and interdependence are important characteristics of social systems, because what goes on within one institution influences how the others function. For example, if political or social strife occur within society, families may turn to their religion for sustenance and guidance, which puts greater demands on religious institutions. Houses of religion all over the United States reported increased attendance in the aftermath of the September 11, 2001, tragedies in New York City, Washington DC, and Pennsylvania. When there are periods of high unemployment and family members lose their jobs, health insurance, and other benefits, there is pressure on the political system to bolster the economy. Sometimes this pressure is responded to by enacting social policy that creates jobs so that people can get back to work.

Few families can be completely shielded from the consequences of major events that occur or from the values that dominate the larger social environment. An obvious example is the outbreak of war taking family members away from each other. A less obvious example would be community support for the traditional gender roles of women as wives and mothers making it difficult for them to achieve their full potential in the world outside the family. Such community values are seen when a local school district is unwilling to offer extended-day programs in the schools, making full-time work difficult for mothers who cannot find half-day childcare for their kindergartners.

Just as a social system is characterized by interrelatedness and interdependence, so too is a family system. Common goals, values, responsibilities, and a family identity are the consequence of the close interconnectedness of family members. If interdependence fails to develop within the family and partners experience too much autonomy, the danger is an insufficient degree of togetherness and commitment to the marriage and family. A husband and wife who fail to cultivate interdependence may find that after a few years they have little in common. Spouses who compete with each other over whose job takes primary importance rather than acknowledge an appreciation for and sharing of each others' successes are more likely to seek approval in other relationships and rely less on each another. Surra (1988) found that the development of strong, independent friendship networks interfered with the development of commitment between partners; such friendships were fostered at the expense of the marriage.

Another example of interdependence is a family's investment of time, money, and energy to ensure that a child prodigy's talent is developed to the fullest degree. Doing so may mean paying a high cost to send the child away from home in order to be coached or taught by an expert, leaving less money for the rest of the family and an absent parent who travels with the child. Another example may be the stay-at-home parent who decides to take a job so that the children can attend private school. Such sacrificing for better schooling could have the inadvertent consequence of altered family roles and less time together for husband and wife. There are multiple other ways that interrelatedness and interdependence are experienced at the microsystem level. Husband-wife or parent-child relations may be negatively affected if a wage earner brings home the stress and tension associated with problems in the workplace. When children are upset by continual conflict between parents, poor grades in school or behavior problems often result. The concept of interdependence focuses attention on the obvious fact that family behavior cannot be understood without examining the interrelationships between family members.

Wholeness

Systems are characterized by **wholeness.** That is, when all elements are combined, the system is more than the sum of its parts. For example, one entertainment venue consists of wild animals and their trainers, flying trapeze artists, clowns, music, and an announcer. Each of these components is a complete entity, yet together they make up what is called a circus: something that is more than the mere addition of the various acts. So, too, do the exchanges and interactions that occur within a family result in a larger, coherent entity with the characteristic of wholeness. In this case the whole—the family system—is greater than the sum of its parts, its individual members. The concept of wholeness is manifest when a family differentiates itself from others when parents tell their children "That is not the way our family does things."

When conceptualizing family system wholeness, you must consider the impact of all members' behavior on the system. Family environments are settings in which children are reared according to parental values, goals, and ambitions: in which they develop a character and a personality. In the process they also change their parents by exposing the family to new people and ideas and pushing the family to participate in an evolving culture that exists outside of the family. Ask your grandparents or parents how the Beatles were perceived by the younger and older generations in your family during the 1960s. Do you think grandparents appreciated hip hop music as much as teenagers did in 2003?

The family setting is a context for growth and development for the adults in the system as well as the children. Family relationships change when a change occurs in any one individual member's behavior. For example, if one partner decides to quit work, go back to school, change jobs, or adopt a different religious faith, the whole family will be affected. Thus, individual members' behavior affects the entire family, and the totality of change that occurs creates a fluid yet coherent (or incoherent) family system.

Organization

A system is *organized*. A system must have some arrangement of parts placed into a structured whole. For example, the arrangements of the nine planets that orbit our sun plus some smaller bodies (asteroids, meteoroids, and comets) make up the solar system. Human social systems similarly involve the organized arrangement of parts. Universities and corporations, for instance, are social systems, arranged and organized into discrete parts. Specific concepts, including positions, roles, norms, values, and status hierarchies, help determine or define the parts. Thus, within each family system every family member assumes a **position,** defined as a status or place in a social group. Wife/husband, mother/father, child/sibling are social positions in the family.

Family positions are interrelated and interdependent: A woman cannot assume the position of mother unless there is a child. **Roles** are culturally defined and recognized ways of behaving that are associated with each position. Roles change over time as family members grow, develop, and change. For example, the position of father has a number of roles (protector, teacher, provider) that are related to, and interdependent with, the position of child. Roles are reciprocal (child misbehaves—parent disciplines), and the behaviors associated with them change over time as family members age (time out sitting on a dining room chair may be an effective technique for disciplining a 3-year-old but not a 17-year-old). Roles also change over time because of change at the macro level. Expectations of how a wife and husband should act toward each other have changed as men and women's positions in society have become more equal.

Specific positions and roles may not pertain to all families. Some couples never have children, so the parent position (and roles associated with it) is irrelevant to them. Increasingly, many parents are raising their children alone, as single parents. In such families there is no husband/father or wife/mother position (which means the associated roles must be assumed by only one parent or not performed at all). Some couples do not marry although they may live together for a lifetime, so they cannot, by law, be called husband and wife despite assuming the position of partners and acting their roles toward each other as legally married husbands or wives do.

Another concept associated with family organization is **norm,** defined as a societal rule that is devised or adopted as a standard for how to behave. Norms govern the interaction between position incumbents and guide the way that roles are enacted. They define the limits of acceptable behavior. Wide variation exists in the way members in individual families behave. The norms that family members adopt are probably the greatest source of this variation. What are some of these norms? Look at the list of family types you made when you began to read this chapter. For each of the family groups you listed, examine the family's norms by answering the following questions: Is there a difference in the amount of talking that goes on between family members? (Some families are silent as they eat their evening meal, while in others it is hard to get one's opinion heard in the ongoing conversation.) Which parent disciplines the children (if there are children and if they are disciplined)? How outwardly affectionate are family members with each other? How much quarreling or bickering goes on between family members? Did you find differences between the families of your friends and kin?

The transition from an only child to a 'big sister' brings more than just a change in family position. What other aspects of family organization change for an older sibling after the birth of a baby?

Values are an important aspect of social organization because they influence the content of norms. That is because values have to do with modes of conduct. According to one scholar, values are abstract ideas, and when they are internalized, become a standard of action or "a criterion for guiding action, for developing and maintaining attitudes toward relevant objects and situations, for justifying one's own and others' actions and attitudes, for morally judging self and others, and for comparing self with others" (Rokeach, 1970, 160). Within the larger society, values define attitudes and behaviors toward morality, sexuality, equality, democracy, achievement, competition, and so on. Within families, societal values define members' orientations toward right and wrong, religious involvement, which political party to support, and the socialization of children, to name only a few.

There are many differences in the expression of values among families. Did your parents encourage you to be politically active or do they seldom pay attention to political events? Do your values reflect those of your parents regarding the marriage of gays and lesbians? I suspect there are wide differences between your views and your classmates on these issues, partially depending on such factors as social class standing, race, and ethnicity. Differences in values are the source of many arguments and heated debates between people.

Over time most groups, including family groups, develop a **status** and power **hierarchy** that acknowledges an order or rank among members. In families, parents are usually at the top of the status and power hierarchy. Sometimes this hierarchy is obvious, as when the father is clearly seen by all members as the "boss." It can also be subtle—as when parents always discuss issues related to the children but the children know it is mom's view that usually prevails when it comes to child rearing. The concept of a power hierarchy may also be applied to the sibling group when the oldest, the smartest, or the most manipulative gets his or her way most of the time.

Structure

All systems have a **structure** that is determined by size, organization, composition of positions, and patterns of interaction (communication, power, affection, and so on). It is primarily a family's structure that determines how it is labeled. In the United States we have a variety of family structures. Child-free, first-married, remarried, stepfamily, single-parent, gay, lesbian, foster, adoptive, widowed, and children living with relatives other than their parents are the primary ones. Each of these family structures has distinct characteristics that set it apart from the others. We illustrate with two characteristics: size and complexity. The number of children in a family affects structure insofar as a greater number of children is associated with a more traditional gender-segregated division of household labor, decreased partner companionship, and decreased parental satisfaction (Teachman et al., 1987). Complexity is introduced when two remarried adults bring children from previous unions into their new marriage, also (often) bringing along relationships with an ex-spouse/nonresidential parent, grandparents, and extended kin of the former spouses who may feel they have a legitimate voice in the new marriage. These topics will be explored in depth in subsequent chapters.

Boundaries

All systems have boundaries and families are no exception. **Boundaries** are invisible barriers that separate a system both physically and symbolically from the outside environment. Boundaries in families regulate the movement of people and resources (such as information, knowledge, values, and property) into and out of the family. By separating the family from the external environment, boundaries help protect it from harmful environmental stresses. They also help create a sense of a unique family identity for family members ("That may be how the Johnsons do it but in our family . . ."). The family system also has internal boundaries that separate individual family members and subgroups of members—called **subsystems**—from one another. Three principal family subsystems have been identified: spousal (the marital subsystem), parent and children (parent-child subsystem), and brothers and sisters (the sibling subsystem). The characteristic of hierarchy is often used to describe subsystems because of the nesting feature of systems (i.e., smaller groups existing within the context of the larger group). Thus, a family consists of several subsystems, each with varying characteristics (power, authority, status, resources), and all with boundaries that vary in the ease with which they can be penetrated.

How do you know there are subsystem boundaries? Think of examples from your own experience. Sisters keep secrets about their boyfriends, or their smoking behavior, from parents. Parents rarely share information about their sex life with children. Boundaries may be characterized by fear or by trust. If a brother reads his sister's diary and shares her personal information with his friends, a boundary has been penetrated and trust violated. Family boundaries are identified by rules, both spoken and unspoken. For example, families have rules about acceptable ways of behaving that encourages or discourages warmth or coldness, privacy or openness, distance or connection between family members. These rules indicate the separateness, or boundaries, around people. There are rules about touching: Do family members hug and kiss each other? Under what conditions is such physical contact encouraged or discouraged? There may be rules about topics that children are not allowed to discuss (such as sex, Aunt Heidi's odd behavior). There may be privacy rules that discourage curiosity about what is happening within the family. Or there may be cover-up rules—never talk about daddy's drinking or mention momma's afternoon friend. Such rules are designed to keep information away from those not in the family or within a subgroup in the family.

Sometimes family rules are not clearly stated or spelled out, but members are nevertheless expected to obey them (covert rules). In some families, when a parent is drinking heavily it may be expected that children go to their room, yet such an expectation (rule) has never been openly stated. Unspoken rules can cause confusion in families. If children do not ask questions about parental behavior, problematic issues may never be confronted and thus will remain unresolved, and the meaning of some behaviors can become distorted. The popular literature and motion pictures are filled with stories of families with unspoken secrets and rules that are rarely openly discussed but become exposed in indirect and at times pathological ways. Can you think of any novels, plays, or films that dramatically portray the consequences of family secrets?

Boundary rules define which behaviors are appropriate and permissible, what is or is not expected and accepted. Boundaries also help define who is and is not considered a member of the family. For example, some children fail to identify a stepfather, stepmother, or stepsiblings when asked to name the members of their family, placing them outside the family's boundaries and thus outside the system. This omission is evidence of the way the family system may be perceived by its members. For a father, his new bride is an integral part of the system, while to his teenage children she is merely "our dad's new wife"—not really a family member.

Family scholars use several adjectives to describe family boundaries. The most noted of these are *rigid* (I can never enter my parent's bedroom without knocking), *clear* (my mother lets it be known that if my father ever messes around, he's history), *flexible* (both of my grandmas came to live with us before they died), and *permeable* (Buddy's probation officer always stops by quite unexpectedly). Relatively permeable family boundaries can be beneficial in some situations and detrimental in others. To illustrate, in one study of rural families (Robertson et al., 1991), some of whom were undergoing severe financial distress, the effects of wives seeking emotional support and help in decision making from persons outside the family varied depending on their husbands' employment situation. In situations where husbands were experiencing unstable work conditions and heightened economic stress, their wives' willingness to seek support from persons outside the nuclear family boundaries resulted in stronger feelings of marital negativity among the husbands. However, when husbands had stable employment, support seeking outside the family by wives was associated with enhanced marital quality. Perhaps when their wives were too open to outsiders about the family's difficult economic situation, husbands experienced feelings of shame and failure for not adequately fulfilling the breadwinner role.

Stability

Human behavior is organized in patterned, routine, expected ways; it tends toward being relatively continuous and stable over time. This maintenance of pattern is called **homeostasis.** Homeostasis reflects family behavior as well as individual behavior. Stability and continuity help foster a unique worldview for each person's perception of his or her family, creating the notion that each family has unique characteristics that make it different from the neighbors, and different from other kin in the extended family—grandparents, aunts, uncles, and cousins.

A family worldview stems from events, stories, rituals, and secrets that develop over time as the family grows. Stories of Mom and Dad's courtship, trips to the hospital for a child's birth, and family vacation (mis)adventures all contribute to a family history and a shared picture of what the family "is." Families tend to maintain this picture of their family and the patterned routines associated with it because it provides a sense of comfort that stems from familiarity. Familiarity in turn contributes to a sense of **cohesion** between family members: the extent to which they enjoy one another, are close to one another, and take pleasure in time spent together.

Family unity and solidarity are created in many ways. At least part of this family's 'worldview' centers around their allegiance to a special university. What are the unique characteristics of your family's worldview?

Equilibrium

Related to homeostasis is the fact that all systems have the tendency to maintain an established balance, or **equilibrium.** In a family, for example, when a member becomes ill or severely depressed, other members may take on the tasks or duties of the ill member until health (and equilibrium) returns. Or, if conflict within a family is rare, a fight between partners can create great discomfort and generate strong efforts to resolve the issue in order to reestablish equilibrium. On the other hand, a state of equilibrium may involve constant conflict as exemplified by couples—referred to as "conflict-habituated couples"—whose quarrels are part of their routine relationship pattern (Cuber and Harroff, 1965). If the quarreling stops, tension is generated.

In extreme circumstances, the establishment and maintenance of equilibrium can be pathological, such as when conflict between parents is so threatening that it is displaced onto a child who is scapegoated within the family. The scapegoat mechanism is functional in such a family in that it establishes family equilibrium and unity, but at the expense of the psychological health of the child (Vogel and Bell, 1985). Even when family organization and family rules are dysfunctional or unhelpful for achieving system goals, once begun, expectations become embedded and the tendency is to maintain the status quo. Behaviors may consciously or unconsciously be reenacted to repeat negative patterns and expectations in relationships and situations both inside and outside the family. For example, if a bright child is constantly told by her parents and siblings that she is "dumb," that she "never does anything right," it is likely she will carry this perception into the classroom and, quite unconsciously, prove them right!

Adaptability

Adaptability refers to the capacity of those within a system to adjust to new events, behavior, information, crises, or stress. In spite of the importance of continuity and stability in families, changes in a family system are inevitable and necessary. Individual family members generally change their behavior when faced with new or different interpersonal or social conditions. Change may originate from many sources, such as the birth of a child, the unexpected and sudden unemployment of a spouse, a child entering a new developmental stage, a divorce, or a death in the family. When family members have difficulty adapting, the family system is viewed as rigid or closed and resistant to change. The inability to adapt is associated with closed family boundaries and evidenced by rigid family rules. On the other hand, a family displaying too much adaptability may have members who are unable to focus or function effectively. When all information brought into the family is absorbed and acted upon, when any outsider can enter the family and be claimed as an intimate, the family cannot provide the stability and familiarity that makes members feel secure and comfortable.

Open Versus Closed

Another important characteristic of a system, one closely related to system boundaries, is the idea that it falls along a continuum from **open** to **closed.** Very few systems are totally open or totally closed, but some institutions do fall near the extreme ends. For example, a cloistered monastery lies closer to the totally closed end of the continuum, while a political party (at least at the local level) lies near the totally open end. One reason family members are able to adapt and incorporate change without a major disruption to the family is because it is a *semi-open* system. That is, it is a system that can maintain its coherence and identity even though it is in flux and its parts occasionally change. How can that happen? It is accomplished by taking in information and resources (called a **stimulus input exchange,** in system theory terms) that identify a problem or clarify a situation to help family members respond to external and internal conditions. This process also involves sending information and resources back into the environment (**stimulus output exchange**).

What exactly does this mean? Consider the situation of an aging widowed parent who is diagnosed with Alzheimer's disease and where children must make a change in the parent's living situation (external condition). A family physician, the Internet, or friends and neighbors may provide information on the medical needs of people with Alzheimer's (stimulus input). Information on support groups and adult care facilities may be sought.

The parent may be moved out of his home, and it may be put up for sale to pay for institutional care (stimulus output), or the father may move in with an adult child (boundary flexibility; internal conditions). Families are called "semi-open" because they are rarely totally open or totally closed. Variation in openness is associated with the degree of permeability of family boundaries.

Feedback

Closely associated with the openness and closedness of a system is feedback. This concept is important for an understanding of how systems gain, maintain, or lose stability. **Feedback** refers to the transmission of information, energy, or services/goods across system boundaries. Feedback processes involve the stimulus input exchanges (coming into a system) and stimulus output exchanges (leaving a system) mentioned above. Internal feedback processes also describe information transmission *within* a system. Feedback implies a two-way communication process, within or internal to a system and between a system and its external environment. It is nearly impossible for a system to function without feedback processes, and family systems are no exception.

Individuals in a system have a limited number of options or behavioral choices when faced with feedback that upsets the stability of a system. They can (a) change the system, (b) change that part of the environment that is causing disequilibrium, (c) withdraw from the environment and look for a more favorable one, or (d) alter their expectations in terms of the original stable state of the system, to make them compatible with the change that has occurred (Miller, 1978). Let's go over that again.

The following example illustrates the relationship between feedback and stability/change in a family system. Suppose a spouse discovers (receives feedback) that his or her partner has been systematically lying about money matters: This information results in a confrontation and, eventually, marital separation and divorce (changes the system). Managing debt and hiring attorneys involves stimulus input and output exchanges. If children are involved, divorce changes the family structure from a first-married family to a single-parent household. It alters family relationships because now one parent no longer shares a common residence with the rest of the family. Consequently, patterns of interaction and communication must be reorganized: Telephone or e-mail may be the principal means of interaction between the nonresident parent and the children. New ways of coordinating family affairs are necessary if the system is to function smoothly. How will the oldest child get to school and the baby to childcare when the resident parent must begin work by 7:00 A.M.? In this case, feedback transfers in the form of information and resources are important factors in adapting to instability and change. This spouse could have overlooked or denied the lie (changed expectations) instead of changing the system. Changing the environment or leaving it would not have solved the problem in this case, because the source of the problem was internal to the family system.

Families as Small Groups

Characterizing families as systems is compatible with viewing them as small groups. But does small-group analysis add to an understanding of family systems? The answer is yes, because findings from small-group research provide knowledge about human interaction processes, such as commitment, communication, cohesion, conflict, cooperation, competition, and the division of labor. Understanding how these processes are established, are maintained, and deteriorate within small groups, including family groups, reveals important information about how families function. Four processes in particular contribute to an understanding of family systems: commitment, consensus, conflict, and communication.

Commitment

One of the problems all small groups face is the need for its members to develop a strong degree of **commitment.** The commitment of both partners to each other is usually necessary for the family to remain intact. Children's commitment to the family is also important, if only because it enhances family satisfaction. All family members benefit when each member is satisfied with being part of the family system. The detachment of one member from family activities can strain other relationships in the family and create discomfort among members (disequilibrium). For example, a stepchild's hostility and withdrawal can detract from the enjoyment derived from family activities involving the child's parent, stepparent, and half-siblings.

It is worth mentioning that commitment to an ongoing partnership may not always be desirable. As we conceptualize commitment, it does not require that couples stay together to honor a promise once made. There are some conditions under which relationships may be harmful and commitments are best broken. We reiterate that commitment is almost always necessary for a couple's relationship to survive—not that it must survive at any cost. The concept of commitment is so important that it is the topic of Chapter 2.

Consensus and Conflict

It is obvious that a family's physical needs—for food, shelter, and clothing—must be met for the family to survive. Less evident, however, is the need for family members to establish **consensus** about its most important values, its goals, and the distribution and enactment of roles and responsibilities. Consensus about role expectations for family members must be reached if *interpersonal conflict* is to be reduced. Who in the family is responsible for what tasks? What constitutes an acceptable task performance? Unresolved disagreements over the division of labor, standards of hygiene, or other family matters often result in quarrels, hurt feelings, or withdrawal. An effective family organization therefore requires interpersonal conflict to be controlled, at least minimally.

The need to control conflict does not mean that conflict is bad per se; effective problem solving requires an airing of differences. However, conflict can be minimized and interpersonal differences resolved more easily when (a) there are shared understandings between family members; (b) consensus is achieved about who does which tasks, when they are expected to be done, and what standards are to be upheld; and (c) all members know who has the responsibility for making final decisions. If consensus is not developed, power struggles continue, conflict tends to be high, boundary maintenance becomes difficult, and family unity is weakened. The worse case scenario is that offspring may disengage from family participation or that the partnership may dissolve because interactions are so dissatisfying.

Communication

Consensus requires a satisfactory system of **communication.** For partners to understand their common goals and values, these ideas must be communicated, clarified, and agreed upon. In many families, decisions concerning finances, friends, in-laws, domestic responsibilities, and so on are made jointly between partners rather than by each one independently, and joint decision making requires high levels of communication. As children grow older they may be consulted and their input considered. Joint family decision making fosters a shared interpretation of permissible behaviors and a shared understanding about behavioral expectations. If, for example, after a family discussion a list of each child's daily chores is posted on the refrigerator, there can be no misunderstanding about whose turn it is to do the dishes, thereby avoiding endless hassles ("It's your turn," "No, it's your turn"). Several styles of marital communication have been documented. These are discussed in Chapter 4.

In the chapters that follow, these four concepts will be discussed at length, as will others from small-group research, including the development of self-awareness, power, authority, socialization, and role strain. These concepts are introduced in the course of discussing the topics of love and mate selection, power relations in the family, parent-child relationships, household division of labor, and the connections between work and family.

The Family as an Institution

To review a key concept, a *social institution* consists of a set of behaviors that are patterned, repeated, and expected, and that encompass specific *positions, roles, norms, values,* and *status hierarchies* that serve an acknowledged purpose for a society. Once behavioral patterns are established and positions, roles, and so on become routine (normative), they are "institutionalized." That is, people know what to expect. Here is an example: Walk into a public school in any city and you will almost always find classrooms (settings) with a single teacher (position) instructing (role) a given number of children. Teachers are supervised by a principal (status hierarchy, power differential), whose work may in turn be evaluated by a superintendent. While these settings may vary somewhat (rural/urban differences), parents generally know what to expect if they transfer their child from a public school in one state to a school in another.

Institutions are the essential elements of any society; they include religious centers, agencies that provide medical care, law and government administrations, schools and universities, and, in developed countries, corporations and businesses that provide and distribute the products and services used in everyday life. The family is among the most basic and universal of institutions. In the following section we stress how families differ within society as well as how they change through time.

Societal Differences

Not all families have the same institutional affiliations, and this variation accounts for some of the differences found between families in terms of their values, beliefs, and behaviors. What does this mean in everyday terms? Using religion as an example, adherence to a fundamentalist Christian doctrine influences parenting practices and gender roles within marriage in ways that differ from those for families who do not espouse fundamentalist views. A family with fundamentalist beliefs is more likely to adopt a patriarchal organization, for example, in which wives perform the housework and devote more time to "female-typed" labor (Ellison and Bartkowski, 2002) while husbands focus on the provider role.

At the institutional level, kinship relations, residence rules, and norms for appropriate husband-wife behavior differ among societies around the world as well as among subgroups within any one society. In Saudi Arabia, for example, women who go out in public are expected to be accompanied by a male relative—a husband, father, son, or brother. They are not permitted to drive a car. In America there are no such expectations. In addition to intersocietal differences, myriad intrasocietal differences occur among subgroups within our society, reflecting diverse family norms and values. For example, in American Amish communities, marriage can take place only after baptism and can only be with another church member (Meyers, 2003). Compare two popular films depicting the courtship/marriage process in two subcultures in the United States. *My Big Fat Greek Wedding* comically portrays the norms and traditions associated with marriage within a stereotypical Greek-American subculture, while *The Wedding Planner* portrays the arrangements made for an upper-middle-class Anglo wedding. These films illustrating lifestyle differences based on race, ethnicity, and a family's position in the economic structure account for variation in family behaviors and traditions.

Changes in the Family Institution

At the institutional level it takes time (usually decades, sometimes centuries), to demark the ways families change. Consider the age at which people marry for the first time. A substantial change has occurred in this aspect of family behavior over the past 400 years. Among European immigrants to Plymouth Colony, for instance, the mean age of marriage for men born between 1600 and 1625 was 27 and for women it was 20.6 (Demos, 1973). In Andover, another Massachusetts colony, the second generation of men married at an average age of 27, and women, at 22.8 (Greven, 1983). By 1950, for the entire United States, the median age of marriage had dropped to 22.8 for men and 20.3 for women. Fifty years later, in 2000, the median age of marriage had increased again: For men it was reflective of the Colonial period, 26.8, while for women it had reached 25.1, higher than either of the earlier periods (Wright, 2003c).

Why is this statistic important? What implications does age at marriage have for a society? One effect is on the fertility rate. Late marriage for women reduces the potential number of children born, and a generation of smaller families affects the economic and educational institutions, among others. A dramatic change in the number of births in a community eventually affects the number of schools and teachers needed to educate young children. Ultimately, employment opportunities and the economy are affected.

Thus, time is a relevant variable when studying the mutual impacts of social systems and family systems.

The Interrelatedness of Institutions

As we've already mentioned, institutions, including families, have positions, roles, norms, and values that govern the behavior of those associated with them. These elements are meant to guide people in their daily lives by offering standards of behavior and rules to live by when interacting within these institutions. Further, there is always some degree of reciprocity between institutions. Thus, the values and norms to which particular families adhere are strongly influenced by the institutional organizations in the society and culture in which they are embedded. Some institutions, such as religious organizations or neighborhood associations, engage families directly through membership and active participation. Others (the law or the mass media, for example) may not involve direct family participation but nevertheless exert an influence on family life. Married couples, for instance, cannot divorce without following the guidelines set by the laws of their state. Television programs watched by young children provide behavioral models that may or may not be acceptable to parents (Zillmann, Bryant, and Huston, 1994).

We mentioned the relationship between age at marriage and fertility as one example of how the family institution exerts an influence on other social institutions. It is also true that what happens in the social, political, or economic realms has direct effects on individual family members and family systems. State laws tell individuals whom they cannot marry (someone of the same sex, siblings, parents, and in some states, cousins) and how old they must be before marriage can take place without parental consent. Laws have been passed and policies enacted that facilitate (for some families) greater access to education, health care, and social services. Taxation rates vary according to marital status. Some corporations have policies that encourage employees to further their education and training, often providing opportunities within the workplace itself. Other companies offer benefits such as on-site childcare. Thus, actions taken by legislators, corporate executives, and others in positions of power have consequences that affect America's families by enhancing or inhibiting their functioning. What happens in the labor force, schools, politics, and religious institutions cannot be ignored when studying the family. These institutional contexts in which families are embedded are the essence of ecological systems theory.

Ecological Systems Perspective

The family systems perspective focuses on how family members interact, how they define themselves as a unit, how they differentiate themselves from those outside the family, and how individuals who make up subsystems within the family relate to one another and change in response to internal and external feedback. The ecological systems perspective provides a framework and an analytical approach that describes how physical and social settings (neighborhood, school, workplace, etc.) influence families and their members, and how families may influence these settings.

A focus on ecology provides a second set of concepts that emphasize—at the small-group and institutional levels—the environments and social settings that are integral to family well-being. The ecological framework, as conceptualized by Bronfenbrenner (1979, 1989), consists of five systems, each potentially influencing individuals or families. These are the microsystem, mesosystem, exosystem, macrosystem, and chronosystem. They are differentiated by the extent to which individuals and families interact directly or indirectly with them (see Figure 1.1).

We will describe these systems at length because they constitute the framework within which we place the research presented in the chapters that follow. The ecological systems

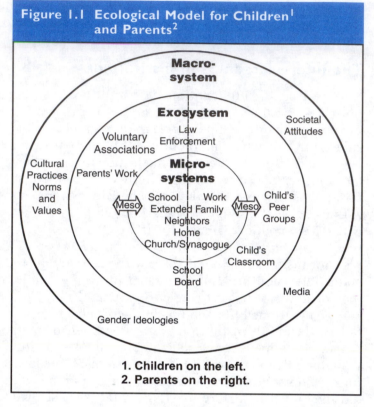

Figure 1.1 Ecological Model for Children[1] and Parents[2]

1. Children on the left.
2. Parents on the right.

perspective is the framework that will best help you analyze and interpret family behavior at both the micro-level and macro-level.

Ecological Systems Concepts

Microsystem. The environmental settings in which individuals participate directly and are most immediately involved in face-to-face interaction are referred to as **microsystems.** For preschool-aged children, for example, possible microsystems are their families (both nuclear and extended), childcare settings, and play groups. Children interact directly within these settings and are influenced by their social and physical characteristics. Adults have a larger number of microsystems directly influencing their lives than children do. These microsystems include other families, friendship groups, workplaces, volunteer organizations, religious organizations, and neighborhoods. What is important about these settings is the extent to which they promote or hinder growth and development and how much they contribute to the needs and goals of individuals and families.

Mesosystem. **Mesosystem** is the term Bronfenbrenner uses to represent the connections between the various microsystems in which individuals are involved. The exchanges between school and family are usually the most important mesosystem for children, just as work-family exchanges tend to be the most meaningful for employed adults. One aspect of mesosystems important for family members' well-being is the extent to which the behaviors that are enacted in the separate microsystems are compatible. Consider the situation of two parents who do not have a television set in their home because they do not want to deal with media influence on their child. The only available source of childcare for their daughter, Sally, is a program that schedules children to watch cartoons every afternoon for an hour. Is Sally to be the only child in the group who cannot spend an hour in front of the TV? Or do these parents compromise their values and permit the TV viewing? When microsystems (home and childcare in this case) provide inconsistent expectations for behavior, children and adults may be more stressed when making decisions about how to behave, and the exchanges and interactions (the mesosystem) between the two microsystems will be less satisfying and not mutually supportive.

When microsystems fail to reinforce each other (e.g., when children's peer groups encourage ways of behaving that are at variance with their parents' values) problems may arise. Similarly, when a man's friends promote one set of behaviors for him (hang out and shoot pool with them after work) and his spouse expects another (go home and start dinner), conflict or stress is likely to occur. If this man opts for the pool hall, he may not fully enjoy this leisure time because he is worried about how his partner will react when he arrives home later than expected. These reactions are likely to affect his satisfaction with marriage and family life. It is at the mesosystem level that some of the most interesting and serious challenges for families exist.

Exosystem. Individuals are also influenced by environmental settings in which they do not directly participate. Bronfenbrenner classified these social settings as the **exosystem.** Some exosystems affect the entire family because they involve at least one family member whose experiences in two or more settings are intertwined and interdependent. For example, a parent's workplace is a microsystem for the adult but typically not one for a young child, because the child does not directly participate in that setting. However, the child is affected by what happens there. A job requiring that Mom or Dad go out of town on business presents a separation that may create adjustment difficulties for the child. A trucker who is on the road for days at a time leaves the day-to-day management of the household to his spouse, but on the days he is home the family has to adapt because the daily routine is not "normal." The same holds for the military father who may be gone for months at a time.

The exosystem also includes significant social institutions (justice system, government) and other settings that may not directly involve any single family member but whose actions can nevertheless affect family life. For example, if a neighborhood association passes a curfew for minors who live in the neighborhood, it will affect all the families, not just those who play an active part in the governing body that passed the rule.

Macrosystem. The outermost level of the ecological system that influences individuals and families is the **macrosystem.** This part of the system encompasses social, cultural, and subcultural components such as ideologies, values, attitudes, and norms that shape the society, including individuals and families. Individual life chances and perceptions of family responsibilities, for example, are influenced by societal attitudes about the proper roles for men and women. Should married women with children work outside the home? That question may seem silly today, but in 1950 a white, middle-class wife and mother working full-time in the paid labor force implied that her husband could not afford to support his family. Because it was nonnormative, the husbands of working wives in the 1950s might have felt inadequate as breadwinners, and these feelings may have contributed to hostile interactions within the marriage and family. As this example shows, societal values, norms, and beliefs may influence family roles, relationships, inter-actions, and satisfaction. Elements of the macrosystem do change over time, some rap-idly, some more slowly, and such change affects families at both the small-group and the institutional levels.

Chronosystem. To account for the importance of historical time, Bronfenbrenner re-fers to the **chronosystem.** This component of the ecological perspective describes the dy-namic, ever-changing aspect of social systems. The chronosystem provides a basis for de-scribing, for example, how schools are more age segregated now than they were 100 years ago and how the ways Americans spend their leisure time has changed in the past five de-cades. Clearly, macrosystem forces, such as attitudes and values, change over time. The settings that constitute a family's micro-, meso-, and exosystem change as well. A child's school environment changes as he or she moves from elementary to middle school to high school. Parents' microsystems change when they switch jobs, alter their involvement in nonfamily activities, and reduce or expand their circle of friends.

Integrating Family and Ecological Systems

All the concepts we presented as integral to analyzing family systems are appropriate to an ecological systems analysis. The micro- and exosystems in which family members participate are settings that consist of behaviors and relationships that cluster in mean-ingful ways; they are organized in ways that reflect the interrelatedness and interdepen-dence of the elements of the family system (i.e., positions, roles, norms, values, and hier-archies); they encounter periods of stability and change over time; and they adapt to change through feedback mechanisms. The contribution of combining family systems theory with ecological theory is that such a union brings important external forces and factors directly into an analysis of family issues. As a result, the dimensions of space, con-text, and time become important features of this approach to understanding families.

Diversity Among Families

Any discussion of families in the United States is inadequate unless race, ethnic back-ground, and socioeconomic standing are considered. The cultural beliefs that are rooted in a racial or ethnic heritage, the subcultural values family members hold and attempt to pass on to the next generation, and the amount of discretionary money families have are the principal factors that create diversity among families. You should keep in mind the difference between the concepts of *race* (physical traits that are inherited) and *ethnicity* (cultural values, practices, traditions). Ethnic identification may fade or diminish over several generations, but racial features remain a source of distinction (Halle, 1984). We caution you to remember that both of these concepts are social constructs and there are in fact few biological distinctions between groups of people. Further, the manner in which society constructs the idea of race has social consequences and strongly affects the oppor-tunities and interactions available to individuals and families.

Race and Ethnicity

Racial and ethnic diversity has been an integral aspect of the American experience since the nation's inception. The United States tends to allow more immigration than most countries, even though it favors some groups over others. The experiences of Irish, Italian, British, Chinese, Japanese, and Mexican immigrants have been historically different, yet none were comparable to the forced immigration of blacks, most of whom suffered the legacy of slavery, and the experience of Native Americans, the original inhabitants who struggled against genocide brought by guns and disease from European settlers. The various ethnic and racial groups have held diverse worldviews and followed honored traditions embedded in their original culture. Over time, these traditions have been modified as succeeding generations have been assimilated into the American culture. The ease of assimilation has varied depending on skin color, sponsorship, individual and family economic resources, and skill levels. For example, Mexican families who illegally crossed the border into the United States and disappeared into the barrios of California, Texas, and Arizona faced different assimilation problems and challenges than Laotian or Cambodian families who came sponsored by religious groups that provided initial housing, jobs, and moral support.

Immigration is not just a historical phenomenon. Between 1981 and 1998, almost 15 million people immigrated to the United States. This influx was greater than during any previous period (U.S. Department of Justice, 2000). By 2001 more than 11 percent of the population had been born outside the United States (Seabrook, 2002). The chapters that follow will consider, whenever possible, the impact of racial and ethnic background on families, emphasizing commonalities across groups as well as differences among them.

The racial groups that are studied and compared most frequently by social scientists are whites, blacks, Latinos, Asian Americans, and Native Americans. Native Americans and Alaskan natives made up 0.9 percent of the U.S. population in 2000. This compares with 3.7 percent for Asian and Pacific Islanders, 12.5 percent for those of Hispanic origin, 12.3 percent for blacks, and 75.1 percent for nonHispanic whites (Wright, 2003d).

One of the greatest sources of diversity among families is not cultural background but socioeconomic status. Wealthy blacks and whites are more similar in the values they hold and the family experiences they have than are wealthy blacks and poor blacks, or wealthy and poor whites.

An important point to be made regarding race and class is that the media tendency to write about blacks that are poor, homeless, or criminals detracts from the large number of middle-class or wealthy blacks who do not fit those categories. For example, current census figures show that 47.9 percent of black families are headed by married couples, 10 percent of blacks work in executive or managerial jobs, and 48 percent of blacks own their own homes (U.S. Bureau of the Census, 2003). Some of the more salient characteristics associated with social class are discussed next.

Social Class

It is a human tendency for people to observe and compare themselves to others. Physical appearance, intelligence, power, wealth, control over resources—these are the typical bases of comparison. The tendency to compare coexists with the tendency to categorize or rank: Am I more or less attractive? Is my family more or less well off? Does my tribe have more or fewer resources, better or worse technology? Among social scientists, the concept of social class is used to epitomize one important basis for comparison, socioeconomic status. **Social class** is defined as a ranking, or stratification system, associated with the distribution of valued resources such as wealth, power, or prestige within a social structure. Those at the higher end generally have more of these resources than those at the lower end.

How is rank in a social class hierarchy determined? Family scholars typically assign rank on the basis of three variables: education, occupation, and income. In the past, a family's rank was based primarily on the characteristics of the male head of household. In today's complex world, however, many families have two wage earners who may have different levels of education, occupation, and income. This means that determining a family's social class status is somewhat more difficult than it was in the past, because it involves balancing two individual rankings (Sorensen, 1994).

Your image of a class system should not resemble geological strata that, once laid down, is preserved until some catastrophic event hurls the levels upward or downward. Instead, conceptualize social class categories as fluid—merging and blending at the margins (rather like a lava lamp that sends blobs of glop floating up or down, depending on the temperature). In America, a strongly held belief is that individuals can improve their life circumstances (class standing) with perseverance, hard work, and a little luck.

A family's social class status is displayed in many ways: through the clothes worn, the number and types of cars driven, and the home in which a family lives. Can you identify at least five ways in which these homes differ from each other?

One strategy for classifying socioeconomic standing is on the basis of occupation. That is the strategy adopted by the U.S. Bureau of the Census. Table 1.1 shows its categorization system. Another strategy combines the three key resources that contribute to social class standing—education, occupation, and income—to assign people and families to one of several hierarchical categories. The most common categories that emerge from this technique are (1) wealthy/upper class/elite, (2) upper middle-class/middle-class/white collar, (3) working class/blue collar, and (4) lower class/poor/homeless.

Table 1.1 Socioeconomic Categories Used by the U.S. Bureau of the Census
Managerial and Professional Specialty Occupations
Executive, administrative, and managerial occupations
Professional specialty occupations
Technical, Sales, and Administrative Support Occupations
Technicians and related support occupations
Sales occupations
Administrative support occupations, including clerical
Service Occupations
Private household occupations
Protective service occupations
Service occupations, except protective and household
Precision Production, Craft, and Repair Occupations
Precision production, craft, and repair
Mechanics and repairers
Construction trades
Other precision, craft, and repairs
Operators, Fabricators, and Laborers
Machine operators, assemblers, and inspectors
Transportation and material moving occupations
Handlers, equipment cleaners, helpers, and laborers
Farming, Forestry, and Fishing Occupations
Farming, forestry, and fishing

1980 Standard Occupational Classification System. U.S. Census Bureau, Bureau of Labor Statistics. *Statistical Abstract of the United States, 2001*, 363.

Needless to say, a person's education, occupation, and income levels are not usually constant over the course of a lifetime; individuals and families often move across class boundaries (Newman, 1988). Winning millions of dollars in a state lottery may move a family from working class to wealthy, but would you describe the newly rich family as elite or upper class? Probably not. Will a family whose current fortune is small but whose past is characterized by generations of vast wealth still be called elite? Probably. Assigning placement in a social class category, therefore, is confounded by individual and family life experiences.

We caution that stereotypical conceptions regarding the interconnectedness of race and poverty be laid aside. The temptation to assume that most minorities are poor and most whites are middle class must be put to rest. In 1998 no fewer than 22.6 percent of all black married couples had an annual income of $75,000 or more, and another 25.2 percent earned between $50,000 and $74,999. The corresponding figures for nonHispanic whites were 32.9 percent and 25.1 percent. The connection between being poor and black stems from the number of single black women who are heads of households: 66.8 percent of these women had annual incomes of less than $25,000 in

1998, compared to 9.3 percent whose income was over $50,000 (U.S. Bureau of the Census, 1999a).

A confounding factor in defining and assigning a social class position to individuals or families is that different levels of education, occupation, and income are associated with distinct social and cultural characteristics. These characteristics include a set of values held in common with others at the same level; a network of associates and friends whose values, beliefs, and attitudes are shared; and access to opportunities that benefit the life chances of individuals and help shape their family organization. We discuss the ways these characteristics vary between different class levels next.

Upper Class/Elite. In a recent documentation of wealth in America, Phillips (2002) profiled the wealth accumulation of America's richest individuals and families. Many of the families whose fortunes were gained in the nineteenth century, or earlier, continue to be listed among the top 30 families with enormous wealth concentrations in the twenty-first century: the Rockefellers, Mellons, Vanderbilts, duPonts, Phipps, Gettys, and so on. Families such as these, viewed as "old money," are very aware of the boundaries that separate them from other classes. Old money families made up the classic upper class, or elite, of American society.

Among members of the upper class, family connotes "history." In old money families, the achievements of family founders are revered, and genealogies, biographies, and the records of ancestral accomplishments are carefully collected and maintained with pride. There is a strong kin-based family structure, and extended family members keep in close contact. This structure serves to preserve inherited wealth through such strategies as a family office or family trust (Allen, 1987; Lenzner and McCormack, 1998). A *family office* protects heirs yet to be born by preserving family wealth. It is a trust set up to pool resources and follow an aggressive investment plan to increase capital over time. The trust may also distribute dividends and handle legal affairs such as drawing up prenuptial agreements, advising on insurance policies, and handling divorces. By pooling or consolidating their money into a common trust, wealthy families are able to take advantage of aggressive investment strategies, which require large amounts of money. Phillips (2002) writes: "The Pratt family of Standard Oil . . . with a family office serving 250 kin, found that many of the youngest Pratts couldn't access high-quality management and had their money in mutual funds. A captive trust company solved the problem" (117).

Because of their important and prestigious ancestors, old money family members care about who comes into the family to produce the next generation and share in its wealth and status. Marriage is not only an emotional commitment; it is also a way to concentrate capital and maintain the in-group solidarity of the class (Allen, 1987). To this end, mothers play an important role as gatekeepers for their children's friends, playmates, and potential suitors (Ostrander, 1984). They exert this control by maintaining family memberships in private clubs, attending churches in exclusive communities—usually ones in which the family has lived for decades—and sending children to exclusive private schools and universities. This privileged education not only provides opportunities for their children's future careers but serves to preserve the values and lifestyles of the upper class. Gatekeeping also serves to promote the **endogamous** nature of this class (i.e., the tendency of marrying within the limits of the group). Largely because of **propinquity** (closeness; in proximity), the tendency is for children to marry someone of their own class. Controlling access to peers also controls the marriage choices of children. Children from wealthy families do marry outside their "circle," but often their choice of mate comes from a family that is socially prominent. Allen (1987) notes, however, that the further removed a new generation is from the founding ancestor, the greater the likelihood that marriages will take place with persons of more modest means.

In addition to raising children to carry on the traditions associated with the management of wealth and privilege, women of the elite class spend much of their time in volunteer activities that support the arts and culture of the larger society. They lend their family name and prestige to these activities, as well as give large financial contributions to functions that promote the arts and charitable organizations (Daniels, 1988). These female-sponsored activities underscore the gender segregation of the upper class. Thus, even though wives may be independently wealthy (a result of equal inheritance norms), they are seldom found in the boardrooms of the family corporations that are the basis of their wealth.

Upper-class men are the power brokers in American banking, industry, insurance, and manufacturing. In Marxian terms, they own and control the means of production (Marx, 1977), making rules and establishing policy. Most are hardworking, but they are able to reap the rewards that come with their privileged educations and access to a large network of influential associates. Their goal is to maintain, and hopefully increase, the family's wealth. This goal is not always adopted by offspring, however. In the Rockefeller family, for example, college professor and social welfare agency worker were occupations of the fourth and fifth generations (Thorndike, 1976).

Middle Class/White Collar. The middle class in America is said to be the stronghold of individualism, achievement, privacy, familism, consumerism, and conventionality (Archer and Blau, 1993). Generally, members of the middle class tend to be active in politics and in voluntary associations, service clubs, churches, and similar organizations. They tend to be work oriented, working long hours as lawyers, executives in large corporations, doctors, architects, scientists, college professors, and high government officials. In these jobs they have an advantage of earning salaries that provide a stable income rather than an hourly wage. This stability cushions the family from unanticipated crises, such as a sudden illness. Middle-class jobs tend to be highly competitive and are represented by career "ladders" in which each step involves personal achievement and evaluation by others in order to succeed. It is characteristic of those in the middle class to be future oriented, to *defer gratification* by putting off marriage until their education is complete and delay having children until they are established in an occupation. The payoff is an occupation that provides enough discretionary income for luxury goods and leisure activities and important benefits such as medical coverage, paid vacations, sick leave, and pension or retirement payments.

Members of the middle class often move for better job prospects, but as a group they tend to be relatively geographically stable (Archer and Blau, 1993). Members of the middle class generally have many friends but see them less often and are less close to them than are members of other classes. Ties with extended kin are important, and members of the middle class tend to keep in touch with relatives even though they may no longer live in their childhood communities. The experience of geographic mobility encourages members of the middle class to place greater emphasis on the **conjugal unit** (the marital couple) than is found in the working class or among the elite. Mobility creates a dependency between husband and wife that is reinforced by an ideal of gender equality. However, gender equality is a philosophy that does not always get put into practice (see Chapter 7, "Work and Families").

The child-rearing values of the middle class differ from those of the working class and the poor in several ways. Studies by Kohn and his colleagues (Kohn, 1977; Kohn et al., 1986) documented some of the differences between middle-class and working-class values related to raising children. These differences are elaborated in Chapter 5 so they will not be discussed here except to say that middle-class parents tend to emphasize personal autonomy, self-determination, and the ability to develop and carry out rational plans and these beliefs are reflected in the way children are disciplined. Reason and the withdrawal of rewards are used more frequently as punishment strategies than is typical of working-class parents. Discipline is more likely to be prompted by parental assessment of a child's motives for misbehavior as opposed to the consequences of the misbehavior. Self-direction, initiative, creativity, self-control, and individualism tend to be the characteristics most valued in children by middle-class parents.

The middle class is a broad category, and some members are close to the ranks of the upper class, holding values and behaviors reflective of those family patterns. Others are closer to the lower end of the category in terms of their levels of income, occupation, and education; their behaviors reflect the values and lifestyles of the working class. For this reason, some early stratification scholars expanded class categories to six: upper upper class, lower upper class, upper middle class, lower middle class, upper lower class, and lower lower class (Warner and Lund, 1941).

Working Class/Blue Collar/Lower Class. Members of the working class are employed in jobs that pay hourly wages. These jobs tend to be in factories, construction, auto shops and similar settings and involve skilled or semi-skilled work, such as machine operation, assembly work, inspection, transportation, plumbing, and so on. Since the middle of the twentieth century a category of "service worker" has emerged that characterizes more and more working-class jobs. This service category includes jobs such as salesperson, bank teller, teachers' aide, barber, childcare worker, and domestic servant, to name a few. At the beginning of the twenty-first century, manufacturing jobs—stereotypically working-class occupations—are fast disappearing, and service jobs are on the increase.

The working-class category is a broad one, and there are real differences among blue-collar workers. Many hold well-paying jobs and never experience unemployment. Others are employed in the kinds of jobs that depend on swings in the business cycle, and layoffs are common. For the most part, hourly wage jobs provide for enough money to meet minimum family needs, with some exceptions for union workers. Some working-class occupations, however, pay more than some middle-class jobs. For example, in 2003 prison guards in California earned more than some California college professors when overtime pay was considered. Remember that occupation, education, lifestyle, values, and attitudes, as well as income, determine class placement.

Education for members of the working class generally ends with high school or trade school. Their work careers begin earlier than those for middle-class workers, and early entry into the labor force means wages reach a peak by middle age. Further, an early start in the labor market is usually accompanied by early marriage. Both working-class males and females marry earlier than those in the middle and upper classes. Because working-class youth tend to live at home with their parents until they marry, marriage is often seen as an escape, a route to independence and freedom from parental supervision and control (Rubin, 1994).

Working-class husbands and wives don't go out together as a couple very often. Instead, visiting with friends and relatives is the source of most of their social life. Women depend on their sisters, mothers, other female kin, and friends for emotional support and conversation, usually visiting in each other's homes. Working-class jobs are not jobs that require men to identify with them. Halle (1984) described men's work as often being physical, dirty, dangerous, and mostly dull, with limited prospects for promotion. Consequently, men put less emphasis on their jobs and more on leisure activities, hanging out with their buddies, male relatives, or friends from work. Male companionship takes place in bars or while engaging in some kind of sport—playing or watching baseball or basketball, soccer, bowling, hunting, fishing, golfing, and so on. Thus, the social life of married working-class husbands and wives involves few shared activities. This is one of the factors that lead to strong feelings of dissatisfaction among wives who report feeling trapped and unhappy (Rubin, 1994).

Children born to working-class parents come relatively early in the marriage, which puts a strain on young couples who may already be experiencing economic insecurity. The young husband's low-paying job is vulnerable to layoffs, and any second income contributed by the wife usually ends after the birth of a baby. The baby's needs and fatigue often lead to a neglected sex life, adding more stress to the family situation. While the kin network can be a source of social and economic support during this time, separation and divorce are not uncommon among young working-class couples (Rubin, 1994). According to Kohn and his colleague (1977, 1983) the conditions that working-class parents face in the workplace influence the child-rearing values they develop, just as in the middle class. Because blue-collar jobs require close supervision, standardization of work, the manipulation of physical objects, and fewer interpersonal skills, working-class parents are more likely to value obedience, orderliness, neatness, and conformity in their children.

Poor/Homeless. Poor families often find it impossible to maintain independent households. One solution is to pool resources with kin or others in need. While this pooling may help meet their immediate material or social needs, it makes the family boundary more permeable. This means less privacy and more intrusions into family life by those with whom they share living quarters. Because poor families' boundaries are more permeable and they are more dependent on social agencies, the police, social workers, government personnel, and social scientists have greater access to them.

People designated "poor" are those whose family incomes fall below the **poverty line,** defined as a dollar figure based on an index created by the federal government. The index is calculated based on minimum food costs for a family of a particular size. In 2003 a family of four with a total family income at or below $18,400 lived below the poverty line (Federal Register, 2003). Many families are "working poor." In 2000, for example, 3.5 percent of householders who were employed full-time for the entire year still lived below the poverty line (U.S. Department of Labor, 2002). The working poor are those who must make choices between paying rent, paying bills, and buying food. Full-time workers can fall into this category because minimum-wage jobs don't pay enough to allow a family to meet all its expenses. Food banks across the nation have seen a rise in the number of families seeking food aid. According to Robert Forney, the president and CEO of Second Harvest, the largest hunger-relief organization in the United States, more than 40 percent of

America's hungry are working poor. Demand for emergency food in food banks, pantries, and soup kitchens rose 25 to 30 percent between 2001 and 2002 (Marks, 2002).

The poor tend to be the elderly, female-headed householders, members of minority groups, and those living in southern rural areas (Rank, 1994). Divorce is one of the most significant life events that place families (usually women and children) below the poverty line. Likewise, remarriage usually improves women's economic status and raises them back above the poverty level (Duncan and Hoffman, 1985). Discrimination within the exosystem is another source of poverty, especially for women and minorities. When people are denied access to education, job training, work opportunities, and equal pay, the odds of improving their living conditions are low.

The consequences of sustained poverty are harsh. The poor experience more health problems and have a higher mortality risk than those in other classes (Oh, 2001). McDonough et al. (1997) found that living on an income of less than $20,000 for four to five years was associated with a significantly higher likelihood of dying. Those living below the poverty line also have more psychological problems, such as depression, anxiety, and poor self-images, and a higher rate of divorce. The poor who live in urban areas tend to live in high-crime areas, move often, have higher school dropout rates, and higher rates of infant mortality (Sampson, 2001). In sum, mental illness, health problems, disability, divorce, drug addiction, teen parenting, and discrimination practices within the exo- and macrosystems are all associated with living at or below the poverty line.

One important point to note about the poverty level is that most measures of poverty report about the same *number of people* living under the designated level year after year. However, the *same people* are not usually counted each time. One study of the poor in 1993 and 1994 estimated the exit rate from poverty to be about 24 percent (Naifeh, 1998). A nationwide representative study by Rank and Cheng (1995) found that three-fourths of the then-current welfare recipients did not grow up in a household that received welfare.

Movement in and out of poverty is a notable characteristic associated with being poor. One study found that 27 percent of persons who rose above the poverty level for at least one year subsequently fell back below it (Stevens, 1994). This movement into poverty is called a **poverty spell.** Oh (2001) cites research indicating about 75 percent of poverty spells last for one year or less, and about 13 percent last for more than two years. According to Oh, the first poverty spell is the most "potent," accompanied by the highest mortality risk. The negative consequences of subsequent spells appear to be modified by adaptation techniques of families as they learn to accommodate, reorganize, and reallocate resources.

For some families, poverty is intergenerational, because chronically poor families require their children to make financial contributions to the family. This means dropping out of school as soon as they can legally do so and going to work at low-end, low-paying jobs. Thus, available opportunities that might end the poverty cycle for them are few.

A general lack of knowledge about available resources and opportunities in the environment is another way poverty is transmitted between generations. Parents socialize children when they effectively deal with the world around them. If a language barrier interferes with communication between home and school, or the inability to read blocks a parent from taking advantage of community resources, poverty is harder to mitigate. Overcrowding and poor health also perpetuate poverty across generations.

Many of the urban working poor cycle in and out of the workforce because of health concerns, either their own or those of family members. Others ignore a health problem because it requires time off from work that they cannot afford because they are the only income provider in the family (Burton, et al., 2002). Many working poor families have no health insurance or else social programs provide coverage only for children in the family. The Children's Health Insurance Program (CHIP) is an example of such a program. CHIP was passed in 1997 by Congress to provide an option for health care coverage to the children of parents who are working but do not have health insurance. Some parents lost health benefits when the 1996 welfare reform act created the Temporary Assistance to Needy Families program (TANF). TANF severed Medicaid (formerly the primary health insurance program for the poor) from other benefits. Family members with income, housing, health, and childcare problems, who can barely hold their families together, find it difficult to negotiate multiple bureaucracies to find programs that can help them.

As in urban areas, the rural poor are more likely to be minority families. In 1990 the poverty rate for rural whites was 14 percent while it was 41 percent for blacks, 32 percent for Latinos, and 30 percent for Native Americans (Ginsberg, 1998). Almost 62 percent of poor rural children live in single-parent families (Poverty and Well-Being in Rural America, 1999). Despite some similarities, the rural poor face a different set of problems compared to the poor in urban areas. Welfare reform requiring recipients to find employment when cash assistance ends created great challenges. Population density is lower and work opportunities fewer in rural areas, and reliable transportation, quality childcare, job training, and educational opportunities are limited. In spite of positive attitudes about the opportunity to work and move off cash assistance, the reality of the situation is bleak. Rural employment is characterized by jobs that are not as likely to provide steady employment. They often are part-time and pay minimum wage (Henderson et al., 2002).

The homeless might be viewed as a special category of the poor. It is nearly impossible to determine the precise number of homeless families in the United States, because homelessness is a temporary situation for many. Some homeless families live with friends or relatives for varying periods of time; others live in their car. Women and children living in domestic violence shelters are counted among the homeless. To understand the extent of the problem of homelessness in general, consider the following figures. A study of major American cities made by the Department of Housing and Urban Development on one night in February 1996 determined that only about one quarter of all the people who were homeless at any time during the year were included in the count of 470,000 people on that single night. Of these people, 66 percent were single, 69 percent male, 41 percent white, 40 percent black, and 11 percent Latino. Over half of these homeless persons said they had suffered from mental illness at some point in their lives (39 percent within the last month), 38 percent said they were or had been addicted to alcohol, and 25 percent had problems with drug addiction (Wright, 2002a). About a third of homeless men in the United States are Vietnam veterans (Hurwitz, 1994).

Although homelessness is a problem for individuals, it also involves families. Approximately 36 percent of the homeless population are families (Lindsey, 1998; U.S. Conference of Mayors, 2000). Eviction is one of the principal causes of homelessness in the United States. A 1990 study of homeless families in Los Angeles found that many had lost their housing because their Aid to Families with Dependent Children (AFDC) allotment was discontinued, an exosystem factor. These families were spending about two-thirds of their monthly income on rent and utilities, and the loss of their monthly AFDC funds pushed them into homelessness (Wood et al., 1990). Eviction may affect an individual family or an entire neighborhood. It precedes the gentrification of poor neighborhoods. With gentrification, dilapidated but affordable houses are replaced with office complexes, luxury high-rise apartments, or renovated and upgraded homes that increase the value of a neighborhood. However, when neighborhoods are upgraded, low-cost homes for the poor are taken away. The shrinking supply of affordable housing has caused a large gap between the number of people needing homes and the number of available units, estimated to be at 4.4 million. In 1998 the average waiting time for public housing was about 33 months. These long waits mean that families must remain in shelters, live in shared quarters, or live on the street for long periods of time (National Coalition for the Homeless, 2001).

Another cause of homelessness also resides in the exosystem. The numbers of families who were in poverty and who were homeless increased with the implementation of the TANF act that replaced AFDC. TANF has time limits and restrictions on assistance that did not apply to AFDC recipients. Other causes of homelessness for women and their children include abusive family relationships, conflict with friends or family with whom they are living, and job loss (Lindsey, 1998). Some research shows that mothers in homeless shelters are more likely to have lived in foster care, group homes, or an institution, to have run away from home, or to have been sexually or physically abused when they were young (Shinn, Knickman, and Weitzman, 1991).

The consequences of homelessness for children are harsh. Homeless children have higher rates of asthma, ear infections, stomach problems, and speech problems. Compared to nonhomeless children, they experience more anxiety and depression and are more likely to have delayed development. For school-aged children, obtaining appropriate clothes for school is problematic, as is transportation to get there, and parents often have no money for school supplies. When children change schools, parents often have trouble obtaining previous school records. Some parents leave their children with relatives or friends so the children can continue to attend their regular school (Homes for the Homeless, 1998).

Family Structure

In addition to differences in race, ethnicity, and social class, much diversity exists in the structure (composition, size, organization, interaction patterns) of American families. At the beginning of the twenty-first century fewer families than ever before could be considered "traditional"—that is, a first-married couple with biological children and only one spouse (the husband) in the labor force. Here are some statistics from the 2000 U.S. Bureau of the Census that illustrate the structural diversity of current American families (Wright, 2002b):

> There were 4,736,000 households inhabited by cohabiting (unmarried) couples in 2000. Thirty-five percent (1,675,000) had children under the age of 15 living with them.
>
> Almost 27 percent of children under the age of 18 are being reared in single-parent households. This percent varies by race: the figure is 21.6 percent for whites, 53.3 per-

cent for blacks, 29.5 percent for Latinos. Nearly half (46 percent) of U.S. marriages each year are remarriages for one or both partners.

About 17 percent of children are living in families with one biological parent and a stepparent. However, there is no way of knowing the actual number of children who have stepparents because a child living with a single parent may have a remarried parent whom they may or may not visit. A large number of children have two remarried parents and thus two stepparents.

Nearly 4 million children live in homes maintained by their grandparents. Thirty-five percent of these children are being cared for by grandparents with neither parent present in the home. These "skipped generation" households occur most often when the grandparents' adult children are unable to assume parental care of their own offspring, usually because of substance abuse, divorce, teenage pregnancy, or incarceration.

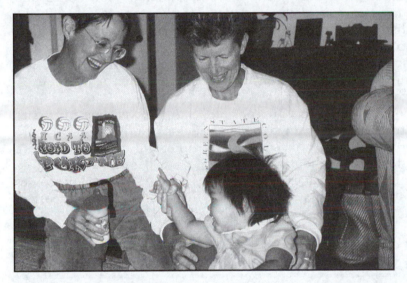

The joy of parenthood is enjoyed by many same-sex partners who adopt their children from foreign orphanages.

Increasingly, gay or lesbian couples with children are recognized as a "family." We do not know how many lesbian women are mothers, but some researchers estimate that there are 2–8 million in the United States (Patterson, 1995b). A landmark study by Blumstein and Schwartz (1983) reported that about one-third of lesbians are mothers and about 10 percent of gay men are fathers. A more recent figure from the popular press claims 6–9 million gay or lesbian couples are raising children (Ford, 2002).

Some of these parents bore or fathered children in previous heterosexual marriages, some women became pregnant by artificial insemination, and some gay partners adopted their children.

All couples, regardless of their sexual persuasion, race, ethnicity or social class, who live in an intimate relationship must confront the same processes of maintaining boundaries, finding the optimum level of interdependence and autonomy, and establishing adequate levels of commitment and consensus to maintain their relationship. Thus, there are many similarities among families no matter what their social standing, sexual composition, race, or ethnicity. We will make an effort to disentangle these similarities and differences in the chapters that follow.

Sex and Gender Differences

Physiological, sociocultural, attitudinal, and behavioral aspects of human beings have all been investigated in an attempt to discover the similarities and differences between the sexes. For example, studies show that infant mortality rates are lower for females than males; females are more prone to report physical and mental disorders and use health services more than males; females are more likely to attempt suicide, but males are more likely to succeed; and in almost every society females outlive males (Lindsey, 1990). Political scientists report that men and women differ in their voting behavior (the "gender gap"). Despite these well-documented differences, the most common conclusion is that there are more similarities than differences between the sexes. Further, it is generally agreed that the debate over nature versus nurture is outdated: Heredity *and* environment, biology *and* society, nature *and* nurturing are responsible for the differences that exist.

Sex differences, yes—but what about gender differences? What is the difference between the terms—sex and gender? *Sex* refers to biological or physiological characteristics that differentiate males from females, including chromosomes, anatomy, hormones, and reproductive processes. *Gender* refers to socially constructed (rather than biologically determined) differences that distinguish males from females. The best way to distinguish between these two terms is to know that gender is learned. How to behave, think, and feel as a male or female, how to act masculine or feminine—these are learned in social institutions and in the cultural contexts in which children are reared: in the micro-, meso-, exo-, and macrosystems within which people interact.

The meaning of what is considered "gender appropriate" changes over time and varies among societies and subcultures. Gender-related artifacts such as clothing, social manners or customs, and gender-acceptable words change over time, and these changes are demarked by the chronosystem. Throughout this text, gender will be discussed more often than sex because the roles, norms, values, beliefs, statuses, positions, and processes that are the core of the family institution are our primary focus, and these are learned within a social environment.

Methods for Studying Families

You are exposed to family research all around you. Just open a newspaper or popular magazine and you will find mention of studies that have investigated family-related issues. Your authors' own local newspapers have recently run stories about the sexual content of television programming, the decline in births to teenagers, and the impact of welfare reform on children's well-being. As a student of the family and an educated consumer of the media, it is critical for you to have a basic understanding of how such research findings, and knowledge about families in general, are obtained.

Research and the Scientific Method

We all do research. Have you ever gathered product information from *Consumer Reports* or another publication when you were thinking of purchasing a big-ticket item? Or gone to the library or onto the World Wide Web to gather material for a paper assigned in one of your classes? Research merely means "to investigate thoroughly" (Olson and DeFrain, 2000), and such investigation can be done many ways.

The goal of family research is to gather information so that conclusions and generalizations can be formulated about what families look like—their structure and composition, and how they live, their interactions, functions, relationship patterns, and so on. Research involves asking questions and then using established, systematic methods to gather evidence that will provide answers to those questions. Three scientific processes underlie nearly all of the research that is done when studying families: description, explanation, and prediction.

Sometimes students comment that the topics and findings of family research seem to be common sense; why do researchers spend time and money studying questions for which the answers seem so obvious? The fact is that conventional wisdom or personal experience is not always an accurate reflection of how things work on a larger scale. Scholarly research that uses established systematic methods to gather evidence is a necessary step to knowing, with a high degree of confidence, how a particular phenomenon looks or works. For example, as rates of nonmarital cohabitation rose in the 1970s and 1980s, the view of many who selected this living arrangement was that it would serve as a "trial" for marriage. By living together before marriage, partners would be able to determine whether they were compatible so that if they married, their marriage would have a greater chance of success than if they had not engaged in cohabitation. Yet, research on cohabitation during this period found that couples who had lived together prior to marriage actually had a higher rate of marital disruption than couples who had not cohabited (Booth and Johnson, 1988)—a finding that strongly contradicted conventional wisdom. This is just one example of why systematic methods of data gathering and analysis are needed to scientifically address issues of relevance to families, despite popular beliefs about how families work. The remainder of this chapter considers a variety of methods used by family researchers.

Descriptive Studies. In family research, descriptive studies focus on compiling accurate accounts of how families live and extensive detail on how they are organized and structured. For example descriptive studies might ask:

- What percent of families live in poverty today?

- How are household chores divided in two-parent families?

- How do stepfamilies differ from first-married two-parent families?

Description asks the key questions: who, what, when, where, how?

Explanatory Studies. Explanatory research builds on descriptive studies by identifying the reasons why certain structures or processes exist:

- Why do wives still perform a greater share of the housework than their husbands even when both are employed outside the home?

- Why is marital conflict troubling for children, even when parents do not divorce?

Understanding the processes and reasons behind certain phenomena makes it possible to try to intervene or change the situation.

Prediction. The purpose of some scientific studies of families is to generate highly accurate predictions about family life. Predictive statements identify likely outcomes associated with various factors. In considering risk factors for divorce, for example, research indicates that a relatively young age at marriage increases a couple's subsequent risk of divorce (Heaton, 1991; South, 1995).

The scientific method is widely used in family research. This method rests on the assumption that society, social relationships (such as those in the family), and human behavior in general can be studied just as other phenomena in fields such as chemistry and physics. A **positivistic** approach to science, which dominates family research today, claims that human and social life are logically ordered and that by applying precise, systematic methods in an objective and consistent way researchers can identify or discover that objective, ordered reality, and the regularities or predictable patterns of behavior and interaction that exist in life (Babbie, 2002). With such information theorists will then be better able to describe and understand our world and gain a sense of predictability about it. A central tenet of positivism is **objectivity**—the belief that research can be conducted in an unbiased, neutral manner and that a researcher's own views will not influence the research process or findings.

Not all family researchers accept the notion of objectivity and the view that the world and social life are orderly and predictable. Therefore, in recent years a number of **post-positivistic** approaches to research have risen in rejection of these views, including feminist, interpretive, and phenomenological approaches. In general, these approaches reject the notion of objectivity and argue that it is impossible for researchers to do their work without being biased by their own personal life experiences and values. In addition, a shared goal of such approaches is to develop a deepened understanding of how individuals interpret and make sense out of their lived experiences. Postpositivists believe that it is impossible to find uniform, predictable patterns of behavior and interaction in a constantly changing world, in a world where individuals are heavily influenced by their unique context and experiences. As Rubin and Rubin (1995, 35) argue, "There is not *one* [emphasis added] reality out there to be measured." Given this view of the world, postpositivists use research methods that are extremely sensitive to context (such as naturalistic observation) and that allow for in-depth consideration of individuals' perceptions and interpretations of events and situations (such as unstructured interviewing). These methods are briefly described in the next section, along with others more often used by researchers who hold a positivistic orientation.

A Sampling of Research Methods

Researchers can address the questions they have about families by using evidence and information that already exists—known as **secondary** data—or by collecting new data—known as **primary** data collection. A distinguishing characteristic of primary data is that the researcher using the data is involved in gathering it. This involvement includes planning what kind of data are to be collected, deciding how they are to be collected, and participating in the actual data-gathering process.

Collecting Primary Data. Family researchers often involve themselves in primary data collection to obtain new information that will help them address a specific research question. Primary data collection can take either an insider or an outsider perspective (Olson, 1977). The insider perspective is largely based on *self-reports*, in which the individuals directly experiencing the situation provide their subjective accounts or report of it. For example, parents may tell a researcher how they discipline their children. The outsider perspective involves someone outside of the situation looking in and trying to report objectively on what is seen in the situation. One example might be a researcher who watches parent-child interaction and records information about the discipline that was observed. Although most studies use only one of these approaches, Olson (1977) argues that family research would benefit from combining the two orientations. The following sections describe several insider approaches, followed by a few outsider methods.

Questionnaires and Surveys. Structured questionnaires are designed and used by family researchers to elicit information on a specific topic, such as parenting, or marital interaction, with a series of questions related to that topic (Babbie, 2002). Generally, along with carefully worded questions, the researcher provides numerous response choices that have been determined from preliminary work. This type of structured data collection is extremely uniform. It is expected that each person will be given the same questions and response choices, in the same order. Consistent with the positivistic approach to science, it is also assumed that each person will interpret the questions in the same way. Researchers have many options for administering surveys and questionnaires, including telephone, mail, in person, and, most recently, e-mail and the Internet.

The term **survey research** is most appropriately limited to primary data collection, using structured questionnaires, from a group of people who represent a larger population of interest. Careful methods (referred to as *sampling methods*) are used to select a group (*sample*) for study that will be representative of (very similar to) the larger population of interest. It is assumed that a well-conducted survey that uses careful sampling methods will produce findings that can be generalized or extended to the larger population of interest. For example, during political campaigns, surveys of registered voters (usually a few hundred or thousand) are taken to determine who is leading in a particular political contest. Although only administered to a portion of the voters, the findings from these surveys are extended to the larger population of registered voters in a particular geographic area.

Interviews. Primary data can also be collected through interviews. In the interviewing process, a researcher asks the questions of interest directly to the study participants, either by telephone or in person. Interviewing can be used to obtain the answers to structured questions, or the researcher can ask open-ended questions that require the participants to respond in their own words rather than with responses from a list of choices provided by the researcher (closed-ended) (Babbie, 2002). Many researchers, particularly postpositivists, believe that open-ended interviewing is a preferable method for capturing individuals' experiences as they were lived and as they were responded to. Through considering the participants' own words, researchers believe that they can more meaningfully assess individuals' actual experiences, perceptions, and feelings, thereby gaining a richer understanding of the phenomenon of interest.

Observation. Observation is a form of data collection that involves a researcher or "outsider" watching the behaviors and listening to the interactions of the individuals of interest rather than asking them direct questions about their experiences. Sometimes individuals are observed without being aware of it. This type of observation, known as **unobtrusive observation,** is the purest "outsider" approach. Typically, such observation is done in public places because of the unrestricted access researchers have to such situations. Amato (1989), for example, observed adult caretakers' interactions with children in public settings (malls, restaurants, and parks) to address several questions about gender differences in caretaking behavior. Through his unobtrusive observations he found that men were more likely to display caretaking behavior with boys than girls, with older than younger children, and in recreational settings rather than other settings. A drawback of the outsider approach is that the observer does not know why such behaviors are engaged in or how people feel and think about them. Often, observational researchers are left to speculate about such issues without solid evidence.

A more common approach used by family researchers who do observational research is to conduct observations in which the individuals of interest know they are being watched and studied (which could affect how they act). This type of

Researchers learn a lot about family behavior just by observing it in public places. Parks, airports, and shopping malls are some of the places utilized for 'unobtrusive observations.'

observation is often structured or set up by the researcher in a laboratory setting. By organizing the setting in a specific way, the researcher can isolate the factors being studied and increase the chances of observing the behavior(s) of interest. The "strange situation," for example, is an observational laboratory procedure used by psychologists to study child-parent attachment relationships. In the strange situation, the laboratory observation room is highly structured: The chairs for the adults (caregiver and a stranger) are arranged in a particular way, the toys that are available for the child are designated by the procedure and arranged in a particular way, and how the actual observation procedure progresses is highly scripted in order to produce increasing discomfort in the child so that the researchers can observe how the child reacts to it and then uses the caregiver to regain comfort and security.

Although structured laboratory observations are widely used in family studies, some researchers question their usefulness. A major concern with highly structured observations is whether the same behaviors would be observed if people were going about their daily lives in a more natural, real-life setting. In response to this concern, an increasing number of family researchers now use **naturalistic observation,** in which individuals and families are observed in naturally occurring settings such as their homes. Vuchinich, Emery, and Cassidy (1988), for example, videotaped dinnertime conversations in the home to assess family conflict processes. One of their findings was that daughters were more likely than sons to intervene in parental disputes. Hochschild (1989) is well known for the observations (and interviews) she made of dual-earner couples negotiating household tasks in their homes at the end of their workdays. (See Chapter 7 for more discussion of her research.) It is generally assumed that observations made in more natural settings are a better reflection of how people really behave and interact than those made in more artificial, structured settings.

Another type of observational research used by family researchers is *participant observation*. This process involves the researcher becoming fully engaged in a relatively long-term relationship with the persons and settings being studied to better understand them (Lofland and Lofland, 1984). Stacy's (1991) book *Brave New Families* describes a variety of new family forms and relationships, distinct from the traditional nuclear family, that emerged in the late twentieth century. Stacy's analysis of these family forms is based on her extensive participant observation, which she describes:

> I accompanied family members to church services and on shopping excursions, hospital visits, and missionary work. I attended a variety of family gatherings and events, occasionally celebratory ones to honor marriages, births, job promotions, or anniversaries. Far more often, however, I found myself witnessing or commiserating over family crises and tragedies, including deaths, severe illnesses, layoffs, evictions, suicide attempts, infidelities, and problems with drugs, alcohol, physical abuse, and the law. (33)

Because of their belief that one's subjective experience is critical to understanding a given situation, postpositivists are likely to use observational techniques that require their full involvement with a particular setting or group of persons. Moreover, observations that permit interaction and discussion (such as unstructured interviewing) with the research participants (such as participant observation and naturalistic observation) are also favored. In contrast, more structured observations, in which the researcher merely observes and records the overt behavior exhibited and then makes interpretations and conclusions based on that "outsider" observation, are more consistent with the positivistic approach to research.

Secondary Data and Analysis. Not all researchers engage in data collection. Often, family researchers have no role in the collection of the data that they analyze. When researchers analyze such data it is known as *secondary data analysis*. Secondary data exist in many forms. One form used extensively by family historians is human documents—written documents that individuals produce in their daily lives, including personal diaries and letters. Such documents are extremely useful for historians because these researchers are unable to go back in time to gather primary data about people who lived long ago. An example of research on human documents is Stone's (1993) study of marital life and marital breakup in seventeenth- to nineteenth-century England. His conclusions about marriage and divorce for that period were heavily based on written courtroom depositions that included accounts from servants who observed their masters' marriages (and sometimes adulterous acts) and husbands' and wives' reports of their own and their spouses' marital behavior. Human documents are also used to study contemporary families. Milkie, Simon, and Powell (1997) examined letters submitted by children to a local newspaper for "Mother of the Year" and "Father of the Year" contests to explore the characteristics that children value most about their parents.

The government and other organizations gather information that is used for a variety of purposes and that may later become secondary data for family researchers. For example, the U.S. Bureau of the Census conducts the national census every ten years to determine legislative representation. The Census Bureau, however, does much more than just count the U.S. population; it also gathers data on the characteristics of U.S. households (household members' ages, race/ethnicity, relationship to one another, income, etc.).

Family researchers access these secondary data to study a variety of family issues and occasionally to inform public policy and programming. The 2000 census, for example, revealed that a greater percentage of U.S. households include grandparents and grandchildren, compared to prior census years (Wright, 2003c). Based on this finding, some states are considering policies and programs aimed at providing economic support and services to this emerging family form.

Some researchers address new research questions and use new analytical methods with data that were previously collected by other researchers. This too is known as secondary data analysis. Generally, the data sets that lend themselves to wide use by many researchers are based on large national surveys (usually involving thousands of participants) that address a broad range of family issues. The National Survey of Families and Households (NSFH) is one study of this kind. Researchers from the University of Wisconsin-Madison designed an extensive survey of over 13,000 adults who were systematically selected from across the entire country. The NSFH has now collected data three times, once in the mid-1980s and again approximately five years and ten years later, from the same individuals and their spouses or cohabiting partners. Because such research efforts are costly and time-consuming, the government agencies that fund such research want the data to be widely disseminated and used so that the study's impact is worth the investment. The amount of knowledge the family field has gained from the NSFH alone is extensive. A recent sampling of articles printed in the top journal for family research, *Journal of Marriage and the Family* (since 2001 titled *Journal of Marriage and Family*) indicated that one of every ten articles published in the journal during the 1990s was based on NSFH data (Milardo, 2000).

Using secondary data like that from the NSFH can be extremely efficient. This is especially true when researchers have questions about how families change over time, either across historical time (How have gender roles in the family changed since the 1970s?), or across their own lifetimes (How does marital satisfaction change over the course of marriage?). To answer such questions, longitudinal data are needed. **Longitudinal data** are gathered from the same group of individuals at more than one point in time (see Figure 1.2). These data allow for a more accurate assessment of change over time than **cross-sectional data,** which include information collected from a sample at only one point in time. Using cross-sectional data, a researcher interested in marital satisfaction over the course of marriage might study a group of couples and compare satisfaction levels for

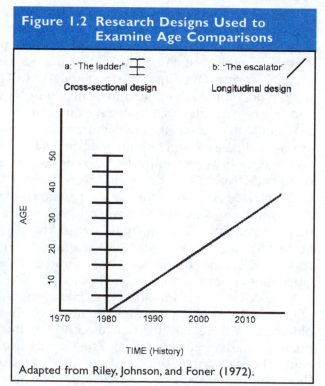

Figure 1.2 Research Designs Used to Examine Age Comparisons

a: "The ladder" Cross-sectional design

b: "The escalator" Longitudinal design

AGE

TIME (History)

Adapted from Riley, Johnson, and Foner (1972).

those married 5, 10, and 20 years. Although this comparison may reveal differences in marital satisfaction for couples of the various marital durations, such differences do not necessarily reflect change patterns. That is, if the couples married for 20 years were found to have higher satisfaction scores than those married for 5 years, the researcher cannot assume that the couples in 5-year marriages will become more satisfied over time. The couples in the 20-year marriages are likely to be those who were happier to begin with, because they are the couples that stayed together over 20 years without divorcing. If these exact couples were to be followed over time (longitudinally) many of the least-satisfied couples among those in the 5-year married group would no longer be together 15 years down the line. Their exclusion from the group would likely raise the average marital satisfaction score for their group over time. This example illustrates that cross-sectional data may not reflect true change over time, which is why longitudinal data are so important in answering many research questions.

Data like the NSFH findings are also beneficial because they save researchers money. Most researchers do not have the financial resources to do a nationwide study of their own, so having access to the NSFH is extremely beneficial. A disadvantage of such data, however, is that secondary researchers are limited to examining the issues and specific questions that were included in the original study. Sometimes this limitation requires that they modify their research questions or adjust the way they would like to examine a particular topic.

Summary

The family can be examined from many perspectives. Our approach adopts two of these, one micro and the other macro. In each of the chapters that follow, the family is studied not only as a small group of people that form an intimate union within a larger social context but also as part of a larger environment, a social institution, in which they act and are studied in the aggregate. The idea that links these two views is the concept of system. Families are small-group systems that exist within larger social systems. We presented many of the concepts from systems theory that aid in understanding family behavior: interrelatedness, interdependence, wholeness, organization, structure, boundaries, stability, homeostasis, equilibrium, adaptability, openness, and feedback. Commitment, consensus, conflict, and communication are processes that occur within small groups that are especially applicable to the study of family systems.

Bronfenbrenner's ecological systems perspective bridges the micro and macro elements of the family by placing family interaction processes within the context of neighborhood, community, and society. The system levels used to construct this bridge are the micro-, meso-, exo-, macro-, and chronosystems of ecological systems theory.

Families are diverse in their structural, racial, and ethnic characteristics, and they all benefit from or are handicapped by their placement within a conflux of systems. Factors associated with diversity (race, ethnicity, class, gender, and sexual preference) affect this placement and therefore must be taken into account when trying to understand how families function and how family members behave. Individuals within families, families within neighborhoods and communities, and communities within a larger society are the systems we want you to understand. These ideas will be developed and integrated into the chapters that follow as you are introduced to salient information derived from research on American families.

There is no preferred or perfect method for studying families. A variety of accepted and established methods exist; which method a researcher uses depends on that researcher's view of the world (e.g., is it orderly and predictable or primarily shaped by unique contexts and situations?), as well as on the particular questions being asked in the study. At this point in your study of families it is important to be aware of these varying perspectives on research and approaches to data collection. As you read the results from studies on families, think about the advantages and disadvantages of collecting information in various ways, how data collection methods may affect the evidence that is collected, and how researchers interpret the evidence they have. All of these issues are central to research on families.

Endnote

1.   "Marriage promise" differs from cohabitation in that it denotes a committed relationship. Cohabitation is often a matter of economic convenience, or a "try" at a relationship. It is often of short duration, and some couples have no intention of making a commitment to each other. Cohabitation will be discussed in Chapter 3.

Chapter Concepts

adaptability: the ability to react to the environment in a way that is favorable to the continued existence of a system.

boundary: something that fixes a limit, or the point or degree to which something extends. Family boundaries are demarked by rules and by common understandings such as who is "in" and who is "out" of the family. Boundaries can be rigid, clear, flexible, or permeable.

chronosystem: the time dimension of a system. The use of this concept permits the measurement of change in social institutions or behaviors.

cohesion: the degree to which family members spend time with each other, enjoy one another's company, work well together, and care for one another.

commitment: an agreement, promise, or pledge; a willingness to give energy and resources to a particular person, group, or activity, and the behavior consistent with such a gift or agreement.

communication: an exchange of information (facts, ideas, beliefs, attitudes, etc.) through speech, writing, and nonverbal gestures.

conjugal unit: a kinship group composed of husband, wife, and children.

consensus: group solidarity of sentiments and beliefs; a general agreement that exists among family members.

cross-sectional data: information collected from a sample at only one point in time.

endogamous: refers to marriages formed by partners of the same group with similar background characteristics.

equilibrium: the tendency to maintain balance in a system—to keep or restore things as they are/were.

exosystem: an environmental system with which individuals do not directly participate but that nevertheless influences them. For example, a change in health care policy by an insurance company will affect all the families and individuals covered by that policy.

extended family: the nuclear family plus other family members, such as in-laws, parents, siblings, cousins, nieces, nephews, and so on.

family: a group of two or more persons related by blood, adoption, marriage, or marriage-promise who live together, or have lived together at one point in time, and who share the expectation and obligation to care and provide for one another.

family of orientation: the family one is born in or adopted into.

family of procreation: the family one establishes through marriage or marriage promise.

feedback: the process through which behavior or information is fed back to its source, or a preceding stage, to affect subsequent behavior. Such information or behavior is called "input" or "output" depending on whether it is entering or leaving the system.

hierarchy: a degree of prestige or esteem that accompanies a place, position, or rank.

homeostasis: a relatively stable state of balance or equilibrium, or a tendency toward such a state. Homeostasis is a process by which members of a family maintain its structure and the internal state necessary for the family's survival in the face of change or disruption in the environment.

interrelatedness and interdependence: the degree of mutual interaction and dependence among members of a system.

longitudinal data: information gathered from the same group of individuals at more than one point in time. These data allow for a relatively accurate assessment of change over time.

macrosystem: the cultural and subcultural components of a social system. The macrosystem includes values, ideologies, norms, laws, and so on.

mesosystem: the interaction that occurs between systems, such as the exchanges between family and school or family and workplace.

microsystem: environmental systems in which individuals participate directly and most immediately, such as family, childcare, occupational settings, and so on.

naturalistic observation: individuals and families are observed in naturally occurring settings such as their homes.

norm: a standard of behavior; a widely accepted and understood rule about how to behave.

nuclear family: two adult partners and their biological or adopted children.

objectivity: the belief that research can be conducted in an unbiased, neutral manner and that a researcher's own views will not influence the research process or findings.

open versus closed system: the degree to which people, information, or resources penetrate a system.

position: a place in a social hierarchy.

positivistic approach: a view of the world asserting that human and social life are logically ordered and that by applying precise, systematic methods in an objective and consistent way researchers can identify or discover that objective, ordered reality and the regularities or predictable patterns of behavior and interaction that exist in life.

postpositivistic approaches: orientations to research and science (such as feminist, interpretive, or phenomenological) that reject the idea of objectivity and the idea that the social world is characterized by patterned regularities. This approach aims to develop a deepened understanding of how individuals interpret and make sense out of their unique lived experiences.

poverty line: a figure calculated by the federal government based on the annual income of families (or unrelated individuals) as a group and the number of people in the group. It is measured by calculating the estimated annual cost of a minimal food budget designated by the U.S. Department of Agriculture and multiplied by 3. In 2004 a family of four with a total family income below $18,725 lived below the poverty line.

poverty spell: a (short) period of time in which a family lives in poverty.

primary data: newly collected information that the researcher was directly involved in gathering.

propinquity: being in close physical proximity; nearness.

role: the expected behavior associated with a specific position.

secondary data: existing information that is used by researchers but that they had no role in collecting.

social class: a ranking or stratification system associated with the distribution of valued resources such as wealth, power, or prestige within a social structure.

social institution: a stable set of positions, roles, rules, values, norms, statuses, and expectations that define a subset of behaviors associated with a specified unit of society, such as religion, politics, recreation, or education.

social system: a behavioral system—an organized set of behaviors of persons interacting with each other; the totality of social institutions within a given society.

status hierarchy: a set or series of places or positions ranked according to some standard; often associated with the distribution of power within a system.

stimulus input/stimulus output exchanges: *see* feedback.

structure: something that is made up of interdependent parts with a definite pattern of organization.

subsystem: subgroups of family members within a family system. Three subsystems are recognized: spousal, parent-child, and sibling.

survey research: most appropriately limited to primary data collection, using structured questionnaires, from a group of people who represent a larger population of interest.

system: a configuration of parts that are in a dynamic relation of interdependency.

unobtrusive observation: observations conducted without the awareness of the persons being observed. They typically are done in public settings.

value: an abstract idea; a standard or criterion for guiding action that infers a commitment to a highly esteemed or honored object or idea.

wholeness: the idea that the family as a group has its own identity and is more than the sum of the individual members.

Suggested Activities

1. Choose a motion picture or novel containing a story line that revolves around a "family secret" (e.g., *Inventing the Abbots, Secrets and Lies, Long Day's Journey into Night, Who's Afraid of Virginia Woolf?*). In a short essay interpret how family boundaries are evident as members try to keep the "secret."

2. Think about the concept of family structure. Write a short essay detailing how differences in family structure might be reflected in family behavior. For example, how would family interaction be different in a family with seven children compared to a family with only two? How might family behaviors be influenced by a divorce, when one person leaves the household? How might remarriage change family interaction patterns? Save your essay and later in the course compare your "speculations" in this essay with the chapter information that deals with these topics.

Suggested Readings

Demo, D. H., Allen, K. R., and Fine, M. (eds.). 2000. *Handbook of Family Diversity.* New York: Oxford University Press.

Franklin, D. L. 1987. *Ensuring Inequality: The Structural Transformation of the African American Family.* New York: Oxford University Press.

Mintz, S., Kellogg, S. 1988. *Domestic Revolutions: A Social History of American Family Life.* New York: Free Press.

Rubin, L. B. 1994. *Families on the Fault Line: America's Working Class Speaks About the Family, the Economy, Race, and Ethnicity.* New York: HarperCollins.

Thorndike, J. J., Jr. 1976. *The Very Rich: A History of Wealth.* New York: American Heritage/Bonanza Books. ✦

Chapter 2

Commitment

To Self, Family, Community

Did You Know?

- In terms of self-concept, does it surprise you that famous, talented, or wealthy individuals do not always feel confident of themselves or their abilities? Here is what actress Halle Berry remarked after receiving an Academy Award for Best Actress in 2001:

    I never expect people to like [a film]. . . . After I finish a project I say, Okay, how am I going to defend this? What am I going to say when they say they hate this? I wish I weren't that way.

    —Halle Berry, 2002

- Some states have created a new type of legal marriage, called *covenant marriage*. The legislation in one such state, Louisiana, reads:

    We do solemnly declare that marriage is a covenant between a man and a woman who agree to live together as husband and wife for so long as they both may live. We understand the nature, purpose, and responsibilities of marriage. We have read the Covenant Marriage Act, and we understand that a Covenant Marriage is for life. If we experience marital difficulties, we commit ourselves to take all reasonable efforts to preserve our marriage, including counseling. With full knowledge of what this commitment means, we do hereby declare that our marriage will be bound by Louisiana on Covenant Marriage, and we renew our promise to love, honor, and care for one another as husband and wife for the rest of our lives. (House Bill No. 756, State of Louisiana, 1997, New Louisiana Covenant Marriage Law)

    Arizona and Arkansas passed similar legislation.

- How many Americans do you suppose give their time to community activities? A recent national survey found that 56 percent of adults in the United States report doing occasional volunteer work in their communities (Independent Sector, 1999).

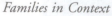

Things to Think About

- What was the very first "lesson" (in manners, dress, etiquette, whatever) that you remember your parent(s) teaching you? Do you still follow that teaching?

- Have you ever made a conscious decision to change your behavior, your attitude, or your outlook? Why did you want to make that change?

- Imagine what a society would be like if there were no common rules, laws, and normative behaviors that everyone must abide by (e.g., obeying traffic lights, honoring others' private property, etc.).

- Evaluate this decree that comes from one of the oldest sets of laws discovered by archeologists in the area of ancient Babylon, The Code of Hammurabi, written in the 18th Century B.C., which had this to say about commitment:

  > If a man's wife be surprised having intercourse with another man, both shall be tied and thrown into the water, but the husband may pardon his wife and the king his slaves. (#129)

The Importance of Commitment

In this chapter **commitment** is the concept we use to bridge the otherwise separate entities of individual personality or self, the attachment of that self to a group of intimate others we call a family, and the behavior of families within the larger environment (community, society) in which they live. Without commitment, marriages would not endure. Without commitment, the socialization of children (and hence their self-development) would not take place. Without commitment, neighborhoods and communities would not be able to provide the services and activities that make life satisfying for families and enhance their well-being.

The most important and necessary ingredient for the maintenance and survival of a marriage and a family relationship is the desire of family members to commit to each other and to stay in the relationship. At first glance, this statement seems self-evident. We form a marriage partnership and create a family because we want to be together. Further, although none of us chooses our biological parents, most people are glad they belong to the family they were born into and go to great lengths to stay attached to that family.[1] Although commitment is necessary for a marriage/family to survive, this concept receives scant attention in most family textbooks. Perhaps that is because it is so salient that authors don't see the need to discuss it. Without the desire to make and maintain a commitment, family relationships would be ephemeral.

In our view, knowing that a commitment is an agreement to "be there" (or "not there") is insufficient for a true understanding of this important aspect of family life. Rather, we believe that knowledge of the processes by which commitments develop, grow, and diminish is essential for understanding both the beginning and ending of relationships. Further, whether one places a high or low value on commitment, such a value is learned behavior, and it originates in small groups, called **primary groups,** such as the family.[2] Understanding the family's influence on the development of commitment provides

'Diamonds are forever' is a well-known slogan, but can we say the same of the marriages that put a diamond on the bride's finger? This couple married in the 1930s and remained together for over 50 years, until the bride died. Only about one in two couples can expect to have a lifelong marriage in 2004.

insight into a wide variety of individual and family behaviors. Because agreeing to make a commitment is the foundation for the establishment of a family, we will discuss this aspect of commitment again in Chapter 3 when we explore the behaviors that bring people to the point of coupling—that is, dating, mate selection, cohabitation, and marriage. Further, after a commitment is made, it must be continually reinforced to maintain ties to the chosen relationship, or it will not last. Separation and divorce are a consequence of diminished commitment. These processes are the subjects of Chapter 8.

In this chapter the meaning of commitment at the individual level—associated with the emergence of a "self" and the ways a person develops a position or place within a network of other individuals—is explained. Expressed another way, we show how personal relationships are grounded in the process of personality development. People learn "who they are" vis-à-vis their relationships with others. We discuss the formation of the self, examine how the self is related to "identities" and "self-esteem," and elaborate on how the self, identities, and self-esteem develop through processes of socialization. We admit that the linking of commitment to personality development and the emergence of the self is a relatively new idea (Adams, 1999) and may be challenged. However, we adopt it because it is a device that allows us to incorporate into the same discussion the self-development processes that place individuals at the center of their family and the processes that place the family at the center of the larger community. Emphasizing the contribution of commitment to the self and the family expands the discussion at the microsystem level. Unless members are committed to the family group, consensus is difficult to achieve, and shared understandings are unlikely to develop. At the meso- and exosystem levels, some degree of commitment on the part of residents to their neighborhoods and communities is necessary in order for society to function.

Commitment to Self

What exactly do we mean by "commitment"? As is true with most complex concepts, commitment is defined by family scholars in a number of ways. Here are three that are frequently used. Gecas (1980) defines commitment as the willingness of social actors to *give energy and resources* to a particular course of action. (Paul writes a check for $50 to his favorite environmental cause; Maria works every other weekend each spring with a group of activists to pick up trash along the streams and creeks in her county; Peter is arrested for protesting the policies of the World Health Organization.) Tallman and his colleagues (1991) define commitment as a *promise*—as a desire or obligation to remain in and maintain a relationship over time. ("With this ring I thee wed . . ."; a nun takes a vow of chastity, promising her love and service to a higher being rather than a mortal one.) Becker (1960) places commitment within an economic framework. He defines it in terms of behaviors (which he calls side-bets) that are based on a person's *assessment of costs and rewards*. (Debra and Roger invest all their savings in a country home that they both dearly love. Subsequently, an office flirtation is stifled because it could not only jeopardize the relationship but might ultimately mean having to move from the home.) We can combine these ideas to conceptualize commitment as an agreement, pledge, or behavior that involves a willingness to give something to, or take action toward, other people, objects, goals, or groups and whose basis may at times be built on perceived costs and/or rewards.

A commitment to others—or to something beyond the individual—is difficult to make if there is not first a commitment to the self. In our analysis, **self** is defined as a combination of physical, mental, emotional, and psychological aspects of an individual that create a unique personality. Gecas and Burke (1995) link self to commitment by defining commitment in terms of a *set of self-meanings* that are relatively stable over time. They argue that a person's behavior results from these self-meanings. The notion of looking at commitment to the self in terms of self-meanings was first put forward by Stryker and Serpe in 1982. These social psychologists link self-meanings and commitment in terms of the degree to which a person's relationships with others depend on his or her being a particular kind of person—for example, loyal, truthful, beautiful, rational, brave, emotional. For example, Lois is known in her neighborhood and among her friends as a "saint" because she is always looking out for the welfare of others. In this view, commitment to certain behaviors (which in totality constitute a "self") that others learn to know and expect is the web that binds people to their friends, colleagues, parents, and partners.

It follows that commitment to self leads to a degree of behavioral *congruity* that others come to depend on (Burke and Reitzes, 1991). This interpretation is important because it stresses the importance of social networks to the formation of the self, identities, and commitments. Thus, commitment to one's self and self-meanings implies being tied to a *network of relationships*. Accordingly, commitment can be understood by focusing on (a) how many people there are in a person's social network, (b) how important these people are to the person, (c) how intertwined everybody is, and (d) what they expect from the person. It is within one's social networks of family, friendships, and so on, that self-meanings are first formed. Social networks influence how individuals behave. Behaviors, values, attitudes, and sentiments create a conception of who one is—one's self-meanings, or *sense of self*. Self-meanings are the source of subsequent behaviors, including the commitments one makes.

Adding the idea of congruity (relatively stable and compatible behaviors that are enacted to meet the expectations of people in one's social networks) to the previous ideas, we define a **commitment to self** as the sum of forces, pressures, or drives that influence people to maintain congruity between their identity in a particular situation and their perceptions of the impression others form of them (Burke and Reitzes, 1991, 243). This commitment includes the will to give time, energy, and resources to a particular course of action or to particular people, objects, goals, or groups.

Identities

A concept closely associated with commitment to the self is **identities.** Identities are a composite of the behaviors, attitudes, and moods individuals adopt and the various meanings they attach to themselves and to others (Gecas and Burke, 1995). Identities influence how one labels oneself and how others label one at any given time and place (this specificity is why people have more than one identity). Identities help establish one's place in the social structure. For example, a star athlete on the high school basketball team may think of himself as generous, gregarious, and self-confident (self-identity). His fellow classmates talk about his team spirit, leadership on the court, and willingness to share the ball with his teammates (others' labels). These "self" and "other" assessments reinforce one another and serve to place this athlete securely within the top echelon of high school popularity (social placement).

How do self and identities differ? Whereas self refers to a combination of physical, mental, emotional, and psychological aspects of a person, identities represent the ways that "self" is located in relation to other people. Identities refer to the processes by which people place themselves in a network of social relationships. But a person cannot do this alone: Social placement involves the active participation of all others with whom the person interacts. The self comes to be defined by behaving in consistent and anticipated ways that those in one's **social network** come to expect. When the high school basketball athlete is rewarded by the coach for his teamwork and leadership on the court, his opinion of himself is reinforced.

Because identities are a composite of the various behaviors, attitudes, and moods influencing how we label ourselves, and how others label us, they vary with time and from situation to situation. This is why they are seen as a *social product*. Further, even though identities are distinguishable from the feelings we have about our personal value or worth (our self-esteem), what we think of ourselves plays a vital part in influencing the way we go about establishing and revising our identities.

An important aspect of identities is the expectation of consistency that allows individuals to assume they know themselves and other people. This knowledge permits people to make reasonable predictions about their own and others' behavior with a minimum of concern and ambiguity. Of course, identities are not necessarily permanent; events happen to people that change their identities. For example, an automobile accident can dramatically disfigure or disable a teenager, causing a change in behavior, attitudes, and moods. A woman's husband may leave her for a much younger woman, stripping her of her valued identity as wife. Alternatively, people may decide to make fundamental changes in themselves that will alter their identity: for example, an obese man might take action to lose weight, or a housewife might go back to school to complete a degree. The consequences of these actions bring about changes in their social networks, self-meanings, and self-concepts. To quote Tallman:

For most of us identities are never complete, but are always in the process of changing. We view ourselves as products of the past with a transitory present and a probabilistic future. Thus, although we may cling almost desperately to some aspects of our identity, in other aspects we anticipate change. Identity, then, has a temporal dimension. At any time our identities include the past, present, and future. These "tenses of the self" (Gordon, 1968) allow us to see ourselves in process and transition. Our identity includes who we were, who we are now, and who we think we will be. Like all aspects of identity, the tenses of the self cannot be created in isolation, but are products of interactions with others. (1976, 91)

Any one of several identities may be called upon depending on the person's social situation. Does a teenager decide not to get into a car driven by a friend who has been drinking heavily because she remembers her parents' admonitions (dutiful daughter identity)? Or does she hop in the backseat and hope for the best so her friends don't think she's a dork (cool kid identity)? An important dimension that determines which identity is invoked in any particular situation is **identity salience.** According to some writers (McCall and Simmons, 1966; Thoits, 1992) various identities are ranked hierarchically within the conception of self, and any one is more or less likely to be invoked depending on the situation. Identity salience is important when considering family-related behavior because it helps predict behavior and explains a person's choices. For example, why does Joe bother to arrange to switch his work schedule so he can attend his son's soccer games two afternoons a week during the summer months? Such behavior is an indication that Joe's identity as a parent is more salient than his identity as an employee who works an eight-to-five schedule. Or consider Jamilah, who sees it as her role to care for her aging mother stricken with Alzheimer's rather than institutionalize her. To fulfill this role she must move back to her childhood hometown, quitting a satisfying job. Jamilah's loving daughter identity is more salient than her occupational identity.

The Development of Identities, the Self, and Self-Meanings

The idea of the "self" was first discussed in the social psychological literature by the philosopher William James (1892). He made the point that each of us has many selves. Each role we play in a group is a different self; therefore, we have as many selves as we have roles to play. James's idea was that a significant segment of personality is rooted in interactions with others via role relationships.

Had James been writing about the notion of people's many selves at the end of the twentieth century instead of the nineteenth, he might have referred to people's many identities. As individuals grow older and begin to interact with a wider variety of people—teachers, peers, friends, enemies, strangers—they learn to enact a wider range of behaviors, selectively chosen depending on the circumstances. In the presence of parents one might not use the same swear words used with one's friends; in school one may behave differently in front of girls than in front of boys. In adolescence this "trying on" of different identities is expected, and the personality traits that are most lasting and permanent are those that are reinforced or that provide the most satisfaction. The development of who one is—one's self and one's self-meanings—is linked to a network of relationships and the roles and expectations that exist within one's family, community, subculture, and society.

The interdependence between the individual, the family, and the larger society is revealed through the development of an individual **self-concept** (the beliefs, attitudes, knowledge, and ideas an individual has about himself or herself). According to Charles Cooley and George Herbert Mead, the self and society are two sides of the same coin. The self can develop only in a social milieu, and the social milieu is made up of the many selves that live within it. These theorists suggest that the growth and development of the self results from the process of *interpersonal communication* within the social environment. Individuals share feelings and ideas through the *mental images* they form of one another and their communications, both verbal and nonverbal, of those images. Particularly important is how people perceive the ways in which others see them. Whether a person is pleased or disappointed with his or her appearance or behavior is a result of whether others are seen to be approving or disapproving. Charles Cooley (1902) calls this aspect of the self the **looking-glass self.** A classic example of this concept occurred during the 1979 Academy Awards ceremony when Sally Fields received an Oscar for Best Actress in *Norma Rae.* As she clutched her award, her jubilant response "This means you like me, you really, really like me!" brought laughter, but it clearly illustrated the link between her sense of self and her need for approval from the academy voters.

Cooley's looking-glass self has three essential elements: the *imagination of the self to another*; an imagination of the other person's *judgment* about the self; and some sort of *self-feeling* accompanying that judgment. This reflective process involves the mental processes of perceiving, attributing, judging, and then feeling—pride, shame, embarrassment, joy, and so on. How does this process play out? Here is an example: "I think I look really great in the new dress I bought for my first day on the job. As I walk in the door I think, oh my God, my boss thinks my skirt is way too short. I'm so embarrassed." The self develops as a result of this reflective process over the course of a lifetime. Because a person's first "looking glass" rests within the family environment, we elaborate on the relevance of Cooley's concept in the section on family socialization processes.

George Herbert Mead (1934), one of the first writers to discuss the self, noted that a self does not exist at birth; it comes into existence as people learn to view themselves from the point of view of others. Human beings have the capacity to assume another's role and in their mind see the self from the other's perspective. Mead called this **taking the role of the other.** When an individual can take the role of the other and *see the self as an object* like any other object in the environment (e.g., a toy, bottle, mother, crib), the individual self has emerged. This means one can see oneself through another's eyes, judge one's own behavior according to what one sees and interprets from their reactions, and behave accordingly. Like Cooley, Mead saw the self as a product of social processes, developed through thinking, language, communication, and the ability to take the role of others in the community. Note that this concept of taking the role of the other differs from the everyday use of putting yourself in others' shoes and "feeling their pain," so to speak. Mead is explicit in emphasizing that his definition of taking the role of the other means to *see the self as an object*, as one of many objects in the social environment.

When does this process begin? According to Mead, it begins very early. When the hungry infant sees his mother approaching with a bottle (or breast) and stops crying, he can already imagine the relief from hunger that will soon follow. By associating the bottle, the mother, and the pleasure of the milk, he sees him*self* as soon to be satisfied. He is beginning the process of seeing himself as an object, differentiated within the environment of other objects including bottle, milk, and mother. However, the self-formation process only starts in infancy. Mead outlined how it develops throughout childhood.

Mead's theory of the development of the self centers on language development as the child learns the meanings of symbols, gestures, and social stimuli that make up the content of a particular language. That is, using our earlier example, the objects of bottle and milk and the gestures of mother are imbued with symbolic meaning. Barring physical impairment of the child (lack of sight or hearing), all social stimuli begin to take on meaning and value from birth onward. The music played when the child is put down to sleep, the barking of a dog, smiles and coos and sounds of familiar voices, a favorite blanket or pacifier—as these sounds, behaviors, and objects take on meaning the child begins the process of learning roles (her own and those of others) and in turn cognitively associates these roles with specific behaviors, responses, moods, attitudes, and so on.

Initially, learned roles are limited, and they must become organized in the child's mind in such a way that she is able to "pretend" to play them. Mead calls this the **play stage.** Two-year-old Megan goes to her father's underwear drawer and puts all his jockey shorts over her head, surrounding her neck up to her nose. She comes out to announce proudly to her parents and their dinner guests, "I'm Daddy." Indeed she does look like she has a bushy beard just like her father. When a child goes beyond the ability to assume one role and puts meaning and action into a number of roles at the same time, he or she has progressed to the second stage of the development of the self, the **game stage.** Mead used the example of the baseball game to illustrate this stage, when knowing the rules is a requisite. When a player comes up to take a turn at bat, she knows what the consequences of a hit to left field means; what the situation "two strikes, three balls" means; the difference between a fair and a foul ball; and what the jobs (roles) of the positions of umpire, coach, pitcher, and catcher are and what each will do under specific conditions, according to the rules.

The final stage of the development of the self is reached when a child (usually by now a teenager) understands all the roles that are played out within the community (storekeeper, police officer, movie manager, priest) and the larger society (president of the nation, sports hero, etc.). The rules (or laws) of the community/society have been learned and, hopefully, *internalized*—incorporated as part of the self.[3] This is the stage of the **generalized other.**

By the time children are in middle childhood they have learned the game rules and are well on their way to learning the rules and norms of their community.

This term encompasses the larger social and cultural environments in which the child lives. By the time individuals reach adulthood they have had experience with a wide range of rules and roles, understand how the rules and roles are organized and enacted (at least cognitively, if not in actuality), and know the behavioral expectations and meanings associated with role relationships (for roles always have a reciprocal content). In Mead's terms, the self is fully emerged.

We can add that as the self progresses through these stages of development, the self-concept emerges, which we previously defined as the beliefs, attitudes, knowledge, and ideas an individual has about himself or herself. A related concept—**self-esteem**—involves an *evaluation* of the traits, abilities, characteristics, and so on that one possesses. Self-esteem is a personal judgment of worthiness based on an assessment of the degree that one is (in)capable, (in)significant, (un)successful, or (de)valued (Meese, 1997). Such judgments come from past relationships and the reactions of others, and they help individuals predict how others will react to them in the future. Have you ever wondered why one friend continues to deny his potential for excelling in a particular activity, why another doesn't believe others who tell her she is attractive, or another intends to marry a woman who constantly belittles him and puts him down? It is as if they need to hear they aren't good enough to compete, have bad looks, or are socially inept. In line with the ideas of Cooley and Mead, *self-verification theory* (Swann, 1990) suggests that people with negative self-concepts have a strong desire to have their mental picture of themselves verified by others. This is true regardless of whether the information they receive is positive or negative. Swann, Hixon, and De La Ronde (1992) conducted a study supporting this idea. They predicted and found that research participants who held the most positive self-concepts were more committed to their marriage when their spouses thought well of them. Participants who held negative self-concepts, on the other hand, were more committed to their marriage when their spouses thought poorly of them, (i.e., rated them lower on measures of intellectual capability, physical attractiveness, social skills, etc.).

How was this anomaly explained? Consistent with Cooley and Mead, Swann and his colleagues assumed that the "key to social relations is the capacity for people to recognize how others perceive them" (118). When people's social relations in the past have been more negative than positive and a negative view of the self has crystallized, they tend to seek and embrace partners who validate their negative self-image and commit themselves to persons who think poorly of them. They look for support for their self-concept. For both men and women, self-verification is more important (and psychologically easier) than trying to accept a new view of the self. Swann et al. sees this situation as negative crossfire between a desire for positive feedback and a desire for self-verifying feedback (120).

Adams (1999) sums up the importance of the process that links the development of the self to ties with others: "An individual's capacity to commit to personal relationships is grounded in the process of personality development" (514). That is, developing the ability to commit to another is concomitant with the development of the self.

From the perspective of the family, the most important factor associated with identities, the self, self-concept, and self-esteem is that their development begins with the very first interactions between infant and caretaker(s), within a family, among parents and siblings. Much of the behavior incorporated in these interactions is called *socialization*.

Socialization: The Creation of Identities and the Self

Elder (1968) provides one of the most general definitions of socialization, referring to it as the process through which a human being becomes a functioning member of society. **Socialization** is a process that occurs throughout the life span as individuals assume new roles (parent, worker, grandparent, retiree), but in this chapter we focus on the socialization of children.

Socialization involves the transmission of traditions, knowledge, and values of a culture. It involves learning the skills necessary for successfully achieving the tasks associated with each of life's developmental stages. **Developmental stages** are periods in an individual's life that are crucial in that person's development. Not necessarily based on age, but often closely related to it, a stage is a time for growth and development; a time when new behaviors are learned. For example, kindergartners are expected to be toilet trained, parents and other role models are expected to help adolescents learn to take responsibility for their sexual behavior, and retirees are encouraged to develop new interests to take the place of their former work-related behaviors. Each stage is qualitatively different from the last one and reflects the adoption of more mature behaviors. **Developmental tasks** include the roles, norms, and behaviors all family members are expected to accomplish as they age and move through developmental stages. Learning to use the toilet is a developmental task for a toddler; selecting and preparing for a vocation is a developmental task for an adolescent. Socialization ensures that appropriate learning takes place, ideally at the appropriate ages, and takes into account a vast number of experiences. We summarize these ideas with the following definition: ". . . socialization is the sum total of ways people learn from a variety of sources what is expected of them and how they can deal most effectively with others in society" (Tallman, 1976, 150). In Elder's (1968) terms, it means to become a functioning member of society.

Within any given society, **socialization agents** (parents, teachers, religious leaders, bosses, supervisors) are assigned the responsibility of teaching the values and norms of the culture and the behaviors that are expected of individuals as they move through life. The family is the first of many institutions that socialize a child. Educational and religious institutions, a variety of other formal and informal organizations, teachers, peers, and other individuals soon begin to add their influence (Boy/Girl Scouts, soccer coaches, debate clubs, etc.). However, it is the family that first sets the child on a course to grow up to be an adult who adopts (or not) the values of the larger society: to be a citizen who votes, who carries on cultural traditions, fulfills personal potential, or contributes to the community and society's goals. It is in the family that children first learn to assess and evaluate their looks, incorporate or reject their family's values, and learn (or fail to learn) to recognize and take advantage of opportunities. (What did you answer to the question at the beginning of this chapter about the first "lesson" you learned from your parents?)

Within the family context both children and adults continue to grow and change their behaviors, attitudes, and outlooks, while urging other family members to accept a new conception of themselves. How many examples of this process can you think of? Do you know a 13-year-old who came home from a sleepover with her hair dyed green? A 19-year-old who hid his new tattoo from his mother? A mother who decided to go back to college and posted a new "housekeeping schedule" on the refrigerator for all to follow? Think back on the question set forth in the "Things to Think About" section of this chapter. What did you come up with when you thought about personal change? What were your friends and family's reactions?

The socialization that takes place in families is reciprocal, meaning that family members socialize each other in multiple ways throughout the life of the family (Gallagher and Gerstel, 2001; Glass et al., 1986). One example comes from a study that looked at which parental behaviors are correlated with children's self-esteem. When Demo and his colleagues (1987) examined a variety of family variables, they found that family conflict, parental support, parental disciplinary techniques, acceptance by family members, family communication, participation in joint activities, and shared family satisfaction were all influential factors associated with adolescent self-esteem. Of these, positive parent-child communication and frequent shared family activities were the two most important variables associated with high self-esteem. However, these same factors were also related to parents' self-esteem. Especially fathers' self-esteem was higher if they perceived that they received support from, and could communicate with, their sons and daughters.

Gender Socialization

One of the most salient identities a person negotiates is his or her status as a male or female, and this identity begins first within the family context. Parenting is seldom a gender-neutral endeavor. A child's first observation of gender roles occurs in the family (for example, in traditionally gendered families men mow the lawn, take care of the car, and take out the trash, while women clean bathrooms, iron clothes, and shop for the kids' clothes). The parents' perception of their child as male or female begins at birth—or even before, if the sex of the fetus is known. The name given a child at birth labels it as male or female, with few exceptions. (In 1969 Johnny Cash had a hit song, "A Boy Named Sue," that described the consequences of incongruous gender naming.) In addition to naming, the clothing chosen for the child, the way parents talk to a child, how they play together, and the attributions they make about behavior all involve a gendered attitude toward the child (Crouter, Manke, and McHale, 1995).

Studies that look at the actual behaviors of parents toward children have had mixed results. According to Peterson and Rollins (1987), female infants receive more attention, vocalization, and smiles from mothers, and males receive more vocalization and stimulation from fathers. Older boys receive less support, higher levels of punishment, and more coercion from parents than older girls do. The differential treatment of children based on their sex has been a topic of study since a seminal book by Maccoby and Jacklin in 1974. After a thorough review of the extant literature, these psychologists found only a few differences in child-rearing practices. Principal among these were that boys received more physical stimulation and encouragement (as infants), were punished more frequently, and received more praise and encouragement for gender-appropriate behaviors and more discouragement of cross-gendered behavior than girls did.

Recent reviews of the child-rearing literature continue to find "few patterns of consistent sex-determined socialization practices by parents" (Peterson et al., 2000, 91). Parents do foster the adoption of gendered behaviors in their children in subtle ways, such as by the decor of the child's bedroom, the Barbie doll or the Mega-Super Action toy given on birthdays, or dance versus Tae Kwon-do lessons. But such parental behaviors are often based on the child's individuality and his or her interests and preferences more than on his or her sex (Fagot, 1995). It is hard to disentangle innate from learned preferences. For example, son Miguel's first word (sound) is "ball," and at seven months he holds a rubber ball and throws it strong and straight with great delight. His father begins to think of future basketball in the backyard, and buys a small hoop and hooks it on the back of a dining room chair.

As a child matures, household responsibilities assigned to boys and girls are clearly gendered. As we will discuss in Chapter 7, girls are expected to assume traditionally female household chores (doing the dishes, doing laundry, shopping, and taking care of young siblings), while the tasks assigned to boys include doing yardwork, removing snow, taking out the trash, and washing the car. Family socialization involving the production of gender-typed behaviors led Berk (1985) to refer to the family as a *gender factory.*

In addition to the family, other social institutions follow the cultural paths that differentiate males from females. Hospitals foster the gender identification of infants in the way they cap and wrap newborn girls and boys with different colors—some continue to use

Gender socialization begins at very young ages for both boys and girls.

pink for girls and blue for boys, traditional sex-linked colors. Toymakers develop different kinds of toys for boys and girls. Even Legos, toys that seem gender neutral, are made in either bold primary colors or soft pastels. Walk into a toy store and rediscover the way boy and girl toys are displayed, or look at a mail-order toy catalog. Other early socialization environments may include childcare settings, play groups, or religious centers.

At the societal level, socialization into gender identification has been associated with negative outcomes. When a rigid system of conceptualizing appropriate gender roles becomes institutionalized it can result in sexual discrimination. Consider the following examples:

- The daughter of President Lyndon Johnson, Luci Baines Johnson, was refused admission to Georgetown University's school of nursing after her marriage in 1966 because the school did not permit married women to be students.

- Swimmer Donna de Varona could not obtain a college swimming scholarship after winning two gold medals in the 1964 Olympics. Scholarships were not awarded to women.

- In 1972 a Connecticut judge commented, "Athletic competition builds character in our boys. We do not need that kind of character in our girls." (Title IX: 25 Years of Progress, 1997)

In 1972 the Education Amendments Act Title IX was passed by Congress. This law mandated that "no person in the U.S. shall, on the basis of sex be excluded from participation in, or denied the benefits of, or be subjected to discrimination under any educational program or activity receiving federal aid" (Title IX: 25 Years of Progress, 1997). The law pertains to a wide range of educational activities, including admission standards and women's participation in athletics. Vocational education was addressed in 1976 when the Vocational Act of 1963 was amended to eliminate sex bias, stereotyping, and discrimination in vocational education. There are still many instances of sex discrimination in American society and there is much work left to do to ensure equal opportunity, but there is no denying that a great deal of progress has been made since Title IX was passed.

Before Title IX was enacted, fewer than 300,000 high school girls played competitive sports. By 2002, that number was more than 2.8 million.

To summarize, it is through the continuous process of negotiated interpersonal interactions with others within a person's environment that the self is created and re-created. Interpersonal interactions are characterized by resistance, acceptance, struggle, cooperation, conflict, and compliance. They make up what are called socialization processes that involve the teaching and learning of cultural and subcultural values, attitudes, and behaviors. In most societies there is a developmental timetable for self-development and status passage throughout the entire lifetime. This timetable is usually based on age, sex, or family status, but it can be altered by unique biological and personality characteristics (such as mental, physical, or medical disability or precocious talent). This cultural timetable structures the pace and pattern of development through infancy, childhood, adolescence, adulthood, and old age. Children are shaped at different ages by specific socialization practices and specific socialization agents (Hagestad and Neugarten, 1985). Socialization experiences across other stages of the life span will be discussed in Chapter 5 when we address parenting and in Chapter 6 when we consider aging family members.

Commitment to Family

As mentioned earlier, interpersonal commitment reflects the desire to devote energy and resources to a particular relationship and to see that relationship continue. The survival of any marriage and family depends on adult members' determination to remain within its boundaries (the "family circle") and to expend resources in order to feed, clothe, and house its members. A family will not survive unless its members are willing to work to maintain its viability. In a married family, spouses are the most important of these members; for other types of families (cohabiting adults, gay or lesbian parents, three-generation households, or single-parent homes) the principal adult caregivers are the most important.

The Commitment of Children

The role of children in the family is a complex one with regard to commitment. Infants and young children are heavily dependent—emotionally and physically—on their caretakers to provide a secure and nurturing environment in which they can thrive. As children approach adolescence the developmental tasks they face require that they lessen this dependency and increase their capacity to be autonomous and independent (Erikson, 1968). In our society most children eventually establish their individual identities and modify their commitment to their family of orientation. Author Kathleen Norris describes the route she took in this process:

> By the time I was 15, I was turning to poems and rock-and-roll lyrics for spiritual sustenance. I was looking for help on my quest to forge my own identity out of the raw materials of family and inheritance, and poems and song lyrics expressed the things I longed to say but could not articulate. (Norris, 2001, 36)

Parents and children begin this process of loving yet "letting go" at a relatively young age. When children live in the household, a family is constantly challenged to open its boundaries, to increase the permeability of the family circle. Children's activities—childcare, school, organized community activities, part-time work, volunteer activities—bring strangers, friends, neighbors, teachers or other school personnel, and sometimes medical or police personnel to the doorstep. This exposure, this entry across the threshold, potentially or in fact threatens the ability of family members to maintain the family as they know it at the time (homeostasis), and in the process, exposure to outside influences may weaken the commitment of family members. Teenagers, by virtue of their growth and development, add peer influence to the authority and influence of their parents. They work in jobs outside the family that expose them to people and experiences that parents do not know about (and might not approve of, should they find out). These influences, both positive and negative, are strong or weak depending on the teen, the family environment, and the effectiveness of the family's socialization processes. But they are necessary for youths to achieve independence from the family. This gradual withdrawal and emerging autonomy is viewed as normal and is usually approved of by parents (even though they may bemoan the "teenage years"). The interdependence among family members forces parents to change as adolescents change. More will be said of this in Chapters 5 and 6 when we discuss parent-child relations at different stages.

Note that the changing commitment to the family in which one is born does not always follow the normative path. Examples may come to your mind of friends or relatives who never left their parents' home or who stayed in such close contact with parents after their marriages that their spouses became frustrated by the perceived interference of their in-laws. This is not a new phenomenon. A noteworthy example is evident in the life of the English philosopher John Ruskin. His marriage to Effie Gray was annulled in 1854 after six years of an unconsummated marriage. Much of the trouble, according to Effie, was that John could not cut the ties to his parents. According to one biographer, "The elder Ruskins were determined to get rid of her in order to have John to themselves. On the afternoon of New Year's Day 1854, she and John visited his parents [where the three] planned a trip abroad in which she was not included" (Rose, 1983, 83–84). You can read the advice columns of "Dear Abby" or "Annie's Mailbox" to get up-to-date examples of such behavior.

Remarriage and the formation of a stepfamily is a situation in which the establishment of family commitment may be difficult to achieve. One reason is that family relationships are strongly interdependent. The noted psychologist Kurt Lewin wrote over 50 years ago: "Every move of one member will, relatively speaking, deeply affect the other members" (1948, 84–88). This statement reflects the interdependence and interrelatedness of family systems. When divorced spouses remarry, it is not always in the emotional interests of the children of the newlyweds to welcome the new stepfather or stepmother into the family. Research indicates that children frequently have a lingering desire to see their biological parents reunite (Wallerstein and Blakeslee, 1989; Ganong and Coleman, 1994), so they resist the adaptation to a new stepparent and stepfamily. Further, while children seldom have a say in whether or to whom their parent(s) remarry, they do have incredible power to cause trouble for the new marriage. They can create divisiveness between the adults, between themselves and the new stepparent, or between themselves and new stepsiblings. They can bring home "stories" from their other parent's household and make uncomfortable comparisons. They can refuse to participate in family activities—activities designed by parent and stepparent to bring the family together, to help forge a new family identity (Ihinger-Tallman and Pasley, 1987). Such an identity is essential to engender and maintain commitment in family members.

Family Behaviors That Forge Commitment

Bolea (2000) discusses the importance of developing a **family identity** during the transition to parenthood. We would argue that the process of developing a family identity (also called a family "heritage") begins when a couple first makes a commitment. This identity begins with shared experiences, shared definitions, and negotiated conflicts. It involves mutual acceptance of how tight or loose the boundaries around the couple will be. Who has access to information or "secrets" about the relationship? How easily does the relationship incorporate and include each partner's friends and family members? A family identity begins to develop from the rituals and stories (sometimes called "myths"), which are based on the events and experiences of daily life together, those things that make each family unique (such as repeated stories of how mom and dad first met, the troubles with a neurotic grandma). **Family myth** is defined as "a set of images that are accepted by the whole family together, giving each person an allotted pattern of interaction" (Bolea, 2000, 48). Family myths help prescribe the ways that members behave, which also helps them define who they are. For example, shared experiences and stories about their courtship help newlyweds adapt their individual identities to a new living arrangement. By creating memories of pregnancy and childbirth through stories that are told and retold to the children, a family identity is forged.

Family rituals foster a collective identity and grow out of the special ways in which the family creates traditions. How are holidays celebrated? Is there much or little emphasis on Easter baskets, new clothes for church, or an Easter egg hunt? Will Ramadan or Passover be observed? How much fuss will be made for the birthday child? Will Mom get breakfast in bed on Mother's Day? Will the house be decorated for Halloween? Christmas? Hanukkah? While adults may be more conscious of creating these traditions

Marriage ceremonies often involve a great deal of symbolism. Lighting a unity candle from two flames symbolizes the commitment of two individuals to one union and begins the 'nomos-building' process.

after children enter the family, expectations and behaviors associated with them begin to crystallize at the beginning of a relationship. The creation of "we-ness" that results largely from conversations is called **nomos-building,** according to Berger and Kellner (1964). They use this term to refer to a process of shared social construction that takes place within marriages and families. Nomos-building "constructs, maintains and modifies a consistent reality that can be meaningfully experienced by individuals" (2). This reality or understanding of the world, according to Berger and Kellner, results from talking through experiences with family members.

Also related to the development of a family identity is the creation of **family scripts.** According to Bolea, family scripts "prescribe the pattern of family interaction in particular contexts" (2000, 48). What does this mean? Bolea believes family scripts are like blueprints or outlines that define how a person is supposed to behave or react under certain conditions, how he or she deals with adversity or good luck, and so on. These response patterns are learned at an early age within the family circle. An excellent example of this process comes from an article in *Parade* magazine, in which actor David Spade (then starring in the TV series *Just Shoot Me*) attributed his positive attitude and ability to cope with the many negative experiences in his childhood and adolescence (his father abandoned the family when David was 4 years old, his high school friend died in an automobile accident, his stepfather committed suicide, two other friends died, one by suicide) to his mother:

> She is the most solid, strongest person around. I learned everything from her—especially how to treat people . . . she could not have had more stuff thrown at her, and she'd just start over each time. It's always a new day (Buchalter, 2001, 5).

Family scripts may have originated generations ago (when grandparents or great-grandparents modeled a response to crisis), or they might be negotiated in a new marriage when the expectations and behaviors that partners bring to the union do not match. Partners bring different histories to a new union, and if these histories prove to be problematic, differences must be negotiated and a new script developed.

Types of Commitment

Commitment is a complicated construct, as we mentioned at the beginning of the chapter. However, not being able to say precisely what it is or how it functions does not keep scholars from recognizing its importance in interpersonal relationships and trying to measure and explain it (Adams and Jones, 1999). In terms of commitment to the family, Johnson's ideas are particularly relevant. He identified three types of commitment: **attraction commitment** ("I really love my spouse and children and cannot bear the thought of living apart from them"); **moral commitment** ("I made a promise and now I must keep it; I must stay for the sake of the children"); and **constraint commitment** ("It would cost me a fortune to get a divorce; I'm Catholic, after all; What would my mother think? Who else would want me?") (Johnson, 1991, 1999; Johnson, Caughlin, and Huston, 1999).

The new Marriage Covenant Law cited at the beginning of this chapter adds the clout of the law as a constraint. For those who live in Louisiana and choose to make a covenant marriage, divorce is not impossible, but the law lengthens the time between separation and the granting of divorce, mandates counseling for a couple before a divorce can be granted, and reintroduces a "fault" notion (i.e., blame is attributed to one of the parties, who is seen as responsible for the breakdown of the marriage). Under the covenant, divorce will be granted only under the conditions of adultery, commitment of a felony, abandonment for one year and refusal to return, physical or sexual abuse, and separation (living apart) for a period of one year from the time the judgment of separation is signed. The new marriage covenant is optional: Louisiana couples can still choose to wed under the conventional law that make them eligible, if the marriage does not last, for a faster, no-fault divorce. But an assumption lingers: If a couple rejects making a covenant marriage, does that mean they anticipate a divorce? Does it mean they take their marriage vows less seriously?

Several factors are associated with the desire to begin, or stay in, a relationship. These are viewed by some scholars as the sources of commitment and by others only as correlates. These factors include love, satisfaction, trust, dependence, and attractive personality traits. Whether commitment stems from these factors or is only associated with them, we cannot say for sure. What we can say at this point in the study of commitment is that people make commitments to each other for a variety of reasons, and once committed, they stay in the relationship because of personal attraction, because they feel their moral or ethical values give them no other choice, or because they perceive that there are too many barriers to ending the relationship.

In spite of an initial genuine commitment, many people do leave relationships. Some of the reasons couples give for forsaking their marital commitments include communication problems, general unhappiness, growing apart, problems associated with money, drinking, drugs, infidelity, incompatibility, sex, in-laws, and mental, emotional, or physical abuse (Amato and Previti, 2003; Cleek and Pearson, 1985). However, problems in marriage tend to cluster, and there is seldom a single cause of divorce. You will read about them in Chapter 8.

There remains much to be learned about the processes associated with making commitments. We do not know precisely how or why changes in commitment occur in a relationship over time (Adams, 1999). Within any one relationship the strength of commitment may be stronger or weaker at various times. What holds it together during periods of vulnerability? What makes it disintegrate altogether? One insightful reason was offered by an elderly woman as she commented on why her long marriage had endured: "We were never out of love at the same time."

The Big Picture: Commitment to Community

What does it mean to have a commitment to one's community? Why are such commitments necessary? As we begin a discussion about commitment to communities it will be helpful to keep in mind the concepts of the ecological systems perspective. They will help orient you to the research findings presented. Neighborhoods and communities are environmental settings in which individuals participate both directly and indirectly. They are both microsystems and exosystems. When we report on research that treats communities as social relationships (Small and Supple, 2001), it will help if you conceptualize them as mesosystems. An important contribution to the quality of life of families in neighborhoods is the extent to which mesosystem interactions are compatible and have consistent expectations (Bronfennbrenner, 1979).

Community

Scholars who write about community generally have three characteristics in mind. A **community** consists of (a) social interaction among people who live (b) within a given geographical area and (c) share one or more ties to one another. There is some debate about the issue of geographical area. Within a highly urbanized and mobile society, community can be obtained outside any given spatial boundaries. For example, children still remain members of a community after they move away to go to college. Total strangers who become regular members of an Internet chat group say they form a "community." However, our discussion puts this possibility aside and focuses on individuals and families embedded within a local area that includes an economic and political base as well as other social institutions, such as the workplace, schools, religious centers, law enforcement, health care, recreational facilities, service clubs, and so forth. This is labeled a **geographic community** (Bowen, Richman, and Bowen, 2000). Communities are social institutions and settings within which adults and children participate (families, schools, peer groups, youth programs, childcare facilities), as well as the influences of and relationships among them.

Compared to neighborhoods, communities are not only physically larger but generally include many more subsystems (such as the economic, political, religious, educational, and legal institutions) that serve, and affect, the resident population. The subsystems within a community tend to be *formal*, with organizational structures that are deliberately and rationally designed to achieve specific objectives. They are characterized by rules, norms, and a hierarchical authority structure. Communities also include *informal* or voluntary organizations such as bowling leagues, book clubs, and self-help groups.

However, informal systems tend to be more important to neighborhoods (Bronfenbrenner et al., 1984).

All of the settings and institutions within a community affect families, both directly and indirectly, in multiple ways. Just as a family helps to make a "self," a community helps to mold a family. And just as commitment is the necessary ingredient that keeps a family together, the commitment of families to their communities and neighborhoods is what makes it possible for them to function. Certainly society as we know it could not exist without individuals and groups working together in communities and neighborhoods with common purposes to achieve shared goals.

Communities offer an array of human and personal social services that benefit families. These services include programs and organizations geared toward protecting or restoring the lives of individuals and families by providing income, education, housing, employment, and personal services (Kahn, 1979). Garbarino (1995) suggests that an important goal of community and government intervention should be to increase the safety of children, particularly in high-risk urban neighborhoods.

Some service agencies (such as family planning organizations) stand on their own in the community, while others originate in or are delivered through community institutions that have other primary missions. For example, education classes to prepare expectant parents for childbirth and parenting are offered through hospitals. Homeless shelters, soup kitchens, and childcare services are offered through religious organizations. Some people advocate that such faith-based charities or services should replace human services offered by the government (Olasky, 1997). The dialogue that emerges between proponents and opponents of this idea illustrates the sometime controversial nature of community mesosystems.

Neighborhood

Small and Supple (2001) define a **neighborhood** as "a *physical place* which is defined by socially shared boundaries, that includes a *population of people* who usually share similar life chances, socioeconomic status, and physical proximity" (162). Their interpretation of a community refers to "*social relationships* that individuals have based on group consensus, shared norms and values, common goals, and feelings of identification, belonging, and trust" (162). Gusfield (1975) refers to such groups as functional communities. In our terminology, this view of community reflects the mesosystem.

The neighborhood is a source of social influence on families as well as an important microsystem for family members. As a smaller part of the geographic community, the neighborhood includes the people and institutions in the immediate geographic area in which a family resides (Sampson, Raudenbush, and Earls, 1997). Measures of neighborhood size consistently show that people perceive their neighborhood differently from one another. Survey responses by people of differing age, sex, race, and ethnic groups lead us to understand that the concept of neighborhood is *socially constructed*. For the very young and the very old, a neighborhood may be much more constricted than for a working middle-aged person because of a limited ability to get around within it. A teenage girl may view her neighborhood as smaller than her teenage brothers do, especially if parental supervision is stricter about her comings and goings than about theirs. Some urban neighborhoods are dominated by a single ethnic group (Irish, Greek, Italian) and the boundaries of the neighborhood are the blocks where members of other ethnic groups begin to reside. The same might be said of neighborhoods dominated by a single religious group (Jewish, Catholic, Mennonite).

Some aspects of a neighborhood (synagogue, recreational centers) are utilized by some but not all families. For example, homeowners tend to become more invested in neighborhood associations than renters do. Race also influences the degree of involvement with neighbors. In one study of an integrated Nashville, Tennessee, community, blacks had neighbor networks that were narrow but deep. In other words, families were close or intimate with only a few neighbors, but these ties were long lasting and used often. This pattern contrasted with the neighborhood networks of whites, which were broad and shallow and very rarely used as a source of support (Lee and Campbell, 1998). The implications of such different patterns of neighboring are clear. Having close ties with neighbors makes them a part of one's personal social network. Having a person nearby who will watch your children in an emergency, or who will share a cup of coffee, a beer, or gossip or discuss personal problems provides neighbors with a sense of security, physical and emotional safety, and personal investment in one another. This type of neighboring builds a psychological sense of community (Brodsky, 1996).

The physical dimensions of a neighborhood, such as the quality and type of housing, patterning of roadways, and zoning regulations are referred to as **neighborhood infrastructure.** The physical aspects of a neighborhood determine more than the aesthetics of an area; they also enhance or restrict opportunities for specific kinds of social interaction and neighborhood activity. For example, neighbors are more likely to know one another and socialize when there are safe public spaces to meet and visit in the neighborhood or when they reside in a home with a front stoop or porch rather than a high-rise apartment building. The presence of certain types of neighborhood meeting places may provide opportunities for trouble as well. Brantingham and Brantingham (cited in Sampson, 2001) found higher rates of delinquency to be associated with the proximity to fast-food restaurants in an area. Sampson suggests that it is the unsupervised nature of such meeting places that contributed to the increased delinquent behavior that occurred.

It is noteworthy that poor neighborhoods are less likely to have ordinary conveniences such as postal drop boxes and banks. In addition to the increased likelihood of danger arising from violent incidents and illegal activities, poor neighborhoods also are more likely to be close to aversive environmental conditions such as hazardous waste facilities (Spencer, 2001).

Why Are Neighborhood and Community Important?

Individuals and families benefit from a commitment to and involvement in neighborhood and community activities. What are these benefits? Community networks have been found to be the basis of support in alleviating stress, diminishing the effects of illness, assisting the elderly and others in need, and guarding against social isolation that fosters domestic violence and child abuse. Research findings suggest that involvement in organizations outside the family fosters individual well-being and increases the quality of marital life (Amato and Booth, 1997; Holman, 1981). For children, there is evidence that where good communication exists between teachers and parents children perform better in school (Epstein, 1990). Bronfenbrenner and his colleagues (1984) found communities with adequate childcare facilities had lower rates of child abuse and neglect than areas where community support for children was lacking.

What are the factors that promote commitment to and involvement in community activities? Decades ago, Greer (1960) found that living in a low-density urban area with children present facilitated community involvement. More recently, owning a home and having young children were found to foster involvement (Lee, 2001). Other relevant factors that promote the community involvement of families are the length of a partnership or marriage, ages of family members, church membership, socioeconomic status, and employment status. Middle-aged parents of school-aged children are the most likely to engage in volunteer activities (Putnam, 2000).

Families living in poor neighborhoods characterized by high levels of unemployment, violence, and high crime rates are less able to protect and promote their children's life chances. Living in a poor neighborhood creates conditions that have *concentration effects*: disadvantages above and beyond individual and family problems (Wilson, 1987, 1996). In terms of specific outcomes, young people are more likely to drop out of high school, give birth while in their teens, and engage in delinquent activities when they reside in disadvantaged neighborhoods where parents are disengaged from and uncommitted to the community (Rosenbaum and Harris, 2001).

Many community and neighborhood organizations depend on volunteer help. When families are committed to their neighborhoods, these types of organizations flourish.

When neighborhoods are dangerous and deteriorated, the co-socialization of children by parents and community institutions and agencies is rare. In these environments parents tend to rely on their own strategies (close supervision, restricted access to the neighborhood) to protect their children and thus they may become isolated from community institutions available to help them. However, these same strategies, when joined with community programs, have been identified as ways families exemplify *resiliency* when living under conditions of risk (Spencer, 2001). Some coping and problem-solving behaviors are associated with positive adult outcomes and upward social mobility that help end the cycle of poverty for young people. These behaviors include stringent monitoring of children's activities (including sending younger sibling to tag along with adolescents), keeping children away from neighbors who do not share similar ideologies, providing a supportive adult network for children (preferably one that can offer resources parents do not have), making close alliances with neighborhood schools and churches, and providing opportunities to engage in activities that teach skills, competencies, and responsibilities

(Jarrett, 1995). The best conditions, of course, allow children to grow up in neighborhoods that are socially and economically advantaged, with well-functioning parents.[4] In neighborhoods where resources are invested in youth programs, such as after-school programs and recreational facilities, children exhibit more pro-social behaviors. Parents are willing to entrust their children to these community-based programs, which in turn foster neighborhood characteristics of social trust and cohesion (Furstenberg, 2001; Furstenberg et al., 1999).

One finding reported in a number of studies is that no matter what the condition of a neighborhood (i.e., wealthy or poor), families *within* any one neighborhood differ more in their involvement with neighbors and community organizations than do families across neighborhoods that are very different in organization and structure. In a study of Philadelphia neighborhoods, Furstenberg (2001) found as much variation within them as he did between them. Even in the most deprived neighborhoods there were families who located and identified community resources, programs, and services to support their own and their children's well-being. These behaviors were linked to a family's management skills and the strategies they devised to garner social support. These skills and strategies were evident in families at all socioeconomic levels.

How Do Neighborhoods Benefit?

Thus far we have enumerated some of the benefits and costs that families derive from their neighborhoods and communities. What are the benefits and costs for neighborhoods when families make a commitment to them? Earlier in the chapter we discussed the processes through which the self, self-concept, self-esteem, and identities are created. One important characteristic that individuals develop to enhance these elements is **efficacy**—the degree to which one sees oneself as able to bring about a desired effect. A related concept, **collective efficacy,** is important to understand when analyzing the costs and benefits that neighborhoods derive from engaged and committed families. Collective efficacy is defined as a shared belief among residents that they can come together to bring about some desired action and have the ability to achieve a desired, intended effect in their neighborhood. Collective efficacy

Communities are changed, or are able to resist change, because of the activism and involvement of neighborhood residents. Shared values about growth and concern over the loss of a community's small businesses often stop corporations such as Wal-Mart from building large superstores in an area.

joins mutual trust with a willingness to intervene for the common good (Sampson, 2001). An excellent example of collective efficacy occurred in East St. Louis. In 1999, a group of 12 grandmothers got together and decided to organize to improve their neighborhood and make it a better place for children. They began by raising money, through church cookie sales and other fund-raisers, and eventually earned enough money to have a playground built on an empty neighborhood lot. These women served as important role models within their community encouraging others into action.

The collective efficacy demonstrated by these St. Louis grandmothers shows how positive change can be effected even in the poorest neighborhoods. How does collective efficacy develop? At least four influences must be present. According to the theory of Small and Supple (2001, 172) there must be:

1. A sense of shared values and goals around which the community will unite.

2. A belief in and commitment to a common good.

3. A sense of cohesion and mutual trust among citizens so they are willing to work together.

4. Human and material resources to draw on to bring about community action.

According to Small and Supple, for values, goals, shared beliefs, cohesion, and mutual trust to develop, there must first be shared life experiences and some similar personal histories to create a sense of solidarity among community residents. These commonalities ensure that neighbors can be counted on to look out for one another and their neighborhood. These characteristics in turn help develop a sense of community identity and shared group membership. Some community groups create and promote experiences and activities that cultivate this identity. These activities include street fairs, block parties, parades, picnics, firework displays on special holidays, and so on. Identification and satisfaction with the institutions, settings, and members in the community generate feelings of ownership and belonging and create an emotional connection to others in the community. When this happens, "personal identity becomes defined in part by the community in which one is a member" (171). The last step of the process brings these processes together as neighbors feel an emotional connection to one another, develop group membership and a shared identity (commitment), and incorporate what they perceive as a set of common norms, values, and goals. They share a collective sense about what is expected, valued, and desirable, which in turn is seen to be the core values and norms "of what the community represents and what it desires for its members" (171). These ideas can be summed up with a concept formulated by the sociologist James Coleman (1988): **social capital.** Social capital refers to nonmonetary resources that are acquired by forming relationships with others who share similar values and that are used to promote the achievement of group-supported goals.

A neighborhood is dependent on the development of this identification and commitment along with the accompanying emotions and ties among its members, just as members of a community are dependent on community institutions and settings for their overall well-being. Neither can thrive without the other. This mutual relationship has a downside, however. For families to bring about desired change in their neighborhood (to improve the schools, fill the potholes in the street, build a playground), they must first

ssary resources. "Agency [action] without resources has limited effective-
nberg, 2001, 158). However, resources are least likely to be found in the com-
t most need them: those with high family instability, a large percentage of
ed households, high residential turnover, more renters than homeowners,
rty, and greater economic dislocation. Commitment is weakest in these
neighborhoods. These characteristics must be taken into consideration when policies and
programs designed to strengthen neighborhoods and communities are formulated.

Summary

Most people live the greater portion of their lives within the context of a family system. In their parents' home children begin to develop a sense of who they are in relation to
significant others (parents, siblings, extended kin). Children learn appropriate roles, behaviors, and expectations (for themselves and others) in this first important microsystem.
For the most part roles, behaviors, and values are adopted and internalized as scripted behaviors and are retained until some event or situation necessitates change or modifica-
tion. Identities, a self, and self-worth learned in the family context are enhanced, modified, and changed in new socialization settings such as play groups, schools, workplaces,
and religious centers that lie within neighborhoods and communities.

Neighborhoods and communities exert both direct and indirect influences on the
families that reside within them. While the consequences of living in poor, high-risk
neighborhoods are well documented, not all families experience deleterious effects. Resiliency is evident when parents utilize strategies to keep their children safe and help them
develop a sense of efficacy and a positive self-concept. Stable, loving relationships can
mute the ill effects of poverty (Seccombe, 2002). Family protective factors include cohesion, commitment, warmth, affection, and emotional support, as mentioned in earlier
sections of the chapter. Also important are clear-cut expectations and predictable routines, shared values, family celebrations, and traditions (McCubbin et al., 1997).

We discussed these phenomena in terms of developing commitments: to self, family,
and community. We used the concept of commitment as an overarching rubric because it
embodies action, motivation, choice, giving, agreement, trust, and change: the basic
building blocks of human interaction. Further, commitment is a variable, meaning that
degrees of it (ranging from none to highly committed) are bestowed on people, places,
and things. Finally, the concept of commitment captures behavior at both the small-group
and institutional levels. In Chapter 3 we continue the discussion of commitment by examining the processes by which people decide who they will (or won't) be intimate with, who
they will (or won't) commit to, and which lifestyle choices they will make.

Endnotes

1. Of course there are exceptions to this statement: Some children run away from home, and others develop
   an intense dislike of a parent or sibling(s).
2. According to Charles Cooley (1902) primary groups include the family, children's play groups, and the
   neighborhood. Primary groups shape human nature. To the extent these groups share a common culture
   and value system they are the basis for similarity between members of a society. Primary groups are slow
   to change and serve to connect human beings to each other within a society. They are the source of indi-

vidual ideals, they foster role taking, and are built on a general and diffuse rather than specific solidarity. Finally, primary groups are characterized by personal, face-to-face interaction, harmony, conflict, competition, and social unity. One caveat should be noted: Out-of-home childcare settings often do not offer the continuity implied in the concept of primary group because of the high turnover of personnel within a care setting and parental decisions to move children between settings. The consistency and continuity that helps to develop trust and personal security may be missing in some childcare centers. Nevertheless, when infants and small children have caretakers with whom they spend the greater portion of the day, these persons need to be included as significant others who nurture the child's development of self.

3. Internalization is a process whereby behavior that begins as public and overt becomes an integral and inner part of the self.

4. The key variable might well be "a well-functioning" parent. Parenting characterized by neglect, harshness, drug or alcohol use, coldness, or other measures of dysfunction jeopardize children's well-being and healthy psychological development no matter what kind of neighborhood they grow up in.

Chapter Concepts

attraction commitment: commitment founded on the premise of wanting the relationship with a person, object, action, or group, to continue because of its reward value.

collective efficacy: shared beliefs in a neighborhood's conjoint capability for action to achieve an intended effect—an active sense of engagement on the part of residents; the shared willingness and belief of a group that they can act together to achieve an agreed upon goal.

commitment: an agreement, pledge, or behavior that involves a willingness to give something to, or take action toward, other people, objects, goals, or groups.

commitment to self: the sum of the forces, pressures, or drives that influence people to maintain congruity between their identity in a particular situation and their perceptions of the impressions others form of them. This commitment includes the will to give energy and resources to a particular course of action.

community: social relationships of individuals that are based on group consensus, shared norms and values, common goals, and feelings of identification, belonging, and trust; the social institutions and their settings within which these relationships exist.

constraint commitment: the presence of external factors that make it difficult to leave a relationship, give up on a goal, or break a vow.

developmental stages: periods in an individual's life that are times of growth and development; a time when new behaviors are learned.

developmental tasks: role expectations that arise at a particular time in an individual's life. Integration and temporary equilibrium result from successful incorporation of task behavior. Lack of integration and normative pressure to change occur if there is a failure to incorporate the expected behavior.

efficacy: the motivation to perceive oneself as a causal agent in the environment—to experience the self in action terms.

family identity: a sense of uniqueness that develops within a family that characterizes its heritage.

family myth: a set of images, rituals, and stories that make up a family's history and are accepted by all family members. Family myths call for predictable behaviors, responses, and patterns of interaction among family members.

family scripts: programs of action (or blueprints) that outline how family members are expected to behave in specific situations—how they are to act and react under certain circumstances.

game stage: the second stage of George Herbert Mead's theory of the development of the self during which children learn that rules are fixed, roles are consistent, and social life is organized. It involves the capacity to simultaneously take into account the roles and perspectives of all participants in a social setting.

generalized other stage: the third stage of George Herbert Mead's theory of the development of the self, during which people learn to generalize from their immediate social setting to the larger social world.

geographic community: a local area that includes interactions among social institutions such as businesses, government, schools, religious centers, law enforcement agencies, health care centers, recreational facilities, service clubs, and so on.

identities: shared social meanings that persons attribute to themselves in a role. They determine how people place themselves in a network of social relations.

identity salience: the probability of a given identity being invoked in a given situation. Salience refers to the subjective importance a person attaches to a particular role identity.

looking-glass self: a term coined by Charles Cooley to indicate social interaction that acts as a mirror in which people observe the reactions of others to their own behavior.

moral commitment: commitment based on a person's internalized values regarding the inherent importance of a relationship, group, or goal that is associated with a feeling of correctness and an obligation to maintain it.

neighborhood: a physical place defined by socially shared boundaries that include a population of people who usually share similar life chances, socioeconomic status, and physical proximity; a smaller part of a larger community.

neighborhood infrastructure: the physical dimensions of a neighborhood, including quality and type of housing, patterning of roadways, and zoning regulations.

nomos-building: a process in which family members create meanings from their everyday life experiences. This process helps create the social organization from which family social order evolves, from which family members make sense of their lives.

play stage: the first stage of George Herbert Mead's theory of the development of the self, during which children learn to put themselves in one specific role. For example, a very young child can pretend to be momma and feed a doll or be a Power Ranger and fight the bad guys. Through this play they begin to see the world from another's viewpoint.

primary group: a small group in which interactions take place face to face and relationships are characterized by intimacy, conflict, and cooperation.

self: a combination of the physical, mental, emotional, and psychological aspects of an individual that create a unique personal identity. It arises only through social interaction and experience.

self-concept: beliefs, attitudes, knowledge, and ideas people have about themselves.

self-esteem: a personal judgment of the value, worth, or regard a person places on his or her abilities, talents, traits, character, and so on.

social capital: advantages that are acquired through the establishment of relationships with others. Assets gained as a result of the structure of relationship networks, often including kin.

socialization: the sum total of ways by which people learn, from a variety of sources, what is expected of them and how they can deal most effectively with others in society. Socialization is the process through which people become functioning members of society.

socialization agents: persons assigned the responsibility of teaching the norms and values of the culture and the behaviors that are expected of individuals as they move through life.

social network: a group or system of interconnected people who exchange information, contacts, and experiences. Kin, friends, acquaintances, and fellow workers make up a person's network.

taking the role of the other: learning to view the self from the perspective of others; the ability to see the self as an object like other objects in the environment by assuming another's role and seeing the self through the other person's eyes.

Suggested Activities

1. Go to a public place (mall, grocery store, park, library, airport, etc.) and observe the way parents deal with children. How do parents differ in their control methods for girls as compared to boys? Do the parents of very young children use different control methods than parents of older children? Pick one family and listen to the words parents use with their child(ren). What conclusions would you draw about the self and identity formation of the children as judged by the way their parent(s) talk to them?

2. Write a short paper doing a "self-analysis." Describe the trait, characteristic, or quality that you like best about yourself. When did you first observe that you had that characteristic? Was it associated with someone else's comment or behavior? How do you feel when your family and friends act as if you do not have that quality?

3. Conduct a systematic social observation of two neighborhoods. First, observe the "built environment" of your own neighborhood. That is, note the degree of social and physical order, the status of buildings (business or residential), the general condition of the buildings, the presence of security precautions (bars on windows, grates), and the presence of litter, garbage, graffiti, abandoned or nonworking cars, and so on. Then travel to a neighborhood that has a different socioeconomic environment. Make the same observations in this neighborhood. Draw conclusions about the general quality of life for the families who live in the two neighborhoods. Would it be more rewarding for a resident to commit time and energy to one versus the other of these neighborhoods?

Suggested Readings

Adams, J. M., and Jones, W. H. 1999. *Handbook of Interpersonal Commitment and Relationship Stability.* New York: Plenum.

Booth, A., and Crouter, A. C. 2001. *Does It Take a Village? Community Effects on Children, Adolescents, and Families.* Mahwah, NJ: Erlbaum.

Mead, G. H. 1934. *Mind, Self, and Society.* Chicago: University of Chicago Press.

Pleck, E. 2000. *Celebrating the Family: Ethnicity, Consumer Culture and Family Ritual.* Cambridge, MA: Harvard University Press. ✦

Chapter 3

Developing Close Relationships

Making Lifestyle Choices

Did You Know?

- Most college romances end because of "someone else." Approximately 60 percent of students report that their last romantic relationship ended because either they or their former partner were interested in or involved with someone else (Knox, Gibson, Zusman, and Gallmeier, 1997).

- A national poll indicated that the majority of teens approve of interracial relationships and over half have dated a partner of a different race or ethnic background. (Peterson, 1997).

- In 2002, over 16 million computer users visited Internet dating sites (O'Connell, 2003).

- The 2000 U.S. Census revealed that about 5 million U.S. households included unmarried partners of the opposite sex and about 593,000 households included same-sex persons who identified themselves as partners (http://factfinder.census.gov, February 2004).

- A *Time* magazine survey found that 8 percent of never-married women and 9 percent of never-married men plan to remain single for life (Edwards, 2000).

Things to Think About

- What is love? Talk to your friends and find out whether they define it the same way you do. How do you and your romantic partner (if you have one) define love?

- To what extent do you think individuals in this country have "free choice" in whom they date? Whom they decide to marry? If you don't believe people have free choice, what do you believe stands in the way of free choice?

Chapter 2 introduced the concept of commitment and discussed its role in building a strong sense of self-identity, family, and community. We addressed the importance of feeling connected to others and the community, and we discussed how individuals define themselves, in part, according to their relationships with others and their perceptions of what others expect of them. In this chapter we consider the intimate couple in greater detail because it is, for many, the foundation for building a family, at least initially. We examine the components of intimate relationships and how they contribute to the formation of a strong, unique psychological and emotional connection between two people. Further, we discuss the social processes through which individuals form unions, including dating and mate selection processes that narrow down the field of eligibles to a selection of that one special person. We also consider how the dating and mate selection processes have changed over the past 100 years. A theme throughout much of this chapter is that the intimate, seemingly personal processes of dating and mate selection involve a great deal of outside influence—from family, friends, and society. We end the chapter by discussing how some twentieth-century social movements, such as the women's rights movement, civil rights movement, and sexual revolution, have altered the formation of intimate relationships in recent decades. The powerful impact of HIV/AIDS is also considered.

Building Intimate Relationships

People are involved in numerous social relationships across their lifetimes. Yet the relationships people most value and enjoy are those from which they derive feelings of warmth and closeness and a strong sense of personal connection. These emotions are the basis for **intimacy,** and they are what distinguish close personal relationships from other social relationships such as ones with teachers, service providers, and neighborhood acquaintances. In this section we explore what contributes to feelings of intimacy in personal relationships, the association between intimacy and romantic love relationships, and cultural ideals regarding romantic love. This discussion leads to consideration of the social and behavioral processes that facilitate the development of romantic relationships and the lifestyle choices individuals make in pursuing intimate, romantic relationships.

Experiences and Emotions That Promote Intimacy

Intimacy is fostered by five important factors: shared experiences, self-disclosure, trust, respect, and empathy.

Shared Experiences. The development of intimacy depends heavily on shared experience. The intimacy felt in many family relationships comes from years of shared family history (Rubin, 1985). Individuals tend to feel connected to family members, such as parents or a particular sibling, because they have interacted closely for a long time, have shared many unique experiences (family celebrations, deaths, crises), and possess similar values, backgrounds, and outlooks on life. Because of the extensive knowledge and deep understanding family members have of each other, they often derive great warmth, comfort, and satisfaction from spending time together. Shared experiences are critical to the development of intimacy in romantic relationships as well as among kin. By spending time together, two people come to know each other better, feel more at ease with each other, and accumulate experiences that make them feel united. These shared experiences make this particular relationship unique among their entire set of social relationships.

Self-disclosure. Spending a great deal of time together usually leads individuals to share personal information and private feelings. This act, known as **self-disclosure,** is a strong predictor of the level of intimacy felt in a relationship (Waring, 1988). However, the link between self-disclosure and intimacy appears to be bidirectional: Self-disclosure not only leads people to feel more intimate with each other, but as a result of such intimacy they are likely to engage in even more self-disclosure.

Trust. For individuals to feel comfortable and willing to engage in self-disclosure, trust is essential. **Trust,** according to Rotter (1980), is "a generalized expectancy held by an individual that the word, promise, oral or written statement of another individual or group can be relied on"(1). Theorists contend that trust consists of three components: predictability, dependability, and faith (Rempel, Holmes, and Zanna, 1985). Predictability and dependability are feelings people come to attribute to another based on past experiences with that person. After repeated observations of another's behavior in a given situation, people develop a sense of predictability about how that person behaves. Consequently, over time, they shift from thinking about that person's behaviors in particular contexts to generalizing particular qualities, such as his or her dependability. To illustrate, initially Joel may share some of his goals and fears with his new girlfriend, Sharon. She always listens well and responds in a respectful way to his disclosures. Over time, Joel begins to think of Sharon more generally as a respectful person. So, in new situations he expects that she will act respectful—he sees her as dependable in that way, based on past interactions.

As partners develop trust, they engage in deeper self-disclosure, which builds intimacy. What types of feelings and experiences do you think are the most difficult to share with an intimate partner?

However, another component of trust, faith, is not based as much in past experiences but in future expectations. It involves "an emotional security on the part of individuals, which enables them to go beyond the available evidence and feel, with assurance, that their partner will be responsive and caring despite the vicissitudes of an uncertain future" (Rempel et al., 1985, 97). Therefore, even though particular events may not be part of a given couple's past experience with each other, each partner has faith in knowing that the other one will always be there for him or her. The phrase often used in traditional wedding vows, "in sickness and in health, through richer and poorer . . ." conveys such faith.

Of the three components of trust, faith is the one with the strongest connection to attributions of love, for both sexes. Moreover, researchers find that men do not associate the other two, predictability and dependability, with love, whereas women hold them to be important. The higher value women place on dependability compared to men makes sense, given the reliance many have on men for economic security (Rempel et al., 1985). Using evidence from a creative study comparing personal ads placed in magazines and newspapers by men versus women, Fisher (2004) found this situation to still be the case today. Women were twice as likely as men to state a preference for a partner who is financially secure. This is an issue we will return to later when we discuss the relative costs and benefits of marriage for men and women.

Respect. Another critical dimension of intimate relationships is **respect.** To feel intimate with another, it is necessary to believe that the other holds you—your views and behaviors—in high regard. Closely related to respect is *affirmation,* in which acceptance is conveyed through interaction and communication with a partner. By supporting and recognizing the importance of a partner's activities (job, interests, and friendships), one affirms who that person is and how he or she views himself or herself. When a husband buys his professional wife a beautiful briefcase for her birthday, he affirms her view of herself as a businesswoman. Such behavior shows respect for another's choices and reaffirms that person's sense of self. In conversation with others, whether they are friends, classmates, or intimate partners, a person shows affirmation and respect or disaffirmation and nonacceptance. By listening to and recognizing what others say (with nods, for example), one displays respect for their feelings and views. If instead one looks away when they talk, rolls one's eyes, or mutters or chuckles under one's breath at what is said, the message is being sent that the expressed thoughts and feelings are not important or valid. Displaying a lack of affirmation or showing contempt (that follows from lack of respect) for one's partner is one of the most destructive behaviors contributing to marital breakdown (Gottman, 1994).

Empathy. Interacting with others is especially fulfilling when their behavioral and verbal responses convey understanding and consideration of one's own beliefs and feelings—what we call **empathy** (Hubbard, 2001). The perception that another understands how one feels—that the person can meaningfully relate to what one's experience is like—helps build a connection with that person. Empathy is critical in close relationships.

What Is This Thing Called 'Love'?

The meaning of love and the images associated with love (and being in love) have varied greatly across place and time. Sternberg (1998), a leading scholar on love, points out that

> In some periods, people have believed that love includes a sexual component, whereas in other eras people have believed that it is a lofty, asexual experience. In the past two centuries, love has become a foundation for marriage. . . . In the past, and even today in many cultures, marriages are arranged without any thought as to whether the two members of the to-be-committed couple will eventually experience intimacy or passion to each other. (61–62)

Much of the scholarly thinking and theorizing about love today is based on the notion that love assumes several forms. One popular conceptualization is based on the work of Lee (1973), who concluded, after an extensive review of literary and historical sources dealing with love, that there are six distinct styles of loving:

- *Eros*—a passionate love characterized by intense physical and sexual attraction.

- *Agape*—an altruistic love focusing on what can be given to or done for the partner.

- *Mania*—a love characterized by high levels of physical and sexual attraction, along with possessiveness and jealousy.

- *Ludus*—a fun-loving, "free" style of love that avoids long-term commitment.

- *Pragma*—a practical love based on rational decision making about the relationship's rewards and costs.

- *Storge*—a less intense but potentially intimate love, in which warmth and closeness develop gradually as the two parties share and interact over time.

Lee contends that most people are unlikely to adopt a single style of loving. Rather, they probably combine several styles across various love relationships.

Both friendship and passion contribute to long-term relationship satisfaction. This couple derives high levels of enjoyment and intimacy from their relationship.

Since Lee's conceptualization was introduced, scales have been developed to assess these different types of love. In addition, researchers have tried to assess whether particular types of love are more or less likely to be part of satisfying romantic relationships. In a small study of dating couples, Hendrick, Hendrick, and Adler (1988) found that for both men and women, high levels of *eros* and low levels of *ludus* were more predictive of relationship satisfaction than other types of love. These researchers questioned whether different styles of love were predictive of dating couples' relationship outcomes. In a two-month follow-up to their study, they found that the 23 couples from their original sample of 31 who were still involved with each other had initially scored higher on *eros* and lower on *ludus*-type love than couples who had split up (Hendrick et al., 1988). While we can't generalize from this study, we can hypothesize that sexual and physical attraction and passion, mixed with low levels of fun-seeking or noncommital love, are critical to high satisfaction and maintaining relationships over an extended period, at least within dating relationships.

A less complex two-class categorization of love was proposed by Hatfield and Walster

(1978). **Passionate love,** as they define it, is heavily focused on physical attraction and arousal. This type of love appears to develop relatively quickly (maybe even as "love at first sight") and is the least enduring of the two forms (Money, 1980). **Companionate love,** in contrast, develops through close interaction and growing interdependence over time. Although sexual intimacy and physical attraction may be part of companionate love, they generally are not the driving force behind it. According to Hatfield (1988), these two very distinct types of love can occur together within a given relationship. People often want to experience both the excitement of passionate love, and the security that comes from companionate love with the same person. Moreover, it is not uncommon for partners to describe themselves both as lovers and best friends (Hendrick and Hendrick, 1993; Sprecher and Regan, 1998). Even in long-term marriages involving middle-aged or older adults, both friendship and passion are highly valued and significant predictors of marital satisfaction (Grote and Frieze, 1998; Inman-Amos, et al., 1994; Montgomery and Sorell, 1997).

The triangular theory of love (see Figure 3.1) developed by Sternberg (1986), is another conceptualization of love that has been validated in several empirical studies. Sternberg contends there are eight kinds of love, distinguished by varying levels of three key components: intimacy, passion, and commitment. We've already discussed how *intimacy* encompasses feelings of connectedness and warmth in a relationship and described the behaviors that promote such feelings. *Passion* is associated with physical and sexual attraction and arousal, as described in some of the theories covered earlier. *Commitment,* according to Sternberg, involves the cognitive process of deciding to maintain and stay in a loving relationship (which is consistent with relational commitment defined by other scholars and noted in Chapter 2).

Four of the more commonly recognized types of love that Sternberg proposes are infatuated love, empty love, companionate love, and consummate love. A young teen who has a crush on a teacher may feel "in love," even though the two of them may have had little meaningful interaction. This is a good example of *infatuated love*—a feeling of love based solely on passion (attraction), without any real intimacy or commitment. *Empty love,* in contrast, combines limited passion and intimacy with a high level of commitment. This type of love characterizes a long-term married couple who no longer feels attracted to each other, who report they've grown apart and feel distant, yet they stay together out of obligation to each other or their commitment to the institution of marriage. *Companionate love* is somewhat similar to, but also different from, empty love; although both reflect

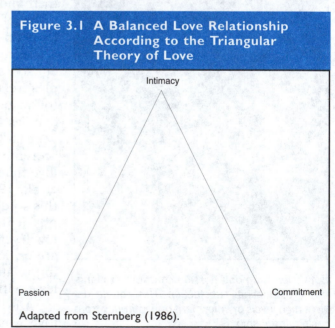

Figure 3.1 A Balanced Love Relationship According to the Triangular Theory of Love

Intimacy

Passion   Commitment

Adapted from Sternberg (1986).

high commitment and low passion, companionate love involves a high level of intimacy that is not present in empty love. The couple who feels intense love and togetherness—like best friends or compatible roommates—yet who've lost the physical/sexual spark in their relationship (or never had it), exemplifies companionate love. *Consummate love,* in comparison, involves high levels of all three components. Consummate love is viewed as "complete" love by Sternberg (1986). Indeed, American culture seems to agree. Television programs, movies, songs—all these cultural forms promote this type of love as the true love, the kind of love everyone should seek in romantic relationships. What do you think?

The Romantic Ideal

The media and other cultural forms contribute heavily to the views that individuals have about love relationships. Much social commentary and scholarly discussion focuses on how cultural images of love relationships are overly romanticized and highly unrealistic. One concern is that when people approach relationships with such unrealistic beliefs about what love is like, they are likely to be severely let down when reality hits in their relationships (Glenn, 1991). As a result of violated expectations and dissatisfaction, idealistic individuals may easily give up on their relationships and keep looking elsewhere for satisfaction and happiness.

What are some of the beliefs that make up the romantic view of love? Sprecher and Metts's (1989) assessment of romantic beliefs is based on a series of items that address agreement with the following statements:

- There is such a thing as love at first sight.
- Love conquers all.
- Every person has a true love in the world.
- Love is perfect.

Another approach to assessing romantic, idealized views of relationships is offered by Epstein and Eidelson (1981). They focus on unrealistic beliefs about behaviors that supposedly occur, or are avoided, in ideal love relationships. Among these beliefs are the following:

- Disagreement is harmful.
- Partners should be able to read each other's minds.
- Partners cannot change over time.
- Perfect sex is possible.

What about you? To what extent do you think the above beliefs reflect idealistic or realistic notions of love relationships?

Although idealized views of love are generally attributed to inexperience and youth, some married adults are known to have overly romanticized views of love. Research indicates that married individuals who report extremely strong romantic beliefs report more marital problems, conflict, and dissatisfaction in their relationships. They also are at greater risk for divorce (Baucom and Epstein, 1990; Glenn, 1991). Thus, while passion and attraction are important for relationship satisfaction and success, couples must recognize that all relationships encounter challenges and change and that these issues need to be actively addressed for any given relationship to remain stable and satisfying. Furthermore, it is useful for individuals to realize that passion or romance is just one aspect of satisfying love relationships and that even if these dimensions wane over time, levels of intimacy and commitment may remain stable or change in positive ways, contributing to the continuance of this feeling called "love."

Social and Behavioral Processes That Bring Couples Together

So far we've discussed the components of love as identified by contemporary theorists. The theories presented thus far, however, are not process oriented, meaning that they don't necessarily address *how* the various dimensions of love and intimacy develop over time in a relationship. In this section we examine the processes through which couples come together and develop intimate relationships.

The Wheel Theory of Love

One process theory that focuses primarily on the psychological processes of relationship development is the wheel theory of love (see Figure 3.2), developed several decades ago by Reiss (1960). He proposed a four-stage interpersonal process (rapport building, self-revelation, forming mutual dependency, and intimacy-need fulfillment) through which two persons develop feelings of love for each other. It works this way: After meeting, extended interaction between two individuals may result in a feeling of comfort with each other. Being together and communicating with each other contributes to **rapport.** Once the couple develops good rapport, they may progress to the point where they feel comfortable engaging in **self-revelation** (disclosure). Earlier we discussed factors that contribute to self-revelation, such as trust and understanding. Over time, the couple becomes behaviorally and emotionally dependent on each other (**mutual dependency**). Certain activities become contingent on the other (e.g., "She always plans our evenings out and organizes our time with friends"), and the partners' lives become tightly connected. Finally, as a result of these processes, the partners' respective needs for intimacy (and other things, such as economic security, social connectedness, and status) are fulfilled through the relationship (**intimacy need fulfillment**). When partners meet each other's needs in a highly satisfactory way, the relationship is difficult to replace.

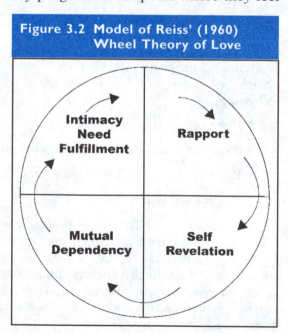

Figure 3.2 Model of Reiss' (1960) Wheel Theory of Love

Intimacy Need Fulfillment

Rapport

Mutual Dependency

Self Revelation

The Filter Theory of Mate Selection

Other theories dealing with the process of mate selection and relationship development focus more heavily on social factors than psychological and interpersonal ones. Although love and intimacy are psychological states, social processes do influence their development, and relationship formation more generally. Certain social experiences and forces either provide opportunities for or create barriers to the development and pursuit of love relationships. The filter theory of mate selection is one such theory that deals primarily with social forces as they shape mate selection, although it does address some interpersonal and intrapersonal issues as well. According to the filter theory, individuals search for and select their intimate partners by engaging in a series of steps (field of eligibles, propinquity filter, attraction filter, homogamy filter, compatibility filter, trial union—see Figure 3.3) that progressively weed out potential partners, thereby narrowing the field of eligible mates (Kerckhoff and Davis, 1962). This theory can be connected to the ecological perspective. The theory starts by considering microsystems, which are important because they allow individuals to meet and get to know potential partners. As couples progress through the filter, exosystem factors come into play. Legal systems and religious institutions, for example, may support policies that control or limit choices in the mate selection process. Furthermore, we see the influence of macrosystem factors, especially in the form of social norms that dictate to members of society acceptable and unacceptable partner choices.

In the broadest sense, we could pair off almost any two people in the world. The population includes all eligible partners, as noted at the widest end of the funnel in Figure 3.3. However, numerous factors reduce the field of eligible partners for each person. *Propinquity*, which means geographic closeness, is a major influence on whom one has the opportunity to meet, date, and possibly marry. It is most likely that a person will become acquainted with and get to know someone with whom he or she shares a microsystem. Perhaps it might be another student in a class, or someone at work, or someone who works out at the same gym. Most married couples report that they met through family, friends, classmates, coworkers, or neighbors (Michael, Gagnon, Laumann, and Kolata, 1994).

Sometimes the demographics of a particular geographic area present challenges for individuals who are looking for a partner because the field of eligibles in that locale is extremely limited. For example, in Alaska, where the sex ratio is heavily male, heterosexual males have a relatively hard time finding available, desirable women. As a result, some savvy businesspeople have capitalized

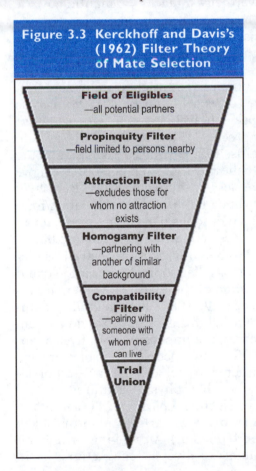

Figure 3.3 Kerckhoff and Davis's (1962) Filter Theory of Mate Selection

Field of Eligibles
—all potential partners

Propinquity Filter
—field limited to persons nearby

Attraction Filter
—excludes those for whom no attraction exists

Homogamy Filter
—partnering with another of similar background

Compatibility Filter
—pairing with someone with whom one can live

Trial Union

on this situation with the publication of *Alaska Men*, a magazine targeted to single women that features available Alaskan men. What is the sex ratio on your college campus? Have you noticed whether it affects the field of eligible partners available to you?

For a large number of individuals, the Internet has reduced and perhaps even eliminated the importance of geographic proximity in dating and relationship formation. Interacting over the Internet is different from interacting in person, especially for people who have trouble with traditional social interactions because of speech problems, shyness, concerns about their physical appearance, or other issues. These individuals are likely to feel more comfortable "meeting new people" when the situation is not face to face. Research conducted by McKenna and colleagues (2002) found that individuals displaying high levels of anxiety in traditional social situations were more likely to disclose personal information to others over the Internet than in typical social situations. As a result of such self-disclosure, those who freely shared on the Internet were more likely than those who were somewhat reserved about sharing personal information to form deep, intimate ties with Internet acquaintances. Relationships tended to develop more quickly when self-disclosures were forthcoming, and a large share of these relationships progressed beyond the Internet interaction. Among the 568 persons who responded to the Internet study conducted by McKenna et al., 54 percent had eventually met the person face to face. (However, not all the relationships were classified as "romantic" by the respondents.)

The attraction filter comes into play once potential partners are exposed to each other in a social situation. Certainly, people meet and interact with many more individuals than they care to get to know better. Physical attractiveness is an important feature during this part of the filtering process. Research shows that physically attractive individuals get asked out more than persons rated as less attractive (Berscheid and Reis, 1998). People not only prefer attractive dates for their aesthetic appeal, but by being seen with attractive others, they believe they gain status (Hatfield and Sprecher, 1986). Additionally, a "halo effect" appears to accompany good looks (Benokraitis, 1999). That is, people attribute positive characteristics to good-looking individuals, believing that such persons are more sensitive, sincere, kind, exciting, and interesting than less-attractive persons (Berscheid and Reis, 1998). Thus, looks appear to matter greatly at certain points in the dating/mating process. Indeed, not knowing what a potential partner looks like is a major factor in individuals' skepticism about using online dating services (Donn and Sherman, 2002).

Looks, however, are not everything to everyone. Women, for example, place less emphasis on physical attractiveness than men do in choosing a date or partner (Hatfield and Sprecher, 1986; Roscoe, Diana, and Brooks, 1987). Some of the features women are attracted to in men include similarity in interests (Roscoe et al., 1987), dependability, maturity, intelligence, and a pleasing disposition (Buss, Shackelford, Kirkpatrick and Larsen, 2001). Also, as interaction between two people increases, the importance of physical appearance wanes (Hatfield and Sprecher, 1986). Therefore, two people who share microsystems and interact often may over time become attracted to each other as a result of desirable personality factors (e.g., humor, kindness) rather than physical features.

Homogamy factors are also an important issue in selecting a partner, as noted in the next layer of the filter. **Homogamy** refers to a similarity between partners in terms of key social characteristics (race, age, social class, education, religion). Although we live in an increasingly heterogeneous society in which individuals of diverse races, ethnic backgrounds, and religions are likely to interact on a daily basis, there are still a number of reasons that partner homogamy with regard to certain social characteristics is still common. Racial similarity between partners, for instance, is an aspect of homogamy still widely practiced today, although most people now approve of mixed-race relationships. However, members of mixed-race couples still report that they experience social disapproval and prejudice (Forman, Williams, and Jackson, 1997). Religious homogamy may also be important to some people, especially if their religion is linked to a strong cultural and lifestyle component. Social class homogamy is also an issue for some families. Goode's (1959) classic writing on the social control of love argued that parents in the upper classes are most concerned that their children marry within their social class. The wealthiest group in society is highly invested in protecting the advantage they have in terms of resources and power; one way they do so is by closely monitoring the mate selection choices of their offspring. As a check on whether homogamy within close relationships still matters, scan the personal ads in your local newspaper. Our guess is that it's not uncommon for those ads to mention the social attributes of either the person writing the ad or the preferred respondents. Here is an example of what we mean:

> Beautiful, retired doctor 43, 5'6", 120 lbs. Seeking intelligent, handsome, tall man, 38–50, European background a plus. High education would be gladly appreciated. (*Pacific Sun* Personals, March 19–23, 2003)

Why does homogamy matter? We already mentioned one reason (guarding wealth and power) that social class homogamy is emphasized. Other than that, it is generally believed that key social characteristics—such as ethnicity, race, religion, and social class—heavily shape a person's personal values, attitudes, and view of the world. Consequently, it is assumed that marriages will be more harmonious and serious conflict will be minimized when partners share key social characteristics (Ortega, Whitt, and William, 1988). This is especially likely to be the case if a particular characteristic is salient to one of the partners or to his or her family. For example, if one's parent is a member of the clergy, the religious practice and beliefs of a potential partner are likely to be more important selection criteria than they would be to a person whose family is not religious or does not hold any strong religious views.

Ultimately, according to the filter theory, movement into a more formal union, whether cohabitation or engagement followed by marriage, will be based on a compatibility filter. For example, do the two individuals share similar values (money doesn't matter all that much), have similar life goals (a big family), enjoy some of the same activities (sports, hobbies), have compatible living habits (smoker versus nonsmoker), and desire the types of roles that the other expects of them ("I'm looking for someone who wants to focus on being a wife and mother"). As noted above, homogamy in social characteristics is assumed to maximize compatibility on a number of these dimensions. But even beyond similarity at the level of social characteristics, these deeper, more important personal and lifestyle issues matter. One of your authors is reminded of a college roommate who was devastated when her long-time boyfriend broke up with her. The roommate admitted, teary-eyed, that after several years of dating she had become aware of the fact that her boyfriend did not share her dream of someday having a houseful of children. Although this realization was difficult to accept at the time, she eventually realized that finding a partner who shared her family goals was critical for her long-term relationship success.

Dating

The social process through which a couple initially comes together, gets to know each other, and possibly ends up united in marriage has changed dramatically in the past century. Over the last 100 years a shift has occurred in terms of where the courtship or dating process occurs, as well as who controls it. As Bailey (1988) argues in her cleverly titled book *From Front Porch to Backseat: Courtship in Twentieth Century America*, prior to the twentieth century a young couple often became acquainted at public gatherings such as town picnics or church socials. Then, if interested, a young man might request to spend some time with a young women by coming to call at her home, which generally required her parents' permission. These visits usually took place in the safe confines of the female's home—usually in the parlor or on the front porch—under the close supervision of her parents. Although lower-class and working-class couples had more freedom to go out alone in public and get to know each other without constant parental supervision (mainly because their homes did not have parlor space for visitors), the widespread practice of couples dating alone in public places did not take hold until the early 1900s. Both urbanization and the invention of the automobile contributed to this change. Having a speedier source of transportation and somewhere to go for entertainment altered the landscape of courting/dating in the United States. So did the growth of public schools and manufacturing jobs, because they brought more young men and women together (Bailey, 1988).

The movement of dating out of the supervised family home and into public also increased couples' opportunities for physical intimacy. Although sexual intercourse was not a common part of dating during the early to mid-twentieth century, heavy necking and petting ("making out") was. Make-out parties were popular, and out-of-the-way spots that young couples reserved for parking (the "backseat" reference in Bailey's book title) were well known during the mid-twentieth century (Rothman, 1984).

Another major shift that occurred in the courtship process in the last century involved who was in control of the situation. When courting took place in the home, it was largely up to a young woman's parents to decide whom they would allow to call on their daughter. However, as dating moved into public spaces, the young man assumed increasing control. It was up to him to ask a young woman for a date, and although her parents might set the time when their daughter was due back, responsibility for initiating, planning, and paying for the date was largely the young man's. Throughout the twentieth century, until the last few decades, male control over dating grew (Bailey, 1988).

Today it appears that dating has become less formal, and the rules about who initiates a couple's time together and takes responsibility for the costs have changed. Both males and females take the lead in initiating dates and may alternate or share financial responsibility for expenses. Moreover, dating has become less focused on finding a marital partner and more focused on recreation and socialization. Teens today often hang out together in large mixed-sex groups, putting less emphasis on one-on-one formal dates, at least early in adolescence, before proceeding to more romantic, private personal encounters (Connolly, Furman, and Konarski, 1995).

Breaking Up Is Hard to Do (For Some)

It is important in discussing the development of romantic relationships to also address their dissolution, because most romantic relationships do not endure. Much of what we know about break-ups in dating relationships comes from a Boston study of college students conducted in the 1970s by Hill, Rubin, and Peplau (1976). These researchers followed over 200 white couples over a period of two years with the goal of examining predictors of couple break-ups, as well as partners' perceptions of the break-up and their adjustment to it.

One interesting focus of this study was the timing and progression of break-ups. The investigators found that for college students, break-ups tended to coincide with other clear transitions, such as the end of academic semesters and the start or end of vacation periods. This finding highlights how the progress of relationships is influenced by both internal "couple" events and external, contextual factors. These researchers also found that when couples broke up, the split was initiated by the partner who was less involved. This finding relates to a principle of close relationships known as the **principle of least interest.** According to this dictum, in any social relationship the party who has made the smallest investment in the relationship—whether it is an emotional, time, or even material investment—possesses the most power or influence over what happens to that relationship (Waller, 1951). Therefore, the partner who has been less involved has much less to lose by breaking up.

Another key finding about the break-up process was that partners had discrepant views of how the event occurred. Each respondent tended to report that he or she was the party responsible for ending the relationship. Additionally, partners showed fairly limited agreement in their views of whether the relationship ended suddenly or gradually (Hill et al., 1976). Regardless of who was seen as the initiator of the break-up, women clearly identified more relationship problems than men did, suggesting that women monitored relationship interactions more clearly than men did. Finally, in terms of post–break-up adjustment, these investigators found that men had a harder time than women getting over a failed relationship; men reported higher levels of depression and loneliness after the break-up than women did. Moreover, when the woman ended the relationship, the chances of the couple "remaining friends" were much greater than when the man initiated the split (Hill et al., 1976). It appears, therefore, that men and women experience different feelings of loss when their relationships fail. It may be that men depend more heavily on their dating partners to meet their emotional and intimacy needs than women do. Later in Chapter 4 we will discuss how marriage can also result in two very different experiences for men and women.

Network Influences on Relationship Formation

As noted, some theories of relationship development focus narrowly on the emotional and psychological processes involved in a couple's developing relationship, paying little attention to the social processes that come into play. Although we discussed the filter theory of mate selection and noted several social structural factors considered to be influential in the mate selection process (e.g., the norm of homogamy), this theory does not really articulate how such factors operate.

The way that one's close social networks react to a particular relationship is partly shaped by societal norms that prescribe acceptable romantic pairings. We live in a society that is generally more supportive of couples when the partners are of a similar age and of the same race. Within some families, similarity in religion and ethnicity may also matter greatly. In response to societal norms about mate selection, individuals may convey support for or discourage particular romantic pairings. Sometimes these actions are very direct, such as when parents outright instruct their offspring about what types of people are and are not considered acceptable dates or mates. An obvious way in which social networks directly affect relationship development is by facilitating introductions between two individuals. Friends set their friends up with persons they think will be a good and acceptable match. Beyond the introductions, however, networks can also facilitate the development of a couple identity by labeling the pair a couple and engaging in actions that reinforce their identity as partners (Milardo and Allan, 2000). By inviting two individuals to a "couples only" weekend trip together, a network not only sends the message that these two persons are considered a couple, but it also promotes their togetherness. Alternatively, when the network disapproves, their actions (e.g., criticism of the partner) and discouragement of the relationship can lead to dissolution.

There are indirect, subtle ways that networks influence dating and mate selection. Parents may choose to send their child to a church-affiliated college so that the child only meets and interacts with persons of a particular religion. Ultimately, the parents are trying to limit the field of eligibles for that child. Similarly, friends may arrange a blind date with an acceptable partner as a way of discouraging or interfering with a less acceptable budding romance that a close friend is having.

Others outside an individual's personal social networks also convey their views about the appropriateness of the romantic relationships he or she pursues. Gay and lesbian couples (Auger, Conley, and Gardner, 1997) and mixed-race couples, for example, are sometimes subjected to the harassment of others who choose to comment in public on their relationships. An important factor in how stigmatized relationships are affected by social disapproval is how the couple manages and deals with the stigma. Among some of the strategies that Datzman and Gardner (2000) found in their study of mixed-race couples were attempts to ignore or repress public disapproval, avoidance of situations in which harassment was likely to occur (which could mean staying home more, or carefully selecting whom to socialize with), and going out in groups rather than alone as a couple.

Even in what may be viewed as socially acceptable relationships, social network reactions and behavior can affect the quality and progress of the relationship. Sprecher and Felmlee (1992) followed 101 dating couples, mostly college students, over an 18-month period to study the impact of social network influences on relationship stability. Specifically, they examined partners' perceptions of social reactions to their relationship (e.g., approval or disapproval of friends and family), the degree of overlap in the partners' social networks, and how much each partner liked the other's family and friends. The researchers found that an individual's ratings of relationship satisfaction, love, and commitment were significantly associated with the support that person perceived for the relationship from his or her social network. Additionally, levels of perceived social support for the relationship early on were predictive of increased feelings of satisfaction, love, and commitment over time. Although no differences were found in the impact of social networks on men's versus women's reports of relationship satisfaction, women noted more

The public is increasingly accepting of mixed-race couples, however such couples still experience occasional social disapproval. How do you think negative social reactions affect a couple's interactions, lifestyle, and relationship satisfaction and stability?

disapproval of the relationships from their parents than men did. The authors suggest that this finding (which has been corroborated by other studies) indicates that parents attempt to control their daughters' dating behavior more than their sons' (Sprecher and Felmlee, 1992). Also considered in this study was whether the support (or lack) of one's social network affected the continuance of the dating relationship over time. The data suggested that it did, but only for women. The less social support that a young woman reported for her relationship, the greater the risk that the relationship would end. Such findings validate Lewis's (1973) contention that significant others play a critical role in people's romantic relationships. Felmlee and Sprecher (2000) cast network influences on romantic relationships in ecological terms when they concluded:

> The social network is an arena in which the effects of meso- and macro-level factors on dyads often are realized. . . . Family relationships and friendships also are likely to be central in the transmission of macro-level societal values and norms that affect existing or prospective pairs. Social networks . . . provide information regarding who is an appropriate partner. (368)

Another study reported by Umana-Taylor and Fine (2003) compared factors influencing the commitment to wed, including family influences, for a sample of college couples, many of whom were of Latino background. Their findings revealed no ethnic group differences in terms of the level of family influence on relationship outcomes. There were, however, differences for Anglo and Latino women in the association between family support for the relationship and the women's own commitment to getting married. Although the authors anticipated that family support would contribute more positively to marriage intentions for Latinos than Anglos (because of the greater emphasis on familistic thinking and collectivist values in Latino families), the results showed just the opposite. As family support increased, Latino women expressed less commitment to getting married. These authors speculated that perhaps in Latino families, family support is accompanied by extremely high levels of family involvement, which reduces the couple's feelings of freedom and satisfaction with the relationship (Umana-Taylor and Fine, 2003). Too much family support may be interpreted as relationship interference. These results, along with those of Felmlee and Sprecher, add to our understanding of the various ways in which social networks play a role in the filtering processes of mate selection.

Lifestyle Choices

Once individuals meet and develop an interest in each other, they have various choices to make about how to proceed with their relationships. In this section we focus on the various lifestyles that individuals can select as they pursue intimate relationships in adulthood.

Sexual Orientation

Although images of homosexual love and relationships are scattered throughout history, at no other point in time has public recognition and discussion of such relationships been as widespread as it is today. Estimates of the size of the gay and lesbian populations vary considerably, as do figures regarding the number of individuals who have had same-sex sexual experiences or been involved in same-sex intimate relationships at some point in their lives. Yet, it is safe to say that more individuals in this country today than ever before acknowledge being bisexual or homosexual and pursue an openly gay or lesbian lifestyle. These experiences fall under the umbrella of "alternative" lifestyles because even today they are not dominant themes in discussions of intimate relationships and unions. Moreover, the majority of Americans still believe that sexual relations between individuals of the same sex are wrong (Smith, 1994).

When Kinsey and his colleagues (1948) conducted their classic study of male sexuality in the 1940s, homosexuality was classified as a mental disorder by the American Psychiatric Association. (It was not removed from the APA list until 1973.) Surprisingly, given the heavy stigma attached to same-sex relationships at the time, nearly half of the men Kinsey studied reported having experienced sexual feelings toward other males, one-third admitted to having at least one sexual encounter with another man in their lifetime, and about 10 percent were considered homosexual (i.e., they reported either predominant or exclusive involvement in same-sex relationships). This estimate of the homosexual population is much higher than those made in recent years. This difference isn't totally surprising, given that Kinsey was criticized as having oversampled homosexuals. Indeed, Kinsey used a volunteer sample rather than randomly drawing men from the population at large, so there may have been a bias toward homosexuals in his study. Research conducted during the 1990s using the General Social Surveys, annual surveys conducted with a representative sample of the U.S. population, found that 3.6 percent of women and 4.7 percent of men reported having had a same-sex partner in adulthood. Not all of these experiences necessarily continued, however, as only 2 percent of women and 3 percent of men had engaged in same-sex relationships in the past year (either exclusively or in combination with heterosexual experiences). Still fewer—only 1 percent of women and 2.5 percent of men—self-identified as gay, lesbian, or bisexual (Black, Gates, Sanders, and Taylor, 2000)—levels similar to those found in a national survey by Michael and his colleagues (1994). It therefore appears that most adults in the United States still engage nearly exclusively in heterosexual relationships.

Despite criticism of Kinsey's sampling methods, his work is still considered valuable. One important contribution was his conceptualization of sexual orientation as ranging along a continuum, rather than being strictly heterosexual or homosexual. This view is consistent with recent discussions of sexual experiences and sexual preference as being heavily shaped by social context and circumstances and therefore being malleable and fluid (Fowlkes, 1994). The ecological perspective is useful in considering this notion. Macrosystem views about the appropriateness or acceptability of same-sex behavior have varied across time (Smith, 1994). Therefore, someone may have grown up with the feeling that he or she was attracted to persons of the same sex but, because of societal views at the time, may have suppressed those feelings and pursued heterosexual relationships. This was true for Richard Chamberlain, the famous actor who played the heartthrob Dr. Kildare on a 1960s television series. In his biography, *Shattered Love: A Memoir* (Chamberlain, 2003), Chamberlain discusses the self-contempt and personal dissatisfaction he felt both while growing up and in adulthood because of his homosexual feelings and society's negative view of homosexuals. For some time he involved himself in relationships with women because it was expected of him and socially acceptable.

At the exosystem level, laws and institutional policies and doctrine varied as well, and not always consistently across geographic areas. For example, half of the states still had laws on the books in the 1990s barring sexual behavior between individuals of the same sex. In many states persons could be arrested in their own homes for having homosexual sex, although such laws were not widely enforced (Cherlin, 2002). In June 2003, however, the U.S. Supreme Court ruled in *Lawrence v. Texas* that laws against same-sex sodomy are unconstitutional. Some institutions may also have policies that support or discourage individuals' acknowledgment or pursuit of same-sex relationships (e.g., the U.S. military). When city governments offer partner benefits to same-sex partners (such as health insurance) or offer marriage licenses to same-sex couples (something San Francisco's mayor Gavin Newsom started doing in defiance of California's Defense of Marriage Act in February 2004), individuals may be more willing to follow their desire to form such unions. Alternatively, if an organization does not protect the individual choices and rights of gay or lesbian members (e.g., the Boys Scouts' rule against homosexual participants), such behavior may be concealed or avoided.

Microsystems may also shape an individual's current sexual experiences and preferences. If a friend acknowledges sexual interest in his or her same sex, or if friends or family members discredit persons with such preferences and interests, one's own behavior may be profoundly affected, despite the types of relationships and experiences that are desired.

The fact that individuals may have different types of sexual experiences at different points in their lives and engage in both same-sex and cross-sex relationships, either concurrently or over time, is evident in most studies of persons currently labeled gay or lesbian. Bell and Weinberg's (1978) report of research with homosexuals claimed that 20 percent of the white males and somewhat fewer of the black males they studied had been in a heterosexual marriage earlier in their lives, as had one-third and nearly one-half of white and black lesbians, respectively. Moreover, 20 percent of the gay men in their study had fathered children, and 40 percent of the lesbians had children in a heterosexual relationship.

That more males than females have had same-sex experiences, and that more lesbians than gay men have arrived at their homosexual lifestyle after being in heterosexual relationships, is attributed to the different sexual socialization experiences for males compared to females. Starting at a relatively young age, teen boys engage in more sexual experimentation outside of intimate relationships than girls do, and much of this is auto-erotic activity that may involve same-sex peers. For young girls, sexual fantasy dominates over experimentation, and such fantasy is predominantly heterosexual. Therefore, males have more opportunities for same-sex encounters than females, and at much earlier ages (Fowlkes, 1994). Males also regard sexual preference as more fixed than females do, according to sexuality experts (Gagnon, 1990).

Nonmarital Cohabitation

Since around 1970, the United States has seen a growing number of couples living together as intimate partners outside of marriage, a situation known as **cohabitation.** Gay men and lesbian women make up a portion of nonmarital cohabitors, although they differ from heterosexual cohabitors in that they do not have access to legal marriage. Moreover, prior to 2000, when the U.S. Census provided estimates of the number of households that included nonmarital cohabitors, they were referring only to housing units consisting of an unmarried male and female. This changed in 2000, however, when new formatting of householder information by the U.S. Census Bureau permitted identification of both same- and opposite-sex partner households.

A Profile of Cohabitors. Aside from becoming more common in the last few decades, cohabitation has involved an increasingly diverse group of people. Here are some of the descriptive facts that we have about cohabitors today:

- There is substantial age variability in persons who cohabit:

    Over half (59 percent) are between the ages of 25 and 44.

    About one in five are under age 25.

    About one in five cohabitors are 45 to 64 years old.

    Few persons over age 65 cohabit.

- Divorced persons are more likely to cohabit than never-married individuals (Bumpass and Sweet, 1989). Couples who remarry are about 30 percent more likely to live together prior to marriage than couples forming a first marriage.

- Blacks cohabit at a rate about three times that of whites (Bumpass and Lu, 2000).

- Cohabitors tend to be overrepresented by persons with relatively low social class standing. A 1995 study (Bumpass and Lu, 2000) found:

    Sixty percent of females with only a high school education had cohabited outside of marriage.

    Less than 40 percent of their same-sex college-educated peers had done so.

A fairly new trend among cohabiting couples today is the increasing presence of children in their households. In 1980 only about one in four households with nonmarried couples had children under 15 residing in them, whereas in 1998 the figure had jumped to

36 percent. About twice as many of these situations involve children from a former relationship rather than the current cohabiting one. Estimates are that 40 percent of nonmarital births in this country today actually occur within an established cohabiting relationship (Bumpass and Lu, 2000).

The Connection Between Cohabitation and Marriage. An important question for family scholars is, what role does cohabitation play in relation to marriage? Is it a new phase in the transition to marriage (a trial marriage phase—occurring prior to or just after engagement), is it an increasingly common alternative to marriage, or is it something else? Viewing cohabitation as an alternative to marriage seems like a plausible explanation in light of the concomitant changes that have occurred in rates of marriage. During approximately the same period that cohabitation rates increased, marriage rates fell. Population experts estimate that about two-thirds of the decline in marriage for people in their early twenties is due to nonmarital cohabitation (Bumpass, Sweet, and Cherlin, 1991).

When married and cohabiting couples are compared, however, the two groups appear to maintain very different types of unions. Casper and Bianchi (2002) argue that one significant way cohabiting couples differ from married couples is in the gender roles they display in their relationship. For instance, data from the Current Population Survey of 1998 show that:

- Cohabiting couples are more likely to include a situation where the woman is more educated than the man (21 percent versus 16 percent for married couples).

- Cohabiting couples are more likely to include two earners (77 percent versus 60 percent for married couples).

- Cohabiting couples are more likely to include a woman who works more hours than her male partner (24 percent versus 16 percent for married couples).

- In cohabiting couples, women contribute a greater share to household income (41 percent versus 37 percent for married couples).

Casper and Bianchi note that the differences in gender roles suggested by these facts are partly due to average age differences in cohabiting and married couples. However, besides being younger, it also appears that cohabiting couples are generally less conventional than married couples.

Another study compared married and cohabiting persons with single persons and concluded that cohabitors more closely resembled single persons than married persons in terms of plans for having children, financial dependence on their parents, home ownership, and school and work activities (Rindfuss and VandenHeuvel, 1990). Therefore, from an outsider's view, cohabitors appear less ready for and currently less interested in establishing a family.

From an insider perspective, the same picture emerges. When asked to classify the nature of their cohabiting unions, only one in ten cohabiting respondents selected the "alternative to marriage" choice as how they viewed their living situation. Instead, nearly half of cohabitors classified their arrangement as a step in the marriage process, with another 15 percent seeing it as a trial marriage (Casper and Sayer, 2000). The remaining couples viewed their situation as part of dating. Interestingly, those viewing cohabitation as a precursor to marriage were most likely to be married when studied five years later. Meanwhile, half of those in what were labeled "trial marriages" were no longer together (Casper and Sayer, 2000).

Half of cohabiting unions do not last beyond a year because either the couple breaks up or they marry (Bumpass and Lu, 2000). Thus, cohabiting unions do not seem to be a replacement for marriage.

Why has cohabitation become such an important step in the marriage process for so many individuals? Indeed, more than half of marriages formed in the 1990s were preceded by the couple's cohabitation (Bumpass and Lu, 2000), and the vast majority of cohabitors believe they will marry their partner (Bumpass et al., 1991). One likely influence is the tremendous rise in divorce that has occurred in the United States over the past 30 years. As a result, many people today have serious concerns about the potential stability of marriage and see cohabitation as a way to test their compatibility with a partner before legally tying the knot (Bumpass et al., 1991). This reasoning may also partly explain why adults whose parents divorced are more likely to cohabit than those whose parents are not divorced (Bachrach, Hindin, and Thomson, 2000). This group, especially, may worry about their potential success in marriage. It is also the case that more young people whose parents have conflicted intact marriages believe cohabitation is a good idea than do those whose parents appear relatively happy (Kozuch and Cooney, 1995). Cohabitation is considered by many as a way to check things out before making a legal commitment.

The Big Picture: The Influence of Macrolevel Forces on the Formation of Intimate Relationships

Despite the fact that intimate, romantic relationships are considered part of one's private life and have deep personal significance for most individuals, they are still influenced by societal forces and institutions. How individuals view intimate relationships, what they expect from them, and the ways in which they pursue and establish them are just a few of the specific aspects of relationships that are subject to societal influences. Here we briefly explore how such social changes and situations as the women's movement, improved contraception, and the emergence of the HIV/AIDS virus have shaped the way individuals think about and approach the formation of intimate relationships at the start of the twenty-first century.

Social Change in Views and Behaviors Regarding Sex, Sexuality, and Gender Roles

The 1960s and 1970s were characterized by immense social upheaval. The civil rights movement, the gay rights movement (which began with the Stonewall riot in Greenwich Village in 1969), the women's movement, and the sexual revolution all had an impact on intimate relationships in this country.

The civil rights movement's push for equality and acceptance for minorities raised questions about the intolerance for interracial dating and marriage that existed in the United States at the time. A powerful movie in the 1960s, *Guess Who's Coming to Dinner?* debated this issue, as two sets of parents considered why they had such problems with the proposed marriage of their daughter (who was white) and son (who was black). These fictional parents came to realize that what really mattered was the feelings these two individuals had for each other; yet, the parents worried about the social stigma and pressure their offspring would face in an interracial marriage. This fear accurately portrayed what was happening at the societal level at that time. Even though many states rescinded laws banning interracial marriage in the latter half of the twentieth century, interracial relationships still face social challenges today, as was discussed earlier in this chapter.

Just as the civil rights movement pressed for the end of racial discrimination, the gay political movement challenged societal discrimination against homosexuality and same-sex couples. Changes in views of homosexuality were evidenced by the declassification of homosexuality as a mental disorder by the American Psychiatric Association in 1973. Legally, states started to remove or ignore laws that dealt with sexual relations between same-sex partners in the privacy of their homes. Gays encouraged each other to be more open about their sexuality and lifestyles, and for many formerly closeted homosexuals, this change allowed for consideration of different lifestyle choices and family arrangements.

The sexual revolution of the 1960s and early 1970s also reshaped how many people approached and engaged in intimate relationships. Encouragement of more open expressions of sexuality—whether one was straight or gay—and a push for increased acceptance of sexual relations outside of marriage were fueled by young adults. However, persons in their late twenties and thirties were also affected by this movement, as growing numbers of them divorced during this historical period and were cast into a new world of dating, relationships, and sex. Medical advancements played a key role in this movement as well, because without the improved contraception that came available in the 1960s (birth control pills), women would not have felt as comfortable being sexually active outside of marriage. Indeed, part of the sexual revolution was a push to revise the view of sex as an act of procreation, which many people held, to an act of emotional expression or recreation.

Sexual expression was affected more recently by the emergence of the HIV/AIDS virus in the early 1980s. This deadly virus is transmitted by the exchange of bodily fluids, such as blood and semen, and most often it is spread through sexual intercourse, blood transfusions, or use of contaminated needles. Initially, the AIDS epidemic was a major concern for gay men, and many believed that the disease could be spread only through homosexual contact. But today, just over half of AIDS cases in the United States are estimated to be the result of homosexual sex (U.S. Centers for Disease Control, 2000). A rising number of heterosexuals have also been infected. As a consequence of the disease, and a rise in other sexually transmitted diseases, emphasis today is placed on "safe sex." This term refers to using condoms to protect against the transmission of bodily fluids, encouragement of communication between sexual partners about their past sexual partners and activity, and caution about the number of partners individuals have.

Michael et al.'s (1994) sex survey found that about one-third of adults reportedly altered their sexual behavior because of fear of AIDS. (Note: only five individuals in their sample said they were infected with the virus.) Those most likely to report exercising greater caution were black (46 percent) as opposed to white (26 percent), and nonmarried (40 percent of cohabitors, 32 percent noncohabitors) rather than married (12 percent). Thus, it appears that society's experience with AIDS has altered the expression of sexual intimacy for a sizeable portion of the population.

As the major social movements described above were occurring throughout the 1960s and 1970s, the United States was also experiencing a wide-scale women's rights movement. Although its major emphasis was on equal opportunities for women in the public domain, especially in terms of education, employment, and income, the debate about equality spread to the family and interpersonal domain as well. Just as the civil rights movement, gay liberation, and the sexual revolution had altered formation of and interaction within intimate partnerships in this country, so, too, did the women's movement.

One study that reflects historical changes in gender-role expectations for intimate partners was conducted by Buss and his colleagues (2001) using archival data gathered beginning in 1936, along with their own primary data collection conducted in 1996. These researchers compared data drawn from college student samples at six distinct historical periods. Their analysis of the most favored qualities in a partner (number 1 denotes the top quality of 18 characteristics that were ranked) reveals some interesting gender and historical differences, as can be seen in Table 3.1.

There was substantial historical consistency over the 60-year period in a few of the most valued partner characteristics. Having a partner who was dependable and mature, and who had a pleasant disposition, mattered greatly to both men and women at each survey point. Mutual attraction/love was also valued highly by both sexes, and over time this factor assumed increasing importance in mate selection. For males, mutual love jumped from a low ranking of number 4 in 1936 to number 1 by the 1980s; for females the low point of number 6 for mutual love came in 1956, but by 1977 it had climbed to number 1 and has remained in that top position.

Table 3.1 Rankings of Preferred Characteristics in a Mate, by Sex, 1939 to 1996

Characteristic[1]	Men's Ranking						Women's Ranking					
	Year						Year					
	'39	'56	'67	'77	'84/85	'96	'39	'56	'67	'77	'84/85	'96
Dependable	1	1	1	3	3	2	2	1	2	3	3	2
Stability/maturity	2	2	3	1	2	3	1	2	1	2	2	3
Pleasing disposition	3	4	4	4	4	4	4	5	4	4	4	4
Mutual love	4	3	2	2	1	1	5	6	3	1	1	1
Desire for home/children	6	5	5	11	9	9	7	3	5	10	7	6
Good cook/housekeeper	8	7	6	13	13	14	16	16	16	16	16	16
Ambitious	9	9	8	8	11	10	3	4	6	6	6	7
Chastity	10	13	15	17	17	16	10	15	15	18	18	17
Good looks	14	15	11	9	7	8	17	18	17	15	13	13
Good financial prospect	17	17	18	16	16	13	13	12	12	11	11	11

[1]This is a partial list of the 18 characteristics that were studied by Buss et al. (2001).

Notable historical shifts can be seen in preferences for a partner who desires a home and children, who is a good cook and housekeeper, who is ambitious, who is good-looking, or who is a good financial prospect, although these historical changes differ somewhat by gender. While women have fairly consistently put more emphasis than men on finding a partner with a desire for home and children (their number 3 characteristic and men's number 5 in 1956), the gender gap has been greater at more recent survey points than in the 1950s, '60s and '70s. The historical trend is reversed, however, in the shifting value of ambition as rated by women relative to men over time. In 1936, an ambitious partner was the number 3 choice for women but only the number 9 choice for men. Men's rankings of this characteristic wavered only slightly over the past six decades (most recently number 10), while women's ranking of this characteristic dropped significantly—in the 1996 survey, ambition only garnered a ranking of number 7. Good looks, on the other hand, is a characteristic that has mattered more to men than women in mate selection at each survey. Although both sexes rate the physical attractiveness of a potential spouse more highly today than in the past, the gap has grown substantially, with men rating it number 8 in 1996, compared to women's ranking of number 13. Men have also rated chastity as a slightly more preferred mate characteristic than women have, but its importance for both sexes has fallen somewhat over time, with a slight increase (from 17 to 16 for men and 18 to 17 for women) between the 1980s and 1996. Finally, despite the fact that over time women have valued the favorable financial prospects of their potential mate more than men have, the gender gap in preferences for this factor has significantly narrowed in recent decades. In 1967 this characteristic was rated last in men's view of what they were looking for in a spouse, whereas today it is number 13, just a few places behind women's historically consistent rating of 11.

Most of these changes in mate selection preferences make sense in light of numerous societal transformations that occurred in the twentieth century. Buss et al. (2001) note for example that the declining value of chastity may be partially linked to increasing availability of effective contraception in the past several decades, as well as to the sexual revolution of the 1960s. For both sexes, the 1969 to 1977 drop in chastity's ranking was most notable, and this was the period right after the sexual revolution and widespread access to birth control pills. The small climb upward in the importance of chastity between the 1980s and 1996 survey may reflect the growing concern over the risk of HIV/AIDS during that period, although it is somewhat surprising that the increase was not greater. This may reflect the misconception held by many that heterosexuals are at low risk for contracting the disease. The higher premium placed on a partner's good looks, especially by men, also is understandable given the surge in sales and advertising for beauty products, which have been heavily targeted toward women (Buss et al., 2001).

The most dramatic changes in mate selection preferences over time appear to be those related to gender roles, such as the declining preferences for women to be good homemakers and cooks and for men to be successful breadwinners. The women's movement, which spurred the growing presence of women in higher education and the workforce, appears to have forced a shift in both men's and women's thinking about the roles they want their future spouses to assume. While modern men seem less interested in selecting a woman for her cooking and housekeeping skills than was true of their peers a few decades ago, modern women consider ambition in a husband as less important than their predecessors do. Interestingly, however, both men and women are now more likely to look for a spouse who has good financial prospects. Perhaps as American women have assumed greater economic independence and earning power, they are less willing to have a partner who is not financially independent and secure, just as men are less willing to carry the economic breadwinning role on their own.

Finally, the heightened importance of mutual love and attraction in partner selection for both sexes in these surveys is interesting to consider in light of historical change. This historical shift is likely a result of the increasing emphasis on individualism believed to have occurred in the United States during the twentieth century. **Individualism** is an approach to family—and to life more generally—that emphasizes individual opportunities, rights, and choice and self-expression and fulfillment, rather than obligation and duty to others and self-sacrifice for others (Bellah, Madsen, Sullivan, Swidler, and Tipton, 1985). It appears that as adults contemplate marriage and the kind of partner they desire to share their life with, their top priority is (and has been since about 1980) finding a partner that satisfies their personal, emotional needs. This shift is consistent with changes in the meaning and focus of marriage over the last century, an issue we address in the next chapter.

Summary

This chapter examined the natural desire that all humans have for intimacy, which we defined as special feelings of warmth, closeness, and connection to another. Such feelings are based in shared experience and self-disclosure. Individuals come to know one another and feel a unique connection to that person through the mutual experiences they share and the information and feelings about themselves that they disclose to each other. What helps people feel comfortable engaging in new experiences with another person and sharing their deepest thoughts and feelings with that person is the conveyance of trust, respect, and empathy in the relationship. When individuals feel confident in how another will respond to them (trust) and believe she or he accepts and understands them, they are more likely to share with that person and feel close to him or her. Shared experiences, self-disclosure, trust, respect, and empathy are at the core of intimacy, which is the one relational component that is most consistently present across various types of love relationships, whether love for a parent, sibling, best friend, or romantic partner (Sternberg and Grajek, 1984).

Intimate unions play a central role in how individuals see themselves, and they contribute in significant ways to individual life satisfaction and well-being. In this chapter we examined the development of intimate relationships, including both psychological and social components of that process. We briefly explored how several major social movements of the last part of the twentieth century are likely to have altered intimate relationships for individuals in the United States. In the next chapter we will discuss some of the central behavioral processes involved in intimate relationships (communication, task sharing, sex) and consider how intimate interactions and relationships are maintained over time.

An important point to keep in mind when considering intimate relationships is that they develop and exist in a complex social and cultural system. Because individuals simultaneously occupy several interdependent roles in their lives—intimate partner, worker, student—and these roles are defined and shaped by societal values, institutions, and conditions, historical or chronosystem changes have repercussions for how these personal, private relationships are experienced over time.

Endnote

1. Developmental scholars report that intimacy is generally not part of most early teen romances. One theory contends that adolescents go through four phases (initial infatuation, affiliative romantic relationships, intimate romantic relationships, committed romantic relationships) en route to eventually forming mature love relationships. It isn't until the third phase, intimate romantic relationships, generally occurring in late adolescence, that teens report high levels of intimacy (Connolly and Goldberg, 1999). The first phase, infatuation, is characterized by limited interaction with the other person. The second phase, affiliative romantic relationships, involves more interaction with the other party, yet little deep sharing and self-disclosure, largely because of the centrality of the peer group for early to mid-adolescents. Young teens hang out in same-sex or mixed-sex groups, and they depend on their friends to meet most of their intimacy needs. As teens mature and gain confidence and comfort with the opposite sex, they begin to engage in more intimate behavior with romantic partners. In young adulthood, they move into the fourth stage of romantic relationships, which involves consideration of commitment issues (Connolly and Goldberg, 1999).

Chapter Concepts

cohabitation: sharing of a household by an unmarried couple who are intimately involved with each other.

companionate love: a type of love that involves fulfillment and enjoyment of time spent together and that develops through close interaction and growing interdependence over time.

empathy: an understanding of another's experiences and feelings as if they were one's own.

homogamy: similarity between partners in terms of key social characteristics, such as race, age, social class, education, and religion.

individualism: an approach to life that emphasizes individual opportunities, rights, and choice and self-expression and fulfillment, rather than obligation and duty to others and self-sacrifice for others.

intimacy: feelings of warmth and closeness and a sense of personal connection that exists between two persons.

intimacy need fulfillment: the stage in the wheel theory of love marked by partners having their respective needs for such things as intimacy, economic security, status, and companionship met through the relationship.

mutual dependency: the stage in the wheel theory of love in which partners become emotionally and behaviorally dependent on each other and their lives become tightly connected.

passionate love: a type of love that primarily involves physical attraction and arousal.

principle of least interest: the idea that in any social relationship the party that has made the smallest investment in the relationship has the most power or influence over what happens to that relationship.

rapport: comfort in interacting and talking with another that comes with time together and trust. Rapport building is the first stage in the wheel theory of love.

respect: holding another's views and behaviors in high regard.

self-disclosure: the act of sharing personal information and deep, private feelings with another.

self-revelation: the second stage in the wheel theory of love, in which partners become increasingly comfortable with disclosing personal feelings and information to each other.

trust: the expectation that another's word or behavior can be relied on.

Suggested Activities

1. Look in the Personals section of a newspaper and clip out or copy several of the ads. After reading them, summarize the qualities that seem to be preferred by those persons posting the ads. Do you see any similarities in what they are looking for? Are the preferred qualities different depending on whether a male or female posted the ad? Do you notice any differences in what heterosexual advertisers mention compared to gay or lesbian advertisers? Which level of the filter theory do most of these ads address?

2. Think about how you have been socialized in terms of the types of people considered acceptable partners for you. Have others (parents, other family members, friends) explicitly discussed with you the characteristics of others they consider acceptable dating or marriage partners for you? Have you noticed implicit influences regarding this issue? Ask some of your friends the same questions.

Suggested Readings

Cooney, T. M., and Dunne, K. 2001. "Intimate relationships in late life: Current realities, future prospects." *Journal of Family Issues 22*:838–858.

Popenoe, D., and Whitehead, B. D. 2002. "Should we live together? What young adults need to know about cohabitation before marriage: A comprehensive review of recent research." (A report from the National Marriage Project.) In E. Schroeder (ed.), *Taking Sides: Clashing Views on Controversial Issues in Family and Personal Relationships* (5th ed.), (pp. 212–236). Guildford, CT: McGraw-Hill/Dushkin.

Solot, D., and Miller, M. 2002. "What the research really says about cohabitation: A report of the Alternatives to Marriage Project." In E. Schroeder (ed.), *Taking Sides: Clashing Views on Controversial Issues in Family and Personal Relationships* (5th ed.), (pp. 212–236). Guildford, CT: McGraw-Hill/Dushkin.

Sprecher, S. 2002. "Sexual satisfaction in premarital relationships: Associations with satisfaction, love, commitment, and stability." *The Journal of Sex Research 39*:190–196. ◆

Chapter 4

Maintaining Intimacy

Marriage and Enduring Unions

Did You Know?

- Most men and women do marry. In 1998, only 7.7 percent of U.S. women and 10.6 percent of men 35 or older in the United States had never married (Current Population Survey 1998, as reported in Casper and Bianchi, 2002).
- Marriage seems to buffer both men and women from health problems and risk of mortality. Unmarried persons have a risk of mortality up to 10 times greater than their married counterparts of the same age (Hu and Goldman, 1990).
- Men and women differ in their approach to relational conflict. According to one study using a national sample, 40 percent of men but only 25 percent of women reported they withdraw from interaction when conflict occurs in their relationship (Stanley and Markman, 1997).

Things to Think About

- Despite high divorce rates and a growing number of socially acceptable alternatives to marriage, why do you think most Americans still marry?
- What factors do you think contribute most to whether intimate partners feel satisfied with and happy in their relationship?
- How do couples determine who makes the critical decisions in their relationship?
- Why is it that some couples seem to stay in love forever while for others love fades?

arriage is a highly valued institution in American society. Fowlkes (1994) claims that "it is the American way to treat adult intimacy as synonymous with marriage" (151) and that as a society we "continue to impose marriage as the standard by which all sexual and intimate relationships are evaluated" (151–152). She notes that even among social scientists, the term *nonmarital* is commonly used to denote relationships that are totally independent of marriage, which seems to imply that marriage is the norm and all other relationships are considered variations from that norm.

The public also sees marriage as a key marker of adult status in American culture, and most adults in this country expect and want to marry some day. Certainly the media, especially reality television in 2003–2004, have become consumed with intimate partnering and marriage. Several popular reality programs, such as *The Bachelor*, have focused on finding the perfect marital partner for the man or women of interest. Marriage and weddings also contribute to big business in the United States. Couples often spend months planning for their special day, and some hire professional wedding planners to help them with the job. Besides the huge time investment devoted to planning for their wedding day, many couples (or their families) make a substantial financial investment as well. The average price of a U.S. wedding was estimated at $19,000 in 2004 (<www.Wedsite.USA.com>). Based on Americans' fascination with marriage and the customs and celebrations around marriage, our society holds marriage in high regard and values it greatly.

This chapter begins with a macro-level review of historical changes in marital patterns and racial differences in marital behavior. It then considers microlevel issues within marital relationships. Specifically, we explore the central behavioral processes involved in intimate unions, including communication, conflict, decision making, power dynamics, and sexual expression. We examine the role these processes play in committed, enduring relationships and in couple stability and satisfaction. Additionally, we address how intimate partners maintain their relationships over time, and we identify specific behaviors they engage in to sustain their connection to each other. Of particular interest is how men and women compare in terms of these relationship processes, as well as how these processes vary across heterosexual and same-sex couples. When considering same-sex relationships in this chapter, we focus primarily on those in which the partners are living together as a couple. This type of situation is more common among lesbians than among gay men: About two-fifths of lesbian women and just over one-quarter of gay men are living in such unions (Black, Gates, Sanders, and Taylor, 2000). Although not recognized by law, these same-sex committed relationships constitute a salient family form to many adults today.

This chapter concludes by examining societal changes that have occurred since the middle of the last century and the impact these changes have had on the establishment and maintenance of intimate relationships. We use the ecological perspective as our tool for considering societal transformations such as exosystem changes in laws (e.g., those pertaining to same-sex relations) and macrosystem changes in values (e.g., greater acceptance of divorce). We discuss the role of these changes in reshaping intimate relationships in American society in recent decades.

Marriage Patterns: Historical Trends and Racial and Social Class Differences

First marriages are occurring later today than at any other point in the past 150 years. During the late 1800s, the median marriage age (age at which half of the population had married) was approximately 26 for white men and 22 for white women. Blacks married two years earlier, on average, than their same-sex white counterparts. Throughout the early part of the twentieth century, age at marriage gradually declined, primarily because of industrialization and the rise in nonagricultural jobs that afforded young people the opportunity to start and support their own families at a younger age. During the economic boom period following World War II, a decline in the age at marriage became particularly pronounced, for whites especially. By 1960, half of white men and women were married by the ages of 22 and 20, respectively. About this time, the age at marriage began to climb for blacks, with the median ages rising above those of whites. In the last few decades the age at marriage has also increased for whites. Today, the median ages of marriage for white males and females are 27 and 25, respectively. Comparable figures for blacks are 29 and 27, respectively (Fitch and Ruggles, 2000).

Although the age at marriage is climbing, the likelihood that individuals will marry has not changed dramatically for Americans. Estimates are that approximately 90 percent of all American adults can expect to marry at some point in their lifetimes. The probability of not marrying is about twice as great for blacks than for whites (Fitch and Ruggles, 2000).

Consistently, studies reveal that racial differences in marriage behavior are not the result of differences in expectations or preference for marriage. This fact was evident in a multicity telephone interview study conducted in the mid-1990s, with 3,407 respondents ages 18–55 (40 percent African American, 7 percent Latino, and 53 percent white) (Tucker, 2000). Data from this study revealed no racial/ethnic differences in expectations for marriage, the value that individuals placed on marrying some day, or how important respondents thought it was to be married when they had children.

How Economic Factors Contribute to Marriage Behavior

Although there appear to be no racial differences in adults' *preferences* for marriage, substantial racial variability exists in the value placed on having a good income before one marries (Tucker, 2000). In the multicity telephone survey, blacks were the group most likely to express the view that having adequate income is critical to marital success. Moreover, when an analysis was done to identify the factors that contribute to adults' expectations for marriage, economic issues were particularly salient for blacks. Among white men, higher education and income predicted significantly higher expectations to marry. For black men, income was the only one of these two variables to matter. Finally, if black women perceived marriage to have economic benefits, their expectations for marrying were greater. This factor also had an effect on white men (Tucker, 2000).

Other studies have highlighted the importance of economic security for the marital decisions of blacks. One national survey found that single black women were more likely than never-married white women to report that a potential spouse's establishment in a job was critical in their decision to marry (Bulcroft and Bulcroft, 1993). Qualitative interviews with low-income single black mothers have richly illustrated this same point. Sharp and Ispa (forthcoming, 2005) share the comments of a young woman, Sherryce, whom they interviewed in their research on low-income families:

> He [a potential boyfriend] has to bring something to the table. I have a full table. You know, he need to bring something, he just can't bring himself and then go live off me 'cause that ain't right. (8)

Sharp and Ispa's research also showed that black men often share a similar concern about being able to contribute to marriage. Tejon, the partner of one of the women they studied, explained:

> We got plans on getting married; I'd like to be married and have a little comfortable life, just real comfortable. I want to be married and living comfortable. When asked about barriers to marriage, he responded, 'Man, jobs. You know, just finding one; it is hard finding a good job.' (8)

Because most individuals marry within their own race, population researchers try to understand marriage patterns by examining the pool of eligible partners within a given race. This pool of eligibles is part of the **marriage market,** a term that refers to the supply of eligible marital partners. A marriage market is determined by examining the sex ratios of persons of approximately similar ages, within race, within a specified geographic area. Researchers have discussed the competitive marriage market that exists in the black population and the consequent "female marriage squeeze" for women (Crowder and Tolnay, 2000). In part, the marriage market for black women is limited by the absolute difference in the size of the female and male populations for young blacks. Table 4.1 shows the relative numbers of single men to women, of selected ages, within the black, Latino, and white populations. At younger ages we would expect more single men than women because, as noted already, men usually wait to marry at a slightly older age than women. This pattern, however, is not evident in the ratios for blacks, due in large part to high mortality rates among young black males. Additionally, a growing percentage of black men are choosing to marry nonblack women, thereby taking them out of the pool of eligibles for black women. Intermarriage is most common for well-educated black men who are economically successful (Crowder and Tolnay, 2000).

We've already mentioned that a man's earning potential and employment status are of particular concern for black women in their decisions about whether to marry. This factor narrows the field of eligibles for black women even more, because of the high rates of black male unemployment. Such rates are more than twice those for white men (U.S. Department of Labor, 1999). Lichter and his associates (1992) report that for

Table 4.1 Number of Never-Married Men Per 100 Never-Married Women at Select Ages, by Race/Ethnicity, 1998			
Age	**Whites**	**Latinos**	**Blacks**
20–24	121	152	93
25–29	135	177	90
30–34	157	154	75
Source: U.S. Bureau of the Census (2004a).			

every unmarried black man who lives above the poverty line, there are three unmarried black women in their twenties. Such statistics suggest that the competition for marrying income-earning black men is particularly stiff for black women.

Social Class and Marriage Patterns

Whereas racial differences in marital behavior pertain primarily to the *likelihood* of marriage, social class differences in marriage are found in terms of marital *timing*. A direct relationship exists between age at marriage and social class. That is, as social class goes up, the age at marriage also increases. (Note, however, that median age at marriage represents the age at which *half* of a population group had made the transition to marriage. Because low-income blacks have such low rates of marriage, the age by which half will have married is higher than for high-income blacks.) Much of this association is the result of the strong connection between education level and marriage; increased educational attainment is one of the best predictors of a delayed age at marriage, especially for women. Expectations for when young adults anticipate marrying are closely tied to their educational aspirations (Hogan and Astone, 1986).

Transition to Marriage

Marriage is a social transition—marking a change in social status from being "single" to being "married"; this transition comes with a variety of new roles and expectations. Knox and Schacht (2002) point out three public or social commitments that accompany marriage: person-to-person commitment, family-to-family commitment, and couple-to-state commitment.

Levels of Commitment Symbolized by Marriage

An obvious commitment that comes with marriage is the person-to-person commitment that intimate partners make to one another (Knox and Schacht, 2002). Through their marriage vows and the legal recognition of their marriage, marital partners declare to society that they have a special, unique relationship to each other, one that comes with unique responsibilities and expectations. While the specific expectations that partners hold for their marriage are likely to vary from couple to couple, the social and legal recognition of their union is still important to many. Even among gay and lesbian couples who cannot legally marry, increasing numbers are choosing to have their unions recognized through public ceremonies.

Marriage also creates family-to-family commitments (Knox and Schacht, 2002). When couples marry, each partner assumes a special connection to a family of in-laws. New relationships are forged with brothers- and sisters-in-law, parents-in-law, and many others. One of the ideas behind the wedding ceremony and celebration is the opportunity to bring the two families together so they can become better acquainted and feel united. Although seating arrangements at wedding ceremonies traditionally separate the bride's and the groom's relatives, most postceremony celebrations try to integrate the two families.

From a systems perspective, this blending of two families can be extremely challenging for the new couple. Newlyweds must work hard to clearly delineate the boundaries of their new family unit and their own routines and rituals. Partners must negotiate how much influence they want their respective families to have on their marriage, as well as how much involvement in their lives. They may struggle to determine such things as:

- How permeable are the boundaries around their marriage going to be?

- Will they discuss relational issues with their parents and other family members?

- Is it acceptable to run home to Mom when they have a serious argument?

This negotiation process can create some tensions within the couple ("That's not how my family does it!"), as well as between the couple and their two families of orientation ("But my parents expect all of their children to be together with them on Passover"). Newly married couples handle this transition more smoothly when each partner has developed a good balance of autonomy and connectedness in his or her own life prior to marriage (Peterson, Madden-Derdich, and Leonard, 2000).

Finally, marriage involves a couple-to-state commitment (Knox and Schacht, 2002). By legally marrying, couples accept requirements and expectations for legally married persons. Although laws vary from state to state, in most places they include such commitments as financial responsibility to each other (e.g., assuming the partner's debt) and the obligation to formally dissolve the marriage through the courts if the marriage fails. All of the types of commitment potentially influence the level of commitment partners feel to their marriage. The degree to which couples believe that their marriage will continue into the future and feel invested in it may be influenced by family or in-law pressure to stay married, the divorce laws in their state, and the personal or moral obligation they feel to maintain the promise they made to their spouse in their public wedding ceremony.

Weddings bring family and friends together to witness marriage partners' commitment to each other. As an observer, do you have different behavioral expectations for a recently married couple than a couple that is dating or cohabiting outside of marriage?

Psychological and Relational Changes Accompanying Marriage

The transition to marriage involves a number of interpersonal and psychological transitions. Two individuals now become part of one couple. Much of one's life that was formerly "me-centered" now becomes "we-centered." As such, newly married partners face the challenge of figuring out how to meet their individual needs and maintain their individual identity while at the same time developing and maintaining connectedness to each other (Cowan and Cowan, 2000). There is no ideal or standard balance between autonomy and connection that can be learned and copied by watching other couples. Rather, "Each couple must find the *balance* between the two orientations that creates an atmosphere conducive to the development of the individuals and the relationship" (Cowan and Cowan, 2000, 189).

Part of the identity change that comes with marriage is captured in the family name that the couple chooses to use and how women prefer to be formally addressed. Some women may feel quite comfortable being referred to as "Mrs. John Smith" in the traditional manner, whereas others might feel such a title suggests a loss of self and individuality—as if the wife's identity now comes totally from her spouse. A study of female psychology students at a major American university (Twenge, 1997) considered the issue of marital names and found that:

- 60 percent preferred to assume their future husband's last name.

- 10 percent preferred to maintain their own last name in all situations after marriage.

- 14 percent preferred using their own last name professionally but their future husband's socially.

- 13 percent preferred to use a hyphenated name (his and hers), but most didn't expect their future husbands to do the same.

- Less than 1 percent preferred to select a new family name with their future husband.

Clearly, women today have a variety of opinions about this important issue.

Another critical issue in many new marriages is figuring out how the couple will socialize with others. Will they socialize only as a couple, or will they conduct some aspects of their social lives on their own? Furthermore, how much of their social and leisure time will be spent with extended family—his or hers? Different couples, or even the two partners within a couple, may have contrasting views about what they need and what's preferred in their marriage. It may take a great deal of emotional energy and time to resolve these issues within a marriage.

Unpublished data from a study of newly married (less than nine months) couples illustrates this idea. The following example involves a husband who is a 23-year-old short-order cook and a wife who is a 19-year-old student and part-time clerk (Tallman, Burke, and Gecas, 1998):

Husband: I went to the bar with my friends to play darts. I went and played and had a good match. We had our millionth argument about how she thinks I don't spend enough time with her.

Question: What did you do about this?

Husband: I tried to ignore her because she complains about this all the time. She always gets upset.

Wife: We argued about not going out very much and not having time with one another. We argued over him never having time with me and me feeling ignored and left out.

Question: What did you do about this?

Wife: I became really upset and felt like crying. He just got angry. He acts as he usually does, like nothing bothers him. I became very upset as usual and I'm sick of feeling unimportant.

As this example shows, establishing an acceptable balance between autonomy and connectedness in a marriage can be a major issue that is not always easily resolved. This issue also can create highly charged emotions within the couple.

His and Hers: Are the Costs and Benefits of Marriage Different for Men and Women?

Since the earliest European settlers arrived in this country in the 1600s, marriage has entailed different rights and responsibilities for men and for women. **Coverture,** a feudal doctrine based heavily on biblical and church teachings, had a particularly strong influence on marriages formed in the early years of North American family life. According to this doctrine, marriage united man and woman into one entity, with the husband gaining full control over a wife and her property (Liss, 1987). Liss quotes from an 1854 document by Blackstone in which this law is described:

> By marriage, the husband and wife are one person in law . . . the very being or legal existence of the woman is suspended . . . or at least incorporated and consolidated into that of the husband, under whose wing, protection and cover she performs everything. (769)

Stemming from this early doctrine, numerous laws were written over the years that continued to restrict the rights of married women. For example, a husband's residence was considered the married couple's legal residence, and women often lost their right to independently obtain credit. In addition, a variety of social practices reinforced the notion that women came under their husband's authority with marriage, such as the practice of a married woman giving up her surname for that of her husband and husbands being designated as "head of household" by the U.S. Census Bureau (until 1980). At the same time that the law required women to forfeit many of their individual rights in entering marriage, it awarded them the economic protection of their husbands, which to some was interpreted as the trade-off women made in marriage. Most states imposed strict support obligations on husbands. The higher marriage age requirement imposed on men than women and divorce laws requiring men but not women to pay alimony were offshoots of such laws (Nock, 1998). In the last 30 years, however, essentially all states have changed their marriage and family laws to make them more consistent with a gender-neutral view of marriage.

Bernard's Views on Marriage. As a result of forces such as religious teachings, laws, and social norms, traditional marriage (even into the twentieth century) posed very distinct roles for men and women. To many observers, the costs and benefits of marriage differed widely for the two sexes. Sociologist Jessie Bernard argued in her now-classic book

The Future of Marriage (1972) that the meaning and experience of marriage is so distinct for men versus women that we must distinguish between "his" marriage and "her" marriage. Bernard contended that traditional marriage required much greater personal sacrifice on the part of women compared to men. With entry to marriage, women gave up their names, their career or work ambitions, and their pursuit of personal happiness. In essence, traditional marital roles called on women to sacrifice their wants and needs for those of family members, whose well-being and happiness were to be of primary concern. The "his" marriage, in contrast, required men to play the "good provider role," in which they were solely responsible for the provision of food, shelter, and clothing for their families (Bernard, 1981). Although such expectations could place a great deal of pressure on husbands to be successful, the opportunity for men to achieve a profound sense of pride and fulfillment in such a role was emphasized (Komarovsky, 1940). Moreover, in return for their hard work in the marketplace, married men were not only rewarded with the status gained from career success but received the constant care and concern of a loving wife who created a comfortable home for them and took primary responsibility for raising their children.

Bernard's reference to a "his" and "hers" marriages also reflected a set of research findings indicating that husbands and wives often interpreted their interactions and the quality of their marriage very differently. For example, some early research indicated that women were less satisfied in their marriages than men were, and perceived more problems (Gurin, Veroff, and Feld, 1960). Additionally, Bernard argued that the "his" marriage is much more beneficial for men than the "hers" marriage is for women. Even though many married women claimed to be happy with their lives, Bernard contended that, in fact, they were merely reconciled to their fate in marriage. She believed that because women had so few alternatives in society besides marriage and motherhood, and because socialization for the wife role was so strong, perhaps many women hopelessly abandoned their dreams and ambitions and passively accepted their roles in marriage as satisfying and fulfilling. (An example of how it was not always possible to do so is found in the role of Laura in the novel and film *The Hours*.)

New Evidence on the Costs and Benefits of Marriage. Recent scholarship revisited this issue of a his and a hers marriage, examining the benefits of marriage for men and women with contemporary data. Nock (1998) analyzed longitudinal data collected from a nationally representative sample of youths (who were followed into adulthood) to consider the effects of marriage on economic and career achievement and community and family involvement. His analyses revealed that, averaged across age, transitioning from single to married status was associated with a $4,200 annual increase in income for men, as well as substantial change in occupational prestige. Similar gains were not realized by men making other transitions (such as cohabitation). Married men worked more each year than single men, however, which could account for some of the income difference. Transition to marriage was also associated with men's increased involvement with relatives and with religious and community groups. However, married men reported reduced contact with friends and less socializing in bars and taverns relative to when they were single.

Nock (1998) reports that he replicated these analyses with women in his sample and found results similar to those for men. However, the positive effects of marriage for women were not as sizable as they were for men. He speculates that perhaps "his" marriage is still better than "hers."

Waite (2000) analyzed nationally representative cross-sectional surveys from 1972 to 1996 to consider the benefits of marriage for men and women. Similar to Nock's, her analyses suggested that married men have an earnings advantage relative to unmarried men. (However, Waite used cross-sectional data, so she was not comparing the same men before and after marriage. An alternative explanation is that the most successful men are "selected" into marriage because they are viewed as good catches. This idea contrasts with the view that marriage somehow makes men more productive.) Waite did not find an earnings benefit to marriage for women. Yet compared to unmarried women, married women reported greater satisfaction with their work. Waite speculates that perhaps this finding is due to the more voluntary nature of employment for married than unmarried women.

In terms of subjective ratings of life quality, Waite found numerous advantages for married persons. Married men and women reported that they derived more satisfaction from family life than unmarried persons did. Specific questions about marital satisfaction revealed small gender differences. In nearly every survey year, a higher percentage of married men than women claimed to be "very happy" in their marriages, yet these differences (although statistically significant) were never more than a few percentage points (e.g., in 1996, 60 percent of women were very happy versus 64 percent of men). In terms of general happiness, married men and women were the most likely to report being "very happy" relative to all other marital status groups, across all survey years. Waite found no substantial gender difference in what she calls the "happiness gap" between married and unmarried persons. Thus, many of the previous claims that Bernard so strongly championed—that marriage was damaging for women and that it only benefited men—are now widely discounted.

Other costs or benefits of marriage might be expected in the domains of physical and mental health. The analyses conducted by Waite (2000), which used a basic self-rating of general health status, found no apparent health benefits of marriage for either men or women. However, studies that examined specific health-related behaviors, such as drinking and smoking, indicate that married persons engage in healthier lifestyles than unmarried persons (Umberson, 1992) and are more likely to detect and seek treatment for symptoms (Joung et al., 1997). A recent study of over 10,000 people in Australia revealed that both married women and men appear advantaged relative to their same-sex single and divorced peers in terms of mental health as well. This study reported that 13 percent of married men and 13 percent of married women have emotional disorders, compared to 22–26 percent of single and divorced men and women (Ross, 2003). What is not evident from many of these studies—especially the cross-sectional ones—is whether marriage is a "cause" of positive health or just a related factor. That is, might there be some other factor, such as a personality low in risk taking, that increases one's chances of marriage and contributes to positive health status as well? Finding the answer to this question requires long-term longitudinal data.

The Internal Dynamics of Marriage

How do couples interact and negotiate their day-to-day lives once they've made a commitment to each other? What are the key dimensions of their relationships? In this section we look more closely at the interpersonal processes that occur within marriage and enduring unions—specifically, couple communication, conflict resolution, sexual relations, and power dynamics. We begin by discussing the concepts of marital satisfaction and stability, then throughout the section we address how specific couple dynamics contribute to these global evaluations of marriage.

Marital Satisfaction and Marital Stability

Marital satisfaction is an evaluative, subjective judgment that individual partners make about their relationship. Typically, researchers use multidimensional scales (with more than one question) of marital satisfaction to assess marital quality. A popular and widely used example of such a scale is the Dyadic Adjustment Scale (DAS), developed by Spanier (1976). The DAS is based on the view that marital satisfaction, or adjustment, is made up of four components:

1. *Dyadic satisfaction*—one's general happiness with the relationship.

2. *Dyadic cohesion*—one's feelings of togetherness gained from the relationship.

3. *Dyadic consensus*—perceived agreement with one's partner on important issues.

4. *Affectionate behavior*—perceived agreement on and engagement in affectionate expression and sex with one's partner.

As a quality indicator of marriage, satisfaction differs from what is referred to as **marital stability,** which is the likelihood that a marriage will remain intact. Researchers assess this component of marriage by asking partners such questions as "Have you ever thought that your marriage might be in trouble?" and "Have you or your spouse ever seriously suggested the idea of divorce?" (Booth and Edwards, 1985, 70). It is important to understand that marital stability and marital quality are distinct, independent assessments. A couple may be very dissatisfied with their marriage yet have no intention of divorcing, thereby having a very stable marriage. One major review article of marital outcomes concluded that, over time, partners' satisfaction with marriage declines although the stability of most marriages actually increases (Karney and Bradbury, 1995). The decline in marital satisfaction for both spouses appears steepest in the first four years of marriage (Kurdek, 1993a; Karney and Bradbury, 1997), with satisfaction leveling off or declining more gradually thereafter. (See Chapters 5 and 6 for added discussion of marital satisfaction and change at specific points in the life cycle.)

What contributes to high marital satisfaction and stability for couples? Karney and Bradbury (1995) reviewed over 100 longitudinal studies of marriage and concluded that among the key factors predicting marital satisfaction are the following:

- Sexual satisfaction.
- Positive couple behavior.
- Similarity of the partners' personalities.

Marital stability, on the other hand, appears to be strongly influenced by:

- Marital satisfaction.

- Similarity in attitudes.
- Sexual satisfaction.
- Family income.
- Partners' education levels.

Although employment also plays an important role in stability, its effects vary based on whose employment is considered. Husbands' employment contributes to the stability of marriage, whereas wives' employment appears to undermine marital stability. A common explanation in the literature is that women's employment reduces their economic dependence on their husbands and facilitates their leaving a marriage if it is troubled or unhappy.

Ethnic and racial differences in marital quality are an area of interest to family scholars. Evidence from some studies based specifically on black couples shows that blacks generally have high levels of marital satisfaction. Thomas (1990) studied 41 black dual-career couples; 98 percent of husbands and 93 percent of wives expressed happiness with their marriage. Moreover, marital satisfaction was the strongest predictor of partners' global life satisfaction in this study, even stronger than partners' satisfaction with work, children, finances, and other family relation-ships. In contrast, research that directly com-pared black and white couples has concluded that black couples report less marital happi-ness, on average, than white couples. Oggins, Veroff, and Leber (1993) did racial compari-sons with newlyweds and found that nearly all the same factors contributed to happiness in white and black marriages (including sexual satisfaction, supportiveness, and affect affir-mation from the spouse), yet overall satisfac-tion scores were lower among black couples. Quite possibly, external stressors, such as eco-nomic and work issues and racial discrimina-tion, place greater pressure on black than white marriages (Oggins et al., 1993). Indeed, marital quality in black couples is heavily influenced by partners', especially husbands', perceptions of the couple's income adequacy, but this find-ing applies only to lower-class couples (Clark-Nicolas and Gray-Little, 1991). Perhaps the relatively high socioeconomic standing of the dual-career couples studied by Thomas (1990) insulated them from such marital stress.

Less is known about predictors of relation-ship satisfaction and stability for same-sex couples than for heterosexual couples. Blum-stein and Schwartz (1983) examined what they

Same-sex couples report more companionship than heterosexual couples, which seems to con-tribute to intimacy, as well as relationship stabil-ity and satisfaction.

referred to as "relationship centeredness" in their study of heterosexual, gay, and lesbian couples, which denoted how each partner balanced relational or family issues with work issues and other roles, such as leisure. The happiest couples in their study were those in which both partners were relationship centered. This pattern was most common among lesbian couples and least common among heterosexual married couples. In particular, the lesbian couples seemed to have made decisions about the work-family balance that pleased both partners. Additionally, gay and lesbian couples were more likely to share leisure time than were heterosexual couples, perhaps because of greater similarity in interests and activities between same-sex than opposite-sex partners. Same-sex partners, therefore, appeared to find greater companionship in their relationship than heterosexual partners, which contributed to the development of greater intimacy and relationship satisfaction (Blumstein and Schwartz, 1983).

Power in Interpersonal Relationships

Relationship partners of every type exert influence over each other. Sometimes that influence occurs in a fairly passive way, such as when one person's language begins to influence the way his or her partner talks, or when partners adopt new interests as a result of spending time with each other and being exposed to each other's interests. At other times partners influence each other in more direct and explicit ways, and this influence is difficult to resist. **Power** is the ability of a person to affect the behavior or thinking of another (Cromwell and Olson, 1975), even in the face of resistance. Within marriage, many issues require decisions, and partners sometimes compete to gain power over decision-making. Most couples have to negotiate:

- Where they are going to live.

- Which house to buy.

- Whether they will have children, and if so, how many.

- How free time will be spent.

- What they will do with disposable income.

- How they will celebrate particular holidays.

Some of these issues are less important than others, but the decision making surrounding all of them is affected by patterns of power distribution within the family.

Which Partner Has More Power? One of the earliest research projects on marital power was conducted by sociologists Blood and Wolfe (1960). They presented married women with a list of issues that may arise in family life (what car to buy, where to go on vacation) and asked who generally had the final say on the issue—their husbands, themselves, or the two of them together. These researchers concluded that men had more power in the family than women based on the fact that wives reported that their husbands dominated decision making on these issues. Blood and Wolfe theorized that men's greater marital power was due to the fact that they controlled more of the resources within the marriage—a theory labeled **resource theory.** Specifically, this theory contends that whoever earns more money, has greater occupational and social prestige, and more education will generally be more powerful at home. The more resources a wife brings to the marriage (such as higher pay), therefore, the more power she gains in the relationship.

Newer studies that considered the role of resources in determining relationship power reveal mixed support for the theory. Rank's (1982) work found that high-earning wives did wield more influence in their marriages relative to women with fairly low levels of resources. However, in their study comparing heterosexual, gay male, and lesbian couples, Blumstein and Schwartz (1983) found that each partner's level of earnings mattered only some of the time. In heterosexual marriages, power was more often attributed to husbands in situations where they earned substantially more than their wives, compared to situations where spouses' earnings were about equal. Among gay male couples, the partner with the greater income was viewed as the more dominant partner in most cases. No support for resource theory was found among lesbian couples. Blumstein and Schwartz argue that to men money represents power, whereas to women money is linked to security and autonomy. Additionally, because of male dominance in society at large and the efforts of many women, and lesbians in particular, to promote egalitarianism, lesbian couples may work particularly hard to maintain equality in their relationships and avoid the display of dominance and power. In fact, other research indicates that when a power imbalance occurs in lesbian relationships, increased conflict is likely (Kurdek, 1994a).

Beyond the balance or imbalance in resources for a given couple, however, other factors are likely to contribute to patterns of power and dominance in intimate relationships. One such influence is the cultural norm of male dominance and authority within marriage, exhibited in the view that the husband is the head of the family and he should be the primary decision-maker. If members of a couple accept this cultural norm, which some have labeled "sex role traditionalism" (Peplau, Hill, and Rubin, 1993), this belief will influence their decision-making. Several studies with college samples have found this situation to be true. In the Boston Couples Study introduced in Chapter 3 (the study that provided data on the break-up process), it was revealed that men who adhered to traditional norms were more influential in relationship initiation than their partners, had greater influence over how time together was spent, and appeared more powerful on a global measure of relationship power, regardless of the partner's relative income. Furthermore, Pyke (1994) and Hochschild (1989) argue that the earnings and status that women derive from work do not necessarily represent a resource for all women; in situations where wives work despite the disfavor of their husbands, or where their income is viewed as a threat by their husbands—both of which may be the case if the husband rates high on sex role traditionalism—earnings may actually come to be regarded as a "gift" for women (i.e., something their husbands are graciously giving them the permission to have). In such cases, these wives may forfeit power to their husbands in exchange for being allowed to work and earn money.

Marital Power or Family Power? A major criticism of research and theorizing about marital and family power is that a male bias has prevailed. That is, power is assumed through the measurement of such resources as income, wealth, prestige, and occupation—all the things that males possess in a male-dominated, capitalistic society. Similarly, assessment of marital power has focused on the types of family decisions that deal with instrumental and material issues, such as what car to buy or where to live. Kranichfeld

(1987) is among the critics who have called for a rethinking of the concept of family power. She claims that one area that has been totally ignored in the power literature is that involving parenting, particularly socialization practices. She defines **family power** as changing and shaping the behavior of other family members. This is the domain where women dominate in families. Through the extensive time and effort they devote to child rearing, women become the major force in influencing and essentially shaping the next generation. As Kranichfeld (1987) puts it:

> Women's power is rooted in their roles as nurturers and kinkeepers, and flows out of their capacity to support and direct the growth of others around them throughout the life course. (48)

One of the long-term rewards of so powerfully shaping their children and helping to develop their family relationships, according to Kranichfeld (1987), is that women gain "the provision of support, and the opportunity for care and connection at deep emotional levels throughout the lifespan" (52). Their heavy influence over and involvement with their children essentially guarantees them their children's care and concern (perhaps out of attachment, but possibly obligation) throughout later life.

Approaches to Gaining Power. Power tactics can characterize the interactional tone in couple relationships. In trying to influence or manipulate another, one of two approaches can be taken: **indirect power tactics,** including such behaviors as whining, hinting, or withdrawing; or **direct power tactics,** involving such behaviors as threats, demands, and physical violence (see Chapter 9). Although it was originally assumed that in couple interactions females used more indirect power tactics and men used more direct ones, most recent research finds no substantial gender differences (Steil and Weltman, 1992). However, it does appear that the type of tactics that partners use to influence each other may depend on their relative power in the relationship. Among heterosexual, gay male, and lesbian couples, the more powerful party more often uses direct tactics in influencing the other, whereas the more dependent partner, who is operating from a position of weakness, more often opts for indirect attempts at manipulation (Kollock, Blumstein, and Schwartz, 1985; Howard, Blumstein, and Schwartz, 1986).

How Power Affects Other Aspects of Intimate Relationships. The importance of power in couple interactions is evident from the fact that much of the conflict that couples report involves power issues. Kurdek (1994) conducted a study with 75 gay male, 51 lesbian, and 108 heterosexual couples in which he compared the prevalence of power-related conflict issues relative to other areas of conflict. Within each relationship type, power and intimacy issues dominated most couple conflicts. Furthermore, Kurdek's analysis revealed that conflicts over intimacy and power uniquely affected couple satisfaction and that over time conflicts regarding power predicted decreasing levels of relationship satisfaction. In the Boston Couples Study, Stewart and Rubin (1976) also found that if men reported a high need for power, both they and their partners expressed less love and relationship satisfaction and anticipated more relational problems. These researchers also found a connection between high need for power and relationship dissolution. Some studies have linked men's pursuit of relational power to physical violence, both in dating and marital relationships (Mason and Blankenship, 1987).

Sexual Relations

The sexual bond that exists between married or cohabiting partners is one of the main ways in which they express intimacy and affection for each other. Sexual interaction can also facilitate the development of greater intimacy within the couple. We have noted above that sexual satisfaction is central to marital stability and happiness for heterosexual couples. To understand this factor, it is important to get a better sense of the sexual activity that occurs for couples and how they feel about it.

In this section we rely heavily on findings from two studies of sexual behavior. One was a national study, focused exclusively on sexual behavior, conducted around 1990 by researchers at the University of Chicago (Michael et al., 1994). Using random sampling methods, these investigators surveyed nearly 3,500 adults, ages 18–59. The other study, known as the American Couples Study, was conducted by Blumstein and Schwartz (1983) in and around three major cities—Seattle, San Francisco, and New York—around 1980. Using convenience sampling methods, they canvassed these cities trying to recruit couples to participate in their survey dealing with money, work, and sex issues. In addition, couples in other parts of the United States heard about the research and requested to participate. In all, these investigators distributed 22,000 questionnaires, with 12,000 people (representing 6,000 married, heterosexual cohabiting, gay male, and lesbian coresident couples) participating.

At What Point Do Couples Become Sexually Intimate? A good place to start this discussion is with the timing of sexual intercourse in relationships. When do most people incorporate sexual activity into their relationships, and what factors contribute to the timing of sexual intimacy for couples? An interesting finding from the Michael et al. (1994) study is that the timing of sex in a relationship appears to vary with regard to the potential stability of the relationship. That is, when individuals share social characteristics—for example, approximate age, education, and social class—they tend to wait longer to become sexually involved than couples who are relatively mismatched on these factors. Additionally, couples who become acquainted through friends or family members are slower to engage in sexual intimacy than couples who meet in bars and through other processes not involving their social networks. Michael and his colleagues speculate that when it appears that a relationship may have some staying power and may potentially lead to a long-term union (e.g., partners are homogamous and they have the support of their social networks), couples wait longer to have sex. In contrast, if the potential for a long-term relationship isn't there, a couple may proceed with casual sex because any other type of relationship isn't likely to occur.

To illustrate, these researchers found that less than 2 percent of married couples became sexual within two days of meeting, whereas 14 percent of persons in partnerships lasting less than a month initiated sex that quickly. Half of married persons knew their spouse over a year before having sex and over 40 percent had sex between one month and one year after becoming acquainted. These investigators also addressed the issue of virginity at first marriage. Is it at all common, or is the image of the virgin bride just an ideal that no longer exists in reality, or never did? Michael and his colleagues report that 7 percent of married men in their survey and 21 percent of married women were virgins until their wedding night. Not surprising, the percentages were higher for older persons in their sample compared to younger ones.

Overall, Michael's research team found that most Americans have had few sexual partners. Across all ages in their survey, from age 25 to 59, the majority (more than 72 percent) of persons had had only one sexual partner in their lifetime. It is thus not surprising that the vast majority of Americans also report being sexually faithful in their marriages.

The Frequency of Intercourse in Established Relationships. How often does sex occur in marriage and other established romantic unions? The earlier study by Blumstein and Schwartz (1983) reported that sexual frequency varied over the course of a relationship and by the type of couple relationship. In general, both married and cohabiting heterosexual couples reported the most frequent intercourse, the majority having sex weekly or more, regardless of whether they were together less than two years or 10 or more years. Over the first two years of their union, gay men were the most sexually active with 94 percent reporting sexual activity once a week or more. Sexual activity within gay couples dropped dramatically over the course of their unions, however, with fewer than half of the couples reporting weekly or more frequent sex after 10 years together. The more recent study by the Chicago investigators reveals slightly lower frequency of sex within couples. The modal frequency for sexual intercourse for married couples in that survey was "a few times per month," with about 45 percent of men and women reporting this level of activity. Cohabitors reported slightly more frequent sexual activity, with a mode of two or three times a week for intercourse. Interestingly, single persons had sex less frequently than partnered individuals (Michael et al., 1994). This last finding contradicts the popular notion of "swinging singles" conveyed in television shows such as *Sex in the City*.

Reasons for Reduced Sexual Activity Over Relationship Duration. Why does sexual activity decline over the course of marriage, and does it matter for satisfaction in the relationship? It is likely that the drop in sexual activity over the course of a relationship is partially a result of the couple becoming occupied with other things (work, children) that cut into their energy level and time together. Some of this drop is also due to simply becoming used to each other and seeing sex as less urgent in the relationship (Blumstein and Schwartz, 1983). However, health status is a major predictor of older adults' reported interest in sex (Mooradian and Greiff, 1990) and the frequency of sexual intercourse among older couples (see Table 4.2). Clearly, health problems may interfere with the frequency of intercourse, but they don't prevent older persons from being sexually intimate or satisfied. Data from a community-based study of persons aged 70 and older found that about 30 percent had engaged in sexual activity in the past month, yet two-thirds were reportedly either "very satisfied" or "satisfied" with their level of sexual activity (Matthias, Lubben, Atchison, and Schweitzer, 1997). Thus, most older adults appear to take the reduced frequency of intercourse in their relationships in stride and do not become overly alarmed about it. Over the years couples find additional ways to demonstrate intimacy and feel close to each other. In one study, a male respondent who had been married 35 years noted:

> When you are young, love is predominantly influenced by sexual activities. In later life, you still relate love to sex-but other things become more important. These things are companionship, doing things together, communicating [with] and relating to your wife. (Brecher, 1991, 188)

Clearly, the drop in sex within marriage doesn't lead most partners to look elsewhere for sexual gratification. A mail survey of persons over age 50 found that 23 percent of men and 8 percent of women were reportedly involved in an extramarital affair after age 50 (Brecher, 1991). Similarly, using data for a wider age range, the Michael et al. study (1994) found that 80 percent of women and the majority of men reported having no sex partners other than their spouse since they married. Based on the reasons heterosexual couples give for seeking divorce, it would appear that when adultery does occur and is discovered, the consequences are severe (see Chapter 8). That may explain why most long-term married couples report high rates of monogamy. Finally, there is some suggestion that among gay male couples who have been together for a while, seeking sexual partners outside the union is considered more acceptable and is practiced more frequently than is the case for heterosexual couples (Blumstein and Schwartz, 1983).

Older couples in long-term unions report relatively high levels of satisfaction with the physical intimacy in their relationships. What do you think these couples do to keep this aspect of their relationships interesting and satisfying?

Who Initiates Sexual Activity in Relationships? Another issue of interest to researchers is who initiates sexual activity within couples and what that says about the relationship. Blumstein and Schwartz contend that initiation and refusal patterns are indicative of who has more power within a relationship and who is more emotionally expressive. Although in a sizeable portion of both heterosexual marriages and cohabiting relationships (30–40 percent) the woman and man nearly equally initiate sex, there is still a tendency in heterosexual unions for males more often than females to be the initiators. Similarly, in heterosexual couples women more often tend to be the "refusers" in sexual situations. Blumstein and Schwartz discuss how these patterns follow the traditional sexual scripts that most males and females have been raised to follow, with males being the sexual aggressor and females being more passive and resistant. Homosexual couples, however, follow a more equitable pattern, in which sometimes one is the initiator and

Table 4.2 Sexual Activity Among Married Couples, Aged 60 and Older, by Health Status		
Health Status	**Percent Having Intercourse in the Past Month**	**Average Frequency of Intercourse Within the Past Month**
Poor/very poor	36%	2.97
Fair	45	4.60
Excellent/good	58	4.27
Source: Adapted from Marsiglio and Donnelly (1991).		

sometimes that same person is the refuser. However, these researchers conclude from their data that the more powerful person in both heterosexual and same-sex relationships is likely to assume the "refuser" role in sex. In this way, that person controls sexual activity. Additionally, they found that the more expressive partner is the one who is likely to initiate sex. However, these authors concluded that the happiest couples they studied were those in which partners assumed about equal responsibility for initiation and refusal of sex. When such patterns exist, guilt and control are unlikely to surface within the sexual relationship.

Communication

Although it probably seems obvious that good communication is essential for a successful relationship, it is still important to identify research that shows that high-quality communication contributes to marital happiness (Thomas, 1990). Communication problems are a key issue for couples seeking therapy (Geiss and O'Leary, 1981) and divorce (Gottman, 1994).

Communication is an interpersonal process through which individuals use symbols to convey ideas and meaning to others (Galvin and Brommel, 1986). Communication can occur verbally when words are used to express ideas, or through nonverbal symbols such as smiles or tears. The tone used in speaking, facial expressions, proximity to the other, and body language all send a message. Generally, the meaning of particular words and symbols are widely known by most people who interact in a specific context, yet sometimes couples develop their own private communication system (Fitzpatrick and Ritchie, 1992). One woman confided that if her husband indicated he wanted a cup of coffee after dinner, he was also telling her he wanted to have sex that night. Parks (1997) describes a few of the increasingly specialized and unique communication patterns that occur in intimate relationships. For example, a couple may have words that they've made up to refer to situations or objects, or they may use existing words in a way that is unique and meaningful only to them. Also, they may use what Parks calls *code abbreviation*, in which they can provide understandable explanations or descriptions without elaborate verbalization because they are so familiar with each other's life experience. *Code substitution* is also common, in which couples replace verbal communication with nonverbal cues (Parks, 1997). Couple communication patterns illustrate the systems concept of interdependence. Specifically, the give-and-take and pattern of stimulus and response that develop over time through repeated interaction shows how each partner's behavior is dependent on that of the other and influences the other (Anderson and Sabatelli, 1995).

Some of the aspects of communication that couples highly value are honesty, self-disclosure, supportiveness, listening, understanding, and affection (Boland and Follingstad, 1987). These dimensions contribute significantly to marital happiness. One large national study that compared happily married and unhappily married couples found that the former were much more likely to feel understood by each other, comfortable sharing their feelings, and satisfied with the amount they talked and the quality of listening in their relationship (Olson and Olson, 2000). Furthermore, other studies indicate that happily married partners are more accurate in interpreting messages and nonverbal emotion from each other than partners in distressed unions (Noller, 1984; Guthrie and Noller, 1988). Clearly, skilled communication is essential to the development and maintenance of a happy marriage, and communication problems predict future marital distress (Markman et al., 1987).

Both classic and contemporary studies suggest that communication is a stronger predictor of marital satisfaction for women than for men (Komarovsky, 1962; Rubin, 1976; Thomas, 1990). Cancian (1986) claims that women's conception of love is more heavily based on intimacy and self-disclosure than men's; therefore, women often demand greater openness and sharing in communication with their partners because they consider these things vital to a loving relationship. However, men often react to such demands by withholding their feelings more. According to Cancian (1984), when women demand openness and intimate disclosure from men, they threaten men's independence and relative power. One way men maintain power over women is by avoiding emotional dependency on them. This struggle over intimacy can create a great deal of conflict in marriage.

Men's and women's communication also differs on dimensions other than self-disclosure. It is generally acknowledged that men are more likely to use language and communication to compete with others and achieve their place in the world or a specific social situation. Women, in contrast, tend to use language and communication to connect with others and to maintain those connections. Personality theorists argue that these distinct communication and interaction styles illustrate the broad orientations to living that distinguish males and females. According to Bakan (1966), men's personalities are focused on "agency," which emphasizes self-protection, self-assertion, and self-expansion; women's personality is focused on "communion," which emphasizes connection to others. These approaches to the world and relationships get played out through specific interpersonal behaviors. For example, females tend to facilitate relationship development and connection to others by using enabling forms of communication, such as agreeing with another, acknowledging another's comment, or being especially attentive. On the other hand, males are more likely to interrupt conversation, disagree with others, or switch the focus of conversation to themselves—all behaviors that restrict and inhibit the input of others and which allow them to dominate (Maccoby, 1990).

Olson and DeFrain (2000) believe that underlying many of these gender differences in communication and interaction styles is a basic struggle between intimacy and independence that everyone experiences. Feminine gender-role behaviors promote intimacy, but sometimes at the expense of independence. Being too accommodating or agreeable, for example, may result in women forfeiting their needs and views and depending on their partners to make all the decisions. However, because independence is so central to many masculine gender-role behaviors, it may interfere with men's ability to be intimate. For example, when a man refuses to talk about a personal problem and insists instead on handling it himself (i.e., showing his independence), he discourages emotional connection and intimacy. In approaching long-term, romantic relationships, it appears that both sexes would benefit from finding a comfortable balance between intimacy and independence.

Conflict Resolution

Conflict seems inevitable in relationships where individuals spend a great deal of time together, have a strong emotional connection, and share mutual goals that require cooperation as they live together over time. According to a survey of over 500 newlyweds,

Disagreements are not necessarily harmful and may actually be beneficial for a relationship. Think of some reasons why handling conflict directly might be better than trying to avoid it by pretending an issue does not exist.

weekly arguments are experienced by about 40 percent of couples, and 70 percent reported conflict monthly or more (Arond and Pauker, 1987). Marriage and family life present a wide assortment of issues and decisions that require a couple to work together and deal with potential differences. The topics that create the most conflict for marital couples are money, family issues, communication, and housework (Arond and Pauker, 1987).

Approaches to Conflict Resolution. The approach couples take to resolving their conflict can be either constructive or destructive. **Constructive** or **functional strategies** involve behaviors that directly address the issue at hand (Cahn, 1992), including expressing one's opinions or ideas, using reasoning and problem solving to propose and discuss alternative solutions, and showing support of the partner and his or her ideas by listening, questioning, agreeing or compromising (Schaap, Bruunk, and Kerkstra, 1988). Such behaviors are beneficial because they can lead to problem resolution and may promote and maintain intimacy within the couple (Noller, Feeney, Bonnell, and Callan, 1994). Specific behaviors that are common to constructive problem solving and conflict resolution are summarizing, paraphrasing, and clarifying what the other has said. These behaviors show that active listening is occurring in the conversation, and they validate the speaker's feeling and ideas (Ting-Toomey, 1983).

Destructive conflict strategies include behaviors such as coercion (using threat, blame, or sarcasm) or manipulation (gaining control by false or indirect means) that are used to influence the other or gain control over the situation (Schaap et al., 1988). Confrontation, complaining, and defensiveness are also considered destructive in conflict resolution (Ting-Toomey, 1983). Withdrawal or avoidance of the issue is also believed to be destructive, according to most experts, because such behavior does not facilitate resolution of the issue. Researchers have labeled a particular form of interaction **demand-withdraw behavior.** This pattern involves one partner demanding more contact or pressuring the other to discuss and deal with a particular issue, and the other partner retreating from the situation (Sullaway and Christensen, 1983). Notice that this is the situation exemplified by the newly married couple's quarrel described earlier in this chapter.

5 to 1: Balancing Positive and Negative Communication. Gottman, a marriage therapist who studies couple interaction, classifies communication as negative and positive.

Among the negative behaviors that he considers most dangerous to a relationship, especially when they become routine, are these:

- Defensiveness.

- Contempt for the partner.

- Criticism.

- Stonewalling (becoming silent and disengaging from the discussion).

Gottman (1994) and his colleagues speak of what they call the *5 to 1 ratio*—a pattern documented in their research with couples. They find that in most stable satisfying marriages at least five positive behaviors/communications occur for every one negative communication. When the number of negatives in that ratio increases, these researchers predict a higher risk of divorce. Some of the positive behaviors that couples are encouraged to engage in more frequently include the following:

- Being empathic and understanding of the partner.

- Validating the partner's views and feelings.

- Laughing and keeping a sense of humor.

- Putting disagreements into perspective.

- Taking a time-out from interaction when things get too heated.

Problems are sure to come up in relationships that last over time. What research clearly indicates is that disagreements are not destructive to relationships if couples can approach them in a constructive way, keep things in perspective, and communicate their respect and understanding for each other as they work on the issues at hand.

Gender and Sexual Orientation Differences in Conflict Resolution.

Men and women generally approach conflict and its resolution differently. In discussing problems, women appear to be more direct than men, regardless of whether they are expressing negative or positive feelings; they are also more critical than men (Hahlweg, Revenstorf, and Schindler, 1984). In contrast, much research suggests that men are more likely than women to avoid or withdraw from conflict, especially when their partners are demanding their attention to an issue. Christensen and Heavey (1990) claimed that in 60 percent of couples, the wife-demand/husband-withdraw pattern was evident. This pattern has been attributed to women's stronger need for intimacy within relationships and men's need for independence, an issue we discussed earlier. Others contend that this pattern occurs because of the difficulty men have dealing with high negative affect, which results in physiological discomfort for them (Gottman and Levenson, 1988). More recent investigations, however, indicate that both men and women are likely to assume the demand position when dealing with an issue that is particularly salient to them, and the partner in such cases will more likely withdraw (Klinetob and Smith, 1996).

It is interesting to consider how gendered interaction affects dynamics in same-sex couples. According to a few studies, gay men do use "masculine" styles of communication and conflict resolution in their relationships. For example, they are more likely to use relatively low levels of self-disclosure when discussing problematic issues. When this form of avoidance is practiced, critical issues may go unattended, resulting in built-up anger and resentment. Gay men are also more prone to directly challenge their partners without listening to their views, which can derail conversations and attempts at problem solving (Rutter and Schwartz, 2000). In a study by Kurdek (1994b) that compared heterosexual, gay male, and lesbian couples, however, the approaches to conflict resolution used by these three groups were very similar. Kurdek used self- and partner-report measures that assessed four styles of problem solving: positive problem solving (which included such constructive behaviors as compromise and negotiation), conflict engagement (characterized by such things as personal attacks), withdrawal behavior, and compliance (passively giving in to the other). The various types of couples exhibited no differences in their use of ineffective problem-solving strategies. Furthermore, for each type of couple, ineffective arguing was predictive of relationship dissatisfaction.

The Impact of Conflict Resolution on Marital Quality. A great deal of research evidence links communication patterns and conflict resolution strategies to relational and marital satisfaction. In one study that assessed couples' communication and satisfaction just prior to their marriage, and then twice in the first two years of marriage, destructive communication, including high negativity and low positivity, was linked to lower satisfaction. Compared to happily married couples, those couples who were less satisfied with their relationships were more aggressive in their communication, used more threats, avoided issues, and engaged in more demand-withdraw behavior (Noller et al., 1994). In another study that examined conflict resolution and marital satisfaction over the transition to parenthood, slightly different results were found (Crohan, 1996). This research, which compared black and white couples, found that destructive conflict was predictive of lower marital happiness for both wives and husbands. Avoidance behavior, however, had different consequences depending on its style. When couples used what was labeled *passive avoidance behavior,* they seemed to maintain higher levels of happiness. Therefore, in some cases—for example, when an issue did not appear to be easily resolved or was resulting in increasing anger and intensity—it seemed beneficial for couples to become quiet and to withdraw from the conversation. *Active avoidance,* however, which occurred when one of the partners physically left the scene of the disagreement, was associated with lower marital satisfaction. The author of this study proposed that active avoidance suggests to the other partner that the avoidant one has neither the time and emotional energy or willingness to deal with the situation. Additionally, the emotional intensity of the situation might go unresolved for quite some time (Crohan, 1996). An interesting result of this study was that over the transition to parenthood, white couples, but not black couples, increased their use of passive avoidant behavior. Crohan (1996) speculates that the new demands of parenthood probably left couples feeling less able to deal with conflict resolution. It is not clear, however, why this change did not occur for black couples.

Maintaining Relationships Over Time

As intimate unions extend over time, couples are likely to experience challenges and changes in their relationships. Promotions and added responsibilities at work or having children may impinge on the time partners have to be alone together. Financial pressures may upset how the couple prioritizes spending. The needs of each partner's extended family may require role changes in the couple relationship. Even stable and happy marriages are confronted with such challenges and change over time. How do couples sustain their relationship in the face of such challenges? Moreover, how do couples stay intimate and satisfied over the long haul, day in and day out, even in the absence of major life changes?

Managing the balance between individual autonomy and couple connectedness is one process that contributes to relationship maintenance (Cowan and Cowan, 2000). Partners are continually faced with the challenge of staying intimately connected while at the same time allowing enough separateness and independence to promote personal growth and fulfillment for each partner (Van Lear, 1998). Even though a couple may have achieved a satisfying balance between these dimensions at one point in time, life changes may occur that upset the situation. If one partner assumes a new role it may affect expectations the two have for each other and their relationship and reduce their time together. An illustration of this is research showing that women who were married before entering professional training (college or professional school) were at greater risk for divorce than those who established their marriages already having assumed these other positions (Houseknecht, Vaughan, and Macke, 1984). It appears that in the former situation, a wife's new interest in and pursuit of education or career may threaten her connectedness to her husband, or his perception of that connectedness.

Another issue involved in maintaining a close relationship is dealing with the tension between predictability and novelty—stability versus change. Healthy relationships need both of these qualities; predictability provides a sense of security for partners, but too much of it without change or novelty can lead to relationship stagnation (Van Lear, 1998). In long-term relationships this balance is particularly important as partners come to know each other well and can sometimes even anticipate what the other is going to say or do in particular situations. Such predictability may be reassuring, but it also can become monotonous. Therefore, it is desirable for partners to introduce some novelty and surprises into their relationship occasionally. One of your authors has a friend who's been happily married for well over 25 years. To this day, the friend makes small gestures to her husband that keep him guessing about what's to come in their relationship. For example, when he travels on business she sometimes puts a handkerchief sprayed with her perfume in his suitcase, or writes him a note about some surprise she's planning for when he arrives back home. Such novelty has spiced up their marriage and kept it interesting for over two decades!

Maintenance Behaviors. Relationship scholars also discuss specific behaviors that couples use to preserve and enhance their relationships and to deal with and avoid relationship distress. These are known as **maintenance behaviors.** Stafford and Canary (1991) identified five common types of maintenance behaviors:

- *Positivity*—Keeping the tone of the relationship upbeat and cheerful, and being polite to each other.

- *Openness*—Willingness to share thoughts and feelings with each other.

- *Assurances*—Behaviors and comments that reflect optimistically on the future of the relationship by conveying hope for the future and a partner's intent to continue the relationship.

- *Shared tasks*—Contributing to feelings of cooperation and fairness. Because couple-centered time declines and time devoted to instrumental tasks increases as couples progress from dating to marriage (Huston, McHale, and Crouter, 1986), sharing tasks provides added opportunity for being together.

- *Social network engagement*—Engaging in activities with friends and family, which contributes to support for the relationship and reinforces couple identity.

Investigators have recently considered whether these same types of maintenance strategies are used in long-term same-sex unions (Haas and Stafford, 1998). What they found is that these strategies were common in gay male and lesbian couples. In fact, the most common maintenance strategy identified among both gay and lesbian couples was shared tasks, which has also been found to be most common in heterosexual samples (Dainton and Stafford, 1993). Two maintenance strategies, however, appear unique to same-sex couples: involvement with gay/lesbian supportive environments, and being "out" to persons in the social network. Haas and Stafford (1998) speculate that these two strategies are important to same-sex couples because they support rather than discourage the relationship, and they help to enhance the couple identity of the partners. In light of the broader social disapproval or stigma homosexual couples may face, having supportive microsystems is especially important to maintaining the relationship.

Women as 'Relationship Mechanics.' According to research, women engage in relationship maintenance behaviors more than men (Bradbury and Karney, 1993; Huston et al., 1986). They are the ones who typically bring up sensitive issues, want to talk about the relationship, and, when there are problems they want to fix them. It is not uncommon for relationship researchers to hear men say something to the effect of, "She always wants to talk about the relationship—why can't we just have the relationship?" Women's efforts in this area are probably the result of their being more sensitive or attuned to relationship dynamics and more invested in addressing them (Acitelli, 1992).

We've already discussed how females are socialized with an emphasis on establishing and maintaining connections to others. Other research suggests that women's engagement in maintenance behaviors is associated with their views of the relationship and their perceptions of their partner's feelings. Weigel and Ballard-Reisch (1999) found in their study of heterosexual couples that wives who reported being more in love, more committed, and more satisfied with their marriages were more likely to use maintenance behaviors. Additionally, if they perceived their husbands were satisfied with the marriage, they also engaged in more maintenance activities. However, husbands' use of maintenance behaviors was solely predicted by their own marital satisfaction.

Do Maintenance Behaviors Predict Future Marital Outcomes? Finally, researchers have explored whether the use of maintenance behaviors contributes to having a better marriage in the future. That is, if couples use maintenance strategies early in their relationship, are they better off later? Based on findings from a short-term longitudinal analysis, Canary and his colleagues (2002) would say "no," unless the maintenance strategies are maintained over time. They found that maintenance behavior is highly predictive of couples' *current* relationship satisfaction and feelings (i.e., liking spouse, feeling committed to spouse). However, the performance of relationship strategies at one point in time did not significantly predict feelings about the relationship one month later or beyond. Therefore, these researchers conclude that to positively affect their unions, "spouses need to engage continually in maintenance activities" (403). Satisfying long-term relationships require continued attention and work from both partners.

The Big Picture

In Chapter 3 we discussed how societal forces such as the civil rights movement, the women's movement, and value changes such as the rise in individualism have influenced partnering and the formation of intimate relations in this country over the last half century. Some of the same forces clearly play a role in marriage, both in terms of affecting specific marital processes (such as power and conflict) and contributing to marital stability. Here we discuss some of the repercussions that the societal shift toward women's increasing economic independence (which resulted in part from the women's movement) and heightened individualism have for marriage.

Women's Employment and Marriage

Huge numbers of married women moved into the labor force in the 1970s (see Chapter 7 for more discussion), which altered family roles. One specific consequence was that many American wives became less dependent on their spouses for economic security. Between 1960 and 1980, the percentage of both white and nonwhite women who totally depended on their husbands' earnings dropped nearly 50 percent. By 1980 only 27 percent of nonwhite women and 31 percent of white married women were totally dependent on their husbands for economic support (Sorensen and McLanahan, 1987).

As discussed earlier in the chapter, the resources that women bring to marriage affect the balance of marital power and women's life alternatives. Data analyzed by Amato and his associates (2003) indicate that women's increased labor force involvement may actually have *both* benefited and hurt marital relationships. On the one hand, these researchers found that greater work hours and job demands for wives were associated with reduced couple interaction and heightened risk for divorce. Clearly we can imagine how spending more time at work would leave a wife with less time for her husband, especially given that other things in her life, such as housework and parenting demands, still exist regardless of how much she works. However, these researchers also found that higher total family income and more equal decision-making between spouses—two things that may result from wives' employment—were associated with reduced chances of divorce and greater marital interaction (Amato et al., 2003). Thus, different dimensions of the work situation (pay, hours, stressors) had distinct effects on marital relationships. From this study we can conclude that married women's greater presence in the labor force and increased earning power have had mixed effects on marital dynamics and stability.

Second, the educational and occupational gains that women secured as a result of the women's movement had an impact on their lifestyle choices and decisions about entering and maintaining intimate relationships. Because of greater access to education, a broad range of careers, and more economic independence, women now have more options to consider when thinking about the adult roles they could pursue. For many, these choices involve delaying marriage, or perhaps even forgoing marriage altogether to pursue an education and career (Gerson, 1985). Even for women who have chosen to marry, these options contribute to the decisions they make regarding separation or divorce. That is, because of their reduced economic dependence on their husbands, married women today may feel more able to leave an unhappy marriage and make it on their own compared to women 40 years ago.

Changes in Views of Marriage: The Rise of Individualism and the Culture of Divorce

Couples' experiences with relationships and marriage, including what they expect from them, how they assign marital and family roles, and how they evaluate their relationships over time, are significantly influenced by cultural values and ideologies at the macrosystem level. In Chapter 3 we introduced the term *individualism,* which we defined as a focus on individual opportunities, rights, choice, and self-expression. We argued that such a focus may have altered what adults look for in a partner today, leading them to heavily emphasize emotional fulfillment and love more than ever before.

Some social commentators believe that the rise of individualism that has supposedly taken hold in American culture has hurt marriages and families. Popenoe (1994), one of the strongest proponents of this view, claims that "recent changes in marriage and divorce are fundamentally rooted in the cultural shift from a collectivist to an individualist ethos" (18). He and others believe that individualistic values prioritize personal choice and devalue the importance of strong social bonds and family responsibility. Popenoe cites evidence that between 1962 and 1985 the percent of Americans who agreed that couples should remain together for the children's sake fell from 49 percent to 18 percent. As a consequence of this value change, he believes that children's attachments have suffered. What do you think?

Other empirical data reveal that Americans' experiences within marriage have changed over the past few decades. Studies focusing on the period from about 1970 to 2000 show a decline in marital happiness (Glenn, 1991) and couple interaction over these years, and heightened marital conflict and problems as well (Amato, Johnson, Booth, and Rogers, 2003; Rogers and Amato, 1997).

Some theorists believe that marital dynamics have changed because the meaning of marriage and what men and women expect from it have changed. Hackstaff (1999) conducted interviews with couples married in the 1950s and couples married in the 1970s, then compared their attitudes about marriage. She found that attitudes have changed and that these changes have influenced the evaluations partners make of their unions and their marital commitment. Her theory is that American society shifted from viewing "marriage as forever" to viewing "marriage is [as] contingent." This societal shift, she believes, influences how couples think about the institution of marriage, how they approach problems, and the decisions they make in their marriages. When marriage is seen as contingent on personal happiness (consistent with increased individualism), partners may be less inclined to try to deal with, or put up with, problems in their marriage, opting instead to divorce and search for personal happiness elsewhere. In contrast, couples with a "marriage is forever" mindset may feel the need to stick it out, regardless of their levels of happiness.

Additionally, macrosystem views about the institution of marriage, along with high rates of divorce, can prompt changes in couple behavior even *prior* to marriage, according to Hackstaff (1999). In her view, in a period when divorce rates are high and confidence in marriage is shaky—which is characteristic of the current "culture of divorce"—couples may more seriously consider such precautions as premarital counseling, living together before marriage in a "trial" arrangement or writing prenuptial agreements to protect their assets should they divorce. These chronosystem changes in how couples approach marriage are heavily shaped by macrosystem views about the permanence of marriage.

Summary

Intimate unions play a central role in how individuals see themselves, and they contribute in significant ways to adults' life satisfaction and well-being. Relationship dynamics are fluid over the course of a union. As partners develop and grow older, encountering new stages of family life, their relationships are affected. The key to their handling these changes is the process of relationship maintenance. In this chapter we discussed in detail the specific behaviors (communication, sexual intimacy, conflict resolution) that contribute to the stability of intimate unions over time.

Intimate relationships are formed and maintained within a broad social and cultural system. Women's labor force patterns and earnings potential have given them many more lifestyle options to consider than their mothers and grandmothers had. For those opting to marry, macrolevel changes have altered their roles in marriage (as well as those of their husbands) and with it the dynamics of couple interaction and negotiation.

Marriage also changed as a result of a heightened emphasis on individualism in American culture. Giving priority to one's own wishes, goals, and happiness over those of the family may affect whether someone marries, the age at which she or he marries, who she or he marries, and if she or he stays married or divorces over the long term. Complaints are made that Americans have become too focused on individualism at the expense of child and family well-being. A new culture of divorce is said to have emerged.

In the next chapter we consider childbearing and parenting and address some of the implications these aspects of family life have for the parents' intimate relationship.

Chapter Concepts

communication: an interpersonal process through which individuals use symbols (words, facial expressions, physical actions) to convey ideas and meaning to others.

constructive/functional conflict strategies: behaviors used to effectively address a problem, such as sharing one's opinions or ideas, considering and reasoning about alternative solutions, and being supportive of the partner by listening, questioning, agreeing, or compromising.

coverture: a feudal doctrine based heavily on biblical and church teachings that viewed marriage as uniting a man and a woman into one entity, with the man gaining full control over the woman and her property.

demand-withdraw behavior: situation in which one partner demands more contact or discussion of an issue and the other partner retreats from the interaction.

destructive conflict strategies: behaviors such as complaining, defensiveness, coercion, or manipulation that are used to influence the other or gain control over a conflict situation.

direct power tactics: overt behaviors such as threats, demands, and physical violence that are used to gain power over one's partner.

family power: power used to change and shape the behavior of other family members.

indirect power tactics: behaviors such as whining, hinting, or withdrawing that are used to more covertly gain influence over one's partner.

maintenance behaviors: actions that couples engage in to preserve and enhance their relationships and to deal with and avoid relationship distress.

marital satisfaction: an evaluative, subjective judgment that individual partners make about the quality of their relationship.

marital stability: likelihood that a marriage will remain intact, not necessarily correlated with marital satisfaction.

marriage market: the supply of eligible marital partners in one's geographic area.

power: the ability to affect the behavior or thinking of another, even in the face of resistance.

resource theory of power: theory contending that the partner who earns more money, has greater occupational and social prestige, and more education will be more powerful in the relationship.

Suggested Activities

1. Rent the 2003 Academy Award winning movie *Far from Heaven*, which portrays a 1950s marriage. Discuss the "his" and "hers" marriage that the main characters had. What were their unique marital roles? What did each partner give up in marriage? What were the benefits each derived from marriage? Some people consider the 1950s marriage as the ideal, believing marriages at that time were happier than marriages today. In a short essay express your views on this issue, keeping in mind the marriages portrayed in this movie.

2. Interview a couple that has been together for over 25 years and that appears to be happy and stable. (They may be heterosexual or same-sex.) Ask them to reflect on the following issues: What do they identify as the major transition points in their relationship—events or life changes—that have affected interactions and dynamics in their relationship? What kind of maintenance behaviors do they use to keep their relationship strong? What advice would they give to new couples that have just formed a committed relationship? Finally, discuss any differences the two partners expressed in answering these questions.

Suggested Readings

Gottman, J., and Carrere, S. 2000. "Welcome to the love lab." *Psychology Today* 33:42–47, 87.

Schwartz, P. 2002. "Love is not all you need." *Psychology Today* 35:56–58, 60–62.

Tannen, D. 1990. *You Just Don't Understand: Women and Men in Conversation.* New York: Ballantine. ✦

Chapter 5

Moving Through the Life Cycle

Family Experiences in Early to Middle Adulthood

Did You Know?

- Nonmarital childbearing has increased dramatically since the mid-twentieth century. The percent of births that occurred to unmarried mothers in 1995 was 25 percent for whites, 41 percent for Latinos, and 70 percent for African Americans (Teachman, Tedrow, and Crowder, 2000).
- In 2000, the U.S. Department of Agriculture estimated that a moderate-income family would spend $165,500 to raise a child to the age of 18 (Schrader, 2004).
- Mothers of children ages 5 to 17 spend an average of 6.4 hours per week alone with their children, compared to 4.8 hours for fathers. Watching TV is the activity most frequently shared by parents and children (Chadwick and Heaton, 1999).
- In the United States, 80 percent of children have siblings (Dunn, 1996).

Things to Think About

- What do you think are the reasons adults give for choosing to have or not have children?
- What factors influence how couples adjust to being new parents?
- How do society's views about childbearing and parenting affect the institutional practices surrounding childbirth (such as the rules hospitals have about delivery)?
- What are the main functions of parenthood? How do they change as children develop?
- What roles do siblings play in each others' lives? How are sibling relationships, parent-child relationships, and marital relationships interconnected in the family?
- How do you think a person's background (race, social class, religion) influences his or her parenting?
- How do you think American child-rearing values have changed in the past century?

Although families in the United States have fewer children today than was the case during most of the twentieth century, having children of one's own is still something the majority of Americans choose to do (U.S. Bureau of the Census, 2002a). This chapter explores parenthood, examining individuals' preferences for and planning about this status, factors affecting individuals' adjustment to the demands of parenting, and the central tasks of parenting children from birth through adolescence. We examine how the birth of the first child alters the family system and affects parents. A key concern is how the identities and roles of men and women change with parenting and how couple interactions are affected by the emergence of parent-child subsystems. Further expansion of the family system occurs with the birth of subsequent children; thus, we will consider the dynamics of the sibling subsystem, as well as the potential interdependence of the sibling, parent-child, and couple subsystems.

The complexity of parenting is evident throughout the chapter as we discuss the many forces that shape this important behavior. Along with discussing the personal characteristics and experiences of parents and their children that influence parenting behavior, we consider aspects of the family system and the broader social context such as childbirth policies and practices. Parenting is presented as a dynamic process in which parents' behavior is expected to change as their children grow and their needs and resources change. We close the chapter by considering how parenting is affected by macro-level societal change, as we look specifically at how parenting beliefs and behaviors change over time in response to shifting values and the expanded role of the media in family life.

The Transition to Parenthood

Being pregnant and having a child is not a uniform experience. Consider these four scenarios:

Simone, an unwed 16-year-old, is expecting her first child in six months. The child's father is 17 and his parents are strongly discouraging their marriage. Simone does not intend to complete high school after the baby is born.

Vivian, a 20-something secretary, lives with her 30-year-old boyfriend. They just learned she is pregnant. He is not sure he is ready for marriage and children.

Makisha is a 30-year-old social worker who married her husband, an attorney, after they graduated from college. They are expecting their first child in three weeks. She plans on being an "at home" mom.

Charlotte, almost 40, is a vice president for a high-tech company. She is five months pregnant after she and her husband spent almost $16,000 on surgery and fertility treatments to conceive their first child. They were lucky: the procedure worked the first time.

We begin this chapter by addressing some of the major changes individuals experience in their lives when they assume the status of parent. Our discussion here focuses primarily on the transition to parenthood for traditional married dyads—husbands and wives. Despite the fact that childbearing is increasingly occurring outside of marriage (to single women and cohabiting couples) across all racial and ethnic groups, little is still known about how single individuals experience the transition to parenthood. Moreover, although extended family members often provide substantial support for unmarried, teenage parents, research has largely ignored how others in the family besides the mother and father deal with this family transition (Merriwether-de Vries, Burton, and Eggeletion, 1996). When possible, however, parenting experiences for nontraditional families (such as Simone's and Vivian's) are noted.

Contemplating Parenthood

Parenthood is a status most individuals assume at some point in their lives. About four out of five women over age 35 in the general population have had children, with the likelihood of childbearing being even greater among minority women (approximately 85 percent of black women over age 35 are mothers) (Chadwick and Heaton, 1999). Becoming a parent today involves far more individual choice and control than ever before in U.S. history. Technological, medical, and social developments have not only resulted in highly effective ways to limit human fertility but also produced more alternative routes to parenthood for couples experiencing fertility problems. However, the options available to people who are looking to become parents through nontraditional means (such as adoption or in vitro fertilization) largely depend on the couple's economic resources. In vitro fertilization may cost tens of thousands of dollars, and the adoption of a healthy infant (which many people favor) can be nearly as expensive.

Despite the fact that most married couples become parents, not having children is an increasingly acceptable option today as societal pressure to assume the parental role has weakened over the past several decades. Currently, the majority of American adults believe that both men and women can be happy and successful without becoming parents (Chadwick and Heaton, 1999). Thus, individuals and couples today have many decisions to make about parenthood. This decision making can focus on questions of *whether* to have children, *when* to have them, and *how many* to have.

Although the vast majority of adults today voice a strong desire to have children, marked variations still exist in childbearing preferences. One factor that exerts a strong influence on these preferences is education level, especially for women (Spain and Bianchi, 1996). Given the high demands of professional life, it is not surprising that married women with high levels of education, such as professional or graduate degrees, have fewer children compared to married women in the general population. Rates of childlessness among married, female college professors, lawyers, and physicians, for example, are two to three times greater than the childless rate in the general population, and total fertility for highly educated women who have children is also lower (Cooney and Uhlenberg, 1989). In understanding such variations, it is useful to explore the reasons people give for having or not having children and the specific factors that contribute to this decision.

Factors Influencing the Parenthood Decision. One factor considered in fertility decisions, particularly by middle-class women, is how parenthood will affect their career, and vice versa (Gormly et al., 1987; Schoen et al., 1997). This issue influences the childbearing decisions of white women more often than of black women (Schoen et al., 1997), although the reason is not apparent. In addition to job-related opportunities, couples who choose not to become parents also cite concerns about social and lifestyle costs they would incur if they were to have children, such as altered and restricted activities, and what they perceive as unfavorable changes in the couple relationship (Fawcett, 1988). A father interviewed by Bolea (2000) shared this concern when he reported on some of the changes in interaction and closeness with his wife that he experienced on becoming a parent:

> I was married at 29. My wife was 24 at the time . . . the first two or three years we had a carefree type of existence—going to plays in New York . . . getting to know each other . . . anticipating that when the children came . . . this would end abruptly, which it has. (52)

Conversely, the most common reasons for *having* children center on the fulfillment of a variety of psychological and social needs. Adults (and often teenagers as well), anticipating parenthood, expect that having a child will provide them with a special, close, affectionate relationship—someone to love and care for (Williams, 1991). One 24-year-old expectant father interviewed for a study by Cowan and Cowan (2000) noted this reason for having children when he said, "I see having a child as a chance to shape the life of another human being—someone who will be very important to me and who I can teach about my view of the world" (36). These same views are shared by many unmarried teenagers who carry their pregnancies to term. The comments of one black teen mother interviewed by Williams (1991) illustrates this:

> My mother thought it [the pregnancy] was on purpose because I talked about it [babies] a lot . . . because I wanted to have a baby so bad . . . it would be something I could call my own . . . I know I was real young . . . I wanted someone to love, feed them, and tell them what to do, give them advice. Somebody to love; somebody to love you back. (69–70)

Such positive expectations about parenting may be more common among teen parents today than in the past because they have more options for pregnancy resolution. Those young women who choose to carry their pregnancies to term and keep their babies may be the ones who are most optimistic about the changes that parenthood will bring to their lives.

In choosing to become parents, many individuals are also trying to fulfill broader social goals. Carrying on the family line or family name, strengthening the connection to one's family of origin, and providing grandchildren for one's parents are common reasons given for having children (Cowan and Cowan, 2000; Schoen et al., 1997). These same social goals may put pressure on individuals to have children even when they are uncertain they want to make this status transition. It is not uncommon for childless persons who are in their late twenties and beyond—especially married ones—to have parents and other family members inquire about *when* they are going to have children and to feel pressured about assuming this role.

Heightening one's social status is a social factor that seems to affect the parenting decision of gay men. Bigner and Jacobsen (1989a) compared the motives that gay and heterosexual fathers gave for wanting children. One difference they found between the two groups was that gay fathers were more likely than heterosexual fathers to believe that having children provided them a higher status in society. Perhaps having children, a status that is highly valued in American society, reduces some of the stigma and devaluation that homosexuals feel in the dominant culture. Other research (Beers, 1996) also suggests that gay men who choose to become fathers may already be comfortable with their sexual orientation and feel more positive about their gay status in society than gay men who don't assume a parent status. Beers's research with a sample of gay men who were not parents found that those in the group who desired to become a father (half of the group) exhibited higher levels of identity formation and psychological development.

Surprisingly, economic factors play a limited role in couples' decisions about whether to have a child, even though having children is a costly undertaking. According to one national survey, finances are a significant factor in decisions about having *more* children after the first one (Schoen et al., 1997). Relative economic stability is seriously considered by couples in their decisions about *when* to have children. Most adults favor postponing parenthood until they feel able to financially support a child (Gormly et al., 1987). However, studies examining this issue have focused primarily on middle-class couples.

Planning for Parenthood. When parenthood does occur, it is not always the result of clear decision making and careful planning, despite improved contraception that makes it more possible today to actively plan for parenthood than ever before. Indeed, among women ages 15 to 44, approximately 33 percent of Latinos, 25 percent of whites, and 42 percent of African Americans have had an unintended birth (Chadwick and Heaton, 1999). Yet, as Williams (1991) found in her research with young black mothers, even though pregnancies may be unintended, especially for unmarried or young couples, the children are generally *wanted*.

Research clearly demonstrates that planning for parenthood does affect the experience individuals have as parents. Nearly twenty years ago, Cowan and Cowan initiated an informative longitudinal study of two groups of couples—expectant parents and nonparents—to examine planning and decision making about parenthood and the transition to parenthood process. Their sample of approximately 100 couples spanned a broad range of socioeconomic statuses and included couples of diverse racial/ethnic backgrounds, although the majority (75 percent) was white. In terms of planning, they found that about half the couples had actively planned and discussed the parenthood decision. Not all of these "planners" decided to have children; some reached an agreement *not* to have children, at least temporarily, after extended discussion. "Ambivalent" couples constituted another group in the Cowans's research; they were characterized by both partners experiencing a range of feelings about possible parenthood—at times positive and at other times negative. Interestingly, of the 72 *expectant* couples in their sample, one out of five fell into this ambivalent category, suggesting a lack of clear planning for this important life change. Nearly half of nonexpectant couples were ambivalent about possible parenthood, which may explain why they postponed it. For some couples, their ambivalence about parenthood was so strong that each month raised the dilemma of whether to risk an attempt at conceiving. One woman in the study said, "Every month we had to 're-choose.' Were we still going to do it? Should we change our minds?" (Cowan and Cowan, 2000, 59).

The remaining couples in the sample were classified as either "acceptance of fate" or "Yes-No" couples. The former group consisted of expectant couples, (14 percent of all expectant couples in the sample). These couples, the Cowans report, were generally pleased with the situation fate had dealt them. The last group—the yes-no couples—were those in which one partner clearly wanted children and the other did not. Although only 5 percent of nonexpectant couples fit this description, 13 percent of expectant parents disagreed about the parenting decision! These findings reveal the planning process couples go through en route to parenthood, as well as the wide diversity that exists in their decision making.

Changes in Self With Entry to Parenthood

Part of the adjustment that comes with parenthood involves changes in how parents see themselves (i.e., their identity) and the roles that they consider to be central to their identity. Galinsky (1981), of New York's Families and Work Institute, theorizes that even before the baby's first cries are heard, expectant parents enter into the first stage of parenting that involves what she calls **image making.** The focus at this stage is for soon-to-be parents to begin thinking of themselves as parents, with all the new responsibilities and life changes this status entails.

Identity Changes in Heterosexual Parents. To assess changes in parents' identities over the transition to parenthood, Cowan and Cowan (2000) used a research task that required soon-to-be-parents to divide a pie chart into the various social positions that they had in their lives. Each position was represented by a piece in the pie, with the size of the piece varying according to the investment or involvement that particular position claimed in their lives. Results from this task revealed that one's identity as "parent" does emerge before the birth of the child, just as Galinsky (1981) theorized.

Both men and women in the Cowans's study included parenthood in their prebirth pie charts, although expectant mothers allotted a greater portion of their identity to parenthood than expectant fathers did. This sex difference increased dramatically after the birth of the baby. When the identity task was given again six months after the baby's birth, the average size of the slice women devoted to motherhood—34 percent of the pie—was three times larger than the average slice that men attributed to fatherhood. Being a parent, therefore, is a more salient position for most new mothers than fathers, which probably isn't surprising. More interesting is the question of why this difference exists. Is it a result of women's closer connection to their babies during pregnancy, of their greater input toward baby care after the birth, or of society's unequal emphasis on the importance of parenthood for woman compared to men (Oakley, 1974)? In all likelihood, it is due in part to all three of these factors, and probably others.

Although both mothers and fathers integrate the position of parent into their perceptions of self, objective personality assessments reveal no significant changes in personality as a result of parenthood (Sirignano and Lachman, 1985). But it was evident in the Cowans's work that the importance of the parental position within one's complete set of positions affected parents' self-esteem and their marital relationship. For mothers, when the slice of the pie representing parenthood far exceeded the average "parent" slice for women, self-esteem was low. The Cowans suggest that women who devoted an exceptionally large portion of their identity to motherhood (and homemaking) left little room in their lives for anything else. One mother in their study spoke of feeling trapped by her new, demanding roles:

It seemed like all my waking hours were spent on caring for Amy [baby], caring for Daniel [husband] and thinking about him, caring for the house and thinking about the house. There was no time for myself, absolutely none. And I was just really feeling boxed in. (Cowan and Cowan, 2000, 78)

On the other hand, men who devoted a disproportionatcly large part of themselves to fatherhood compared to other men reported greater self-esteem. These findings say a great deal about the importance of finding a balance in one's life roles, which can be especially challenging when one becomes a parent and assumes responsibility for the care of a totally dependent child. But, as noted, mothers who were able to have a variety of positions, rather than being dominated by motherhood, appeared to be most mentally healthy. On the other hand, fathers who allowed parenthood to assume a central part of their lives, along with paid work, were better off psychologically.

Lesbian parents appear to balance their parenting roles more evenly with other life roles (e.g. work) than do heterosexual parents. Why do you think this happens and what might the benefits be for the parents, their children, and the couple relationship?

Additionally, the Cowans's research highlighted the need to include the partner role in this balancing act. With entry to parenthood, both men and women reported that being a partner was less salient in their identities, and this change was substantially greater for women than for men over the course of the transition to parenthood. However, partners who reserved a relatively large slice of the pie for being a partner reported greater self-esteem and less stress than those who saw the marital aspect of their lives as less central. Additionally, husbands and wives who reported the greatest marital satisfaction after becoming parents were those who had achieved a similar balance (as demonstrated by approximately equal slices of their pies being devoted to parent roles) in their views of parenthood and its importance in their lives.

Lesbian Parents' Identity Changes. A study of lesbian couples' adjustment to parenthood, conducted by Mitchell (1996), used the same psychological task (the pie chart) to assess possible variations in the way nonheterosexual parents balance their various life roles with parenting. Mitchell found that lesbian mothers attributed approximately the same portion of their pie to parenting, on average, as the heterosexual mothers in the Cowans's study. The partner position for lesbian mothers consumed just less than a quarter of the pie, which again was similar to that found for women in the Cowans's study. The striking difference between Mitchell's data and those compiled by the Cowans was the average size of the worker position for parents in the two studies. The lesbian mothers studied by Mitchell devoted substantially more of their self space to being a worker than heterosexual mothers on average but dramatically less space than heterosexual fathers.

The lesbian parents studied by Mitchell, therefore, seemed to strike a healthy balance among their various life roles. This balance, according to Mitchell, provided a unique strength for the lesbian families she studied, which she sees as "an asset for the child in that it brought freedom from traditional models, a very close relationship with two people, and a firsthand appreciation of differences and diversity that were not tied to gender" (353). Other research comparing heterosexual and lesbian parents reports similar role patterns, with heterosexual fathers viewing their work as more salient than heterosexual and lesbian mothers do (Hand, 1991). Thus, gender appears to have a strong influence on how one's view of oneself changes with the transition to parenthood.

Changes in Couple Roles and Relations With Entry to Parenthood

The birth of the first child creates two new subsystems in the traditional family system of wife and husband: the baby and mother, and the baby and father. Because subsystems in the family system are interdependent, the emergence of these new parent-child subsystems affects functioning in the marital couple subsystem. Figure 5.1, adapted from Belsky (1981), displays not only the bidirectional influences of the parenting and marital subsystems on each other but the additional effects that the child's behavior and development have on both of these subsystems, and vice versa. Throughout the next few sections, we'll discuss evidence of such connections in the family system.

Who Does What at Home? Behavioral changes are likely to occur in the family system during the transition to parenthood because the addition of a totally dependent third person alters the workload in the home and the time parents have available for other activities. Longitudinal studies following couples through the transition to parenthood usually show that the proportion of time spent in joint recreation and couple-focused activities declines significantly with the birth of a child (Belsky and Pensky, 1988; McHale and Huston, 1985). A couple's time together becomes more focused on instrumental tasks, such as caring for the home and yard, rather than centering on activities that enhance the couple relationship, such as talking or spending leisure time together. This same pattern occurs across the early years of marriage even when children don't enter the

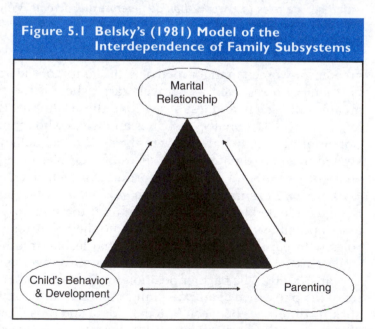

Figure 5.1 Belsky's (1981) Model of the Interdependence of Family Subsystems

scene, but the shift is particularly strong for couples who become parents (McHale and Huston, 1985). One new mother interviewed by Colarossi and Lynch (2000) reported that as she and her husband left their home heading to the hospital to deliver their first child they "both knew it was the last moment we would ever be alone together" (128). While her remark is somewhat exaggerated, this expectant mother was realistically anticipating a noticeable change in time spent with her partner after the birth of their child.

Typically, parenthood brings marked changes in the distribution of household tasks among couples. Numerous studies indicate that the division of household labor becomes increasingly traditional with the transition to parenthood (Belsky and Pensky, 1988). Regardless of how couples divided household work prior to parenthood, once children come along women generally assume an increasing proportion of traditionally "female" tasks (laundry, cooking), while men take on a greater share of "male" tasks (yardwork, taking out the trash). And, because children create more work *inside* the household than outside (they contribute to the speed at which the laundry piles up but don't make the grass grow faster!), new mothers experience a greater increase in household work than new fathers do. The workload assumed after the birth of their first child may also seem especially large to new mothers because most of them cut back on housework during the final trimester of their pregnancies (Belsky and Pensky, 1988).

As noted earlier, research on lesbian couples reveals that after transitioning to the position of parent, lesbian mothers generally rate the salience of their parenting roles similar to those of heterosexual women, and the worker or provider role assumes less importance in their lives than it does for heterosexual fathers. Consistent with these strong parenting orientations, data presented by Mitchell (1996) indicate that parenting tasks among lesbian mothers are shared nearly equally in most cases. Specifically, Mitchell found that when presented with a long list of tasks in the domains of childcare, parenting, and decision making, lesbian couples reported near-equal sharing for 80 percent of the activities. An exception to such reports of shared parenting, however, is noted in studies of lesbian couples in which one of the partners is the biological mother of the child(ren). Research with lesbian couples fitting this description notes that the biological mother generally assumes more responsibility for care of the young child, while the nonbiological mother devotes more time to employment (Osterweil, 1991; Patterson, 1995a, 1996). This division of tasks, and the even more important issue of *which* woman will become the biological mother in a lesbian couple who want to give birth to a child, requires extensive negotiation (Reimann, 1997).

The limited research on gay parents also indicates that same-sex male couples more equally share household duties and childcare tasks than heterosexual couples do. McPherson (1993) studied 28 gay and 27 heterosexual sets of parents and found that the gay parents noted a more equal division of labor around the home and were more satisfied with the division of labor they had established than heterosexual couples were.

Pressure on the Father to Be the 'Good Provider'

The increasing gender-role traditionalism in new parents' roles is especially evident in the heightened commitment to paid work that many new fathers report (Belsky and Kelly, 1994). In trying to be the "good provider," many men devote more hours to their paid jobs once they become fathers. Unfortunately, men sometimes feel as though the financial support they provide to their families isn't recognized or appreciated as much as direct types of paternal involvement, such as diaper changing, feeding, and bathing their babies. Some family scholars argue that there has been an overemphasis on the physical care and emotional nurturing involved in parenting that neglects other important aspects of parenting such as economic providing, which is a major contribution that many fathers make to their children's care (Christiansen and Palkovitz, 2001). This feeling was evident in the comment of one father interviewed by the Cowans (2000):

> Most of my responsibility for the family is providing the bread. You know, Daddy is at work, Mommy is at home. Daddy makes the money, Mommy makes the house and takes care of Faith [the baby]. I get really pissed off at Celie's friends. They're always asking her, "How come Ray doesn't look after Faith more?" Man, I'm looking after Faith six days a week, ten hours a day, busting my ass at the plant. (104)

This theme was also conveyed in a study of working-class fathers conducted by Rubin (1994). One father in Rubin's study noted, "Women complain all the time about how hard they work with the house and kids and all. I'm not saying it's not hard, but that's her responsibility, just like the finances are mine" (85). Although there are two earners in most working-class families today, many working-class men still see themselves as the primary breadwinner. Moreover, their wives are less likely than middle-class wives to expect a lot from their husbands in terms of involvement with childcare. Yet working-class men in several studies voiced the feeling that their wives failed to appreciate the pressure that financial providing creates for them.

Maintaining this image of the male provider can create serious problems for men's psychological well-being, especially if a steady, well-paying job is difficult to find and keep. One study of unmarried black fathers found that those who believed they had failed to meet their families' wants and needs reported significantly lower self-esteem and quality of life (Bowman and Sanders, 1998).

Even though low-income black men may feel frustrated by their inability to fulfill the provider role expectations that society poses for men, it appears that their children's mothers often adopt a more flexible paternal role for them. In a study conducted by Jarrett (1994), low-income unmarried black mothers reported a fairly relaxed view of the traditional male provider role. This attitude was because of the high levels of unemployment that many black men face. Instead of demanding economic support from their children's fathers, many of the mothers appreciated and welcomed whatever efforts the men made to show care and support for their children. Therefore, fathers who were unsuccessful in finding steady work that paid well were nonetheless valued for their job-seeking efforts and noneconomic child support. One mother was quoted as saying, "Even though he [the father] don't have a job, sometimes what counts is he spends time with his child" (Jarrett, 1994, 42). Another mother added:

> If he ain't out there trying to find a job doing something . . . he can be there with that baby, holding that baby, changing that baby's Pampers and let that mommy get rest or let her go out there and do what she have to do to support that baby. (43)

Changes in Couple Relations

Beyond the behavioral changes couples experience with parenthood, changes are likely in the emotional nature of their relationship and their feelings about the quality of their relationship. The early years of marriage are usually marked by reductions in relationship satisfaction and positive interactions and increase in conflict and negative emotion (Kurdek, 1998a; McHale and Huston, 1985; White and Booth, 1985). However, parenthood seems to intensify and accelerate such changes. This pattern is evident among couples of various race and ethnic backgrounds (Crohan, 1996).

Studies of heterosexual couples reveal that new parents experience greater conflict, larger reductions in positive interactions, and more significant drops in marital satisfaction compared to couples not entering parenthood. This finding is especially the case in studies that focus on the mothers' perspective. Belsky and Pensky (1988) partly attribute such changes to the altered division of labor discussed earlier, which puts a greater burden on new mothers than fathers. The sharper drop in marital satisfaction experienced by new mothers than fathers may be due to numerous other changes that mothers go through with parenthood as well. Besides having another person in the family, new mothers often have to adjust to physical and hormonal changes, physical fatigue, altered employment status, and increased social isolation that may accompany staying home with a newborn baby (Cowan and Cowan, 2000).

As noted at the beginning of this chapter, little is known about how young, unmarried couples make the transition to parenthood. One such study, however, gathered longitudinal data from teen couples, ages 14–19, and examined how their relationships changed with parenthood and how their relationship affected the parenting behavior of both young mothers and fathers (Florsheim et al., 1999). The researchers expected that parenting might be particularly challenging and stressful for these young people because of their lack of interpersonal and psychological maturity and the low socioeconomic status that characterizes many teen parents. Additionally, many young men who become adolescent fathers have a record of antisocial behavior, which could contribute to problems for both parenting and the couple relationship. To address these issues, these researchers used a unique research design, in which they included two geographically distinct samples: half of the 70 couples were from Salt Lake City, Utah, most of them white and lower middle class; the other 35 couples resided in the Chicago area, most of them black and from low-income or impoverished backgrounds (Florsheim et al., 1999).

As expected, this study found that teen fathers with previously high levels of antisocial behavior had more negative transitions to parenthood. Specifically, the more antisocial behavior the fathers reported at the start of the study, the more likely that problems (e.g., conflict, lack of support) were reported in the couple relationships after the baby's birth. In addition, fathers' earlier antisocial behavior predicted less nurturance toward their babies.

Also of interest in this study were the differences associated with geographic region. Most notable was the finding that fathers' hostility levels and antisocial behavior had a stronger and more significant negative effect on mothers' nurturing behavior and ratings of the couple relationship in the Salt Lake City sample than the Chicago one. In part, the researchers attributed these differences to the fact that more of the Salt Lake City than

Chicago couples were living together after their babies' births. Shared residence likely increased the potential for the fathers' behaviors and feelings to have an impact on the mothers. Another possibility noted by the researchers was that young, low-income blacks might be better prepared to handle the transition to parenthood than their white age peers because of cultural differences in the meaning and context of teen parenthood. Indeed, the Salt Lake City teens reported feeling more stigmatized by their parenthood status than did those in the Chicago sample, which contributed to their reports of greater stress and more problems (Florsheim et al., 1999). Moreover, it is evident from other research that black families generally are supportive of teen parents and willing to provide substantial back-up assistance during the transition to parenthood (Merriwether-de Vries et al., 1996). Such support may reduce the stress felt by young parents. These differences in the cultural context of teen parenthood suggest why adjustment processes vary by race and socioeconomic level.

The unique demands on the couple relationship produced by the transition to parenthood for gay or lesbian couples have also received only limited research attention. One study found that lesbian couples experienced reduced sexual intimacy in their relationships after having children (McCandlish, 1987). In terms of relationship satisfaction, studies reveal similar (Osterweil, 1991) or slightly higher levels of overall relationship satisfaction for lesbian (Patterson, 1995a, 1996) and gay couples (McPherson, 1993) than heterosexual couples after the arrival of children. A slight advantage in couple satisfaction during the transition to parenthood for same-sex parenting couples compared to heterosexual couples may be due to several of the issues discussed earlier, such as the greater similarity in lesbian partners' identity changes with parenthood, or to the more equitable distribution of household chores for gay and lesbian couples compared to heterosexual couples.

Factors Influencing Positive Adjustment to Parenthood

The general trends we have reviewed paint the picture that intimate couple relationships are severely altered by parenthood, and not in a desirable way. At this point, it is insightful (and *hopeful*) to look beyond these general patterns and identify factors that contribute to couples effectively weathering the transition to parenthood. Among the influences known to make a difference are aspects of the couple relationship (planfulness and marital quality), individual partner factors, child characteristics, and aspects of the broader ecological/environmental system.

Was Parenthood Planned? Especially predictive of how couples' relationships will hold up during the transition to parenthood is the decision-making and planning process that occurs in relation to this life change. Returning to the topic of planning reported from the Cowans's (2000) research (remember the couples categorized as planners, ambivalents, acceptance of fate, and yes-nos?), we see that *how* couples reached the parenthood decision is critical in their subsequent adjustment to the transition. Cowan and Cowan (2000) found that the new parents who had been labeled planners, as well as the acceptance-of-fate parents, maintained relatively steady levels of marital satisfaction over the early years of parenthood. In contrast, marked declines in marital satisfaction occurred for those partners with conflicting feelings about parenthood—whether both partners vacillated between viewing parenthood positively and negatively (the ambivalents) or the two disagreed on their individual feelings about parenthood (yes-no couples). Evidence of the destructive effect childbearing can have on a relationship when partners disagree about becoming parents is the fact that all of the yes-no couples in the Cowans's research had divorced by the time their children had entered school (although certainly other factors may have contributed to these break-ups)!

Other researchers report findings about the importance of planning for children that are similar to the Cowans's findings. Using a primarily white sample from a rural area (instead of an urban area like the Cowans did) and a sample with a more variable range of educational backgrounds, Cox and her colleagues (1999) also found that one of the strongest predictors of increased negative marital interaction over the transition to parenthood was having an unplanned pregnancy.

How Strong Is the Couple Relationship? Adjustment to parenthood is easier for partners who establish a good, stable relationship before starting a family (Cowan and Cowan, 1988; Russel, 1974). Communication is probably more honest and frequent in good marriages, providing opportunities for partners to discuss their fears, hopes, and expectations for parenthood prior to its occurrence; once the child is born, parenting and couple issues that arise can also be dealt with more constructively if the couple has good communication. A practical lesson gained from the literature on this topic is that having a child does not fix a troubled marriage!

Individual Expectations About Parenting. Beyond couple communication, research shows the important role that individual expectations play in new parents' adjustment and relationships. Work by Kach and McGhee (1982) found that mothers reported the roughest adjustment to parenthood when their actual motherhood experience differed from the expectations they had previously held about parenting. Although most new mothers in this study of middle-class parents reported overall positive feelings about becoming parents, their expectations about the demands of childcare and the opportunities they would have for time with their partners were highly unrealistic in comparison to what actually occurred (Kach and McGhee, 1982).

Women's marital satisfaction after becoming parents also relates to whether their prebirth expectations for their partners' involvement in childcare are met. Understandably, the most dissatisfied mothers are those who report the largest discrepancy between how much they anticipated their partners would contribute to home and childcare and what their partners actually did once the transition occurred (Belsky, Ward, and Rovine, 1986; Cowan and Cowan, 2000). One angry mother in the Cowans's (2000) study shared her feelings about violated expectations:

> I just didn't expect it to take so much work. We planned this child together, and we went through Lamaze together, and Jackson [her partner] stayed home for the first two weeks. But then—wham!—the partnership was over! (98)

The powerful, often unrealistic expectations that many expectant couples have about parenthood and family life have led to a call for programs for expectant parents that provide information on changes likely to occur with this transition. Adding such content to already popular childbirth preparation classes seems feasible (Belsky and Pensky, 1988), and such efforts are currently under way (see Gilliland, Hawkins, Christiaens, and Carroll, 2002). Even nonexpectant couples considering this family change should be exposed to realistic information about parenthood and the family changes that generally accompany it. Such information might help couples determine whether they are ready to take the parenthood plunge.

The Role of Child Characteristics. One significant influence on parents' adjustment to their new roles is the particular characteristics of their newborn child. Researchers often cite the temperament of a child as a key characteristic—referring to the child's behavioral style, which is characterized by eating and sleeping patterns, general emotion, attention level, and activity states (Lerner, 1993). Children may be labeled as difficult or easy, depending on the general style of such behaviors. Irregular sleeping and eating, and not being easily soothed, are behaviors typical of *difficult* babies, although many indicators contribute to this classification. Babies who eat and sleep on a regular schedule and soothe easily when distressed are classified as *easy.* Having a difficult baby, not surprisingly, is associated with heightened parental stress and adjustment problems (Russel, 1974; Sirignano and Lachman, 1985).

Other child factors, such as a premature birth or health or developmental problems, affect parents' adjustment too. Roach and her colleagues (1999) found that parents of young children with Down syndrome felt more stressed and less competent in their parenting than parents of nonaffected children. Studies of children with serious illnesses also suggest the negative effects such child conditions have on the parents' marital relationship. One study with parents of pediatric cancer patients found that such consequences as reduced sexual desire and heightened couple communication problems were common in reaction to the stress of having an ill child (Hughes and Lieberman, 1990). These are a few examples of how the characteristics of the child can affect the parenting and marital subsystems, as previously depicted in Figure 5.1.

Ecological Factors. The parenthood transition is heavily shaped by societal and institutional factors that exist in the broader ecological system. Some examples are given in Figure 5.2.

Microsystems. Microsystems that expectant and new parents participate in, such as childbirth preparation classes and the particular childbirth and delivery setting they choose, are important aspects of the parenting experience. The settings in which the delivery occurs vary tremendously, for example, in terms of the persons involved and the

Some of the most dissatisfied new mothers are those whose pre-birth expectations for their partners' post-birth involvement with the baby and housework were not met. How do you think new parents, like this one, develop an awareness of their partner's expectations so that the transition is more satisfying to both of them?

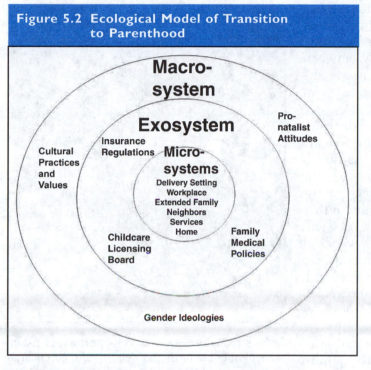

Figure 5.2 Ecological Model of Transition to Parenthood

roles expected of them (Garbarino and Benn, 1992). Sometimes the delivery microsystem includes the mother, father, and medical staff, while in other cases it excludes the father. In some settings, such as a home delivery, fewer medical staff and more family members are included in the birth experience. These situations influence how parents think about themselves as parents and their views of parenting more generally.

Exosystems. Factors at the exosystem level, including institutional policies and procedures, insurance regulations, and availability of delivery options in the community, largely determine what the delivery microsystem will be like. Do hospital policies or arrangements accommodate the psychosocial needs of the expectant couple and new family? Are fathers permitted and encouraged to be involved in the delivery experience, assuming such tasks as cutting the umbilical cord after the baby's birth, helping to clean the newborn, and presenting the new baby to the mother? If a mother requires a Caesarean section or if a medical emergency arises, is the father allowed to remain with her? After the birth, does the baby room-in with the mother (and possibly father, if he's allowed to stay at the facility) so that the parents, and perhaps other family members, can see, hold, and feed the baby when they wish? How many days of hospital care does the insurance company typically cover for a new mother and baby?

These issues may seem minor, yet research suggests that they play a critical role in facilitating bonding and providing other early parenting opportunities. Such involvement may prepare parents for the childcare tasks that they will assume upon going home and may affect their feelings of confidence or anxiety about their new roles. A study comparing the early parenting experiences of two sets of couples—those where the husbands were and were not present during a Caesarean section procedure—provides an illustration. Fathers who were allowed to be with their wives during the Caesarean birth of their children handled their babies more in the postdelivery period, and they and their wives reported more positive feelings about parenting than their counterparts in the father-absent group (Cain et al., 1984). Such feelings and experiences are a significant part of parents' introduction to their new roles.

Mesosystems. In addition to the delivery microsystems, the mesosystems that exist between the hospital and home are critical for the adjustment of new parents. Garbarino and Benn (1992) point out that many hospitals expect fathers to be removed and passive during delivery and immediately afterward, yet the father's input is often expected by the mother once the new family returns home. Such incongruity between the expectations of the two microsystems does little to facilitate positive adjustment for either parent.

Another critical mesosystem in the transition to parenthood is that between the hospital, home, and community. As hospitals and insurance companies push for speedy discharge of mothers and their newborns, a growing expectation is that either nurses or other community workers will visit new families during the early weeks of parenting to provide information and help if questions and problems arise. Research by Olds and his colleagues (1986) revealed that if families receive nurse home-visitors throughout the infancy period, parents are able to establish stronger ties to community resources that can later assist them in parenting. Thus, exosystem resources, policies, and practices (such as home-visiting nurses) enhance mesosystems that contribute to positive parental adjustment.

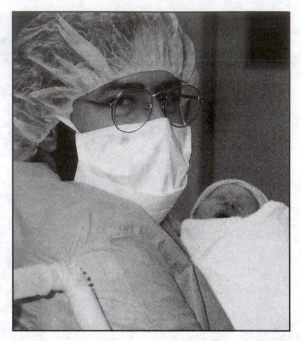

Fathers today are given more opportunities for involvement in the birth and delivery of their children than their own fathers were. In what ways might this early involvement influence their later parenting?

Macrosystems. The impact of macrosystem values and beliefs on the experience of new parenthood cannot be overlooked. Cultures differ, for example, in their perceptions of childbearing, the roles they expect for new fathers and mothers, and what is expected of extended family members during this transition. In some cultures childbearing is considered a natural occurrence that is integrated into daily life, while in others, such as our own, it is viewed more as a medical event (Lozoff, Jordan, and Malone, 1988). One of your authors knew a woman who, once she became pregnant, requested and received from her employer a parking tag for disabled persons, even though she had no special medical condition that threatened her health during pregnancy. Consider what this says about her perception of pregnancy and childbearing and how that perception might affect adjustment to her new parental roles.

Other aspects of how society views parenthood are also critical, including the evaluation of and beliefs about mothering and fathering. This issue was widely debated in 2001 when a psychologically distressed Texas woman drowned her five young children, ages 6 months to 7 years, in the family's bathtub (*Newsweek*, 2001). Much of the early discussion about this case centered on how society idealizes motherhood, neglecting the psychological strain that many new parents and parents of toddlers feel. (In this case, the mother reportedly suffered bouts of severe postpartum depression and possibly even schizophrenia throughout her childbearing years.) Some believe that parents who need help would be more open and willing to seek it if society were more open about the challenges that parenthood presents and the negative emotions many new parents experience (Quindlen, 2001).

This returns us to the issue of expectations about parenthood and parent roles. These expectations exist at both the individual and societal levels, and both sets of expectations affect how parents adjust to their new roles. One of the most controversial topics ever covered on the Oprah Winfrey television show detailed the negative side of motherhood. Thousands of e-mails, faxes, and letters responded to the women who reported on the show that being a mother was frustrating, tough, depressing, and tiring. The woman who said that 80 percent of the time being a mother stunk was harshly condemned (What mothers honestly think, April 16, 2003).

Adoption. Our discussion of the adjustments that new parents face with the arrival of their first child largely assumed that the child is a biological child. Although most want-to-be parents probably expect that the children they eventually raise will be their biological offspring, many American couples do adopt children within the United States or from abroad each year. Adoptive parenting, however, is still considered by many as a fall-back or second-choice substitute for biological parenting. Bartholet (2001) claims that many adults see adoption as a "last resort" and that adoption is being considered less and less today because of the growing number of reproductive technologies available to couples who for some reason have been unable to conceive or give birth to biological offspring.

Many of the transitions and adjustments that new adoptive parents face are similar to those experienced with the birth of a biological child. Like other parents, they will experience change in their financial situation, their marital and family roles, and their views of themselves as people once they become parents. In addition, adoptive parents need to adjust to the fact that now they are intimately connected to another family—the child's birth family (Bartholet, 2001), and with this fact comes a number of unique parenting issues that require attention. One issue that adoptive parents may struggle with is whether they have a legitimate right to behave as the full parents of the child they have adopted (Smith, 1991). The courts confer their legal rights, but adoptive parents themselves must come to terms with their psychological or emotional right to feel like and consider themselves the parents of the adopted child (Reitz and Watson, 1992). Their parental identities are likely to be influenced by societal views about adoption (such widely used terms as "real parents" surely interfere with adoptive parents' feelings of legitimacy) as well as the supportiveness and acceptance of persons in their microsystems.

Another issue in the adjustment of adoptive parents is the fear that the birth mother will reclaim the child. Between 40 and 60 percent of adoptive parents report this concern at some point in their transition (Grotevant, McRoy, Elde, and Fravel, 1994). Such fears are probably exaggerated, yet their existence is understandable given the publicity that such cases receive when they do occur. Finally, adoptive parents may question the permanence of their parenting situation. How will their adopted child feel about them if and when it becomes known that they are adoptive parents and that the biological parents are somewhere out there in the world? Adoptive parents question whether their child will still love them and feel attached to them in the future. All of these issues can affect how adoptive parents adjust to their new parenting situation.

A major influence on how adoptive parents experience and deal with these issues is the degree of openness that exists in their adoption. Adoption procedures can be classified along a continuum of openness, ranging from those that are not open at all, which are labeled **confidential,** to those that are completely open, referred to as **fully disclosed adoptions.** Between these two types are **mediated adoptions.** Traditionally, adoptions were confidential and the birth parent(s) and the adoptive parents and child were denied access to much information about each other because records were private and sealed. Over the past few decades in the United States, there has been movement toward more openness in adoption. Mediated adoptions offer some nonidentifying information on the other party to the birth mother or adoptive family, through agency personnel or an attorney. However, direct contact between the involved families never occurs.

In the case of more open adoptions, such as fully disclosed adoptions, all information about the other party is shared, and direct contact may occur between the parties. Such contact may include calls, letters, and visits (Grotevant et al., 1994). Research conducted by Grotevant and his colleagues (1994) demonstrates that adoptive parents who are involved in open adoptions generally report a greater sense of permanence in relation to their adopted child, and they experience less worry that their child's birth mother will try to reclaim the child than parents who know little about the birth parents and the child's birth situation. Therefore, at least from the perspective of adoptive parents and their adjustment to their parenting situation, the movement toward more openness in adoption in this country seems to have advantages.

Another unique issue adoptive parents face, especially when they participate in an international adoption (see Table 5.1 for statistics on such adoptions) or a U.S. adoption of a child of a different race/ethnicity, is promoting and maintaining the child's cultural heritage within the adoptive family environment. Increasingly, community resources, such as "culture camps," are becoming available to assist families in this effort. Evidence of children's adjustment in mixed-race/ethnicity families is equivocal. One study found no problems with the self-esteem and confidence of transracially adopted children yet claimed that identity issues were a problem for such children (McRoy, Grotevant, and Zurcher, 1988). Other research (Feigelman, 2000) found that children in mixed-race adoptive families did not exhibit high rates of problem behavior; in fact, they adjusted particularly well when they lived in heterogeneous neighborhoods. Such findings highlight the importance of microsystems beyond the immediate family for children's well-being and adjustment.

Table 5.1	International Adoptions by American Families in the Year 2000, by Child's Country of Origin
Country	**Number of Adoptions**
China	5,053
Guatemala	1,511
Rumania	1,144
Russia	4,269
South Korea	1,794
Source: Adapted from Snider (2001).	

Parenting

In this section, our goal is to provide an overview of parenting—the types of behaviors it involves and the purpose these behaviors serve for children's development from infancy to adolescence. Information comes primarily from research on two-parent families, although we do review the limited information available on single, teen parents. (For more discussion of single parenting, particularly after divorce, see Chapter 8.) Where possible, we address important variations in parenting that exist for families of different social classes, racial/ethnic groups, and religions.

Parenting Stages

Although one doesn't officially assume the "parent" status until the actual birth of a child, men and women usually assume a parental identity during pregnancy, as discussed above. Even prior to conception, however, some want-to-be parents engage in what is called **anticipatory socialization** for parenthood, where they begin imagining and anticipating what parenthood is like. Through such activities as babysitting for the children of friends or family members, talking with others about their parenting experiences, and reading books on pregnancy, childbirth, and parenting, nonparents rehearse for the parent role. Such anticipation and preparation usually focuses on the very early years of parenting and the parenting of young children.

The demands and responsibilities of parenting change over time as children develop and their exposure to the world increases. Changes in the biological, psychological, cognitive, and social needs of children across childhood require different forms and levels of parental input. According to Galinsky (1981), after the stage of image making during pregnancy, parents go through five more stages over their parenting careers, with each stage involving a different emphasis. Galinsky labels the second stage of parenting the **nurturing stage** because parenting a young baby focuses on meeting the child's basic care needs, as well as forming a close emotional bond with the child. Once children become mobile and begin to use language to express themselves, around age two, parents enter the **authority stage.** Besides nurturing their children, parents now have to set and enforce rules for their behavior. We will cover the balancing of authority and nurturance in parenting later when discussing parenting styles. The **interpretive stage** of Galinsky's parenting framework begins when children enter a school setting and become involved in microsystems beyond the family, usually at around age 4 or 5. With the expansion of their social world, children are exposed to many new experiences, ideas, behaviors, and views. Part of the parents' job is to assist their children in interpreting and understanding this world and to determine how their own values fit into this bigger picture.

For minority families, it is especially likely that the interpretive stage involves efforts centered on racial or ethnic socialization. Minority children have to figure out how to function in a majority culture that may differ dramatically from the culture that characterizes their home and family life. Research indicates that one of the things minority parents emphasize with their children is how to deal with societal prejudice and discrimination. Additionally, many minority parents stress knowledge and appreciation of their heritage and culture, and maintenance of cultural values. In so doing, minority parents attempt to facilitate the development of self-respect among their children, which will help them deal with a society that may devalue them and discriminate against them because of their minority status (Hurd, Moore, and Rogers, 1995; McAdoo, 1992).

Stage five, the **interdependent stage,** emerges as children enter adolescence and parents grant them more power and privileges, along with expecting more responsibility from them. The parent-child relationship assumes more give and take than it did earlier in childhood when parents assumed nearly total responsibility for their children's well-being. Finally, Galinsky refers to stage six, the **departure stage** of parenthood, when offspring reach adulthood and leave home to venture out on their own. During this stage, according to Galinsky (1981), parents evaluate how their children have turned out and how they have done in their job as parents.

Galinsky's is an especially useful framework for viewing parenthood because it emphasizes how parents must adapt their parenting behavior to the changing needs and abilities of their children as they grow. It also highlights how the challenges of parenting change as the boundaries between the family and the outside world become more permeable for the child, calling for changes in family system rules and ways of behaving.

Parenting Functions and Styles

Parenthood is generally viewed as involving two main functions. One involves limit setting, guidance, and control of children. In the early literature on parenthood this was referred to as the permissiveness-restrictiveness dimension of parenthood (Becker, 1964). Today, researchers generally use the term **demandingness** to describe this dimension. The other function of parenthood centers on emotional nurturance and responsiveness and was described originally along a warmth-hostility continuum (Becker, 1964). This dimension is referred to as **responsiveness** in the literature today. Children's healthy development and socialization for society requires that parents set limits on behavior (e.g., "You can't just take toys from your sister because you feel like it") and institute rules for their children to follow. At the same time, parental support and warmth is necessary to foster children's feelings of security, self-worth, and confidence, which will facilitate their exploration of and involvement with the larger social world. We discussed this process in Chapter 2.

The two basic dimensions of parenting—demandingness and responsiveness—can be combined in various ways to create four styles of parenting (see Table 5.2). However, the parenting styles most widely used in research and theory today are based on the work of Maccoby and Martin (1983), and Baumrind (1971). **Authoritative parenting,** according to Baumrind (1971) is a style involving high levels of both demandingness and emotional responsiveness to children. Authoritative parents establish clear rules and expectations for children's behavior but foster independence as well by encouraging children to express their opinions and discuss rules and regulations with them. **Authoritarian parenting,** in contrast, is a style that places high demands and control on children's behavior, combined with low levels of emotional support and parental responsiveness. As a consequence of this parenting style, children are likely to comply with adult demands, but they fail to develop much independent thinking and self-competence. Parenting may also be identified as **indulgent-permissive,** a style in which parents have few demands for children's behavior but are extremely responsive to and supportive of them (Maccoby and Martin, 1983). Finally, the **rejecting-neglectful parenting** style consists of extremely low levels of both parental demandingness and responsiveness (Maccoby and Martin, 1983).

Initially, researchers espoused the benefits of authoritative parenting styles for children's optimal development (Baumrind, 1967). Authoritative parenting appeared to lead to self-confidence, mastery, and self-control in children. In contrast, children raised in an authoritarian manner were considered somewhat more withdrawn and hostile, and the

Table 5.2 Parenting Styles as Classified Along the Dimensions of Demandingness and Responsiveness		
Level of Responsiveness	**Level of Demandingness**	
	Low	**High**
Low	Rejecting-neglectful	Authoritarian
High	Indulgent-permissive	Authoritative

children of permissive parents tended to be immature and overly dependent on adults. More recent research, however, suggests that the value of various parenting styles for children's successful development depends on the context in which they live. For example, in families of some Asian Americans, where cultural beliefs emphasize strict obedience and respect for adults, authoritarian parenting may not lead to problematic outcomes (Harrison et al., 1990), and authoritative parenting is not necessarily associated with good outcomes. To test this hypothesis, Chao (2001) studied the connection between parenting style and school performance for Euro-American compared to Asian American adolescents. She found that authoritative parenting predicted better school performance in the Euro-American group but not in the group of first-generation Asian Americans. Additionally, authoritarian parenting had a negative effect on the school effort of Euro-American adolescents only. Thus, Chao suggests that parenting styles reflect different qualities and meanings for different ethnic groups. Some research indicates, for example, that in Asian families, youth associate parental control with warmth and concern rather than with hostility or rejection (Rohner and Pettengill, 1985).

Studies that focus on low-income black children, particularly those living in dangerous urban settings, also call into question the value of particular parenting styles for children's outcomes in different ecological contexts. Apparently, authoritarian parenting that is more controlling and is accompanied by firm discipline—referred to as *no-nonsense* parenting (Peters and Massey, 1983)—may benefit children in these settings. Children's safety and well-being may be maximized when parents control and monitor their behavior under conditions of high risk. In addition, firm parenting may instill greater self-control in the children, which will contribute to positive outcomes (Baumrind, 1972; Brody and Flor, 1998; Pettit, Bates, and Dodge, 1998) and reduce adjustment problems (Brody, Dorsey, Forehand, and Armistead, 2002).

Predictors of Parenting Behavior

By comparing your own family experiences with those of close acquaintances, you can see great variability in how individuals parent and relate to their children. Parenting has been referred to as a "multiply determined process" (Belsky, 1984), meaning that more than one factor influences how a person parents. In his now classic piece on parenting, Belsky (1984) identified six major domains of influence that affect parenting and ultimately child outcomes:

- Parents' developmental history.
- Parents' personality.
- Characteristics of the child.

- Social support and/or relationships of the parent.

- Parents' marital relationship.

- Parents' work situation.

Parent's Developmental History. Developmental history refers to parents' past life experiences that may affect their parenting. Of great interest, for example, is how individuals' experiences in childhood with their own parents influence their parenting in adulthood. Research has shown that women who recall positive, secure bonds with their own mothers in childhood, for example, tend to be more responsive and sensitive mothers themselves (Gara, Rosenberg, and Herzog, 1996). Similarly, fathers whose own fathers were involved with them as children spend more time with their children, exercise more control in parenting, and take more responsibility for the care of their children, according to a recent study (Hofferth, 2003). On the other hand, mothers and fathers who recall harsh parental treatment in childhood use harsher parenting methods themselves, according to their offspring (Simons, Whitbeck, Conger, and Chyi-In, 1991).

Educational attainment is also part of parents' developmental history and is associated with their subsequent parenting. Studying a sample of black mothers, Bluestone and Tamis-LeMonda (1999) found that while many mothers used an authoritative approach to parenting their 5- to 12-year-olds, a significant predictor of their parenting style was education level. More-educated mothers generally used a child-centered, supportive, yet directive approach to parenting their offspring than less-educated mothers did. Thus, developmental history influences on parenting originate either in parents' families of origin or in their own past experiences in other areas of their lives, such as education.

Developmental history also includes the accumulated experience and maturity that one gains with age, making age an important influence on parenting. Compared to older mothers, adolescent mothers have been shown to provide less supportive or stimulating home environments for their children. Specifically, very young mothers tend to display relatively low emotional and verbal responsiveness to their children, which can have detrimental consequences for the child (Darabi et al., 1984; Coll, Hoffman, and Oh, 1987). The less-than-optimal parenting found among some adolescent mothers may be due, in part, to related problems such as stress, depression, and low self-esteem, which are part of the personality dimension in Belsky's model. There also is a connection between unwed teen childbearing and low educational achievement. As was noted for our hypothetical teen expectant mom, Simone, at the beginning of the chapter, having a child is correlated with early school departure and high school incompletion. Using nationally representative data, Pirog and Magee (1997) demonstrated that the chances of graduating from high school on time are reduced 25 percent for young women and 12 percent for young men who become teen parents, compared to their nonparent age peers. Furthermore, by age 26 rates of nongraduation are still 6–8 percent higher for males and females, respectively, who became teen parents (controlling for several other background variables such as socioeconomic status). Not completing high school, or delaying completion, has serious negative consequences for young parents' employment potential and economic situation, which in turn interferes with their ability to support their young children.

Clearly, added stress is an issue for teen parents, many of whom come from low-income, disadvantaged families. Lack of resources, unsolicited and unwanted advice, perceived loss of personal control, and conflicted interpersonal relationships are among some of the specific stressors noted in one study of mostly nonwhite, unmarried teenage mothers (Schinke, Barth, Gilchrist, and Maxwell, 1986). Research suggests that the stress experienced by adolescent mothers and fathers may be greater among whites than blacks (Thompson, 1986; Florsheim et al., 1999). As noted earlier, black teens may experience less social and family stigma and greater social support than white teens when they become parents. Research demonstrates that social and family support does have a positive impact on adolescent mothers' adjustment (Unger and Wandersman, 1988).

The parenting problems and economic vulnerability that exist for many teenage parents has raised a great deal of social concern over the issue of teenage childbearing. Yet, since 1991 there has been a steady decline in births to teenagers. In 1998, birth to girls between 15 and 17 years old dropped 5 percent, falling to a record historic low of 30.4 per 1,000 girls (National Center for Health Statistics, 1999). Thus, while there still is concern about teenage pregnancy and parenting, what some referred to as the "epidemic in teen childbearing" has passed.

Parental Personality and Belief Systems. The personality dimension in Belsky's model refers to a parent's current psychological well-being and personality attributes. One variable in this domain that is consistently related to parenting is depression. In the Bluestone and Tamis-LeMonda study (1999), the strongest predictor of parenting style was a mother's emotional adjustment. The most depressed mothers in this study were the least likely to report authoritative-type parenting behaviors that involve consideration of the child's perspective and needs or use of reasoning rather than strict control in discipline. A variety of negative outcomes are associated with parental depression, primarily because of the insensitive parenting that typically accompanies it (Hops, Sherman, and Biglan, 1990).

Although Belsky's model does not explicitly refer to cultural values and beliefs about children, they could be classified as part of either developmental history (e.g., the values one was socialized with early in life and cultural experiences one has had) or personality factors (e.g., belief systems). A central theme in the literature on ethnic minority families, for example, is the way that minority parents, especially Latino, black, and Asian parents, socialize their children toward interdependence rather than independence (Harrison, Wilson, Pine, Chan, and Buriel, 1990). Instead of raising their children to be increasingly independent and focused on individual achievement—which many Anglo American parents do—minority parents generally emphasize family and group interdependence in their child rearing, with a focus on collective actions and the collective good. This approach to child rearing appears to promote behaviors such as cooperation with others in childhood (Delgado-Gaitan, 1987) and the feelings adult children have about caring for aging parents (Pyke and Bengtson, 1996).

Differences in parental values and subsequent parenting practices are linked to parents' social class, an important part of one's developmental history. Kohn's (1969, 1976) theories of the connection between social class (education and occupation) and parenting values have been particularly influential in explaining social class differences in child-rearing. Kohn proposed that middle-class parents, who are typically more educated and hold jobs requiring more independent thinking, decision-making, and responsibility, tend to value independence and self-direction as goals for their children. In contrast, working-class parents, with lower levels of education and jobs that demand less independent thinking and involve routine tasks, and whose job success depends more on following orders, strongly value and emphasize conformity and obedience to authority in their children. Research shows that these values do translate into actual parenting behaviors. Parents who highly value conformity report more controlling and less supportive parenting (see Gerris, Dekovic, and Janssens, 1997), while those favoring independence and self-direction in their children encourage exploration of the environment and report less restrictive parenting (Luster, Rhoades, and Haas, 1989).

Parents' religion, more specifically their religious beliefs, is also associated with parenting practices. A comprehensive review of the influence of religion on family life recently concluded that conservative Protestant parents—those who accept a more literal interpretation of the Bible—are more likely to view physical punishment, such as spanking, as acceptable and effective in achieving parenting goals. Conservative Christians are less likely to think that corporal punishment has negative consequences for their children, and they feel less guilty about using physical punishment on their children (Mahoney, Pargament, Tarakeshwar, and Swank, 2001). One study involving parents of three-year-olds found that conservative Protestant parents were more likely than parents with other religious beliefs to endorse the idea that spanking is a necessary and effective way of achieving valued parenting goals (Gershoff, Miller, and Holden, 1999). Use of spanking and firm discipline is consistent with the belief held by many conservative Christian parents that obedience is an important trait to instill in children (Ellison and Sherkat, 1993).

With increasing religious heterogeneity in the United States, it is becoming more important to explore how parenting is influenced by religious belief systems, such as Buddhism, Hinduism, and Islam, which are present but less common in Western societies. Unfortunately, research on family life and its links to religions outside the Judeo-Christian tradition is absent in the literature, according to a review of nearly 100 studies on religion and family life (Mahoney, Pargament, Tarakeshwar, and Swank, 2001).

Another characteristic associated with parenting behaviors, but in just one study, is sexual orientation. Based on self-reports of their own parenting, gay fathers in Bigner and Jacobsen's (1989b) study were more likely than heterosexual fathers to report high levels of responsiveness, limit setting, and control behavior with their children. What might account for more authoritative parenting behavior on the part of gay fathers than heterosexual fathers? Perhaps gay fathers devote more time to reading and studying the material available on parenting than heterosexual fathers do because of the negative reactions they anticipate from a disapproving public. As noted, authorities on parenting often tout authoritative parenting as the preferable approach to parenting, despite some of the exceptions from research that we have noted.

Child Characteristics. Characteristics of the child are a major factor affecting parenting, which is a key reason that a parent may treat two children in the same family very differently. An obvious child characteristic that shapes parenting is the child's sex. Although extensive reviews of the parenting literature reveal few consistent differences in the parenting of boys versus girls (Lytton and Romney, 1991), scattered evidence suggests that parents use harsher discipline with boys (Simons et al., 1991) and require girls to do more household work (Gager, Cooney, and Call, 1999). Differences in parenting based on the sex of the child appear to be more acceptable in some cultural groups, for example among Mexican Americans (Sanchez, 1997), than others. In many Mexican American families parents grant boys much greater indulgence than girls and accord them higher status, and this sex-differentiated parenting supposedly increases as children move into adolescence (Locke, 1992). Variations in parental treatment also relate to age differences in children. This topic is discussed later in the chapter.

Parents' Social System. Belsky's (1984) model addresses the importance of the *social context* in which parenting is embedded, focusing on key parental microsystems: the workplace, the marriage, and social networks. In Chapter 7 we discuss in some detail the effects parents' work settings have on parenting and children. Therefore, in this chapter we focus primarily on social networks and their impact on parenting.

Aside from our immediate families with whom we live, one of the most important microsystems, and the one we interact with most, is our **personal social network.** Cochran and Brassard (1979) use this term to refer to relatives, friends, neighbors, coworkers, and professional helpers outside the household who engage in activities and exchange support on a regular basis with family members. Personal social network members do not necessarily live nearby; regular interaction, rather than geographic proximity, is required for inclusion in this system.

Members of one's personal social networks can contribute to individual and family well-being, but they can also detract from it. Sometimes the term *social support network* is used to refer to individuals in one's personal networks from whom one benefits by receiving nurturance, assistance, and support. Parenting is one area of family life that can benefit greatly from the help and support of others outside the family. Yet there are situations in which members of one's personal social networks behave in ways that interfere with family life and optimal performance in the parenting domain. For example, sometimes network members demand too much of one's time and energy, which detracts from personal happiness (Antonucci, Akiyama, and Lansford, 1998). It is critical to recognize both the positive and negative effects personal social networks have on families.

Personal social networks can have both indirect and direct influences on children. *Indirect* effects of parents' social networks on children result from network circumstances or situations that have an impact on the children without directly engaging them in the situation (Cochran and Brassard, 1979). (In such situations, the personal social network is a microsystem for the parents, and an exosystem for the children.) Cochran and Brassard (1979) identified three pathways through which parents' personal social networks indirectly influence children.

One way is through the role demands the parents encounter in connection with their network members, which ultimately may affect their parental role performance. In Chapter 7, we discuss how the demands that parents experience as workers may interfere with their parental role performance. Another example comes from Riley's (1990) work on men's participation in parenting and the influence of what he refers to as the *male network*—the percentage of a father's network made up of men. Interestingly, he found that among men who were the sole earner in their families, the more "male" their support network, the less time they spent playing with their children. In interpreting his finding, Riley speculates that a predominantly male peer group "maintains activities and attitudes in competition with the father's home role" (150). The friendship demands parents face sometimes interfere with the parenting role, thereby affecting their children.

Parental network members also affect children through the opportunities they provide parents that also benefit the children. For example, if a friend helps a parent find a better, higher-paying job or a safer home, the children are likely to experience positive outcomes as a result.

A third way parents' social networks influence their children indirectly is when network members shape the parental role by serving as parental role models (either good or bad!), setting standards for and controls on parenting behavior, and providing emotional and material support. Crnic and Greenberg's (1990) research on mothers of preschool children confirms the positive value social network members may have. They found that mothers who experienced high stress from the daily hassles they experienced with their children (such as children's whining and arguing) exhibited more positive interaction with their children if they had high rather than low levels of emotional support from network members. Therefore, even in situations where children do not have direct interaction with parents' social networks, these systems influence them in both good and bad ways because the parents are affected.

The potential also exists for children to be *directly* influenced by parents' personal social networks when they come in contact with them (in which case the network then becomes a microsystem for the children, too). Cochran and Brassard (1979) emphasize how children can broaden their range of cognitive and social stimuli through exposure to their parents' social networks. By observing and interacting with persons in the parents' network, children are introduced to a variety of interaction styles from which they may learn, especially if the behavior modeled by network members differs from that which the children have observed in the family. Participation in these social settings may also expose children to rules of social convention as they start to distinguish private from public behavior (it's all right to eat french fries with your fingers at home, but in a fancy restaurant a fork is used) and to distinct ways of talking and acting that are reserved for certain people (we call the babysitter by her first name but not the minister at church). Through observation and participation in these groups, children are essentially building their own social skills and possibly even components of their own social networks (e.g., children of their parents' friends). One situation in which children can be observed practicing the social skills they've picked up from adults is in their dramatic play at home or school. Listen to how children talk as they play house or market—they closely mimic the interactions modeled by the adults in their social world.

Children may also be exposed to novel activities and settings through their parents' networks, all of which broaden their base of experience. When network members are of a different ethnic or religious group from the family, for example, children may learn about and have the opportunity to participate in new rites and rituals. Or, city children may gain new experiences and knowledge by spending time with family friends who live in the country. Such experiences contribute to children's development across many domains.

Personal network members may also affect children directly through the exchanges of support they offer parents and children. In Mexican American culture such parenting supports are formalized in the **compadrazgo** relationship (somewhat like godparents), which is established through religious ceremonies. The comadre (co-mother) and compadre (co-father) provide support and assistance across the child's life (DeGenova, 1997). In other cultural groups, parenting support generally is temporary and supplements the care and resources the parents provide, as in situations where relatives or friends occasionally offer babysitting services. At times, however, parents' network members become more extensively involved to secure the welfare of children. In her classic work in a lower-class black community, for example, Stack (1974) observed the practice of "child-keeping," in which parents (typically single mothers) would temporarily send their children to reside with relatives to get a break during a particularly stressful period. Clearly, parents' personal networks can meet a wide range of direct support needs for their children as well as having a much broader impact on family life, family role performance, and family relationships.

The Marital Relationship. The quality of a couple's marriage is an influential force that shapes their parenting. Research demonstrates that a good couple relationship, involving harmony and support, provides a scaffold for positive parenting (Belsky, 1984; Parke and Tinsley, 1987). Indeed, parents benefit when they have good communication with their partner regarding the children and their respective experiences with them. For example, a traditional father who spends less time than his partner does with the children may be less aware of their specific likes and dislikes, habits, and schedules. Sensitive and responsive parenting on his part, therefore, may heavily depend on input from his wife—a process called **parenting facilitation**. When this dad fixes Saturday lunch for his young sons, he will surely avoid problems and be viewed more positively by them if his wife has warned him that their sons prefer grape jam over strawberry and insist that their sandwiches be served whole, rather than cut in half. The fact that fathers depend on parenting facilitation from their wives more than mothers depend on it from their husbands may partly explain why the quality of the couple relationship is a stronger predictor of parent-child relationships and parenting behavior for men than for women (Howes and Markman, 1989). Compared to mothering, fathering is more contingent on the marital relationship and input or assistance from a spouse.

Marital quality may also influence the extent to which partners support each other's parenting. **Co-parenting** refers to the process by which two parents either work together to support and reinforce each other's parenting or else work against each other, thereby undermining the parenting of the other (Gable, Belsky, and Crnic, 1995). Supportive co-parenting is considered critical for children's well-being because it provides them with clear, consistent messages and guidelines for behavior (McHale and Rasmussen, 1998). In contrast, inconsistent parenting is confusing for children, and it appears that when a marriage is highly conflicted, parenting (especially discipline) is likely to become less consistent (Fauber, Forehand, Thomas, and Wierson, 1990). Other aspects of parenting, such as parental monitoring of children, may also be compromised if parents have a distressed relationship.

Several explanations have been proposed for the connection between marital quality and parenting. Some theorists argue that parents who are in distressed marriages are less sensitive to their children's needs (Goldberg and Easterbrooks, 1984) because they are less emotionally and behaviorally available to their children than less-conflicted parents. It also appears that conflict between parents, especially conflict that is aggressive, may lead to harsh parenting practices (Fincham, Grych, and Osborne, 1994). Or, rather than parents actually transferring aggressive behaviors from their marital relations to their interactions with their children, the negative emotion from the conflicted, unhappy marriage is what spills over into parenting (Kerig, Cowan, and Cowan, 1993). Finally, marriage theorists claim that compared to other men, fathers in conflicted marriages are relatively withdrawn from parenting (Howes and Markman, 1989). This withdrawal is viewed as a generalization of the marital withdrawal that often characterizes men's reactions to marital conflict (Christensen and Heavey, 1990).

In sum, there are several ways in which parents' marriages may affect the interactions with their children, illustrating the interdependence that exists between marital and parent-child subsystems in the family. The explanations generally posit that marital discord leads parents to be less available, sensitive, or responsive to their children and their developmental needs. Ultimately, these parenting behaviors affect the children's well-being.

Parenting Changes From Childhood Through Adolescence

The time and energy demands of parenting young children are obvious because of the dependency of young children. Parents are not only the primary sources of physical and emotional nurturance, intellectual stimulation, and guidance regarding social rules and skills, but often companions and playmates as well. The focus of parenting changes as children age. Parents' concerns about their children, how they distribute their time among the numerous demands of parenting, and the specific activities involved in parenting shift as children develop. These changes are necessary for parents to stay attuned to their children's developmental needs. When parents understand children's development and respond sensitively to their current needs, the children benefit. In contrast, when parents have age-inappropriate expectations because of a lack of knowledge about child development, problems can occur. For example, the fact that children of teen parents are more often victims of physical abuse has been considered a possible consequence of young parents' relatively limited knowledge of children's abilities. As a result, they may mistake developmental immaturity with purposeful misbehavior, leading them to punish a child who actually does not know any better (Dallas, Wilson, and Salgado, 2000). The following sections review how the aims and activities of parenting change as children develop from birth through adolescence.

Infancy

The immediate experience of most infants is restricted to just a few microsystems, including interactions with family and close friends in their own homes, and possibly a childcare center or the homes of relatives and friends. Parents provide the bulk of care to most infants. During infancy, parental care falls into four main categories, according to Bornstein (1995). **Nurturant caregiving** involves fulfilling the physical needs of children—ensuring their survival through the provision of food, shelter, clothing, and a safe environment. **Material caregiving** extends beyond basic survival needs to how parents structure and organize their infants' physical world. This type of caregiving includes the level of stimulation that parents provide in the environment, with toys, books, art, and music. **Social caregiving** is focused on the interpersonal aspects of parenting, such as visual and physical contact, vocalizing, smiling, hugging, and kissing. Such behaviors contribute to the affective and social development of the infant. Finally, parenting infants requires **didactic caregiving,** in which parents stimulate children's interaction and understanding of the world outside the caregiver-infant pair. Focusing young children on objects and events in the environment, and mediating their interaction with the environment, is a key component of didactic parenting behavior that heightens near the end of infancy—after around age one (Bornstein, 1995). Around this age, for example, parents might try to interest their child in animals or nature. Pointing out the colorful birds that are perched on the birdfeeder and helping the child to pet a dog for the first time are examples of how a parent gradually and safely introduces him or her to objects in the outside world.

The Toddler Years

During toddlerhood (approximately ages one to three) and early childhood, children develop the capacity to function more interdependently and independently of parents because of heightened physical skills and enhanced verbal and cognitive abilities. Not only do toddlers not need their parents' constant help and guidance to explore the world, they often don't want it. The fact that the word "no" is used so much by toddlers is evidence of that! The enhanced capacity of toddlers to explore the environment around them and manipulate objects requires parents to monitor them more and employ more authority with them than when they were infants. To illustrate, it is much safer to leave an infant in a room alone for a few minutes than it is to leave a two-year-old who has become mobile and can climb and grab at objects. Finally, increasingly during the toddler years, parents need to guide their children's interpretation of the outside world, because they now have more interaction with that world and the cognitive capacity to reflect on it. This challenge was described in Galinsky's (1981) authority and interpretive stages.

The heightened activity and abilities of toddlers and young children present both fun and frustration for parents. Indeed, parents feel great pleasure and pride as they watch their young ones take their first step, learn to peddle their tricycles, and perform daily care tasks, such as toileting and feeding themselves. Yet parenting young children also involves the stress of what Crnic and Greenberg (1990) label **daily hassles.** These are "irritating, frustrating, annoying, and distressing demands that to some degree characterize everyday transactions with the environment" (p. 1629). Parenting hassles frequently reported by mothers of youngsters include the following:

- Cleaning up repeated messes.
- Listening to children's whining, nagging, and complaining.
- Children not listening to parental requests.
- Children interrupting adult conversations.

Though bothersome when they occur, such hassles are likely to decline in number as children enter school and their parents' time with them is reduced by about half (Hill and Stafford, 1980).

Early Childhood

Between the ages of two and a half to five, children's cognitive capacity grows dramatically. Unlike toddlers, whose world is comprised largely of immediate experience, preschoolers begin to explore the workings of the world at a deeper level. The *how* and *why* of events and experiences become of greater interest to them, and children of this age attempt to construct their own understanding of the world (Sroufe, Cooper, and DeHart, 1996). Language development also occurs at an accelerated rate during this period. The vocabulary of an average preschooler triples between ages three and five (Brooks, 1999). The ability to meaningfully connect several words to convey thoughts also emerges during this stage.

All of these changes have important implications for parenting. Thus, one significant change that occurs in parenting from the toddler to preschool or early-childhood period is that communication with the child becomes much more verbal. Instead of showing children of this age how to do something, or doing it for them, parents can now verbally instruct their preschoolers. This ability eventually reduces the number of tasks that the parent has to do for the child, and it also contributes to the child's sense of independence. Also, parents can share clear rules and expectations for behavior with their preschool child, and the child is able to consider the explanations that are given for why certain rules exist. The establishment of clear rules, along with the child's expanded ability to think about the events he or she experiences, means that consistency in parenting behavior becomes especially important during this period. Inconsistencies in how their world operates create great confusion for preschoolers (Sroufe et al., 1996).

Another aspect of verbal communication with a child that becomes especially important in the preschool period centers on the child's emotional experiences. Because preschoolers are developing a deeper understanding of the connection between their behavioral experiences and feelings and have the ability to regulate and control emotion and behavior better, it is valuable for parents to talk with their children about feelings and the appropriate expression of them. This activity, labeled "coaching," includes talking with the child to help him or her identify the emotions that are being experienced and then assisting the child in figuring out what to do to express those feelings and feel better. Children who received emotional coaching from their parents tend to experience less stress, and over time their adjustment and social relationships are more favorable than those of children whose parents did not coach them in dealing with their emotions (Gottman, Katz, and Hooven, 1996). Additionally, the preschooler's increasing ability to understand emotion and to think about

Despite some of the daily hassles children present during the toddler and early childhood years, they bring great joy and pleasure to most parents.

how others may feel—to be empathetic—contributes to greater care and concern for others during this period (Bigner, 1998).

Middle Childhood

The middle-childhood years, spanning from approximately ages six to twelve, present many new challenges for parents. Maintaining responsibility for children and monitoring their behavior can be difficult for parents during this stage, as children become more engaged in settings outside the family system and spend more time away from their parents in microsystems such as the neighborhood, school, and peer group (Collins, Harris, and Susman, 1995). Children's involvement in the bigger social world also requires parents' help in navigating and interpreting the expanding world outside the home and family. Parents engage in more **co-regulatory processes** with their children across middle childhood, gradually transferring greater responsibility for self-management to their children. In the process, however, it is critical for parents to maintain an oversight function (Collins, Harris, and Susman, 1995). For example, allowing children more input into the clothes they buy and wear is appropriate; however, parents will still want to monitor their children's selections to ensure that the clothing is appropriate for their age, the weather, and settings in which the clothes will be worn.

Family boundaries may also change during this period. With more people becoming involved in the lives of children as they age, the flow of information between the family system and the outside world will likely increase. Parents, for example, may tell a teacher about a family problem they are having, because they want their child to be treated sensitively at school and to be understood. For example, an aging grandparent's move into the home can be disruptive for a child if mental or physical disabilities need to be accommodated, or parental separation or divorce can present stressful changes. The family's physical boundaries may also shift as the child's social world expands. Openness of family boundaries to nonfamily visitors in the home generally increases as children bring friends home to visit or play.

Families will vary in how they respond to these boundary changes. More than likely, a family will experience both positive and negative consequences to the increased permeability of family boundaries. At times, more-permeable family boundaries may threaten the maintenance of family rules, routines, and togetherness. However, at other times, family members may benefit from heightened contact and openness with others, perhaps gaining new and additional sources of support and companionship. Many parents, for example, claim their closest and most supportive friendships came from the contacts they made with other parents when their children were young.

Because of the many new academic and social experiences that children encounter during middle childhood, parents are also likely to assume a key emotional support role for their children as they deal with the stress of these new experiences. Levitt and her colleagues (1993) studied a sample of black, Latino and white children, ages seven to fourteen, to determine how the parental support role differed for children of various ages and ethnic backgrounds. They found that across these ages, close family members were the most frequent source of emotional support for children in all three racial/ethnic groups. The importance of friends in children's support systems, however, increased substantially across these ages. By age fourteen, friends assumed as much importance in the support network as close family members.

Adolescence

As just noted, a major change that occurs in relations between parents and their children with the onset of the younger generation's adolescence is that friends become more supportive relative to parents; additionally, friends become more influential—at least in certain domains. The total time children

Even for children approaching adolescence, parents continue to play the main support role in their lives. Most parents and children report good relationships at this point in development.

spend with their parents is cut in half between elementary school and junior high (Larson and Richards, 1991). For adolescents, time with parents is replaced largely by more time with friends and hanging out in their rooms alone (Larson and Richards, 1991). The role of parents as sources of influence also weakens as children become adolescents. Friends are favored when it comes to talking about personal issues such as relationships and sex, yet teens still prefer parental rather than peer input on serious issues regarding values, future goals, and school performance (Youniss and Smollar, 1985).

Given parents' reduced importance as sources of companionship and influence for their children as they move into adolescence, it is not surprising that conflict between the two generations rises during this period. Despite what the media and popular views of adolescence suggest, most parent-adolescent relationships are not dominated by conflict. Fewer than one in ten families experience serious relationship problems during adolescence, and most of these troubled relationships were already problematic during childhood (Holmbeck et al., 1995). The disagreements that do occur between parents and teens generally involve issues such as household chores (Barber, 1994; Larson and Richards, 1994) and other fairly mundane issues that are part of daily life. Of course, parents and adolescents do disagree and argue about more serious topics, such as sex, drugs, and drinking, too. However, these issues are not discussed nearly as often as relatively minor ones (Barber, 1994).

Mothers seem to be the favored opponent in parent-teenager disputes (Steinberg, 1990). Perhaps mothers are more "at-risk" for conflict with their teens than fathers because of the extended time they spend with and the higher number of activities they share with their offspring (Collins et al., 1995). Alternatively, teens may feel safer disagreeing and arguing with their mothers than their fathers because they usually feel closer to and more understood by their mothers (Youniss and Smollar, 1985).

A final point about parent-teen conflict is that it is not necessarily undesirable. For teens, experiencing some conflict with their parents may actually be beneficial, because it can help them develop conflict-resolution skills, increase their tolerance of different views and opinions, and contribute to the individuation process, in which they begin to see themselves as distinct from their parents. For parents, conflict can signal a need for reflection about and possible changes in how they are parenting their adolescents (Holmbeck at al., 1995).

One of the most significant challenges for parents of adolescents—and one that often creates conflict between parents and offspring—is the teenager's demand for added independence and freedom from parental monitoring. The dilemma for parents is figuring out how to provide increased opportunities for responsibility and autonomous decision making for their adolescents while remaining emotionally supportive and physically available to them and ensuring that they are safe and out of trouble. In the next chapter, we'll explore some of the factors that contribute to how both offspring and parents adjust to this process of independence granting in families during the late teen and early-adulthood years.

In sum, parenting across childhood is a dynamic process that requires rules, roles, and routines within the family system to change in response to children's growth and development from infancy through adolescence. The connection between the family system and the outside world changes across this period as well; the developing child's expanding social world creates new tasks and roles for the parents. For young children, parents are usually the center of their universe and parental input is required almost constantly, across nearly all life domains. But when offspring reach adolescence, many parents struggle to maintain even a small part in their children's lives. Their companionship and input is not needed, or wanted, nearly as much as when the children were young. Thus, as children's needs for constant attention and extended time from their parents decline, the older generation has to shift the balance of their lives. The next chapter discusses in more detail how parents do this. Finally, it is important to note that, in addition to the child's development, changes in family life and parenting over time are also motivated by situational changes in the parents' lives and their own development. Divorce or separation, a serious illness or accident, or even the death of a parent radically changes the nature of the parent-child subsystems. Although research on these issues is limited, they will be explored in more depth in the next chapter.

Sibling Relationships in Childhood

Family systems experience dramatic change when additional children enter the system. Each new birth creates additional parent-child subsystems and sibling subsystems, with all of these subsystems potentially affecting one another. In this section, we discuss how the birth of a sibling alters family life for the firstborn child, the various dimensions of the sibling relationship, and how parenting influences and is influenced by sibling relationships.

The Firstborn's Adjustment to a New Sibling

The birth of a sibling creates significant changes in the life of a child. Most research has considered this family transition for preschool-age children, with the results showing at least temporary changes in the firstborn's behavior after a sibling's birth. Sleeping, eating, and toileting problems usually increase, along with moodiness, aggression, naughtiness, and withdrawal behavior. However, positive developments, such as accelerated language development and heightened independence, are also noted among firstborn children during this family transition (Dunn, 1996).

The variety of behavioral changes observed in children on the birth of a sibling is understandable, given the extensive disruption that occurs in the life of a firstborn child when a sibling is born. Remember, the experiences of most very young children occur in just a few microsystems, with the home being their primary environment. Thus, when a sibling is born, nearly every setting the firstborn child participates in is likely to also involve the sibling. Positive parental interaction and attention for the firstborn child drops significantly when a second child enters the home; in response, the older child may act out to gain extra parental attention. Some firstborn children alternatively withdraw or act more independently to meet their own needs when parents become less available. Similarly, parents' mood changes, brought on by heightened fatigue and stress, may elicit undesirable behavioral responses from the firstborn child, as might the child's witnessing parental interaction with the new infant (Dunn, 1996). At least initially, the firstborn child is likely to perceive that much is lost and little gained by the birth of a new brother or sister. This feeling results primarily from changes in the firstborn child's relationship with the parents.

Sibling Influences and Relationships

Over time, as siblings increasingly interact and a bond between them grows, the relationship can become extremely important for the development of both children. In comparison to other family relationships, the sibling relationship is especially salient. More time is spent in one-on-one interaction between siblings than between parents and children (Dunn, 1996). Also, within the family, the relationship between siblings is the longest. Another unique aspect of the sibling bond compared to other relationships in the family system—most notably the parent-child connection—is that it is reciprocal and symmetrical. That is, siblings are generally close in age, share similar experiences, and have fairly equal status and power. This symmetry can result in both negative and positive emotional expressions and interactions between siblings (Brown and Dunn, 1992). Similar status, age, and experience can contribute to deeper understanding and empathy in the relationship, as siblings face many of the same challenges and share many of the same joys and disappointments in life. Yet, because siblings are often dealing with the same challenges and goals, they frequently compete for the same set of resources (parental attention, favor among neighborhood friends), which can create conflict or other negative emotions in the relationship.

It is the negative interactions and emotions experienced between siblings that seem to get the most attention from the public as well as scholars. Sibling rivalry, for example, is a popular media topic, although it is actually reported less often by parents than other types of sibling problems (Felson, 1983; Raffaelli, 1992). The concept of rivalry is based on the notion that siblings must compete for their parents' attention and love and that parents may treat some children in the family more favorably than others. There is limited evidence, however, that children perceive significant levels of parental favoritism in their families. In one study of adolescents and young adults, similar parental treatment for respondents and their siblings was noted by half the sample, while another third claimed there was "a bit" of difference. "Much" difference in how parents treated the various children in the family was reported by fewer than 10 percent of respondents (Daniels and Plomin, 1985).

Moreover, other research indicates that even when children do perceive that their parents treat the children within the family differently—(referred to as **parental differential treatment—PDT**)—it is not necessarily problematic. Rather, if children can justify why the parents treat siblings in the family differently, they usually accept it and do not feel terribly bothered (Kowal and Kramer, 1997). This understanding was reflected in the comment of six-year-old Erica, who was asked to reflect on her feelings about her younger brother, Jake, who is autistic:

> I get mad when Jake draws on my walls and makes dark marks on them. Mommy cleans it up. If I did that I would have to clean it up! But, I guess it's all right that Jake doesn't have to clean up because he doesn't understand. (Meyer, 1997, 7)

If it isn't competition for parental attention and affection that leads to the sibling conflict most of us probably remember experiencing, at least occasionally, what is it? Studies of preschool-aged siblings (Dunn and Munn, 1987) and older ones (Goodwin and Roscoe, 1990; Raffaelli, 1992) report that conflicts commonly occur over property (e.g., toys, television) and individual rights and privacy ("stay out of my room"). Among older children, verbal insults and household duties and chores get added to this list (Goodwin and Roscoe, 1990; Raffaelli, 1992). Therefore, most of the issues siblings fight about are fairly minor, and the intensity of their battles is low, although more serious aggression is not unheard of in sibling relationships (Felson, 1983). Abusive sibling relationships are discussed in Chapter 9.

Several facts suggest that perhaps too much is made of sibling conflict. We know, for example, that

These siblings vary widely in age. How might each benefit from relating to the others? In particular, think about what older siblings, like this boy, gain from their relationships with very young siblings.

conflicts between siblings are typically short-lived, with most problems being resolved within minutes, and almost all within one hour, even for siblings who habitually fight (Raffaelli, 1992). Also, some developmental psychologists argue that children may learn valuable lessons about conflict resolution and negotiation in the problem situations they encounter with their siblings (von Salisch, 2000). The developmental benefits children gain from their sibling relationships go beyond lessons in conflict management. Indeed, Dunn (1996) argues that social understanding is facilitated through both positive and negative sibling interactions. Through experiences with their siblings, children learn how to determine what others are thinking and feeling, they discover what behaviors are expected and accepted in social interactions, and they learn important physical skills and knowledge. These lessons are likely to benefit siblings in their interactions with peers and others throughout life.

Interactions Among Sibling, Parent-Child, and Couple Subsystems

We have already addressed how the parent-child subsystems affect one another in our discussion of the birth of a sibling and the subsequent changes that occur in parents' time and interaction with the firstborn child as a consequence of their relationships with the new baby. The interdependence of family subsystems is also evident in considering how parent-child subsystems influence, or are influenced by, sibling subsystems. For example, Brody and his colleagues (1992) had parents and their school-aged children engage in a problem-solving task that the researchers observed and coded for quality of sibling and parent-child interactions. The researchers found that parents' unfair treatment of their children in the problem-solving situation (e.g., one child being unfairly blamed for something) predicted greater conflict and negative behavior between siblings one year later when the tasks were repeated. Research with younger sibling pairs documents similar consequences. Dunn and Kendrick (1981) found that when mothers devoted a relatively high proportion of their time to playful interaction with the younger infant, the siblings' relationship was less positive and more problematic months later.

Additionally, interactions between siblings can influence the parent-child subsystems. One explanation for this connection, according to Furman (1995), is "behavioral contagion," in which siblings' conflict may spread and produce parent-child conflict as parents grow increasingly agitated by the negative sibling interaction. Also, the disciplinary approach parents choose to use with their children may be influenced by the siblings' interactions with one another (Furman, 1995). Parents use more physical punishment with their children when siblings engage in more verbal and physical conflict (Patterson, 1986). Because most studies on this topic are cross-sectional, however, it is unclear whether the influence of parent-child relationships on sibling relationships is stronger or whether the reverse is true. In all likelihood, these influences work in both directions.

Finally, there is evidence that the sibling subsystems in the family interact with the marital subsystem and that these effects too may work in both directions. In the longitudinal study mentioned earlier, Brody and his colleagues (1992) examined the connection between parents' reports of marital conflict and observed sibling interaction. These researchers found that the more overt conflict the parents reported, the greater the level of negative behavior and conflict observed between siblings one year later. These investigators theorize that interparental conflict probably creates a hostile environment for children, contributing to their heightened distress and aggressive behavior. Eventually, such negative emotional reactions may spread to the children's relationships with each other, creating sibling conflict and tension. Alternatively, Brody and his associates suggest that heightened sibling aggression may result from children simply observing and modeling the aggressive interactions of their parents. Research by Stocker and Youngblade (1999) with 7- to 10-year-olds supports this idea. They too found a significant association between parents' marital conflict and troubled sibling relationships. Moreover, they discovered that this connection was dependent on levels of both paternal and maternal hostility: As overt hostility in the home environment increased, it served as a catalyst to tension in sibling relationships.

Parental marital problems, however, can sometimes contribute to positive sibling relationships. Jenkins (1992) claims that siblings sometimes turn to one another for confiding and support under conditions of high marital conflict; in such situations, strong sibling bonds can buffer the negative impact of an unpleasant home environment. One study of family relationships following divorce found that young adult offspring often felt closer to and more responsible for younger siblings after their parents divorced (Cooney, Smyer, Hagestad, and Klock, 1986). These alternative outcomes reveal the variation in family dynamics that is possible as subsystems come together and interact over time. The addition of each new sibling to the family system makes the potential for change and variation in family dynamics even greater.

The Big Picture: Historical Change Affecting Young Families

This chapter addressed a number of issues surrounding parenting roles and practices, parent-child and sibling relationships, and the factors that influence them. We have not yet touched on how historical and social change at the macrosystem level affects family life, and parenting specifically. Two major societal changes that have produced widespread consequences for family life and roles in this country (and most Western nations) are the marked reduction in fertility and the huge influx of married women into the paid labor force, both beginning around 1960. Specifically, the number of births per thousand married women in the United States dropped from approximately 160 in 1960 to around 90 just 15 years later (Farley, 1996). Since 1975, the fertility rate for married women has remained steady at about 90 births per thousand. The jump in the employment rate for married women was also dramatic. Between 1960 and the 1990s it climbed from approximately 30 percent to nearly 70 percent (Spain and Bianchi, 1996).

The connection between these population trends is interesting to consider and is widely debated (see Spain and Bianchi, 1996). Our concern here, however, is their implications for family life, especially parenting. Chapter 7 provides an extensive discussion of how women's employment has altered the roles women and men perform in families. Here we speculate about the impact of reduced fertility, women's employment, and other related trends on macrosystem parenting values and practices. In addition, we briefly address the explosion in media and technology that has occurred over the last 50 years in this country. How does the presence of television in virtually all homes in the United States, and children's exposure to nonfamilial influences via television, the Internet, and other media forms (CDs, videotapes, DVDs) affect parenting and young families? Related to the issue of changing values, we briefly consider the question of whether media depictions of families affect family values and orientations or whether such media forms reflect existing societal values.

Shifts in Parenting Values

Classic research conducted by Lynd and Lynd (1929) during the 1920s (known as the Middletown Study), was probably the first study to ask a sample of American parents about the characteristics they valued most in children and the goals they emphasized in child rearing. Using the Lynds' findings as a comparison, Alwin more recently addressed this same issue with data gathered in the 1950s, 1970s, and 1980s.

Alwin's sociological research (1984, 1988, 1990) considers how Americans' views of "preferred parenting" (or socialization values) have changed over time. His central finding is that since early in the twentieth century substantial growth has occurred in the percentage of Americans who value independent thinking or autonomy in children and a significant decline has occurred in the percent valuing obedience. One illustration of this change is evident in the classic Middletown Studies. When the Lynds first conducted their research in 1924, approximately 45 percent of parents placed "strict obedience" among the top three characteristics emphasized in child rearing, whereas 25 percent included "independence" among the three most important characteristics to emphasize. In contrast, a 1978 follow-up study showed 17 percent of parents listing obedience among the top three characteristics to be emphasized in child rearing and 76 percent naming independence (Alwin, 1988).

Alwin also examined these parenting values with cross-time data from the Detroit Metropolitan Area survey, which asked parents to rank several values from 1 to 5, with higher numbers indicating greater importance of a particular value in child rearing. Table 5.3 illustrates how obedience declined in importance to parents, whereas independent thinking gained in importance over several decades. Note that in the Detroit studies "to think for self" was most important of these five values across all years while obedience moved from second place in 1958 to fourth in 1983 (Alwin, 1990).

An important contribution of Alwin's research is that it explored historical changes that might explain this shift in child-rearing values. He notes, for example, that reductions in fertility during the last century may have influenced parents' shifting orientations. Research from the 1960s and 1970s indicated that smaller family size usually resulted in parents placing fewer restrictions on children's behavior and relaxing their demands for obedience to rules (Clausen and Clausen, 1973; Nye, Carlson, and Garrett, 1970). Cer-

Table 5.3 Average Rankings* for Values Emphasized in Parenting, From the Detroit Metropolitan Area Surveys

Trait	Year of Study		
	1958	1971	1983
1. To obey	3.19	3.00	2.81
2. To be well liked	1.76	1.57	1.38
3. To think for self	4.14	4.24	4.40
4. To work hard	2.73	2.92	3.21
5. To help others	3.15	3.26	3.20

*(1=least important to 5=most important)

Source: Adapted from Alwin (1990).

tainly having more children in a home requires having more rules so that things run smoothly and some order is maintained (Bossard and Boll, 1956). Thus, historical decline in fertility may partly explain the reduced emphasis on obedience in parenting that Americans now report.

The heightened presence of women in the workforce could also explain some of the change in parents' expectations for children. With more families today consisting of two working adults (see Chapter 7) or single parents (see Chapter 8), children may be expected to assume more responsibility for themselves and make more decisions on their own at an earlier age. Rather than emphasizing obedience to authority figures, it may actually serve children and families better to encourage independent thinking and autonomy in children so that they become less dependent on adults at earlier ages. Research on children in single-parent families does show that they assume more household responsibility than peers in two-parent families (Gager et al., 1999).

Other societal changes that occurred with modernization, such as increased levels of formal education and a shift toward more highly skilled jobs, could also account for the changes in child-rearing values that Alwin documented. Because more jobs require the manipulation of ideas, technological skills, and creativity, parents may consider it important to emphasize independent thinking and decision making in their children as a way of preparing them for the work world they will enter in adulthood. Alwin (1984) demonstrated that increasing educational attainment in this country accounts for a major share of the growth in independence as a child-rearing value for Americans.

Media Influences on Family Life

Media and communication systems have greatly expanded in the past half-century. Television, CDs, videotapes, Internet resources, and print material have assumed a growing presence in American family life. Today, over half of homes in the United States have a computer and direct Internet access (National Telecommunications and Information Administration, 2002). Not having a television is almost unheard of in American households, as 98 percent of families report having at least one TV, which is more than have telephones or indoor toilets (Dorr and Rabin, 1995). It is estimated that the average American watches approximately 30 hours of television a week (Kellner, 1990) and that the television is turned on about 7 hours per day in American households. Because of its almost continual operation during a family's waking hours at home, television has become part of much of family life, including leisure, homework, play, socializing, and mealtime (Dorr and Rabin, 1995).

Just think about your own experience and how concurrent television viewing affects your conversations with family members, attentiveness to others (e.g., listening to a family member talk about an important concern or event in his or her day), and the time you devote to family and household chores or studying. Larson and Richards (1994) found that television watching was the most frequently shared activity between adolescents and their parents. In fact, 40 percent of the time teenagers in their study spent with their fathers was in front of a television. Is this quality time, and does it produce positive interactions and feelings? Larson and Richards's study indicated that teens and their parents appeared to be emotionally numb while watching television. That doesn't say much for the emotional side of family life, given that watching television consumed the largest piece of shared family time in these households.

Studies on the impact of computers and the Internet on family interaction also reveal some distressing results. Early research found that when families purchased computers and access to the Internet, the amount of time family members spent communicating with each other went down (Kraut, Patterson, Lundmark, Kiesler, Mukophadhyay, and Scherlis, 1998). Observational research confirmed this general finding, as it revealed that the majority of the time children ages eight to seventeen spent online was devoted to solitary activities, such as playing games, exchanging e-mail, and visiting chat rooms. Indeed, parents and children rarely communicated when the children were on the computer (Orleans and Laney, 2000). Surprisingly, few parents reported concern over their children's computer use and activities on the Internet (only 6 percent) in a recent study (Livingstone, 2002).

But it appears there is a positive side of the Internet for family life as well. In terms of contributing to exchange and communication with family members beyond the household, the Internet may indeed be a valuable tool. In one study, the majority of Internet users (60 percent) claimed that the level of communication they had with relatives and friends had increased since they obtained

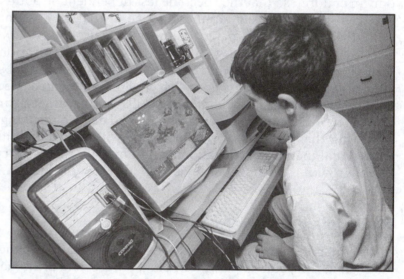

Many homes now have computers and children often choose to spend free time on the computer. How can parents monitor computer (especially Internet) use and ensure that it does not become a problem that interferes with other valuable learning and recreational activities for children?

access to e-mail (Howard, Raine, and Jones, 2001). This appears to be the case with older adult family members as well, who are increasingly becoming Internet users (Fox et al., 2001). Overall, research suggests that use of the Internet may enhance contact with family members and other network members who live outside one's own household (Wellman, Haase, Witte, and Hampton, 2001).

Beyond their role in family interaction, media forms (the lyrics of songs, magazine advertisements) may potentially shape how people think about their world. Some social scientists believe that television is *the* socializing agent that competes most with traditional forms of socialization. One authority notes:

> Messages and images of television consciously and unconsciously compete with and challenge the teachings in the home and other institutions concerned with the growth and development of young people. (Berry, 1998, 234)

A number of studies examining media portrayals of males and females, and of persons of different racial and ethnic groups, have found that current daytime television still reflects stereotypical images and roles (Coltrane and Messineo, 2000; Kaufman, 1999). What effects do such images have for viewers? For example, when viewers see women, rather than men, providing the majority of care to children (Kaufman, 1999), or whites more often than blacks assuming positions of authority (Coltrane and Messineo, 2000), does it affect their behavioral goals and views of what is appropriate behavior in families and the larger society? How much does the type or quality of parenting observed on television programs affect viewers' own parenting or beliefs about appropriate parenting? Studies from the 1980s and 1990s (Dail and Way, 1985; Scheibe and Grossman, 1993) revealed that fictional parents on television—at least those enacted by real people rather than cartoon characters—were largely portrayed as authoritative rather than authoritarian or permissive in their parenting styles. (Remember the Cosby parents?) Unfortunately, there is no evidence showing whether these portrayals influence the parenting of the viewers who watch them. However, it is hypothesized that children may be heavily influenced by the family images they see on television, because they have relatively few opportunities to experience families other than their own (Olson and Douglas, 1997). Indeed, research suggests that children consider real-life families to be very similar to the families portrayed in the television series they watch most often (Dorr, Kovaric, and Doubleday, 1990).

There has been a great debate about how television relates to the ideals Americans have for family life. Historians have written widely about how the idealistic family life portrayed in 1950s television programs (*Leave It to Beaver, Father Knows Best*) created a pervasive myth regarding what families were really like in the 1950s, a myth that persists to this day (Coontz, 1992). A more recent debate regarding television centers on whether current programs reflect accurate images and values Americans have about families or whether these programs actually shape new beliefs and values about families. Results based on nationally representative data from the 1980s and early 1990s showed that the more television adults reported watching, the less traditional they were in their beliefs about appropriate family structures and roles (Morgan, Leggett, and Shanahan, 1999). Although the authors of this study contend that these results support the notion that television shapes the values of its viewers—in this case, making their values less traditional—other interpretations are possible. For example, given the cross-sectional design of their research, it could just as easily be argued that persons with less traditional values are more likely to watch heavy amounts of television.

Another study that focused on the impact of television viewing on teenage girls' goals for family life found a contrary finding. In this study the girls who watched the most television were the ones most likely to express more traditional values, such as a preference toward assuming traditional family roles in adulthood, including being married to the same person for life and being a parent (Signorielli, 1991). Therefore, it seems reasonable to expect that the media play some role in shaping family interactions and ideals, although more research is needed to understand the specific connections. In all likelihood, media images in society today both reflect *and* shape people's views of family life.

Clearly, historical and societal events and social movements filter down to influence family interaction, roles, relationships, and family life in general. To understand the dynamics and workings of an individual family system, we must consider the broad social context in which the family system exists. That includes paying attention to such factors as the values that exist within a community and culture, the symbols and images that are emphasized and conveyed through society's media forms, current demographic patterns, and historical changes in the institutions in which people engage in everyday life. These are some of the powerful social forces that contribute to family life as it is experienced every day.

Summary

The majority of American adults will assume the position of parent at some point in their lives. A common reason adults take on the parental role is the psychological and emotional rewards they anticipate. Many adults and teens expect that parenting will provide a special loving relationship for them and will give them someone to care for and teach. More practical rewards are not usually considered, nor are the economic costs of parenthood, although women are more likely than men to consider the career implications of parenthood. This sex difference is consistent with the fact that once women become parents, they generally invest a greater share of their identities and time in parenting than fathers do.

Planning carefully for parenthood, having realistic expectations about what parenting will be like and the childcare contributions each parent will make, and having a strong couple relationship are all critical predictors of a relatively smooth adjustment to parenthood. In addition, the wider ecological context influences what the birth and early parental experience will be like. Hospital policies surrounding delivery, insurance regulations addressing the length of stay that mothers and their new babies are allowed, parenting/family supports that exist at the community level (such as visiting nurses, parenting education programs, childcare options), as well as societal attitudes about the nature of children and men's and women's parenting roles, all contribute to the early parenting experience. Policies and programs that support parental involvement and competent parenting and that contribute to the development of strong mesosystems benefit both parents and children.

Parenting behaviors involve two key dimensions—demandingness and responsiveness—that combine to form unique styles of parenting (authoritative, authoritarian, permissive, and neglectful). Parenting behaviors are determined by multiple factors, including (a) the parent's own developmental experiences in childhood (how he or she was parented) and adulthood (educational achievements); (b) the parents' personality (beliefs and values) and psychological/emotional adjustment; (c) characteristics of the child (sex, health status); and (d) the parents' social roles, relationships, and supports (marriage, work, social support networks). These factors may change over time, thereby altering parenting behavior, just as parenting changes as children develop from infancy through adolescence. Indeed, parenting is a dynamic process that must respond to a child's changing developmental needs.

Sibling relationships are a central aspect of early family life. The entry of a new child into the family system not only alters the preexisting relationship between the first child and each parent but may affect the couple subsystem as well. Thus, it is critical to recognize the interdependence of subsystems in the family during the family building years, as well as the bidirectional nature (marital interaction influencing sibling interaction, and vice versa) of subsystem interdependence.

Finally, the impact of large-scale societal forces and change on parenting and family life cannot be overlooked. Such things as shifts in macrosystem parenting values over the twentieth century and the technology revolution that created an influx of televisions and computers into American households are influential forces shaping the socialization of children and interaction among members in families. Moreover, they play a role in how families interact with their personal networks and the world at large.

Chapter Concepts

anticipatory socialization: preparing for and practicing the behaviors involved in a role that will be assumed in the future.

authoritarian parenting: a parenting style that includes high demands and control on children's behavior and low levels of emotional support and responsiveness.

authoritative parenting: a parenting style involving high levels of both demandingness and emotional responsiveness to children. Parents maintain clear rules and expectations for children's behavior but encourage them to express their opinions and discuss rules and regulations with them.

authority stage: the third stage of Galinsky's six stages of parenting, from the child's ages two to four; as children become mobile and begin to understand language, parents set and enforce structure and guidelines for behavior.

compadrazgo: godparent-like relationships established through religious ceremonies in the Mexican American culture, which provide regular support to parents in raising children across their lives.

confidential adoptions: adoptions in which each party (the adopting family and the birth mother) are unaware of the identity of the other. These are sometimes referred to as "closed" adoptions.

co-parenting: the process by which two parents either work to support or back up each other's parenting (positive co-parenting), or work against each other, thereby undermining the parenting of the other (negative co-parenting).

co-regulatory processes: processes, usually beginning in middle childhood, in which parents begin to gradually transfer increasing responsibility for self-management to their children, although they maintain an oversight, supervisory function.

daily hassles: relatively minor, bothersome, and frustrating interactions parents have with their young children on a regular basis, such as the children making messes, whining, and interrupting, that can create stress.

demandingness: the aspect of parenting that involves limit-setting, guidance, and control of children.

departure stage: the sixth stage of Galinsky's six stages of parenting, which occurs when offspring reach adulthood and leave home; parents evaluate how their children have turned out and the job they did as parents.

didactic caregiving: parental behaviors that stimulate children's interaction and understanding of the outside world.

fully disclosed adoptions: adoptions that are completely open, with each party (adoptive family and birth mother) knowing the other's identity.

image making: the first stage of Galinsky's six stages of parenting. It involves expectant parents' thinking of themselves as parents and the changes in themselves and their relationships that will come with parenthood.

indulgent/permissive parenting: a parenting style characterized by few parental demands for children's behavior and extremely high levels of parental responsiveness and support.

interdependent stage: the fifth stage of Galinsky's six stages of parenting; it starts when children enter adolescence and parents allow them more power and privileges, along with expecting more responsibility.

interpretive stage: the fourth stage of Galinsky's six stages of parenting, which begins when children enter preschool or school. It requires that parents help their children interpret and understand their expanding social worlds.

material caregiving: that aspect of parenting that involves structuring and organizing the child's physical world.

mediated adoptions: adoptions that fall between confidential (closed) and fully-disclosed (open) adoptions, in that a mediator (usually an attorney) knows information about both parties (the adoptive family and the birth mother) but does not reveal the identities of each to the other party. The mediator may facilitate communication between the parties by exchanging information for them.

nurturant caregiving: meeting the basic care needs of children, including provision of food, shelter, clothing, and a safe environment.

nurturing stage: the second stage of Galinsky's six stages of parenting, which extends from birth to the child's age of eighteen to twenty four months. It involves meeting the child's basic care needs and the formation of a close affectional bond to the child.

parental differential treatment (PDT): parents' treatment of children within the same family as different—not necessarily as the result of favoritism, but perhaps because of age or other differences in child characteristics.

parenting facilitation: phenomenon that occurs when the parenting behavior of one parent depends on input (information about the child, mediating the relationship, behavioral assistance) from the other parent.

personal social network: persons outside the household who regularly engage in activities and exchanges with family members.

rejecting/neglectful parenting: a parenting style characterized by extremely low levels of both parental demandingness and responsiveness.

responsiveness: parental behavior aimed at meeting the emotional support needs of children.

social caregiving: parenting behaviors focused on the interpersonal domain, such as visual and physical contact and vocalizing.

Suggested Activities

1. Go to a card shop and study the messages included in cards for parents. Write down the exact messages from a few cards that exemplify typical themes in these cards. What do the themes you've identified say about societal views or ideologies about parenthood? How might these views affect the adjustment of new parents?

2. Select a television program that involves a family with children (cartoon or real characters). Categorize the parenting style of each parent. Be sure to give a few specific examples of behaviors that you observed that illustrate this style.

Suggested Readings

Belsky, J., and Kelly, J. 1994. *The Transition to Parenthood. How a First Child Changes a Marriage: Why Some Couples Grow Closer and Others Apart.* New York: Dell.

Cochran, M. M., and Niego, S. 1995. "Parenting and social networks." In M. Bornstein (ed.), *Handbook of Parenting* 3:393–418. Mahwah, NJ: Erlbaum.

Dunn, J. 1996. "Siblings: The first society." In N. Vanzetti, and S. Duck (eds.), *A Lifetime of Relationships* (pp. 105–124). Pacific Grove, CA: Brooks/Cole.

Luster, T., and Okagaki, L. 1993. *Parenting: An Ecological Perspective.* Hillsdale, NJ: Erlbaum. ✦

Chapter 6

Moving Through the Life Cycle

Family Experiences in Middle to Late Adulthood

Did You Know?

- The exchange of support in families flows primarily from parents to children until the children reach about age 40 and parents reach approximately age 75 (Cooney and Uhlenberg, 1992; Spitze and Logan, 1992).
- Approximately 40 percent of parents with children under age 5 receive occasional babysitting or childcare assistance for their children from their own parents (Eggebeen and Hogan, 1990).
- Half of adults have at least monthly contact with a sibling, and two-thirds count a sibling among their closest friends (White and Riedmann, 1992b).
- Over half of women aged 45–49 with a living parent can expect to provide parent care sometime in the future (Himes, 1994).
- By the age of 62, 75 percent of adults have experienced the death of both their parents (Winsborough, Bumpass, and Aquilino, 1991).

Things to Think About

- What do you think are the positive and negative role changes that parents experience when their adult children leave home?
- What kinds of behaviors characterize the interaction that occurs between adult children and their parents? How do these behaviors change as both generations age?
- How do you think families plan for and decide how parents will be cared for in old age and by whom?
- What types of transitions do family members face in mid- to late adulthood?

This chapter addresses the family transitions and experiences that typically occur around middle age and beyond. It begins by examining the dramatic transformations that occur in parent-child relations as offspring mature and move into adulthood. The discussion builds on several of the ideas about adolescence presented in Chapter 5. We consider how the younger generation attempts to gain independence from parents and how parents respond to these changes. Growing independence from parents, along with a shift in social roles and legal emancipation, requires young adults and their parents to renegotiate many aspects of their relationship. We are interested in how these processes work in families.

This chapter also examines the importance of adult children, siblings, and spouses for middle-aged and older adults. We explore patterns of interaction among these various family members and what they do for one another. Additionally, we consider how specific relationships are affected by changes in family subsystems and roles. For example, how does the death of aged parents alter sibling relationships? How does retirement affect a marriage? As in other chapters, this approach recognizes the interrelatedness and interdependence of family systems. Throughout the chapter we address how race and ethnicity influence these family situations and transitions. We conclude by considering how macro-level forces influence families during the second half of the lifespan.

Renegotiating Parent-Child Relationships in Late Adolescence and Early Adulthood

A central challenge of late adolescence and early adulthood is to successfully establish a unique, independent identity distinct from that of one's parents (Josselson, 1988). Although this process, known as **individuation** (Grotevant and Cooper, 1982), is a critical aspect of individual development, it has a significant impact on parent-child relationships as well. As offspring work to form an independent identity, they often become less accepting of their parents and more critical of their views. At the same time, it is not uncommon for adolescents to push for greater emotional distance from their parents so that they can make more objective assessments of themselves and their parents as unique individuals with distinct views (Nydegger, 1991).

These changes in interaction patterns with parents can be particularly upsetting to the older generation. In an essay titled "One Week Until College," Sandi Kahn Shelton (2001), a mother who was soon to experience her daughter's departure for college, painfully described her daughter's obvious distancing behavior:

> Her feelings have gone underground, where to reach over and touch her arms seems an act of war. She pulls away . . . she turns down every invitation I extend . . . instead of coming out with me, she lies on her bed reading Emily Dickinson until I say I have always loved Emily Dickinson, and then—but is this just a coincidence?—she closes the book. (38)

This passage reflects the conflict and tension that may develop between parents and young adult offspring as the younger generation strives to be different and to achieve a unique identity apart from the parents. Additionally, parents' own developmental concerns may add to the tension that forms when offspring challenge their views and experiment with new ways of thinking and behaving. Many parents of adolescents are middle-aged; at this point in life it is fairly typical for individuals to reassess life goals and priorities and to think more introspectively about themselves—who they are and what meaning their lives have. Therefore, as children begin to emotionally distance themselves and challenge their parents' thinking and lifestyle, the older generation may become defensive or somewhat ambivalent about their own life situations (Farrell and Rosenberg, 1981).

Acting on One's Own

Dealing with their children's desire for greater behavioral autonomy presents challenges for many parents. Yet it is critical for parents to encourage and allow more independent decision making on the part of their maturing offspring and to grant them greater behavioral freedom and privacy (Aquilino and Supple, 2001; Petronio, 1994). By expecting their children to be more accountable for their behavior, parents contribute to their increasing responsibility and maturity. However, it's not uncommon for parents to worry that allowing their children too much independence might result in their struggling, failing, or getting into trouble. Even more serious for parents is the possibility that, in several states now, they can be held civilly, and/or criminally, responsible for their children's delinquent or illegal behavior (Parental Responsibility Laws, 2003).

Bengtson and Kuypers (1971) argue that an issue that contributes to the tension young adults and their parents have regarding autonomy versus dependence is the competing developmental needs of the two generations. As noted, young adults are pushing for greater independence from their parents because of their developmental need to form a separate, unique identity. At the same time, their parents—many of whom are middle-aged—are often struggling to achieve a sense of generativity, which according to Erikson's classic theory involves leaving one's mark on the world by closely guiding and influencing the next generation. Parents may, therefore, try to stay heavily involved in their children's lives because of their own development needs, just as offspring are trying to pull away and become more independent. Not surprisingly, tension can result. Relationship tensions that emerge from the competing developmental needs of family members have been labeled **developmental schisms** in the literature (Fingerman, 1996).

Despite young adults' demand for increasing independence from parents, research indicates that it is important for youth to maintain a good, supportive connection to their parents (Grotevant and Cooper, 1982). The back-up support that parents can offer during the transition from adolescence to adulthood is especially valuable because most of the typical sources of support that youth rely on are in a state of flux. For instance, friendship networks are likely to change as young people leave high school and enter work or college. Therefore, at a time when they are faced with assuming greater responsibility and new, more demanding social roles, many young people perceive a loss of support. If parents are available and supportive, these transitions may be less stressful. This was evident in a study of new college students by Holahan and his colleagues (1994). They found that a positive, supportive relationship with parents was highly predictive of adjustment for students over a two-year period after entering college. Not only was parental support directly related to student well-being, but students with good parental relationships were more social, which contributed to their long-term adjustment.

Even for working-class and poor youth who are unable to leave home and enter college, gaining autonomy from parents and demonstrating their growing maturity is critical. For these youths, work plays a central role in this transition. Using data from a qualitative study of approximately 200 young people living in two poor, predominantly minority neighborhoods of New York, Newman (1996) examined the role of low-wage employment in the transition to adulthood. For many poor youth, being able to maintain a low-wage service-sector job allowed them to be independent and financially responsible for their own needs, even if they still resided in their parents' home. An adultlike commitment to the workforce—even if only to low-paying "McJobs," allowed low-income youth to contribute to the basic needs of others in their households. Newman points out that for many of these young people, the lack of more-promising economic opportunities in the segregated neighborhoods where they live may prevent them from ever being able to leave home and establish an independent residence. Certainly within their families, however, their responsible work behavior gives them adult status and the associated privileges. Much more research is needed, however, about family role changes that accompany the transition to adulthood in families other than the middle class.

When offspring transition to college, the parent-child relationship is likely to change. What kind of changes did you experience with your parents at this point in your life?

Adjusting Family Boundaries

A major task of late adolescence and early adulthood is to redefine existing boundaries between parents and children within the family system. Boundaries surrounding the flow of information, for example, change as maturing offspring demand greater privacy and independent decision making. Youth on the brink of adulthood consider fewer and fewer of their own issues and decisions as warranting parental input and negotiation (Greene and Boxer, 1986). Therefore, many young adults believe the boundaries around their personal lives should now be less permeable. A related issue was recently debated at the university where one of the authors teaches. University officials were considering a policy that would permit parental notification when a student violated residence hall drug and alcohol policies. One view of the students opposed to the proposed policy was that students, not parents, should be the ones taking responsibility for inappropriate or illegal actions. Such a policy, they believe, would cloud the issue of who is responsible for student behavior (Flory, 2001).

At this point in family life it is also common for the boundaries around parents' lives to become more permeable to the maturing offspring, especially boundaries around such topics as the parents' work, marriage, and family relationships. As the younger generation moves into adulthood, parents generally expect more give and take in their relationship, in terms of both sharing work around the home and emotional support. Upon becoming adults, offspring may hear family secrets for the first time, or they may be elevated to the status of "friend" or even "counselor" to their parents. Renegotiation of boundaries between the generations requires caution, however. Too much privacy and extremely rigid boundaries may result in each generation feeling isolated from the care and potential support of the other. On the other hand, too much permeability, especially in terms of the parents' sharing their issues, can threaten the sense of security that the younger generation continues to look for from their parents at this point in life.

Evidence of the potential problems that extremely open boundaries can create comes from research by Silverberg and her colleagues (1998). Studying a sample of divorced mothers and their adolescent daughters, these researchers found that the majority of mothers had discussed financial issues and concerns and had shared complaints about their ex-husbands with their adolescent daughters. These more permeable subsystem boundaries had serious consequences for the adolescent offspring. Mothers' disclosure of such information was highly predictive of increased depression among the daughters, regardless of their age. Parents' openness about their own personal and private situations, even with their older adolescents, thus needs to be carefully monitored.

The negotiation of family boundaries can take many forms during this period in the family cycle. Sometimes families develop clear, yet implicit boundaries around sensitive issues. According to Hagestad (1979), some families establish **demilitarized zones (DMZs)** in their communication. That is, certain topics are off limits because of the intense conflict that might develop if they were open for discussion. Topics that are likely to be DMZs in some families include sexuality, religion, money, and politics. Other families, however, deal openly with heated issues and generational differences in points of view and behaviors. **Boundary recognition** refers to the process in which parents and offspring acknowledge their differences through communication but accept, rather than try to change, the other party's point of view (Greene and Boxer, 1986).

These two processes reveal very different approaches to handling conflicting views within the family, yet both reflect the great effort family members make to nurture close, harmonious relationships, despite their differences. Because it is often during young adulthood that significant differences between parent and child lifestyles and beliefs first become evident, the use of these processes becomes especially important during this period.

Adjusting to the Empty Nest Period

Research on the transition from adolescence to adulthood has concentrated heavily on the changes experienced by the child generation, largely ignoring the adjustments that parents make as their children mature. One exception is the literature produced in the 1960s and 1970s on the **empty nest stage,** which discussed parents' personal adjustment to the life stage that occurs once all of the children have reached adulthood and left home.

In general, the early literature on the empty nest depicted this life stage as a time of dread and crisis for parents, particularly mothers. Supposedly, women experienced serious problems after all of their children had moved away and their active mothering role, which had encompassed a large part of their lives, was no longer needed (Bart, 1972). However, the empirical evidence of parents' troubled adjustment to the empty nest period was never totally convincing. Most early studies were based on parents who sought professional help (referred to as *clinical samples*) during this transition. When nonclinical samples were studied, negative effects associated with the departure of children from the home were minimal and time limited, if evident at all.

More recent studies using representative samples of families have failed to find serious adjustment problems for most empty nest parents. In fact, it appears that when couples move into the empty nest stage they may experience some positive changes in their lives, specifically in regard to their psychological health (Harkins, 1978) and marital happiness (White and Edwards, 1990). Especially when earlier parenting was problematic and stressful, parents seem to respond very positively to their children leaving home (Wheaton, 1990). One factor that contributes to parents' positive adjustment to this transition is the departed children's maintaining frequent contact with their parents (White and Edwards, 1990). In sum, parents seem to welcome the empty nest period because they feel relieved of the demands and challenges of daily, hands-on parenting. Furthermore, by maintaining ongoing relationships with their departed children, parents have the opportunity to support that piece of their identities that is still tied to parenthood yet have extra time and energy to pursue other aspects of their lives with renewed vigor.

Nydegger (1991) claims that parents' positive adjustment to the increased independence of adult offspring is facilitated by what she labels **parental maturity,** a process in which parents work to establish some distance between themselves and their children. This process benefits offspring because it facilitates their independence, and it helps parents because it forces them to reshape their identities to make parenting a less central component. Commitments outside the family may also contribute to this process for parents—especially mothers. A study conducted by Silverberg (1996) found that mothers adjusted more positively to relationship changes with their adolescent offspring if they were emotionally invested in work outside the home. The importance of achieving a healthy balance between various life roles—inside and outside the family—appears to be crucial at this stage, as it was during the transition to parenthood, which we discussed in Chapter 5.

What helps the offspring generation adjust to the transition to adulthood and leaving home? Research again points to the importance of balance—in this case the balance between parents' support and control of their maturing offspring. Aquilino and Supple (2001) studied a large sample of young adults, ages 18 to 24, to explore predictors of positive adjustment in adulthood. They found that young adults who reported better adjustment (measured as low depression, high self-esteem, and personal efficacy) tended to have parents who used an authoritative parenting style (highly supportive, high levels of monitoring and supervision) during their adolescence. Other researchers concur that when parents foster independence but remain available and supportive, offspring adapt better to the challenges of early adulthood (Kenney, 1987; Rice, Cole, and Lapsley, 1990).

Parents and Children in Middle to Late Adulthood

Generally the term *parent-child relationship* conjures up an image of a fairly young parent and small child because we assume the term *child* refers to chronological age rather than to a position in a family constellation. However, with the average life span now exceeding 75 years, most people will actually spend more time relating to their parents as adults than as children. Individuals today will likely live over 40 years as adults with at least one surviving parent (Watkins, Menken, and Bongaarts, 1987).

Research on the relationships between parents and adult offspring paints a fairly positive picture. Most of these relationships are characterized by:

- High levels of contact between adults and their parents.

- Regular exchanges of support between adults and their parents.

- Reports of warm, affectionate relationships with one another. (Lye, 1996; Suitor, Pillemer, Keeton, and Robison, 1995)

Still, substantial variability exists in the ways in which the generations connect and interact.

Types of Parent-Adult Child Relationships

To understand the key elements of the relationship between parents and offspring in adulthood, Bengtson and his colleagues (Bengtson and Schrader, 1982; Silverstein and Bengtson, 1997) developed the family solidarity framework. **Family solidarity** refers to family unity or integration, which Bengtson describes as having six dimensions. **Associational solidarity** is family unity as demonstrated through shared interaction and contact. A family in which the adult offspring gather every Sunday evening at their parents' home for dinner would rate high on this dimension. **Affectional solidarity** refers to the emotional bonds that exist between family members. Despite seldom seeing a parent, an adult child may still feel great affection for and emotional intimacy with the parent, which would be indicative of high affectional solidarity. **Attitudinal solidarity** addresses the amount of agreement between family members on important issues. A family in which members share political or religious views would rate high on this dimension of solidarity. **Functional solidarity** pertains to exchanges of assistance and resources between the generations in the family. Family members who are high on functional solidarity would depend heavily on each other for instrumental assistance and practical support, such as childcare or help with chores. Finally, **structural solidarity** involves demographic factors (e.g., marital status) or geographic factors that constrain or facilitate intergenerational relationships, and **normative solidarity** deals with feelings of obligation toward family members.

Using data from a 1990 nationally representative survey of 1,500 adults ages 18 to 90, Silverstein and Bengtson (1997) demonstrated high levels of family solidarity based on reports from adult children. In relation to their aging mothers, these adults reported high levels of associational, attitudinal, and affectional solidarity. Most reported relationships with their mothers that were characterized by:

- At least weekly contact (69 percent).

- Somewhat/very similar views on important issues (69 percent).
- Strong emotional closeness (73 percent).

While relationships with aging fathers did not reflect equally high levels of solidarity, they too were generally positive: About 60 percent of adults reported high levels of associational, attitudinal, and/or affective solidarity with their fathers.

Levels of functional solidarity, measured by the provision of instrumental assistance such as running errands and doing repairs, were relatively low. Thirty-five percent of adults reported regularly giving such help to their mothers and only 29 percent gave such help to their fathers (Silverstein and Bengtson, 1997). One explanation for these findings is that many aging parents do not require substantial assistance from their adult offspring. Indeed, when researchers ask older adults about *potential* support from family members, including their children, if they needed it, rates of support are much higher (Hogan, Eggebeen, and Clogg, 1993). It appears, therefore, that generally adult offspring act as a safety net for aging parents, in case the need for help arises, but most older individuals are able and prefer to function independently as long as possible.

Using all of the solidarity dimensions except normative solidarity, Silverstein and Bengtson (1997) analyzed data from the national survey to determine how the various dimensions of solidarity fit together. They were interested in whether there were distinct types of adult child-parent relationships characterized by different degrees of solidarity. Table 6.1 shows the five types of intergenerational relationships they identified for mothers and fathers separately.

A few general findings regarding variation in adult child-parent relationships, as revealed in the Silverstein and Bengtson (1997) study, are important to highlight. First, the fact that adult child-parent relations vary considerably between mothers and fathers is obvious from the substantial differences between the percentages shown in Table 6.1. Whereas the most common type of relationship adults have with their mothers is "tight-knit," characterized by high solidarity on all dimensions, the modal type of connection to fathers is "detached," which involves low levels of solidarity across all dimensions. A second important finding is that adult child-parent relationships take many forms, yet de-

Table 6.1 Types of Parent-Adult Child Relationships, Their Definitions, and Frequency

Type	Definition	With Mother	With Father
Tight-knit	High solidarity on all dimensions	31%	20%
Sociable	High solidarity except for functional	28	23
Obligatory	Medium to high functional and associational solidarity, but low affective and attitudinal solidarity	16	16
Intimate but distant	High affective and attitudinal solidarity and low functional and associational solidarity	19	14
Detached	Low solidarity on all dimensions	7	27

Adapted from Silverstein & Bengtson, 1997.

spite these different styles or types of relationships, most adults consider their intergenerational relationships to be of good quality—a perception that we'll return to later.

The Influence of Sex and Race. Silverstein and Bengtson (1997) also tried to discover what factors predicted the type of relationship a parent and grown child reported. Two of the best predictors turned out to be gender and race:

- Daughters were more likely than sons to report tight-knit relations with their mothers.

- Sons were more likely than daughters to be classified in the obligatory category in relations with their mothers.

- Blacks were less likely than whites to report detached relations with their mothers.

- Blacks and Latinos were less likely than whites to be classified as having obligatory relationships with their mothers.

The authors speculate that altruism more strongly guides adult relations in minority families, whereas utilitarian or obligatory motives may be more apparent in white families (Silverstein and Bengtson, 1997). Neither race nor gender was associated with relational outcomes with fathers.

Researchers often hypothesize, however, that race and ethnicity distinguish family relations in aging families. Cultural differences in obligation to aged family members are one explanation they offer for this expectation. Others cite the relatively low income of minority families compared to whites and how this factor may affect family relations in later life. One argument is that disadvantaged economic conditions create stronger familial support systems in minority families. Alternatively, some believe that the limited resources of minority families interfere with their ability to engage in as much helpful, supportive behavior as white families (Hogan et al., 1993; Lawton, Silverstein, and Bengtson, 1994).

The empirical evidence examining race and ethnicity differences in adult child-parent relations is inconsistent across studies. While some studies suggest that minority families, especially blacks (Chatters and Taylor, 1993; Raley, 1995) and Mexican Americans (Dietz, 1995), have especially high contact and close proximity between adult family members, other studies that directly compare whites and minorities do not fully support these findings (Hogan et al., 1993; Lye and Klepinger, 1995). Discrepant findings are also common in regard to intergenerational helping and feelings of closeness. Some of the inconsistent research findings are due to varying approaches by researchers in how to account for factors that may be associated with race and ethnicity, such as income, educational achievement, cultural assimilation, and geographic proximity. That is, a Mexican American family with older parents still living in Mexico may be very different from one in which all family members have immigrated and parents live nearby. Also, some studies combine exchanges received or given across *all* family members, rather than just parents and children. This approach clouds the issue of parent-child exchanges, especially in minority families where households and kin support systems are more likely to include other relatives. Thus, it is difficult to draw firm conclusions about racial and ethnic variability in adult child-parent relations.

The Effects of Parents' Marital Status. An important predictor of relationship solidarity with mothers and fathers in late life is parents' marital status. Silverstein and Bengtson (1997) found that when parents were divorced or separated, the chances that their offspring reported detached relationships with them were significantly greater. For fathers, detached relations were also likely following widowhood, perhaps because widowed men have lost wives who likely played the family's **kinkeeper role**—the person (usually a female) who works to bring the family together, maintain family traditions, and watch over family relationships. However, for mothers, widowhood and divorce both raised the chances that offspring reported obligatory relations with them.

These findings and others suggest that parental divorce often strains relationships between parents and their children, even in adulthood (Cooney, 1994). However, the real source of strain is probably the marital conflict that preceded the divorce. This is evident from research showing that if adult children recall a childhood scarred by parental conflict and family problems, they report less contact with their aging parents (Webster and Herzog, 1995) and less concern about their well-being and care (Whitbeck, Hoyt, and Huck, 1994), even if their parents never divorced.

Most adults have either tight-knit or sociable relationships with their mothers. How do you think the activities and interactions that you share with your parents will change as they age?

Conflicting Needs and Views of Parents and Adult Children

Although most adult child-parent relationships are characterized by positive feelings, conflict and tension do occur, and in a small number of relationships they occur often. Fingerman (1996) claims that many of the conflicts that surface in relationships between aged mothers and adult daughters (although the same could be said of other dyads as well) are the result of developmental schisms, a concept we introduced earlier in this chapter. Fingerman (1996) reports that sometimes middle-aged daughters feel that their mothers intrude too much in their lives, whereas older mothers may feel excluded from their daughters' lives. For middle-aged daughters who are juggling multiple roles and relationships (daughter, wife, mother, grandmother, worker), however, more distance from their mothers may be necessary to adequately handle all of their responsibilities. At the same time, however, older parents are likely to desire more contact and companionship from their children because personal networks become smaller as individuals age. This tension was illustrated convincingly in a quote from one 47-year-old daughter in Fingerman's research:

> I was annoyed when I saw her [mother] on Thursday, she asked if I would see her again on Sunday. And it's kind of this ongoing theme in our relationship, her insatiable desire to be with me. I'm her number one choice: she chooses me all the time. She sucks me dry. (109)

The relationships that are maintained in late life are mostly close family members and friends (Carstensen, 1992). That the conflicting needs of aged parents and busy midlife offspring may create some tension and conflict in the relationship is not surprising. Still, it is an issue many families feel uncomfortable acknowledging.

Aged Parents and Adult Children

Although most parents and their offspring maintain relatively high levels of contact and emotional closeness across adulthood, extremely high levels of instrumental exchange do not typically exist in American families. Throughout most of adulthood, when instrumental assistance is given, it is more likely to be from parents to offspring than the other way around (Eggebeen and Hogan, 1990; Spitze and Logan, 1992). Parents help their children by providing, for example, babysitting and loans for such things as the purchase of a first home. However, as Figure 6.1 shows, once adult offspring reach their forties they are likely to experience a marked drop in their receipt of parental support (Cooney and Uhlenberg, 1992; Eggebeen and Hogan, 1990). One of the strongest predictors of this reduction in parental assistance is parents' declining health (Cooney and Uhlenberg, 1992). Health changes of aging parents also give rise to their increased need for assistance and care.

How families respond to the declining health of parents in very old age appears to vary substantially based on race and ethnicity. Elderly blacks are more likely than whites to be receiving care from family members (White-Means and Thornton, 1990) and to be residing in the same household with them (Angel and Angel, 1993). Similarly, Latino (especially Mexican Ameri-

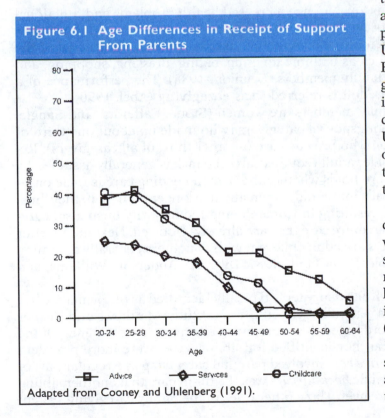

Figure 6.1 Age Differences in Receipt of Support From Parents

Adapted from Cooney and Uhlenberg (1991).

can) and Chinese American elders report higher rates of contact and coresidence with adult offspring than nonLatino whites (Lubben and Becerra, 1987; Angel and Angel, 1992). Within the Mexican American community, however, frequent contact and closeness does not appear to indicate high instrumental assistance to elderly family members. Dietz (1995) analyzed nationally representative data from the 1988 National Survey of Hispanic Elderly People and found that despite close proximity and frequent contact with family, about one-third of Mexican American elders with functional needs (housework, bathing, cooking) did not get help from their family members. Dietz cites the severe economic constraints and inadequate resources of many Mexican American immigrants as a possible reason for this problem. The reality of limited economic means may leave some Mexican American families unable to be as supportive as they would like to be given their cultural emphasis on familism values and beliefs regarding responsibility for the maintenance of family members' needs (White-Means and Thornton, 1990).

The severity of this issue is pronounced for older minorities who are recent immigrants to this country. Angel and Angel (1992) note that minority elders who have immigrated to the United States after age 50 generally have not worked and contributed long enough to Social Security (10 years are required) to draw on this system. Family support thus becomes one of their few options for obtaining an adequate livelihood and needed assistance with care.

Caregiving for Older Adult Family Members

As individuals age and begin to experience increased health problems and functional impairments, their situation not only alters what they do for their adult children, but what they need *from* them. When frail elders require assistance with some or all of the basic activities of daily living, such as bathing, toileting, eating, dressing, shopping, and cooking, they typically turn to family members (Scanlon, 1988). The performance of a routine set of tasks for an older adult is referred to as **caregiving** (Abel, 1990).

Most caregivers to older family members are women (Stone, Cafferata, and Sangle, 1987). This is the case among both spousal caregivers (who made up about one-third of all caregivers) and adult children who provide care (another third of all caregivers). Research indicates that when an older adult requires care, the task is generally assumed by the spouse, if present. This pattern holds whether the person needing care is male or female. Yet, because women typically marry older men and live longer than men, their husbands usually require care first, resulting in women being the majority of spousal caregivers. By the time most women require care they are already widowed. Next in line after a spouse to serve as care providers are adult children, with daughters generally assuming primary responsibility for the role (Stone et al., 1987; Dilworth-Anderson, Williams, and Cooper, 1999).

Sharing the Caring. Although one daughter is typically identified as the primary caregiver for an aging parent, others generally help out. In one study, Matthews and Rosner (1988) explored how siblings coordinated their caregiving efforts for aged parents. Of the five possible caregiving roles that they identified for siblings, two were more prevalent among daughters than sons. *Routine care* involved parental caregiving as a regular part of the adult child's daily schedule, while *back-up care* was the fill-in care that another sibling provided to assist the routine caregiver. Three other roles in the family caregiving system were more typically occupied by male than female offspring. Some male offspring provided *circumscribed care* by helping with a limited number or types of tasks, such as handling financial matters. Other siblings engaged in *sporadic care* that involved providing occasional assistance, but only when it was most convenient to them. Finally, male offspring were more likely than females to practice *dissociation*, which was characterized by noninvolvement in parental care (Matthews and Rosner, 1988). These findings are important because a great deal of research on caregiving considers only the situation of a single caregiver—usually the primary caregiver—and neglects to recognize that siblings can and do work together to create a caregiving network for aging parents.

Dilworth-Anderson and her colleagues (1999) addressed this same issue of how families distribute elder caregiving by studying older blacks who had some functional limitations. In the majority of cases in her sample, primary care responsibilities also were assumed by middle-aged daughters. However, other family members usually contributed to caretaking, similar to what Matthews and Rosner's findings indicated. In addition, the Dilworth-Anderson study identified the factors that predicted the size of the caregiving network for these older adults. Why did some elders rely solely on a *primary caregiver*, and others use what she referred to as *secondary caregivers* (doing the same tasks as the primary caregiver but with less oversight responsibility), or *tertiary caregivers* (those who perform specialized tasks) in addition to the primary caregiver? Elders who used a wider caregiving network tended to have fewer economic resources and greater physical care needs. But, geography mattered as well, with those elders who had children living in closer proximity having larger caregiving structures. These authors conclude that the use of extended caregiving structures to provide caregiving for older adults in black families is consistent with the black cultural legacy that emphasizes the collective role of the family in providing support for its dependent members.

Explaining Caregiver Selection. Beyond *who* provides parental care, little is known about *why* families make particular caregiving assignments and *how* this process works. Brody (1990), a leading authority on caregiving, claims that the adult child with the fewest competing demands generally becomes the caregiver. We know, however, that many women who do elder care also work outside the home (like most men) and have other demanding roles as well. Yet it is women who must often become caregivers. It may be that gender-role expectations and associated lifetime "practice" with nurturing and caregiving (e.g., caring for youngsters and the ill) contribute to women's overrepresentation among caregivers.

Merrill (1997) conducted a qualitative study of approximately 50 caregivers to explore the process through which they assumed their role as caregiver. In nearly one-third of the cases she studied, no family deliberations occurred regarding the selection of a caregiver, and the role was essentially assumed by default by one of the adult children. Sometimes this situation happened because no one else volunteered for the job or appeared to be available. In other cases, unspoken family expectations were the reason care was assigned a particular way, as noted by one caregiving daughter:

> I am from a big Italian family—the oldest of nine. It is expected that the oldest son or daughter will take care of the parents. . . . Now I do most of what gets done or make arrangements. . . . (Merrill, 1997, 37)

In 20 percent of the cases Merrill studied, family meetings were held to discuss the "choice" of caregiver, but this did not usually occur until a medical emergency was imminent. At that point, only one child was typically viewed as "available" to take on the task. Another 20 percent of cases involved the parents making a choice as to which child they wanted as their caregiver. Finally, in the rest of the families, the caregivers merely assumed the role over time through their continued involvement with the parent (e.g., they had been living together) or because they volunteered for the task (Merrill, 1997).

From Merrill's work it is obvious that family members rarely discuss and plan for the current or future care of aging parents. Aging parents and their offspring probably find it uncomfortable or difficult to discuss that time in the future when the parents' health will begin to fail and care will be required. Additionally, siblings may avoid such discussions because they anticipate that conflict will erupt. Merrill (1997) found that tension over unresolved family issues, such as parental favoritism, often prevented siblings from acting together to address their parents' needs.

Coordinating Other Roles With Caregiving. The research literature and the popular press frequently refer to adults who provide care to aging family members as the "sandwich generation," or, when referring only to the women in these roles, to "women in the middle." These terms create images of women *caught* between the competing care demands of frail, aged parents and dependent, young children. In fact, adults who are of the typical age to be providing parent care (beyond age 50) usually do not have dependent children still in the home and thus are not balancing two sets of caregiving demands (Rosenthal, Martin-Matthews, and Matthews, 1996; Soldo, 1996; Spitze and Logan, 1990). Table 6.2 presents figures from a Canadian study of role occupancy at midlife illustrating the low probability that midlife adults will be called on to provide care to older parents when they are also parenting children in their home *and* employed in a job. From these data it is apparent that caregiving is more likely to require coordination with employment than raising one's own children. Family caregivers who are married also face the challenge of balancing the caregiving role with their marital roles. In the next sections we consider how elder caregiving may influence marital and work positions.

Table 6.2 Multiple Role Occupancy by Middle-Aged Persons

Role	Age 50–54		Age 55–59		Age 60–64	
	Women	Men	Women	Men	Women	Men
Have a living parent	53%	58%	39%	37%	20%	17%
and						
Offspring home/no job	13	2	8	2	2	2
Offspring home/have job	11	29	4	15	<1	3
No offspring home/have job	13	18	10	13	3	5
No offspring home/no job	13	1	14	4	12	5

Source: Adapted from Rosenthal, Martin-Matthews, and Matthews (1996).

Marriage and Caregiving. Consistent with the family systems framework, caregiving responsibilities assumed by a family member are expected to affect others in the family as well as family relationships and functioning. Whether in-home or out-of-home care is being given, caregiving places severe restrictions on the time and activities that married caregivers engage in with their spouses. A common complaint heard from caregivers is that their responsibilities interfere with their ability to have an evening out with their partners or to take a family vacation (Kleban et al., 1989; Merrill, 1997). Although about half of the husbands of caregivers in one study reported that they argue with their wives about the caregiving situation, surprisingly, only a few reported that the situation had hurt their marriages (Kleban et al., 1989). Another study actually followed caregivers over the course of a year and found that 15 percent of the caregivers experienced substantial decline in marital satisfaction during this period, while another 21 percent noted significant increases in marital satisfaction, despite the demands of caregiving (Suitor and Pillemer, 1994). This study found a strong connection between marital satisfaction changes, as reported by the female caregivers, and wives' reports of their husbands' supportiveness. Women who noted higher levels of emotional support from their husbands not surprisingly tended to experience increased marital satisfaction over the year of the study. In contrast, those reporting high levels of spousal hindrance (husband placing new demands on them or complaining) were more likely to reveal a decline in satisfaction with their marriages over the year. The authors of this study noted that husbands who hindered their wives' caregiving efforts tended to be unhappy with changes in their own lives and saw their wives' responsibilities as reducing the couple's social time or intimacy, or perhaps demanding more contributions from them to do household chores (Suitor and Pillemer, 1994).

Not only does spousal support affect the caregiver's marital satisfaction, it can also contribute in positive ways to the actual caregiving situation. Being married and having another adult in the household may lighten the care load. In fact, about half of married caregivers get occasional help with caregiving from their spouses—more than they get from their adult offspring (Penrod et al., 1995). Spouses can also serve as a buffer when stressors build up. Aside from actual participation in the care of the older person, husbands' emotional support to their caregiving wives reduces the wives' feelings of caregiving strain (Kleban et al., 1989).

Caregiving appears to be more disruptive for family and marital life when the elderly parent shares a home with the caregiver (Kleban et al., 1989). In such cases, husbands of caregivers report greater interference of caregiving with their own social lives; time with their wife, children, and other relatives; and family vacations. These men also perceive a greater caregiving burden for their wives than men whose wives are providing out-of-home care (Kleban et al., 1989). What is obvious from several studies is that many of the added family disruptions and tensions associated with in-home elder care are a result of the more demanding care that someone who can no longer live independently requires (Kleban et al., 1989). In racial and ethnic groups where co-residence of extended kin is fairly common, as in the black population, providing in-home care for an older family member is less stressful and burdensome for caregivers and their families than in the white population (Dilworth-Anderson et al., 1999).

Employment and Caregiving. Because most caregivers are women and the majority of women today are in the paid labor force (see Chapter 7), caregiving has potential consequences for work roles outside the home. Combining a job with parent care is most common for women ages 40 to 54. During these ages, 8–13 percent of women report that they provided help to parents monthly or more, as well as work outside the home. For men, around 10 percent report a similar combination of work and parental assistance roles, and this percentage holds up through age 59 (Rosenthal et al., 1996). Of course, many fewer adults are likely to be providing extensive, ongoing day-to-day care. A few studies have focused only on persons in the workforce to determine how prevalent elder care is for them. One study concluded that 7–12 percent of *all* employees also assume responsibility for some elder care (Gorey, Rice, and Brice, 1992). Take note, however, that surveys of current workers underestimate the problem of work-caregiving interference because such surveys do not account for those caregivers who have left their jobs because of the demands of the caregiving role (Neal, Chapman, Ingersoll-Dayton, and Emlen, 1993). This situation applies more to female caregivers because they are more likely than men to adjust their work schedules to accommodate caregiving responsibilities (Mutschler, 1994).

The more demanding the caregiver role in terms of number of hours devoted to care, and the severity of the care recipient's impairments—especially cognitive impairment—the greater its impact on the caregiver's paid job. Specifically, as caregiving hours increase, workers are more likely to need to arrive late at work or leave early, miss work, or turn down job promotions (Franklin, Ames, and King, 1994). Stress associated with caregiving is also associated with work adjustments, such as taking time away from work during the day (Starrels, Ingersoll-Dayton, Dowler, and Neal, 1997). The good news is that when a more flexible work environment exists, such as one where the person has some choice over where the work can be done (e.g., home or office) or can be accessible to family calls, caregivers report less interference of caregiving with work and less chance of leaving their jobs (Scharlach, Sobel, and Roberts, 1991).

These findings point out the importance of having workplace policies and procedures (part of the exosystem) that facilitate the coordination of work and caregiving roles. (The Family Medical Leave Act, discussed in Chapter 10, is one policy that affects such coordination.) This need will be even greater in the future, as more of the workforce will face caregiving responsibilities because the huge baby boom cohort will be elderly and possibly needing care. Since baby boomers had their children relatively late compared to earlier cohorts and had fewer children, the demand for care they will place on their offspring is expected to be particularly great.

The 'Uplifts' of Caregiving

A critical point to emphasize about caregiving for aged parents is that such situations are not always interpreted negatively. When researchers have been attentive to a wide range of caregiving outcomes—both positive and negative—they have uncovered several potential benefits to the caregiver role. Sometimes caregivers report, for example, that they derive pleasure and honor from caregiving, and feelings of worth and fulfillment (Kinney and Stephens, 1989). John Daniel, who cared for his frail mother in her later years, reflects back with newfound appreciation at what he had once viewed as a burdensome task—assisting his mother with her showers:

I guess I came out of the bathroom cleaner of spirit myself. Soap or no soap, whatever the tenor of our conversation, I appreciate now what a privilege it was to help my mother with her shower. I wish I'd seen it more clearly at the time. (Daniel, 2001)

The response of a participant in the Generations Study at the University of Southern California also illustrates the positive reaction to caregiving that some people experience:

After my mother developed Alzheimer's I became closer to her. At last I felt that I could do something meaningful for her, something that approached what she had done for me over the years. (Bengtson, 1993, 19)

Evidence from a recent study suggests that experiencing positive outcomes as a caregiver to an aging parent might depend partly on the history of the parent-child relationship. Based on data he collected from an equal number of white and black caregiving daughters, Carpenter (2001) found that caregivers who recalled secure, positive attachments to their mothers were more likely to provide emotional care (e.g., affection, comfort, sympathy) to them. However, the provision of instrumental, practical care (e.g., grooming, preparing meals) was not associated with their past relationship dynamics. Moreover, Carpenter (2001) found that daughters who reported more positive, secure attachments to their aged mothers reported less caregiver burden. Perhaps daughters who devoted emotional energy to caring for an aged mother with whom they had a positive, secure relationship were able to derive more emotional fulfillment and satisfaction from the experience. In such cases, this emotional lift may have reduced the burden they had during the caregiving experience.

While Carpenter's study did not find differences in the caregiving experience for blacks and whites, other research suggests that blacks are more likely than whites to experience the "uplifts" of caregiving and less likely to report negative experiences (Lawton et al., 1992). Black caregivers perceive caregiving responsibilities to be less intrusive in their lives than whites do (Lawton et al., 1992) and report less emotional upheaval and role strain in association with caregiving (Farran et al., 1997; Martin, 2000). Minority caregivers seem to utilize a wider and more diverse network of additional supports (Dilworth-Anderson, Williams, and Gibson, 2002), which may buffer some of the stresses of caregiving, resulting in racial and ethnic differences in caregiving reactions.

Race and ethnic differences may also be the result of cultural values. In summarizing the literature on cultural differences and assistance to aged family members, Martin (2000) notes that blacks are more likely than whites to consider providing help to family as normative and to show special respect for older family members. Historically, black families have also developed a value system and coping strategy that involves working together as a family to overcome hardship and problems. Cultural variations like these may shape the different experiences blacks and whites have with elder caregiving.

Marital Relations in Middle to Late Adulthood

As couples age and experience altered family living arrangements and roles, their marital relationship also changes. In Chapter 5 we discussed some of the ways in which marriages change when children enter the family. We described how that change in the family system affects the time partners have together, the activities in which they engage, and their reports of satisfaction with their marriage. As noted, many couples report a downward shift in their marital satisfaction across the very early years of marriage, although levels of satisfaction remain moderate to high (Kurdek, 1998a).

Marital Satisfaction

For a long time, family scholars discussed changes in marital satisfaction over the life course by referring to a "U-shaped" curve in marital happiness. This pattern reflected an alleged drop in marital satisfaction over the early years of marriage, followed by a leveling off during the middle years, and then a rise in satisfaction in late life (Orbuch, House, Mero, and Webster, 1996; Vaillant and Vaillant, 1993). Work and parenting roles were proposed as two factors critical to the decline in satisfaction early in marriage and then a reversal in the trend late in marriage (Lee and Shehan, 1989; Orbuch et al., 1996; White, Booth, and Edwards, 1986). These roles were believed to place excessive demands and stress on partners during early to middle adulthood, thereby limiting the time and energy they had to devote to their relationship and detracting from the satisfaction they felt. When children eventually left home and husbands and wives retired in late middle and old age, however, it was assumed that they again had time and opportunity to nurture their relationship and regain higher marital satisfaction.

Such thinking has been refuted by at least one recent study using longitudinal data. VanLaningham, Johnson, and Amato (2001) used data from a national longitudinal study to document couples' changes in marital satisfaction over nearly two decades. They found that satisfaction in marriage declines fairly continuously and that particularly steep drops occur in early marriage and again in the later years. Several processes may contribute to the decline in marital satisfaction. One possibility is that early in marriage, partners become disenchanted with each other and marriage as they experience some of the mundane activities of daily life. Additionally, over time, partners may begin to formulate more realistic images of each other than they had while dating (Huston and Houts, 1998), which creates some disillusionment. Satisfaction and excitement with the union may also decline because the novelty of the relationship and marriage may wear off as time passes (Call, Sprecher, and Schwartz, 1995). Finally, people grow and change over time, and some of the personal characteristics that the partners valued in each other, and that may have figured heavily in their decision to marry, may disappear or change (Pineo, 1961).

VanLaningham and her colleagues (2001) did find that the addition of children to the household predicted an accelerated decline in marital satisfaction, and the departure of children was linked to some slowing of the decline in satisfaction. However, the empty nest period was not associated with an upswing in marital satisfaction and sudden marital renewal, as earlier research had suggested. Although individual factors, such as health impairments and illness, were not considered in this study, they are known to contribute to reduced marital satisfaction in late life (Williamson and Schulz, 1990; Wright, 1991). For example, studies indicate that when one spouse has Alzheimer's disease, the couple's marital satisfaction is much lower than that for healthy couples (Cavanaugh and Kinney, 1994). Other less critical health impairments are known to jeopardize the level of marital companionship and intimacy that is experienced, at least from the perspective of the caregiver. Even the short-term care required when one spouse is recovering from hospitalization puts strain on a marriage (Johnson, 1985).

Marital Roles and Issues

Besides marital satisfaction, what else changes over the course of marriage? Based on a study comparing couples—both satisfied and dissatisfied ones—in their 40s (married at least 15 years) with those in their 60s (married at least 35 years), a group of psychologists found differences in such behaviors as couple disagreement and shared enjoyment, affection, and intimacy (Levenson, Carstensen, and Gottman, 1993; Carstensen, Gottman, and Levenson, 1995). Middle-age couples reported more disagreements than older couples, particularly regarding money, religion, children, and recreation. They were also less likely than the older couples to say that they enjoyed conversing about such topics as children, activities together, dreams, and vacations. (Not surprisingly, dissatisfied couples were least likely to report pleasure from discussions with their spouses!) The researchers concluded that, as marital partners age, their children become less a source of conflict and more a source of pleasure (Levenson et al., 1993). For example, older couples appear less conflicted over day-to-day hassles related to time and money, to which minor children can contribute. For long-term married couples, then, communication appears more focused on the joys of life—taking pleasure in the activities and accomplishments of adult children and grandchildren, planning and reminiscing about vacations, and shared couple activities, especially if partners have maintained good health. Moreover, older couples in this research reported more affection, intimacy, and marital pleasure than younger couples (Carstensen et al., 1995).

In terms of marital roles, substantial stability exists across adulthood in the marital subsystem (Lee and Shehan, 1989). Similar to most couples in early to middle adulthood, those in later life generally adhere to a traditional pattern of household roles, even after retirement. (See Chapter 7 for discussion of the division of household labor.) In retirement, women typically continue to do a majority of the traditionally female chores (cooking, cleaning), even though their husbands are around more and have more time available to contribute (Lee and Shehan, 1989). This situation doesn't appear to reduce wives' marital satisfaction, however, unless they are still employed and their husbands have retired (in which case they may feel it is even more unfair that they are doing the second shift!).

In addition, when both spouses are retired and spend more time at home, marital satisfaction is compromised if they feel like they are getting in each other's way (Alford-Cooper, 1998). This is especially the case for women who have not worked outside the home, be-

Compared to middle-aged couples, those in old age seem to take more pleasure in the joys of life and report less conflict. What do you think explains the relatively high marital satisfaction that couples like this one usually report?

cause they may feel their autonomy at home is threatened once their husbands retire (Brubaker, 1985). Maybe the presence of husbands in the home after retirement threatens their wives' feelings of control over the domestic sphere. Whether such findings will hold true in the future is interesting to consider, because future cohorts of older adults will have experienced less traditional marital roles as a result of the gender revolution and women's increased employment.

Adult Sibling Relations

As noted in Chapter 5, sibling relationships are usually the longest-lasting relationships in the family system, yet relatively little is known about them during adulthood. How central are sibling connections in adulthood, especially if siblings get married and/ or have children, thereby expanding relationships and responsibilities within their families of procreation?

Variations in Sibling Ties in Adulthood

One national survey suggests that strong ties exist between adult siblings. White and Riedmann (1992b) report that half of adults have monthly contact with a sibling, and a majority of adults consider one of their siblings amongst their closest friends. Although the likelihood of exchanging help or support with adult siblings declines across the young- to middle-adult years as individuals marry and have children, exchanging practical and emotional assistance increases in late life, especially if siblings live in close proximity (White, 2001). Nearly half of adults report exchanging support with siblings, and about one-third report that a sibling is the person they would turn to for help in an emergency (White and Reidmann, 1992b).

Several factors contribute to variations in adult sibling relations. White and Riedmann (1992a) show that other family relationships place demands on adults that take precedence over maintaining active sibling ties. Having grown children, therefore, is associated with less sibling contact and exchange of support. Parents may use their extra resources, free time, and vacation opportunities to assist their offspring in establishing their families and homes once they have reached adulthood and moved out on their own. Such assistance leaves less time and fewer opportunities for visiting with their siblings. Ties to one's siblings, therefore, appear secondary to other close family relationships. Added support for this conclusion comes from research indicating that adults who have never married or had children and those who are widowed have particularly strong ties to their siblings in later life (Campbell, Connidis, and Davies, 1999).

Other consistent predictors of contact and support between adult siblings are the sex composition of the sibling group and geographic proximity (Lee, Mancini, and Maxwell, 1990; White and Riedmann, 1992a). Living within a 300-mile radius of siblings significantly improves the chances of having frequent interaction with them (White and Riedmann, 1992b). Having a sister is also an important factor, because it contributes to more frequent sibling interaction, greater emotional closeness, and more support exchanges. The presence of a sister not only appears to intensify sibling relations for both women and men (Lee et al., 1990; White and Riedmann, 1992b), but in late life it also contributes to happiness and positive morale, especially for men (Cicirelli, 1989).

Adult Sibling Types

Gold (1989) depicted the variation seen in adult sibling relationships by classifying sibling bonds into five distinct types, based on interaction and feelings of attachment or closeness. The first three of the five types listed below represent fairly positive relations, whereas the last two do not:

- Loyal—available, but not deeply involved or close.

- Congenial—friendly and somewhat close.

- Intimate—very close and heavily involved.

- Apathetic—indifferent and limited contact.

- Hostile—negative feelings and limited contact.

Race Differences in Sibling Relationships

In subsequent work Gold (1990) considered racial variations in the prevalence of the sibling relationship types she defined. She found that black adults were much less likely than whites to be categorized into the negative (apathetic and hostile) relationship types. About one out of four whites reported negative sibling relationships, compared to only one of twenty blacks. Envy and resentment toward siblings were not typically expressed by black adults.

White and Riedmann (1992a) indicate that compared to whites, blacks in their study also had more contact with siblings in adulthood, although greater association did not translate into higher levels of emotional closeness or exchange. In part, this could be due to the overrepresentation of blacks in lower-class families, who are, according to these researchers, significantly less involved in sibling exchanges. White and Riedmann note that even though the need for outside support may be substantial in lower-class families, the expectation for reciprocal exchanges in many families prohibits those with few resources from asking for and receiving, help because they won't be able to repay such favors.

Family Structure Influences on Sibling Relationships

Type of family structure also is associated with adult sibling relationships. In considering the influence of step- or half-sibling status on sibling relationships, White and Riedmann (1992b) found that although contact is maintained between step- and half-siblings, it is at a much lower rate than with full siblings. This reduced contact may be due to the fact that step- and half-siblings generally live farther apart than do full siblings. Finally, White and Riedmann (1992b) assessed whether variations between adult step/half siblings and full siblings differed based on race. Past research had suggested that blacks were less likely than whites to emphasize biological relatedness in their family relationships (e.g., treating nonrelatives like family—seeing them as *fictive kin*), yet this did not appear to be the case in these national data. Even for blacks, involvement was more limited among half- or step-siblings than among full siblings.

Grandparenting

The likelihood that individuals will grow up knowing at least some or all of their grandparents is much higher today than it was 100 years ago, when the average lifespan was about 50 years (Uhlenberg, 1980). Grandparenthood is an interesting social position because it comes with no clear rules or guidelines for how the role is to be enacted. Should a grandparent be like an adult playmate, an advisor, a source of knowledge and wisdom, a surrogate parent, or some distant authority figure? It's just not clear. In part, the reason grandparent roles are so ambiguous is that grandparents are a highly variable group in terms of their key personal characteristics. For example, the age of grandparents may range from around 30 (if a grandparent was a young teen parent, as was his or her child) on up into the 80s and 90s. Based on age alone, it is obvious why the behaviors of grandparents can vary dramatically.

Styles of Grandparenting

In one of the earliest studies on grandparents, Neugarten and Weinstein (1964) interviewed 70 pairs of middle-class grandparents about their roles, classifying their behaviors into several distinct *styles* of grandparenting, which included:

- *The formal role*—Grandparents who assume a distinct, formal role with their grandchildren that is clearly discernable from parenting. They are visible but do not interfere with the parenting. They occasionally indulge the grandchildren.

- *The fun seeker*—Grandparents who assume an informal, playful role with grandchildren and for whom grandparenting is a source of leisure. Mutuality is central, meaning both the grandparent and grandchild derive satisfaction from the relationship.

- *The reservoir of family wisdom*—Grandparents as a formal authority who bestow knowledge, wisdom, and skills on the grandchildren, who assume a subordinate position.

- *The distant figure*—Grandparents who have limited contact with grandchildren on special occasions. Interaction is remote and formal.

- *The surrogate parent*—Grandparents who assume caretaking responsibilities for the grandchildren.

Several factors influence the particular type of grandparent role that is assumed. Geographic distance between the generations, age and sex of the grandparent and grandchild, and grandparents' health are a few central factors that determine the style of the relationship. Another influential factor is the grandparent's relationship with the grandchild's parent—the adult son or daughter (Kahana and Kahana, 1971). This is a critical dimension, because the middle-generation grown child assumes a mediator role in the relationship, serving as the gatekeeper to the grandchild, intervening in the relationship and influencing the quality of the grandparent-grandchild bond (Hagestad and Burton, 1986).

Grandparents as Surrogate Parents

One type of grandparent that has become more typical in the past few decades is the surrogate parent. According to Census data, nearly twice as many children under age 18 now reside in a home with a grandparent than was the case just 30 years ago (Bryson and Casper, 1999). Figure 6.2 (next page) illustrates the growth in this family structure over the past 30 years. This figure also details the percent of children who reside in three-generation households (with at least one parent and one grandparent) and those who reside in **skipped-generation households,** where there is no parent present and the grandparent is the primary caregiver. The reasons that grandparents assume primary responsibility for grandchildren in skipped-generation households are many, but some of the most common ones are that the parent is (Jendrek, 1994; Minkler, 1999):

What relationship style do you think this grandmother has with her granddaughter? Do you think this will change as time passes and they both get older?

- Mentally unstable.

- Addicted to drugs or alcohol.

- Abusive/neglectful to the child.

- In jail or in trouble with the law.

- Having job or money problems.

- Working in another location.

Research is just beginning to examine how these situations affect grandparents, grandchildren, and other relationships in the family system.

Experiencing the Death of Family Members

Prior to the twentieth century, extremely high mortality rates—especially infant and child mortality—made death and bereavement a fairly common experience for young families. In 1900, children in the United States had a one in three chance of losing a young sibling to death and a one in four chance of experiencing the death of a parent. Furthermore, by age 15 half of all U.S. children had a death occur in their nuclear family (Uhlenberg, 1980). But for modern families, adjustment to the death of a loved one assumes a less central part of family life, especially early family life. The death of family members today is more often experienced in one's middle to later years, and it usually involves older family members.

Parental Death

In middle age, parental death becomes a common, somewhat expected, experience. By the time individuals reach age 65, most do not have surviving parents (Winsborough et al., 1991). Even though middle-aged and older adults may anticipate their parents' death, the event still has a marked impact on personal well-being. One large longitudinal study found that the death of a mother was associated with significantly higher levels of psychological distress among adults, whereas the death of a father predicted increased alcohol intake and physical health problems (Umberson and Chen, 1994).

Substantial variation exists among adults, however, in their adjustment and reactions to parental death. For example, daughters tend to report more emotional distress than sons following parental death (Moss, Resch, and Moss, 1997), and adult children's reactions appear more adverse if the deceased parent was relatively young and if the parent-child relationship had been particularly close (Moss et al., 1997; Umberson and Chen, 1994). According to Umberson and Chen (1994), the adult offspring's past experience with an

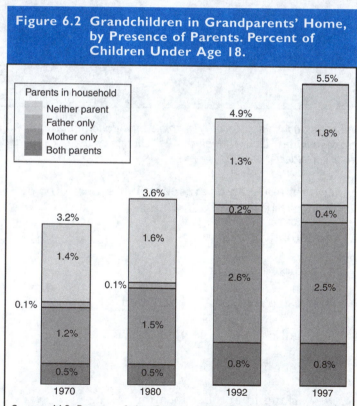

Figure 6.2 Grandchildren in Grandparents' Home, by Presence of Parents. Percent of Children Under Age 18.

Source: U.S. Bureau of the Census, 1970 and 1980 Censuses and 1992 and 1997 Current Population Surveys as reported in *Marital Status and Living Arrangements*: March 1992, Table H and *Marital Status and Living Arrangements*: March 1997, Table 4.

aging parent, such as providing care if the parent was ill or frail, also shape their reactions to death. Specifically, in cases where a mother had been in poor health and was functioning at a low level prior to her death, adult daughters reported lower levels of emotional distress after the death. In contrast, sons in such situations reported greater distress when compared to men who reported that their mothers had functioned well prior to death. One interpretation of these reactions focuses on the different roles daughters and sons are likely to have assumed in the care situation preceding maternal death. Caregiving daughters may feel some relief when the demands of caring for a dependent mother are eliminated, whereas sons may feel some added guilt, especially if they had not participated in parental care for an ailing mother, which is more often the case for sons than daughters.

Another common reaction to parental death is the recognition by offspring of their own impending mortality (Moss et al., 1997). This reaction is more typical when the last surviving parent has died. At this point, adult offspring are confronted with the fact that their own generation is "next in line," which often prompts serious reconsideration of their lives and accomplishments. In addition, these experiences may lead to a restructuring of how individuals think about their lifetimes—shifting from a time-since-birth to a time-left-to-live orientation (Neugarten, 1979).

Because of the interdependence of family subsystems, the death of a parent is also expected to affect relationships between adult siblings. One common reaction is for adult siblings to rally together and bond more closely when a parent dies (Gold, 1996; Scharlach and Fredriksen, 1993), taking comfort in their shared experience. However, a parent's death also can lead to greater sibling conflict, especially if the parent mediated sibling relationships. One-fourth of the adults studied by Scharlach and Fredriksen (1993) reported such responses following parental death. Another possibility, however, is that the loss of the parent generation (when both parents have died) may lead to reduced interaction and closeness between siblings because they have lost the *kinkeeper* in the parent generation (Connidis, 1992). In research by Gold (1996), one man described his family's situation when the kinkeeper died:

> We [siblings] didn't deliberately try not to be close once our parents died. But no one organized holidays and family celebrations for the group, and each of us began to be with our own families. (239)

An important point about relationship changes that follow such family transitions as parental death is that, when they occur, they are usually consistent with past interaction. Thus, if any substantial changes in sibling relations result from parental death, it is likely that close siblings will become closer, and distant ones may grow even further apart. Sibling relationships characterized by fairly neutral ties may change in either direction, if at all (Connidis, 1992).

Widowhood

The death of a spouse in mid- to later life also is likely to spur a number of life changes and create marked distress for both men and women. Bereaved persons typically report higher levels of emotional distress and depression than nonbereaved peers, with several studies documenting more negative outcomes for men than for women who lose a spouse (Lee, Willetts, and Seccombe, 1998; Lee, DeMaris, Bavin, and Sullivan, 2001).

Research has identified some of the specific factors that make the loss of a spouse difficult for the surviving partner. Newly widowed men are often challenged by the new domestic roles they are left to assume, such as cooking and cleaning. Also, because wives often assume the role of facilitating and organizing social activities and family gatherings in couples (playing the kinkeeper role), widowed men often find it difficult to maintain social ties once their wives are no longer around to do so. Indeed, widowed men have substantially fewer friends and social contacts than widowed women (Hatch and Bulcroft, 1992). These types of life changes are predictive of increased depression for widowed men (Umberson, Wortman, and Kessler, 1992). Specifically, Lee and his colleagues (2001) found that the greater depression in male versus female widows was largely the result of altered day-to-day activities after the spouse died. Many of the men they studied reported less frequent church attendance, greater dislike of household tasks, and less ability to assist their adult children after they lost their wives. These factors were significant predictors of heightened grief and depression.

For older women, the challenges of widowhood are slightly different. Research shows that a key factor contributing to their greater emotional distress is economic stress (Umberson et al., 1992), which is understandable, as older-generation wives are still heavily dependent on their spouses for financial security. Carr and her associates (2000) reported that among the widowed men and women they studied, adjustment to spousal death was contingent on how dependent the surviving spouse had been on the deceased spouse. For wives especially, greater dependence on the husband for instrumental support (financial management, household repairs) predicted greater anxiety and yearning for the spouse. An additional finding of this longitudinal study was that the emotional quality of the marriage prior to the death also affected the surviving spouse's adjustment. Widowed men and women who had greater marital conflict in their marriage were less likely to report high levels of yearning for a now-deceased spouse compared to those who had noted marital closeness prior to widowhood.

Another factor that theorists have considered in trying to understand adjustment to widowhood is whether the death was anticipated or sudden. Some researchers hypothesize that the grief process should be less severe when the death was anticipated, because the widowed spouse had time to emotionally disengage from the now-deceased spouse and to psychologically prepare for the loss (Carr et al., 2001). For example, a woman who is providing care to an ailing husband may anticipate and prepare emotionally for his death, making the transition somewhat less difficult when it actually occurs. However, one study that addressed this issue found that having some forewarning of the death did not reduce the grief men and women experienced when their spouses died (Carr et al., 2001). Thus, it appears that the roles and dynamics that existed in the marital subsystem—the extent to which spouses derived instrumental support and emotional closeness from their relationship—is the strongest predictor of the loss they feel and adjustment problems they face once they experience widowhood.

Death of an Adult Child

While death of a parent or spouse is a common transition of mid- to late adulthood, the loss of an adult child is not expected by most parents. Yet, demographically, it is known that among older mothers (over age 65) with sons, one in four will experience the death of a son. This situation is the result of fairly profound sex differences in mortality rates (Moss and Moss, 1995). The limited literature on aging parents' reactions to the death of offspring suggests that it is probably more devastating than even spousal or parent death. Some of the reactions to such a loss that have been identified among bereaved parents are (Moss and Moss, 1995):

- Threat to or loss of parental identity.
- Feelings of guilt over surviving.
- Concerns about one's future security because of the loss of support and assistance from the adult child.

Death of a Sibling

The death of a sibling is also a significant event for individuals in middle to later adulthood. This, too, is a topic that has received minimal attention from researchers, and little is known about its effects on personal adjustment. One common view is that an adult sibling's death symbolizes to a person that his or her own death is nearer (Moss and Moss, 1995). Furthermore, when a sibling dies, the surviving siblings may be drawn closer together, at least initially, as they gather to reminisce about the lost loved one (Moss and Moss, 1995). Given the longevity and salience of sibling relationships in an aging society, more research is certainly needed on this topic.

The Big Picture: Societal Influences on Family Relationships Across Adulthood

As is the case earlier in the family life cycle, how families function and interact during middle to late adulthood is affected by the broader environmental context in which they live. Although we touched on some of these influences in this chapter, this section deals more directly with a few specific ways in which the exosystem, macrosystem, and chronosystem affect the situations of families across the adult years.

Societal Context and Parent-Child Relationships in Adulthood

The nature of relationships between young adults and their parents is highly contingent on the socioeconomic context. In the 1950s, when the country was in the midst of the postwar boom and the economy was experiencing tremendous expansion, it was not unusual for young people to leave home to establish an independent residence and begin their own families by their early twenties. Indeed, as noted in Chapter 4, over half of young men coming of age in the 1950s were married by age 22, and for women the median age at marriage was even younger (Fitch and Ruggles, 2000). With no more than a high school degree, it was possible for young people to find steady employment that paid a livable wage and to buy a first home with government-financed loans. For many young couples just barely out of their teens, economic and instrumental independence from parents was a possibility and a reality in the 1950s.

Fifty years later, however, economic and labor force changes have created a dramatically different world for young people. Although most youths today still aspire to someday marry and start a family, they expect to defer marriage until a much later age than youth did just 25–30 years ago (Schulenberg et al., 1995) and to wait longer to form their own households apart from their parents (Hill and Yeung, 1997). In part, this delayed entry to marriage and independent living is due to greater caution in approaching marriage. Even more important, however, is that the economy today, compared to 50 years ago, includes a greater proportion of skilled jobs that require college or other types of extended training, and fewer unskilled jobs. Today unskilled workers with limited postsecondary training face an unemployment rate five times higher than that of college graduates. They also face declining wages (Blank, 1995; Diebold, Neumark, and Polsky, 1997). Therefore, young people and their parents today expect the transition to adult roles to occur later and parents to continue supporting their offspring, at least partially, as they move into adulthood. For some, this will involve providing financial support for advanced schooling and/or covering the living costs incurred while attending school. For others who move into the world of work, parental assistance (either financial or housing) may be needed to supplement the limited income that accompanies unskilled jobs.

Another way parents offer continued support to adult offspring is to act as a safety net when emergencies arise (as discussed earlier in this chapter). An increasingly common practice in the last few decades has been the return of adult children to the parental home after making their initial departure (Goldscheider and Goldscheider, 1994). Population researchers demonstrate that returns to the parental home by adult offspring are usually a response to unexpected, disruptive events in their lives, such as marital break-up, dropping out of college, or single-parenthood (Goldscheider and DaVanzo, 1985). The bigger picture suggests, therefore, that greater adult child-parent interdependency (or dependency) is more common, and perhaps more acceptable, under historical conditions that demand extended educational preparation and job training for young people. In addition, when newly established families of procreation are less stable (because of high rates of divorce and rates of nonmarital childbearing), and governmental support is hard to come by (because of welfare reform), informal sources of support such as one's family will be expected to provide assistance. Thus, expectations for and the dynamics of adult child-parent relationships heavily depend on social and economic conditions.

Societal Context and Aging Families

Several large-scale social trends have been identified as potential influences on the relationship between adults and their aging parents. One theme evident in commentary on aging families today is how recent family changes, such as women's increased labor force participation (Stone et al., 1987) and rising divorce rates will affect the ability of families to meet the care needs of their elderly members. This is a critical question because, as noted, families are the frontline of support to aging individuals in our society, and women occupy the top positions in the hierarchy of caregiving. An added concern is decreasing family size and its implications for later life parent-child relations and elder support (Uhlenberg and Cooney, 1990). As Preston (1984) noted, we face a situation in this country where the average middle-aged couple has more surviving parents than children. Because the large baby boom cohort had significantly lower fertility than recent cohorts of elderly, policymakers need to seriously consider whether families will have the necessary human resources to provide elder care in the future as the babyboomers reach old age.

Formal services and supports, some of which are partially funded by the government, are considered the main alternative or supplement to informal care provided by family members. However, serious doubts exist regarding the future availability of government resources because of the rapidly increasing size of the older population in this country relative to the working-age population. Kinsella (1995) illustrates this concern by showing that the ratio of U.S. elderly to adults of working age was 15 to 100 in 1950, was 20 to 100 in 1990, and will reach 25 to l00 in 2020. Not surprisingly given these trends, both Social Security and Medicare, which the older population depends on, are likely to be seriously threatened in the next 20 years.

Even if public resources remain available, Wolf (1999) argues that families still provide the most appropriate and efficient care for their aging members. One reason is that family members have personal knowledge of the specific needs of the care recipients. Wolf also notes that when family members engage in caregiving tasks, others in the family may also benefit. For example, when a meal is prepared for the aged person needing care, others in the family can also be fed, which meets joint needs in the family. Formal providers, however, would not meet family needs in this way. Aside from the question of whether family members are the best source of care for elders, the bigger question in the future is who will have the most human or financial capital to provide support—families or the state? Clearly, both entities face tremendous pressures as we move into the twenty-first century.

As we look to the future, creative solutions are needed to deal with the challenges of an aging population. Government can certainly play a role in supporting aging families, through both programs and legislation. Beyond its direct impact on individuals' situations, government action can stimulate investments in the well-being of individuals and families by others. Some argue, for example, that by enacting federal legislation like the Family and Medical Leave Act (see Chapter 10 for details), the government demonstrated support and leadership for the issue, which subsequently encouraged similar changes in policy and programming at the corporate level (Wilcox and O'Keefe, 1991). Thus, policies implemented in one area of the exosystem may be a catalyst to nonmandated changes in other domains of the exosystem, eventually creating microsystem changes for individuals. Similarly, such exosystem initiatives can alter how people think about particular issues, even to the point of shifting macrosystem ideologies.

While it may seem easy to shrug off the large-scale concerns of government as something we as individuals and families need not worry about, in reality the macro and micro issues go hand in hand. Macro-level policy decisions have direct and significant effects on family relationships. When the state tries to reduce its financial responsibility to vulnerable populations such as the aged, children, or the disabled, it adds to the responsibility that families must shoulder. Such care potentially alters family functioning more generally, as well as the relational bonds between family members.

Summary

Family relationships and roles continue to change throughout middle and late adulthood. As offspring in the family move toward adulthood and transition into adult roles, their relationships with parents change dramatically. The boundaries around the parent-child subsystem and other subsystems (e.g., marital) in the family undergo major changes, as each generation reassesses the information that can and should be shared with the other generation, and the roles they are expected to play in one another's lives.

The family solidarity perspective that was introduced in this chapter emphasizes the key relationship dimensions that characterize adult family life (consensus, association, affect). Significant variation exists in adult child-parent bonds, despite the general conclusion that most adults report good or close connections within these relationships. Several factors distinguish adult child-parent relationships, ranging from individual characteristics (sex/gender), to past family experiences (history of parental divorce), to social structural characteristics (race and social class).

Throughout adulthood, a number of predictable, yet potentially stressful, situations occur that require reorganization and renegotiation of family roles. Most adults, for example, anticipate the time in their lives when their parents will become frail or ill and possibly require greater support and care from them. Or, middle-aged and older adults think about retirement and how it will affect their relationships and interactions with their spouses, children, and grandchildren. When such events or situations actually occur, families are faced with difficult decisions ("Who's going to take Mom into their home?" "Should I retire now just because my husband's health has forced him to retire?"). The solutions they choose are likely to have widespread consequences for the entire family system.

In thinking about family life in middle age and beyond, it is important to recognize the numerous broad societal forces that influence how families live. Cultural expectations for when young offspring should become independent of their parents, and who is responsible for aging family members are just two of the macrosystem forces that filter down to influence family roles, relationships, and experiences for adults. The dynamic nature of these larger social and economic forces contributes tremendously to family change across time.

Chapter Concepts

affectional solidarity: emotional bonds between family members.

associational solidarity: family unity characterized by shared interaction and contact.

attitudinal solidarity: consensus between family members on important issues.

boundary recognition: the process in which parents and offspring communicate their differences but accept, rather than try to change, the other party's point of view.

caregiving: the performance of a fixed set of tasks for an older adult, including some of the basic activities of daily living, such as feeding, dressing, and toileting.

demilitarized zones (DMZs): in communication, implicit barriers established around sensitive topic areas (e.g., money, sex, religion) so that conflict can be avoided.

developmental schisms: tensions that exist between the generations because of their differing developmental needs.

empty nest: a period in family life when all of the adult children have left the parental home.

family solidarity: family unity or integration.

functional solidarity: exchanges of assistance and resources between family members that generate family unity or integration.

individuation: the process in which adolescents and young adults attempt to establish an independent identity distinct from that of their parents.

kinkeeper role: the role usually assumed by one of the older females in the family that involves fostering family relationships, such as remembering and acknowledging anniversaries and birthdays, maintaining family traditions, and organizing celebrations.

normative solidarity: feelings of obligation toward family members that generate family unity and integration.

parental maturity: a process in which parents work to establish some emotional distance between themselves and their adult children.

skipped-generation household: a home in which a grandparent and grandchild live together without the middle-generation parent(s) being present. The grandparent is usually assuming the position of surrogate parent for the grandchild.

structural solidarity: family unity and integration that is constrained or facilitated by demographic or geographic factors.

Suggested Activities

1. Talk with some young adults about recent renegotiations they have had with their parents regarding the boundaries and expectations of their relationship. What are the main issues that they felt needed to be renegotiated? Who tended to raise the issue of renegotiating these aspects of the relationship? Try to compare and contrast young adults in different situations, such as some who are living away at college and some who are co-residing at home, either as students or as workers. Do the answers of these different groups vary?

2. Interview a professional (clergy member, funeral home director, nurse, hospice worker) who serves families dealing with parental death in late life. Question them about the key issues, concerns, and responses they have witnessed among families. Compare and contrast these with the issues discussed in this chapter.

Suggested Readings

Allen, K. R., and Walker, A. J. 1992. "A feminist analysis of interviews with elderly mothers and their daughters." In J. F. Gubrium, K. Daly, and G. Handel (eds.), *Qualitative Methods in Family Research* (pp. 198–214). Newbury Park, CA: Sage.

Brody, E. M. 1990. "Role reversal: An inaccurate and destructive concept." *Journal of Gerontological Social Work 15*:15–22.

Cooney, T., and Dunne, K. 2001. "Intimate relationships in later life: Current realities, future prospects." *Journal of Family Issues* 22:838–858.

Nydegger, C. N., and Mitteness, L. S. 1991. "Fathers and their adult sons and daughters." *Marriage and Family Review 16(3/4)*:249–266. ✦

Chapter 7

Balancing Work and Family

Did You Know?

- It wasn't until 1841 that the word *housework* was introduced into the written English language (Hodson and Sullivan, 1990).
- Fifty-six percent of married couples in the United States have both husband and wife in the labor force (U.S. Bureau of the Census, 1996).
- Sixty percent of married women with preschool children are employed (Drobnic, Blossfeld, and Rohwer, 1999).
- A 1999 poll among workers found a growing resentment over the special treatment for parents in the workplace. Some workers said that when there was an urgent deadline, those without children were asked to stay, whereas parents were able to leave when the workday was over. The "family-friendly" benefits offered were only considered useful to parents or married workers (*USA Weekend*, 2000).

Things to Think About

- From a systems perspective, what links the family to the workforce?
- What values are transmitted within families that prepare family members for the workforce? What are the sources of these values? How are they transmitted? What are the costs of not being able to live up to these values?
- What experiences did you have with work, both paid and unpaid, as a teenager?
- Think about the retirement experiences of your family members (parents, grandparents, great-grandparents). How has the concept of retirement changed over time? Do you think at all about your own retirement?

What was the first job you ever had outside your home for which you got paid? It would be surprising to find anyone over the age of 19 (healthy and without disabilities) who has not worked for wages at some time in their lives in either the private or public sectors of the economy. Babysitting, mowing lawns, delivering papers, and cooking/serving in fast-food restaurants are some of the typical ways teens earn money. Those of you who are older no doubt have extensive job experiences, having moved in and out of a variety of positions. For all of you, these jobs brought more or less satisfaction or frustration with your fellow workers, employers, or work environments. So most of you have some knowledge of the work world, a sense of how working affected your family relationships (and vice versa), and how it benefited or handicapped you personally. This knowledge is what you bring to a study of the topics covered in this chapter. What we hope you will take from this chapter is information that extends beyond your personal experience and gives you an understanding of work and family dynamics that involve various ages, classes, races, and both sexes.

No other institution affects family life like the economy does. The coordination of time, energy, and effort by at least one family member in the labor market is necessary for a household to survive in our society, for few families in our country are fully self-sufficient. In our consumer-based economy, money is brought into the home and is eventually exchanged for food, clothes, housing, and the nonessentials that add to the quality of life. In this chapter we explore how the labor force participation of men and women affects families in terms of the division of household labor and family members' life satisfaction. We compare the work experiences of men, women, and children, and the impact of these experiences on family life. We describe the effects of unemployment and retirement on family relationships. At the end of the chapter we examine the intersection of the two microsystems of family and work at the institutional level.

Labor Force Participation

What does the picture of American workers look like? There is no significant difference among racial groups in terms of percentage working: among whites, 66.8 percent of the civilian population is in the labor force, as are 69.1 percent of Latinos and 64.8 percent of blacks. Looking across all racial/ethnic groups, 59.6 percent of females are in the labor force, compared to 74.1 percent of males (Wright, 2003a). Twenty-five percent of women work part-time—that is, less than 35 hours a week (Drobnic et. al., 1999).

At the beginning of the twenty-first century, jobs were plentiful and the unemployment rate reached a low of 3.9 percent (U.S. Bureau of Labor Statistics, 2000a). However, by 2003 it had risen to 6.4 percent as a result of the economic downturn that began in 2001 (U.S. Bureau of Labor Statistics, 2003).

How Employment Affects Adults' Lives

The positive effects of employment are manifest in greater mental and physical health of working Americans. Studies that compare working women with those who are full-time homemakers show, on the average, that housewives are worse off in terms of depression, self-esteem, and anxiety (Sloan, 1985; Tallman, 1995). However, this finding is qualified by attitudes toward working. Mental and physical health is negatively affected when women who stay home would rather be working or when they are working and would rather stay at home. Husbands' mental health also suffers if their wives work yet they prefer that she stay home and care for the family (Ross, Mirowsky, and Huber, 1983). Paid employment appears to help women cope with raising adolescent children when they have a positive orientation toward their work. Such women are better able to deal with teens that are pulling away from the family, demanding more independence, and challenging parental authority (Silverberg, 1996). Perhaps this is because their work role provides fulfillment at a time when parenting roles are losing some of their importance to their offspring.

American workers are not always a contented lot. Many newspapers include a "work" section that features job opportunities, workplace issues, and management skills. Does your newspaper have such a feature? Many men and women turn to these pages seeking information about a more satisfying or better-paying job, trying to learn about the possible effects of two working parents on a newborn infant or preschooler, or trying to figure out how to do a better job at balancing work/family responsibilities. These are also topics of "conversation" in Internet chat rooms.

Advice columns and work-related articles are not new. However, what seems to characterize the nature of many current advice seekers is a sense of frustration associated with the expenditure of time. Research shows that the biggest problem for married couples is money (a work-related issue), followed by who does what around the house (a home/work issue), and interpersonal interaction problems (communication) that could involve arguing about money and home tasks (Gottman, 1999; Tallman, 2003). With the increasing number of two-earner families, the time couples have available to spend with each other and with their children is reduced. One recent survey asked two-career couples about the biggest challenge they faced, the majority answered "too little time" (Hunter, 1999).

A recent United Nations study of the number of hours spent working reported that Americans work the longest hours of persons in the industrialized world (International Labor Organization, 2003). Since 1970, American workers have worked increasingly longer hours. The average worker worked 148 more hours in 1996 than his or her 1973 counterpart (Collins, Leondan-Wright, and Skalar, 1999). This increase includes fewer paid and unpaid absences from work and 14 percent less time taken for vacations. Galinsky and her colleagues at the Families and Work Institute (1993) studied the amount of time spent in work-related activities (including commuting and overtime work) and found that men averaged 48.8 hours of work a week and women, 41.7. Increased time spent at work means less time at home for both parents. This is a relatively new experience for mothers beginning in the second half of the twentieth century.

The problem of a shortage of family time for middle-class women was exacerbated when mothers began to enter the paid labor force. Although unmarried middle-class women participated in the paid labor force in the past, the majority quit after they married. However, women of color and some white working-class wives continued to work outside the home after marriage because their families needed their financial contributions. Almost a third of married nonwhite women worked in the paid labor force in the 1920s and 1930s compared to less than 10 percent of married white women (Cherlin, 1996).

The participation in paid work by all wives and mothers increased gradually over the course of the twentieth century, especially during the last four decades. In 1960, 37.7 percent of women were in the workforce, compared to 60.2 percent of women in 2000 (U.S. Bureau of Labor Statistics, 2001). Women's increased participation in paid labor was a result of changes in society (such as the expansion of the service sector of the economy), which in turn brought about other changes. For example, many scholars attribute delayed marriage and a higher divorce rate to women's entry into the labor force (Cherlin, 1992).

What other consequences does paid work have for families? When women work outside the home their "family work" waits to be done, and the amount of time they spend on it drops (Coltrane, 2000). The amount of time available to spend with children lessens. Instead of children having the day-long presence of a mother, both must be content with what has come to be called "quality time." Note that being in the "presence" of children during the day and time spent in actual interaction may not necessarily be the same.

For men, a shortage of family time is associated with overtime work, moonlighting, and professions or careers that absorb more than a standard 40-hour workweek, such as law, academics, medicine, and some business positions. Between 1998 and 2000 many "dot.com" workers might have been placed in this category. Some occupations, such as firefighters, necessitate round-the-clock work (several days and nights on followed by several off), while others demand graveyard or evening shifts. Some occupations put workers on the road for long periods of time (sales, truckers, railroad engineers, airline pilots). Increasingly, workers spend more of their time in the daily commute to and from work, estimated to be 45 minutes a day (Bond, Galinksy, and Swanberg, 1998), which represents time taken away from family, home, and leisure activities.

Further, some careers are so absorbing and stimulating that workers are drawn away from their families. Within a gender-traditional framework, men are congratulated for working hard to provide for their family while actually spending little physical time with them. This approval stems from the belief that providing financially comes before providing time and attention. These same beliefs admonish a dedicated career woman for not being at home raising her children.

Workplace Versus Home-Work

A relative of one of your authors worked out of her home when her children were small during the 1930s, doing detailed embroidery beadwork for Hollywood dress designers. Before she died, she owned her own embroidery business, hiring dozens of women who worked either in her shop or in their homes. Such "home-work" is not a new phenomenon, especially for recent immigrants to America. Today, home-work is still part of low-tech industries such as the apparel business (Fernandez-Kelly and Garcia, 1998) and increasingly it is a desirable situation for workers in high-tech industries as well.

Working from home is sometimes called a **cottage industry.** A cottage industry is one in which the creation of products or services is home based rather than factory or office based. Technological telecommuting, or telework, is an example of a high-tech cottage industry. Telework is a solution to the dilemma of parents who want to be at home with preschool children and at the same time want or need to earn a wage. Computers and the Internet enable them to work as accountants, bookkeepers, medical transcribers, and so on from home. Research on teleworking will be reviewed later in the chapter when we discuss work/family spillover.

Part-Time Workers

Consider the following case study about a friend of one of your authors:

Melanie is a young mother who lives with her husband and two preschool sons. When her first boy, Henry, was born, Melanie gave up her job in an insurance company to stay home and raise her son: she wanted to be an "at home" mom. Soon after Henry was born, a former coworker and friend at the insurance company prevailed on her to take care of her 10-month-old grandson, Wally. Since money was short, and since she had a degree in psychology and training in child development, this was something Melanie felt she could do and still stay home. Soon Wally's cousin, Nate, and another cousin, Sara, joined the group. All three of the children's mothers worked full-time. Within two years Wally had a new baby brother. Melanie was an at-home mom "parenting" a newborn, three two-year-olds (she called them the triplets), and a 4-year-old, earning enough to make the car and insurance payments and a little extra for miscellaneous spending.

Three years later, Melanie still cares for Sara each day, and Henry has a new little brother. She is also earning a part-time wage from her church, organizing childcare for the various church activities each week. Last fall she started working several weekends a month selling merchandise at the team shop in the city's Sports Arena. In March she signed up with a local marketing group to test and critique products such as baby diapers, salad dressing, or other food products and to participate in marketing focus group discussions. She is paid $40 to $50 for each test or focus group in which she participates. Melanie still sees herself as an at-home mom, although by all accounts, she is working four jobs.

Melanie is not alone. In 2001 almost 20 percent of Americans worked at jobs considered to be part-time employment. Women are most likely to work less than full-time because shorter hours at work permit them to earn a wage while leaving them time to care for their family. About 70 percent of part-time workers are women (Lovell and Hill, 2001). On the other hand, some part-time workers hold down a full-time job in addition to their part-time work; 13 percent of workers hold two or more jobs in order to make a living for their families (Hunter, 1999). Men are more likely to hold a part-time plus a full-time job, and women are more likely to hold two part-time jobs (Uchitelle, 1994). This additional work shift is yet another factor explaining why spouses/parents feel they do not have enough time to spend with each other and their families.

Childcare Arrangements

Most recent research on out-of-home childcare indicates few negative effects on preschoolers over the age of two (Peth-Pierce, 1997). Still, there is some ambivalence in women's attitudes and behaviors about whether to return to work right after the birth of a child. For many women, guilt accompanies both of the two possible outcomes: stay at home and forgo a wage that contributes to the family's financial well-being, or return to work and place the infant in someone else's care. Before a child is conceived or born, many women will say the former decision is the best, yet after the birth they are soon back at work. In 2000, a Census Bureau report indicated that 59 percent of women who gave birth between July 1997 and June 1998 returned to the workforce within a year. The corresponding figure in 1976 was 31 percent.

Contributing to the distress associated with leaving an infant in the care of others in order to reenter the workplace is a lack of confidence in the quality of that care. A report in 1998 described the various kinds of care provided for children of mothers who work: 22 percent of children were in childcare centers and 21 percent were in home care provided by nonrelatives, such as Melanie's care for Sara and the other children in the example of part-time workers. In the report another 19 percent of children were cared for by their fathers, 16 percent by grandparents, and 9 percent by other relatives; 8 percent were in preschool, and 5 percent were with their mothers at work (U.S. Bureau of the Census, 1998).

Contributing to the time problem discussed earlier, in 1997, 25 percent of two-earner couples worked a split shift, usually so that parents could care for their children. Most of these were parents with preschool-aged children (Presser and Cox, 1997). Some differences exist between low-income and higher-income families. An Urban Institute report (Capizzano and Adams, 2004) indicates that low-income children under the age of five are less likely to be cared for in a center-based childcare arrangement and more likely to be cared for by a parent or relative than are higher-income children of the same age. See Table 7.1 for these differences.

Low-income families often call upon adolescent daughters for their childcare needs. There are high costs for adolescents of this sibling childcare, including a detour "from education, extracurricular experiences such as athletic activities, school clubs, and the arts, and perhaps most important, the chance to cultivate a dream about the future" (Dodson and Dickert, 2004, 26). Minority mothers are also more likely to use full-time grandparent care than whites are, but they are not more likely to use them for part-time care, or sporadically (Vandell et al., 2003).

The questions researchers have begun to ask is not whether non-maternal childcare is good or bad for children but, rather, what aspects of care contribute to children's social, psychological, cogni-

Table 7.1   Primary Childcare Arrangements for Children Under Age 5 With Employed Mothers, by Family Income

	All Children Under 5	
	Low income*	Higher income**
Nonparental	68.7%	74.6%
Center-based	24.9	31.2
Family child care	10.7	14.2
Nanny/babysitter	3.5	5.3
Relative	29.5	23.9
Parent/other**	31.3	25.4

Adapted from *2002 National Survey of America's Families, No. 16, Series: Snapshots of America's Families*, 111. Urban Institute (2004).

*Low income is defined as below 200 percent of the federal poverty thresholds and higher income as 200 percent of the federal poverty thresholds and above.

**Parent/other category contains children whose mothers did not report the use of any regular childcare arrangement while they worked.

tive, and language development and their overall well-being? What seems to matter, at least in the case of infants under the age of one year, is the *quality* of the care. Is it consistent? Is it stable? Is it characterized by sensitivity to the infant and frequent language stimulation? These characteristics indicate high-quality childcare. In a major study funded by the National Institutes of Health (which examined many kinds of childcare, including father care, grandparent care, nonrelative care in the child's home, childcare homes, and center-based care), it was reported that children performed better on measures of cognitive and language development when their caretakers spoke frequently to the children, asked them questions, and responded to the children's vocalizations. Children in quality settings with higher amounts of provider-child interaction resulted in better language abilities at ages 15, 24, and 36 months and greater positive engagement at 3 years of age. The researchers who conducted this study found that the quality and amount of childcare was also associated with the quality of mother-child interaction. However, other variables—family environment, mother's education level, and family income—had the greatest effect on mother-child interaction (Peth-Pierce, 1997).

Many children with two employed parents spend their days in out-of-home childcare. Can you think of any negative effects such settings might have on children? What about positive effects?

One negative finding from these same data was released in 2001 in a highly publicized report. It indicated that while language and memory skills were greater in children cared for in nonmaternal care settings, children cared for by persons other than their mother also tended to be more aggressive, demanding, and defiant by the time they reached kindergarten age. The researchers qualified this finding by saying that almost all the aggressive children behaved within the "normal" range for 4-year-olds. As you might imagine, this report was very controversial (Gibbs, 2001). This controversy is an example of how the systemic connection between two microsystems (family and childcare givers) is influenced by information originating from and disseminated by other parts of the exosystem (the government and media), causing parental and caregiver concern.

Recent analyses of these data are more reassuring for working mothers. Booth and her associates (2002) found that when they compared children at 15 months of age who were in childcare for 30 or more hours a week with children who stayed home with their mothers (i.e., comparing working versus nonworking mothers) no differences were found for cognitive development, early language development, mother-infant interaction, and infant-mother attachment. Some other interesting findings also were reported:

1. At-home mothers spent significantly more time in instrumental care (dressing, feeding, supervising, disciplining) and social interaction (talking, teaching, helping) on weekdays than working mothers (no surprise).

2. There were no differences between mothers in the amount of time spent in these activities on weekends.

3. The quality of parenting did not differ between the two groups of mothers.

4. Employed mothers measured significantly higher on separation anxiety and beliefs that their working might be detrimental to their child.

5. Fathers of children whose mothers were employed were more involved (bathing, feeding, reading to the child, giving attention to a crying child) than fathers of children with at-home mothers.

For at-home mothers, it was determined that they did not invest the majority of their "extra" time in social interaction with their children. Further, the more children the at-home moms had, the less time they spent in social interaction with the child who was the focal point of the research.

The reassuring conclusion of this report for employed mothers was that, at least at 15 months of age, there were few "costs" to children of working mothers as a result of reduced mother-child interaction time, and the quality of mother-child interaction did not appear to be influenced by hours at work.

Work Schedules: How Shift Work Affects the Family

If spouses work alternate hours, does it affect their marriage? Only a few researchers have tried to answer this question, but the uniform answer is "usually." A study by White and Keith (1990) found that over a three-year period the probability of divorce increased from 7 percent to 11 percent when one or both spouses had work schedules involving shift work (defined as spending more than half of their job hours outside the traditional 8 A.M. to 4 P.M. shift). This study focused on such factors as the degree of marital happiness, number and frequency of disagreements, how much time spouses spent together eating, shopping, and so on, the extent to which they had problems with their spouse's behavior or personal traits, the extent of their sexual happiness, jealousy, spouse's faithfulness, and child-related problems. Overall, the findings showed modest but consistent negative effects of shift work, as evidenced by lower marital happiness, greater sexual problems, and more child-related problems. Statistical analysis ruled out the possibility that the findings were attributable to other characteristics of the spouses' jobs, or whether it was the husband or wife who worked the alternative schedule.

Presser (2000) examined whether shift work affected marital instability. Her data revealed that only night shift work (where at least half of the hours on the job were between midnight and 8 A.M.) served as a predictor of divorce or separation. Her comparison was with day, evening, and weekend shifts. Results varied depending on the duration of marriage, the presence of children, and whether the worker was the husband or wife. Specifically, women who had children, were married more than five years, and worked a night shift were three times more likely to divorce or separate than women with equal status characteristics who worked days. Men who were more vulnerable to divorce or separation worked a night shift, were married less than five years, and were fathers. These men were six times more likely to divorce or separate than those who worked days. Presser was able to test whether spouses in troubled marriages were the ones most likely to take a night shift job; her analysis indicated that this was not the case. Thus, it appears that shift work leads to marital problems.

A third longitudinal study focused on the interpersonal and psychological well-being of husbands and wives when one of them worked an alternative shift from the other. Perry-Jenkins and her colleagues at the University of Massachusetts–Amherst (2000) studied working-class families in which both partners worked. The study was conducted from the time the couples were expecting their first baby to one year following the birth. The findings clearly supported the negative effects of shift work on the couple relationship. Comparing those in same-shift versus alternating-shift relationships, Perry-Jenkins and her colleagues found the following:

- Feelings of belonging, closeness, and attachment to partner (love scores) significantly declined over time for both husbands and wives. Wives in relationships where one spouse was in an alternating shift job had scores on these variables that declined more than all other spouses.

- Wives reported significantly higher levels of marital conflict than husbands, and those in alternating-shift families reported more than wives in same-shift families. This finding was still evident at the end of the study. However, when husbands spent more time in solo care of the child, conflict was reduced.

- Wives reported greater levels of depression than husbands, but their depression levels decreased across the three time periods of the study more than husbands' levels.

- Wives reported more **role overload** (as measured by time pressure and too many commitments) than husbands did, and wives in alternating-shift families reported higher levels of role overload than wives and husbands in same-shift families. This was especially true immediately after the baby was born. By the time of the one-year follow-up interview, however, husbands but not wives reported more role overload, especially husbands in alternating-shift families. Interestingly, the more solo time fathers put into childcare, the less role overload they reported.

The question of the effects that shift work has on children has largely gone unanswered. Children living in these arrangements have a special type of "single-parenting family" (Presser, 1988). They may lose time with both parents, but is there an advantage to having time alone with one? Children may experience higher-quality child-parent involvement when fathers or mothers must prepare supper, give baths, and read bedtime stories because they are the sole parent on duty. Or quality may be lower because the parent is tired from working all day and just feeds the kids and sends them off to bed. Considering that approximately one-third of dual-earner couples with children use an alternating-shift work schedule as a means to manage childcare, the prospects for quality family life for millions of workers are dimmed. When parents see each other for only a few minutes a day at a halfway-home freeway rest stop while they exchange children, kisses, and quick comments on their day, the quality of the marital relationship suffers (Perry-Jenkins, 2000). Children end up seeing their parents in shifts, the time for intimacy between partners is reduced, and family activities must be curtailed when parental work shifts alternate. One outcome is a greater likelihood of separation or divorce.

Commuter Marriages

Another type of situation that is reflective of shift schedules occurs when spouses live apart for work-related or school-related reasons and one or the other "visits" whenever possible. This situation is referred to as a "commuter" marriage and is usually viewed as temporary (although sometimes it lasts for years). Gerstel and Gross (1984) characterized commuter marriages as partnerships in which both partners are equally committed to their careers and two separate households must be established because one workplace is too distant for commuting. For many couples the separation is viewed as permanent, but they nevertheless wish for a shared life together. They look forward to the day when the time, energy, and money spent to be together can be used for other purposes. Most couples choosing this situation agree that it is psychologically stressful. One college instructor described her situation as follows:

> My husband quit his job and moved out of state to go to medical school. My first daughter was two years old and stayed with me. This continued all through my second pregnancy (we wondered if he would make it to the birth—he was there!). It was stressful and difficult for the adults, but particularly on our child. Adults understand deferred gratification, but a two-year-old doesn't. We were creative about language, calling one residence our "Arizona house" and our regular residence our "Utah house." We never told her that daddy was "visiting," since that made it sound like he didn't live with us. Thank goodness it was a temporary phase.

This example sums up the positive and negative aspects of having a long-distance relationship. Separation may enhance one partner's career, but it comes at the cost of day-to-day family relationships. Some of the problems encountered include short-circuited conversations about daily work and family experiences, the absence of shared leisure events, a restricted sex life, unproductive periods of work because of loneliness, and, if children are in the family, losing out on their growth and development (Gerstel and Gross, 1984). On the other hand, living apart may be the only solution for the maximization of career potential for partners who truly love their work. So they strive to make the time they have together high quality and satisfying.

Work-Family Spillover

The microsystems of work and family reflect two important domains, both highly important to individuals' self-esteem and sense of well-being (Thoits, 1992), which means the mesosystem connections between family members' work environments and family take on added importance. Two ways of conceptualizing this connection are the **spillover** (sometimes called the **crossover**) **model** (Staines, 1980) and the **interactive model**

(Chow and Berheide, 1988). These concepts—spillover and interactive—refer to work and family conditions or experiences in one setting that affect those in the other. The spillover model emphasizes an asymmetrical relationship, stressing one-direction effects, whereas the interactive model emphasizes the mutual interdependence of family and workplace, "acknowledging their independent as well as their joint effects, directly and indirectly, on the psychological state and social conditions of individuals" (Chow and Berheide, 1988, 25).

Both models recognize three important system characteristics:

- There is boundary permeability within and between systems.
- Individuals have memberships in multiple systems.
- There are social psychological consequences of simultaneous membership.

So, what are the consequences of simultaneous membership in two important systems, and what are the various ways and circumstances in which family and work roles intersect?

The Interdependence of Work and Family

The family variables most often thought to affect the realm of work are family and marital conflict, distress, or discord. One study found that marital distress was negatively associated with work performance and productivity for men who were married 10 or fewer years. This relationship did not hold for women or for men married longer than 10 years (Forthofer et al., 1996). Family conflict decreased work performance and was associated with withdrawal from work in a study conducted by Frone, Yardley, and Markel (1997). Another study looked at marital discord and women's income. (Discord in this sample of 455 women was measured by asking how stable the marriage was perceived to be, the number of relationship problems, and the amount and severity of spousal conflict.) Marital discord and women's income were related, but discord pushed women to earn more money and not the reverse. Women apparently increased their income when they perceived marital discord was increasing. The opposite was not true. Increased income did not increase marital discord (Rogers, 1999).

Barnett (1994) studied husbands and wives in dual-earner families where both worked full-time. She found for both men and women that when marital and parental experiences were positive, the quality of perceived work roles (how rewarding their job was, their level of job security) did not influence their level of psychological distress (depression, anxiety levels, and negative moods). However, when marriage and parental quality was low, the quality of work roles did affect psychological health. This study showed how family life can serve as a buffer between a difficult work environment and any mental distress that might accompany it.

Dilworth (2004) searched for the family factors that predicted negative spillover from family to work with a sample of 453 full-time employed mothers and fathers. Negative spillover in her study was determined by asking whether the respondents' family or personal life kept them from getting work done on time, kept them from taking on extra work, interfered with doing a good job at work or concentrating on work, or caused them to feel drained of energy. She found for both fathers and mothers, negative spillover to work was high when satisfaction with family life was low. Negative spillover was not affected by the number of hours spent doing housework or caring for children, for mothers or fathers. Higher education did predict negative spillover from home to work for fathers more than for mothers. It was speculated that fathers with higher education held jobs that may have involved greater responsibility and commitments. Mothers experienced increased negative spillover from family to work when they worked more hours per week and had young children in the home. White mothers experienced greater negative spillover than nonwhite mothers. Dilworth speculated that this might be because Latino and black husbands of working mothers are more likely to help with housework and child care.

Grzywacz and Marks (2000) investigated work-family and family-work spillover by focusing on adult drinking behavior. They found among a national sample of over 1,500 middle-aged adults that both negative and positive spillover from work to family was associated with greater odds of problem drinking. As a response to negative spillover from work to home, drinking problems were explained in terms of high levels of pressure on the job. As a consequence of positive spillover, problem drinking was explained in terms of the acceptability of social drinking at lunches and parties that was thought to be associated with highly satisfying and rewarding jobs. Looking at the reverse relationship, spillover from home to work, positive family relationships were associated with lower odds of problem drinking, whereas conflict at home (negative spillover) was associated with a greater likelihood of having a drinking problem.

Rogers and May (2003) studied a sample of 1,065 husbands and wives (not married to each other) who were questioned four times over a 12-year period. Job and marital satisfaction measures were obtained at each survey point. Analyses established that the most influential spillover relationship was from family to work rather than the reverse: Marital satisfaction contributed to increases in job satisfaction and marital discord contributed to declines in job satisfaction for both husbands and wives. This otherwise excellent study did not include the number of work hours or the flexibility of work schedules, both important variables when examining work-family and family-work spillover. As we mentioned earlier, there is some evidence that marital instability is increased when either spouse works nonstandard hours (Presser, 2000; White and Keith, 1990). Similarly, work stress and psychological stress, two of the most studied variables in the work-family mesosystem, were left out (Perry-Jenkins, Repetti, and Crouter, 2000). The effects of stress are discussed next.[1]

The Effects of Stress

What are the consequences to the family when stress is experienced at work? Research indicates that work stress contributes to less sensitive and fewer responsive family interactions, a withdrawal from interpersonal interaction with family members after a high-stress day, and the expression of negative emotions, including irritability, impatience, and a greater number of power assertions ("Go back to bed! You've had your last drink of water!") (Repetti, 1989; Matthews, Conger, and Wickrama, 1996).

Many studies report marked differences between mothers and fathers in the transmission of stress from work to family, with fathers' stress having the strongest effects on children Repetti (1989, 1993). Fathers' stress at work affects their emotional state at home. A bad day at work is associated with withdrawal behavior, expressions of anger, and being more punitive when disciplining children. However, negative transmission of stress does not hold for mothers (Larson and Richards, 1994). Further, wives are often able to moderate their husbands' moods; if they discover their husband had a bad day at work, they take on more of the evening household tasks and permit him to withdraw to have some quiet time alone (Repetti, 1989). The lack of wives' transmission of negative emotion from work to home is explained by a greater capability of women to "leave the job behind" or, once they get home, to give priority to the situation they find there over whatever occurred at work that day (Larson and Richards, 1994).

Larson and Gillman (1999) propose a gendered explanation for fathers and mothers' differing emotional states. They suggest that for fathers, home and work are different emotional experiences. While fathers may feel stressed at work because of perceived competition, coworker stress, and so on, they typically consider home a relaxed setting where they report much "down-time." Basically, home is their haven or retreat. For working mothers, the time at work is dominated by more positive than negative emotion, relative to home. At work, mothers feel cooperative, friendly, social, and less isolated, and in the Larson and Gillman study none felt guilty because they worked. Compared to fathers, they find work an emotionally positive setting compared to their experience at home. The authors suggest, "For many of these women, work provided social rewards they did not get at home. Their labor was not taken for granted; they got appreciation from others; many of them also received social support" (65). Work provided an "emotional buoyancy." In essence, aside from whatever stresses and negative moods spill over from work to home, work has apparent positive consequences for women's emotional well-being and development. A similar idea will be discussed later when we present the results from Hochschild's (1997) research.

Telecommuting and Work-Family Balance

Does working from home contribute to a satisfactory work-family balance? Hill and his colleagues (1996) attempted to answer this question with an exploratory study comparing 149 teleworkers and 100 traditionally employed office workers (all IBM employees). Not surprisingly, the teleworkers reported more flexibility in the timing and location of their work. However, they were not more likely to report that they had more time for home and personal life, and it was no easier for them to balance work and personal/home life than the traditionally employed workers. No gender differences were found; however, workers who were parents of preschool children evaluated telework more positively than those who did not have preschoolers, reporting they could more easily balance work and personal/home responsibilities.

Written comments provided clues regarding the benefits and costs of telecommuting. The benefits included more time for the family ("I have time to take my child to his basketball practice in the middle of the day") and more time for household chores ("I can do laundry while writing a report"). What were the costs? The study found that for some, the lack of defined workspace at home had a negative effect on family life (telework blurs the boundary between work and family), while for others a home office with a door contributed to less time for family life (they worked too many hours behind the door). Some teleworkers reported that they never seemed to get away from work and thus were not psychologically available to their families. A majority of teleworkers reported having a "difficult" or "very difficult" time balancing personal/home life. The researchers surmised that some flexibility is helpful but that some people need more structure in the workplace, such as colleagues who will tell a workaholic it's time to go home!

Another study (Hill et al., 2001) using the same methodology but a larger sample of IBM employees (6,451) also found no gender differences: Men and women reported similar levels of work-family balance and held similar perceptions of job flexibility (although men worked longer hours and women spent more hours in domestic labor). Results showed that perceived job flexibility (flexible work hours and telecommuting) was positively related to work-family balance even when job

Some women pay a high career price when they stay home to care for children. To avoid these costs, parents work out creative solutions, involving mom or dad working full- or part-time from home.

hours, household work hours, gender, marital status, and occupational level were controlled. Occupational rank was the biggest contributor to perceived work-family imbalance: The higher the rank, the more difficult it was to achieve work-family balance. Among those who were able to telecommute and who worked a reasonable number of hours per week, 71 percent had no difficulty with work-family balance, compared to 60 percent of those who traveled to traditional workplaces.

Considering the hours spent working, this study found that when employees worked at home or were able to take advantage of company flextime, they worked longer hours before experiencing difficulty in balancing work and family life than those who did not perceive they had job flexibility (Hill et al., 2001). Not having to commute every day in rush-hour traffic, the option of living further from one's workplace (e.g., in rural areas or small towns), being able to schedule work hours more closely aligned with school-aged children's schedules, being available for quality family time when family members need attention (not just before or after an 8 to 4 daily working schedule), and being home for ill children, dependent elders, or monitoring adolescents are some of the benefits of telework suggested by these researchers. These benefits are perceived by a growing number of workers and employers. In 1990 there were 4 million employees telecommuting; in 1997 there were 11 million (Kee, 2000).

Workplace Appeal for Women

As mentioned earlier both men and women are spending a greater number of hours in the workplace. One indirect indicator of this change comes from a recent Nielsen rating showing the 5:00 A.M. radio listenership is up 25 percent since 1994 (Tronner, 2000). Why has this happened? Aside from more time needed for the daily commute, one hypothesis (Hochschild, 1997) is that the workplace is becoming so hospitable and supportive that many workers are heading to work early, finding it a great source of emotional satisfaction, competing with home life as a major system of support. Hochschild (1997) studied men and women working in a "family friendly" midwest industry. In her study, more than a few men and women dropped off their children at school or childcare earlier than necessary in order to get to work and talk with coworkers over a cup of coffee or to get a head start on organizing their day; and they often stayed on the job until long after the dinner hour. One respondent described the start of her workday:

> We sit there and chit-chat for five or ten minutes. There's laughing, joking, fun. My co-workers aren't putting me down for any reason. Everything is done with humor and fun from beginning to end, though it can get stressful when a machine malfunctions. (38)

This same respondent described what happens when she does get home: she is met by a demanding teenager who needs to talk while complaining about her stepfather, a baby that should have been in bed two hours ago, a husband who jealously criticizes his stepdaughter for monopolizing his wife's time, and dirty dishes in the sink that nobody bothered to clean up. For this woman, "Home had become work and work had become home" (38). Hochschild explains: Women are experiencing a level of satisfaction at work that many men found long ago. For them, the workplace had become a source of personal value, appreciation, pride, and friendship.

Friends in the workplace tend to make it a supportive environment for workers.

It is not possible to generalize from Hochschild's qualitative study because it represents only one company and she interviewed a relatively small sample of workers. However, her observations are consistent with the research by Larson and Richards (1994) reported earlier. These data lend support to the **compensation theory** of work and family (Zedeck, 1992), which argues that individuals invest themselves differently in work and family settings. What a person finds missing in one setting is made up for by what is offered in the other.

When home competes with a work environment for the time and attention of women, it is easy to understand how it can lose out in terms of valuation and appreciation. Fixing dinner, shopping, picking up the cleaning, and doing the laundry are "expected" female tasks for which women rarely receive thanks. Thankless jobs that are routine and never-ending, such as picking up the mess left by others and listening and attending to the emotional problems of children and partners, are what women are supposed to do. If, in the workplace, their jobs also entail listening, attending, or repetitive tasks such as filing papers or soldering electronic components, at least their time and effort is recognized with a salary, paid vacations, and for some, recognition or awards for outstanding work.

The benefits of paid labor are clear-cut. The benefits of unpaid housework are less obvious. Moreover, the evidence is strong that women who engage in paid work are still responsible for doing the majority of unpaid household work (Noonan, 2001). Hochschild (1989) called this women's **second shift.** The total number of hours worked by women must include the time they spend in the labor force as well as the hours doing childcare and household tasks before, and after, their hours spent in paid employment. Larson and Richards (1994) discovered that whereas the early evening hours were a time for husbands to relax and recover from the stresses of the long workday, this period was a time for wives to focus on housework and childcare.

A study by Barnett and Shen (1997) indicates that the idea of a second shift may be overstated, at least among white, middle-class, dual-earner couples. They analyzed *total* work time and concluded that in the 300 families they studied, the gender gap in total work hours was closing. When total hours of work were added together (full-time work and housework), the results were similar for men and women. However, women still did more of the housework. The similarity came because the amount of time women spent in the paid workforce was slightly less than that of their spouses. Both husbands and wives spent about 65 hours in a combination of paid and unpaid work. Barnett and Shen did not include childcare tasks in their analysis. However, they noted that when children were under the age of five, wives did more childcare than husbands. After children started school, husbands and wives put in the same number of hours. Thus, the conclusion that the second shift is exaggerated may be premature when all aspects of maintaining a household are considered.[2] Let's look at the costs and benefits of doing housework.

Household Division of Labor

Looking at "who does what around the house" is one way to examine the relationship between home life and labor force participation. During World War II, women in all social classes, married and single, worked for the war effort. Some joined the military; others worked in the defense industry, in factories and shipyards; some cared for the children of industry workers; and others volunteered in fundraising efforts. However, once those in the armed forces returned to take back their places in the workforce, women were expected to resume their prewar status at home as well. After an initial postwar exodus from the labor force, a growing number of women began to enter the labor force as the service sector grew. In 1960, 37.7 percent of women over the age of 16 worked. This figure increased to 59.6 by 2002 (U.S. Bureau of Labor Statistics, 2003). Since this movement included married women and mothers, the obvious question is, if wives are working outside the home in increasingly greater numbers, has there been any change in who does the work *inside* the home? As it turns out, the answer is: very little.

The past 40 years have seen a slight decrease in married women's responsibility for housework, although wives still do significantly more than husbands. Since 1965, time spent doing housework has declined for women, especially those who are employed. Robinson (1993) found young women spend about nine fewer hours a week doing housework than they did in the past. For older women the decline is somewhat less, about six hours. This amounts to about a 40 percent reduction in household labor for working women. A quip from one dot.com company employee illustrates how this reduction in housework combines with the increased number of hours spent on the job: "Cleaning up the dining area means getting the fast-food bags out of the backseat of your car."

The number of hours spent doing housework increased for men. One study found men's housework per week increased from an average of 4.6 hours in 1965 to almost 10 hours 20 years later (Gupta, 1999). What jobs do husbands do? In addition to the traditional "male" chores such as yardwork and household repairs, they do the dishes and shop for groceries more consistently than they do the laundry or clean the bathroom. Twiggs, McQuillan, and Ferree (1999) call doing dishes a **boundary task.** A boundary task is a task that acts as the gateway to doing more housework. That is, if men do any housework, it is usually the dishes. If they do other household tasks, they also do the dishes. Twiggs and her colleagues found that not as many husbands prepared meals as did the dishes, but those who cooked also washed dishes. Those who did dishes were likely to do other household chores, such as the laundry. For men, washing dishes is the line in the sand, so to speak, that when crossed means they are likely to do more, not less, housework.

Some men are 'helpers' with domestic tasks while others share the household and childcare work with their partners. In one family we know the parents split the work equally (shop, cook, clean-up, childcare), taking turns every other day. This frees up time for career-related tasks on the day they are free of childcare and household tasks. On weekends they clean the house and do the laundry and other household jobs together. How is the household work distributed in your family?

Husbands' household work typically tends to be male gender-typed, such as taking out the trash and washing and maintaining the car. These kinds of tasks are considered to be "occasional" rather than "routine"— and hence less tedious and boring. They are also tasks that can be deferred to a "later" time when other, more pressing demands stack up. These types of tasks have been called *high-schedule-control* because they can be done when you want to and not according to some predetermined schedule, such as fixing dinner, which is a *low-schedule-control* task (Barnett and

Shen, 1997). Working wives are responsible for the routine and repetitive household chores 70–90 percent of the time, and these chores tend to require fairly constant attention (Twiggs et al., 1999).

Housework in Different Types of Families

Who do you think contributes more to household help: black, white, or Latino husbands? You'd be correct if you said black men do more housework than white men, with Latinos falling in between. It is hypothesized that the black/white difference stems from greater egalitarian attitudes, and employment and earnings equality, between husbands and wives in black families (McLoyd et al., 2000). What accounts for these egalitarian attitudes? Scholars speculate that the legacy of slavery among blacks fostered role reciprocity because of the economic equality between the sexes under slavery (Taylor, 2000). Current economic conditions for blacks help maintain gender-role equity. According to Scott-Jones and Nelson-LeGall (1986), blacks "have not experienced as strong an economic basis for the subordination of women, either in marital roles or in the preparation of girls for schooling, jobs, and careers" (95). The consequence of this is a more egalitarian division of household labor.

Among white men, Cunningham (2001) hypothesized that paternal role modeling influences the degree to which men help with the housework. He found that for men, having a father who participated in a greater share of stereotypically female tasks (cooking, doing the laundry, shopping for groceries) when they were young children influenced their relative participation in such tasks as married (or cohabiting) adults.

There is some variation among Latino husbands' contributions to household tasks (Baca-Zinn and Wells, 2000). Cultural underpinnings are deeply gendered in Latino households, yet when wives work outside the home their economic contributions bring them somewhat greater power within the family, including more help with family tasks from husbands. Wives with middle-class jobs receive more assistance than wives with lower-paying jobs (Coltrane, 1996). Coltrane interviewed a small number (20) of Latino dual-earner couples. While we cannot generalize to all Latinos from his small study, he did discern a trend in husbands' helping behavior. When husbands earned considerably more income than their working wives, wives readily accepted the responsibilities for managing the household and husbands saw themselves (and were viewed by their wives) as "helpers." Both spouses accepted this division of household labor as normal. When husbands and wives had incomes that were more nearly equal (although most men still earned a greater proportion of the total family income), husbands tended to share family work and childcare. They washed dishes and played with the children (the least burdensome tasks), and their overall contribution level was more equal. Those spouses admitted that sharing household tasks was the result of continual bargaining and negotiation. Coltrane (1996) observed that these middle-income Latino families might represent a trend toward the increased sharing of household labor. A more cautious view comes from Baca-Zinn and Wells (2000), who suggest that structural and cultural aspects of Latino family life (such as dense social networks of extended families, ideals about male and female roles) may impede the development of egalitarian relations.

Although gay and lesbian couples have not been studied to the same extent as heterosexual couples, their division of household labor is reported as more egalitarian than that for heterosexual couples. This finding is reported in studies of gay/lesbian families with and without children (Patterson, 2000). However, gay and lesbian couples tend to spend more time and energy on negotiating the distribution of roles, responsibilities, and resources than heterosexual couples (Schwartz, 1994). A study by Kurdek (1993b) found lesbians to be more sensitive to equality and likely to share all tasks. Gay men focused more on an overall equal distribution of tasks, and they tended to specialize task performance, depending on the skill and interests of the men. As with heterosexual couples, the division of household tasks is reported to be one of the greatest sources of conflict for gays and lesbians.

Cohabitation, Marriage, Remarriage, and Housework Contributions

When women marry for the first time, they increase the time they spend in household work. First-married women also spend more hours on housework than cohabiting women do (Shelton and John, 1993). Leaving a cohabiting relationship does not affect the time women spend in household work, but housework time is reduced for women leaving a marriage. Entering into marriage or cohabitation for men results in a decrease in time spent doing housework. Conversely, if men leave a marriage (but not a cohabiting relationship), the amount of time spent doing household chores increases (Gupta, 1999).

Another structural variable that affects a family's division of labor is whether the marriage is a first or second (or higher) marriage. Some researchers have looked at marriage order and found that remarried couples have the most equitable division of household labor. Sullivan (1997) reported remarried women spend less time doing housework compared to first-married women. There were no differences for the men in her study. On the other hand, Ishii-Kuntz and Coltrane (1992) found remarried men were slightly, but significantly, more likely to spend time cooking, cleaning up after meals, housecleaning, shopping, and doing laundry than men in first marriages. Remarried men contributed about 8–10 hours per week, about 20 percent of the total couple housework time. These researchers caution that it is important to consider the variations in family structure—stepfather family, stepmother family, and combinations of the two. That is because stepfamilies with children living either outside or inside the home present different possibilities when assigning and carrying out family tasks.

What happens to the division of housework when children come into the family? Not surprisingly, the number of hours wives spend doing housework increases. The data from one national study show that each child from birth to age four adds more than three hours a week to women's housework time (Gupta, 1999). Men tend to devote more hours to paid work when children come, while women spend fewer hours on the job but do significantly more at home. (In Chapter 5 we made the point that many men feel as if their enhanced workforce contributions are ignored when parenting contributions are considered.) There is one qualification to this trend if childbearing is delayed. Coltrane (2000) reports that when men over the age of 28 become fathers, there is a more equitable division of childcare and housework among couples.

The Fairness Issue

A question frequently addressed by researchers concerns the perceived fairness of the distribution of housework. The most frequent response reported by women when asked about the division of housework is that they are satisfied with the contribution their own spouse makes to the household when compared to what they think is contributed by the spouses of friends, relatives, and "husbands in general." However, this finding is qualified: It does not pertain to women who hold nontraditional views on gender roles and those who spend more hours in paid work. Women with these characteristics are less likely to be satisfied with their partners' contributions if they perceive inequity (Robinson and Milkie, 1998).

In spite of *actual* inequality in the distribution of housework, researchers find that satisfaction with the division of household labor is associated with greater marital happiness and lower marital conflict across all stages of the family life cycle, for both spouses (Suitor, 1991; Blair, 1992). Perceived equity is also associated with less depression in women. Time spent in household chores is positively associated with marital disagreements for those who perceive unfairness in the distribution of housework (Voydanoff and Donnelly, 1999). A recent study conducted by Tallman (2003) found that "who does what around the house" is the issue that generates the second most intense arguments among husbands and wives during the first two years of marriage ("money" generated the most intense conflict).

In the following example, a discussion between Jan and Sam, a newly married couple, calls attention to the principal issues associated with "who does what around the house." As you read their conversation, look at the way they indicate their perceptions of "fairness." Which partner is "keeping score"? Prior to this discussion, Sam gave the magnitude of their conflicts over housework a score of 80 (on a scale of 1 = low to 100 = high); Jan rated them 20.

Sam: It seems like I'm always doing a little bit more than half of the housework in addition to doing most of the job work and most of the outside work.

Jan: You're right. Lately you have been doing most of the housework but keep in mind that school is tough and I spend a lot more of my day, every day at school or on school work than you spend at a job . . .

Sam: Um.

Jan: . . . earning income, plus I, that's probably why I don't feel it's a, there's a problem, because I feel that my time is very well occupied.

Sam: Yeah, but. You are busy, but, half the time when I come home from work, even if it's only a four- or five-hour shift, you know, it's a real effort to get up and do the housework. And, you know, sometimes I'm a tired ole dog but I know that, you know, for instance, the house needs to be straightened and the dishes washed . . .

Jan: Um hum.

Sam: And it takes 45 minutes and I'll go and do that. And you know, maybe, once in a while, having my little wife . . .

Jan: Yeah.

Sam: . . . offering to do it or help me with it would be nice.

Jan: I try to do that too. But think about last week, how many days over the last week and how many hours did you spend at work?

Sam: It's about 20.

Jan: Twenty hours?

Sam: Um hum.

Jan: And how many days?

Sam: Three, four, probably three.

Jan: Seems to me you only went to work a couple of days.

Sam: Hmm, no, I, I've figured it out. I worked, I've been working 20–22 hours is all.

Jan: I spend . . .

Sam: It's not much, but still . . .

Jan: In mine, I spend five days a week.

Sam: Um hum.

Jan: I spend about six hours at school, then I come home and I've got approximately two to four hours of homework every day.

Sam: Um hum. Well, what's on my mind . . .

Jan: And that, you know, I mean, doesn't leave me with a lot of energy . . .

Sam: Um hum. Well, like the other day when we got in the big argument cuz you wanted to play on the couch. If you would've said, you know, and I said "No, we can't cuz I gotta do the housework," you could've said, "Well, I'll take that excuse away; I'll do the housework afterwards." And if I thought you were sincere, I probably would have . . .

Jan: You're right.

Sam: . . . You know, it's just . . .

Jan: That never even occurred to me.

Sam: Yeah, it's just, sometimes, it would be nice to have an offer of help doing what I am doing. Like today. I was tickled . . .

Jan: Yep.

Sam: . . . you tidied up the kitchen before I got out there and started because I was figuring . . .

Jan: Um hum

Sam: . . . that would be awful nice while I was in the shower if little muffin would go ahead and straighten up the kitchen for me. At least we'd get that out of the way. And you did. And I was happy.

Jan: Well, I do try. I do try. Sam, think back to when, when we had the same schedule when we were working together . . .

Sam: Um hum.

Jan: . . . and we had the same amount of time off and so forth. Wasn't it a lot more equal doing . . .

Sam: Um.

Jan: . . . housework back then?

Sam: I suppose it was. I was . . .

Jan: So, a lot of it really is the amount of time we've got to dedicate to other things outside of our house. And right now, I've got more responsibilities outside of the house. Just because of school.

Sam: Well, it makes me wonder, though, and it's been on my mind lately, if, you know, when I go back to school and you're working, is the house gonna turn into a pigsty or am I gonna not only work part-time, take a full load of very hard classes, but also do most of the housework, too.

Jan: What I'm trying to do . . .

Sam: Or is our house just going to end up being a pigsty?

Jan: . . . is get enough money. What I'm trying to do is get enough money into the bank so that when you go back to school you're not gonna have to work. I'll be working. I'll insist on working . . .

Sam: And, work . . .

Jan: It's not a matter of whether I, whether we need it . . . And what I'm talking about Sam, is work . . .

Sam: . . . or what, you know, it's a matter of pride.

Jan: . . . work can be a second priority and school your first priority when you go back to school. Get enough money in the bank that the working won't be necessary. You can work like what I do now, when you've got the time, if it doesn't interfere with school. Do you see what I'm saying? And then I would assume that I'd take it on, you know. It's I think it's whoever's got the most amount of free time should try to pick up the slack. Anyhow, that's, you know, I, I do understand what you're saying and I can try to do more around the house.

Sam: Hmmm. I guess I just . . .

Jan: If you understand where I'm coming from, too . . .

Sam: Um hum.

Jan: What were you gonna say?

Sam: Well, I'm just saying, I remember back when you had your own place and it's like, uh, you were working, what, two hours in the morning was all . . .

Jan: And I was . . .

Sam: Seven days a week?

Jan: And I was spending most of my time at your house and we were spending most of our time together playing.

Sam: Um hum.

Jan: You know, so . . .

Sam: I guess, even though we were spending most of our time playing, I still kept my house spotless. So . . .

Jan: Forget about what my place looked like before we moved in together and think about the things since we have been together, sharing an apartment together . . .

Sam: Um hum.

Jan: . . . think about how we worked things out there. And because everything before we lived together doesn't matter.

Did you notice the many issues related to housework that are evident in this conversation? First is Sam's perception of inequality and an accompanying feeling of unfairness because he's always "doing a little bit more than half" of the housework. Second is Jan's focus on the issue of time: her perception of which of the two is the most overworked and has less time to do household chores. Third, Sam underscores two different standards for household cleanliness, twice comparing Jan's standard to a "pigsty." Underlying the discussion are feelings of self-worth (which of the two do you think feels a greater sense of worth at this early stage of their marriage?) and the denial of sex (refusing to "play") to get even.

The gender roles of this couple are reversed. The husband is responsible for doing the majority of the housework, he is the one that perceives inequality and unfairness, and he considers their conflicts over housekeeping to be greater than his wife does. Yet the issues they argue over are typical of intimate relationships that are founded on a belief in an egalitarian standard: Is the load shared, who has the time, and are housekeeping standards similar?

Changing Norms: What Has Changed?

If fewer hours are spent cleaning and maintaining homes these days, are our homes dirtier than those of our mothers? If so, how do we feel about it? Robinson and Milkie (1998) looked for the answers to these questions. They found that women's attitudes toward housework in 1995 were similar to, or *more* positive, than attitudes held in 1975. These researchers used a nationally representative sample and found that women have not given up the responsibilities of maintaining a clean home. In 1995, 62 percent of younger women reported they cleaned because they "felt good about having a clean house" (compared to 54 percent of middle-aged and 64 percent of older women). All the younger women thought that (1) their housekeeping standards were higher than those of their own mothers, (2) the typical American home is less clean than their own, and (3) typical American homes were cleaner in 1980 than in 1995, indicating a perception that homes are less clean today than they were in the past. Among these women, perceptions about cleanliness were not influenced by their ability to hire help because there was only a small difference in the percentage of women who reported having some paid help: 18 percent in 1975 and 22 percent in 1995.

In this study several factors mediated satisfaction with household cleanliness. If women were married, if they had children, and if they worked outside the home, they reported less satisfaction with household cleanliness than if they were single, childless, or homemakers. Their level of education did not influence their perceptions, but when the family household income was higher, women reported more satisfaction with the cleanliness of their homes. What is intriguing about these women's attitudes is that being married and having a husband decreased satisfaction with the cleanliness of the home, but overall, wives did not blame husbands for not contributing more to the maintenance of the home. Are gender-specific socialization patterns and normative expectations so strong as to erase blame?

Berk (1985) and DeVault (1991) are two scholars who attribute gender relations and the gendered nature of housework to the acceptance of inequality. According to this view, housework is not a neutral activity but rather is fundamentally tied to gender relations in the home. In Chapter 4 we discussed power relations between partners and how inequality may be tolerated in spite of a strong value of gender equality (Knudson-Martin and Mahoney, 1998). Women are supposedly socialized to want to serve and care for the members of their family. One of the ways this is done is through effort spent in cleaning the house, cooking, and taking care of others. When women feel that the quality of the care and service they provide does not meet their standards, they may feel dissatisfaction, frustration, guilt, or anxiety.

Children's Work

Children's Contributions to Housework

As you may have learned from your own experience, children's household work is gender typed, just as it is for adults. Gager, Cooney, and Call (1999) analyzed data from a large longitudinal study that attempted to sort out the confusion and contradiction in the literature about high school students' time spent in household labor. For example, boys and girls under the age of 19 spend about three to six hours per week on household chores according to a study by Demo and Acock (1993), and ten or more hours according to the Gager and colleagues (1999) study.

Gager and colleagues demonstrated significant gender differences in time devoted to household tasks (which included babysitting siblings): boys gave 87 percent as much time as girls when they were in the 9th grade and only 68 percent by the time they were high school seniors. Phrased another way, boys averaged two hours less per week of household work than girls in the ninth grade and almost four hours less when they were in the 12th grade. Other findings from this study include: (1) teenagers from families with three or more children spent more time in housework than teens from smaller families; (2) 12th graders living with a single parent spent about three hours more a week doing household chores than teens living with both biological parents (this finding was the same for teens living in stepfamilies, except for taking out the trash and doing yardwork, which they did less often); (3) mother's employment had no significant effect on the amount of time spent doing household chores for either 9th or 12th graders; and (4) hours spent in household work decreased for both boys and girls across the four years of high school, but the decrease was greater for boys.

Contributions to some household tasks vary by the season. For example, sibling care may increase during the summer months for youth with two working parents, and yardwork increases in the fall when there are leaves to rake (Crouter and Maguire, 1998). Regardless of the type of work, the most frequently reported conflict by parents with their teens has to do with adolescents' help with housework (Barber, 1994).

What household chores did you do while you were growing up? The primary chores children perform include washing dishes, cleaning the house, cooking, doing laundry, and caring for brothers and sisters. Preteen boys and girls both help with yardwork. Goldscheider and Waite (1991) examined data from a national sample of youth and found teenage girls did more household work than their younger sisters and brothers. When daughters were older than 18, they changed the type of work they did to include grocery shopping, childcare, and laundry, and they helped less frequently with the dishes and cleaning. When sons were age 18 and older, they contributed less help than they did when they were younger, doing less cooking and childcare than children ages 6–12. You might think that older sons paid money into the household in exchange for not helping out, but there was no evidence that older sons contributed financially to the family. Goldscheider and Waite would agree with Berk (1985) that the family is a "gender factory." Within it children perform gender-traditional tasks, learning to do—and to like doing (or not)—the tasks typically assigned to adults of their own sex.

To test whether gender differences were attributable to time spent in paid work, Gager et al. (1999) compared the amount of time teenagers spent earning money each week. As it turns out, girls spent more time in paid work than boys. Paid work made up 6.9 and 13.8 hours per week for 9th and 12th grade girls compared to 3.5 and 12.1 for 9th and 12th grade boys. Mortimer (2003) also reported that girls are more likely than their male age peers to be employed. What can we conclude? Girls do more total work, household and paid, than boys. Is that fair? Does it train females as adults to shoulder more of the housework than their male partners?

The chores children and adolescents do at home can be grouped into two categories: self-care and family care. Parents' assignment of these chores to children serves several purposes. Most obvious is the fact that having children do chores helps get the housework done. But parents also assign self-care chores because they believe children's participation in such work (making their own lunch, cleaning their room) helps develop self-worth, independence, and a sense of responsibility. Family care tasks such as babysitting siblings or setting or clearing the dinner table demonstrate care and concern for others, and parents encourage such tasks because they promote prosocial behavior (Cooney and Gable, 2001).

A parent's ideas about task allocation do not always turn out for the best, however. One of your authors remembers that when her children were school-aged she got the bright idea that every morning a different child (there were five) would make *all* the lunches, one for each child. Five children, five days, everything evened out. But you can guess the outcome. Every day there were complaints: "You didn't put enough peanut butter in my sandwich"; "I hate mayonnaise"; "I wanted Doritos instead of potato chips!" Within two weeks the children were packing their own lunches.

Adolescent Employment

The literature regarding teenage employment is ambiguous. For example, *The Report on the Youth Labor Force* (U. S. Bureau of Labor Statistics, 2000b) found among the teens they surveyed (15 to 17-year-olds), an average of 28 percent of white, 13 percent of black, and 15 percent of Latino teens worked during the school year. Manning (1990), on the other hand, reported that about 90 percent of U.S. adolescents in the 11th and 12th grades worked for pay some time during the school year. Mortimer (2003) reported that 63–65 percent of boys and girls ages 14 to 18 in her study worked during their high school years. These reports differ because each study is based on a different methodology: The questions asking about employment are different, the age range of the teenagers in the studies differ, and in some studies adults were asked about the teens' employment and in others only teens themselves were queried. Most studies agree with the higher number, estimating that 80–90 percent of high school youth are employed at some time during the school year (Mortimer, 2004, personal communication).

Working means adolescents have less time for family and friendships. Teens who work long hours or night shifts may experience chronic fatigue and exhaustion. These youths are more independent of their parents and more likely to increase their use of alcohol, cigarettes, and illegal drugs (Bachman and Schulenberg, 1993). The primary factors affecting positive versus negative outcomes for working youth seem to be the number of hours spent in actual work. Generally, the optimum threshold of paid work appears to be about 20 hours per week (Mortimer, 2003).

Adolescent employment has benefits beyond a paycheck. Teenagers can develop a sense of efficacy, enhance their self-esteem, and learn to deal with challenges and obstacles as they make the transition to adulthood.

Does working affect the parent-teen relationship? One longitudinal study found the benefits of work experience for boys included greater feelings of closeness to their fathers, especially if they were learning skills that would be useful in their future employment. Closeness to fathers was not evident for girls, who, in some cases, grew less close to their fathers if they worked long hours (Mortimer, 2003). Some research finds working teens spend less time in contact with family members, spend less time doing housework and have more disagreements with parents if they work long hours. Yet there seems to be no firm evidence that the supportive relationship between parents and their teens is diminished. Most parents feel that their teenagers are enacting appropriate behavior for their life stage when they get a paying job. Children are gaining autonomy and independence from parents and learning life skills. These characteristics give parents a sense of satisfaction about their child rearing strategies.

Effects of Unemployment on the Family

Up to this point we have discussed the effects of employment on family members. But what happens in the family when the primary wage earner experiences sudden and unexpected job loss?[3] A person's status and identity are closely associated with the paid work that he or she performs. If one does not work, status and identity must come from other sources. Are there other sources?

Work as a Source of Status and Self-Esteem

In the not-too-distant past, family lineage was the principal source of a person's status and sense of self. Ancestors, kin, lineage—traditionally, these were the foundation of an individual's self-esteem and status; they provided both the place and the regard held by others within the family's larger community. Former president Harry S. Truman often talked of his grandfather, "the 'big man' in his background who made his own way in the world, on will and nerve, who had seen the Great West when it was still wild, who had played a part in history; and who—of course—came home always to Missouri. With such a grandfather, a boy could hardly imagine himself a nobody" (McCullough, 1992, 42).

Americans have always been a peripatetic people, but during the twentieth century high levels of residential mobility, especially within the growing middle class, helped reduce lineage as a source of status. Greater than that, however, is the particular American ideology that stresses the importance of independence, personal responsibility, and accountability. It is the ideal that if men or women are successful in life (as measured by education, occupation, income, or high regard within the community) it is because of their hard work, intelligence, and personal ingenuity, with a little luck thrown in.

Personal accomplishment, however, is always tied to the social system within which people are embedded. Wilson (1996) argues this connection when he posits that labor-force attachment is shaped by the social conditions affecting specific aspects of the self: specifically, self-worth. Within the framework of American macrosystem ideology, failure becomes personal. It follows that a lack of success can be attributed to personal characteristics such as laziness or low intelligence and, if the critics are kind, perhaps bad luck.

Within this ideological framework, being out of work has devastating repercussions on a person's physical health and self-esteem as well as his or her financial status. When it is the family's primary wage earner who is out of work, the entire family must adjust to the circumstances of loss of income and status. Newman (1988) studied a group of high-status white-collar managers who lost their jobs during the early 1980s as companies downsized or replaced highly paid, middle-aged managers with younger, well-trained, less-expensive workers. Her analysis of downward social mobility described the emotional turmoil that extended periods of unsuccessful job searching created for some formerly successful men:

> Men accustomed to the bustle of the office, the pressure of deadlines, the feeling of purpose and accomplishment, berate themselves for sitting at home 'wasting time' . . . the idleness is paradoxically pressured. Every moment spent 'doing nothing' is a moment in which the clock is ticking. Mortgage payments are due, banks are calling for credit cards in arrears, savings are slipping away. Anxiety alternates with lethargy, sleep disturbance with slow panic. (63)

According to Newman's research, for formerly comfortable families facing sudden unemployment and downward mobility, loss of the family home is the "watershed event" (102). Home ownership is a marker of economic independence and stability, and its loss suggests that all of that is slipping away.

Coping With Unemployment

What are the consequences of loss of esteem and status to the family? What are the adjustments that family members must make to get them through the unemployed experience successfully? Voydanoff (1983) raised these questions in a classic essay on the consequences of unemployment. After studying the hardships associated with unemployment and analyzed their effects on families, she concluded that financial hardship is ameliorated by several factors, including eligibility for unemployment benefits, length of unemployment, and the income of the family prior to unemployment. Was the unemployment unexpected and sudden, as when a manufacturing plant suddenly closes its gates, or was there time to plan and prepare for the job loss, as in the case of a union strike? If health insurance continues or if there is a severance pay package or a pension to draw on, the family's hardship is ameliorated, at least temporarily. If the family has savings, or if it is relatively debt-free, financial stress is reduced.

As important as financial hardship is, one of the most devastating aspects of unemployment is the loss of a major social role for the unemployed wage earner. As we have mentioned, work in America is closely associated with one's identity, sense of social importance, and self-esteem (Rubin, 1994). Voydanoff points out that work is also a major source of social integration. A major portion of every workday is spent with coworkers who are also friends and colleagues. It is the place where one's sense of accomplishment and value are recognized; when a job is lost, friendships suffer.

Are there ways in which family members can protect themselves from the psychological devastation that comes with long-term unemployment? Voydanoff proposes several mediating factors that can help reduce stress and discomfort until new employment is found. One important factor is how the family **defines the situation**. That is, what are the meanings that become attached to the unemployment situation by family members? If the job loss is defined as temporary or anticipated, some preparation time is available. Construction workers in Minnesota, for example, know that during each winter season they may experience a layoff and can prepare for these months of unemployment by saving for the tough times or finding part-time work. Also important in defining the situation is determining who is seen as responsible for the job loss. If the worker is blamed for the job loss and defined by family members—including spouse, children, in-laws, or other relatives—as irresponsible, lazy, or incompetent, family stress will be high and the family's adjustment to the situation will take longer.

Is the job loss accompanied by a personal sense of failure? This self-feeling is a second important factor in the adjustment process. Men whose primary identity comes from a traditional provider role—a strong belief that the husband/father must be the one who provides the family's livelihood—may have deep feelings of failure and shame when this role is lost (Rubin, 1994). On the other hand, men who hold egalitarian gender roles and feel that the family's support is a shared effort are less likely to experience feelings of failure. Many families create a support system around them that helps soften the effects of unemployment. If a network of friends, family members, and neighbors is available to help, it is easier for the family to get through the tough times. A social network can offer moral support and encouragement and assist in practical ways such as giving advice, providing job leads, and providing childcare or transportation to job interviews. If such a network is not available, social isolation exacerbates the family's reduced well-being.

Yet another factor related to successful coping has to do with the characteristics of the family itself: How cohesive is it? How adaptable are the family members? What is the authority pattern within the family? Families in which members share responsibility for the well-being of the family and hold less traditional gender roles are likely to cope with unemployment easier than other families. Stress is less likely to be debilitating if the family is flexible and reorganizes family roles, establishes and maintains cohesiveness, and keeps communication channels open. Finally, those family members who remember that unemployment occurs within a social context that is (usually) beyond the control of any individual person are able to cope best. If unemployment can be viewed as an opportunity to reexamine and adjust personal goals, to take advantage of offers for retraining for a more fulfilling occupation, and is accepted as a growth experience, the stress associated with job loss will be lessened. These qualities contribute to individual and family resilience.

Behavioral Reactions to Unemployment

It is important to note the consequences of family members' behavior during times of economic crisis. When the family's primary wage earner loses his or her job, a change often occurs in the entire family's work effort. For example, a spouse may get a job, or increase the number of his or her work hours. Adolescents in the household may get jobs to help the family's financial situation. Newman (1988) found that children in downwardly mobile families felt the need to tighten their connections to the family. They wanted to support their parents and help out as much as possible. Additionally, they tried to hide their new situation from long-term friends and outsiders because they no longer could meet the standards set by their peers. The number and ages of children mediate unemployment in both negative and positive ways. Having several young children in the family may inhibit a wife from finding employment when her husband loses his job, whereas having teenagers who contribute to the family's resources is a relief.

In a now-classic study of children of the Great Depression, Elder (1974) found that very young children were less likely to be affected by their father's unemployment than older children were. Elder found that there were many confounding effects of deprivation. For example, significant economic loss was associated with irritability and arbitrary disciplinary practices on the part of fathers. Unemployed fathers were more explosive and harsh in their discipline when economic deprivation was great, compared to fathers whose situations were not as bad. A father often lost status and authority in the eyes of his adolescent children if his unemployment was lengthy, the interactions with his children were poor, and older children contributed money to the household from jobs they held. Young school-aged boys expressed hostile feelings toward their fathers if their fathers were erratic in punishing them and their families were undergoing the greatest level of economic deprivation. On the other hand, adolescent boys in the hardest-hit families benefited from new family responsibilities. Overall, sustained unemployment did affect the quality of fathers' parenting, and children whose fathers became depressed and withdrawn from the family had the most difficult time.

Recent research has shown that economic strain disrupts the parenting of both mothers and fathers, an important finding considering the large number of mothers in the workplace today (Simons et al., 1994). This finding calls attention to the effects that one subsystem has on another within the family. Unemployment or economic stress causes hostility or irritability between parents (the marital subsystem) that tends to spill over to their interactions with children (the parent-child subsystem). In turn, children emulate their parents' hostility with each other, and thus the sibling subsystem is affected. The effects of such sustained interaction puts children at risk for developing a hostile interaction style with others, and it increases their feelings of depression and worthlessness (Conger, Conger, and Elder, 1994).

Heightened use of alcohol or illegal substances, an increase in the instances of domestic violence, destabilized self-images, and feelings of failure are often consequences of long-term job loss. Chapter 9 will discuss some of these consequences. Hostility and irritable behavior reduces marital quality and increases marital instability (Conger et al., 1990; Conger and Conger, 2002). Reduced finances often result in increased isolation of the family because the usual recreational activities are no longer affordable. Especially among husbands who hold more traditional and less flexible gender-role attitudes, resentment may arise when a wife goes to work to help meet expenses. A new degree of independence may develop in teenagers who bring money into the household and then resent being told they must still obey the rules for curfew and other parental rules. It takes strong family ties and a high level of cohesion and flexibility among all family members to withstand the stress and negative emotions accompanying a lengthy period of unemployment.

William Julius Wilson (1987) conducted extensive research on high-risk inner-city neighborhoods, where he noted that the lack of jobs and high unemployment denies children the benefit of seeing adults engaged in disciplined work habits and productive routines (including getting up and getting to work on time). Such routines serve to model appropriate behaviors along with their utilitarian function of earning a livelihood. When working adults are absent, street activities and the peer system remain as principal models for children to emulate.

The preceding discussion illustrates how all levels within the ecological systems perspective can be applied when analyzing situations of unemployment. Insofar as the family is successful (or not) in its adaptation and problem-solving processes involving the marital, parent-child, and sibling subsystems, relations in the family microsystem are directly affected by job loss. Mesosystem interactions are involved in understanding the ways work is terminated and the degree of support available to the family. The exosystem can facilitate adjustment through benefits offered and the degree to which institutions (such as state agencies, or religious and other community institutions that offer unemployment insurance or job training) become part of the problem-solving process. Finally, ideologies and values within the macrosystem ("a good man provides for his family"; "a man doesn't do a woman's work") profoundly affect the adjustment that family members make to a long-term job loss.

Retirement

So what happens when a spouse or a couple decide to leave active, paid employment? Leaving the workforce has a variety of repercussions for the family, which by retirement age usually includes the couple and their "launched" children. An increasing amount of information is available on aging family members, and in this section we report the research on the end of employment.

Patterns of Retirement

One contribution to the retirement literature is a typology of retirement patterns developed by Brubaker (1985). He distinguished four patterns of retirement based on the work experience of each spouse. **Traditional retirement** occurs when only the husband was in the paid labor force; **dissynchronized husband initially** is a pattern that occurs when both spouses work but the husband retires before his wife; **dissynchronized wife initially** involves two working spouses but the wife retires first; and the **synchronized** or **dual** pattern occurs when both spouses are employed and both retire at the same time.

Each of these patterns has benefits as well as potential drawbacks for the retired couple. For example, we know that most spouses opt for synchronized or dual retirement if possible, and couples express higher marital satisfaction when both spouses retire at the same time. However, the dual pattern may be problematic if the marriage is not a good one and spouses have all that extra time with each other. In the dissynchronized husband initially pattern, wives' continued labor force participation is associated with elevated levels of conflict for husbands (Davey and Szinovacz, 2004) and wives (Moen, Kim, and Hofmeister, 2001). Further, if wives' work requires long hours (and their pay is good), husbands report lower marital quality after their retirement. According to Myers and Booth (1996), "Any sign of a breadwinning role reversal appears to decrease marital quality when the husband retires" (352). Some wives with traditionally retired husbands report a loss of personal freedom. They find husbands are "underfoot," and they resent the interference and freely offered advice about how to do the household chores they have been doing for years (Clarke, 2003; Ekerdt and Vinick, 1991).

When Smith and Moen (2004) examined retirement satisfaction, they found that the degree to which a spouse was influential in the retirement decision was related to his or her satisfaction with retirement:

- Retired wives reported more satisfaction with their retirement when their husbands did *not* play a key role in their decision to retire.

- Husbands of retired wives reported greater satisfaction when they had *little* influence on their wives' retirement decision.

- Retired husbands were more satisfied when their wives *were* influential in their decision to retire.

- Wives of retired husbands were more satisfied with retirement when their husbands perceived that they *were* influential in the decision to retire.

Based on this study, it appears that women need to make up their own minds regarding if and when to retire, without undue influence from husbands. Husbands, on the other hand, are more satisfied after retirement when wives help make the decision. Three other factors are associated with retirement satisfaction: the couple's good health, an adequate income, and, especially for the husband, plans to do other things after retirement.

Reasons for Retiring

The motives for retiring from paid work vary. Some workers are forced to retire because of a disability or injury (service workers have a particularly high rate of disability) (Hayward, Hardy, and Grady, 1989). Poor health or a spouse's poor health makes retirement appealing or necessary for others. Couples who enjoy each other's company may choose dual retirement in order to spend time together before their health becomes a problem. On the other hand, couples in habitual conflict may delay retirement so as not to have to spend much time together (Szinovacz, 2000). Finally, retirement may be chosen because a couple has accumulated enough resources to finance their old age. Depending on the resources and perceived needs, this choice may occur early in midlife (usually after age 50), or anytime thereafter. Retirement age is correlated with occupational prestige. According to Hardy and Shuey (2000), retirement tends to be delayed for professionals, managers, and salespersons, while clerical workers, skilled, and semi-skilled workers retire earlier.

Retirement and the Quality of Marriage

As long as most couples follow the social norm that women marry men older than themselves, and as long as women enter the workforce in large numbers and have opportunities to develop meaningful careers, the timing of retirement may be problematic. This situation promotes the dissynchronized husband initially pattern of retirement, affecting marital quality in negative ways. Wives may resist leaving the workforce (and all of the social networks, income, prestige, and status accompanying it) when their older and possibly less healthy husbands retire (Cooney and Dunne, 2001) and pressure them to retire also.

The marital relationship improves after retirement for some couples because of (Szinovacz, 1995):

- A reduction in work-related stress.

- A reduction in conflict that was generated by differences in attitudes regarding the wife's working if she was employed.

- An ability to implement long-awaited retirement plans—i.e., to travel or move to a more desirable location now that the couple is no longer dependent on places of employment.

A reduction in commitments and more available time with each other may contribute to greater companionship and intimacy. Contacts with adult children and grandchildren may also increase (Szinovacz and Davey, 2001; Ward, 1993). Moen and her colleagues (2001) found that couples who were retired for two or more years enjoyed higher marital quality than either those who were not retired or those who were recent retirees (less than two years).

Plans to move and change residence after retirement are not uncommon. Among the 108 retired couples studied by Myers and Booth (1996) almost a quarter (23 percent) changed their residence, and 11 percent moved to another community. Where retired couples choose to live after they retire is important to the well-being of both spouses. This is particularly true for women after the death of their spouse. Hong and Duff (1994) studied several retirement communities and found that an important predictor of widows' adjustment and life satisfaction was the marital composition of the retirement community in which the couple had moved. Widows living in communities with a relatively high proportion of nonmarried to married people engaged in more social activities and reported greater life satisfaction than those surrounded by mostly married persons. In general, social ties reduce psychological distress and help maintain physical and psychological well-being during the retirement years (Hays et al., 1998).

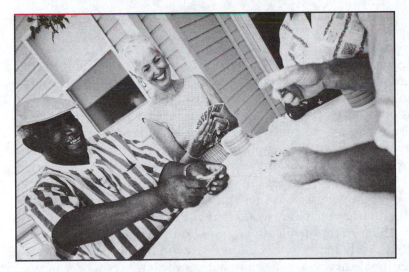

After the death of a spouse old friendship ties may be strengthened and new ones created. Friendship networks provide social support, an important source of well-being and identity reinforcement in old age.

Retired but Still Working

Note that there is a difference between occupational retirement and withdrawal from the labor force (Ekerdt and DeViney, 1990). Many workers leave their place of employment, collecting 401k or pension payments, and happily turn to other employment, retrain for another occupation, or turn their hobby into a business. Military service personnel can retire after the requisite 20 years, at middle age, and begin a second career. During poor economic times or when corporations merge, older workers are the most likely to be downsized, cut back, or let go. These are the workers who are most vulnerable to a forced early retirement. You may find them greeting you in Wal-Mart or bagging your groceries at your local market, replacing the teenagers who worked that job five years ago.

The Big Picture: Family and Work in the Larger Society

Up to this point in the chapter our focus has been on individual families. Obviously, individual families are embedded in a larger environmental context where forces operate that are beyond the control of any one family. Natural disasters such as floods, fires, hurricanes, and mudslides are the first examples that come to mind that can cause devastation to large numbers of families. However, a human-made disaster occurs when the nation experiences an economic recession with consequences that include large job losses from factory closings, downsizing within large corporations, outsourcing of jobs to other countries, or the bankruptcy of family farms and businesses. Our object here is to call attention to the important juncture between the individual family system and the larger environment in which it is embedded—in the exo- and macrosystems. What are these connections, and what are their consequences?

Exosystem Factors

One connection that links individual families with the totality of families is reflected in the kinds of laws and social policies enacted by local, state, and national governments within the exosystem. For example, what would be the consequences of a government policy that adequately funded quality childcare in communities where childcare is scarce? For one thing, children who are currently enrolled in less-than-optimum childcare programs would have quality care within an appropriate learning environment. Single mothers trying to move from welfare to jobs under the welfare reform laws (discussed in early chapters) would have fewer worries about the well-being of their young children, since childcare issues represent a key barrier in their pursuit of work (Arendell, 2000). Parents who seldom see each other because they work split shifts in order for one parent to be at home with preschool children or during afterschool hours would both be able to take day jobs, giving the entire family more time together. How many families would be affected? According to one national survey, among married couples in two-earner households, 25 percent have at least one spouse working in the evening or on a night or rotating shift (Cherlin, 1996).

Corporate Policies. What about family and medical leave programs? Many workplaces strive to facilitate new or growing families. In 2003, for example, the Microsoft Corporation offered women a three-month paid maternity leave with the option of two additional months without pay. Returning at the end of three months meant a woman could return to her specific job; returning after five months guaranteed a job at the same level and pay but not necessarily in the same position. Fathers at Microsoft got four weeks' paid leave. Procter and Gamble Corporation offers employees a childcare leave of absence (unpaid) when maternity leave of absence ends, which can last up through the child's first birthday.

Not all workplaces provide workers with parental leave, whether paid or unpaid. The Family and Medical Leave Act (FMLA), the federal mandate that provides employees with up to 12 workweeks of unpaid, job-protected leave a year, applies only to public agencies, including state, local, and federal employers, local education agencies (schools), and private sector employers who employed 50 or more workers for at least 20 workweeks in the current or preceding calendar year (Compliance Guide to the Family and Medical Leave Act, 2002). This leaves about 59 percent of working mothers and 51 percent of working fathers who do not qualify for FMLA. Even when it is available, 78 percent of workers who needed to take a leave for medical or family purposes in 2002 declined to do so because they could not afford unpaid leave (Henk, 2003).

What about the relationship between the business community and families? The business segment within the exosystem directly influences families through the type and abundance of jobs offered, the requisite training they require, and the wage levels that accompany the jobs. Workplace policies regarding issues such as promotion, vacation and sick leave, relocation expenses, and parental leave affect how workers balance the demands of work, personal, and family life. Some negative repercussions may stem from policies that favor family life if nonparent employees see parental benefits as unfair. One example is reported in the "Did You Know?" section at the beginning of this chapter.

Some workplace policies are regulated by law and do not vary much from community to community (minimum wage, family and medical leave, etc.). Other policies and programs are up to the discretion of individual employers and may be shaped by the geographic location of the community and community characteristics, interests, and goals. One of your authors attended graduate school in rural Pennsylvania where many employers gave workers a day off (and sometimes more) during deer hunting season because of its popularity in that region. Some employers are recognized as being "family friendly" because they offer provisions that benefit families, such as maternity, paternal and family leave, flexible work hours, health insurance for workers and their families/partners, and childcare benefits and supports (e.g., referral services). Many offer discount meals in the corporate cafeteria and free sodas, bottled water, coffee, and so on in the lounge. All of the 2003 top 100 companies surveyed for *Working Mothers* magazine offer flextime, and 98 percent offer elder care resources and references (compared to 20 percent nationwide) (2003, p. 99). Although these types of benefits are expensive for employers, they are thought to pay off in terms of heightened worker productivity and retention, as well as contributing to workers' job satisfaction (Piotrkowski et al., 1993).

The Economy. Economic fluctuations in the larger society leave their mark on families. When the economy booms, jobs are plentiful and the unemployment rate goes down. During boom times, demands for workers increase, drawing wives and mothers into the workforce and employing hard-to-place workers who have limited education levels and job skills. This is what happened in the mid-1990s. Both individual workers and their families benefit from increased cash flow, but so do other systems in the community. For example, families may be more willing to support tax increases for improving schools when they feel economically secure. A good business economy may mean more tax revenue for a community, leading to greater discretionary spending on things such as improving parks, roads, and sidewalks or building recreation facilities.

In other decades (the 1930s and the 1980s), high rates of layoffs, capital reorganization, and downsizing has been associated with a marked downturn in the economy and rising unemployment rates. The early years of the twenty-first century were years of economic downturn, job loss, with a rise in the number of unemployed. A negative aspect of the economic downturn of the early 2000s associated within the exosystem was the decision of a growing number of corporate executives to export production and service jobs to countries where labor costs were low. Many working-class and middle-class workers found themselves unemployed not because of lack of education or training, but because of the lack of actual jobs.

We wrote about how long-term unemployment affects family behavior at the individual and family level. What is its effect on the family as an institution? During the 1930s Depression, the unemployment rate was about 25 percent, the marriage rate slowed, and the birthrate dropped. Such effects are not short-lived. Among cohorts born between 1905 and 1909 who came of age during the Depression, one in five adults ended up childless because of postponing marriage or parenthood during those tough economic times (Wolf, 1999). Today, about 10 percent of elderly persons are childless because many could not or did not marry during their prime marriage and family-building years. These older adults cannot turn to grown children for support and care, as is common for many elderly persons. Even temporary downturns in the economy can have serious consequences that last a lifetime.

Economic downturns affect communities and neighborhoods, too. When businesses fail, young people leave and small communities die. In many rural agriculture communities in Iowa, Minnesota, and the Dakotas, economic downturns changed many exosystems. Some small communities that used to have their own school system were forced to consolidate schools within counties because of the drastically reduced population of children. This consolidation had major and minor consequences. To the sadness of loyal sports fans, it killed old rivalries between communities that had existed for decades, children were bussed farther distances to get to school, and teenagers had to drive longer distances to socialize with friends and participate in afterschool activities. These kinds of changes affect family life as well as impair residents' sense of community.

At the end of the twentieth century, retirement was taking place at earlier ages because of government policies that funded Social Security and corporations that offered what were thought to be solid pension (401k) plans. However, the downturn of 2001–2003 brought many retired workers back into the workforce as they watched their pension funds decline along with the stock market. While many couples begin to plan and save for their retirement years during the early years of their working lives, doing so does not always prove to be a safety net. It is possible for families to suffer severe economic loss when the retirement plan they depend on dissolves because the company they invested in declares bankruptcy or suffers great losses due to fraudulent business practices, as did the Enron Corporation at the end of 2001.

The effects of policies designed to help troubled families cannot be judged to be beneficial and effective or negative and harmful until some time has elapsed after they are enacted. For example, it will be a few years before the actual benefits (or costs) of the 1996 welfare reform that was designed to get recipients off welfare and into the workforce are forthcoming. In the interim, family members must change their behaviors to cope with and adapt to the new policies, rules, requirements, opportunities, or burdens posed within their community. Such changes, in turn, have consequences that are the cause of further change. If welfare policies encourage and pay workers to retrain or obtain a GED (or higher) degree even though benefits are reduced, eventually a more qualified worker will enter the labor force. However, if retraining policies and opportunities once begun are discontinued, if there are few jobs available in the community for undertrained workers, and if welfare benefits are discontinued, hope is dispelled and the well-being of families is jeopardized. People living in small towns in rural America are especially vulnerable because of reduced opportunities (Henderson et al., 2002).

Why is the family the most important institution connected to the nation's economy? Because it is within the family that individuals are socialized and learn to be workers. Our capitalist economic system cannot function without some ancillary institution that "prepares" workers, that is, teaches them the importance of promptness, dependability, and in some cases passivity and acceptance. That institution is the family. (In American society the educational system also does this—but its role is to supplement what the family does or does not do.) Ruling out the choice of engaging in illegal behavior, one of the strongest motivations people have to engage in work-related behavior is to earn a wage, for individuals must find a way to feed, house, and clothe themselves and those they love. However, success in the modern work world cannot be achieved unless people behave in certain ways. Have they learned self-discipline? Have they learned to be responsible (e.g., show up on time, put in the required amount of hours, etc.)? Do they take pride in the job they do? To have these characteristics means that workers have adopted a "work ethic." American families have succeeded for the most part in transmitting such an ethic to their children across many generations. So much so that in our modern age, American workers put in more hours at work than workers in Japan, Norway, France, and Germany (International Labor Organization, 2003, 90).

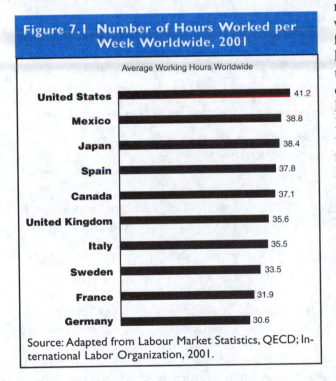

Figure 7.1 Number of Hours Worked per Week Worldwide, 2001

Average Working Hours Worldwide

United States	41.2
Mexico	38.8
Japan	38.4
Spain	37.8
Canada	37.1
United Kingdom	35.6
Italy	35.5
Sweden	33.5
France	31.9
Germany	30.6

Source: Adapted from Labour Market Statistics, QECD; International Labor Organization, 2001.

Social Class Differences

An important aspect of all social systems is their social class composition. A discussion of the connections between family and work cannot overlook the differences between and within these groups. Scholars have spent a great deal of time studying the poor and the middle class, have given less attention to the working class, and have pretty much ignored the rich. Perhaps the lack of investigations of the wealthy in America is because the rich can successfully protect their families from the observant eye of the researcher. Family members in the middle class have been more willing to provide information for scholarly research—a welcome, if limiting, base of information.

What we do know about the wealthiest families in America is that their economic position has improved over the past two decades. In 1980, the richest 20 percent of families earned 41 percent of all income; in 1996 this figure had risen to 46.8 percent. Contrast this to the poorest 20 percent of families, who earned 5.3 percent of all income in 1980. By 1996 this figure had decreased to 4.2 percent (Teachman, et al., 2000). Look at what has happened to the richest of Americans, the top 1 percent: Between 1995 and 1997 their average after-tax income increased by 31 percent, while the after-tax income of the bottom 90 percent rose less than 4 percent (Center on Budget and Policy Priorities, 2000). Table 7.2 shows this income discrepancy for each income quartile for the years 1977 and 1997.

While much progress was made during the last half of the twentieth century to mitigate gender, race, and ethnic inequity, class divisions have deepened. One reviewer sums up this situation: "To predict the life chances of a child born in the United States in 1998, it is more important to know the parents' socioeconomic status than the child's race or gender" (Bogenschneider, 2000, 1148).

Table 7.2 Income Disparity, 1977–1999			
Household Groups	**Average After-Tax Income (Estimated)**		**Change***
	1977	**1999**	
One-fifth with lowest income	$ 10,000	$ 8,800	12.0%
Next lowest one-fifth	$ 22,100	$ 20,000	9.5
Middle one-fifth	$ 32,400	$ 31,400	3.1
Next highest one-fifth	$ 42,600	$ 45,100	5.9
One-fifth with highest income	$ 74,000	$102,300	38.3
(1% with highest income)	$234,700	$515,600	119.7

*Figures are adjusted for inflation.
Adapted from Phillips, K. (2002).

A now-classic study of working-class families was conducted by Lillian Rubin in 1976 and updated in 1994. The new publication contained a discussion of the changes that took place in the social context for working-class families from 1972 to 1992. Her data, collected from face-to-face interviews with working-class husbands and wives, brings into sharp focus the hardships associated with the uncertainties of working as unskilled (sometimes skilled) laborers and the misfortunes associated with unemployment. Values, traditions, and behaviors of those in the working class (such as less emphasis put on educational attainment) serve to reinforce the tenuous position they hold within the American economy. Working-class jobs are seldom viewed as "careers" (a term that implies the possibility for movement up to or near the top of a profession or field). Working-class jobs may be skilled or unskilled, but they are jobs that rarely change from the time one is hired until one quits or is fired (included are plumbers, electricians, painters, roofers, garbage collectors, etc.).

In the past decade many excellent books have been written on the American poor. Several of these are listed at the end of this chapter, as suggested readings. In 2001, 11.7 percent of Americans were living below the poverty line. This figure varied by race, however: 9.9 percent of whites lived below the poverty level, as did 22.7 percent of blacks, 21.4 percent of Latinos, and 10.2 percent of Asians (U.S. Bureau of the Census, 2001a).

Poverty as a Result of Structural Factors in the Macrosystem

Who are the poor in America? Those most likely to be "living on the edge" (Rank, 2001) include children living in single-parent families often headed by women, the elderly, and those who are poorly educated, have low job skills, have ill health, have work disabilities, are cognitively impaired, or are drug and alcohol abusers. Societal factors within the macrosystem (such as racism, sexism, and capitalism) are thought to contribute as well. In what ways, you ask? Corporations that move their manufacturing centers from the inner city to the suburbs, or to less-developed countries where wages are lower, take away jobs—jobs ordinarily held by the working people of those cities. If a wage-earning worker cannot travel to a job because the community lacks an adequate mass transportation system, and few job opportunities are available where he or she lives, normative life course events such as getting married and having children are likely to be postponed. When there are few opportunities for work and normal life events are deterred, deviant behavior is likely to increase. What was once a viable community suffers from lack of resources, and middle-class residents move to more desirable places. Thus important role models and community leaders are lost as well (Wilson, 1987, 1996).

An excellent example of this situation comes from the research that William Julius Wilson conducted on the West Side of Chicago. Writing about a black neighborhood in the inner city, here is what he reported:

Two large factories anchored the economy of the West Side neighborhood in its good days—the Hawthorne plant of Western Electric, which employed over 43,000 workers; and an International Harvester plant with 14,000 workers. The world headquarters for Sears, Roebuck and Company was located there, providing another 10,000 jobs. The neighborhood also had a Copenhagen snuff plant, a Sunbeam factory, and a Zenith factory, a Dell Farm food market, an Alden's catalog store, and a U.S. Post Office bulk station. But conditions rapidly changed, Harvester closed its doors in the late 1960s. Sears moved most of its offices to the Loop in downtown Chicago in 1973; a catalog distribution center with a workforce of 3,000 initially remained in the neighborhood but was relocated outside of the state of Illinois in 1987. The Hawthorne plant gradually phased out its operations and finally shut down in 1984.

The departure of the big plants triggered the demise or exodus of the smaller stores, the banks, and other businesses that relied on the wages paid by the large employers. . . . It has been estimated that the community lost 75 percent of its business establishments from 1960 to 1970 alone. . . . In 1986, North Lawndale, with a population of over 66,000, had only one bank and one supermarket; but it was also home to forty-eight state lottery agents, fifty currency exchanges, and ninety-nine liquor stores and bars. (Wilson, 1998, 168)

Racism and sexism work to suppress the talents and opportunities for minorities and women (sometimes men) of all racial/ethnic backgrounds because these prejudices influence who gets hired, who gets promoted, who gets to live in the neighborhood, and so on. This is not to say that there have not been advances in alleviating racism and sexism in the past few decades. Just compare the behavior of Americans in 1950 (read some old novels, see some old films, examine the old laws) with behavior today. Clearly, at the beginning of the twenty-first century Americans are more likely to espouse and uphold the values of freedom and equality that they cherish for all people. But while norms, laws, and behaviors are becoming less racist and less sexist, class differences are widening. The gap between the wealthy and the poor grew during the past two decades, as the wealthy increased their riches and the poor lost out.

It is possible for an individual or family to be poor after having once lived in more affluent conditions. For instance, middle- and upper-class youth may become addicted to drugs or alcohol and slip into a lifestyle not commensurate with their family of orientation. Or a once stable middle-class family may experience job loss or health problems and suddenly lose their home, car, and other valued possessions. A major motion picture released in 2001, *John Q*, tells such a story. Rank (2001) has calculated the odds of such a slide into poverty based on the Panel Study of Income Dynamics (PSID) data obtained from a national longitudinal study. He reports that two out of three Americans will experience at least one year of poverty during adulthood (between ages 20 and 85), with a higher rate for blacks. This experience will typically last for one or two consecutive years. Unfortunately, he also predicted that once a person has experienced poverty, he or she is likely to be poor again at some point in life.

About one in three (34 percent) American children under the age of 18 will experience at least one year of poverty during their lifetime. This figure is higher for nonwhite children. In 1998, 10.6 percent of white, nonHispanic children under the age of 18 were poor, as were 36.7 percent of black children, 34.4 percent of Latino children, and 18 percent of Asian and Pacific Islander children (Seccombe, 2000). At the other end of the life cycle, Rank (2001) reports that 40 percent of those between ages 60 and 90 will experience at least one year of poverty.

It is true that one could say "there is poverty, then there is poverty." For example, a college student living on $8,000 a year in a scummy apartment, eating mostly carrots and potatoes while working her way through school, lives in poverty. However, she is gaining the education that will likely keep her from a similar lifestyle in the future. A divorced mother or an unmarried teen mother may also experience years of living poor before being able to increase her education level, get a well-paying job, or (re)marry. While most people are poor for relatively short periods of time, it was learned from the PSID data that 4.5 percent of the participants lived below the poverty line for each of the study's 13 years (Blank, 1997). These were people who had low levels of **human capital** (the resources that facilitate interaction within social institutions). Education, job skills, job training, and personal characteristics all help create an individual's human capital. Research findings show that the effects of human capital on the risk of poverty are substantial. When workers lack marketable job skills and have low levels of education, they are at a much greater risk of experiencing poverty.

Summary

This chapter presented an analysis of family behavior associated with paid work in the labor force and unpaid work at home. What is the greatest change in the last four decades related to work and the family? There is a simple answer: Wives and mothers have entered the paid workforce in large numbers. At the end of the twentieth century 59 percent of women worked outside the home for pay, and 72 percent of employed mothers of children under the age of 18 worked full-time. We discussed the childcare options for mothers who are in the paid labor force and learned that many suffer from guilt and anxiety over the well-being of their children when in actuality research shows that children rarely suffer negative consequences from nonmaternal childcare.

What are some of the consequences that follow women's entry into the workforce? For some, housework standards have lowered (but not necessarily the desire to have, and the pleasure taken from, having a clean house). Wives spend fewer hours each week cleaning and cooking, while husbands' time spent on household chores and childcare increased. However, the feminist ideal that an egalitarian norm would emerge between two wage-earning spouses concerning "who does what around the house" has not yet materialized.

The reciprocal nature of two microsystems, work and family, is conceptualized as "spillover" or "interactive." The effect these two systems have on each other is incontrovertible. What happens at home affects the workplace, and vice versa. This mutuality is as true for adolescent workers as it is for adults. When teenagers work, they have the opportunity to learn valuable skills and values. If they work too many hours, however, these benefits may be overshadowed by the adoption of risk behaviors, including too much independence and use of illegal substances.

Family boundaries do not keep outside influences from penetrating the attitudes, emotions, and behaviors of individual members. When the state or national economy improves, everyone seems to benefit, even those who find it hard to get a job under ordinary conditions. When the economy declines, many individuals and family members are affected. Parents may lose their jobs; some young people delay marriage or childbearing or may move back with their parents and give up the apartment they rent; others quit school. Job loss has debilitating effects on self-esteem, the marital relationship, and parent-child relationships.

When it comes time to leave the paid labor force, couples have several options. Partners can retire in tandem or stagger their retirement, with either husband or wife retiring first. The dual option tends to lead to the most satisfying marital relationship (as long as the couple has good feelings toward each other). The circumstances of retirement—such as age, health, amount of savings or pensions, whether retirement was forced, and the ability to take early retirement—contribute to the degree of satisfaction with retirement experiences.

Corporate and government policies can ease job loss or they can exacerbate it. Policies related to health care, childcare, and retirement affect individual families. Laws passed within separate states and by Congress bring changes that individual families must adjust to. Two of the most relevant are the Family and Medical Leave Act of 1993 and the 1996 reform of Aid to Families with Dependent Children, the public assistance program popularly known as "welfare."

Socioeconomic status is as important a structural variable as race and ethnicity when examining micro-, exo-, and macrosystems. Race and class are often so intertwined that it is difficult to disentangle them. Wilson's (1998) description highlights the effects of the exosystem on a working-class neighborhood that experienced devastating losses resulting from the withdrawal of businesses from the area. Corporate decisions to close factories sent a formerly active and energetic neighborhood into ruin and most of its residents who could not move from the neighborhood into poverty. Such practices demonstrate how the interaction between the family system and its larger environment is reciprocal and unending.

Endnotes

1. Stress variables are usually measured as role overload, role strain, negative work climate (low morale, interpersonal conflicts), depression, poor marital relations, and conflict in the family or at work. Variables associated with stress levels include the degree of commitment to, and the level of involvement in, a role or roles, the level of perceived spousal support, and marital quality.
2. The key dependent variable in Barnett and Shen's study was psychological distress. When they examined its association with the performance of household tasks, they found that the amount of time and the proportion of time (relative to spouse) spent in housework was unrelated to distress. However, if tasks needed to be performed according to a time schedule (such as fixing dinner), the amount of time spent performing these tasks was related to distress. This was not the case with tasks such as looking after the car, taking out the trash, caring for the yard, and doing repairs.
3. The unemployment rate is a measure of the number of active (last four weeks) job seekers as a proportion of the total labor force. It is an indirect measure of the number of people without jobs. The rate reached 9.6 percent during the 1982–1983 recession and was 3.9 percent in 2000. In July 2003 it was 6.4 percent.

Chapter Concepts

boundary task: a household chore that, if performed consistently, serves to demark the performance of a larger number of chores. Washing the dishes is a boundary chore. That is, if a husband washes the dishes, he is more likely to do the laundry. He is less likely to do the laundry if he does not do the dishes.

compensation theory: a theoretical explanation of the relationship between work and family hypothesizing that individuals make differential investments in the two microsystems. If work is unsatisfactory, it may be compensated for by greater participation in nonwork activities.

cottage industry: an industry in which the creation of products or services is home based rather than factory or office based.

definition of the situation: a concept introduced by W. I. Thomas, who wrote "If men [sic] define situations as real, they are real in their consequences" (Thomas and Thomas, 1928). This idea embodies a "self-fulfilling prophecy" insofar as people can be labeled (by self or others) and, by behaving in such a way as they are labeled, makes the definition that was asserted come true.

dissynchronized husband initially: a type of retirement in which both spouses work and the husband retires first.

dissynchronized wife initially: a type of retirement in which both spouses work and the wife retires first.

human capital: the resources that people have, innate or acquired, that facilitate their interactions within social institutions. Examples include gender, education level, cognitive ability, level of attractiveness, and family background.

interactive model: a theoretical explanation of the relationship between work and family that recognizes the mutual interdependence between the family and the workplace; each has independent as well as joint effects on workers.

role overload: a psychological state that develops when there are competing demands from too many roles.

second shift: a term that refers to the household and childcare tasks that working women engage in after a day of paid work.

spillover/crossover model: a theoretical explanation of the relationship between work and family that recognizes that either system may have consequences that transfer to the other. Positive and negative feelings, attitudes, and behaviors that emerge in one sphere are carried over into another.

synchronized/dual retirement: a type of retirement in which both spouses are in the labor force and both retire at the same time.

traditional retirement: a type of retirement in which only the husband worked and retired.

Suggested Activities

1. Choose a movie or novel that deals with any of the work-related topics of this chapter. Two excellent examples are *Erin Brockovich* (2000, 131 minutes, rated R) and *Baby Boom* (1987, 103 minutes, rated PG). List the work issues the film or novel presents. Write a short analysis of how the characters deal with or brought about change regarding the issues you identify.

2. Talk to three people about their post-labor force experience. At what age did they retire? How have they adjusted to retirement? Did they experience any problems? If you pick a married couple, be sure you interview each spouse separately, in private.

3. Select a corporation (or small business if you are not in an urban area) and interview the director of human services (or equivalent) and find out what services or benefits the company offers employees. For example, in 2003 State Farm Insurance Corporation's Operations Division offered a variety of programs, including job sharing, a compressed workweek, flextime, onsite mammograms, and dry cleaning services. How new to the company are the programs that you learned about? In what ways did the company think they would benefit employees, and why did it feel the need to benefit them in the first place? Alternatively, did the company cut benefits after the economic downturn in the early 2000s? If you were king or queen of the world, what would you mandate that companies offer their employees? Why?

Suggested Readings

Conger, R. D., and Elder, G. H., Jr. (eds.), 1994. *Families in Troubled Times: Adapting to Change in Rural America.* New York: Aldine De Gruyter.

Crouter, A., and McHale, S. 1993. "The long arm of the job: Influences of parental work on childrearing." In T. Luster and L. Okagaki (eds.), *Parenting: An ecological perspective* (pp. 179–202). Hillsdale, NJ: Erlbaum.

Liebow, E. 1993. *Tell Them Who I Am: The Lives of Homeless Women.* New York: Penguin.

Seccombe, K. 1999. *So You Think I Drive a Cadillac? Welfare Recipients' Perspectives on the System and Its Reform.* Needham Heights, MA: Allyn and Bacon.

Wharton, A. 1998. *Working in America: Continuity, Conflict, and Change.* Mountain View, CA: Mayfield. ◆

Chapter 8

Family Transitions

Divorce, Single Parenting, Remarriage

Did You Know?

- The divorce rate has fluctuated over the past 30 years. In 1970, it was 3.5 per 1,000 members of the population; in 1980, 5.2; in 2000, 4.1 (U.S. Department of Health and Human Services, 2002).

- Divorce rates vary across the 50 states; they are highest (above 6.0) in Arkansas, Nevada, New Mexico, Oklahoma, Tennessee, and Wyoming. They are lowest (3.0 or below) in Massachusetts, Maryland, and New Jersey (U.S. Bureau of the Census, 2001c).

- In single-parent households, custodial fathers develop parenting styles that are different from those of custodial single mothers. For example, both are equally warm and nurturing, but single fathers have more problems with communication and supervision and fewer problems with control (Hetherington and Stanley-Hagan, 1999).

- Almost half of all current marriages involve one or both spouses who are in a second, third, or higher marriage (U.S. Bureau of the Census, 2000b).

Things to Think About

- One explanation for the decreasing divorce rate is the delayed age at marriage associated with a reduction in the number of teenage marriages. Recent census data reported that only 4.5 percent of 15- to 19-year-olds were married in 2000 (U.S. Bureau of the Census, 2000c). After you finish reading this chapter think of other changing societal factors that might be associated with divorce and explain how they might inhibit the divorce rate.

- The quality of parenting goes down during the divorce process and, for some, stays down long after divorce. Mothers are particularly vulnerable during this time. Do you know of any social services or programs designed to help single parents cope with this change in their life situation?

The nation's tragedy at the New York World Trade Center on September 11, 2001, created thousands of widows and widowers who unexpectedly and without warning made a transition from marriage to singlehood. In one shocking moment a major life change occurred for the surviving spouses and children—without planning, thought, or preparation. Death, however, does not end the majority of marriages these days. Rather, it is divorce—a slow and, for most people, painful process—that is the primary cause of marital dissolution in the United States. In the millennium year, 2000, 19.9 million divorced people lived in the United States—9.8 percent of the total adult population over the age of 18 (Wright, 2002a). Most of these were women (11 percent compared to 9 percent of men) because women are less likely than men to remarry after divorce. The majority of divorced women and men, however, enter another marriage within about four years of their divorce. Are higher-order (second, third, etc.) marriages more stable than first ones? Not exactly. The divorce rate is higher for second marriages than for first. For example, for couples marrying between 1980 and 1985, the divorce rate was 25 percent higher for those in remarriages compared to first marriages (White, 1990).

We discussed in Chapter 3 the processes of courtship and partner selection. In this chapter we consider three more individual and family transitions: from marriage to divorce; from a two-parent to a single-parent household after divorce; from singlehood following divorce or widowhood to remarriage. We'll answer the following questions: What individual and marital factors are associated with greater probabilities of divorce? What do divorced couples say are the reasons for their marital break-up? How does the experience of divorce affect adults and children—physically, psychologically, and behaviorally? Why do children reared in single-parent households fare more poorly than children in two-parent situations? We will also explore the pleasures and problems associated with family re-formation: remarriage and stepfamilies. Who remarries? What are the different "types" of remarriages/stepfamilies? What are the costs and benefits of remarriage for adults and children? Why does it sometimes happen that one child loves a stepparent but a sibling hates him or her? Do stepgrandparents behave any differently toward their stepgrandchildren than they do toward their biological grandchildren?

The chapter ends with a look at the big picture. Do the values, attitudes, norms, and social meanings found in the larger culture influence individual decisions to divorce and remarry? Does the neighborhood in which a family resides affect whether a couple divorces? What laws and social policies in the exosystem are designed to assist (but instead sometimes hinder) individuals as they struggle to legally end marital relationships, and to re-form them?

Divorce

The marriage vow that most couples make to live "joined together until death" is upheld for approximately half of newly married couples. For those who decide they made a mistake, the median duration of marriage is about seven years. However, this seven-year figure has a wide range. Almost one-third of divorces occur within the first four years of marriage (Clarke, 1995). This fact tells us that spouses, one or both, decide early in their marriage that they made a mistake and take measures to bring it to an end. Couples are more likely to end a marriage if they do not have children, which may more often be the case for these shorter marriages. There are many fewer couples that decide after 10, 20, 30, or more years that they do not want to stay married to their partner. An estimated 11 percent of women over the age of 40 will have their first marriage end in divorce (Uhlenberg, Cooney, and Boyd, 1990).

Who Ends the Marriage?

The ending of a marriage is difficult for most people, but one consistent characteristic of a marital break-up is that at least one spouse (sometimes both) has given the decision a great deal of thought and has begun to think about a life without their current partner before the actual decision is made. In the literature, this phenomenon is called a **time advantage.** When a husband or wife has the benefit of time to think about an alternative life outside the marriage, assess the costs and benefits of a marital disruption, and begin to mourn the "lost" relationship even though it is still physically intact, he or she can begin planning for a new life and thinking about alternative identities. The concept of time puts the divorce experience into a process framework rather than a discrete event framework. Divorce as "process" is how many family scholars conceptualize it today (Amato, 2000a; Sun and Li, 2002).

The beginning of the end of a marriage is characterized by a feeling in one or both partners of dissatisfaction and estrangement (Kayser, 1993). When such feelings are acknowledged, spouses often go through a period of renegotiating their relationship, or at least aspects of it. For example, if, like Sam and Jan in Chapter 7, the household division of labor is a source of conflict, partners may spend considerable time talking and trying to renegotiate a new division of labor. Criticizing, complaining, and manipulation are three typically unsuccessful methods partners use to try to get each other to change their behavior. When such tactics bring about no change or lead to a more negative relationship (as they often do), support or advice from others may be sought. Depending on the nature of the problem, the degree to which it causes distress in one or both partners, and the presence of certain psychological characteristics in the partners (i.e., personality clashes), marital conflict has several possible consequences. The problem may be solved and the relationship enhanced. Or it may stay unresolved and remain the source of continued conflict. Alternatively, problems may be ignored or denied, sometimes for years, before the thought of divorce occurs to one or the other partner.

Amato (2000a) points out that negative effects of the divorce process may actually begin years prior to final separation. He also points out that overt adult conflict over a period of years may lead to behavior problems in children—problems that later may be mistakenly associated with parental divorce but that were apparent long before the legal dissolution of the marriage. Other evidence supporting the idea of divorce as a process comes from Kitson's (1992) study of divorce. The respondents in her sample reported that their greatest level of stress occurred before making the decision to divorce: The next greatest came when the actual decision was made, while the least stress was reported after the decision had been made. This process varies, of course, depending on which partner initiates the divorce. Especially when one partner wants the marriage to continue, the degree and the nature of the stress associated with the divorce experience will be different for each spouse.

Accompanying any divorce process are two roles: initiator and noninitiator. In a study conducted by Braver, Whitley, and Ng (1993), their Arizona respondents reported the wife to be the initiator in 63–67 percent of the divorces; in 4–9 percent it was reported to be a mutual decision (the question asked of both husbands and wives was "Which of you was the first to want out of the marriage?"). When Braver and his colleagues examined Petition for Dissolution records, they found that wives were legal petitioners 67 percent of the time and husbands 33 percent of the time, thus indicating some consistency in the self-reports. This finding contrasts with about 26 percent of the 1,215 respondents in Sweeney's (2002) study of divorce, which reported that both partners were ready and willing for the marriage to end: slightly more husbands (32 percent) than wives (21 percent) perceived this mutuality.

When Amato and Previti (2003) asked what or who was responsible for the divorce, 33 percent of the women and men in their study referred to their partner as the cause of the divorce, and 5 percent said they themselves caused the break-up. The others referred to the relationship as cause (27 percent), cited external causes (9 percent), or gave answers too ambiguous to classify (26 percent). Not unexpectedly, men and women differed in their reports of marital breakdown. The women in this study were almost twice as likely to say it was their husband's fault: 40 percent versus 21 percent of men who blamed their wives for the break-up. Hetherington (2003) reported that about 24 percent of the husbands in her study were surprised when their wives wanted a divorce and said they were not sure of the reasons that their marriages fell apart. The typical process of marital break-up, then, involves one partner who initiates a divorce decision and one who reacts. The noninitiator may experience distress even when divorce has been a subject of discussion or argument for some period of time.

Separation and Reconciliation

Divorce follows a period of separation during which the legal business of breaking up can be conducted, but sometimes couples go back to their marriage after a brief separation. An early study found that 11.7 percent of ever-separated women had reconciled with their husbands (Bloom et al., 1977). More recently, Wineberg and McCarthy (1993) analyzed data from a national sample of women and found that 14.3 percent of black women and 9.2 percent of white women had experienced reconciliation in marriages in which the couple stayed married. If the marriage ultimately ended in divorce, however, the percentages were higher: 32 percent of black women and 27.9 percent of white women experienced a separation and reconciliation before finally divorcing.

Further evidence of divorce as process is the finding that multiple separations are common. More than half of the women in the Bloom et al. study had more then one reconciliation (60 percent for blacks and 54 percent for whites). Those with the greatest number of reconciliations were less educated and had married young. About one-third of the women who divorced in this study separated and reconciled three or more times.

Binstock and Thornton (2003) analyzed data from a panel of 800 white adults (all aged 31). Twenty-five percent of those who separated had reconciled at least once. However, more than one-third of those who reconciled separated again within one year. Kitson and Langlie (1984) found that when marriage ended in divorce, 30–44 percent of couples had experienced a separation and reconciliation.

In general, blacks have longer separations before divorce than whites. Some couples never divorce or reconcile. In Watkins, Menken, and Vaughan's (1981) study, 19 percent of white women and 31 percent of black women reported they never intended to return to their husbands or get a divorce. Regardless of their intentions, we do not know how long these women actually retained their married-but-separated status. The actor Will Smith, age 37, told the story (in a television interview) of his parents who had separated when he was a young teenager. He remained in a close relationship with both parents. When Will was 35, his father phoned him, exclaiming he had just been given a bunch of papers to sign. "What kind of papers, dad?" "They're divorce papers. What do I do with them?" "Well, just sign them, dad." Pause. "Yeah, but what do you think she means by it?"

Sociodemographic and Psychological Characteristics Associated With the Probability of Divorce

A neighbor was talking with one of your authors not long ago about a recent accomplishment of her husband. Your author said how proud she must be of him. "Plus, he's so responsible, hardworking, and a really involved father. You're very lucky." "Yes," she answered, "those were the characteristics I noticed when we were going together. I also decided they would make him a good man to be divorced from." The neighbor was being particularly candid (perhaps because, as she confided, she came from a long line of women who had divorced). Although many people might be concerned about the vulnerability of marriage these days, few are so pragmatic as to think about the qualities (unselfish, caring, a generous and devoted parent) that might make someone a good ex-mate as well as a mate. Or, at least, few would admit to it.

Few people enter a marriage with divorce in mind. Then, you ask, what accounts for so many divorces? This question cannot be answered at the personal level. That is, we can't tell you the odds of *your* marriage ending in divorce, or our neighbor's, no matter how happy she may be with her husband at the moment. However, enough research evidence has been gathered over the past four decades to help us understand the characteristics associated with the probability of divorce among the married population as a whole. The odds are highest that a marriage is likely to dissolve if:

1. Wives and husbands marry in their teens.

2. Brides are pregnant or have given birth already.[1]

3. Spouses' income and education levels are low.

4. Husbands' and/or wives' parents were divorced.

5. Couples cohabited prior to marriage, especially with other partners before the person they married.

6. The marriage is not a first marriage for at least one spouse.

7. Religious participation is low.

8. The couple's race is black.

9. The couple has no children.

10. When children are present they are girls rather than boys.

11. The couple does not spend much time together.

Factors 1 through 8 are called **distal factors** by Amato and Rogers (1997) because they represent characteristics that spouses bring to the marriage. Wives' participation in the labor force is thought by some scholars to be a contributor to divorce, but the research findings are mixed. Recent studies generally show the relationship between wives' working and divorce is associated with another variable, earned income. Wives that earn more are at a greater risk of marital dissolution. Further, when wives' earnings are low, the risk of divorce is reduced. This may be because most wives have jobs that are not career based and do not foster job security or career development. Under these conditions, marriages benefit because wives supplement husbands' earnings but their incomes are not large enough for them to become economically independent. Only 15 percent of wives earned at least $5,000 more than their husbands in 2001 (U.S. Bureau of the Census, 2004a).

On the other hand, labor force participation offers wives some degree of financial independence and choice because their income brings assets that the family would otherwise not have. In a recent study the highest risk of divorce was found when wives earned between 50 and 60 percent of the total family income (Rogers, 2004). This situation may shift the balance of power and create tension in a marriage if husbands hold traditional views about their role as provider and "head of household." Men's earnings are consistently shown to have a positive effect on marital stability when wives do not work, while men's unemployment has a negative effect (Ono, 1998). We know that home ownership and high socioeconomic status (as determined by husbands' income) are also key determinants of marital stability for couples of all racial groups (South, 2001).

There are also confounding factors for wives' level of education as a factor predicting divorce. Not completing a high school education is associated with a higher risk of divorce, but so is starting but not completing college. Among a sample of 2,484 women in mid-life, those who had graduated from high school and those who had graduated from college had the lowest risk of marital disruption (Hiedemann et al., 1998). Women with very high levels of education (graduate or professional degrees) also have a high risk of divorce (Cooney and Uhlenberg, 1989).

Some scholars have tried to identify personality factors that foster a high probability of divorce. For example, spouses who are depressed or exhibit mental or psychological problems, who are drug or alcohol abusers, or who are strongly antisocial are more likely to divorce. Family theorists call psychological characteristics such as these **selection factors,** because people with deep personal or social problems are thought to get "selected out" of stable marriages. That is, their problems are often the reason they divorce or are the reason their partners seek a divorce (Johnson and Wu, 2002; Davies, Avison, and McAlpine, 1997). What are the reasons people give when asked the cause of their divorce?

Perceived Reasons for Divorce

The list of reasons people give for divorcing has stayed pretty much the same over the past several decades. Infidelity is one of the most commonly cited problems that lead to divorce. South and Lloyd (1995) calculated that about 31 percent of divorces are preceded by infidelity. This is a conservative number, because their study included only reports from one partner. If spouses' infidelity were included, the number would be higher. For example, 14.3 percent of wives and 16.5 percent of husbands reported that they had been involved with another person before divorcing. However, 40 percent of these respondents (both men and women) reported that their spouse had been unfaithful. It is apparently easier to place the blame on one's spouse for leaving a marriage because of a relationship with another person than to take responsibility for one's own behavior.

Other problems listed as the cause of divorce are incompatibility, communication difficulties, physical and emotional abuse, disagreements over gender roles, sexual problems, substance abuse, irritating habits, and financial problems or disagreements over money (White, 1990). These types of problems are called **proximal factors** (Amato and Rogers, 1997) because they represent features of the marital relationship itself. Interestingly, these marriage-breaking proximal factors are very different from the distal factors cited by researchers. That is, divorced persons do not say their marriage ended because they lived with their partner before they married or that they were expecting a baby before the wedding. What accounts for this discrepancy between the distal factors found by researchers and the actual reasons people give for their divorce?

Several scholars have attempted to answer this question. Some hypothesize that the problems people list as the reasons for their divorce are only seen as problems *after* the couple have already given up on the marriage (Amato and Rogers, 1997), or they are offered as an attempt to reduce the internal tension associated with the decision to divorce (Rasmussen and Ferraro, 1979). In a longitudinal study of 1,189 respondents, Amato and Rogers were able to disentangle these distal/proximal differences as well as test the hypothesis regarding post hoc explanations of why marriages end. They found that the marital problems of couples who eventually divorced had been the source of conflict as many as nine to twelve years preceding the dissolution, thus ruling out "end of marriage" post hoc explanations. They were also able to show that a younger age at marriage, parental divorce, and being in a remarriage were associated with certain interaction or behavioral problems such as jealousy and infidelity. For example, young spouses are thought to more readily enter into extramarital relationships.

One interesting finding from the Amato and Rogers study is based on their analysis of the contribution parental divorce makes toward marital problems among adults. In particular, spouses whose parents were divorced had an increased likelihood of problems related to jealousy, infidelity, irritating habits, and spending money. The authors speculate that divorce during childhood interferes with learning communication skills that contribute to successful marital interaction, which in turn increases marital problems and the risk of divorce.

In general, women tend to report more problems, and different types of problems, than men do. They are more likely to name their husband's drinking or drug use, dominance, abuse, immaturity, personality problems, untrustworthiness, poor money management, lifestyle, or values as the cause of divorce. Men, on the other hand, more often call attention to their own faults (drinking, abusiveness, poor communication) or external factors such as work commitments, problems with in-laws, or wives' unfaithfulness. They are more likely than women to say they don't know why the marriage ended (Amato and Previti, 2003; Amato and Rogers, 1997; Kitson, 1992).

Some men leave the room, or the house, during a confrontation with their partner. John Gottman, a respected marriage researcher, calls this 'stonewalling.' Replacing communication with stony silence or withdrawing entirely. This behavior is predictive of divorce.

One explanation of why marriages dissolve was formulated over three decades ago by Levinger (1965, 1976). He offered a social psychological perspective based on the cohesiveness of the couple relationship, and proposed three key elements. The first is the *attractiveness of the couple relationship* (feelings of pleasure, admiration of one's partner) in terms of met needs and of the costs versus benefits of maintaining the relationship. If a marriage relationship does not serve the needs of both partners, one spouse may simply leave the relationship or find a more attractive partner. This element is elaborated in a set of ideas put forward by Becker and his colleagues (1977; Becker, 1981). Becker's idea is that people marry only if both partners stand to gain from the marriage, and they stay married only if perceived gains are greater than those offered by alternative partners or can be achieved through becoming single. A couple divorces when new information acquired after marriage makes a separation more desirable than remaining together for one or both partners. One kind of new information that may change over the course of a marriage relates to the potential to form more desirable alternative unions. For example, if a wife enters the labor force and becomes acquainted with new people, her opportunity to meet and become attracted to another partner increases.

This parallels Levinger's second element: *alternative attractions*. He hypothesizes that marital interaction may be threatened when a relationship outside the marriage competes with the marriage by consciously excluding the spouse. This might happen if a spouse regularly goes with a work colleague to a bar after work every day instead to going home. Levinger's third and final element involves *restraining forces that act as barriers* that keep the marital relationship intact. Barriers include social norms that emphasize marriage as a life-long commitment, the legality of the marriage contract, a perceived loss of rights and privileges, and a potential decrease in their standard of living should the couple separate. Levinger wrote, "Barriers lessen the effect of temporary fluctuations in interpersonal attraction; even if attraction becomes negative, barriers act to continue the relationship" (1976, 26).

Levinger's social psychological framework includes both family system concepts (such as the role of feedback, interrelatedness of the couple) and ecological system ideas (the mesosystem connections between work and family, the role of macrosystem norms, values, and beliefs). Huston (2000) articulated this blend of social psychological factors and systems perspective when he wrote: "The behavior settings within which people function also provide the medium through which cultural values are articulated, reinforced, or undermined. The link between societal conditions and the marital relationship . . . suggests that the embeddedness of the marriage in a macrosocietal milieu can directly affect husband-wife interaction" (317).

A study by Lauer and Lauer (1986) that looked at long-term marriages (of 15–61 years in duration) provides an indirect test of Levinger's theory. These researchers found that viewing one's mate as a best friend and liking him or her as a person were the two most often listed reasons for staying in the marriage (attraction factors). A belief that marriage was a long-term commitment (barrier) was another reason. Among the respondents who claimed their marriage was unhappy (although of long duration), the reasons for staying together were a commitment to marriage, the presence of children, and the strength of religious or family values—for example, the belief that marriage is sacred (barriers).[2] Of the unhappily married persons in Lauer and Lauer's study, 47 percent reported they stayed together because of the children, and some commented that they may separate or divorce once the children all leave home. As valuable as this study is, we can't generalize these results to the entire U.S. married population because the respondents were mostly white (93 percent) and predominantly middle class or upper middle class, and the study may be biased for those reasons. These characteristics favor long marital duration.

There is some similarity between the framework proposed by Levinger and the material we discussed in Chapter 2 on commitment. Remember Johnson's (1991, 1999) model of commitment that was presented in Chapter 2? It was based on the perspective that couples stay married because of personal commitment (similar to attractiveness), moral commitment (don't seek out alternatives), and structural commitment (barriers).

Reasons for marital breakdown vary by class and race. Moore and Schwebel (1993) reviewed the findings related to these two distal factors and found lower-income spouses complain more about instrumental aspects of marriage, such as household chores, child-rearing differences, financial problems, spouses' behavior (drinking, physical abuse, infidelity), while higher-income spouses complain about interpersonal aspects, such as communication problems, lack of love, or incompatibility. Amato and Previti (2003) also found couples with higher socioeconomic status attributing their divorce to relationship-centered causes and lower-socioeconomic-status couples claiming problem behavior (i.e., abuse, drinking) as the cause. Moore and Schwebel reported racial differences in the reasons respondents gave for their divorce. In their study, blacks were more likely than whites to divorce because of infidelity, the need for personal freedom, or physical abuse. Whites were more likely to list communication and child-rearing problems.

Kurdek (1998b) hypothesized that gay and lesbian couples have no institutional barriers that inhibit ending their relationships. His five-year longitudinal study found this to be the case, with gay and lesbian couples reporting fewer constraints to leaving the relationship than heterosexual married couples. The break-up rate for these respondents was higher for lesbian couples (16 percent) and lowest for heterosexual couples (7 percent). Gay men's dissolution rate fell between the others (14 percent). According to Kurdek's analysis, barriers are lax in the areas of legal constraints (none, since the relationships were not legally sanctioned), religious constraints (none, since most religions condemn homosexuality), and social constraints (few, because family members are not likely to be approving of the relationship in the first place). Not only are there fewer macrosystem forces inhibiting relationship break-ups, it is likely that nonheterosexual couples are less concerned with conforming to existing norms because their sexual orientation puts them at odds with many social norms. This situation may change if state laws are changed in the United States to permit gay and lesbian marriages. However, such marriages are not always enduring when enacted. In the Netherlands, where gay/lesbian marriages have been legal since 2001, the first divorces have also been registered (Associated Press, 2004).

Postdivorce Adjustment

Economic Adjustment. When a marriage ends, the economic well-being and standard of living of both partners generally declines. For most men this decline tends to be temporary, although according to data analyzed from the longitudinal Panel Study of Income Dynamics by McManus and DiPrete (2001), it varies depending on the preseparation household income and family composition. White husbands who had contributed 80 percent or more to predivorce household earnings maintained, or in some cases increased, their standard of living by about 10 percent, even when child support, alimony, or voluntary payments were calculated. Increases in the standard of living were also reported for black men who were primary income contributors of 80 percent or more of household income. White men who contributed more than 60 percent but less than 80 percent of family income and who made child support payments saw a decline of about 5–8 percent in their standard of living postdivorce. However, black men who had contributed more than 60 percent but less than 80 percent to the predivorce household experienced an estimated 20 percent decline in their standard of living. Both black and white men whose household income contribution was less than 60 percent experienced a significant decline. These differences are attributed to the increased number of dual-earner households over the past three decades and the dependency of both partners on having two wage earners.

The heterogeneity that characterizes men's postdivorce standard of living is not evident for women. There are no comparable data showing that women gain financially after separation and divorce (Hanson, McLanahan, and Thomson, 1998; Smock, Manning, and Gupta, 1999). Women's lowered income generally continues for many years if they do not remarry. Because the majority of mothers retain physical custody of children, this forces women and children into distressed economic circumstances at a particularly stressful time in their lives. On average, divorced women have a lower standard of living, have less wealth, and experience greater economic hardship than married women (a finding that is true for some men as well, as mentioned above). Only upon remarriage do most women recoup their losses, so to speak, and gain a better standard of living for themselves and their children (Duncan and Hoffman, 1985).

Health Adjustment. Much research examining the physiological aspects of distress after separation and divorce documents the health consequences of marital disruption. Separated and divorced men have higher rates of pneumonia and death, are more distressed, are lonelier, and report a greater number of recent illnesses compared to married men. Divorced men suffer more from alcohol and drug abuse, sleep disorders, stomach and intestinal problems, and sexually transmitted diseases. Separated and divorced women are more likely to report acute illnesses and increased numbers of doctor visits. Recently divorced women are reported to have more headaches, stomach and intestinal problems, fatigue, infections, flu, and colds than happily married women (Hetherington, 2003). On the other hand, mental health is reported to improve if individuals have left conflict-ridden and low-quality marriages (Aseltine and Kessler, 1993; Booth and Amato, 1991). Who wants the marriage to end is another factor that produces different health consequences. A medical study that examined men who separated or divorced within the past year reported "initiators" were in better health and showed better immune functioning than "noninitiators" (Dura and Kiecolt-Glaser, 1991).

Psychological Adjustment. Divorce has well-documented psychological effects as well. Many studies report greater levels of psychological distress among divorced compared to married couples. Overall, researchers report lower levels of happiness, higher levels of depression, and poorer self-concepts among the divorced. They are more socially isolated, have less satisfying sex lives, and experience more negative life events (Amato, 2000a). Looking at the effects of parental divorce on adult depression, Ross and Mirowsky (1999) analyzed data from a sample of 2,592 respondents. Those who experienced parental divorce in childhood had significantly higher levels of distrust and depression than those from never-divorced families, a finding that held even after adjustments were made for parents' education, parents' death, sex, race, and age. After extensive analyses, these researchers concluded that their findings regarding depression could be explained by the disadvantage these adult children experienced in the aftermath of parental divorce, specifically through lower educational attainment. Less education was associated with respondents' current level of economic hardship. In turn, low education level and economic hardship were correlated with high levels of depression. This finding was the same for men and women.

Postdivorce Attachment. Under what conditions does a continuing relationship with a former spouse constitute a desirable situation? Certainly when former spouses are cordial and cooperative over issues concerning children, a continuing attachment between them could be interpreted as a positive development. Normatively, however, ideal and healthy postdivorce adjustment is defined as one of emotional detachment (Masheter, 1997). So how does a divorced spouse who feels anger, resentment, or even feelings of love for his or her former spouse negotiate a postdivorce relationship and get to the point of "detachment"? Many books address this question, some of which are listed at the end of this chapter.

But what does social science research tell us about former spouse attachment? Most studies find that about 50 percent of recently divorced couples report little distress, preoccupation, or mourning over their ex-spouse, while about 20 percent experience intense feelings. The remaining couples lie somewhere in between these extremes. A study by Masheter (1997) of white, middle-aged, middle-class divorced individuals reported that 87 percent had weekly or monthly contact with their former spouses. Children were the reason given by most respondents for their contact (61 percent), but financial reasons (39 percent) and just being friends (33 percent) were also listed. This contact was not entirely benign; some of it was characterized by anger and hostility. Masheter measured the level of hostility and degree of preoccupation with the former spouse and examined the effects on emotional well-being. She found that preoccupation was associated with being male, with lower well-being, and with lower levels of hostility. Former spouses who measured low on preoccupation and high on friendship scored higher on emotional well-being, as did those who scored low on preoccupation and high on hostility. Evidently, low preoccupation is indicative of a healthy level of postdivorce attachment even when it is accompanied by hostile feelings.

Other research examining contact between former spouses confirms that contact is commonplace for 40–80 percent of formerly divorced couples, at least for the first two years after divorce. By the third year most anger has dissipated. In terms of friendly contact, 12–13 percent of formerly married couples maintain positive attachments (Ahrons, 1994). Amato and Previti (2003) found that divorced men and women were most attached to their former spouses when they attributed the cause of the divorce to themselves. Former spouses also had the poorest postdivorce adjustment when they blamed themselves for the divorce.

Does divorce produce any positive consequences for adults? For some individuals divorce is associated with higher levels of autonomy and personal growth (Costa et al, 2000). It improves the lives of some women by providing them with opportunities to continue their education, enhance their careers, improve their social lives, raise their level of self-confidence, and increase the sense of control over their lives. Some men develop better interpersonal skills and a greater willingness to self-disclose (Amato, 2000a). In other words, identity changes are likely to occur after a divorce experience. Among the divorced couples in Hetherington's (2003) study, at the end of six years over 75 percent of the spouses felt their divorce had been a good thing.

Parenting After Divorce

A new view held by some family scholars shifts the emphasis from the trauma of marital break-up and loss, instability and stress, to give equal attention to the resiliency and the ability of family members to construct their own life course (Elder, 1998). This view does not deny the negative and sometimes destructive aspects of the divorce process for children and adults. Rather, the divorced family is seen as different, not deviant. This approach emphasizes that the primary concern of children is that their parents are emotionally and materially committed to them after separation and divorce (Walker, 2003). Do both parents still love them? How do they show it? Do children have a voice in reconstructing the postdivorce family? These ideas follow from research evidence showing that although separation and divorce introduce immediate trauma into the lives of the majority of children, most (75–80 percent) grow up to be healthy, functioning adults (Ahrons and Tanner, 2003).

However, while divorce outcomes may diminish over the long term, the information in the following sections discusses the problems and consequences (risk factors) for parents and children in the short term. The final section of the chapter explores some solutions proposed to facilitate a resilient recovery after a divorce experience.

Does It Matter Which Parent Has Residential Custody?

Sanctioning the custody of children is one of the most important tasks undertaken by the legal institution within the exosystem. Several types of custody arrangements have been devised to determine who will have primary responsibility for children after divorce. These include **sole legal custody** (one parent is the primary parent and has full parental authority, such as making school or medical decisions that require parental consent); **joint legal custody** (parents share decision making and responsibility for children, but one parent has primary physical custody), **joint physical custody** (parents share decision making and responsibility and physical custody, but not necessarily 50-50), and **split custody,** in which the children are divided between parents, each of whom has responsibility for at least one child (Price and McKenry, 1988; Ahrons, 1994).

One question divorcing parents sometimes ask is whether children are better off being raised by their same-sex parent after divorce. One major attempt to answer this question analyzed data from a national longitudinal study of 3,892 eighth graders, 3,483 of whom lived with a single mother and 409 lived with a single father (Downey and Powell, 1993). This research analyzed 35 variables, including children's view of self, behavior in school, educational expectations and achievements, extracurricular activities, parent-child interactions and involvement, and parents' interpersonal and economic resources. It took into account a number of relevant structural variables, including parents' education, income, race, and so on. None of the findings indicated that boys and girls had an advantage by living with their same-sex parent. Only two items suggested that boys and girls were advantaged by living with single fathers: if the parents had saved money for their children's college education and if there was a computer in the home used for educational purposes. More than anything, these items likely reflect a higher standard of living offered by many single fathers.

Custodial Mothers. Mothers gain residential custody of children in about 85 percent of divorces, even though the concept of joint physical parental custody was instigated in the early 1980s. In practice, even when joint custody is the agreed on arrangement it does not always mean equal parenting (Ahrons, 1994). Most mothers continue to have primary responsibility for children.

Residential custody of children is primarily granted to mothers, still today. What factors do you think parents and judges consider in making these custody decisions?

One consistent outcome of dissolved marriages is a period of disrupted or diminished parenting (Avenevoli, Sessa, and Steinberg, 1999). In many divorce situations, mothers have difficulty dealing with their own lives and emotions during the divorce transition, and thus their parenting skills and ability to protect children are compromised. Stress may follow from having sole responsibility of children. Numerous studies find that divorced mothers, on average, spend less time with their children, discipline them harsher, have fewer rules, provide less supervision, and engage in more conflict with children than married mothers do. These differences are attributed to the poorer economic condition of the family when a father leaves. Stress associated with the need to manage on fewer resources, to enter the labor force, or to work more than one job takes its toll on patience and the capacity to listen and be understanding. Moreover, these new demands simply take away time that children need from a parent. Added to this stress is a wide range of emotions a divorcing parent experiences, such as anger, depression, irritability, or sadness. Under these conditions, some mothers find it difficult to provide the consistency, routine, and nurturing necessary to meet the needs of children. On a positive note, many adolescent girls and boys in single-mother households develop close relationships with their mothers, slightly more so than those who live with their single fathers. And single mothers, compared to fathers, praise, hug, and talk more with their children (Amato, 2000b).

One mediating factor of distress may be a mother's level of education. There is consistent evidence that mothers' educational attainment is positively associated with children's socioemotional development, academic performance, and global well-being (Amato, 2000b). Higher levels of education are also associated with higher self-esteem and psychological well-being, and better physical health for mothers themselves. However, the majority of single-parent mothers are not well educated. Slightly more than one-third (36 percent) of the single mothers raising children in Amato's (2000b) study had attended college, and only 8 percent had graduated from college. Because level of education is usually associated with income level, educated mothers have a much greater chance of avoiding poverty. Among all single parents in the Amato study, white divorced fathers who were college graduates age 45 or older had the highest standard of living. The lowest standard of living was held by separated black mothers who were high school dropouts, age 24 or younger.

Young, poor, black single mothers have a number of challenges to overcome. Among these mothers, depression stemming from neighborhood conditions (such as gangs, overcrowding, and poverty) is linked to inadequate parenting that, in turn, is associated with poor psychosocial adjustment for children (Jones et al., 2002). On a positive note, several studies report that black compared to white children living with single mothers score higher on measures of well-being, and they seem to adjust better to single-parent family life. This may be because black children may not suffer from the same stigma of living in a single-parent household that white children do because divorced and never-married mothers are more prevalent in black communities. The potential of a larger extended friend and family support system among blacks is another explanation of this finding (Fine, 2000). This extended support network was the subject of a longitudinal study examining changes in the living arrangements of 912 black children in a poor urban Chicago community. About 20 percent of children living in nuclear family households in first grade were living with extended kin (grandparent, uncle, aunt, cousins) by adolescence.

Overall, 75 percent of the children experienced a change in household composition between first grade and adolescence (Hunter and Ensminger, 1992).

Custodial mothers are acknowledged "gatekeepers" of their children. Some nonresidential fathers complain that former spouses bar them from access to their children (Furstenberg, 1995; Arditti, 1995) or complain about their visits. Consequently, some noncustodial fathers choose to withdraw from their children as a way to avoid conflict when the relationships with their ex-spouses are conflict-ridden, noncooperative, and unsupportive (Ahrons and Tanner, 2003). There is little acknowledgment from mothers themselves that they engage is such behavior, however. On the contrary, many custodial mothers say they wished their children's father were more engaged and took a greater interest in his children. They welcome some relief from the responsibilities of child rearing.

King and Heard (1999) tested these conflicting views and found some interesting results. Using mother (1,565 mothers) reports, they examined the relationship between mothers' satisfaction with nonresidential fathers' visitation, frequency of fathers' visitation, parental conflict, and child well-being. Dividing visitation into high and low categories, King and Heard found that when fathers visited often (several times a week) 88 percent of mothers were satisfied; when fathers did not visit at all, 71 percent of mothers were satisfied! The majority of mothers, then, appeared to be satisfied with the current visitation schedule. Looking at the effects of visitation on children, frequent visitation did not benefit children any more than infrequent contact, even when mothers were satisfied with the frequency of visitation. However, in about 10 percent of families where there was frequent father visitation and mothers were dissatisfied with the level of contact, children's adjustment and overall well-being scores were lower and they manifested more behavior problems. Conflict between parents did not influence this finding. To understand this situation King and Heard tested a wide range of variables. They found that although fathers visited their children frequently, they rarely discussed the children with their former spouse and appeared to have little influence in the lives of children. Thus, contact alone was not satisfying for the mothers. Their unfulfilled expectations that fathers would be more forthcoming, intellectually involved, or engaged with them about the children was evidently the source of a great deal of dissatisfaction. These results emphasize that the interrelatedness of family members continues even after marriage ends.

A significant portion of children's pain after a parental divorce is caused by separation from their fathers (and in some cases, mothers). When asked, college students whose parents' had divorced reported they had wanted to spend more time with their fathers. Seventy percent selected "equal time" when asked about the amount of time they wished they had had with each parent (Kelly and Emery, 2003). Gatekeeping may be one strategy used to reduce the number of visits, because mothers feel threatened when children want to spend more time with their fathers.

Custodial Fathers. About 14 percent of parents with residential custody are men (Stewart, 1999). Most fathers gain custody of their children through mutual agreement with their former spouse. Sometimes a transfer of residence happens when children reach adolescence and choose to live with their father. Other situations include mothers who believe the children will be better off financially, or otherwise, living with their father. Or they feel a father is better able to discipline an out-of-control adolescent. Some mothers are addicted, disabled (physically, mentally, emotionally), or incompetent, so children live with their father to have a more stable home environment. The odds of fathers being awarded physical custody of children if they go to court are greater if the children are older and are boys. The chances of paternal custody are also greater if fathers are of a higher socioeconomic class, are older, and have consistently paid child support (Fox and Kelly, 1995; Price and McKenry, 1988).

There appear to be few differences in children's psychological well-being, behavioral problems, and educational attainment when they are raised by single fathers compared to single mothers (Amato, 2000b). Children who live with their fathers tend to fare very well, reporting close relationships with them.

Fathers report better relationship quality with their children when they co-reside when compared to fathers in nonresident situations. However, they are no different from continuously married fathers in their perception of the quality of the relationship with their children. Generally, no differences are seen between resident and nonresident fathers on level of depression, but in one longitudinal study residential fathers reported themselves to be less happy

A growing number of fathers are being granted sole custody of their children. Researchers find few differences in children who are raised by single fathers compared to single mothers.

than both nonresidential and continuously married fathers (Shapiro and Lambert, 1999). Why would single fathers who are raising their children feel less happy than fathers in the other two groups? It was speculated that rearing children takes time and energy from their own personal needs, which contributes to a lower level of reported happiness. Also, raising children may be emotionally challenging for single fathers because they tend to have less experience with parental roles, and men usually have a smaller network of people to use as confidants (Shapiro and Lambert, 1999). Single fathers find being a parent more manageable than fathers who are remarried or cohabiting (Seltzer and Brandreth, 1994). Grief and DeMaris (1995) suggest that a selection effect may be operating in many father custody situations—that is, these dads are likely involved and sensitive fathers to begin with.

What are the characteristics of father-custody families? Fewer children are living with widowed fathers today: 5.7 percent of father-only families compared to 32 percent in 1960. However, a growing number of children are residing in father-custody families, living with fathers who were never married to their mothers (33.2 percent). Father-custody families often include a cohabiting partner (34.7 percent of all children in single-father families) or have other adults (35.3 percent) living in the household (called complex households—e.g., living with grandparents, aunts, uncles, or other unrelated adults). Thus the stereotype of father and child making a life together alone is the least common type, involving only 30 percent of father-custody families (Eggebeen, Snyder, Manning, 1996).

Never-married fathers with custody are more likely to have the lowest levels of education, while widowed fathers have the highest. Divorced fathers fall between these two groups. Similar trends hold for employment: Widowed and divorced fathers are more likely to have full-time year-round employment. Correspondingly, widowed and divorced fathers have the highest median household income ($28,000 each), and never-married fathers have the lowest ($22,700) [in 1990 dollars]. These figures vary, of course, depending on whether fathers and children live in cohabiting or complex households. Never-married fathers who live alone with their children are reported to have the lowest median income of all groups ($14,400) (Eggebeen et al., 1996). In general, father-custody families have higher family incomes than mother-custody families. They are more likely to include boys (56 percent of children in father-headed families, according to data collected in 1990) and older children. About 68 percent of single-father households include children over the age of six (Meyer and Garasky, 1993).

Little is known about minority fathers who have custody of their children. However, a study conducted by Hamer and Marchioro (2002) provides some insights into the custodial experiences of low-income black fathers. These fathers differed from white middle-class fathers in that they usually had never married the mother of their children. Why did they gain custody of their children? According to Hamer and Marchioro, this happened in one of three ways:

1. The children's mother wished to relinquish custody.

2. Child protective services sought out the father as the most viable person to care for the children when the mother could not.

3. The children (usually a preteen or adolescent) indicated a desire to live with the father.

More often than not, these fathers perceived themselves to be unprepared for full-time fatherhood and reported that they initially panicked at the prospect. To cope with their changed circumstances, they developed a support system (their own mothers, sisters, friends) to help them when they needed childcare, to act as a sounding board for questions or decisions about parenting, and sometimes to share housing. The men in this study held low-wage jobs, barely making enough to support themselves. Most of them also found social services personnel to be unsupportive when they sought help. Their motives were mistrusted when they applied for public aid, and some social workers felt it was inappropriate for children to be in their fathers' care. In general, custodial fathers who are poor are less likely to receive public assistance than poor custodial mothers (Garasky and Meyer, 1996).

Noncustodial Fathers. A large number of fathers decrease contact with their children after divorce. In a study of 1,565 families, 59 percent of nonresidential fathers were reported to visit their children only a few times a year or less (King and Heard, 1999). Another study using 1,350 of these same families found that while 25 percent of the children saw their father at least once a week, 30 percent had not seen their father during the past year. Fathers who were never married to the mother of their child were less likely to maintain contact with the child (Seltzer, 1991). Diminished contact is attributed to several factors: geographical distance, time since the divorce, fathers' way of dealing with the pain of losing their children, poor relationships with former wives, poor psychological health, or a new partnership (for either custodial or noncustodial parent) that may or may not include new children or stepchildren.

The complexity of fathers' lives after divorce is said to be a contributing factor to the level of support offered nonresidential children. By five years postdivorce, 70 percent of men are cohabiting or have remarried (Bumpass, Sweet and Cherlin, 1991; Ahrons and Tanner, 2003). These new relationships often involve additional children. Manning et al. (2003) observed that "an intricate web of parenting and family obligations across households" affects the level of support and involvement fathers offer (646). Over time, men may have nonresidential children from several prior relationships that affect the commitments they make and keep (or not) to their children. Manning and her colleagues studied 759 families and found 49 percent of nonresident fathers had complex parenting responsibilities. As expected, nonresident fathers with no competing parenting obligations visited their nonresident children more often than those who had repartnered, and they were more likely to be paying child support. When fathers were responsible for a wider array of children, support payments were less likely, but visitation continued. However, if a new partner had nonresident children, visiting was discouraged but child support payments continued. When children were born to the new partnership, fathers reduced visitation but not payment of child support. New unions, whether joined through cohabitation or marriage, influenced nonresidential fathers insofar as the income of the new partners facilitated the payment of support to children.

Staying in Touch. Several father-related behaviors that benefit children may continue after couples separate and fathers no longer live with their children. Foremost, some fathers continue to support their children financially; maintain contact through visitation, telephone, letters, or e-mail, engage in their children's social/school activities; and participate with their former spouses in discussions and decisions related to the children. However, fathers who do not visit in person rarely stay in touch with children via other means of communication (King and Heard, 1999).

An interesting relationship exists between noncustodial parent contact and child support payments. Seltzer's (1991) study (based on mothers' reports) suggests that fathers who continue to visit are more likely to pay child support and be involved in discussions and decisions concerning the child. However, paying child support, by itself, does not necessarily increase nonresidential fathers' involvement in decision making.

One consistent finding is reported from studies that look at the effects of child support paid by absent fathers. Child support payments, independent of all other variables, appear to have positive benefits. Children's academic success is enhanced, they experience fewer behavior problems at home and in school, they are less aggressive and engage in fewer delinquent acts, they are less depressed or anxious, and they have higher self-esteem when their fathers pay support (Amato and Gilbreth, 1999). Depending on whom you ask, there is some discrepancy over paying support. Fathers tend to overreport the amount of support they give for children by between 15 and 30 percent (compared to mothers' reports). When Sorenson (1997) analyzed data from two separate samples, he found that 46 percent and 54 percent of nonresident fathers in the two samples did not make child support payments; when fathers were asked, only 22 percent and 46 percent acknowledged they did not pay support. Neutral third-party verifications (court collection and distribution data) tended to support the mothers' reports (Braver, Fitzpatrick, and Bay, 1991; McManus and DiPrete, 2001).

Are there identifiable characteristics of nonresident fathers who pay no child support at all? One attempt to answer this question was made by Garfinkel and his colleagues (1998). They concluded that nonpaying fathers were disproportionately poor (30–40 percent had annual incomes below $6,500 [in 1995 dollars]), suffered from alcohol and drug problems, or were in jail or homeless.

What about nonresidential fathers who stay in contact with their children? Nonresident fathers worry about the tenuousness of the relationship with their children and often do not set firm rules or discipline the children for misbehavior—behaviors quite opposite of authoritative parenting (Hetherington and Jodl, 1994). Yet Amato and Gilbreth's (1999) **meta-analysis** of 63 studies that looked at nonresidential father-involvement found authoritative parenting to be the most consistent predictor of positive child outcomes. In the group of studies they reviewed, authoritative parenting consisted of behaviors such as listening to children's problems, giving advice, providing explanations for rules, monitoring children's homework, engaging in projects with children, and using noncoercive discipline to deal with misbehavior. However, because most nonresidential fathers are not involved in the daily lives of their children (because they do not live with them), they are more likely to parent in a permissive and indulgent way, trying to make sure the children enjoy themselves when they are together—hence the term *Disneyland Dads*.

Noncustodial fathers often depend on entertainment venues such as movies or playland attractions when they are with their children. Maybe they are afraid that ordinary life settings bore children. What behaviors have you observed of a noncustodial father, grandfather, brother, or uncle?

Passing time in leisure activities continues even when children are older. Stewart (2003) examined whether shared leisure activities such as shopping, playing sports, and going to see movies, plays, concerts, museums, or sporting events contributed to adolescent adjustment (level of emotional distress, participation in delinquent behavior, and academic achievement). Using national longitudinal data with a sample of 7th through 12th graders, Stewart found that nonresidential father-child participation in shared activities was unrelated to children's academic achievement and their level of emotional distress. Authoritative parenting was also examined (i.e., if fathers talked with adolescent children about dating, parties, or other things they were doing at school, personal problems, schoolwork or grades, or worked on a school project with them). Only one of these behaviors—talking about "other things" at school—had a positive effect on adjustment. Adolescents reported less emotional distress, less delinquent behavior, and better school performance when they talked with their fathers about ordinary stuff happening at school. Interestingly, when youths said they talked to their fathers about personal problems, schoolwork, and grades, their level of emotional distress and their participation in delinquent acts were higher. Stewart surmised that children who faced these problems talked to and sought out advice or counsel from their fathers about them. Or perhaps mothers encouraged children with such problems to talk with their fathers.

Do Children Benefit From Visits With Dad?

Do Children Benefit From Visits With Dad? There is some inconsistency in the literature surrounding the benefits and costs to children of nonresidential father contact. Some studies find that contact is related to an increase in children's well-being, while others find no significant relationship. King and Heard's (1999) study of father visitation and children's well-being found that frequent visitation did not benefit children any more than lack of visitation. This finding corresponds to most other research on the subject. Some studies even find that contact increases problems for children. How can that be? Isn't contact with fathers important? Of course it is. The consistent finding that children living in continuously married families compare more favorably on measures of well-being, academic achievement, and behavioral adjustment than children living in single-parent households is proof enough of that. One explanation for the inconsistent findings regarding father contact is a lack of comparability between studies in terms of sampling (small, convenience samples versus large representative ones) and respondent selection (children versus adults). Amato and Rezac (1994) offer another explanation. They attribute some of the differences to a variable that is often unmeasured: the conflict between former spouses. Intense parental conflict is known to be harmful to children, affecting their psychological adjustment and behavior. The researchers hypothesized that "although continued contact with a nonresident parent may be beneficial for children, continuing hostility between parents may negate any benefits that accrue to children from a high level of input from the nonresident parent" (193). Using a national sample, they tested this idea with a sample of children (ages 5–18). When the resident parent (both nonresidential mothers and fathers were included in this study) reported low levels of conflict with the former spouse, boys who had a high level of involvement with the nonresident parent had fewer behavior problems (e.g., they had not failed a grade in school, been expelled or suspended, run away from home, or been in trouble with the police). However, when contact was high and conflict between parents was high, boys were reported to have a large number of behavior problems. These researchers speculated that the findings were not significant for girls because girls are more likely to manage stress by becoming depressed, anxious, and having low self-esteem, while boys are more likely to act out and get into trouble.

Amato and Booth (1997) studied the effects of conflict on children of divorce. In their longitudinal study, less than one-third of divorced parents engaged in high levels of conflict prior to divorcing, with 28 percent reporting some spousal physical abuse. The children living in the latter households undoubtedly benefited from their parents' marital dissolution. Research generally shows that high parental conflict is associated with stress, insecurity, fear, anger, or the inhibition of normal behavior in children. Amato and Booth's data indicated that children in high-conflict families showed positive outcomes after the divorce. However, they suggest that the 72 percent who did not witness high discord between their parents may have had the hardest time understanding their parent's break-up because they didn't understand the marriage was in trouble. They consequently suffered the most stress during the divorce transition.

Children in Single-Parent Households

One indication that the American family system has changed during the past half century is the fact that 40 percent of all children born during the 1980s are expected to experience their parents' divorce. With another 10 percent born to unmarried mothers, this means that about half of all children in the United States will spend some time living in a single-parent household, usually with their mother (Amato, 2000a). Currently, about 26 percent of children under the age of 18 live in a single-parent home, of these, 22 percent live with their mother and 4 percent live with their father (U.S. Bureau of the Census, 2002a).

There is a growing racial disparity in the number of single-parent households. As Figure 8.1 shows, in 2002, 15.1 percent of Asian and Pacific Islander children, 22.4 percent of white children, 30.1 percent of Latino children, and 53.3 percent of black children lived with a single parent. (The corresponding figures in 1970 were 8.7 percent for whites, 31.8 percent blacks, and 21.1 percent for Latinos. No figures are available for Asian and Pacific Islanders.)

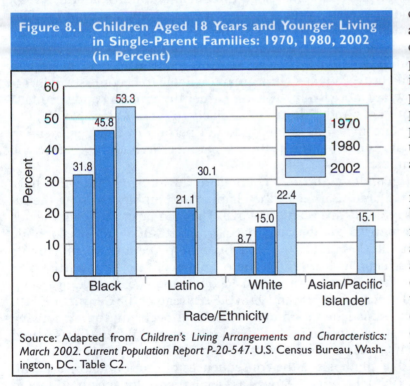

Figure 8.1 Children Aged 18 Years and Younger Living in Single-Parent Families: 1970, 1980, 2002 (in Percent)

Source: Adapted from *Children's Living Arrangements and Characteristics: March 2002. Current Population Report P-20-547.* U.S. Census Bureau, Washington, DC. Table C2.

These figures represent not only a high divorce rate but also a trend of never-married women giving birth and raising their children alone. In 1997, 26 percent of births to white women were to unmarried mothers, compared to 69 percent of births to unmarried black mothers (Caplow, Hicks, and Wattenberg, 2001; Amato, 2000b). With these figures as a backdrop, let us explore the dynamics of single parenting after divorce for children.

The majority of children survive the divorce of their parents with apparently few long-term negative effects (McLanahan, 1999). Children are resilient, and most overcome the difficulties during the period of stressed parenting, conflict between separated parents, and lowered standard of living. They grow up, get a job or go to college, marry, and have children of their own. However, many children are negatively affected and are slow to recover. This includes about 20–25 percent of children who experience divorce (Amato and Keith, 1991; Kelly and Emery, 2003). In this section we discuss the aftermath of divorce for these children.

Negative Impacts of Divorce on Children

Divorce can negatively affect parent-child relations. When divorce occurs during adolescence, daughters' affection for fathers is reduced, as is sons' affection for mothers. When divorce occurs early in children's lives, they express lowered affection for both parents, compared to those whose parents remain married (Amato and Booth, 1997). Father-child interaction does not improve when children grow up: low levels of affection, contact, and exchanges characterize divorced father–adult-child relationships (Cooney and Uhlenberg, 1990; Shapiro and Lambert, 1999).

The research conducted on single-parent families indicates that children growing up in these families are not likely to fare as well as those raised in two-parent families, regardless of race, education, or parental remarriage (McLanahan and Sandefur, 1994). There is a large body of findings showing that children raised in single-parent families (compared to two-parent families) are more likely to engage in delinquent behavior; use drugs, alcohol, and tobacco; have lower self-esteem; drop out of high school; leave home early; and see a mental health professional. They are also less likely to attend college, and when they do they are less likely to graduate. Girls are more likely to become sexually active at an earlier age and boys are more likely to have a harder time finding and keeping a job in young adulthood. Both boys and girls are more likely to work at low-paying jobs (McLanahan, 2002). These outcomes, interestingly, do not pertain to children living in single-parent households that result from the death of a parent (Kiernan, 1992). (We will discuss this later in the chapter.)

The Effects of Lowered Economic Status. Economic disadvantage is known to have negative consequences for children. Earlier in the chapter we emphasized how the income of all family members typically drops after divorce. The income of single mothers is about one-third that of their married counterparts, partially the result of lack of economic support by fathers (Carlson and Corcoran, 2001). Eighty-nine percent of single parents (primarily mothers) were due support in 1997. Of these, 66 percent received partial payment. However, payment itself does not guarantee an adequate income. On average, nonresident parents paid $3,700 for child support in 1997 (U.S. Bureau of the Census, 1999b).

When economic support is inadequate, unmet nutritional needs and poor housing contribute to poor cognitive, social, and emotional development in children (Carlson and Corcoran, 2001). Recall the information on the relationship between depression in adulthood and parental divorce that emphasized the consequences of economic loss after divorce (Ross and Mirowsky, 1999). Low income was associated with low occupation and education. Most of the effects of depression in adults were due to their lower educational attainment.

Psychological Well-Being. There is no doubt that most of those who experience the trauma of marriage disruption feel angry, sad, irritable, or depressed. These feelings tend to dissipate with time for the majority of adults and children, and they recover from the divorce experience within about two years (Aseltine, 1996; Hetherington and Kelly, 2002). Research has discovered, however, that some children experience lingering effects. Both boys and girls have been found to have increased levels of depression when they reach early adulthood (Cherlin, Chase-Lansdale, and McRae, 1998) and some adult children of divorce exhibit jealousy, anger, and domineering, critical, or uncommunicative behaviors (Amato, 1996)—behaviors that inhibit effective interpersonal communication.

Among 522 California teenagers whose parents had divorced, depression was lowest among adolescents when there was consistency and good parenting in both parents' households. When there was a great discrepancy between parenting in the two households, children experienced higher levels of depression and anxiety. These emotions were manifest indirectly. That is, when parenting styles and values were dissimilar, adolescents reported feeling caught between their parents, and this loyalty struggle was associated with depression and anxiety. Discrepancy in parenting styles also led to conflict between adolescents and their residential parent, and that conflict was, in turn, associated with depression and anxiety (Buchanan, Maccoby, and Dornbusch, 1996).

A recent study using a representative national sample of over 2,500 adults (of all races) found adult children of divorce (both men and women) had more unhappy interpersonal relationships, a history of divorce and remarriage, and higher levels of depression and mistrust compared to those who grew up with both parents. They also had lower levels of educational attainment and occupational status, a history of economic hardship, and greater current economic hardships. Analyses indicated that there was no direct psychological harm (depression, lowered trust) to adult mental health because of childhood parental divorce. Rather, it was restricted to educational attainment and economic hardships following divorce that affected adult depression and trust (Ross and Mirowsky, 1999).

Parental Socialization Practices

We mentioned earlier that the divorce transition often brings with it changes in parenting. At the time of the divorce and immediately afterward, both parents tend to be inconsistent in their parenting practices, express less affection for children, and find it harder to control children (Hines, 1997). Other changes have also been noted. Mothers and fathers in single-parent households are more likely to leave their adolescent child home alone (Acock and Demo, 1994), a finding that holds for all racial groups and children's ages (Bulcroft, Carmody, and Bulcroft, 1998). In addition to reduced monitoring, single parents have fewer rules, exert less supervision and control, and are less involved in decision making pertaining to children (Astone and McLanahan, 1991; Bulcroft, et. al., 1998; Dornbusch et al., 1985).

When looking at differences in parenting styles, Kurdek and Fine (1993) found that single-parent fathers were more likely to be judged by their early adolescent children as more permissive than were first-married parents or parents who had experienced more than one divorce. Stepmother families were viewed as the least permissive. Interestingly, single-parent fathers were also reported to be more authoritarian compared to the other three groups (single-mother households, stepfather families, and parents who had been divorced more than once). The permissiveness of single fathers also was reported by Thomson and her colleagues (1992), who found that single fathers allowed children to be left alone at home, knew of their whereabouts less often, and let them stay up beyond their bedtime to a greater extent than did biological parents, parents in stepfather-stepmother families, single mothers, or cohabiting mothers.

In Chapter 5 we stressed that parenting practices have well-documented outcomes for children. That is, in samples that are predominantly white, authoritative parenting is associated with less psychological distress, higher self-esteem, better grades in school, fewer delinquent acts, and less drug and alcohol use (Avenevoli, Sessa, and Steinberg, 1999). Some research shows that an authoritarian style may be more effective when parenting teens in high-risk environments (Baldwin, Baldwin, and Cole, 1990; Deater-Deckard et al., 1996). Following up research conducted by Steinberg et al. (1991), Avenevoli and her colleagues (1999) questioned over 11,000 high school students. They compared youths living in single-parent households with those living with two biological parents, in working- and middle-class families, and in African American, European American, Asian American, and Hispanic American families. Their findings showed that parenting in two-parent families, regardless of ethnicity, race, or class, was more authoritative, more authoritarian, less permissive, and less neglectful. Differences between the two types of family structures were small, but nonetheless evident. No differences in parenting styles were found among whites, blacks, Latinos, or Asian Americans or between middle-class and working-class parents. Regarding parental socialization practices, these researchers wrote:

> Virtually regardless of ethnic or social class background, across one- and two-parent homes alike, adolescents whose parents are warm and democratic and who provide limits and structure report less psychological distress and more positive self-esteem, perform better in school, and engage in less delinquent behavior than peers. (Avenevoli et al., 1999, 87–88)

The Effects of Stress

Death and divorce rank first and second on the list of life events in terms of their emotional intensity and need for time to recover and adjust (Joung et al., 1997). These events bring stressful changes in family positions and roles, sometimes requiring a change in housing, neighborhood, and schools for children. In one study, 30 percent of custodial parents moved out of the area within two years after separation (Braver, Ellman, and Fabricius, 2003). We have already discussed the change in socioeconomic conditions after divorce, but we emphasize here the high stress level that accompanies it. Economic stress associated with divorce may be the strongest explanatory factor related to poor adjustment postdivorce. A study comparing widowed and divorced women reported that although equally large proportions of both groups of women were in the lowest income level, divorced women reported excessive health complaints and had a harder time paying the rent, paying electric bills, and meeting their housing needs. Economic deprivation associated with divorce was the key explanatory factor. This is how the difference was explained:

> Widowed women with the same level of household income as divorced women are actually better off financially. . . . [D]ivorced women often lose their house and generally must divide assets with their ex-husband, but widowed women more often retain the family home and financial assets intact. (Lillard and Waite, 1995, 1154)

A majority of children experiencing parental divorce or death appear to suffer no long-lasting negative consequences. Quite the contrary, research indicates that for some children the single-parent household experience provides the opportunities to develop a strong sense of responsibility, competence, and independence that promotes developmental growth (Demo and Acock, 1988; Hines, 1997). Further, if the parental marriage is excessively conflicted, children are better off in a conflict-free single-parent household.

However, positive outcomes are not merely a function of time. Research has identified three effective **resilience resources** that serve to ameliorate the negative consequences of divorce and living in a single-parent household:

1. Having adults close to children who can act as supportive resources, helping them cope with their emotions and changed family situations.

2. Consistent warmth and discipline provided by the residential parent.

3. The quality of the child-father relationship.

To the degree that fathers participate in decisions involving children, have and take opportunities to visit and stay in contact with their children, and ex-spouses contain the conflict between them, children of divorce will thrive, and the "legacy of divorce" will change (Haine et al., 2003).

Remarriage and Stepparenting

Sixty percent of all Americans are expected to be part of a stepfamily at some point in their lives (Bumpass, Raley, and Sweet, 1994). The majority of us, then, have something to gain from learning about this family structure. Here are some answers to the question we asked earlier in the chapter: Who remarries?

- In about 50 percent of all marriages in 1990, at least one of the partners was entering a remarriage (Coleman, Ganong, and Fine, 2000).

- Overall, two out of three ever-married persons remarry, and 75 percent of divorced persons remarry within 10 years (Coleman et al., 2000).

- Men remarry in greater numbers than women, and whites in greater numbers than blacks and Latinos. Five years after divorce, 32 percent of black women, 44 percent of Latina women, and 58 percent of white women are remarried (National Center for Health Statistics, 2002).

- It does not take long for a person to contract a new marriage: About 30 percent do so within a year after divorce, with an average time of less than four years between divorce and remarriage (Coleman et al., 2000).

- The widowed, both men and women, take slightly longer to remarry than those who are divorced. Widowed white men remarry within 3.6 years after the death of their spouses, while widowed women wait an average of 6 years (Wilson and Clarke, 1992).

- Blacks who are widowed take longer to remarry than whites: 6.1 years for men and 8.9 years for women (Coleman et al., 2000).

• Sixty percent of remarried couples divorce. Divorce rates are 50 percent higher in remarriages in which there are stepchildren compared to those with no step-children (Hetherington and Stanley-Hagan, 2000).

A number of reasons help explain the longer time between divorce (or the death of a spouse) and remarriage for women compared to men. First, as the population ages, the sex ratio changes and there are fewer eligible men for older women to marry. Second, women with very low or very high education levels find it harder to attract compatible mates, while high education level is a desirable characteristic for men. Third, employed women take longer to remarry. However, this association is complex: high-status occupations tend to delay remarriage for younger women but speed it up for older women. High occupational status enhances marriageability for men. Fourth, women typically have residential custody of children after divorce, and having residential children tends to slow (but not block) the path to remarriage.

Remarried relationships are more complex and difficult than first marriages for a number of reasons, which may explain why more than half of second marriages end in divorce. However, the possibility of another divorce is not a deterrent for those who remarry, for the majority of men and women who divorce a second time enter into a third, or higher marriage. The marriage-divorce-remarriage-redivorce experience has led scholars to label the process of marital partnering in our postmodern era as **serial monogamy.** How many people are we talking about? More than one-third of all Americans are expected to marry, divorce, and remarry during their lifetimes (Cherlin and Furstenberg, 1994).

Given the higher divorce rate and the difficulty of helping rear children who are not one's own, it is surprising to find that some researchers find no significant differences in marital satisfaction levels between first-married and remarried couples (Booth and Edwards, 1992; Furstenberg and Spanier, 1984). One study that sought to explain this inconsistency differentiated cross-sectional from longitudinal findings. These data confirmed the similarity in marital quality between first-marrieds and remarrieds but also showed that remarried couples were more likely to report a decline in marital quality over an eight-year period (Booth and Edwards, 1992).

MacDonald and DeMaris (1995) conducted a study demonstrating the complexity of remarriage. In a cross-sectional study of 2,655 couples, these researchers found no difference in the degree of marital conflict when comparing first-married couples and couples in remarriages in which only one spouse was remarried. However, with double remarriage (when both spouses were previously married), less marital conflict was reported than in the other two groups. The researchers hypothesized that double remarriages bring together persons who hold realistic expectations gained from their prior marriage that serve to diminish conflict.

MacDonald and DeMaris found couple conflict to be lower in the first year of remarriage when there were only stepchildren in the family compared to families with only biological children. However, by six and ten years of marriage, stepchildren-only couples were experiencing more marital conflict than those with biological-only children. Two possible explanations for this finding were offered. Stepchildren-only families may have established workable rules and interaction patterns prior to their marriage (perhaps based on those realistic expectations they held) and thus marriage conflict was at a minimum in the first year of marriage. This advantage was lost as couples with biological-only children matured, established homeostasis, and decreased their conflict. Alternatively, MacDonald and DeMaris suggest that remarried couples may hold unrealistic hopes for what family life will be like. They deny the amount of conflict experienced in the early stages of the marriage in order to establish integration, unity, and harmony. Over time, denial diminishes, and as expectations become more realistic, harmony is replaced by conflict. We discuss the issues related to the complexity inherent in remarriage next.

Types of Remarriages

Part of the difficulty of establishing a stable and lasting remarriage comes from the complex family structure that may result from the new union. Nine different remarriage family structures have been documented (Ihinger-Tallman and Pasley, 1987). Table 8.1 elaborates these types.

Couples in Types One and Two resemble a first marriage and experience most family processes, such as establishing boundary maintenance, cohesion, clear communication patterns, and commitment, under the same conditions as first-married couples. However, couples in second marriages without children have a higher risk of divorce than childless first-married couples (Furstenberg and Cherlin, 1991). Types Three through Nine are sufficiently different from a first marriage to introduce complexity into these processes. Research shows that stepfamilies are less close and cohesive than first-married families (Henderson et al., 1996; Ihinger-Tallman and Pasley, 1987). Family boundaries are loosened because there are others (nonresidential children, former spouses, ex-in-laws, adult stepchildren) who may feel they have a "right" to comment on, offer advice, or try to control the behavior, goals, expenditure of resources, and so on, of the new couple. Some scholars have argued that stepfamilies actually benefit from less cohesion and more permeable family boundaries. This is because, if family unity and loyalty (which typify high cohesion) are immediate goals of a remarried couple, they will no doubt suffer from disappointment and unmet expectations. It is generally thought that cohesion and family integration take three to five years to develop in remarried families (Bray, 1999; Ihinger-Tallman and Pasley, 1987). It is this complexity and diversity that can make remarriage problematic.

When divorced women remarry, they improve their economic standing. Accompanying this increase in standard of living, however, is a set of circumstances unique to remarriages. All the system processes of family interaction that must be established when a new partnership is formed are confounded by the presence of a former spouse, children with "outside" parents, and kin from a former marriage. What's more, the remarriage situation varies depending on many factors:

- Do both partners in the new marriage have an ex-spouse?
- Are relations between ex-spouses cordial?
- How far away do ex-spouses live?
- Do they pay child support?
- Do they visit the children?

	Table 8.1 Typology of Remarried Families
1.	Remarried spouses, both are childless. This type of family is not structurally different from a first-married one except that at least one spouse has prior marital experience.
2.	Remarried spouses who only have a child with the current partner—a child-in-common. Again, this type resembles a first-married couple, except for the prior marital experience of at least one of the spouses. The fact of the parent's previous marriage(s) is irrelevant to the child of this union.
3.	Remarried spouses, at least one has an adult child from a previous marriage. Here the differentiating factor is the adult status of the offspring. Remarriage is expected to be somewhat different for couples that are past the age of parenting minor children. This is not to say that older couples do not encounter difficulties pertaining to children. Rather, the issues and problems related to child rearing are not part of their daily lives.
4.	Remarried spouses who have a child in common and one or both partners have a child from a previous marriage who does not reside with the couple. The couple may or may not have the nonresidential child visit. Here the remarried couple approximates a first family by having their own biological child. However the presence of a nonresidential child who occasionally visits his or her parent is a distinguishing characteristic of this remarriage type.
5.	Remarried spouses with no children in common, but at least one of the partners has a child from a previous marriage and the child does not reside with the couple. The nonresidential child may or may not visit. In this case the child is a potential participant in the couple's life but usually only on a visiting basis. Frequency of visits may vary widely, from regular weekly visits to extremely rare ones. However, custody arrangements do change and remarried couples of this type could very well fall into category 6 at some point in time.
6.	Remarried spouses, one of whom has a child from a previous marriage residing in the home. This remarried type is labeled "simple," meaning children of only one spouse reside with the remarried couple.
7.	Remarried spouses, both of whom have a child from a prior marriage residing in the home. This family incorporates stepsiblings as an aspect of its structure. This remarried type is labeled "complex," meaning children of both spouses reside with the remarried couple. The following two types are variations of the complex stepfamily.
8.	Remarried spouses, both of whom have a child from a previous marriage residing with them, plus a child in common. The distinguishing characteristic here is a half-sibling as a member of the sibling sub-system.
9.	Remarried spouses, both of whom have a child residing with them, plus a child in common, plus a nonresidential child of one or both spouses living elsewhere. This type of stepfamily is the most complex of all, incorporating all possible contingencies. It includes stepmother, stepfather, stepsibling, and half-sibling positions, plus residential and nonresidential children.

Ihinger-Tallman, M. and Pasley, B. K. 1987. *Remarriage* (pp. 48–49). Newbury Park, CA: Sage Publications.

- How old are the children?

- Are they boys or girls?

- How do the children feel about the new marriage?

- Have they been able to grieve the break-up of their parent's marriage?

Answers to these questions help determine how well the new couple and family members adjust to one another. Studies that compare different family structures generally find that child outcomes (e.g., staying in school, grades in school, academic achievement, psychological well-being) are better when children are living in stepfamilies compared to single-parent households. However, these children usually do not fare as well as children living in never-divorced two-parent families.

The divorce-remarriage process is intricate. Some attempts have been made to disentangle the effects of these life processes. For example, one study of adolescents in remarriages found that conduct problems were associated with the experience of parental divorce, not remarriage. It was the divorced-couple relationship that accounted for behavioral problems, not the remarriage (Anderson et al., 1999). In the following sections we discuss some of the differences between stepfather and stepmother family structures and describe the effects of living in a stepfamily for adults and children.

Stepfather Families. Fifteen percent of all children in the United States were living with their mother and a stepfather in 1992 (Hines, 1997). Most of the information available on stepfamilies is about stepfather families because the majority of mothers retain physical custody of children after divorce. Scant research has been conducted on minority stepfamilies, but one study comparing black and white stepfamilies found them to be very similar (Fine et al., 1992). One exception was a slightly lower level of life satisfaction among blacks. In Fine and his colleagues' study, adults in both groups living in stepfather families reported that their children's lives were not going well and that the quality of the stepparent-stepchild relationship was poorer (compared to adults in black and white first-married families). However, in both first-married and stepfamilies, white parents perceived their children to be more psychologically distressed than black parents did. This difference might be due to the greater prevalence of divorce and single-parent families in the black community. Alternatively, these researchers speculated that white parents may have a higher likelihood of reporting that their children are distressed compared to black parents (i.e., a difference in response style by race) even when there are no actual differences experienced by the children.

Most studies find that stepfathers have less difficulty rearing their partner's children than stepmothers do. Some data suggest that stepfathers find less satisfaction with their stepchildren after a child is born to the new marriage and they become biological parents for the first time. However, after the birth of a first child, subsequent births to the remarried couple have no effect on satisfaction with stepchildren (MacDonald and DeMaris, 1996).

What is the family climate like in stepfamilies? Stepfather families are perceived to be more permissive than stepmother families, as reported by adolescent stepchildren. Kurdek and Fine (1993) found that teenagers living in stepfather families described their family climate as less warm than did adolescents living in first-married families. However, the climate was viewed as warmer than that reported by teens living in single-parent households and stepmother families.

Probably contributing to teens' perceptions of less warmth, stepfather families are also characterized by less parental involvement and, not coincidentally, are seen as being less cohesive. The level of involvement of stepfathers with stepchildren appears to be an important factor influencing child behaviors. When Amato and Rivera (1999) investigated this factor, they found, compared to first-married families, that children in stepfather families manifest significantly more behavior problems (measured as not attending school, parents required to meet with the teacher or principal, trouble with the police, etc.). This behavior was conditioned, however, by level of involvement. If stepfathers were highly involved in the lives of their stepchildren—that is, they frequently ate breakfast and dinner with them, helped with homework, talked and played with them, and engaged in activities away from the home—children had few behavior problems.

Are Dads Still in the Picture? Approximately two-thirds of children living in stepfather families maintain some contact with their biological fathers. When children develop an attachment to their stepfathers, does this influence the relationship with their biological father? A recent study conducted by White and Gilbreth (2001) found no association between adolescents' evaluations of their biological fathers and their stepfathers. Good relationships with stepfathers were not at the expense of good relationships with fathers, and vice versa. These researchers also found that contact with a biological father was unrelated to the quality of the teenagers' relationships with their stepfathers. They did find that when teens reported good relationships with their stepfathers, they had fewer overall problems (as reported by mothers). When children reported that they had good relations with their biological fathers, they were also perceived to have few problems, but the association was weaker than it was for stepfathers.

These two issues—contact with biological fathers and level of stepfather involvement—may be clues to answering one of the questions posed at the beginning of this chapter: Why does one child appear to thrive in a newly formed stepfamily while a sibling has a much more difficult time? One answer may relate to varying levels of attachment children have to their parents, and vice versa. That is, while most parents claim not to have "favorites," they may find that they resonate to one child more than another, with more shared interests, values, physical resemblance, and so on. Birth order, the sex of parent and child—any number of variables may be the source of partiality. These subtle preferences do not matter in an intact family system that establishes equilibrium and a homeostasis that integrates these differences. However, when the system is disrupted and one parent leaves, more than family structure changes. Parents and children suffer varying degrees of pain. Many complex factors, including identities, resiliency, and dependency, facilitate or hinder the healing and adaptation process. And the outcomes may be different for different children. After a mother remarries, one child may thrive in the new stepfamily, feeling affection and respect for a stepfather and a desire to please, while a sister who was more attached to her father may hate her stepfather. In one case, academic achievement, recognition, and college follow. In the other, the child may turn to illegal drugs and run away from home (Ihinger-Tallman, 1986).

Stepmother Families. About 1 percent of American children lived with their father and stepmother in 1995 (Hines, 1997). Stepmother families have the most difficult stepparent-stepchild relationships. This difficulty is mediated somewhat when fathers have physical custody and children live with their stepmother. Under this condition, stepmothers report feeling more secure and having a closer partnership with their husbands compared to stepmothers with nonresident children (Furstenberg and Spanier, 1984; Quick, McHenry, and Newman, 1995).

In general, more stepfathers than stepmothers assume the parent position and roles with stepchildren. Perhaps this is because it may be more difficult for a stepmother to take on "mother" roles than for a stepfather to become an added "father." Women usually see childcare and homemaking tasks as their responsibility, and these tasks increase their involvement with stepchildren. One must get children to make their bed, do the dishes, clean their room, and so on, if the work is to get done. "Making" a child who is not your own (and who incidentally may resent your existence) do something is fraught with difficulties, and these difficulties tend to decrease satisfaction with the relationship—for both adult and child.

Adolescents living in stepmother families report more conflict in their families than adolescents who live in other family structures, including two biological-parent families, single-parent mothers, single-parent fathers, and those whose parents experience more than two divorces (Kurdek and Fine, 1993). When stepmothers adopt the role of friend with their stepchild, the relationship tends to be more successful than if they try to be a parent (Church, 1999; Coleman et al., 2000). A study comparing parent socialization behavior across a variety of family structures found stepmothers engaged in less praising and hugging as well as less yelling and spanking than mothers in first-married two-parent families, mothers in stepfather families, mothers in families where both parents were stepparents, cohabiting mothers, or divorced or never-married single mothers. It was suggested that stepmothers are less emotionally engaged with their stepchildren, which diffuses both negative and positive responses toward children (Thomson et al., 1992).

There are no clear-cut predictions about long-term outcomes of stepmother-stepchild relationships. Some studies find that this relationship grows more positive over time, while others find a growing distance. In a longitudinal study of stepmother families, many stepmothers reported overall positive relations with their stepchild at the beginning of the study. Over the course of three years, however, the researchers found stepmothers' positive expectations and attitudes, optimism, satisfaction with childcare, whether they liked being a stepmother, and positive evaluations of their stepchild had lessened (Guisinger, Cowan, and Schuldberg, 1989). This decrease in overall satisfaction over time may be the result of unclear roles and norms governing stepchild, stepfather, and stepmother behaviors. A long time ago Cherlin (1978) addressed this phenomenon when he labeled remarriage an **incomplete institution**. A quarter of a century later, researchers still have not documented any clearly established normative behaviors for members of stepfamilies.

Effects of Remarriage on Children

One in seven American children currently lives with a parent and stepparent. This figure varies among racial and ethnic groups: In 1998 the figure was 14.6 percent for white children, 16.1 percent for Latino children, and 32.3 percent for black children (Arnold, 1998). About one-third of all children are expected to live with a stepparent for some time before reaching age 19 (Amato, 2000a). When parents remarry after divorce, the new family has one unique characteristic: the child now has more than two parents. As Coleman and her colleagues (2000) noted, the death of a parent whose spouse subsequently remarries brings a *substitute* parent into the family; divorce and remarriage bring added parents. How does this addition affect children?

For starters, we reiterate that there is a great deal of variation in the way children adapt to parental remarriage. When a stepfamily provides warm, supportive, and involved parenting, children thrive just as they do in first-married families or single-parent households with these characteristics. However, when these conditions are missing, children's relationships with family members may suffer long-term consequences. Ahrons and Tanner (2003) reported on a study of adult children and their relationships with fathers after parental divorce. Adults whose relationships with fathers worsened after the divorce conceded they also had poor relations with their stepmothers, stepsiblings, and paternal grandparents, compared with adult children whose relationships with fathers stayed the same or improved after divorce.

Studies are relatively consistent in showing that stepchildren, compared to children in first-married families, leave home at younger ages, drop out of school, are more likely to experience sexual abuse, are more depressed, have more emotional problems, exhibit more behavioral problems, use drugs and alcohol more frequently, engage in sexual intercourse at younger ages, and are more likely to have children premaritally (Coleman et al., 2000). At the microsystem level, a large proportion of children, between 24 percent and 30 percent, report disorganization and tense relations in their family (Furstenberg and Cherlin, 1991). Others come to feel their family situation is "hopeless" (Quick et al., 1995). Yet, in spite of these negative outcomes, the picture is mixed. Almost half of the children whose parents remarry view their families as close, relaxed, and with a large amount of sharing (Furstenberg and Cherlin, 1991).

Stepfamilies offer the opportunity for a number of complex relationships among children. In addition to their own siblings (in the family of orientation), parental remarriage often brings with it stepsiblings and/or half-siblings, all of whom may live with them full-time, part-time, or never (Ganong and Coleman, 1994). After one or both of their parents remarried, almost 75 percent of children gained a stepsibling and 37 percent a half-sibling, according to one study of adult children of divorce (Ahrons and Tanner, 2003). In some instances children of divorced parents may not learn of the existence of stepsiblings until they are adults, if ever. The grandfather of one of your authors remarried after many years and never told his two sons born to the new marriage of his first marriage and two older daughters. When his 42-year-old daughter and 13-year-old granddaughter came to visit, they were introduced to the teenage boys as "family friends." (Talk about a family secret!) However, even when relationships are acknowledged, children often do not consider stepsiblings as part of their family, indicating how permeable family boundaries can be after remarriage. When Furstenberg (1987) asked children to name the members of their immediate family, 41 percent failed to mention their stepsiblings. This omission was unrelated to the amount of time the children lived together in a stepfamily.

On average, sibling relationships are less close in stepfamilies. Siblings normally tend to disengage from one another during adolescence, and for children living in stepfamilies this distance is maintained during adulthood (Anderson and Rice, 1992; White and Reidmann, 1992a). Siblings in stepfamilies score higher on measures of antisocial behavior, noncompliance, and aggression, but they are similar to children in single-parent families (Anderson et al., 1999). Many factors contribute to the quality of sibling/stepsibling relationships after divorce and remarriage, including the quality of parenting, sex and ages of children, and length of the remarriage.

A longitudinal study by Hetherington (1988) examined all these factors and reported a complex picture of children's behavior. After remarriage, she found sibling relationships were characterized by more rivalry, aggression, and avoidant behaviors compared to nondivorced families (as reported by stepfathers and the children themselves). Mothers saw these characteristics only in sons, but children and stepfathers perceived stepdaughters as more avoidant than stepsons. Stepchildren were viewed as less warm, as less engaged, and as avoiding their siblings more often than children in two other family structures (those living with divorced, nonremarried mothers or with never-divorced parents). After six years in the stepfamily, sibling aggression had decreased to a level similar to that in the never-divorced families, as had rivalry (but rivalry was still higher than in never-divorced families). Girls were more avoidant and disengaged, especially if they had a brother.

Across the three types of families analyzed in this study, sibling relationships were most affected by the quality of parenting. No matter which type of family structure, if parents were punitive, unaffectionate, and unresponsive to children's needs and erratic in the enforcement of discipline, sibling interaction was characterized by hostility, rivalry, and lack of affection. This was especially true if parents favored one child over another. Particularly in stepfamilies, "when there was preferential treatment of children by stepfathers this led to even more dissention and avoidance than was found with preferential treatment by biological fathers in nondivorced families. Moreover, these effects were most marked when both siblings were girls" (Hetherington, 1988, 328).

In spite of the complexity that stepfamily life entails, resiliency is evident in many youngsters. Becoming a stepsibling can be the source of identity change in children. This change can occur when a child suddenly becomes the oldest, or youngest, or gets lost in the middle of a newly combined household. Ordinal positions among siblings have definite roles attached to them, and remarriage brings increases or decreases in status, rights, and privileges. One seven-year-old "only" child we know quickly found a meaningful identity as "older brother" upon the birth of a stepsibling. He continued to move weekly between his two parents' households, but his new and valued position gave his life a structure that it had lacked before the baby came.

Kin and Extended Family

Bengtson (2001) hypothesized that multigenerational (three or more generations) bonds are becoming increasingly important in American society. Intergenerational relationships are highly diverse in their structures and functions and some scholars expect them to become more important for the well-being and support of family members over the life cycle than nuclear family ties. During the past decade, an increasing number of grandparents have become responsible for rearing their grandchildren (Bryson and Casper, 1999). However, we do not know whether this care extends to stepgrandchildren. An estimated 40 percent of all families include stepgrandparents (Szinovacz, 1998).

In their extensive review of remarried relationships, Ganong and Coleman (1994) summarized the involvement grandparents have in the lives of their (step)-grandchildren. Reflecting Cherlin's (1978) incomplete institution concept, they tell us there are few guidelines for grandparents who want a continuing relationship with the ex-spouse of a divorced adult child. How and whether to stay in contact with grandchildren when a divorced child no longer lives with the child's other parent is not yet prescribed in social norms. Therefore, there is great variation in the amount of involvement. Involvement is higher if the adult child has physical custody of the grandchildren. When the former son- or daughter-in-law has custody, the amount of contact depends primarily on that person. If in-laws were close before a divorce, they are more likely to be close after the marriage ends. Even so, contact diminishes, and grandparents provide less social and emotional support as time passes. When a daughter with physical custody of her children divorces, grandparents are likely to be involved with the grandchildren, offering emotional and financial help. When daughters remarry, contact does not diminish but giving help and resources is reduced (Ganong and Coleman, 1994).

When a divorced son or daughter remarries, the relationship between the children of the new spouse and the new stepgrandparents is normatively unclear. Three factors that help determine the kind of steprelationships that evolve are how old the children are, which parent has residential custody, and whether the new marriage is accepted by family members (Cherlin and Furstenberg, 1986). Younger children, children who live with the adult child of the stepgrandparents, and a new marriage that is supported and accepted by both stepgrandchildren and stepgrandparents are the conditions of perceiving the stepgrandparent relation as important as a biological grandparent relationship. For the most part, children have little difficulty accepting a new set of stepgrandparents and view these older adults in their lives not as a "substitution" but as an "augmentation" or expansion of their kin network; "more like an accordion than a pie" (Furstenberg, 1987, 58). With more adults in their lives to offer support and nurturance, children can only benefit.

Analyzing a sample of college students, Sanders and Trygstad (1989) found grandparents had more contact with their grandchildren than stepgrandparents did. This lessened contact had been the case since the children were young, during grade school and high school. Fifty percent of the students rated their grandparents as "extremely important" compared to 6 percent for stepgrandparents. However, a large number—40 percent and 42 percent, respectively—rated both their grandparents and stepgrandparents as "important." Other studies also find relationships between stepgrandchildren and stepgrandparents more distant than those between biological kin (Doka and Mertz, 1988; Henry and Ceglian, 1989).

Looking at this issue from the perspective of the stepgrandparents, one study found 35 percent felt that "there are often problems in getting grandparents to accept stepchildren" (Furstenberg and Spanier, 1984, 153). A second study by these same researchers reported that 33 percent of stepgrandparents agreed with the following statements: "Your stepgrandchild can't think of you as a real grandparent," "It is harder for you to be a stepgrandparent than a grandparent," "You feel differently about your natural grandchildren than your stepgrandchildren," and "It is generally harder for you to love your stepgrandchildren than your own grandchildren" (Cherlin and Furstenberg, 1986, 161).

In spite of any emotional barriers, people may have a self-serving motive for maintaining good relations with stepgrandchildren: it allows them to maintain access to their own adult children (Johnson, 1989). Considering the increase in the number of divorces and remarriages that have occurred since the data for these two studies were gathered, it is not unreasonable to think that stepgrandparenthood has grown more common and is more familiar. There may now be fewer stepgrandparents who have difficulty accepting their new stepgrandchildren.

Death as the Cause of Marital Dissolution

We will end this section on marital transitions as we began: with a discussion about death as the cause of marital disruption. Death ends marriages of all duration, as we noted in the chapter's introduction. However, the odds of becoming a widow or widower increase with age. Widowers have higher rates of remarriage than widows. Widowed women are slower to remarry than divorced women, and they are also less likely to remarry. One explanation is that many widows are attitudinally less disposed to remarriage because they feel they cannot find a mate who compares well to the one they had. In addition to attitudinal barriers, as age increases there are fewer eligible men in the marriage market. Thus, because of the differences in remarriage behavior and in mortality rates, there are fewer men than women among the ranks of the separated, divorced, or widowed at any given time (Morgan, 1991).

Why Do the Widowed Remarry?

Remarriage is an important determinant of physical and economic well-being among the widowed. Among the elderly, there are several reasons for remarriage. They include: loneliness, a desire for a companion and/or sexual partner, a need for greater financial security, and a desire to share household responsibilities. It appears that remarriage among the widowed favors those who have the most resources. Among older widowers, those who are better educated with higher economic status are more likely to remarry. Widows who are black or who have dependent children in the home are the least likely to remarry (Smith, Zick, and Duncan, 1991). Given that the well educated, the healthy, and those with the most resources are the most likely to remarry, three significant variables associated with widowhood among those who do not remarry are, low education level, poverty, and racial minority status. When widowed women do not remarry, their financial situation does not improve over time. About one-third live in poverty, and another 10–15 percent have marginal incomes (Morgan, 1991).

Labor Force Participation

Among the 3,756 women Morgan (1991) studied, 69–78 percent of widows worked full-time (they were followed over a ten-year period), compared to 82–89 percent of divorced and 63–67 percent of married women. She found a general shift in work patterns before and immediately after the death of a spouse. In her study more women left the workforce after becoming widowed than entered it, but after a year or two, these women were once again employed. Five years after widowhood the pattern shifted again, with women once again leaving the labor force. White women were more likely than black women to make labor force changes after the death of a spouse, because black women were more likely to be working prior to the loss of their partner. Older widows were less likely than younger ones to look for employment, especially if they had never worked. Morgan speculated that this was because they more likely held traditional gender-role attitudes that may have inhibited their labor force participation.

Among middle-aged widows, wages make up the larger part of their income. These earnings contribute to greater Social Security benefits when they retire. Some younger widows have survivor benefits from Social Security paid to them because they have dependent children in addition to their earnings. Older widows depend to a greater extent on Social Security benefits, earnings from investments or savings, or public or private pension benefits for their financial security. However, these sources of income are highly dependent on the economic situation within the exosystem. Recessions, depressions, and boom times affect both widowed men's and women's pension payments, employment opportunities, and overall financial security.

Kin Support

What about relationships with adult children after widowhood? Research indicates that children are key players during times of bereavement. After the death of a parent, adult children increase both the frequency of contact and the amount of emotional support they offer the surviving parent (Umberson and Slaten, 2000). Aquilino (1994) found that the relationship between mothers and their children did not change after the fathers' death. However, if the mother died, substantial declines in the father-daughter relationship occurred. Father-son relationships changed only minimally. Chapter 6 discussed several issues related to adult children and parental death.

Children Living in Widowed Single-Parent Households

Children who live in single-parent households formed as a result of the death of their father are more likely to complete high school, enter and graduate from college, gain a higher than average occupational status, and report a higher level of happiness as an adult compared to children of divorce. Only one negative outcome has been noted, and it is a result of comparing children in widowed with those in two-parent families: Children whose parent died are slightly more likely to drop out of high school than teenagers who still have a father (Biblarz and Gottainer, 2000). Another variable accounting for an easier adjustment for children living with widowed versus divorced parents is that they are less likely to have experienced the negative effects of parental conflict, as children of divorce sometimes do. Also, children whose fathers or mothers die do not experience the negative emotions of rejection, hostility, or anger that some children do when one parent leaves the family (Wallerstein and Kelly, 1980).

Because most children of divorce and children whose fathers die live in single-mother families (i.e., the same type of family structure) Biblarz and Gottainer (2000) wanted to account for the differences in child well-being. How did they do this? They first examined the responses of single mothers (1,494 divorced, 960 never-married, and 149 widowed), looking at behaviors and values, including smoking, drinking, and going to bars. They found no differences among the three groups of mothers. They asked for self-rated reports of health and psychological well-being and found no differences. Looking at values, all mothers were equally likely to attend church, value religion, share similar values about rearing children, share values of gender equality, and have a similar general level of optimism. So, could anything explain the differences in widowed versus divorced parent-child outcomes? As you may have guessed, the answer lay in the amount of socioeconomic resources held by mothers. Widowed mothers were more likely to hold higher-status occupational positions (with or without controlling for education), and their earnings were higher. This advantage did not come from higher educational attainment, because there was no difference in the average attainment of the mothers. These researchers concluded that widowed mothers held "an advantaged position in the social structure" (545). Advantage came to widowed parents because of macrosystem and exosystem factors, such as policy decisions and public support that are more favorable to widows and that discriminate against other single mothers. We'll look at some of these system factors next.

The Big Picture: Family Transitions in a Social Context

Divorce has always been a part of the American social structure, even in Puritan New England. Departing from English Law, the Puritans adopted a liberal (for the times) civil divorce policy as a way of ending, albeit reluctantly, living arrangements that were no longer viable (Calhoun, 1945; Demos, 1973). Divorce, like the institution of legal marriage, is a social response. It is a way that society regulates and controls otherwise spontaneous behaviors. Policies and laws regulating divorce and (re)marriage are put into place to serve group needs rather than individual needs. The story of how divorce and remarriage rates and the laws and policies associated with them have changed over time lies within the chronosystem. Figure 8.2 shows a slow but steady increase in the number of divorces obtained between 1900 and 1980 and the gradual decrease over the past two decades. Several explanations have been offered for the decline in divorce since 1980. We'll discuss them later in this section.

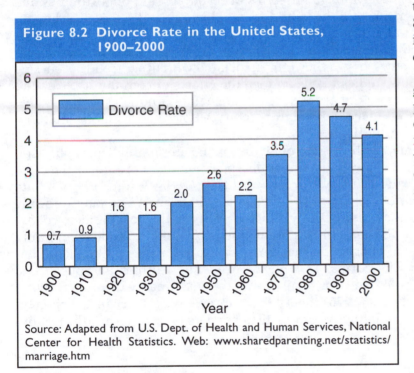

Figure 8.2 Divorce Rate in the United States, 1900–2000

Source: Adapted from U.S. Dept. of Health and Human Services, National Center for Health Statistics. Web: www.sharedparenting.net/statistics/marriage.htm

One pattern is consistent in these rates. There are sometimes small, sometimes large, increases immediately following periods of war: World War I, World War II, and the Vietnam War. According to Price and McKenry (1988), wartime brings briefer courtship leading to quick marriages and long separations, providing opportunities for extramarital involvement. Hasty marriages involving couples with disparate values, attitudes, and ways of looking at the world are likely to be untenable in the long run. Following the end of national conflict, these marriages are at high risk of ending. Bumpass, Martin, and Sweet (1991) found the marriage disruption rate to be twice as high for couples with a husband in the armed forces during the first year of marriage, compared to other couples. Another explanation for a high rate of divorce during or after periods of warfare is that participation in the macrosystem war economy fosters the development of new skills and greater independence for women, which in turn facilitates their leaving an unsatisfactory marriage. There are also stressful effects on couples that accompany long separations during military service. Finally, war experiences exact a psychological toll on men and women in the military. Elder and Clipp (1988) found men that had lingering traumatic memories from combat experience had higher divorce rates. Blankenship (2003) reported that men who saw actual combat duty were 62 percent more likely to divorce or separate compared to men who did not serve in combat.

Exosystem Effects: Does Neighborhood Matter?

Some scholars ask whether the community a family lives in has an effect on the behavior of residents. Mostly, scholars have looked for an answer to this question in urban inner-city communities and neighborhoods. Maybe this is because social norms exert a clearer influence on residents of small towns (Simmel, 1964).

When a neighborhood is disadvantaged in terms of resources and opportunities and those who live there are poor, many of the behaviors that have been discussed earlier are found: Sexual activity starts at a younger age, there are higher rates of premarital pregnancy and childbearing, and there are more single parent households. But are communities the source of these outcomes, or are they only associated with other trends occurring within society? One of the few studies that examined the effects of community structure on divorce rates found that community (measured as the neighborhood's socioeconomic status) had no direct effect on marital instability—poor people divorce more often, no matter where they live (South, 2001).

Another variable associated with the rate of divorce is the amount of geographic mobility that takes place within a community. Generally speaking, the more stable the community, the greater the marital stability (South and Lloyd, 1995; White, 1990). White (1990) has written: "Aggregate-level studies in the United States and Canada uniformly find that community stability, as measured by social mobility, is the best predictor of aggregate divorce rates" (905). The basis of this prediction is twofold: A stable community reflects a high degree of social integration that in turn assumes a strong likelihood that residents will conform to social norms. This means residents will pick an appropriate spouse, fulfill their marital roles, and not "court community stigma by divorcing" (905). These findings support Levinger's (1976) theory that we reviewed earlier in the chapter. Recall that he argued that restraining forces he called barriers (social norms, the legality of the marriage contract) discourage marital dissolution.

Effects of the Exosystem on Family Behavior

The Legal System. Over many years laws and policies in the American exosystem that are related to marriage and divorce (such as no-fault divorce, a shortened waiting period before remarriage) have brought about greater ease in dissolving marriages and entering new ones. Think about the various ways the exosystem affects marriage-related behavior:

1. In order to get married, a couple needs state approval in the form of a legal license (or, in a few cases, common law residence for a specified number of years). Gay and lesbian couples have lobbied for several years for their unions

to be legally recognized. However, in 2004, only one state, Massachusetts, legally acknowledges a gay or lesbian marriage.

2. For a couple to divorce, the state must first decree that the marriage is over. States vary in the required length of separation before a divorce can be granted.

3. The state determines or affirms the amount of spousal support and/or child support that is awarded after divorce. Sometimes this decree confirms an amount agreed on by the divorcing couple; at other times it determines a compromise settlement when an amount cannot be negotiated between spouses.

4. No-fault divorce laws adopted by states between 1969 and 1985 brought an end to the granting of divorce based on identifying one spouse as guilty of some offense (i.e., adultery, cruelty). No-fault means irreconcilable differences (irretrievable breakdown) are the only grounds for divorce.

Sanctioning the custody of children is one of the most important tasks undertaken by the legal institution within the exosystem. The various types of custody arrangements were discussed earlier in the chapter. Joint legal custody is a favorite solution in many states because it is thought that having both divorced parents responsible for making decisions about children will result in better adjustment for the children. As of 1998, 42 states explicitly authorized joint custody (compared to one, North Carolina, in 1975) (Pearson and Thoennes, 1998). In actuality, joint legal custody has not changed the fact that the mother continues to be the primary residential parent who makes most child-rearing decisions. This form of custody does have implications for continued father involvement: Fathers with joint legal custody visit their children more often and are more likely to comply with child support payments. However, an alternative view credits the greater resources of fathers who have joint legal custody as the factor that accounts for greater involvement and postdivorce contact with their children (Seltzer, 1994; Stephens, 1996).

Two other ways the exosystem influences family behavior is through **divorce mediation** and the enforcement of child support. The primary goal of mediation is to help contesting parents resolve their conflicts (dispute resolution), but it can also be seen as a way to improve postdivorce co-parenting. Mediation helps identify and negotiate mutually acceptable settlements. It may be voluntary or court ordered, and it may take place in the court, in social service agencies, or in private practices. The point of mediation is to involve a neutral third party in an attempt to negotiate differences. Lawyers, psychologists, social workers, or professional mediators tend to be facilitators (Emery, Kitzmann, and Waldron, 1999). Mediation does not mean that partners must settle their differences, only that they must try in good faith to do so. The process seems to work most of the time: Former spouses are less likely to go back to court to settle their disputes after mediation (Emery, 1995; Kelly, 1996). Both parents appear to prefer mediation to other adversarial procedures, but mothers report greater overall satisfaction with the process, outcome, and impact of custody determinations than fathers do. Mediation programs reduce the number of court custody hearings, and joint legal custody is the most frequent outcome. Further, former partners comply with mediated decisions to a greater extent than they do with adversarial decisions (Emery, 1988, 1995). Children benefit from mediation as well. Fathers are more likely to comply with child support arrangements and to stay more involved with their children following mediation (Emery, Matthews, and Kitzmann, 1994; Dillon and Emery, 1996).

One of the ways legislators have attempted to ease the negative effects of parental separation and divorce on children is by focusing on the enforcement of child support obligations. The Child Support Enforcement Program (established in 1975) was intended to locate absent parents, establish paternity for children born to unmarried mothers, and establish and enforce child support orders. In 1984 the Child Support Amendments were passed mandating that states pass laws that enforced the collection of support payments. The goals were to reduce the variability of award amounts, ensure adequate levels of payment, distribute the financial responsibility for children between residential and nonresidential parents more fairly, and reduce the child support noncompliance rate. Congress passed the Child Support Act in 1988 in an attempt to strengthen the 1984 amendments. This act required states to (Buehler, 1995):

1. Make child support guidelines mandatory.

2. Have mandatory wage withholding plans in place by 1994.

3. Make it impossible for judges to dismiss parents who are in arrears of payment.

4. Review child support orders every three years (for selected cases).

5. Increase the funding for interstate enforcement.

Today, the federal government finances 77 percent of the states' costs of enforcing and collecting support from absent parents (U.S. Bureau of the Census, 2001e). These legislative attempts have been only partially successful. In 1997, 67.4 percent of all custodial parents actually received some amount of support payment (based on 100 percent of those with a child support agreement or award); 32.6 percent received no payment at all. The full amount was received by only 40.9 percent of parents.

Religious and Educational Institutions. Other formal and informal organizations within a community exosystem are dedicated to help divorcing and remarried parents. Religious institutions, private practitioners, and social service agencies set up counseling or group therapy sessions for divorced and remarried adults and their children. Their goals are to provide support for those going through the divorce experience and help improve family relations, help parents improve their parenting skills, and help adults and children enhance their psychological adjustment and well-being (Emery et al., 1999; Price and McKenry, 1988). Many states now mandate that divorcing parents attend parent-education classes prior to granting their decree to facilitate children's adjustment to the divorce and co-parenting across households after divorce (Fine et al., 1999).

Within the exosystem the educational institution offers programs to alleviate the distress that children experience when their parents divorce. In actuality, these groups create a mesosystem between home and school. When counselors and school leaders have access to information from both microsystems, they are able to coordinate necessary help for children more effectively. Some school-based programs consist of group therapy sessions with children who share similar experiences. The goals of these programs are threefold: to provide support for the children, to dispel the myths and misconceptions surrounding divorce and separation, and to help children develop better coping skills. An implicit fourth aim benefits the school and teachers as well as students. When children understand that their experiences are not isolated and they learn to cope with the challenges and stresses associated with divorce and living in a single-parent household, it is hoped that behavioral and academic problems will decline. Evaluation research examining some of these programs found them to be "a helpful but limited intervention" (Emery et. al., 1999, 331). They are limited because schools are circumscribed in the amount of resources (budgets and counselors) that can be devoted to these programs. Their effectiveness is limited to schools with excess resources to fund the programs and select teachers and counselors who feel comfortable in the role of therapist.

Some in the helping professions are moving away from the view of children as innocent victims (Wallerstein, Lewis, and Blakeslee, 2000) to seeing them, at least older children, as active agents in reconstructing their postdivorce families. Giving older children a voice in the process begins to set a new agenda among counselors, therapists, and child custody evaluators (Walker, 2003). There are both pitfalls and benefits to giving children a say in custody decisions and visitation. Children do not always know what is best for them, and delegating too much authority to children who are too young is ineffective in helping them cope with the distress of family break-up. Care must be taken to avoid putting children in the midst of their parents' disputes. Also, empowering children beyond their capacity to understand can diminish a parent's authority over children (Warshak, 2003). There is an implicit (sometimes explicit), threat: "If you won't let me go to that concert, I'll just go live with dad. He'll let me do these kinds of things!" Nevertheless, there is a growing tendency to "move beyond a child-saving agenda as the guiding framework within which to protect children from the potential negative effects of divorce toward one that respects children and young people as competent social agents, capable of participating in a major life change" (Walker, 2003, 415).

The Economy. During the 1920s and 1930s it was widely believed that divorce rose during times of prosperity and fell during times of depression or recession (Ogburn and Thomas, 1922). South (1985) countered this idea with figures from 1945 to the mid-1980s showing a tendency for the divorce rate to fall when times were prosperous and to rise during economic recessions. This pattern was explained by arguing that divorce is more affordable in prosperous times but there is less financial stress on couples, so relationship tensions are reduced (White, 1990). In the opposite case, when personal relationships are stressed because of financial hardships, a desire to end the marriage appears to override the economic costs of divorce. With more wives in the labor force, the liabilities of staying together are offset by an ability to earn a wage and be self-supporting.

What is happening today? The divorce rate reached an all-time high in 1981 at 5.3 per 1,000 persons and has gradually declined since that date: In 2000 the rate was 4.1. Between 1981 and the early 1990s, the economy experienced a long recession, then a large upturn between 1995 and 2000. During 2001–2003, another economic recession occurred. Given these fluctuations, why does the divorce rate continue to go down? One explanation is the later age at first marriage for both men and women. Marriages contracted when spouses are beyond their teen years tend to be more stable. Another possibility is that a greater awareness of the consequences of divorce for children that is presented in the media deters some couples from ending their marriage. In 1985, South argued that a shift in social context changes the relationship between economic conditions and the divorce rate. We think that argument also holds for the time period from 1985 to 2005. The task is to understand the social context!

Macrosystem Effects on Family Behavior

Sociologists South, Trent, and Shen (2001) proposed a macrostructural theory of divorce that bridges the distal and proximal factors discussed earlier in this chapter. One of the proximal causes of divorce (finding a more attractive partner) is embedded in the social structure, specifically in the opportunities available for spouses to form alternative relationships with others. They cite research suggesting that marriage is more likely to occur when there are relatively large numbers of desirable opposite-sex partners within a given geographic area, and divorce probabilities are lowest when the numbers of males and females in a geographic area are near equal.

South, Trent, and Shen extrapolate these ideas and theorize that the availability of alternative partners might destabilize existing marriages.[3] When they tested this theory, they found that the risk of divorce for their sample of married couples was curvilinear: it was highest in labor market areas with a comparatively high sex ratio (more men than women) and in areas with a comparatively low sex ratio (more women than men). In areas where the sex ratio was nearly equal, the risk of divorce was low, supporting prior research and their theory. When several of the distal risk factors of divorce (age at marriage, education level, number of children) were controlled, the analyses showed a reduced effect but one that was still significant. When specific occupations were analyzed, the researchers found that wives who worked with many men and few women were more likely to divorce than wives who worked with many women and few men. The opposite was not found, however. Husbands who worked with a disproportionate ratio of women to men were not more likely to divorce. The authors speculated that men might find alternative partners in places other than the workplace, such as in bars, at recreational events, and in voluntary associations, whereas for many working women recreational and volunteer opportunities are limited.

The Consequences of Changing Norms and Values. A macrosystem concept, **permanent availability,** lies at the core of South and his colleagues' research. Farber coined this concept in 1964. He hypothesized that in U.S. society, married persons are permanently available for another marriage. His theory states that societal norms that regulate an orderly replacement of values and behaviors to the next generation are eroding. What he calls traditional elements of social structure (such as norms governing class and race status, religion, and kinship), which transmit a way of life from one generation to the next and which help control and facilitate a stable family life, have been reduced. Farber sees significant changes in the American kinship structure over the past several generations. For example, lines of authority and responsibility (via the roles of husband and wife) have weakened, individuals have diminished obligations and commitments to spouses and children, and status boundaries (between males and females, parents and children) have blurred. He finds evidence for this change in the increase (since the 1950s) in singlehood, cohabitation, sexual permissiveness, childlessness, single-parent households, divorce, remarriage, and social movements that blur civil and sexual distinctions.

Farber speculates that in the United States the family is at the center of the debate about our changing values. He writes, "Current conflicts about the implications of such matters as property rights over fetuses, residual rights and obligations after divorce, or the consequences of planned illegitimate births" are only the beginning of an ongoing struggle over changes in status distinctions in family, kinship, and domestic groups

(Farber, 1987, 433). We might point to the heated debate begun in 2003 about whether homosexual marriage should be permitted as another example that the family is at the heart of America's (changing) value system.

The concept of permanent availability reflects Hackstaff's (1999) idea of a "culture of divorce" that was discussed in Chapter 3. It also mirrors Amato and Booth's (1997) conclusion that couples are now divorcing who might have stayed married in an earlier generation. Amato and Booth reason that because a large number of contemporary marriages are not characterized by high degrees of conflict (less than a third in their study) and divorce is now socially accepted, couples today are unwilling to accept a low level of unhappiness that would have been tolerated in the past. Spouses opt for divorce rather than live in a state of what they see as perpetual dissatisfaction.

The Role of Stereotyping. Are there other macrosystem values, attitudes, and belief systems that are related to divorce and remarriage? Stereotypes are pervasive in our culture, and stereotypes of stepmothers, stepfathers, and stepchildren have not escaped this labeling. Teachers, social workers, nursing students, and ordinary citizens evaluate members of stepfamilies less positively than they do those living in other types of families (Ganong and Coleman, 1997). Members of stepfamilies are seen as less happy, less powerful, and less well adjusted. Stepmothers in particular are viewed more negatively (unkind, unreasonable, not family oriented, unskilled in raising children). Stepfathers have not escaped negative labeling, either; they are viewed less favorably compared to biological fathers. Stereotypes such as these are introduced to children through storybooks, DVDs, and videos (Cinderella, Snow White, Hansel and Gretel). They become the first impression a child forms of how stepparents behave.

We have already discussed the concept of permanent availability and described how a "culture of divorce" seems to have become normative in American society. Other cultural values that characterize the last half of the twentieth century and seem to be associated with an increase in divorce include a decline in the value of community, an increase in individualism and hedonism, and a narcissistic focus on the self—collectively called the "Me Generation" (Bellah et al., 1985). Together these terms are used to describe a "flight from commitment" that leads to multiple marriages and divorces (White, 1990). White writes, "distinctions between marital and nonmarital childbearing, marriage and cohabitation have lost their normative force, and marriage and divorce are reduced to mere formalities" (906). She and Farber are in agreement!

Furstenberg and Cherlin (1991) add other factors to this argument, substantiating it. Reflecting White, they argue that personal fulfillment is the standard by which people assess marriage today, and if a marriage doesn't measure up, divorce is sought. These authors explain that this change results from the weakening of religious and other moral constraints, a decrease in the number of single "breadwinner" families (and concomitantly, the increased autonomy of wives), and greater tolerance for the unmarried and the previously married.

Summary

A significant number of Americans of all ages, both sexes, and all racial and ethnic groups will experience a life course disruption because of divorce: either theirs or their parents. The majority of adults and children will recover from this experience within about two years and go on with their lives. For a minority, however, the consequences of divorce are negative and seemingly long-lasting. This group has dramatic obstacles to overcome in the form of a decreased standard of living, decreased educational and economic opportunities, decreased emotional, mental, or physical health, increased stress, and increased conflict in their lives.

In spite of the popularity of joint legal custody in many states, about 85 percent of children of divorced parents are in the physical custody of their mothers. Mothers still make most decisions regarding their children's care and well-being, and contact with fathers is sporadic for many children. Children who live with their fathers fare no worse than those living with their mothers except that their standard of living on average tends to be higher. Parenting after divorce for both fathers and mothers changes, usually for the worse in the short term. That is when supervision tends to decrease, rules are more lax, and discipline is less consistent.

Family lives are significantly more complex when the divorced or widowed remarry (to perhaps redivorce and remarry again). Men tend to remarry more quickly than women, and the divorced remarry more quickly than the widowed. Race, age, level of education, occupation, presence and number of children all affect the speed of remarriage and condition the adjustments that must be made in a remarriage or stepfamily.

When a marriage is disrupted because of death (as opposed to divorce) the negative outcomes are not as dramatic for either adults or children in spite of the loss. When husbands/fathers or wives/mothers die, families of the deceased suffer economically, but on average they fare better than the divorced. Perhaps that is one of the reasons that widows and widowers are less likely to remarry than those who divorce.

When we examine the "big picture" it is clear that the family microsystem does not exist in a vacuum. The community has many organizations whose aim is to help family members adjust and cope after a divorce. Within the exosystem the judicial system adjudicates conflicts between divorcing parents through mediation. Federal legislation involving child support laws was passed in the 1980s to force parents to assume financial responsibility for their children. Many who work within the educational institution assist children who are experiencing divorce and single parenting in afterschool programs.

The economy has a direct effect upon families. Those at the bottom of the income hierarchy have the fewest resources to protect themselves from poverty and are most vulnerable to marital dissolution. They are also the ones who have the most difficulty coping with divorce.

Endnotes

1. Premarital childbearing has been found to be associated with divorce more often among white than black Americans, and it has a stronger effect in the early years of marriage (White, 1990).
2. In general, greater church attendance is associated with fewer marital problems. This association is explained as follows: Frequent church attendance is accompanied by socialization processes that help people internalize norms (such as lifelong marriage), which in turn are supported and reinforced by the church community (Wilcox, 2002).
3. South, Trent, and Shen tested their theory focusing on the sex composition of workplaces using Census data within designated labor market areas. (The scope conditions of their study limited it to nonLatino white couples between the ages of 18 and 44.)

Chapter Concepts

distal factors: characteristics that an individual brings to a marriage (age, sex, family background, etc.).

divorce mediation: a form of dispute resolution that brings couples together with an impartial third party who attempts to help them resolve their differences cooperatively.

incomplete institution: a phrase coined by Andrew Cherlin indicating a lack of social guidelines for solving the problems associated with remarriage. There are no institutionalized solutions to the problems stemming from the complex social role relationships that emerge in stepfamilies.

joint legal custody: custody in which parents share decision making and responsibility for children but one parent has primary residential custody.

joint physical custody: custody in which parents share decision making and responsibility and physical custody.

meta-analysis: the process of analyzing previously collected data (rather than collect new data) based on a systematic organization of the literature on a particular topic. All relevant studies based on predetermined criteria that can be located are included in the analysis.

permanent availability: Farber's idea that married persons are permanently available for another marriage because social norms that regulate an orderly replacement of values and behaviors are eroding.

proximal factors: characteristics of a marital relationship (communication, cohesion, commitment, etc.).

resilience resources: persons, groups, and behaviors that help develop individuals' attributes and capabilities to sustain them in adverse circumstances.

selection factors: aspects of personality or individual characteristics that create a high probability for divorce (antisocial, alcoholic, mentally ill, etc.).

serial monogamy: multiple marriages of one person that occur in sequential order (first, second, third) as opposed to bigamy (more than one marriage simultaneously).

sole legal custody: custody in which one parent is the primary parent and has full parental authority while the other parent has visiting rights.

split custody: custody in which children are split up and reside with different parents. The resident parent has responsibility for care and decision making for the child(ren) living with him or her.

time advantage: phenomenon that occurs when one partner has made a decision to end a relationship before informing the other partner of the decision.

Suggested Activities

1. What motion pictures or television programs can you list that portray a divorced father-child relationship? (*Kramer vs. Kramer* was one of the first movies that we can recall, but there have been many more since that time.) View one of these films/programs and make note of the parent-child interaction. What

kinds of parenting styles are portrayed? How is affection expressed? What kinds of problems or situations do the parents and children experience?

2. Go to the library or online and search for information on the history of divorce and child custody in the United States. When and why did the policy known as the "tender years doctrine" come into being? What does it mean? Did the focus on "equality" that emerged in the 1970s result in policies that are really "equal"? Why or why not?

3. What is your reaction to the statistics that report a decrease in the number of marriages, divorces, and remarriages but an increase in cohabitation? Do you think this trend will continue? Do you agree with Farber's (1987) interpretation of changes in modern cultural norms? What is your interpretation of the way intimate relationships are developing in twenty-first-century American culture?

Suggested Readings

Ahrons, C. 1994. *The Good Divorce: Keeping Your Family Together When Your Marriage Comes Apart*. New York: HarperCollins.

Ganong, L. H., and Coleman, M. 2004. *Stepfamily Relationships: Development, Dynamics, and Interventions*. Thousand Oaks, CA: Sage.

Hetherington, E. M. 1999. *Coping with Divorce, Single Parenting, and Remarriage: A Risk and Resiliency Perspective*. Mahwah, NJ: Erlbaum.

Hetherington, E. M., and Kelly, J. 2002. *For Better or for Worse: Divorce Reconsidered*. New York: W. W. Norton. ✦

Chapter 9

Distressed Families

The Darker Side of Family Life

Did You Know?

- Sexual abuse accounts for about 12 percent of the substantiated cases of child abuse and neglect. The majority of victims are girls, who are more likely to be abused by family members. Boys are more likely to be abused by family friends (Reece, 2000).

- An estimated 1.3 to 2.8 million runaways are on the streets of the United States (National Runaway Switchboard Statistics, 2003).

- The notion that violence is transmitted between generations appears to be overstated. About 20 to 30 percent of children who grow up in violent families are found to perpetrate violence in their families of procreation (Johnson and Ferraro, 2000; Lackey, 2003).

Things to Think About

- Social isolation is a significant risk factor for many forms of family distress. However, the evidence is not clear whether social isolation is a cause or consequence. Which direction do you think the casual relationship goes?

- Several social surveys show that between 84 and 97 percent of parents have used physical punishment at some time in their children's lives. Do you think that when parents spank, slap, or hit their child with a strap or belt they would say they are being violent?

- College campuses are prime settings for physical and sexual abuse. Think about the role male peer groups (such as fraternities) may play in perpetuating sexual violence.

- Do you think forced sex within marriage is rape?

- Why do you think elder abuse is less likely to be reported to authorities than other forms of abuse?

Many American families are characterized by one or more members' alcoholism, substance addiction, psychological abuse, violent behavior, or sexual abuse. Is yours one of them? These situations are not uncommon. For example, Watt (2002) reports an estimated 28 million individuals come from families affected by alcohol. Straus and Gelles (1990) estimate that about 28 percent of couples experience physical violence at some point in their relationship. What causes a parent to hit a child, partners to emotionally abuse their loved one, a spouse to gamble or drink away the family's income, or a teenager to run away from home? What is it like to grow up in this kind of family? What consequences do such behaviors have for family members living in these situations? These are the questions addressed in this chapter.

A family's dysfunction may be revealed through self-disclosure or because of a public agency's (police, school, hospital, child welfare) intervention. Or it may remain hidden. In many families an alcoholic or drug-addicted parent exhibits "normal" behavior outside the front door and holds a respected position in the community. Family members may work hard to keep the family secret. Such secrets have a cost, however. When a mother is addicted to alcohol or drugs, for example, an older child may take over housekeeping tasks and the care of younger siblings, but she will never invite friends over to visit. This child learns responsibilities that are age-inappropriate, and the situation may impair her social development. The coping solutions that are adopted allow the family to continue to function, but the addiction goes untreated and individual members continue to live in a distressed environment.

The problems families face can be placed on a continuum of severity with low and high points at either end. Throughout the life cycle, individuals and families move on and off this continuum, as well as back and forth along it. Sometimes family problems are external, because of events that are well beyond the family's control, that they cannot avoid, but that nevertheless have serious consequences. For example, a crippling accident can incapacitate a spouse, causing the family to lose earning power in addition to incurring high medical costs, or both partners may be out of work for extended periods of time. Such stresses have been associated with inappropriate alcohol or drug use and out-of-control outbursts of violence.

Many parents are unaware that their child is smoking, using drugs, or engaging in early sexual intercourse. What do you think is an appropriate parental response when they find out? Where would you place these behaviors along the distress continuum?

Other problems have an internal source, such as when a wife gradually begins to exhibit schizophrenic behavior or a 4-year-old is diagnosed with autism.

Whatever the source of problems, they all require that families develop adaptive, coping, or problem-solving responses if they are to end the trouble and reduce or eliminate distress. (Chapter 4 covered the topics of communication and problem-solving techniques that help or hinder dealing with problems.) If families are unable to solve their problems, an acceleration of maladaptive behavior may result. Problems may generate strong emotional reactions (anger, depression) and/or destructive behaviors (excessive drinking, violence) that cut off positive responses. The following true story illustrates such a distressed family situation (adapted from Finz, 2002, A23):

> In 2001 Cary Stayner was convicted of the triple murder of Carole Sund, 42, her daughter, Juli, 15, and their 16-year-old Argentine friend, Silvina Pelosso, outside of Yosemite National Park in February of 1999. Five months after killing the three women, he murdered Joie Armstrong, a 26-year-old Yosemite naturalist. Stayner was sentenced to serve a life sentence for killing Armstrong and sentenced to death for the other three murders.
>
> The family in which Cary grew up was characterized by high distress. When he was 11 years old, his 7-year-old brother, Steven, was kidnapped from a Merced, California, street on his way home from school. His abductor kept Steven hidden, and sexually abused him for seven years. At age 14 Steven was able to escape and sought help at a nearby police department. After returning home, however, his problems were not over. He became a promiscuous teenager with an alcohol problem, eventually dying in a motorcycle crash. Steven's story was turned into a television mini-series.
>
> After Steven was kidnapped, Delbert Stayner, Steven's father, became obsessed with finding the boy, neglecting his other four children—especially Cary. "I didn't socialize with him," he said. "I yelled at him a lot." It was common for the couple to load the children in the car and take off in search of a new tip that could lead them to Steven. The trips always ended in a wild goose chase. Steven's mother, Kay, said that family members never talked about their feelings—because in the Stayner home emotions were taboo. Only Kay Stayner's father, who lived in the Stayner home, voiced his opinion. "He said we should be glad that Steven was gone. Now we only had four children to clothe."
>
> Kay Stayner said that although her father molested her and her sister when they were children, she allowed him to live in the Stayner home but kept him away from her daughters. But the girls weren't safe. State authorities reported that they were molested by their father, Delbert Stayner. Cary was reported to have been molested when he was 11 years old (the perpetrator was not identified).
>
> The Stayners admit they weren't always the best parents. But they said they can't imagine losing another son. "We got Steve back, not Stevie," said Kay Stayner, who spent a lot of time telling the jury about the toll her youngest son's disappearance took on the family and how it affected Cary.

This true story illustrates a dysfunctional family that experienced problems at the high end of the distress continuum. It contains examples of both external and internal problems including the kidnapping of a son and the sexual abuse of daughters by their fathers. In the following sections we report on some empirical findings related to the behaviors that place families at the high end of the distress continuum: partner violence, child abuse and neglect, alcoholism and substance abuse, and runaway children.

Partner Violence

Before we begin this discussion, we need to establish a common vocabulary so everyone will be referring to the same behaviors. Following are some definitions found in the literature on domestic violence (Tjaden and Thoennes, 2000; McCauley, et al., 2001; Wilson, 1997).

Physical abuse: any use of size, strength, or presence to hurt or control someone else.

Physical assault: behaviors that threaten, attempt, or actually inflict physical harm.

Emotional (psychological) abuse: any use of words, voice, action, or lack of action meant to control, hurt, or demean another person.

Sexual abuse: any sexual behavior meant to control, manipulate, humiliate, or demean another person.

Child abuse and neglect: at minimum, any recent act or failure to act on the part of a parent or caretaker that results in death, serious physical or emotional harm, sexual abuse or exploitation, or an act or failure to act that presents an imminent risk of serious harm. This definition was established by Congress in 1996 (42 U.S.C. ~5106g[2][1999]).

Prevalence of Partner Abuse

The actual prevalence of intimate violence in the United States is unknown because fear, embarrassment, or shame leads to underreporting. However, the estimated rates of intimate violence range from 20 to 39 percent depending on the relationship and the study (Lloyd and Emery, 2000; Straus and Gelles, 1990). Over the past 25 years researchers have taken two distinct paths to examine partner violence. One path includes surveying relatively large numbers of randomly selected respondents. The other selects the offenders or victims of violence to study. These strategies often produce different results.

One controversial finding reported by researchers who study partner violence relates to gender differences in rates of perpetrating violence. Two large national surveys found that women are as likely to engage in violent acts as men. In the first, Straus and Gelles (1990) reported that 11.6 percent of husbands and 12 percent of wives had committed a violent act against their partners during the prior year. When they examined "severe violent" acts (kicked, bit, choked, punched), the percentages were 3.4 percent for husbands and 4.8 percent for wives. In the second study Swinford and his colleagues (2000) found among young adults (ages 24–29) that women were more likely to perpetrate physical aggression against husbands, cohabiting partners, and steady dating partners and less likely to be victimized by them. The same questions measuring aggression were used in the two studies. A third study looked at the prevalence of aggression in dating relationships. O'Leary and Cascardi (1998) examined three separate studies of New York high school students and found that 15 to 65 percent reported they had engaged in physical aggression against a dating partner in the year prior to the study. Across all three studies, females self-reported engaging in physical aggression more than males. In contrast to these figures, other research reports higher rates of male-to-female violence. For example, The National Violence Against Women Survey reported 24.8 percent of women in a national probability sample said they had been raped or physically assaulted by a current or former spouse, cohabiting partner, or dating partner sometime during their lifetime. Men were not excluded from this survey: The figure was 7.6 percent for them (Tjaden and Thoennes, 2000).

What accounts for these different figures? Discrepancies between study findings are attributed to different interpretations of data and the use of different methodologies. The dispute over interpretation stems from different motives attributed to those engaging in violent behavior. It argues that violence by women is usually committed in self-defense and should not be interpreted in the same way as male violence, which is interpreted as originating from a desire to control.

Methodological differences stem from, first, a decision regarding whom to include as respondents in a study (called *screening questions*). Will both victims *and* perpetrators be questioned, or only victims? You learned in Chapter 1 that *who* answers the question is critical in shaping research outcomes. A greater amount of male-to-female violence is found in studies that gather data from women living in battered women's shelters, from those who participate in clinical or treatment groups associated with domestic violence, from men in treatment programs for batterers, and from police records, family court files, hospitals, and crisis centers. These respondents all have had direct experience with partner violence. The overrepresentation of women victims in all these cases is due to (a) the greater severity of harm to women which puts them in contact with public agencies, and (b) women's greater willingness to admit to abuse than men (U.S. Department of Justice, 2000). On the other hand, researchers who gather data from respondents using random sampling of the general population or who conduct nonclinical surveys find violence rates for men and women to be nearly equal (Stets and Straus, 1990).

Second, methodological differences stem from using different *framing questions* (how the questions are worded), and asking different *substantive questions* (whether the study includes questions about the context in which the violent behavior occurred or ignores the context). Different findings are likely to be reported between two studies when one asks a respondent, "Did you ever commit violence against a partner?" and another asks that question in addition to "Were you ever victimized by a partner?" One study will gauge self-perpetuation as well as partner violence, while the other will only obtain information about victimization (Tjaden and Thoennes, 2000).

A third methodological decision that produces differences in findings is whether the researcher asks a broad question about "any" experience of physical assault or includes a separate item on rape in addition to a question about physical assault. The Conflict Tactics Scale, one of the most commonly used instruments to measure couple conflict, does not include a specific item on rape. Inclusion or exclusion of a rape question produces different findings. One final explanation of differences in rates between male and female violence comes from the fact that men, when asked, tend to underrepresent their perpetration of violence (Swinford et al., 2000).

Johnson and Ferraro (2000) point out that differences in the rates of violence reported in the abuse literature stem from a failure to account for four factors: the **type** of violence engaged in (sexual? psychological? physical? a combination of these types?); the *motives* of the perpetrators (was the violence an attempt to intimidate or harm, or was it enacted in self-defense?); the **social location** of both partners (are partners down and out, living below the poverty line, or are they among the elite?); and the **cultural context** in which the violence occurs (is the couple part of a subculture in which violence is seen as culturally normative and tolerated?) The following sections elaborate on each of these variables. Be aware as you read this material that partner violence occurs in all types of intimate relationships: dating, cohabiting, and married, whether heterosexual or homosexual.

Types of Violence. In 1995, Johnson began to conceptualize ways to identify various forms of violence. In 2000, he and Ferraro reviewed the literature on violence and distinguished between four major patterns of partner violence. First, **common couple violence** describes slapping or hitting between partners. It occurs when partners get angry, argue, strike out, or throw something. Johnson reports that this type of violence is sporadic, is situation specific, seldom escalates into more severe assault, and is generally mutual. A second type, **intimate terrorism,** is the kind of violence associated with battered wives. It is perpetrated primarily by males, it appears to have more per-couple incidents than common couple violence, it is more likely to escalate over time, and physical injury stemming from it is more severe. Intimate terrorism is not usually mutual. It is often associated with psychological violence, an abusive tactic used to control and dominate. Hamby and Sugarman (1999) found that high levels of psychological aggression were associated with high levels of physical violence. The consequence of repeated psychological attacks is low self-esteem, depression, demoralization, and feelings of being trapped. Much of the research that has been conducted on violence in families focuses on this type of violence, studying men as batterers and women as victims (referred to in the current literature as "survivors"). Johnson (1995) insightfully observed that the quarrel over whether women perpetrate violence as much as men is an artifact of what is being measured. He suggests that common couple violence is what is measured in most large-scale surveys, while intimate terrorism is measured in the research on wife battering drawn from public agencies. According to Johnson, these "two information sources deal with nearly nonoverlapping phenomena" (286).

A third type of violence, **violent resistance,** is generally perpetrated by women and occurs when victims strike back. Some women endure repeated episodes of assault by their partners and eventually kill or injure them in order to stop the violence. This type of violence is the subject of newspaper headlines and film plots. For example, in 1993 Lorena Bobbett made headline news for weeks after she ended the violence that her husband had perpetuated for years against her by cutting off his penis with a butcher knife. **Mutual violent control,** a fourth type of violence, is violence that is mutual and potentially equally injurious. It happens when both partners are out of control, struggling to dominate. This form of violence is rare, and there is little scientific empirical data on couples that are mutually violent (Johnson and Ferraro, 2000). A Hollywood depiction of mutual violent behavior is found in the film *War of the Roses.*

The Motives of Perpetrators. When asked why family members are violent toward those they love, scholars offer several explanations. **Interpersonal power theory** focuses on violence as an attempt to exert power and control over another. The concepts of power and control were presented in depth in Chapter 3 where the focus was on developing interpersonal relationships. These are relevant concepts when trying to understand family abuse. **Power,** remember, is the ability to influence the behavior of others and to resist others' influence (Huston, 1983). **Control** is behavior that is directed at getting another to do what one wants (Stets and Hammons, 2002). How are power and control translated into violent behavior? Fathers use harsh physical punishment to make children obey, husbands hit wives to maintain their dominance, wives throw things or assault husbands in a rage when they feel thwarted, and siblings hit each other to get what they want. Males who consistently batter in order to establish or maintain dominance and control have been characterized in two ways: as sociopathic, antisocial, and violent, or as men who are deeply attached to and emotionally dependent on their partners (Holtzworth-Munroe and Stuart, 1994). In the latter case, a complex dynamic of jealousy, arguments, aggression and control are closely interwoven. This combination is not uncommon, especially in young people. In one study of dating relationships more than 70 percent of respondents mentioned a "perceived threat to the relationship as the primary catalyst for aggressive episodes" (Lloyd and Emery, 2000, 52).

A second approach to explaining why men and women abuse each other is a **gender-based theory,** a feminist explanation directed at understanding the motives for wife beating or for violence perpetrated against women (Johnson, 1995). In this macrosystem perspective, violence is viewed as a way that men exert their masculinity and maintain social dominance in a patriarchal society. **Patriarchy** is a system of society in which men hold the power and women and children are generally excluded from it. According to Kirkwood (1993), partner aggression is "an expression and a mechanism of the institutional oppression of women" (21). Gender and power are seen as the basis of family violence and as deeply embedded in a cultural belief system in which men are expected to have authority over women and children within the family microsystem (Yllo, 1993). Some men thus justify the use of violence with their belief in male entitlement (O'Leary and Cascardi, 1998). Macrosystem values and social practices that reinforce male authority and are thought to justify violence against women include (a) a normative sexual division of labor (both in and out of the home); (b) a tendency for men to marry down (i.e., to marry women with less education, income, and occupational achievements than themselves) and women to marry up; (c) more opportunities for men than women in the labor force; and (d) higher wages, on average, paid to men than to women (Anderson, 1997).

The feminist perspective sees these beliefs and practices as being transmitted across generations through gender-role socialization. That is, males learn that masculinity means that to hit in order to protect personal and/or emotional integrity may not always be out of line. Those who adopt this perspective see genuine differences in the ways boys and girls learn (are taught) to communicate, express their feelings, and manage frustration and conflict. One domestic violence counselor described the outcome of such differences: "Women try to keep dialogue going, while men typically walk away and refuse to talk. Men very often say, 'I hit her to make her shut up. She just wouldn't shut up.' Women say, 'I hit him to make him listen to me. He wouldn't stay and listen, he just walks away'" (Thompson, 2002, 16). You may have noticed that the feminist explanation is compatible with the interpersonal power theory mentioned at the beginning of this section.

Finally, a third approach used to explain the motives of abusers is a sociological or **sociodemographic theory** of family violence (Anderson, 1997; Gelles and Loseke, 1993). This macrosystem explanation suggests that structural inequality is the primary motive behind domestic violence. According to this view, race, income, age, employment status, marital status, and couple status incompatibility are the sources of violent behavior. The findings related to structural inequality are tied to social location and cultural context and we'll examine them in greater detail after discussing Johnson and Ferraro's last two factors.

Social Location. Individuals are located within the social system based on their demographic or status characteristics—sex, age, sexual orientation, socioeconomic status, marital status. Because these status characteristics dictate different social opportunities, allocation of resources, and consequences of violent behavior, social location must be considered when analyzing data related to family violence. The explanation for a young son's bruises offered by a member of the town's elite may be more readily accepted than an explanation by a single mother receiving government assistance, even though in both cases the bruises are a result of physical abuse. Perceptions and assumptions related to social class can lead to different outcomes. At the societal level, when income, occupation, and education are controlled, the higher prevalence of violence among certain racial and ethnic groups vanishes (Lockheart, 1991; Straus and Gelles, 1990). Researchers who investigated neighborhood context found poverty level, overcrowding, social disorganization, and high unemployment to be contributing factors to intense male violence (DeMaris et al., 2003).

Cultural Context. Short of personal experience, the instruments of mass culture (novels, popular press, and other media that capitalize on the dysfunctional family experiences of laypersons and celebrities) may be the most common source for knowledge of how things go wrong in families. Newspaper headlines tell the story of Nicole Brown Simpson, Ronald Goldman, and O. J. Simpson, biographies are written about celebrities or they write their own autobiographies telling tales of sexual abuse, family violence between partners, or violence between parent and child. *Mommie Dearest* (Joan Crawford), *What's Love Got to Do With It?* (Tina Turner), and *The Uncommon Wisdom of Oprah Winfrey* (Oprah) are only three of many such accounts. In addition to macrosystem values that are reflected in the gender-based explanation of partner violence, there are subcultural values, beliefs, and practices that sometimes perpetuate a violent ethic.

The subculture in which individuals and families are embedded may include a set of values, beliefs, and traditions that influence male-female and parent-child interactions, including aggressive behavior. For example, among some youth gangs (which serve as substitute families for some children) members' aggressive and violent behaviors are respected (Klein, 1995). Another subculture value that has been theoretically linked to partner aggression and sexual prowess is the concept of *machismo*, a stereotype rooted in Mexican American subcultural values. Machismo stands for male dominance—that is, the father is protector and head of the household, power holder and decision maker, and other family members are placed in a subordinate role. In this situation fathers have the "right" to assert their dominance, even if it involves abusive behaviors. However, stereotypes do not always reflect reality. Latino couples were not more likely to be male dominated or accepting of violence than white couples in a study by Kaufman-Kantor and her colleagues (1994).

Whether male dominance is the norm among Mexican American families depends on a number of conditions, including where the family lives and its socioeconomic standing. Although research generally finds that many Mexican American husbands and wives share family activities and decision making (Baca-Zinn, 1998), the tradition of patriarchy among Mexican Americans lingers. Indicating how complex family behavior can be, while the concept of male machismo emphasizes dominance and protection, it also incorporates family values that foster a strong sense of loyalty, reciprocity, and solidarity. These values result in a close-knit family system in which kin are highly dependent on one another for economic and social support (Asbury, 1999). Apart from cultural values, Latinos as a group experience many of the stress factors associated with family violence. Their median annual income is below that of non-Hispanic whites and Asian Americans, and, compared to these two groups, their educational attainment is lower, their unemployment rate is higher, their families are larger, more of their children drop out of high school, and they are more likely to live in poverty.

When subcultural values define normative behavior as cooperative, cohesive, and committed, with an emphasis on sharing and respect, less violent behavior is likely to be manifest. Traditional Hopi communities are an example of this type of subculture (Lewis, 1981; West, 1998). Because there is such wide diversity among Native Americans, it is difficult to generalize to all groups, yet values of group cooperation (versus individual achievement), interdependence (versus independence), strong family traditions, and harmony with and respect for nature are values they hold in common (Asbury, 1999). On the negative side, there appears to be a greater incidence of partner violence among some Native American tribes than among other groups (Wilson, 1997). A strong familism value within the Native American culture may impede a battered woman's seeking help. As members of a highly valued extended family system, Native American women may be discouraged from leaving an abusive relationship because, when violence occurs, it is the extended family's—aunts, uncles, cousins as well as parents and in-laws—responsibility to handle the matter. A woman may appear to be disloyal to the family as well as the community if she seeks shelter away from home. Further, if a woman has lived on a reservation her entire life, leaving means giving up the only support system she knows (Wilson, 1997).

In the following sections we return to the specific parameters of the sociodemographic explanation that are included in Johnson and Ferraro's (2000) analysis of partner violence. These parameters include race/ethnicity, social class, couple status incongruence, age, marital status, and sex.

The Demographics of Partner Violence

Race and Ethnicity

Generally, few differences have been found in the rate of domestic violence by race or ethnicity, however there is some inconsistency. For example, three national studies report greater family violence among blacks compared to whites (Ellison, Bartkowski, and Anderson, 1999; Gelles, 1997; Salari and Baldwin, 2002). However, another national sample of women who had been "physically assaulted by an intimate partner in their lifetime" placed whites and blacks in the center of the racial distribution. The rates reported in this latter study were 16.6 percent for Asian and Pacific Islanders; 29 percent for whites and Latinos; 33.7 percent for blacks; 35.1 percent for women of mixed race; and 46.6 percent for American Indian and Alaska Natives (Tjaden and Thoennes, 2000). Other research has found no difference among racial groups. For instance, a large study that questioned women living in community shelters found no differences among white, black, and Latino women and the amount of violence they had experienced (Gondolf, Fisher, and McFerron, 1991). Similarly, there were no differences in rates of violence between black and white women within three levels of socioeconomic status—low, middle, and high—as reported by Lockheart (1991). Fox and her colleagues (2001) also reported that after controlling for neighborhood socioeconomic disadvantage, "race became only marginally significant as a predictor of intimate violence" (804). Thus, the strongest evidence seems to indicate that when socioeconomic status is controlled, race and ethnicity cease to be predictors of physical violence.

While few differences in rates of violence are reported between racial and ethnic groups, Latino women who seek help from battering partners differ on some dimensions when compared to white and black women. A study analyzing data collected from 5,708 Texas women over a period of a year and a half who sought help from women's shelters found that Latino women tended to endure the violence longer before getting help. Gondolf, Fisher, and McFerron (1991) credit this difference to a subcultural norm of "loyal motherhood." That is, abused Hispanic women tended to marry younger, have more children, and stay in relationships longer before seeking help than black or white women in shelters. They were poorer, had less education, were less mobile, and had more language difficulties (many were undocumented workers).

Social Class

In a classic piece on family violence William J. Goode (1971) wrote that when people lack other sources of power, such as income or educational status, they are more likely to resort to violence as a means of achieving power within interpersonal relationships. Unemployed men in the United States have rates of spousal assault twice that of employed men (Ellison et al., 1999; Gelles and Cornell, 1990). Frustration and lack of control result from economic stress. Social class is closely identified with family violence, with those of lower socioeconomic status perpetrating more violence than individuals of higher status (Anderson, 1997). Low-income respondents are also more likely to report the most severe forms of violence that involve injury (Salari and Baldwin, 2002). A study of Latino families found that the severe violence rate among unemployed Latino husbands was two and a half times greater than that for men with full-time jobs—16.1 percent compared to 6.5 percent (Straus and Smith, 1990). Thus the link between poverty and physical violence is clearly established. Violence appears to be a consequence of the frustration and lack of control that results from economic stress. Garbarino and Ebata (1983) warned that confounding ethnicity with social class risks confusing actual cultural differences with the harmful effects of socioeconomic deprivation.

Johnson and Ferraro (2000) noted the positive association between family violence and poverty, but they turned the variable on its head by reversing the possible cause and effect. While recognizing that there are higher levels of partner violence among low-income couples and in lower-income neighborhoods, they proposed that for poor women, violence might be a *precipitating* factor of their poverty. Men who "deliberately undermine women's employment by depriving them of transportation, harassing them at work, turning off alarm clocks, beating them prior to job interviews, and disappearing when they promised to provide child care" restrain women from gaining work and income opportunities (958). Johnson and Ferraro point out that these behaviors contribute to women's low self-esteem, poor physical health, low mental agility, poor concentration, and low occupational aspirations, thus keeping them from achieving success in the labor force and gaining greater autonomy from their partners.

Couple Status Incongruence

When partners hold disparate status positions (in terms of income, education, age, or religious affiliation), they experience more partner violence than if their status positions are equal. How is this manifest? If women's educational level is higher than their partner's, the odds of their experiencing violence are higher (Tjaden and Thoennes, 2000). Similarly, when women earn more money than their male partner, they are more likely to experience physical aggression that results in injury (Ellison et al., 1999) or the likelihood of injurious aggression reported by the couple is higher (Salari and Baldwin, 2002). Under these conditions, status incongruity is thought to be the source of aggression in men who use violence to maintain or restore control and dominance over their partners.

A study by Anderson (1997) looked at status incompatibility and the likelihood of common couple violence as reported by both partners. She reported similar findings. Women who earned over 70 percent or more of the couple's income had over five and a half times greater odds of experiencing violence than women whose incomes were similar to their partners. She also found, however, that these high-earning women were more likely to commit violent acts against their partners than women who earned less. In the Anderson study incongruity in education level differentiated the perpetuation of violence when both partners reported violent incidents. Men with lower levels of education than their partners had slightly higher odds of committing violent acts than those with an equal amount of education. Women with education levels lower than their partners had about three times greater odds of committing a violent act against their partners.

What about incongruity in beliefs? One study examining religious differences in partners found no relationship between the degree of denominational dissimilarity or mixed faith marriages and the likelihood of violence. However, there was a higher risk of male violence if men were more religiously conservative in their beliefs than their partners and attended religious services more often (Ellison et al., 1999).

Age

Stated simply, younger people are more violent than older people. Age is one of the key variables predicting the probability of violent behavior, for both males and females. Cross-sectional data show a marked decrease in physical aggression over time. One study of 11,870 white military personnel found that the odds of being severely physically aggressive toward one's wife decreased by 19 percent for every 10-year increase in age (comparing aggressive and nonaggressive men) (Pan, Neidig, and O'Leary, 1994). Longitudinal data, however, indicate that for some couples aggression remains stable, at least in the short term. A study following couples over three years of marriage reported 51 percent of men and 59 percent of women who reported physical aggression prior to the marriage reported the presence of aggression 18 months after marriage. By the end of the three-year study 25 to 30 percent of couples remained physically aggressive (O'Leary et al., 1989). Thus, while the tendency to be violent deescalates over the age cycle, this behavior does not change very rapidly.

The age factor might be questioned when one considers abuse of the elderly by their middle-aged caretakers. Elder abuse is often viewed quite differently than abuse of children and partners. We will take up the discussion of elder abuse in a later section of this chapter.

Marital Status

Dating and cohabiting couples are reported to be more violent than married partners. Perhaps this is because many partners who have experienced violent outbreaks while in the dating stage do not allow the relationship to progress toward marriage. In a nationally representative sample, 24 percent of cohabiting couples reported experiencing physical or injurious aggression compared to 7.2 percent of married couples (Salari and Baldwin, 2002). The National Violence Against Women Survey 2000 also reported that unmarried couples were at a greater risk of intimate violence than married couples. In this study cohabiting couples reported more violence than dating couples—35 percent compared to 20 percent (Tjaden and Thoennes, 2000). Several studies have examined dating aggression among high school students and reported rates ranging from 13 to 25 percent (Bergman, 1992; O'Keefe, Brockopp, and Chew, 1986; Smith and Williams, 1992). In all these studies, females engaged in physical aggressive behaviors more than males. Aggression is also found among dating college couples. Depending on the study, between 20 and 72 percent of students reported that physical aggression occurred in at least one of their dating relationships (O'Leary and Cascardi, 1998).

There is an increased risk of abuse during a transition from marriage to divorce. Perhaps the most publicized example of abuse during and after separation is that of O. J. Simpson and Nicole Brown Simpson.

Sex

As noted earlier, women are reported to be as likely to perpetrate common couple violence as men. This finding is reported consistently in survey research with both small and large samples (Straus and Gelles, 1990; DeMaris, 2000; Swinford et al., 2000). However, many people do not take violence perpetrated by women very seriously. This may be because "minor" violence (pushing, shoving, slapping, spanking) by women is characterized by some as feminine or cute, and under certain conditions it is seen as less objectionable, and even normative (Straus, 1999). Remember in the film *Moonstruck* Cher slapping Nicholas Cage in the face and ordering him to "get over it?" These are the kinds of violent behaviors that we earlier called common couple violence, and both sexes, often mutually, engage in them. Men are more likely to engage in intimate terrorism, causing injury and pain to their partners. The severe violence that women perpetrate against their partners is primarily violent resistance, in which they act in self-defense against assaults by their partner. It is estimated that 10 to 20 percent of women who assault their partner do so for reasons of self-defense (Thompson, 2002).

Some violence perpetrated by women falls into the category of intimate terrorism. Pagelow (1985) estimated that 3 to 5 percent of husbands are battered. However, we know very little about battered husbands. One small exploratory study by Migliaccio (2002) attempted to provide some details of the serious abuse of husbands by wives. Although only 12 men were interviewed in this study, it provides some evidence of the harm men may suffer at the hands of abusive wives. As one husband described his wife's attacks, "She would pull hair. She would pinch me hard until I bruised. She would kick me in the balls or hit me in the balls. Scratching. Hitting. Slapping in the face" (34). Cook (1997) interviewed 30 men who told similar stories of wives throwing things causing physical injury, groin attacks, biting, and use of weapons. In 1993, CBS aired a TV movie entitled *Men Don't Tell* that described a situation of husband abuse.

One reason that a wife's aggression directed toward her husband is unlikely to be reported is the shame of having to admit being abused by a woman. According to Howard and Hollander (1996), "victimization may be so deeply 'female' an experience that a man who is victimized is literally 'feminized' in respondents' cognitive evaluations" (86). Masculine stereotypes belittle the guy who can't "handle" women. Expectations that men are bigger and stronger than women are normative, if not factual, and a masculine identity rests on attempting to maintain a masculine ideal (Migliaccio, 2002). Just as it is difficult for a man to see himself as victimized by a woman, often the police and other officials downplay wife violence or do not believe that a man's injuries were caused by a woman.

Marital Rape

Marital rape is more controversial than stranger, acquaintance, or date rape. That is because public opinion polls indicate that most Americans do not view unwanted sex between husband and wife as rape (Bergen, 1998). This view has its roots in English common law, described as follows: "The implied or irrevocable consent inherent in the marriage contract in which the wife willingly gives herself to her husband negates the possibility of marital rape" (Peacock, 1998, 227). According to this view, husbands are entitled to have sex with their wives, what happens in the bedroom is private, and, ultimately, a wife's sexuality is a commodity that is owned by her husband (Mahoney and Williams, 1998).

Public opinion aside, all 50 states currently have laws that define marital rape as a crime, although definitions, or sexual offense codes, vary across states. Of these, 33 states have some exemptions that protect husbands from prosecution for marital rape. For example, in most states a husband can have sexual intercourse with his wife when she is mentally or physically impaired, asleep, or unconscious without the fear of being prosecuted. Marital rape laws are continually being challenged. In 1997 New Mexico's Supreme Court ruled "that violently forcing a spouse to engage in sexual intercourse is not rape, but 'the undue exercise of a right.'" This ruling was justified on the basis that if one spouse violently imposes on the other normal copulation when the obligation of cohabitation exist, that is not sufficient for the act to be considered rape" (Bergen, 1998, 222).

What are the consequences of marital rape? Perhaps the most benign outcome is that the "violent act of forcing one's spouse to engage in sexual activity without consent destroys the most intimate and trusting relationship of the marital bond" (Peacock, 1998,

226). More damaging outcomes include physical trauma and psychological and emotional scars. Marital rape differs from stranger abuse in that the victim lives with the memory of a horrible attack while a woman who is raped by her husband lives with her rapist (Mahoney and Williams, 1998).

What exactly is marital rape? Women who reported that they had submitted to sexual demands by their partner to prevent a beating or out of fear of their partner did not feel they had been raped (Pagelow, 1984). They felt it is a wife's duty to have sex on demand; it is part of the marital obligation. Marital rape includes acts other than nonconsensual sexual intercourse, including oral or anal sex, or coercion into having sexual relations with someone else. It involves the exertion of power and control, the domination of a husband over his wife, and is often accompanied by other forms of violence (Peacock, 1998).

When is marital rape most likely to occur? Several circumstances have been noted: when a marriage is deteriorating (before, during, or after separation), after long periods of no sexual contact (e.g., after childbirth), when the husband is suspicious of his wife's infidelity, when he is drunk, during a wife's illness, or immediately after release from the hospital (Mahoney and Williams, 1998).

It may be easy to understand why battering or abusive men rape their wives, but why would men in the general population who are not abusive do so? Some suggestion of an answer to this question come from three middle-class men, interviewed by Finklehor and Yllo (1985), who had forced their wives into having sex. These men all said that they felt powerless and emasculated in their marital relationships and felt their contributions went unappreciated. Forced sex was the only way they had to maintain some control. Anger management was a problem for them all, and they used sexual assaults as an outlet. One man said he didn't think his wife was really hurt; another believed his wife sometimes wanted to have sex even when she said "no," and a third thought his wife could have stopped him if she really wanted to. Finkelhor and Yllo call these beliefs common rape myths.

It is difficult to gather data that accurately assess the incidence and prevalence of marital rape, because sometimes researchers group instances of marital rape with incestuous rape or combine it with rape by lovers or cohabiting partners. Two studies using representative samples that focused only on married or previously married women provide the best estimates; they found that 8 to 14 percent of women have experienced marital rape (Russell, 1990; Finkelhor and Yllo, 1985). Several studies report that drug or alcohol use accompanies the incidence of marital rape, and many wives who experience rape in marriage report a history of sexual abuse, indicating they were victims of incest or other forms of sexual abuse as children (Russell, 1990). Compared to marriages in the general population, marital rape occurs at rates that are five to seven times greater in highly distressed families—families characterized by physical violence, substance abuse, divorce, and child maltreatment. As such, the significance of marital rape may be lost among other conditions and symptoms of extreme distress.

Violence Among Same-Sex Couples

Emotional, sexual, physical, and verbal abuse takes place in many intimate relationships, and sexual orientation is not a deterrent. The prevalence of partner violence is reported to be about the same among same-sex couples and heterosexual couples, although exact numbers are difficult to determine. Coleman (1996) reviewed the literature on lesbian abuse, comparing it to the reported heterosexual prevalence of battering. The rate of violence between heterosexual couples was between 28 and 55 percent, while it ranged from 25 percent to 48 percent for lesbian couples. In her 1991 study she found among a sample of 90 white, lower- and middle-class lesbians that 46.6 percent reported repeated acts of physical abuse in their current relationship.

Renzetti (1992) interviewed 100 self-identified battered lesbians and found a large majority (71 percent) reported that the intensity and frequency of battering increased over time. She found psychological abuse was present in all the violent relationships experienced by these women, and dependency and jealousy were the main contributors to battering. In a study conducted by The National Association of People with AIDS, 12 percent of respondents reported they had experienced violence by a partner. Bisexual men experienced more violence (23.7 percent) than did gay men (10 percent). Women were not questioned about their sexual orientation in this study (Hanson and Maroney, 1999). A study by Bologna, Waterman, and Dawson (1987) compared gay and lesbian college students. Fifty-six percent of lesbians reported at least one incidence of violence in their most recent relationship, compared to 25 percent of gay men. In general, men are less likely to define their situation as domestic violence and are less likely to tell anyone or to seek help.

The techniques of abuse by same-sex abusers to maintain control and dominance are similar to those used in heterosexual relationships: isolation, intimidation, and verbal degradation. However, an additional level of intimidation exists among same-sex partners if one threatens to expose the sexual orientation of a partner who has not told family members or co-workers (Leventhal and Lundy, 1999).

There is mixed evidence about the role alcohol and drugs play in lesbian relationships when battering occurs. Some research shows these substances to play a contributing role in violent incidents, while other research finds no relationship between drugs and abuse. Renzetti (1998) concluded from her study that drugs and alcohol were typically used to facilitate or excuse the abuse—"She didn't know what she was doing, she was high," "She only hit me because my drinking frustrated her" (121). Further, drinking or drug use sometimes followed and sometimes preceded a violent episode. Among the group of lesbians in this study, "substance abuse appeared to be neither a necessary nor a sufficient cause of partner abuse" (121).

Bridging a Micro and Macro Explanation

Dutton (1996) points out that the physical abuse inflicted on lesbian partners calls into question one of the key arguments underlying the gender-based framework discussed earlier in the chapter. Violence between women seems at variance with the assumption that the cultural prescription of patriarchy (male domination at the social level) is the foundation of partner assault. A study by Sorenson and Telles (1991) tested this idea by examining wife assault rates among Mexican-born Latinos and nonLatino white heterosexuals. One might expect that the more patriarchal culture of Mexico (exemplified by the machismo stereotype) would produce a higher rate of spouse abuse. However, they found the opposite: The Mexican-born sample reported an abuse rate that was about half that of the non-Latino whites. Dutton further noted that 90 percent of marriages are free of serious assaults (although common couple violence may occur), and this high figure further questions the strength of the patriarchy argument. In a patriarchal society wouldn't you expect more than 10 percent of males to assert their dominance in violent ways? If patriarchy is not the best explanation for partner abuse, does he provide a better one?

Dutton, a psychologist, focuses on individual psychopathology as the most cogent explanation for partner violence. (Note that his attempt is to understand instances of intimate terrorism, not common couple violence.) Dutton does not entirely rule out the contributions made by culture, subculture, and family insofar as "men with severe identity problems and intense dependency on women may seek out aspects of the culture to direct and justify abuse" (141). These aspects include values and attitudes within the culture that may serve to "isolate men emotionally and alienates them from their ability to sense and know their own feelings" (142). However, the thrust of his argument is that the majority (80–90 percent) of men who batter their wives suffer from personality disorders or other diagnosable psychopathological disorders (borderline personality organization, narcissism, antisocial behavior, aggressive-sadistic personality characteristics). Dutton does acknowledge the variation that exists among male batterers in terms of individual characteristics that separate habitual from occasional abusers.

Miller (1996) calls for an integrated approach to the study of partner violence that is gender neutral (bridging the gender-based and psychological arguments) and includes societal, interpersonal factors and psychological characteristics. She suggests that the ways the patriarchal structure of American social institutions create and perpetuate male domination cannot be ignored, nor can the male and female socialization behaviors that are enacted within this structure. For example, she asks: How effective are male peer groups in reinforcing community definitions of masculinity and dominance? Is there inconsistency among community socialization agents and institutions that teach gender-appropriate behavior to young girls? Miller points out that the choices and behaviors of males and females, heterosexuals, gays, and lesbians, are limited by an American capitalist, patriarchal social structure that is the basis of most social relationships and interactions. She emphasizes the importance of resources (particularly control over them) and power in interpersonal relations, both of which know no sexual orientation boundaries. Finally, Miller welcomes individual personality variables into the explanation of partner assault. Learned or innate, tendencies toward the expression of anger and frustration, degree of impulse control, and serious psychological disorders all play a role in the perpetration of physical assault. Factors that influence the development of the self, including family socialization practices, cannot be left out of any explanation of why people who profess to love their partners abuse them in sometimes terrible ways. We will summarize the variety of explanations of family violence in a later section of this chapter.

Child Maltreatment

In 1990 child abuse was declared a national emergency by the U.S. Advisory Board on Child Abuse and Neglect (McCauley et al., 2001, 242). This board determined that an estimated 3 million children in the United States suffer from child abuse and neglect each year. This figure represents only reported cases, however, and the widespread belief is that many cases go unreported (McCurdy and Daro, 1993). Equally unsettling is the information that only 28 percent of cases in which children are reported abused or neglected are investigated by child protective services (McCauley, et al., 2001). The following sections present the research findings relating to various types of child maltreatment.

Child Neglect

Child neglect is the most common type of child maltreatment and accounts for approximately half of the cases of abuse (National Research Council, 1993). A wide range of behaviors constitute child neglect, ranging from educational, supervisory, medical, physical, and emotional neglect to abandonment. According to the National Research Council (1993), emotional abuse/neglect is the least studied type of abuse. That is because behaviors such as verbal abuse, belittlement, threats, or symbolic acts that assault a child's emotional state and that are intended to terrorize are hard to document. When emotional abuse is not accompanied by physical abuse or neglect, it is hard to detect because it leaves no physical mark. Children are unlikely to reveal this kind of abuse, because they become familiar with verbal assaults and may not realize there are alternative ways of being treated.

The consequences of infant neglect are harsh. An infant may die from neglect or fail to thrive because of nutritional neglect. This form of child neglect is called *nonorganic failure to thrive*. Children with this condition have been found to smile less, to have an expressionless face, to exhibit gaze aversion, to have an intolerance of changes in routine, to have low activity level, to have flexed hips, and to engage in self-stimulating behavior (Oates, 1984). The lack of appropriate nurturance and emotional availability of caretakers can result in severe anxiety, depression, withdrawal, or violence directed at others. A lack of appropriate bonding and attachment in infancy may interfere with a child's expectations of adult availability, positive affect, problem-solving behavior, ability to cope, and appropriate social relationships (Drotar, 1992). This situation reflects what you learned in Chapter 2 about how a positive self-image fails to develop when a child's microsystems do not provide warmth, support, and adequate nurturing. Older children who were neglected in infancy may become defiant and hostile as adolescents (Polansky et al., 1981) and suffer delayed intellectual development, poor school performance, and lower levels of academic attainment (Romans, Martin, and Mullen, 1997; Perez and Widom, 1994).

Physical Abuse

Research is consistent in finding that child abuse occurs among all racial and ethnic groups, at equal rates. In the 1970s researchers found an overrepresentation of abuse among minority families, but national studies conducted in the 1980s and 1990s found no racial or ethnic differences (Hampton, Gelles, and Harrop, 1991). As before, methodological issues are cited for the discrepancy. Early studies gathered evidence from clinical samples within medical or social service settings in which minority children were overrepresented. The way children are labeled by health care professionals is another way that race and social class are misrepresented in reported rates of violence. Several studies show that poor and minority children are more likely to be labeled "abused" than children from more affluent and white families who have comparable injuries. Hampton, Gelles, and Harrop (1991) contend that ". . . race and social class are as (or more) important in determining which cases will be labeled child abuse than the nature of the injury or incident" (4–5).

Some adults who have experienced abusive punishment in childhood are likely to perpetrate violence in an intimate relationship (Swinford, et al., 2000; Tjaden and Thoennes, 2000). This "transmission rate" has been found to be between 20 and 30 percent (Johnson and Ferraro, 2000; Lackey, 2003). Some studies find that children who are physically punished during adolescence have an increased risk for alcohol abuse, partner abuse, and child abuse (Straus and Kantor, 1994). Even if they are not abused themselves, the psychological effects on children who witness aggression in their family experience such psychological effects as low self-esteem, anxiety, and depression. According to some reports, children who witness violence in the home also have an increased likelihood of being arrested for delinquent behavior, adult criminality, and violent criminal behavior (Widom, 1989). They are at greater risk for experiencing school, social, emotional, and behavioral problems. Exposure to violence appears to challenge a child's sense of security (Cummings and Davies, 1996). This connection stems from data showing that battered mothers are less emotionally available to their children, are less proactive in avoiding power struggles, and less consistent in their parenting practices (Rossman, 2003).

To add a positive note to this dark chapter, note that the vast majority (between 70 and 80 percent) of child abuse victims do not grow up to be perpetrators of abuse and are not doomed to mistreat their own partners or children. When there is warmth and consistency on the part of some significant adult(s), children can learn to be resilient and grow up to break the "cycle of violence."

Sexual Abuse

Girls are more likely than boys to be the victims of sexual abuse (Sedlak and Broadhurst, 1996). Between 20 and 25 percent of women report being sexually victimized compared to about 10 percent of men (Elliot and Briere, 1995; Epstein and Bottoms, 1998). There appears to be no difference between ethnic groups in the rate of child sexual abuse (National Research Council, 1993). A study of incestuous abuse reported rates to be similar for blacks and whites, lower for Asians and higher for Latinos (Russell, 1984). Boys are more likely to be abused by strangers and girls by family members. Male perpetrators outnumber female perpetrators across all studies. Margolin and Craft (1989) examined over 2,500 substantiated cases of child abuse by caretakers and reported that 85.5 percent of the abuse was perpetrated by males. The average age of the children was 9 and a half. More male perpetrators were nonbiologically related: adoptive father, stepfather, boyfriend (committing 41 percent of reported abuse), than were biological fathers. Nine percent of the abuse cases involved nonbiologically related mothers. Foster parents committed the most severe abuse, followed by siblings, whose average age was 16. The study found that the younger the victim and perpetrator were, the more severe the abuse.

The consequences of sexual abuse include a wide number of potential outcomes: posttraumatic stress disorder, cognitive distortions, emotional distress, phobias, social withdrawal, an impaired sense of self, interpersonal difficulties, runaway behavior, physical health problems, and a greater potential for substance abuse, suicide attempts, promiscuity, binging and purging, and self-mutilation (Briere and Elliot, 1994; Kendall-Tackett and Marshall, 1998). The severity of outcome is related to the use of force, with greater symptoms accompanying force (Kendall-Tackett, Williams, and Finkelhor, 1993). Not all children experience long-term consequences of an abusive experience. Some never show symptoms, others manifest short-term effects, and still others have a delayed response. Some of the conditions that determine abuse consequences include the way others respond following disclosure, whether the abuse happened through persuasive seduction or violent attack, whether the perpetrator assumed responsibility or engaged in denial or blame, whether the abuse was frequent or rare, and whether the child was removed from the home (Morrow and Sorell, 1989). Responses to sexual abuse differ by the age at which the act was committed. Preschool children are likely to become anxious, have nightmares, or act out sexually. Fear, aggression, problems in school, hyperactivity and regressive behavior are more likely to be manifest by school-aged children. Adolescents are more likely to exhibit depression, abuse alcohol or drugs, attempt suicide, or engage in illegal activities (Kendall-Tackett, 2003).

A community's response to violence can help bring about awareness and change. 'Take Back the Night' marches are one example of such involvement and community action.

There is a microsystem-exosystem connection in the perpetration of child abuse, particularly between a family and its level of community contact. Parents who abuse their children tend to be socially isolated and without supportive social networks (Cazenave and Straus, 1990)—a condition that Garbarino and Sherman (1980) label **social impoverishment.** A lack of social networks deprives parents of help in dealing with the stress associated with the correlates of abuse: unemployment, illness, poor housing conditions, childcare problems, large families, a new baby, or a child with physical, mental, or developmental disabilities.

When community contacts are missing, families are unlikely to change their behavior to conform to community values and standards. This makes them more vulnerable to violent responses to stress, while at the same time it inhibits the perception that their behavior is deviant (Steinmetz, 1978). They also miss the input that comes from the community in the form of modeling developmentally appropriate behavior. Such modeling takes place in schools, Head Start programs, childcare centers, and recreational centers. These institutions can provide enriching and protective environments staffed by limit-setting and nurturing adults to children who are exposed to or have experienced abuse (Hardin and Koblinsky, 1999). Also to be considered is the possibility that an abusing parent isolates his or her family purposely, to avoid detection.

Causes of Child Maltreatment

No one risk factor is thought to be a necessary or sufficient cause of child maltreatment. The Panel on Child Abuse and Neglect (National Research Council, 1993) identified a multitude of contributors that lie within the family microsystem, the community exosystem, and the cultural macrosystem. Within the family system, individual factors such as parents' personality attributes (susceptibility to stress, anger, anxiety), parental attitudes and level of cognitive functioning, the use of alcohol and drugs, whether a parent was abused in childhood, mother's age, and characteristics of the child (temperament, ability to be soothed) have been identified as precipitating factors. One source estimates that "30 to 90 percent of all substantiated child maltreatment reports involve families with some degree of adult alcohol or drug abuse" (Harrington and Dubowitz, 1999, 124). Family factors such as marital status, the degree of marital conflict, number of children, and the social isolation of the family are also found to be contributors.

Exosystem factors related to poverty and diminished economic opportunities that lead to unemployment play a large role in creating a context for abuse. For example, while maternal age is one of the risk factors for abuse and neglect, mothers with young children who are living below the poverty line have the greatest risk of behaving violently toward their children (National Research Council, 1993). Community resources in the form of the availability of job training, low-cost housing, educational programs, and home visitation programs to reduce social isolation can alleviate the risk of abuse, as can formal and informal social support for children and parents.

One macrosystem contributor to the maltreatment of children is a strong societal norm of family privacy—the idea that what happens behind the front door is nobody's business. Societal beliefs that view children as the property of fathers or that encourage physical punishment because "if you spare the rod you spoil the child" are also contributors. Violence in the mass media is pervasive. Thus, when searching for causes of child maltreatment, the interaction between micro-, exo-, and macrosystem factors must be examined.

Abuse of Siblings and Parents

Studies of family violence find that the most violence that takes place in families is between siblings. If a 3-year-old throws a block at her 5-year-old brother, a parent typically is not alarmed at the behavior. The situation may be treated as a "teaching moment." Aggression of this type between siblings is a more tolerated and accepted form of violence (Straus and Gelles, 1990). Conflict between siblings that is perceived as "typical" or normal was discussed in Chapter 5. Little research evidence is available on severe violence by siblings, but we know it is perpetrated more often by brothers than sisters. Most of the evidence comes from research on sexual abuse. In the study reported earlier of sexual abuse by caretakers conducted by Margolin and Craft (1989), over 5 percent of the 2,662 abuse cases were perpetuated by siblings: 5 percent by brothers and 0.3 percent by sisters. The average age of these perpetrators was 16, and that of their sibling was 9. Types of abuse by brothers chronicled in this study include the following:

- Indecent exposure (6 percent).

- Nonviolent abuse (19 percent).

- Nonviolent intercourse (30 percent).

- Intercourse with threats (29 percent).

- Abuse with injury (16 percent).

- Intercourse with injury (1 percent).

For sisters, the most frequent type of abuse was intercourse with threats (50 percent) and nonviolent intercourse (38 percent).

Some children perpetrate abuse against their parents, particularly during adolescence. The research suggests that about 10 percent of youth have hit their parents at least once and about 3 percent engaged in severe violence (Gelles and Cornell, 1990; Peek, Fischer, and Kidwell, 1985). Across all ages sons and daughters commit assaults at about equal rates, but when children are younger assaults are aimed more frequently at mothers than fathers. However, older adolescent males (17 and 18) seem to be about twice as likely to assault fathers. Most studies find that white youth are more likely to assault parents than black youth (Cazenave and Straus, 1990; Charles, 1986; Agnew and Huguley, 1989). Social class is generally not associated with child assault of parents, with the exception of findings by Agnew and Huguley (1989), who found more adolescent male violence directed toward fathers with high-prestige occupations. Family structure is also not associated with the incidence of parental assault.

Why do some children assault their parents? Few studies are available to explain the factors involved. According to the American Psychological Association (1996), the rates of parent abuse by children are associated with the frequency of substance abuse and with other forms of violence in the home. Garbarino and his colleagues (1986) also suggest that abuse in the family is a contributing factor. The study by Agnew and Huguley (1989) found no support for the variables most likely to be associated with assaults, such as a lack of attachment to school, drug use, strictness of parents, personal problems, or children's somatic anxiety (headaches, stomach aches, insomnia, and so on). Instead, the significant predictors in this study of violent adolescents were (a) whether the adolescents had friends who assaulted their parents, (b) whether they held values approving of delinquent acts (including assault), (c) whether they were less attached to their parents, and (d) whether they felt there was a low probability of getting caught by the police. Perhaps because of shame or embarrassment, parents who are assaulted by their children tend to deny the problem and work hard to keep it secret. Denial and secrecy, however, interfere with opportunities to solve the problems associated with the abuse of parents, thus preventing effective intervention. Unfortunately, we know very little about the causes and consequences of this particular aspect of family abuse. Much more research is needed to help us understand the family dynamics that turn children against their parents.

Elder Abuse and Neglect

As the number of individuals who live into old age increases, more and more elderly parents (and spouses) will need care and attention to deal with declining physical and mental health. An issue that is receiving growing attention in the popular press is the abuse of older adults who are cared for in institutions or in the family. While the actual incidence of elder abuse is not known, current estimates put the number between 4 and 7 percent annually (Griffin, 1999). The criterion for defining behavior as abusive is whether it "results in unnecessary suffering, injury, pain, loss, and/or violation of human rights and decreased quality of life" (Wolf, 2003, 511). Abuse refers to behaviors such as physical, sexual, emotional or material abuse (such as inappropriate use of the older adult's money), as well as acts of omission, such as neglect of the older adult's need for care (bathing, cooking, getting dressed) (Griffin, 1999; Schiamberg and Gans, 2000). Acts of omission are likely to occur when an elderly person is responsible for the care of his or her aged spouse. Men and women are equally likely to be the victims of elder abuse. Elder abuse crosses class lines, occurring in families across all socioeconomic strata (Boudreau, 1993).

Focusing on domestic abuse occurring in private homes, the National Elder Abuse Incidence Study (NEAIS) (1998) estimated that about 550,000 persons ages 60 and older experienced abuse, neglect, or self-neglect (behavior that threatens one's own safety) in 1996, the year these data were collected. However, these figures may underestimate the real incidence of abuse, because older victims tend to deny that inappropriate actions have occurred, often because they fear institutionalization or out of love for and dependence on their caregivers. Whatever the actual rate of abuse is today, many expect the figure to increase as more adults live into old age, often with chronic disabling conditions that create a need for extensive family care (Schiamberg and Gans, 2000).

Some scholars have identified age and impairment as two strong risk variables for experiencing elder abuse. Persons in the oldest age category—80 years old and older—experience abuse and neglect at a rate two-thirds higher than others in the elderly population (NEAIS, 1998). Older adults who are particularly frail or have severe cognitive impairments are considered to be at greater risk (Wilber and McNeilly, 2001). Because it is the very old, dependent adults who have the greatest risk of being abused, it is not surprising that the most common perpetrators of abuse are the family members who have assumed responsibility for their care (NEAIS, 1998). Decalmer (1993) created a list of characteristics describing the typically abused elderly person and his or her caregiver—see Table 9.1.

Although elder abuse typically occurs in the family, the conventional wisdom regarding why it occurs is dramatically different from that which surrounds other forms of domestic violence. Rather than considering that the perpetrator of elder abuse may be using inappropriate behaviors to control, dominate, and possibly even punish the elderly victim (as is often the case with spousal and child abuse), more often the *stress* of caregiving is used as an explanation (or excuse) for the perpetrator's abusive actions (Brandl and Horan, 2002). Thus two widely accepted theories for elder abuse are "the exhausted caregiver" theory and the theory of "external stressors" (Curry and Stone, 1995). Both these theories address the demands of the caregiving situation and the stress that accompanies the caregiver roles.

According to the exhausted caregiver theory, as the older family member becomes more dependent and impaired, the demands on the caregiver increase, along with the frustration and stress that contributes to abuse. The external stress theory alleges that other events (personal illness, financial difficulties) may occur to exacerbate the strain already imposed by the care situation, thereby heightening the risk of abuse (Curry and Stone, 1995). Solid empirical research provides little validity for these caregiver stress

Table 9.1 Characteristics of a Typical Abused Elder and Abusing Caretaker	
Abused Elder	**Abusing Caregiver**
Female	A relative who has looked after the elder for many years (9.5 on average)
Over 75 years old	Lives with the victim
Physically impaired: chair or bedridden	50 to 70 years old
Mentally impaired	Short of money, stressed
Socially isolated	Socially isolated
Depressed	Past violent behavior—at least to property
Ready to adopt the sick role	Exhibited depression, hostility, or anger
Thwarted many attempts to help in past	Alcohol or drug addicted
Was an abusing parent in the past	Parent-child hostilities early in life
Too poor to live independently	
Stubborn—last attempt to have some independence	

Adapted from Decalmer, 1993, pp. 60–61.

theories of abuse, yet they remain popular (Wolf and Pillemer, 1989). Moreover, the notion that elder abuse perpetrators are "overburdened" caregivers may be a central reason that protective service agencies and other service providers are less likely to prosecute the accused than is true with other forms of domestic violence, such as child abuse (Bergeron, 2001).

Since attention began to focus on elder abuse in the mid-1970s, Congress has held several hearings and passed protective legislation and mandatory reporting requirements (Griffin, 1999). States and local communities within the exosystem have developed services aimed at ameliorating the stress associated with continual caregiving. Some of these services include (Griffin, 1993):

• Shelters for short-term support.

• Counseling that offers information about the physical, emotional, medical and social needs of the elderly.

• Home health care.

• Adult day care, elderly homemaker services.

• Home-delivered meals.

• Medical care delivered by private physicians.

The availability of services does not mean that they are used, however. Some elderly persons avoid reaching out for help even in the worst of situations. They do so out of fear, shame, or embarrassment, reluctant to admit that their child is mistreating them (Tomita, 1990). What kind of parents were they who raised such a child?

There is scant research on elder abuse among blacks, and the answer is unclear as to the differences or similarities compared to whites. It is not known whether the characteristics listed in Table 9.1 represent the profile of abused and caregiving blacks, but there are known subcultural differences that may be applied to the caregiving situation for this minority group. For example, the social networks and household composition of blacks often include both kin and nonkin, and these relationships are a potential source of support and cohesiveness for the elderly. This extended family tradition, attitudes about family closeness, and strong religious beliefs are factors thought to buffer elder abuse among blacks. Yet, it does occur (Griffin, Williams, and Reed, 1998).

Community services and resources for the elderly are not as readily available in black as in white communities, which means that most elderly and their caregivers must depend on the extended family for support. For example, services that whites may come to depend on, such as home health care or adult day care, may not exist in black neighborhoods. As with some white elderly persons, even when services for the abused are available, there is often resistance on the part of elderly blacks to use them because of shame, fear, embarrassment, or the feeling that if they change anything, their situation will worsen. Further, it has been suggested that traditional assessment tools used by agencies to determine need or eligibility services are insensitive to the minority experience and fail to take into account the effects of economic and discrimination factors associated with being black (Gibson, 1989). Further, prior experience with prejudice and discrimination may make blacks suspicious of public or private agencies, so they do their best to avoid them.

Alcoholism and Substance Addiction

Research findings show that alcohol is involved in one-half to two-thirds of homicides, one-fourth to nearly one-half of serious assaults, and more than one-fourth of rapes (Wilson, 1997). Alcohol abuse among batterers varies from 16 to 79 percent, depending on the study. However, abusive men with severe alcohol problems are just as likely to abuse their partners when sober as when drunk. Drug abuse (marijuana, cocaine, opiates, hallucinogens, and stimulants) among batterers is reported to range from 8 to 30 percent (Wilson, 1997). But just how pervasive is the abuse of alcohol and other illegal drugs in the United States? The National Household Survey on Drug Abuse is an annual survey conducted to measure substance use patterns and trends. According to the 2002 report, 19.5 million Americans (8.3 percent of the U.S. population) used illegal drugs at least once during the 30 days prior to the survey. This figure varied by race and ethnicity: 3.5 percent of Asians, 7.2 percent of Latinos, 8.5 percent of whites, 9.7 percent of blacks, and 10.1 percent of American Indian/Alaska Natives acknowledged use in the previous month. A little over 6 percent (6.2 percent) of Americans reported heavy use of alcohol (defined as consuming five or more drinks on one occasion in five or more days during the 30-day period before the survey) (Substance Abuse and Mental Health Services Administration, 2003).

When both partners drink, they usually do so at the same rate, sharing a similar pattern of alcohol use. However, when partners' drinking patterns are *not* shared, serious relationship problems may occur, including alcohol-related arguments and violent behavior. Yet we cannot assume that substance abuse is the cause of domestic violence or child abuse. Gelles (1993) writes that if substance use is linked to violence at all, it is through a complicated set of individual, situational, and social factors. It is thus necessary to consider the issues of substance abuse and domestic violence as related but separate.

Although women drink less than men, they tend to be more susceptible to the physical consequences of drinking. Female alcoholics die at rates 50 to 100 times higher than that for male alcoholics. There are also psychological consequences. Alcoholism is accompanied by low self-esteem, feelings of inadequacy, and depression among women. Female abusers report feeling lonely, isolated from positive support networks, and less worthy of help than do men in similar conditions. The overlap between substance abuse and physical abuse is not great. Approximately 7 to 14 percent of battered women have alcohol abuse problems. Results of a study of battered women seeking emergency room services indicated that battered women have a rate of alcohol abuse 15 times greater and a risk of drug abuse six times greater than nonbattered women (Wilson, 1997).

There are other consequences of substance abuse. The abuse of alcohol and illegal substances takes its toll in terms of financial costs to the family, developmental problems in young children resulting from the poor parenting skills, and damage to infants with fetal alcohol syndrome or other addictions born to alcoholic or addicted mothers. The consequences of prenatal alcohol exposure can include mental retardation, behavioral problems, and/or neurological damage (National Institute on Alcohol Abuse and Alcoholism, 2000). Studies of children raised in families with substance abuse histories find them to have higher levels of depression, aggression, delinquency, hyperactivity, impulsivity, anxiety, and negative affectivity, and lower self-esteem than children without such a family history (Dore et al., 1996; Giancola and Parker, 2001; Maynard, 1997).

What happens to these children when they grow up? Watt (2002) answered this question by analyzing data from a random sample of over 9,000 adults. Comparing those who grew up with a family member who had an alcohol problem with those who reported no such problem, the results were clear. Adult children of alcoholics were more likely to have never married or to be in a cohabiting relationship; if married, they were more likely to be unhappy in their marriages, and they were more likely to have experienced parental divorce. Both men and women scored lower on self-esteem than adults who did not grow up in an alcoholic family. Men but not women reported lower levels of educational achievement, and women but not men were more likely to have a substance abuse problem of their own, were more likely to marry a substance abuser, and were more likely to divorce. If they were married to a substance abuser, they were three times more likely to divorce than women who did not come from alcoholic families but who also were married to substance abusers (261). Watt notes that these data "reveal some truth to the popular conception that alcohol abuse in a child's family of origin can have long-lasting consequences for their future adult partnerships" (263).

Are the 10 percent of children who grow up in alcoholic families fated to become alcohol abusers themselves? Not usually. The literature is consistent about the protective effects of supportive relationships for children living with an alcoholic parent (including the nonalcoholic parent, siblings, or other adults in the child's microsystems). High-quality parenting in the form of parental acceptance and open communication can mitigate some of the negative effects of being raised with an addicted parent (Moser and Jacob, 1997; Walker and Lee, 1998). We have discussed the importance of communication in several sections of this text, and here again we emphasize its importance in developing and maintaining resilience and integrity in the family system. When an alcoholic lives in the family, communication often becomes distorted and dysfunctional. The family is characterized by arguments, nagging, pleading, blaming, and patterns of avoidance and withdrawal (Hayes and Emshoff, 1993). Family boundaries become more rigid and closed, and communication about family problems with others outside the family is discouraged in order to keep the family "secret."

When protective factors are missing, children growing up with an alcoholic parent are more likely to experience other negative and stressful events. For example, 20 percent of 9,346 adults who had at least one alcoholic parent were more likely to have witnessed or experienced at least one of the following: childhood emotional, physical, or sexual abuse; domestic violence; parental separation or divorce; or the mental illness, suicide, or criminal behavior of family members (Anda et al., 2002). It may be that the stress associated with problem drinking is the ultimate culprit. Children who experience none or few negative events, and hence live in less stressful family environments, are likely to be less affected by a family member's alcoholism.

There are no easy solutions for family members living in a distressed environment. Tight family boundaries may operate to keep family secrets, and social isolation tends to be cultivated, depriving members of needed social support. Some partners of alcoholics and batterers minimize the impact of drinking and violence on the family. A denial process of not feeling, not trusting, and not talking dominates the family. Alcoholism, when coupled with violence, doubles the need for denial and creates an even greater sense of hopelessness for family members. Claudia Black (1981), author of *It Will Never Happen to Me* explains it this way: "Remember, the goal of family members in attempting to live through these problems is the same—minimize the conflict, adjust, placate, act-out, drop-out—do anything, but be sure to survive" (150).

Children Who Run Away

Running away from home is one solution that troubled children choose in order to escape home situations they perceive as intolerable. The majority of runaways (74 percent) are between the ages of 12 and 17 and most (75 percent) are female. Most of the 1 to 2 million runaways in the United States each year are gone from home less than 24 hours, and many run to relatives or friends. Most return home within six days and their absence is never reported to authorities (Tomb, 1991). Figure 9.1 lists problems identified by callers who have sought help from the National Runaway Switchboard.

Problems with parents, school, or peers (and the mesosystems among them) are the primary reasons teenage children leave home. These problems include competitiveness between siblings, conflict over parental rules, poor school performance, reprimands for the way the child dresses, conflict over boyfriends, pregnancy, or the perception of unfair punishments (Roberts, 1981; Whitbeck and Hoyt, 1999). Running away may be an attempt on the part of an adolescent to get parents to give in, or at least compromise, on what the child sees as restrictive rules and control. A poor relationship with a child is the most consistent finding reported by parents of runaways. Here is how one adolescent and his parent described their situation:

Son: I didn't think my parents were treating me right. He [dad] doesn't like me going out at night, drinking, partying. He wants me to be a prisoner, to work around the house all the time and talk to him every night.

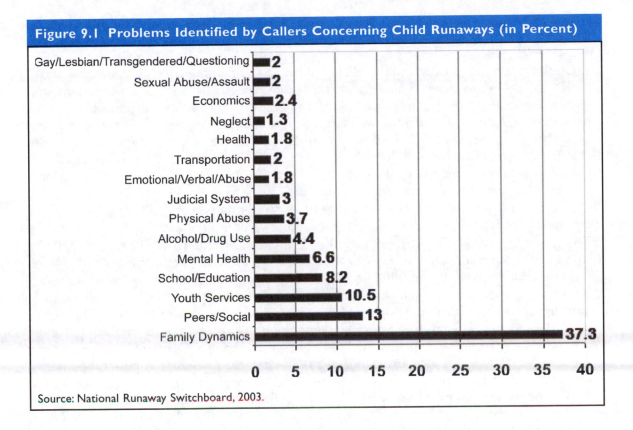

Figure 9.1 Problems Identified by Callers Concerning Child Runaways (in Percent)

Category	Percent
Gay/Lesbian/Transgendered/Questioning	2
Sexual Abuse/Assault	2
Economics	2.4
Neglect	1.3
Health	1.8
Transportation	2
Emotional/Verbal/Abuse	1.8
Judicial System	3
Physical Abuse	3.7
Alcohol/Drug Use	4.4
Mental Health	6.6
School/Education	8.2
Youth Services	10.5
Peers/Social	13
Family Dynamics	37.3

Source: National Runaway Switchboard, 2003.

Father: He lies a lot. He keeps everything to himself. He does everything you ask him not to do—smoking pot, missing school, dressing like an animal, getting to school late, staying out late. . . . (Roberts, 1981,70)

Running away may also be a consequence of great distress in the family lives of adolescents, such as financial troubles, unemployment, illness, divorce, parental drug or alcohol abuse, or a parent or stepparent in trouble with the law. Alternatively, a child's personality characteristics may foster leaving home. Running away may be an indication of rebelliousness, poor impulse control, and a search for excitement and stimulation. Janus and his colleagues (1987) found that adolescents with these characteristics and motives were younger, more impulsive, and more easily bored, with a great need for independence. These children tended to be repeat runaways.

Children who have sporadic fights with their parents but who generally have nurturing and caring parents or caretakers are not the children we are focusing on here. Wiles (1995) reports that the "preexisting attachment between a parent and a runaway child is predictive of reunification" (602). Less-benign family conditions that spur children to run away from home include parental neglect or rejection, verbal abuse, poor parent-child communication, and low family cohesiveness that leaves adolescents feeling powerless, insecure, and vulnerable. These children, and those who flee from physical, sexual, or substance abuse or who have been thrown out of the house (called throw-away children) experience a disruption in their normal developmental growth. Leaving home may be an act of defiance and rebellion for adolescents or an adaptive response taken to save their lives, but in either case these children are often frightened, insecure, and demoralized (Wiles, 1995).

On the street, runaways find themselves homeless and vulnerable to an increased risk for HIV infection and other sexually transmitted diseases, prostitution, rape, assault, and substance abuse. According to Wiles (1995), they are looking for love, attention, and nurturance but are doing so with the wrong tools: low self-esteem, despair, depression, and anger. Runaways are more likely to be sexually active, use drugs, or get into trouble with the law. Running away may be the final step in a coping response to what is seen as an intolerable situation. Roberts (1981) reports that running away may not be the first action a child takes; it often follows a series of maladaptive behaviors such as drinking, taking drugs, or attempting suicide. The runaways in his study shared several characteristics, including school failure, truancy, suspension, and drug and alcohol use.

In an extensive study of runaway children, Whitbeck and Hoyt (1999) enlisted the help of child outreach services in four midwestern states and were able to gather data from 602 children and 201 parent/caretakers. These youth, ranging in age from 12 to 22, were living in shelters, with friends, on the street, or in an institution (juvenile detention, group home, or hospital), and some (14 percent) were back at home with their parents. Most (61 percent) were white, 25 percent were black, and 14 percent were Latino, Native American, or members of some other racial or ethnic group. Over the course of their childhood, these youths had experienced many changes in their living arrangements, some self-initiated and others parent-initiated. The researchers commented: "Life for the majority of the adolescents had been a "revolving door" of various living situations often beginning early in life" (32). When parents initiated a transition they said that it was primarily because of adolescents' behavior problems or their failure to obey rules. These moves included placing the child in foster care, sending him or her to a relative or another parent (in cases of separation or divorce), or just telling the child to leave. When the youth were asked why they left home, most of them gave no definitive reason or said they left because of intolerable or dangerous conditions. One-third reported neglect or abuse, 38 percent reported they left because of arguing or fighting, 21 percent had been threatened with a weapon, 6 percent had been assaulted with a weapon, 18 percent experienced caretaker verbal requests or attempts to touch them sexually, and 21 percent experienced forced sexual activity (three times as many females as males).

Many of the families the children ran from were characterized by alcohol and drug abuse problems. Considering all parents and stepparents, 65 percent were perceived by their children to have an alcohol problem, 21 percent a marijuana problem, and 44 percent a problem with hard drugs. Over half the youths experienced parental divorce or separation (53 percent of boys and 54 percent of girls), and 42 percent lived with a parent or stepparent who had, at some time, serious problems with the law. As we discussed earlier in this chapter, the parenting skills of problem-ridden parents are minimal. This was reflected in the children's reports that parental monitoring, warmth, and supportiveness were low and parental rejection was high (rejection was measured as distrust, blame, lack of caring, unhappiness with the adolescent, and thinking the child caused a lot of problems). Prior to running away, youth were increasingly alienated and emotionally withdrawn from the family; "they were leaving families that had little to hold them" (53).

Alone and on their own, children living on the street are vulnerable to hunger, exploitation, and abuse. Many youth feel, however, that it is better than the conditions they left at home.

Once out of the home, youths tended to follow behavioral paths that were familiar. That is, adolescents whose parents were substance abusers became drug dealers as a survival strategy, and those who had been sexually victimized at home were more likely to engage in survival sex in the struggle for independence and safety. Sexual activity was not always voluntary and there was a good deal of sexual victimization, exploitation, and abuse while on the run. Being robbed (11.2 percent), beaten up (14.4 percent), and threatened or assaulted (23 percent) more than once was not uncommon. More than a quarter (27.9 percent) of these kids went without food for a day more than once. Stress levels were high from fear of being physically harmed. Many suffered from depression and posttraumatic stress disorder. Many adopted antisocial options (drug use, sex exchanged for security, burglarizing or taking money by force) as a solution to the problems they faced. As Whitbeck and Hoyt summarized: "Witnessing violence, avoiding it, and occasionally being caught up in it were part of everyday life when on the streets" (115).

An observation the researchers made about the future of the runaway children they studied was not optimistic. They surmised that the available prosocial options diminished as the consequences of early developmental disadvantages (inadequate parenting and socialization) accumulated and as ties to conventional microsystems broke down (e.g., truancy from school). They felt those youths who had successfully adapted to street life were at a disadvantage, since the skills learned on the street run counter to successful adult development. Rather, runaways who were conventionally "resilient" were those who did not adapt well to street life. These youths maintained ties to some significant adult, if not family, stayed connected to schools, were able to be gainfully employed, and could make realistic and achievable plans for their futures (that is, they did not aspire to be a professional football player, a dentist, or a singer).

If They Are Family, Why Are They Mistreated?

Scholars use a variety of theories to explain family violence. Some of these theories were discussed earlier when we wrote about the motivations of abusers and violence among same-sex partners. Theory, or explanation, is the foundation of social research. Bottom line, we want to know *why* something happens! So, we will devote some space here to review the most widely used explanations of why violence occurs in family relationships, with help from a review by Gelles (1999). He outlines three broad theoretical models under which most explanations fall: the psychiatric, the social-psychological, and the sociocultural.

When we discussed Johnson and Ferarro's (2000) motives of violent abusers at the beginning of this chapter, we touched on three theories: interpersonal power theory (a social-psychological approach), a gender-based theory, and a sociodemographic explanation (sociocultural approaches). Aspects of these theories will be repeated here, as they fit well within Gelles' typology. Also, as we noted earlier, Dutton (1996) postulated a psychiatric approach to explain family violence. Let's begin with that one.

Psychiatric Approach to the Study of Family Violence

According to Gelles, those who adopt a psychiatric explanation point to individual characteristics as the cause of violence: personality or character disorders, mental illness, and addiction to or abuse of drugs or alcohol. This approach starts with the individual and attributes or traits as they currently exist within him or her. However, we know from Chapter 2 that the social and cultural environments that influence the growth and development of self, personality, identities, and character cannot be ignored. Thus the psychiatric approach cannot stand alone. Both Dutton (1996) and Miller (1996) made this clear.

A sociobiological (or evolutionary) explanation of violence straddles the psychiatric and sociocultural approaches. The basic assumption of *sociobiology* is that biology, genes, or reproductive striving lie at the root of *natural selection*, which is the process of differential reproduction and reproductive success. Sociobiologists suggest that aggression is used against females in order to control and intimidate them, thus assuring the male's own reproductive success. Certainty of paternity ensures that males will make an investment in their own children and not those of other males. According to this explanation, offspring who are unrelated (foster, adopted, step) are at greater risk for experiencing aggression and abuse than related offspring. However, this explanation does not tell us why males abuse their own biological offspring. Sociocultural factors enter into this explanation with the knowledge that there are some social conditions under which women and children are protected from male violence. According to Gelles, these include the strength of female alliances within a group, the support women receive from their relatives, male alliances that are weak in strength and importance, a high degree of equality in male-female relationships, and weak control by males of the economic resources within a society (13).

Social-Psychological Approach to the Study of Violence

The social psychology approach blends information from the disciplines of psychology and sociology to account for personal, interpersonal, and social factors associated with violence. General social psychological theories used to explain family violence include learning theory, resource theory, and exchange theory. According to *learning theory*, modeling of violent behavior by parents and siblings makes the home a learning environment for the perpetuation of violence. According to *resource theory*, the lack of personal and/or social resources leads to acts of violence intended to address grievances or restore balance in relationships. The principle is that the more resources a person has, the more power and control she or he has over others. Aggression is a mechanism used to restore or increase one's power/control. *Exchange theory* is based on an assessment of rewards and costs. According to Gelles, the most important rewards are power and control. Violence may be used to gain these rewards if the costs incurred are minimal. The costs of inflicting violence are reduced in our society, because of the private nature of families. For privacy reasons some social agencies and helping professionals are reluctant to intervene in spite of reporting laws that have been enacted. The approval of displays of violence in our culture (at least in the media, in games, and in sports) also reduces the perceived cost of committing violent acts for some people.

Sociocultural Approach to the Study of Violence

Social situational, stress, and coping approaches draw on macrosystem factors of social inequality, patriarchy, and cultural norms that influence attitudes and beliefs about violence. Social location (situational) and the accompanying stress associated with coping with an inadequate income, low education levels, low-paying jobs, or the lack of any employment facilitates the perpetuation of abuse and violence within the family system. The gender-based theory of violence we discussed earlier also falls within this framework. To review that idea, social and economic forces within society serve, directly and indirectly, to support a male-dominated (patriarchal) social order and family structure. These processes serve to subordinate women and children, opening the way for the expression of violent behavior.

The sociocultural approach also includes *ecological systems theory*. It is an integrative theory insofar as it explains family violence by combining the psychiatric, social-psychological, and sociocultural approaches. Using the systems theory you have come to know well, this perspective explains violence by analyzing the relationships among the individual and his or her microsystems, exosystems, and mesosystems and the conditions within the macrosystem. Using this perspective, scholars propose that violence and abuse stem from mismatched relationships between parent and child and between family and neighborhood or community. Violence is highest when parents cannot function well because of undue stress, when they face personal problems, when they have personality problems, or when children have learning disabilities, developmental problems, or physical or emotional handicaps (Gelles, 1999, 14).

The Big Picture: The Social and Cultural Context of Violence

You are aware of the multiple ways in which family behaviors are affected by other institutions in the exosystem. This is especially true for distressed families. One of the most influential of these institutions is the economy. Biglan and his associates (1990) stated it simply, "Poverty may be the single most important cultural factor affecting the prevalence of aversive practices in families" (117). Communities that offer resources to alleviate unemployment and other factors associated with poverty will find that in doing so they also reduce the individual and family distress that leads to intimate violence.

Neighborhoods and communities can also affect the prevalence of child abuse and neglect. By itself, living in a poor neighborhood is not a predictor of the rate of child abuse. However, child abuse rates are higher in poor neighborhoods when social resources are scarce and social organization is weak. Thus, the factors associated with the causes of family distress involve some of the same neighborhood conditions that were discussed in other chapters, such as the availability of social resources in the community, whether parents use these resources in a preventive fashion or as a response to crisis, whether children participate in informal organizations such as scout groups or other youth groups, whether parents exchange services with one another, and whether they take an active and protective interest in all the neighborhood children (National Research Council, 1993). However, a point to remember when considering the impact of communities on distressed families is that many neglectful families are socially isolated, and for that reason the conditions that exist within their community may be less relevant (Polansky et al., 1981).

Violence in the neighborhood is another condition that endangers children. Young children are taught to lie quickly on the floor when they hear gunshots. They see family members, friends, or neighbors killed in drive-by shootings. Table 9.2 indicates the prevalence of children's exposure to community violence, abstracted from a variety of research studies.

Aspects of the community that foster violence are the same as those mentioned above: poverty, overcrowding, unemployment, poor housing, and the presence of drugs and other illegal activities. Macrosystem elements include beliefs that support gun ownership and violence, the glorification of violence in the media, socialization practices based on patriarchal beliefs, and the consumption of child pornography (Jones Hardin and Koblinsky, 1999).

Many experts believe that the most effective prevention programs for families in distress are community rather than federally based, because less stigma is attached to programs devised by the community, and community members organize and staff the social support programs for families. Such programs help increase police involvement in child protection, establish well-baby clinics, and link new parents to community resources (Rabasca, 1999). Community shelters for battered women are available in many communities. Children make up about two-thirds of the residents in most battered women's shelters. (Interestingly, teenage sons of battered women are often barred from battered women's shelters.) Community shelters tend to focus on the needs of heterosexual women. Battered gays and lesbians experiencing partner abuse usually are refused service from these programs (Allen and Leventhal, 1999).

Programs directed toward helping children in families with substance abusers are few. Services offered to domestic violence survivors have a longer history of responding to children than chemical dependency services. In contrast, most drug or alcohol treatment programs for women are not equipped to serve mothers with children. Large cities have shelters and transitional living programs for runaway youth but lack effective ways to track children as they move from foster care to institutional care, out on the streets, or in and out of their family of orientation. Because most of these youths come from severely distressed families, the way to end the problem of chronic runaway children is to begin with early and effective intervention and outreach programs for these families (Whitbeck and Hoyt, 1999). Finally, while they are fewer in number, men who suffer from partner

Table 9.2 Prevalence of Children's Exposure to Community Violence

Study	Sample Age Ranges	Prevalence Rates
Bell & Jenkins (1991)	elementary school-aged children and adolescents	one third witnessed shooting/stabbing; one quarter adolescents witnessed homicide
Berman, Kurtines, Silverman, & Serafini (1996)	adolescents	93% witnessed some form of violence; 44% were victims
Burton, Foy, Bwanausa, Johnson, & Moore (1994)	young adolescents	71% witnessed gang violence; 56% experienced death of a friend; 75% victim of weapon
Campbell & Schwartz (1996)	young adolescents	89% suburban & 96% urban knew victim of violence; 67% urban victims
Dubrow & Garbarino (1989)	preschoolers	100% exposed to shooting
DuRant, Cadenhead, Pendergrast, Slavens, & Linder (1994)	adolescents	85% witnessed and 70% were victims of violent incident; 40% witnessed homicide
Hardin (unpublished paper)	elementary school-aged children	75% witnessed violence
Hausman, Spivak, & Prothrow-Stith (1992)	adolescents	69% witnessed violence; 37% experienced threat
Horowitz, Weine, & Jekel (1995)	adolescents (female only)	65% witnessed shooting; 58% witnessed stabbing; 41% witnessed friend's murder
Marans & Cohen (1993)	elementary school-aged children	40% witnessed violence
Osofsky, Wewers, Hann, & Fick (1993)	older elementary school-aged children	91% witnessed violence
Richters & Martinez (1993a, 1993b)	elementary school-aged	97% older children & 84% younger children witnessed violence
Saltzman (1992)	elementary school-aged children	85% witnessed moderate to severe violence
Schwab-Stone, Ayers, & Weissberg (1995)	adolescents	40% witnessed shooting/stabbing
Shahinfar (1997)	preschool-aged children	74% (by child's report) and 60% (by parent's report) witnessed violence
Shakoor & Chalmers (1991)	adolescents	75% boys and 70% girls witnessed severe violence
Taylor, Zuckerman, Harik, & McAlister Groves (1994)	preschool-aged children	47% exposed to violence

Adapted from Hardin and Koblinsky, 1999, 70.

assault find little assistance or support within the community and have few places to go for help.

The education institution—primarily the public schools—began in the late 1970s to develop sexual abuse prevention programs aimed at teaching children about personal safety, appropriate and inappropriate touching, how to get support from others, and empowering them to say "no." These behaviors are intended to reduce children's vulnerability and potential exploitation and to teach them skills to resist abuse (McCauley et al., 2001). Some programs have expanded to include a curriculum that aims not only at preventing sexual victimization but also at keeping children from abusing others. These programs include lectures, role playing, and the use of puppets and dolls, depending on the ages of children (Kohl, 1993). Many high schools include parenting skills as part of the curriculum, and some elementary schools teach children to use nonaggressive conflict resolution techniques on the playground. The education system is thus working in tandem with other institutions in the exosystem to prevent violent behavior rather than merely respond to violent outbreaks once they occur. Some schools have experimented with programs to help children who live with alcoholic parents, and a number of clinical and commercial programs are designed to help these children (Roosa et al., 1989).

At the other end of the age spectrum, the ecological systems perspective is useful in analyzing and understanding elder abuse. The risk for abuse depends on factors at multiple system levels. Not only do individual characteristics of the recipient (age, disability level) and provider (depression, stress level) contribute to the risk of elder abuse, but so do factors at all system levels. Conditions within the microsystem (co-residence of the care recipient and provider), exosystem (respite services provided through adult day care programming), mesosystem (social isolation from friends and family), and macrosystem (societal prejudice reflected in ageism and the perception of older adults as less valued members of society) all reflect the complexity of caring for dependent or disabled elderly persons (Fulmer, 1989; Schiamberg and Gans, 2000; Wilber and McNeilly, 2001; Wolf and Pillemer, 1989).

At the macrosystem level, laws supporting the death penalty, gun ownership, and an active military are cultural values that promote violence. Physical punishment of children is permitted in some school districts on the belief that it is a deterrent to misbehavior. In many communities the police have been accused of using undue force when making arrests. Throughout society, films and video games stimulate and excite with high-speed chases, killings, and general mayhem and havoc. These are only a few examples that illustrate the value placed on violent behavior in American society.

Summary

This chapter presented data relevant to the causes of violent behavior, the family dynamics associated with living in a distressed family, and the consequences of serious problems that families face, such as partner violence, child maltreatment, runaway children, alcohol and substance abuse, and elder abuse. Common couple violence, intimate terrorism, violent resistance, and mutual violent control are four ways that partner violence is manifest. Identifying which type of violence a couple engages in helps explain contradictory findings reported in the literature. Whether or not individuals are likely to perpetrate violence or mistreat family members has been explained on the basis of socio-economic status, social location, subcultural values, age, sex, marital status, personality characteristics, and gender ideology.

Strong dependency needs and a desire to control are common characteristics of batterers. The consequences of experiencing abuse for wives, husbands, and children are similar: depression, low self-esteem, anxiety, physical ailments, and sometimes injury or death. Living in a distressed family situation is associated with a loss of trust, feelings of insecurity, nonnormative social development, and, in children, maladaptive behaviors such as poor school performance, running away, delinquency, drug use, promiscuity, and attempted suicide. Adults who grew up in alcoholic families have lower self-esteem, have unhappier marriages, and, all things considered, are less likely to marry. Women from alcoholic families are more likely to divorce husbands who are substance abusers than women whose husbands have a similar problem but who were not raised in an alcoholic family.

At the societal level, many social programs are designed to assist distressed families. The most successful are local, originating in the neighborhood or community, although some national sources, such as telephone hotlines (e.g., National Runaway Switchboard), have proved to be successful in providing information to assist families in trouble. However, because of the social isolation of distressed families the availability of these services may be of no help at all. That is one reason that institutions such as public schools that have access to and can effectively reach victimized children are valuable sources of information and help. Unfortunately, in times of deficit budgets and economic downturns, the programs offered at these sites are usually the first to be eliminated.

Families are the foundation of society in terms of socializing the next generation of citizens, and they are ultimately responsible for perpetuating democratic ideals and a valued way of life. Therefore, efforts must be made by people in positions of power, by those who hold decision-making roles, and by neighbors within communities to create the support systems necessary to respond to situations that create or perpetuate family distress.

Endnote

1. In this chapter three possible terms—distress, dysfunction, and crisis—could have been used to describe the family situations we explore. *Distress* is defined as anguish of body or mind; trouble; a painful situation; a state of danger or desperate need. *Dysfunction* means impaired or abnormal functioning. *Crisis* means an unstable or crucial time or state of affairs. We use the concept *distress* because it appears to encompass both dysfunction and crisis.

Chapter Concepts

child abuse and neglect: any recent act or failure to act on the part of a parent or caregiver that results in death, serious physical or emotional harm, sexual abuse or exploitation, or an act or failure to act that presents an imminent risk of serious harm.

common couple violence: violence that includes hitting, slapping, shoving. It is situation specific and usually mutual.

control: behavior that is directed at getting another to do something that the controlling person wants.

cultural context: a set of values, beliefs, and traditions that may or may not foster the use of violence.

emotional (psychological) abuse: any use of words, voice, action, or lack of action meant to control, hurt, or demean another person.

gender-based theory of violence: violence enacted by men in order to perpetuate male social dominance in a patriarchal society.

interpersonal power theory of violence: a theory that explains violence as an attempt to exert power and control over another.

intimate terrorism: violence directed toward a family member that is likely to cause severe injury. With intimate terrorism, physical violence is often accompanied by psychological violence.

mutual violent control: violence between intimates that is mutually and potentially equally injurious.

patriarchy: a system of society in which men hold the most power and women and children are generally excluded from it.

physical abuse: any use of size, strength, or presence to hurt or control someone else.

physical assault: behaviors that threaten, attempt, or actually inflict physical harm.

power: the ability to influence the behavior of others and to resist others' influence.

sexual abuse: any sexual behavior meant to control, manipulate, humiliate, or demean another person.

social impoverishment: a situation in which individuals or families lack strong social connections that can offer standards and guidelines for acceptable behavior as well as support in times of need.

social location: the status a person holds and the status of the community or neighborhood within which he or she behaves.

sociodemographic theory of violence: a theory that explains intimate violence on the basis of structural inequality in society and in the family.

violent resistance: violent behavior that occurs when a battered partner strikes back.

Suggested Activities

1. Visit a local high school and inquire as to whether any programs have been instituted to help students develop nonviolent conflict-resolution skills, learn appropriate parenting skills, and so on. If there are no such programs, ask why there are none. If there are, ask to examine the course of study and determine how much attention is devoted to family behaviors. In class, share your findings and as a group analyze them for their efficacy in reducing family violence.

2. Conduct an observational experiment by viewing and taking notes on at least two films portraying violence between family members of various classes and races. (For example, *La Bamba* is a film about violence in a Latino family, and *What's Love Got to Do With It?* is the depiction of marital violence experienced by a black couple.) Are the class levels of the depicted families in the two films comparable? What micro-, exo-, and macrosystem factors can you identify as

precipitating causes of the partner violence in the films? Following from these observations, which theory (power-based, gender-based, or demographic-based) best explains the family violence depicted?

3. Although the example of Cary Stayner's family was brief, extract from it as many concepts from family systems theory as you can. Make a list of them and in a short essay indicate how these elements were manifest in this family. (Hint: The concepts of family secrets and permeable boundaries are easily identifiable).

Suggested Readings

Bergen, R. K. (ed.). 1998. *Issues in Intimate Violence.* Thousand Oaks, CA: Sage.

Jasinski, J. J., and Williams, L. M. 1998. *Partner Violence: A Comprehensive Review of 20 Years of Research.* Thousand Oaks, CA: Sage.

Pelzer, D. J. 1995. *A Child Called 'It': One Child's Courage to Survive.* Deerfield, FL: Health Communications.

Ryan, T. 2001. *The Prize Winner of Defiance, Ohio.* New York: Simon and Schuster.

Schwartz-Kenney, B. M., McCauley, M., and Epstein, M. A. 2001. *Child Abuse: A Global View.* Westport, CT: Greenwood Press.

Wilson, K. 1997. *When Violence Begins at Home.* Alameda, CA: Hunter House Publishers. ◆

Chapter 10

Families in a Social Context

The Big Picture

Did You Know?

- Parents of adolescents most often make decisions about where to live based upon affordable housing (19 percent), followed closely by the quality of neighborhood schools (18 percent) (Billy, 2001).

- In 1996, the year Welfare Reform was passed, one of every eight U.S. children was on welfare (U.S. House of Representatives, 1998).

- A 2002 survey of American families conducted by the Urban Institute found that 70 percent of the nonelderly who access food pantries had some income in the past year. About half of food pantry customers were working parents and their children (Zedlewski, 2002).

Things to Think About

- In what ways do you think institutions in the community (e.g., schools, work settings) impact family interaction, parenting practices, and children's development?

- What makes a community "family-friendly"?

- What ideologies are reflected in current U.S. family policy?

- Should the business sector or the government be obligated to provide families with parental and medical leave? What are the costs and rewards of providing such benefits?

335

"No man is an island." By replacing the word "man" in this common phrase with "family," you have the theme of this chapter. Although most families would find it nearly impossible to live totally isolated from the social world around them, occasionally news stories tell of families that have either purposefully, or as a result of circumstances, done just that. Inevitably, the problems that result from such isolation are what bring these families into the public eye.

A case in point is the tragic story of the McGuckin family in rural Idaho, who made the headlines in May and June of 2001 (CBC News, 2001). This family experienced serious problems after the father, a lumber mill worker, was stricken with multiple sclerosis and died. In the years preceding his illness and eventual death, Mr. McGuckin had experienced tremendous economic problems to the point where he and his wife were forced into bankruptcy (their eldest daughter claimed that they owed creditors over $400,000, according to ABCNEWS.com, 2001). Additionally, Mr. McGuckin and his wife had become increasingly distrustful of outsiders and the government (they owed large sums in back taxes on their Idaho land). He believed that their phones were tapped and that people were trailing him. Over time, mounting distrust led the family to cut themselves off from the world outside. In fact, at the time of his death, Mr. McGuckin had not been seen outside his home in about five years (ABCNEWS.com, 2001). As a result of isolating themselves from the outside world, the family missed opportunities for help and support during their difficult economic times and the stressful period surrounding Mr. McGuckin's illness and death. For example, they refused to apply for state assistance and they also rejected informal help from their former church. Following Mr. McGuckin's death in early May of 2001, his wife was arrested on charges of felony injury to a child because of suspected child neglect (<showmenews.com>, 2001). Left without either parent and the fear of being separated and sent to different foster homes, the six children who were still at home (ages 8 to 16), barricaded themselves in their house, armed with guns and surrounded by packs of dogs. The situation was partly resolved several days later when the oldest son left the home to talk with legal authorities and find a solution to his family's problems (showmenews.com, 2001).

In hearing about this family and the hardships they experienced, one can't help but consider how things might have worked out differently had the parents been open to receiving services and support from the community. How would the father's coping with his chronic disease been different with more medical support or other social and family services? Might Mrs. McGuckin and her children coped differently with her husband's death if they had not been deprived of the basic necessities of life that a steady income provides? What difference would it have made for the family to have the emotional support of church members and neighbors as they struggled to deal with the challenges confronting them? In sum, could things have ended up better for this family if they had not insisted on going it alone during such difficult times?

This chapter focuses on the larger community and societal context in which families are embedded and examines how supports and services in the community, such as child care, schools, and human service agencies, interact with and impact family life. We include social and human services even though all families do not come in direct contact with such services. For those who do, however, these services may constitute a highly influential microsystem. We also discuss the role of the federal government and policy issues related to family life and closely examine three specific family policies (family and medical leave, marriage policy, and welfare reform) that relate to central topics covered in this book. With attention centered on the community, we forgo our customary chapter inclusion of micro-level elements in the ecological system.

Beyond the Family Microsystem

As family members move beyond the physical boundaries of their homes and families they are influenced by people and institutional forces around them. In Chapter 2 we defined neighborhoods and discussed their importance for families. We noted that a key distinction between neighborhoods and communities is that the latter include the economic, political, and social institutions within a geographic area. The institutions within a community are formal settings, meaning they have an organizational structure that is deliberately and rationally designed to achieve specific objectives. As noted in Chapter 2, **formal institutions** are characterized by rules, norms, and a hierarchical authority structure. Some examples of formal institutions in a community are churches, schools, youth clubs (e.g., Boys' and Girls' Club, Girl Scouts) and the police force (Jencks and Mayers, 1990). Communities also include informal or voluntary organizations, such as bowling leagues, book clubs, and self-help groups, although these informal systems are more salient to neighborhoods (Bronfenbrenner et al., 1984).

Although families contribute to and shape the neighborhoods and communities in which they live through involvement in decisionmaking (e.g., via voting), volunteering, and community participation and leadership, family scholars are most interested in what communities and their various institutions can do *for* families. For example, a series of studies by Garbarino and his colleagues found that communities with adequate childcare institutions have lower rates of child abuse and neglect than areas where community support for childcare is lacking (Bronfenbrenner, Moen, and Garbarino, 1984). These findings demonstrate that some of the everyday challenges that families experience can be buffered by community institutions, and these institutions contribute to individual and family well-being.

Community Businesses and Workplaces

The Direct and Indirect Effects of Business. Businesses and other segments of the labor force within a community directly impact families through the jobs they offer. The number of jobs available in the community, the requisite training they entail, and the wage levels that accompany them (as well as the cost-of-living in the community) will ultimately affect whether community members find gainful employment that provides a livable wage, which in turn determines whether they will be able to adequately support their families. Workplace policies regarding such issues as relocation, vacation and sick leave, and parental leave affect how workers balance the demands of work, personal, and family life. Support programs (e.g., childcare referral) offered by employers and human service agencies in the community also make a difference.

Some workplace policies are regulated by law (e.g., minimum wage and the Family and Medical Leave Act, which will be discussed in detail later), and therefore may not vary much from community to community. Other policies and programs are left to the discretion of individual employers, and may be shaped by the geographic location of the community and community characteristics, interests, and goals. Some employers are recognized as being "family-friendly" because they offer provisions that benefit families, such as maternity, parental and family leave, flexible work hours, health insurance for workers and their families, and childcare benefits and supports (e.g., referral services).

In addition to directly affecting families, businesses in the private sector also influence families in indirect ways (Garbarino, Gaboury, and Plantz, 1992). When a community's businesses are booming, not only do individual workers and their families benefit from the increased cash flow, but so do other institutions in the community. For example, families may be more willing to support tax increases for improving schools when they feel financially secure. A good business economy may provide more tax revenue for a community, leading to more discretionary spending on such things as schools, parks, or recreational facilities. On the other hand, when businesses fail, communities die, as was the case in many rural, agricultural areas of the upper Midwest (e.g., Iowa, Minnesota, and the Dakotas) in the last decade. (See Chapter 7 for more discussion of this.)

The operating practices of public and private sector employers also impact communities and the families in them in noneconomic ways. For example, quality-of-life issues in a community are closely linked to the effect that business operations have on the environment (Garbarino, Gaboury, and Plantz, 1992). Think about noise and air and water pollution that results from airports and factories and their potential influence on families. An extreme illustration is portrayed in the popular movie, *Erin Brockovich*, which told the true story of how many California families suffered severe health and economic consequences from living in close proximity to utility plants that illegally used poisonous chemicals. But even minor issues, such as having a high-traffic business on your street, or *not having* certain businesses available in your community (such as movie theaters or arcades for youth recreation), may affect how families live.

We mentioned earlier how many rural communities in the upper Midwest are faced with a serious decline in population, and how this has affected local schools. Similarly, as people leave their rural communities and businesses die, young people are often left with fewer options for recreation, such as arcades, swimming pools, and bowling alleys. Parents in these communities are concerned about the boredom and restlessness their children experience when there are no places for teens to go and socialize, and they worry that the lack of recreational outlets may contribute to increased rates of teen drinking and drug use. Research also suggests that rural youth foresee assuming adult positions (taking on work and family roles) at earlier ages than suburban youth (Stemmler et al., 1991). This is most likely a result of limited opportunities in these communities for higher-level jobs that require an advanced education.

Childcare in the Community

For many children, an important microsystem is their childcare setting outside the home. Over 60 percent of preschool-aged children are cared for outside their homes by nonrelatives (U.S. Bureau of the Census, 2000a), and 6.5 million school-aged children participate in afterschool programs because of their parents' employment schedules (Afterschool Alliance, 2004). In response to the growing child care needs of families, government support for child care programs burgeoned during the 1990s; 34 of the 50 states funded programs for preschoolers (Knitzer and Page, 1998), and the level of state and federal funding for child care tripled (Kamerman and Kahn, 2001). But local communities also affect childcare.

Community Effects on Childcare. Communities influence and shape the childcare microsystem in several ways (Garbarino, Galambos, Plantz, and Kostelny, 1992). Zoning regulations, for instance, impact the availability and quality of childcare options for families. In some communities, restrictive zoning for home daycares may lead to a shortage of childcare spaces. Lax zoning regulations, in contrast, may not adversely affect availability, but may create safety issues, such as when daycares are permitted to operate alongside busy roadways or near toxic waste areas. How a community distributes local funds from state and federal childcare grants (e.g., Head Start) or from agencies like United Way also shapes the childcare options available to parents.

People are sometimes against having in-home childcare centers in their neighborhood. What do you think their main concerns or complaints are about?

The Infant Care and Incentive program (Long, 1983) provides a useful illustration of how community funds can be targeted to meet unique community needs. This program was created in response to a high demand for infant care in the south side neighborhoods of Minneapolis, Minnesota. The community obtained a Block Grant that was used to subsidize childcare providers who offered infant care, and to offer these providers specialized training in caring for infants. These efforts ultimately benefited families because the program created more high quality infant care spaces in the community (Long, 1983). The businesses of a community (industries, banks, and insurance agencies) may become involved with childcare services by allocating monies for childcare centers through trusts or foundations they establish. These are all ways communities directly shape the childcare system.

A community indirectly affects the nature of its childcare system through demographic characteristics and the businesses and services that provide jobs. Communities that include high proportions of young families are likely to create more childcare options than those with mostly older adult residents. Rural communities tend to have fewer options available than urban ones (Long, 1983). Communities in which a high percentage of workers do shift work (as employees of hospitals, factories, etc.) are likely to have a greater demand for childcare centers with extended hours, or centers located on the job site. To illustrate, one small Minnesota town with a population under 3,000 has at least one childcare center that remains open until 11 P.M.; the largest employer in town is a potato factory that runs shifts around the clock. Clearly, services are most effective when tailored to the unique population they serve.

Schools in the Community

Schools represent an influential microsystem for children and are a central component of communities. Many families select the community or specific neighborhood in which to live based on their perceptions of the quality of the schools in that area (Billy, 2001).

Community Effects on Schools. Communities greatly influence the quality and character of the school systems that exist within their boundaries. The degree to which a community values and supports education may be dependent on its demographic profile; for example, a large older adult population in a community may predict a lower level of support for tax increases that fund education initiatives (Ponza, Duncan, Corcoran, and Groskind, 1988). In addition, a community affects its schools by encouraging and facilitating connections between the schools and other institutions. Community businesses usually become involved in schools in one of two ways: through business-school partnerships wherein companies or corporations "adopt" a community school where employees donate time to such activities as tutoring, or businesses provide occasional monetary support for extra needs the schools may have (Epstein, 1994). For example, in a large city where one of your authors resided, a major local department store provided backpacks one fall to all elementary schoolchildren in the public schools.

Communities also influence schools via the decisions school board members make about the preferred size of schools and the particular residential areas specific schools serve (Garbarino, Galambos, Plantz, and Kostelny, 1992). Some communities promote neighborhood schools that tend to be homogenous, whereas the goal in other communities is to establish diverse schools that include a mix of children from different races and socioeconomic levels, thereby possibly ignoring neighborhood boundaries. In these cases, school bussing is necessary.

The Interface of Schools and Families. Across and within communities, school systems vary in the relationships they establish with students' families. This is referred to as the home-school mesosystem (Garbarino, Galambos, Plantz, and Kostelny, 1992). We already noted how individuals benefit when mesosystems are strong. When parents either directly or indirectly connect with their children's teachers and schools they are building what the late sociologist James Coleman (1988) referred to as social capital (discussed in Chapter 2), which is a nonmonetary resource acquired by forming relationships with others who share similar values and goals. As a result of forming social bonds, parents can work cooperatively with other adults to monitor their children, keep them out of trouble, and guide them toward the goals set for them, such as academic success (Teachman, Paasch, and Carver, 1996). Parents also cultivate social capital that contributes to children's school success by forming close bonds with neighbors and the parents of their children's friends. Again, by working together with these other adults, parents promote common values, such as the view that academic achievement is important. As a result, the values they are trying to instill in their children are reinforced. These ideas are similar to the process of collective action, discussed in Chapter 2. In this case the term **collective socialization** (Jencks and Mayers, 1990) or **co-socialization** (Furstenberg, 2001) is used because the group goal is focused on the proper socialization of the community's children.

Parents' Indirect Involvement With Schools. Indirectly, parents work with their children's schools by engaging in at-home activities, such as talking with their children about school experiences and academic goals, helping with homework, reinforcing their children's school successes, and structuring an environment that facilitates learning. They can also identify and take advantage of learning opportunities (e.g., enrichment classes, music lessons) or services (e.g., reading tutors) in the community. Efforts to promote children's academic achievement will be most successful if parents have established strong and positive emotional connections with their offspring (Crosnoe, 2004).

Interestingly, research indicates that positive family dynamics are more important to the school success of white and Asian students than black students. That is, for black students academic performance is less contingent on family dynamics. Perhaps the largest barrier to academic success that black children, especially low-income black children, must overcome is limited access to high-quality schools (due to high concentrations of blacks living in poor inner-city neighborhoods) and teachers who are not fully supportive and encouraging of their academic achievement (due to racial stereotypes and prejudices).

Children do better in school when their parents are involved, either indirectly by monitoring and helping with homework, or directly by participating at school in parent activities. Think about the ways your school promoted these types of parental involvement, or could have done more in these areas.

Parents' Direct Input Into Schools. Parents can directly engage with their children's schools by participating in parent-teacher organizations and parent-teacher conferences or by volunteering in the classroom. These efforts transform school settings from mesosystems to parental microsystems (Muller and Kerbow, 1993). Parents' involvement in their children's schools demonstrate to the children and school administrators an overall concern about the educational experience, as well as support for the educational process and school as a whole. Attendance at parent-teacher meetings gives parents opportunities to develop relationships with one another as well as with school administrators (contributing to an increase in social capital). Such links are especially valuable when parents want to initiate change in a school and its programs. Through volunteering, a parent can directly "observe the working of the school as a type of participant/observer" (Muller and Kerbow, 1993, 34). Parent volunteers can witness teachers doing their jobs and interacting with students, and students interacting with one another. Through these direct microsystem experiences, parents and teachers become familiar with what is expected and valued in each setting (parent with school, teacher with home) and how the other setting operates. When teachers get to know their students' families better they may be able to bond more closely with the student. Crosnoe's (2004) research found that student-teacher bonding (assessed by adolescents' reports of teachers' fairness, caring, and how well they got along with the student) was a significant predictor of students' academic success.

As explained in Chapter 1, individuals adjust best and have the most positive outcomes when their experiences in different microsystems are coordinated and support one another. The benefits of a strong home-school mesosystem, for example, are evident in the significant positive correlation between parents' school involvement and children's grades (Muller, 1993). It makes sense that parents can better support and contribute to their children's learning when they know what is happening at school and what the teacher expects from the child (and the parents) in terms of school experiences and homework. To facilitate the link between home and school, some teachers and schools post homework assignments on a website so that students and parents can be kept up-to-date. Other schools have homework hotlines that parents can call to hear a listing of the latest assignments.

Teachers, too, are likely to benefit from greater knowledge of their students' home situations. This information helps them to be more sensitive and responsive to students' unique needs. For example, expecting a child to complete a lengthy homework assignment that requires substantial parent supervision or input is probably setting a student up for failure if his or her single parent works nights, or if English is not the parents' first language.

Identifying and Responding to Barriers to Parents' School Involvement. Studies indicate a significant association between parents' social class background and their involvement in their children's schooling. Quite consistently research finds a positive correlation between such social class indicators as education, occupation, and income, and parents' involvement with their children's schooling (Eccles and Harold, 1993; Shumow and Miller, 2001). Experts have proposed various explanations for these findings. Some reasons that parents of lower socioeconomic backgrounds do not actively participate in their children's schools is because (a) they feel uncomfortable and unwelcome in these institutional settings, perhaps due to their own limited achievement; (b) they have unfavorable school memories of their own; (c) they have experienced institutional discrimination; (d) their own lower-class background places little value on education and therefore they consider it less important to be involved with their children's schooling; and (e) there is a lack of flexibility in lower-class jobs such that even when parents with few resources wish to get involved in their children's schools their lower level jobs may keep them from doing so (Muller, 1993).

A challenge for schools with a high proportion of low income families is to find ways to build stronger home-school connections. In the community where one of your authors resides, a local school recently took on this challenge. Teachers in one of the lower-income schools in the community were frustrated because only 75 percent of parents attended parent-teacher conferences (McLaughlin, 1998). What the school determined was that many parents missed conferences because of transportation problems. Therefore, the school planned alternative conferences at churches and apartment buildings in the neighborhoods where many of the students lived. These efforts increased conference attendance to 91 percent and created very positive impressions among the families regarding the school's concern for and sensitivity to their situations. This case reflects how minimal participation on the part of low SES parents might be misinterpreted as a lack of concern or caring, when in fact limited resources create barriers to parents' greater engagement with their children's schools.

In sum, the experiences children and their families have with school systems and the children's ultimate educational outcomes are determined by individual and family factors, as well as forces operating at the school and community level. Indeed, even more distant systems—such as the federal government—play a role in community schools through the policies they institute and programs they support that affect children's school success. One example is the recent "No Child Left Behind" federal legislation, signed into law in 2002, which intends to make schools more accountable for student performance, provide them more flexibility in how they use federal funds, and give parents greater choice in their children's schooling (Thornburg and Brookes, 2003).

Community-Based Services

Family life presents a variety of both expected and unexpected challenges over the course of time. Many of the changes that occur for families are part of normal development, and thus are anticipated. These include the birth of children, coping with age-related changes as children grow and mature, and helping aging parents. Many of these issues were discussed in Chapters 5 and 6. Still, when changes occur in family systems, family members can be left feeling unprepared and needing help. In some families parents may be frustrated and irritable in reaction to the constant defiance of their 2-year-old. In another family, members may be dealing with feelings of helplessness as an aging parent becomes increasingly impaired and dependent. Unexpected situations, such as divorce, serious illness, or unemployment, are harder to anticipate and may also leave family members in need of help. These issues were addressed in Chapters 7, 8, and 9.

Whether stressors are anticipated or not, families can receive help from either informal or formal sources of support in their communities. **Informal support** comes from nonprofessional helpers such as relatives, friends, and neighbors who are part of an individual's ongoing, natural, personal social network. This help includes childcare, transportation, and household care—domains of helping that do not necessarily involve expert knowledge or training. **Formal support,** on the other hand, includes organized services that have been developed to give assistance to individuals in need and that are officially recognized as such. Formal support generally involves trained professionals, although many use a combination of professionals, lower-skilled workers, and sometimes volunteers in their delivery of services. For example, many women's centers have a crisis hotline that women who have been battered can call for help. Often, minimally trained volunteer staff members answer these calls and then provide the callers with referrals to professionals in the community or the center where they can obtain more specialized help. Integration of formal and informal support is considered a more effective and desirable approach to service delivery because the needs of individuals are met by *supplementing* rather than *replacing* the natural, informal helping networks that exist in communities (Garbarino and Long, 1992).

Comparing Informal Versus Formal Support. When faced with challenges in their lives, what determines whether individuals and families rely on informal or formal supports? The preference generally appears to be for informal rather than formal support (Gottlieb, 1980), perhaps because of convenience, comfort, and cost. Because informal supports are part of the personal networks that individuals interact with on a regular basis, they may be better able to provide help than a formal support that requires making an appointment or dropping by an agency's office. Some formal supports involve fees, and may be judged too costly, which makes informal support preferable. Family members may also feel more comfortable seeking help from someone they already know and trust. Support and advice received from a close friend or other informal helper is likely to be perceived as more personalized and sensitive to the unique situation and background of the person in need than formal support might be. This last point is especially relevant for immigrant and minority families, who are known to underutilize available services (Cheung and Snowden, 1990). The son of a friend of one of your authors married a Russian immigrant several years ago. It is a source of unending frustration for the friend that his daughter-in-law never goes outside the Russian community for services or household help. The real estate agent, lawyer, and handyman they hire, are all members of her city's Russian immigrant community. Perhaps such barriers as negative stereotypes about persons of their group, differences in language from the service providers, and cultural differences in styles of communication (Rivers, 1995) make minorities feel uncomfortable in seeking help from formal service providers, especially those outside their ethnic or racial group.

Despite the fact that informal support is generally preferred, in some cases it may not be sufficient and formal help from a community agency is required. One such situation is when the presenting problem involves (or has consequences for) members of the informal network who would be likely sources of help. This often is the case when dealing with family problems. For example, an adolescent who is being abused by his or her parent may find it ineffective to seek help from the other parent or another relative because these family members will likely be affected by the events that would subsequently occur in the family. Seeking help from a school counselor or calling an abuse hotline may be more effective for the child in this case. A second instance when formal support may be preferable to informal support is when the presenting problem is one about which informal helpers may lack the knowledge and understanding needed to effectively help. When a family member is diagnosed with a rare disease or experiences an unusual problem, those in the family may find it necessary to seek out services and supports of health care organizations that are targeted for persons and families dealing with their specific condition. For example, Alcoholics Anonymous and ALANON are two organizations established to help individuals and families with an alcoholic member.

Human Services. Because communities primarily deal with organized and formal services for families, we focus the remainder of this discussion on formal supports, namely human or personal social services. These include programs and organizations geared toward protecting or restoring the lives of individuals and families by providing the following:

- Income.
- Education.

- Health.

- Housing.

- Employment.

- Personal services. (Kahn, 1979)

Some of the service agencies and programs designed to address these needs stand on their own in the community (e.g., family planning agencies), while others originate in, or are delivered through, community institutions that have other primary missions. Classes that prepare expectant parents for childbirth and parenting, for example, generally are offered through hospitals. Many churches and religious organizations also involve themselves in offering an assortment of services to meet human and family needs. Shelters and soup kitchens for the homeless and childcare services are some of these. Such **faith-based charities or services** seem to be increasing, and some of their supporters argue that they should largely replace human services offered by the government (Olasky, 1997).

The Scope of Service Delivery. A critical dimension of human service organizations is their scope (Garbarino and Long, 1992). *Scope* refers to the areas of coverage included in a specific service and may range along a continuum from narrow to broad. Services that are narrowly targeted to a single aspect of a client's life are termed **categorical,** and include such programs as Meals on Wheels, which has the sole purpose of preparing and delivering meals to homebound persons, or GED programs that assist adults in obtaining their high school degrees. **Comprehensive** services are those with a broad scope that provide a wide assortment of services within one organizational unit. The Hawaii Healthy Start Program is an excellent example of a comprehensive service. This program is specifically targeted toward reducing child abuse and neglect, and approaches this goal using a "home-visitor model" whereby trained professionals model problem-solving skills and make referrals for families to receive needed income, housing, child care, employment training, and medical services (Duggan et al., 1999). This comprehensive program recognizes that quality parenting is enhanced when a family's most basic survival needs are met.

Although generally less expensive than comprehensive services, the categorical services approach to helping families may result in a lack of integration and communication across services that could lead to the duplication of services, or to individuals and families not being effectively supported (Garbarino and Long, 1992). A serious weakness of the categorical approach is that various human services in a community may fail to communicate with one another when they come in contact with the same families. This is a major problem when "the sum of the family's problems may put them in real need while no single problem does" (Garbarino and Long, 1992, 236). For example, consider a marginally employed, single mother who only occasionally receives child support, has a child requiring special speech and hearing services, and an aged father with moderate dementia who is living on a low, fixed income and needs round-the-clock supervision. This single mother's earned income and child support may place her above the income level allowed to receive financial assistance for any particular special service. Yet, the sporadic nature of the child support payments she receives, in combination with the costly services she needs for both her child and father, suggests that this mother truly needs some economic assistance. Cases such as this highlight the importance of creating mesosystems of support—connections between human service microsystems that are focused on helping the same families in need. In this way, needy families will not fall through the cracks and service overlap will be minimized.

The Type of Services Provided. Service organizations also can be classified according to the type of help or service they provide clients—personal or social (Garbarino, 1983). Building personal resources is the goal of services geared toward helping individuals help themselves. Education sessions (e.g., sex education) and skills development classes (e.g., communication training for premarital couples), are intended to empower individuals by helping them acquire the knowledge and competencies needed to handle issues and problems that occur in their lives. Other organizations focus on providing social resources for persons in need, such as integrating them into support groups. These services offer individuals a social network in which they can share their experiences and gain nurturance, feedback, and understanding from others in similar situations. A variety of organizations have this focus, such as Parents Without Partners (initially started to serve divorced parents), and PFLAG (Parents, Families and Friends of Lesbians and Gays). By utilizing the help of service organizations to enhance their personal and social resources individuals and families maximize their chances of coping effectively with a variety of life challenges (Garbarino, 1983).

The Timing of Services. A final aspect of human services that we address deals with the timing of services (when services are offered in relation to a problem occurring), and the population that is targeted. **Remediation or intervention approaches** direct services at solving or treating a problem once it has occurred. **Prevention approaches** gear human services toward avoiding the occurrence of a problem before it happens (Mace, 1983). Intervention approaches thus target populations that already have encountered a problem (e.g., family counseling for a drug-addicted teen), whereas prevention efforts either direct services toward the general population or toward persons identified as "at-risk" for certain problems. Hawaii's Healthy Start Program, for example, targets mothers at-risk for child abuse based on established risk factors, such as inadequate income and housing, being single, having a history of substance abuse or depression (Duggan et al., 1999).

The types and number of human services available to families vary from community to community. The spectrum of services offered by a given community depends on the unique challenges of its residents, the resources available to the community, and the priorities the community establishes for using those resources.

Governmental Exosystem and Macro-Level Influences

Even though individuals' daily family experiences occur in the proximal context of their neighborhood and community, family life is shaped by broader societal forces as well. In this final section we discuss governmental policies, which are part of the exosystem, and their potential impact on families. In addition, we consider some macrosystem factors, such as values and ideologies, which heavily influence the norms and institutions that shape everyday family life.

Family Policy

Policies and service programs implemented and supported by governing bodies at the local, state, and federal levels represent important exosystems for families. Although our interest here is primarily **family policy,** defined as planned actions aimed at achieving agreed-upon goals with respect to family problems (Zimmerman, 1995), it represents just one domain of concern for policy makers. There is no need to remind you that decisions made in other policy areas such as business and economics, the environment, safety, health, and education impact families in important ways as well.

In considering family policy, a basic question to start with is *why* should government attend to family issues and concerns when considering and formulating policies? Briar-Lawson and her colleagues (2001) make a good case for such action when they argue that:

> families are comprehensive service, resource and support systems. They continuously care for, and work on behalf of, their members. . . . In most communities families perform, for example, most of the child care, elder care, health care, teaching, counseling, norm enforcement, and justice work. . . . When families are supported, healthy, and strong, many individual needs and social problems are prevented. (51–52)

Bronfenbrenner (cited in Bogenschneider, 2002, 29) asserts that, "The family is the most powerful, the most humane, and by far the most economical system known for building competence and character." Families encourage civic participation and ultimately promote democratic government (Briar-Lawson, Lawson, Hennon, and Jones, 2001).

Compared to other developed nations the United States has relatively few family policies, at least those that would be accurately labeled *explicit* family policies. Such policies are those in which the goals and objectives of the policy for families is outwardly stated (Zimmerman, 1995). The lack of explicit family policy in the United States is consistent with how families have been overlooked in governmental action and policies since its inception. Bogenschneider (2002) illustrates this point by noting that the United States stands out as one of the only countries worldwide that neglects specific mention of families in its constitution. Moreover, she argues that our forefathers' emphasis on the individual, and individual rights continues to shape policy formulation in the United States today.

The argument is also made that not only are family issues overlooked in current United States policy, some policies and services actually work directly *against* families. Bogenschneider (2002) refers to Medicaid regulations as an example, noting that the program usually will reimburse recipients for treatment of mental illness but generally will not cover costs of family or marital therapy. Similarly, she points out that Medicare will cover the costs of visiting nurse care when a homebound older adult is chronically ill, but the program does not provide support for respite care so that family caregivers can be relieved occasionally of their caregiving duties to get much needed rest and relaxation. Policy problems such as these raise the question of *why* U.S. policy seems relatively unresponsive to family needs and issues.

Agenda Setting and Considering Intended and Unintended Policy Outcomes. One possibility is that the agenda setting of policy makers has been inadequate. Agenda setting involves problem identification—figuring out what needs to be fixed (Briar-Lawson et al., 2001) and how to fix it. Are U.S. policy makers aware of the real needs of Americans and their families? (Ask any political candidate and he or she will claim to be the one candidate most in touch with the lives and needs of constituents, although the public may or may not agree.) Do they agree on the root cause of the problem? Bogenschneider and Corbett (2004) argue that most social problems are interpreted as having either an individual or a structural explanation. For example, some see poverty as a consequence of individual shortcomings, such as a lack of motivation or laziness. Others attribute it to an inadequate wage structure in the labor force system. The likelihood that policy initiatives will be created to address a particular social problem depends heavily on which explanation one accepts, according to Bogenschneider and Corbett (2004). They claim that policy initiatives are more likely to be enacted when problems are viewed as having structural rather than individual causes.

Another possible explanation for current policy problems is that although the critical issues may have been accurately identified, the solutions chosen are not sensitive to families. Moreover, policies that are enacted may have unintended and unexpected negative consequences for families. Zimmerman (1995) describes how some policies are designed and implemented to deal with a problem that is not viewed as a *family* problem (e.g., setting the minimum wage), but which has implications for family well-being. Policies that impact families, but the implications and expected outcomes for families are not specifically or widely addressed in the policy decision-making process, are known as *implicit* family policies (Zimmerman, 1995). Occasionally when families are not considered in policy formulation, or when policymakers neglect to ask important questions about the broader family context, unintended negative consequences result (Garbarino, Gaboury, and Plantz, 1992). This is one complaint that has been lodged against the welfare reform policy passed in 1996 by the U.S. Congress, which you will read more about later.

To avoid policymaking that is insensitive to families or possibly harms them, Monroe (1995) suggests that policymakers need to consider how a policy might affect family members' experiences in a variety of key microsystems, such as the home, neighborhood, school, and workplace. Additionally, discussions must address how a given policy may alter the connection between families and other important institutions in society.

Even when the policy consequences for families are taken into account, opinions may differ about whether the expected consequences in fact represent favorable outcomes for families. For example, no-fault divorce laws were enacted so that couples wanting to divorce could do so without having to cast blame and prove wrongdoing by one of the partners. This change was expected to eliminate some of the emotional stress of divorce for couples and their families. Some now believe, however, that deregulation of divorce actually hurts families because couples who in the past might have worked to resolve their problems due to a difficult and adversarial legal process, may now quickly proceed to divorce, thereby contributing to family breakdown (Whitehead, 1996). Values play a large part in this debate.

The Role of Values in Policymaking. Societal values are central to understanding policymaking decisions because we use them to evaluate the expected or observed outcomes of a particular policy (Zimmerman, 1995). Macrosystem beliefs about how the world should be and how it should work (or, in the present case, how families should be and how they should work) provide the blueprints for policymaking (Garbarino and Kostelny, 1995). Consider the following questions:

- Is more or less government better?

- Who is deserving of help (e.g. poor children, the elderly, but not poor, able-bodied adults)?

- Who should provide help (government, religious organizations, family)?

Overarching ideologies and values are at the heart of many policy decisions (Garbarino, Gaboury, and Plantz, 1992; Monroe, 1995). Ideological debates centered directly on family life consider issues such as what constitutes a family (are two parents in the home necessary?) or a marriage (a union involving a man and a woman only?). This latter issue is at the center of The Defense of Marriage Act, discussed later in this chapter. Another salient ideological debate focuses on what is the key to family well-being (is it the maintenance of economic independence?). As noted earlier, views about the importance of individualism versus dependence on, or interdependence with others also contribute to current U.S. policy struggles. Bogenschneider (2002) wonders how growing ethnic diversity in this country, especially increased numbers of Asians and Latinos whose cultures emphasize collectivism over individualism, will impact future policy formulation.

Finally, in understanding policy decisions we cannot overlook where family concerns rank on the values hierarchy of the overall policy arena (Zimmerman, 1995). There is a popular bumper sticker that reads, "It'll be a great day when our schools have all the money they need and the Navy has to hold a bake sale to buy battleships." This message expresses the view of some that family and child-related policy are not positioned high enough in the U.S. values hierarchy.

The Focus of Family Policy. In an attempt to support families and enhance their well-being, those who develop family policy have adopted a number of approaches to dealing primarily with four family functions (Bogenschneider and Corbett, 2004):

- Family formation (e.g., marriage, divorce, childbearing, adoption).

- Economic support.

- Child rearing.

- Caregiving.

Some policies seek to help families through the distribution and redistribution of resources among families. This approach is evident, for example, in tax laws that set different taxation rates for families of different income levels, and in services (e.g., food stamps) that are offered for those who have a minimum income level. Other policies aim to support and help families by regulating behavior, such as laws mandating the use of infant and child car seats, and the reform of marriage and divorce laws (Zimmerman, 1995).

Regardless of the approach taken, however, assessment of the effectiveness of a particular family policy depends on several issues. From the perspective of family researchers who take an ecological view, good family policies create favorable microsystem contexts for family members, and strengthen the mesosystems that connect microsystems (Garbarino, Gaboury, and Plantz, 1992). Effective policies strengthen microsystems by contributing to their stability (e.g., by creating block grants to revitalize run-down urban neighborhoods), and enhance mesosystems by connecting the various settings in which families participate (e.g., establishing visiting nurse programs for new parents). Policies that build and encourage mesosystem connections assist programs and services by more efficiently coordinating their efforts, and in promoting a consistent set of goals and values for their clients. In Schorr's 1988 book, *Within Our Reach,* she describes such a policy at Sinai Hospital, Baltimore's busiest obstetrical service. Here they require that every baby born be assigned to the responsibility of a specific pediatrician. One group of pediatricians working out of Sinai, the Greenspring Group, has its own policies in place that ensure continuity of care for newborns and their families over time. Some of the procedures they follow to maximize services for their patients are a computer-aided reminder system of scheduled immunizations and screenings, active use of outreach workers and home visitors, transportation services for families to get to medical appointments, and after-hour telephone advice lines. The Greenspring Group believes such efforts pay off in terms of building healthier and stronger families (Schorr, 1988). This example is another illustration of the benefit of linking various human services (i.e., building mesosystems) to more comprehensively and efficiently serve families.

Family Policy Examples

Thus far we have discussed aspects of family policy, the values and thinking behind family policy, and the possibility that policies can have both positive and negative effects on families. In this final section we briefly overview three specific family policies that have passed the U.S. Congress in the last decade. We consider these policies important examples to cover because of their recency and because they are closely connected to key areas of family life addressed in this book. The Family and Medical Leave Act is used to illustrate how policy addresses the competing demands that various microsystems (i.e., workplace and home) place on individuals (issues mentioned in Chapters 5, 6, and 7). Welfare reform legislation is discussed because it focuses on family economic issues and the government's recent approach to dealing with families that are economically vulnerable. Welfare reform also involves community supports and services, such as affordable, quality childcare. Finally, we discuss the Defense of Marriage Act, a federal policy that sets restrictions on who is officially recognized as a couple or family and their associated rights and responsibilities. This legislation potentially affects attitudes that individuals hold about intimate relationships, as well as how individuals meet intimacy needs in their lives (which we addressed primarily in Chapters 3 and 4).

Family and Medical Leave Act (FMLA). The Family and Medical Leave Act, signed into law in 1993 by President Bill Clinton, is perhaps the most explicit family policy in the United States. This legislation, which provides short-term leave (up to 12 weeks per year) for workers to attend to various family and medical emergencies (e.g., birth or adoption of a child, care for an ill family member), was the first law established at the federal level that addresses family leave (Waldfogel, 1999). The law mandates that employers must maintain eligible workers' health benefits over the course of a leave, and that the workers be assured a comparable position with their employer on return from the leave. A major drawback of the legislation—at least from the perspective of the worker, is that the leave is unpaid thus providing no cash benefit (Kamerman and Kahn, 1995; Wisensale, 1997). Another feature of FMLA that makes it less than desirable or helpful for many workers is that the policy only covers workers meeting the following criteria:

- Must have worked for the employer for a minimum of 1 year.

- Must have worked at least 1,250 hours in the past 12 months.

- The company may deny leave to employees located at work sites where there are fewer than 50 workers within a 75-mile radius.

About half of female workers in this country are excluded from the policy because they work for small businesses (Kamerman and Kahn, 1995).

FMLA was a long-time coming in this country. In 1985, Congress considered a proposed law offering a 26-week family and parental leave for workers in firms with a minimum of 15 workers; however, the proposal was defeated. A few years later a modified version of the legislation again was proposed. It offered a shorter leave period and set the minimum firm-size exemption somewhat higher than the 1985 legislation. Although approved by both houses of Congress, the law was vetoed by President George H. W. Bush in 1990. The same thing happened again under President Bush before he left office. Still, the issue did not go away, and, in 1993, as one of the first acts of his administration, President Bill Clinton signed the current FMLA into law.

Central in the debate over family and medical leave was the issue of how large firms/employers should be before they would be required to follow the legislation. Table 10.1 presents data on various employer-size thresholds debated over the years and the associated share of workers who would have been covered by the legislation had the employer size dimension alone been altered when formulating the FMLA policy. Cleary, setting the minimum number of employees at 50, rather than 15 as had been initially proposed in 1985, markedly reduced the proportion of U.S. workers covered by this policy. Based on the 2000 Survey of Employees, which interviewed over 2,500 U.S. workers, Waldfogel (2001) reported that only about 46 percent of private sector workers were covered by FMLA.

Table 10.1 Association Between Employers' Firm Size and Employee Coverage in FMLA Legislation Considerations

Number of Workers in the Employer's Firm	Percentage of U.S. Workers That Would Be Covered by FMLA
15	71
20	47
35	43
50	39

Source: Adapted from Kamerman and Kahn (1995).

The passage of FMLA left many supporters of government-mandated family and medical leave dissatisfied. The fact that FMLA was not universally available to U.S. workers, that it was unpaid, and that it only provided a 12-week leave were points of criticism. Many of those critical of the legislation cited how little it had to offer compared to family/parental leave policies in other developed nations. Table 10.2 presents some international comparisons so that you can judge for yourself.

The Impact of Legislated Family and Medical Leave. Prior to the passage of FMLA, 34 states already had enacted some form of family leave legislation, but in about one-third of these states, laws only applied to state government workers (Waldfogel, 1999). Due to the limited coverage that FMLA was expected to have with its firm size limits, and because some states already had provisions in place when FMLA passed, questions were raised about how much impact FMLA would actually have in this country. Waldfogel (1999) reported that between 1991 and 1997, the period during which FMLA passed, the percentage of full-time private sector employees in companies with 100 or more workers that had access to maternity leave coverage increased from 37 percent to 93 percent. Paternity leave coverage increased from 26 percent to 93 percent over the same period. In small companies (<100 employees), maternity leave coverage increased from being available to 17 percent of employees in 1990 to 48 percent in 1996. The percentage rose from 8 percent to 48 percent over the same period for employees with access to paternity

Table 10.2 Basic Job-Protected Maternity/Parental Leaves in Select Developed Nations

Country	Durations (weeks)	Paid Benefit (% of wage)
Austria	16	100
Canada	15	60 (2 additional unpaid wks.)
Denmark	28	100
France	16	84
Germany	14	100
Japan	14	60
New Zealand	6 months	Flat rate allowance
Spain	16	75
Sweden	12 months	80
United Kingdom	14	90

Source: Adapted from Kamerman and Kahn (1995).

leave. Although many more public sector than private sector employees had coverage available before FMLA, there was still growth in coverage for employees in this sector. These findings suggest that FMLA had a substantial positive impact on employee coverage.

Other important questions to ask in the era of relatively new FMLA legislation are whether workers are taking advantage of family and medical leave, why or why not, and how satisfied are they with their leave situation? The 2000 Survey of Employees that Waldfogel (2001) summarizes included some employees who had FMLA access and others who did not (interestingly, about half of employees in covered and noncovered firms were unsure of whether FMLA applied to them). All respondents to this survey were in private sector jobs. Some of the findings reported by Waldfogel (2001) are the following:

- 13.5 percent of men and 19.8 percent of women took a family or medical leave in the 18-month period prior to the 2000 survey.
- 47 percent of leave takers took a break from work due to their own health.
- 7.8 percent of leave takers took a maternity or disability leave.
- 17.9 percent of leave takers used leave to care for a new child (biological, adopted, or foster).
- 11.4 percent of leave takers used their leave to care for an ill parent.
- 34.2 percent of leave takers received no pay during their leave.

- 2.4 percent of employees reported needing a leave but forgoing it due primarily to financial reasons.

- Financial concerns top the list for workers who do take leaves (53.8 percent note such concerns).

- The majority of leave takers reported that taking the leave was a positive experience given their situation. (Waldfogel, 2001)

In summarizing the findings of this survey, Waldfogel (2001) concludes that FMLA is being increasingly used by employees, and with satisfying results for the well-being of workers and their families. Yet, the lack of some income provision during a family or medical leave still interferes with the ability of many workers to assist their families in periods of high need. Efforts to add a provision for paid leave to FMLA are widespread, but according to Waldfogel (2001), such provisions are probably more likely to come from the state than the federal level in the near future.

Welfare Reform. The Personal Responsibility and Work Opportunity Reconciliation Act (PRWORA), commonly referred to as *welfare reform,* was signed into law in 1996 by President Clinton. This legislation ended the welfare program known as Aid to Families with Dependent Children (AFDC), which for over 60 years provided cash entitlements to eligible adults and children who were in desperate financial need. Instead, welfare reform includes a new program, referred to as TANF, which provides Temporary Assistance for Needy Families. This assistance is distributed to an eligible family for a maximum of 24 months, at which point the adult family member must actively engage in search for employment. In addition, TANF imposes a lifetime use limit of five years. These two time-limit features are aspects of welfare reform that never existed with the former AFDC program. Finally, the PRWORA legislation includes some related requirements, such as that states must establish paternity in 90 percent of cases involving an unmarried mother, and that teen mothers must live with their parents in order to receive benefits (Bogenschneider, 2002).

Policy makers and professionals who work with economically challenged families are watching closely to see the impact of welfare reform. Some early indicators suggest that the legislation has had positive effects in the key areas that were targeted for reform. Specifically, states have reported a decline in the number of families on welfare, increased success in the collection of mandated child support payments, and reductions in nonmarital births to teens (Sorenson and Tableman, 2002). In the next few sections we move beyond these general trends to consider how welfare reform has affected the well-being of poor families who are facing new requirements and restrictions in their involvement with the welfare system.

Welfare Reform's Impact on the Families of Preschool-Aged Children. A major concern in response to welfare reform centered on how the stricter time limits and work requirements would ultimately affect poor children—the largest group of welfare recipients. Mandating that welfare mothers (most of whom are single) go to work means that there is a substantial increase in the demand for childcare. Lewin (2000) reported that the new legislation would increase the number of children in childcare in this country by about one million. In urban centers, such as Chicago, where childcare services are limited and the percentages of poor families is high, there was serious concern about the severe shortage of available child care slots, especially for infant care. One early projection was that only 14 percent of the demand for infant care in Chicago would be met once welfare reform passed (Nadel, 1997).

Research conducted post-welfare reform confirmed these early concerns about child-care for families on or transitioning off welfare. A three-state study (California, Connecticut, and Florida), which included nearly 1,000 families with preschool-aged children and mothers who were starting the new welfare program, revealed several problems surrounding childcare issues (Fuller and Kagan, 2000):

- The childcare utilized by these mothers was often of very low quality.

- Few mothers were receiving childcare subsidies, even when they were eligible for them.

- Many single mothers struggled with the challenges of long workdays and solo parenting.

Specifically, Fuller and Kagan (2000) found that the childcare settings these mothers utilized were often substandard. Most had few learning materials available for children, there was limited promotion of literacy through activities such as reading to the children or storytelling, and staff often had minimal training—usually only a high school degree. In the Connecticut sample the majority of mothers had their youngsters in care that was not regulated by the state (Lewin, 2000).

Availability and affordability of quality care explains these findings. Although welfare reform legislation in these three states assures that mothers are eligible for childcare subsidies for two years after entering a job, relatively few program participants actually received these benefits. In Florida, about half of mothers received subsidies, compared to 13 percent in Connecticut (Fuller and Kagan, 2000)—the state where such a small portion of children were in regulated care. It appears, therefore, that program participants are not always alerted to or assisted with obtaining the resources that welfare-to-work programs have promised participants. As a result, their children's well-being may be seriously compromised by substandard care in low-quality care settings.

A serious issue noted by Fuller and Kagan (2000) is the stress and distress felt by many of the young mothers making the effort to move from welfare to work. These researchers report that compared to the national average, former welfare mothers in their study had a rate of depression three times higher; in the Connecticut sample, one in six mothers was seriously depressed. When mothers are not functioning well psychologically, parenting can be especially challenging (as discussed in Chapter 5). Among the California mothers studied by Fuller and Kagan (2000), 39 percent reported that it was tough to be a warm and loving parent when they had to deal with a long workday, too.

The Impact of Welfare Reform for Older Children. Expectations for the impact of welfare on adolescents were not as consistently negative as they were for young children. Some policymakers and researchers, in fact, anticipated that older offspring would benefit the most from seeing their mothers moving from welfare to work, because their mothers would model independence and self-sufficiency for them. Yet, others questioned whether having their mothers in the workforce and away from home would leave older children from low-income families with inadequate adult monitoring, resulting in more problem behavior for this group (Moore, 2001).

Early evidence of the consequences of welfare reform for adolescent offspring suggests small but negative outcomes. Brooks, Hair, and Zaslow (2001) examined data from a few experimental welfare-to-work programs and noted that the adolescent offspring of program participants experienced poorer academic achievement and exhibited more problem behavior, including drinking, smoking and delinquent acts, than adolescents whose welfare mothers were not participating in work programs. They speculated that the negative outcomes might be the result of harsher parenting observed among mothers newly admitted to work programs, or due to elevated levels of responsibility that adolescents in these families were assuming. Adolescents with mothers in the experimental welfare-to-work programs had an increased likelihood of:

- Working 20 hours or more per week themselves.

- Doing more chores around the home.

- Providing care for younger siblings. (Brooks et al., 2001)

Extreme involvement in any one or combination of these activities could place too much demand for autonomy and responsibility on adolescents. Problematic outcomes may result from added stress or adolescents' perceptions that they are adults and thus should be able to engage in adult activities (Brooks et al., 2001). Regardless of the explanation, these early results require attention in future decision making regarding reauthorization of welfare reform.

Welfare Reform—Is It Getting Families Out of Poverty? The goal of welfare reform is to improve the financial well-being of hundreds of thousands of American families who were dependent on government support by getting them into jobs, off welfare, and out of poverty. Today there are approximately two million families receiving welfare benefits, over a 50 percent drop from the 4.4 million families on welfare rolls in 1996 (Kaufman, 2003). This figure alone seems to suggest that welfare reform is working, as many fewer Americans are dependent on a government check to live. Furthermore, the percent of single mothers who are employed is higher today than ever. Between 1994 and 1999, this figure increased from 47 to 65 percent; the figure for never-married mothers—those who struggle most with poverty, increased from 60 to 75 percent (Moffitt, 2002). Still, the number of families receiving welfare and the percent of mothers in the workforce tell only part of the story regarding the outcome of welfare reform and the financial well-being and security of American families.

Although some families have benefited from the changes in welfare legislation by moving into work and raising their incomes, many families have been less fortunate. According to reports issued by the government's own Department of Health and Human Services, between 10–15 percent of former welfare recipients have seen a decline in their financial situation since welfare reform was passed (Kaufman, 2003). For some adults, welfare reform looks promising at first as they accept new jobs and anticipate gaining financial independence. However, a 2002 survey conducted by the Urban Institute revealed that about one-fifth of families who leave welfare "boomerang" back to welfare rolls (Loprest, 2002). Over half of returnees had originally left welfare by taking a job, but they were unable to make it on their own for long because of layoffs, income inadequacy in their jobs, or lack of childcare (Loprest, 2002). Additionally, of those families that left welfare between 2000 and 2002, about one in seven were struggling economically without

Figure 10.1 Problems for Families After Leaving Welfare, by Employment Status

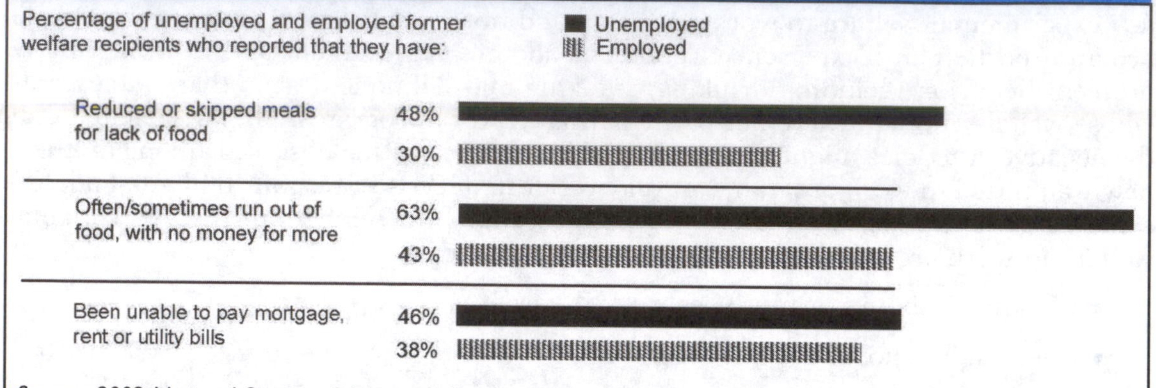

Percentage of unemployed and employed former welfare recipients who reported that they have:

■ Unemployed
▦ Employed

Reduced or skipped meals for lack of food	48%	
	30%	
Often/sometimes run out of food, with no money for more	63%	
	43%	
Been unable to pay mortgage, rent or utility bills	46%	
	38%	

Source: 2002 National Survey of America's Families, Urban Institute.

jobs, spousal support, or other benefits from the government (Kaufman, 2003). As a consequence, day-to-day survival is shaky for many families. Figure 10.1 presents findings from a 2002 Urban Institute survey showing the percentage of former welfare recipients who reported food insecurity and problems with paying for shelter and utilities, based on their 2002 employment status. Substantial portions of both groups report serious challenges with these aspects of daily living; employment status hardly seems to matter.

The report from the Urban Institute indicates that some adults have greater success staying off welfare and establishing self-sufficiency than others. A few of the risk factors associated with a return to welfare are the following (Loprest, 2002):

- Limited education, especially the lack of a high school degree.

- Having mental or physical health problems.

- Being never-married.

- Having young children.

- Not receiving such supplemental benefits as childcare and housing assistance, public health insurance, or food stamps.

Part of the problem in trying to facilitate the economic well-being of families as they move off welfare is ensuring that they are aware of and can access the public benefits for which they qualify. Moffitt (2002) reports that receipt of food stamps and Medicaid (medical insurance for poor families) declines for welfare leavers, although most are still eligible for these supports. Efforts aimed at reducing the administrative processes through which welfare leavers must maneuver to obtain their benefits would help. Loprest (2002) emphasizes that the system needs to become more "worker friendly" so that former welfare recipients can be given a solid chance to benefit from these reforms. Approaching former welfare recipients as "halfway" clients who need to be eased into their new work and economic roles, due to past hardships and possible inexperience in the workplace, is also encouraged (Loprest, 2002).

From 1997 to 2001, Hays conducted research on the impact of welfare reform in two regions of the country, interviewing over 130 welfare mothers about their experiences with reform. Despite the continued hardships they face trying to meet the strict requirements of welfare reform, many of these women agreed with its underlying principles and were hopeful that they will eventually benefit from the legislation, as the quotes below illustrate (Hays, 2003):

> I think welfare reform is there to teach us a lesson, a lesson about taking a little more responsibility. I look at this as a great opportunity. . . . It gives you something to look forward to. (Sandy, 117)

> I think welfare reform is a good way to help people. (Chrystal, 116)

> I think welfare reform is great. . . . They taught me how to do my resume and things like that. And you learn how to feel good about yourself too. (Shannon, 114)

Clearly, welfare reform is still in its early stages and more research is needed to determine whether it will meet its original goals of putting low-income parents to work so that they can gain financial security for their families. In addition, researchers need to continue to monitor unintended consequences of the legislation—an issue that was emphasized earlier in this chapter.

Defense of Marriage Act. In 1996, the United State Congress passed the Defense of Marriage Act. This federal legislation defined marriage as the union of a man and woman for the purposes of receiving federal benefits (e.g., filing joint income tax forms). A second purpose of this legislation was to establish that if any state in the United States ever began to grant same sex partners licenses to marry and actually married them, other states would not be obligated to recognize such unions as marriage. This is an important provision because Article IV, section 1 of the United States Constitution, known as the Full Faith and Credit Clause, directs the states to grant "full faith and credit" to laws, legal decisions, and judicial actions of other states, meaning that marriages legally formed in one state are, by law, recognized in other states. However, this article also allows Congress to decide the "effects" of a state's laws in other states; this is where Congress acted on the Defense of Marriage Act, determining that same-sex marriages need not be recognized (<CNN.com>, 2004).

Since 1996, 38 states have passed Defense of Marriage Acts at the state level to limit state benefits and other privileges to homosexual couples. As of January 2004, only the following 12 states did not have a Defense of Marriage Act on the books: Connecticut, Maryland, Massachusetts, New Hampshire, New Jersey, New Mexico, New York, Oregon, Rhode Island, Vermont, Wisconsin, and Wyoming.

The effectiveness and constitutionality of such laws will certainly come under question soon, as some states begin to allow same-sex marriage. On May 17, 2004, over 1,000 same-sex couples in Massachusetts filed for marriage licenses and were wed as that state became the first in the nation to permit same-sex marriages (Cooperman and Finer, 2004). Four thousand couples in San Francisco did the same earlier in 2004 when the city's mayor defied a state law and gave permission to allow the issuing of marriage licenses. The legality of these licenses is in dispute.

Same-sex couples who are not recognized by law as married couples may, in some places (including New York City, Boston, Tampa, Atlanta, San Francisco), qualify for partner benefits under what are called Domestic Partnership laws. (Unmarried heterosexual couples may also qualify for these benefits in places where they exist.) Such legislation requires couples to register with the city or state enacting the law, and as a result they will have access to health insurance benefits, and other employee benefits, such as family leave, that are typically awarded to spouses/families of employees (Knox and Schach, 2002). Some same-sex couples, however, argue that they deserve more than this, including marriage and the legal rights and responsibilities that come with it. Vermont enacted a Civil Union Statute in 2000 that granted same-sex partners identical benefits, rights and responsibilities that apply to heterosexual married couples. Although civil union couples in Vermont are entitled to state benefits, they are denied federal benefits because of the federal Defense of Marriage Act. (This is no minor issue; over 1000 federal laws base benefits, rights, or privileges on marital status, according to a 1997 Government Accounting Office report (<CNN.com>, 2004)). Moreover, civil unions are not recognized by other states unless they too have such a law (<CNN.com>, 2004). The debate over the morality and legality of same-sex unions is likely to remain strong as an increasing number of individuals establish nontraditional partnerships and seek to gain the rights and benefits afforded members of traditional marriages and families.

Summary

In this final chapter, we elaborated on a key theme of the ecological perspective. Families are embedded within a complex social system; one in which family members contribute to and respond to continually in their everyday lives. From this social environmental context we selected some specific systems to emphasize in terms of what they mean for family life, including workplace and childcare settings, schools, and human services. Our discussion addressed how these organizations or institutions support the needs of families and contribute to their goals. However, we noted that characteristics of families and communities shape these institutions as well: the reciprocal nature of families in context is evident. We concluded with a discussion of the importance of governmental policy in supporting family life and how broad macrosystem values affect what policymakers define as problems, and how they ultimately contribute to policy decisions. This chapter highlighted the interconnections of families and the micro-, meso-, exo-, and macrosystem contexts in which they live and grow.

Chapter Concepts

categorical services: helping services that are narrowly targeted to a single aspect of a client's life.

collective socialization/co-socialization: the process through which adults influence young people in their communities, other than their own children, through shared monitoring and support.

comprehensive services: helping services that are broadly targeted to provide for a wide array of client needs within one organizational unit.

faith-based charities/services: human services that are offered by churches or religious organizations with the intent of helping individuals and families.

family policy: planned governmental actions aimed at achieving agreed-upon goals with respect to family problems.

formal institutions: organizational structures, consisting of rules, norms, and a hierarchical authority structure, which are designed to achieve specific objectives.

formal supports: organizations that have been developed to offer helping services to individuals in need.

informal supports: nonprofessional helpers, such as relatives, friends and neighbors, who function on their own to provide another with assistance and support.

personal and social: programs and organizations geared toward protecting or restoring the lives of individuals and families by providing income, education, health, housing, employment and/or personal services.

personal resources: an approach to human services whereby individuals in need are given information and taught skills so they can help themselves.

prevention approaches: human services geared toward reducing the occurrence of a problem before it happens.

remediation or intervention approaches: human services directed at solving or treating a problem once it has occurred.

social capital: nonmonetary resources acquired by forming relationships with others who share similar values and goals.

social resources: one approach to human services, which provides persons in need with social relationships that offer understanding and support.

Suggested Activities

1. The ecological perspective assumes that intervention and prevention cannot only be directed at the individual level. Describe a social/human service program (for example Planned Parenthood or Head Start) that you are aware of and assess how well it considers the ecology of the family in dealing with the problem it addresses (e.g., teenage sexuality, poverty). For each level of the ecological model (micro, meso, exo, macro) specify what the program does. If it does not consider a particular level, make some suggestions of what could be added to the program to target prevention or intervention at that level.

2. There are several sites on the Internet targeted toward helping people select new places (cities/towns) to live, based on their lifestyle preferences and likes and dislikes. Go onto the Web and search one or more of these sites using such terms as "moving and relocation services" (careful with this one—it'll get you lots of moving help), or "best places to live." Find a site and go through its material: (a) What are the factors they ask their users about? (b) What do they appear to base their relocation recommendations on? (c) Are there subjects they ask about (e.g., weather preferences), or things they left out (e.g., proximity of major league sports teams), that surprised you? (d) Write a brief essay discuss-

ing why the things included on this site are or are not important factors for families to consider in making relocation decisions. (Possible sites: <www.findyour spot.com> or <homeadvisor.msn.com/pickaplace/findcity.asp>.

Suggested Readings

Bowen, G. L., Richman, J. M., and Bowen, N. K. 2000. "Families in the context of communities across time." In S. J. Price, P. C. McKenry, and M. J. Murphy (eds.), *Families Across Time* (pp. 117–128). Los Angeles, CA: Roxbury.

Garbarino, J., and Kostelny, K. 1995. "Parenting and public policy." In M. Bornstein (ed.), *Handbook of Parenting* 3:419–436. Mahwah, NJ: Erlbaum.

Hays, S. 2003. *Flat Broke with Children: Women in the Age of Welfare Reform.* New York: Oxford University Press.

Schneider, B., and J. S. Coleman. 1993. *Parents, Their Children, and Schools.* Boulder, CO: Westview Press. ✦

Photo Credits

Chapter 1

Page 2—Roxbury Publishing; page 8—Corbisimages; page 11—Roxbury Publishing; page 20 (all 3 photos)—Amy Enderle; page 31—Roxbury Publishing; page 36—Roxbury Publishing.

Chapter 2

Page 47—Roxbury Publishing; page 52—Corbisimages; page 60—Roxbury Publishing; page 65—Roxbury Publishing; page 66—Amy Enderle.

Chapter 3

Page 75—Amy Enderle; page 77—Amy Enderle; page 87—Amy Enderle.

Chapter 4

Page 104—Roxbury Publishing; page 110—Amy Enderle; page 116—Roxbury Publishing; page 119—Amy Enderle.

Chapter 5

Page 135—Roxbury Publishing; page 142—Roxbury Publishing; page 144—Amy Enderle; page 158—Roxbury Publishing; page 160—Roxbury Publishing; page 163—Amy Enderle; page 168—Amy Enderle.

Chapter 6

Page 178—Amy Enderle; page 184—Amy Enderle; page 193—Amy Enderle; page 197—Amy Enderle.

Chapter 7

Page 213—Amy Enderle; page 220—Amy Enderle; page 221—Amy Enderle; page 223—Amy Enderle; page 232—Amy Enderle; page 239—Fotosearch.

Chapter 8

Page 258—Amy Enderle; page 263—Roxbury Publishing; page 266—Roxbury Publishing; page 269—Roxbury Publishing.

Chapter 9

Page 298—Roxbury Publishing; page 315—Roxbury Publishing; page 325—Roxbury Publishing.

Chapter 10

Page 339—Roxbury Publishing; page 341—Roxbury Publishing. ◆

References

ABCNEWS.com. 2001. From riches to rags: Family in squalor came from privilege. Found at <http://abcnews.go.com/sections/GMA/GoodMorningAmerica/GMA010627McGuckin_profile>.

Abel, E. K. 1990. "Informal care for the disabled elderly: A critique of recent literature." *Research on Aging* 12:139–157.

Acitelli, L. K. 1992. "Gender differences in relationship awareness and marital satisfaction among young married couples." *Personality and Social Psychology* 18:102–110.

Acock, A. C., and Demo, D. H. 1994. *Family Diversity and Well-Being.* Thousand Oaks, CA: Sage.

Adams, J. M. 1999. "Future directions for commitment research." In J. M. Adams and W. H. Jones (eds.), *Handbook of Interpersonal Commitment and Relationship Stability* (pp. 503–520). New York: Plenum.

Adams, J. M., and Jones, W. H. 1999. "Interpersonal commitment in historical perspective." In J. M. Adams and W. H. Jones (eds.), *Handbook of Interpersonal Commitment and Relationship Stability* (pp. 3–33). New York: Plenum.

Afterschool Alliance. 2004. 15 million youth need afterschool programs, demand high for middle school students, new study finds. News Release, May 19, 2004 (found at <http://www.afterschoolalliance.org>).

Agnew, R., and Huguley, S. 1989. "Adolescent violence toward parents." *Journal of Marriage and the Family* 51:699–711.

Ahrons, C. A. 1994. *The Good Divorce.* New York: HarperCollins.

Ahrons, C., and Tanner, J. L. 2003. "Adult children and their fathers: Relationship changes 20 years after parental divorce." *Family Relations* 52:340–351.

Alford-Cooper, F. 1998. *For Keeps: Marriages That Last a Lifetime.* Armonk, NY: Sharpe.

Allen, C., and Leventhal, B. 1999. "History, culture, and identity: What makes GLBT battering different." In B. Leventhal, and S. E. Lundy (eds.), *Same-Sex Domestic Violence: Strategies for Change* (pp. 73–81). Thousand Oaks, CA: Sage.

Allen, M. P. 1987. *The Founding Fortunes: A New Anatomy of the Super-rich Families in America.* New York: Dutton.

Alwin, D. F. 1984. "Trends in parental socialization values: Detroit, 1958–1983." *American Journal of Sociology* 90:359–382.

——. 1988. "From obedience to autonomy: Changes in traits desired in children." *Public Opinion Quarterly* 52:33–52.

——. 1990. "Historical changes in parental orientations to children." *Sociological Studies of Child Development* 3:65–86.

Amato, P. 1989. "Who cares for children in public places? Naturalistic observation of male and female caretakers." *Journal of Marriage and the Family* 51:981–990.

——. 1996. "Explaining the intergenerational transmission of divorce." *Journal of Marriage and the Family* 58:628–640.

——. 2000a. "The consequences of divorce for adults and children." *Journal of Marriage and the Family* 62:1269–1287.

——. 2000b. "Diversity within single-parent families." In D. H. Demo, K. R. Allen, and M. A. Fine (eds.), *Handbook of Family Diversity* (pp. 149–196). New York: Oxford University Press.

Amato, P. R., and Booth, A. 1997. *A Generation at Risk: Growing Up in an Era of Family Upheaval.* Cambridge, MA: Harvard University Press.

Amato, P. R., and Gilbreth, J. G. 1999. "Nonresident fathers and children's well-being: A meta-analysis." *Journal of Marriage and the Family* 61:557–573.

Amato, P. R., Johnson, D. R., Booth, A., and Rogers, S. J. 2003. "Continuity and change in marital quality between 1980 and 2000." *Journal of Marriage and Family 65*:1–22.

Amato, P. R., and Keith, B. 1991. "Parental divorce and the well-being of children: A meta-analysis." *Psychological Bulletin 110*:26–46.

Amato, P. R., and Previti, D. 2003. "People's reasons for divorcing: Gender, social class, the life course, and adjustment." *Journal of Family Issues 24*:602–626.

Amato, P. R., and Rezac, S. J. 1994. "Contact with nonresidential parents, interparental conflict, and children's behavior." *Journal of Family Issues 15*:191–207.

Amato, P. R., and Rivera, F. 1999. "Paternal involvement and children's behavior problems." *Journal of Marriage and the Family 61*:375–384.

Amato, P. R., and Rogers, S. J. 1997. "A longitudinal study of marital problems and subsequent divorce." *Journal of Marriage and the Family 59*:612–624.

American Psychological Association. 1996. "Violence and the family." Report of the American Psychological Association Presidential Task Force on Violence and the Family. Washington, DC.

Anda, R. F., Whitfield, C. L., Felitti, V. J., Chapman, D. Edwards, V. J., Dube, S. R., and Williamson, D. F. 2002. "Adverse childhood experiences, alcoholic parents, and later risks of alcoholism and depression." *Psychiatric Services 53*:1001–1009.

Anderson, E. R., Greene, S. M., Hetherington, E. M., and Clingempeel, W. G. 1999. "The dynamics of parental remarriage: Adolescent, parent, and sibling influences." In E. M. Hetherington, (ed.), *Coping with Divorce, Single Parenting, and Remarriage* (pp. 295–319). Mahwah, NJ: Erlbaum.

Anderson, E. R., and Rice, A. M. 1992. "Sibling relationships during remarriage." In E. M. Hetherington and G. Clingempeel (eds.), *Coping with Marital Transitions. Monographs of the Society for Research in Child Development 57(227)*:149–177.

Anderson, K. 1997. "Gender, status, and domestic violence: An integration of feminist and family violence approaches." *Journal of Marriage and the Family 59*:655–669.

Anderson, S. A., and Sabatelli, R. M. 1995. *Family Interaction. A Multigenerational Developmental Perspective.* Needham Heights, MA: Allyn & Bacon.

Angel, J. L., and Angel, R. J. 1992. "Age at migration, social connections, and well-being among elderly Hispanics." *Journal of Aging and Health 4*:480–499.

Angel, R. J., and Angel, J. L. 1993. *Painful Inheritance: Health and the New Generation of Fatherless Families.* Madison: University of Wisconsin Press.

Angel, R. J., and Angel, J. L. 1997. *Who Will Care for Us? Aging and Long-Term Care in a Multicultural America.* New York: New York University Press.

Antonucci, T. C., Akiyama, H., and Lansford, J. 1998. "Negative effects of close social relations." *Family Relations 47*:379–384.

Aquilino, W. S. 1994. "Later life parental divorce and widowhood: Impact on young adults' assessment of parent-child relations." *Journal of Marriage and the Family 56*:908–922.

Aquilino, W. S., and Supple, A. J. 2001. "Long-term effects of parenting practices during adolescence on well-being outcomes in young adulthood." *Family Relations 22*:289–308.

Archer, M., and Blau, J. R. 1993. "Class formation in nineteenth-century America: The case for the middle class." In J. Blake and J. Hagen (eds.), *Annual Review of Sociology 19*:17–41. Palo Alto, CA: Annual Reviews, Inc.

Arditti, J. A. 1995. "Noncustodial parents: Emergent issues of diversity and process." *Marriage and Family Review 20*:283–304.

Arendell, T. 2000. "Conceiving and investigating motherhood: The decade's scholarship." *Journal of Marriage and the Family 62*:1192–1207.

Arnold, C. 1998. "Children and Stepfamilies: A Snapshot." *Center for Law and Social Policy* <http://www.clasp.org>.

Arond, M., and Pauker, S. L. 1987. *The First Year of Marriage.* New York: Warner Books.

Asbury, J. 1999. "What do we know now about spouse abuse and child sexual abuse in families of color in the United States?" In R. L. Hampton (ed.), *Family Violence* (2nd Ed.), (pp. 148–167). Thousand Oaks, CA: Sage.

Aseltine, R. H. 1996. "Pathways linking parental divorce with adolescent depression." *Journal of Health and Social Behavior 37*:133–148.

Aseltine, R. H., Jr., and Kessler, R. C. 1993. "Marital disruption and depression in a community sample." *Journal of Health and Social Behavior 34*:237–251.

Associated Press. 2004. "Same-sex marriages are 'totally ordinary' in Netherlands." *Marin Independent Journal* March 5, A1, A9.

Astone, N. M., and McLanahan, S. S. 1991. "Family structure, parental practices, and high school completion." *American Sociological Review 56*:309–320.

Auger, D. G., Conley, C., and Gardner, C. B. 1997. "Lesbian and public harassment: An initial exploration." *Perspectives on Social Problems* 9:281–289.

Avenevoli, S., Sessa, F. M., and Steinberg, L. 1999. "Family structure, parenting practices, and adolescent adjustment: An ecological examination." In E. M. Hetherington (ed.), *Coping with Divorce, Single Parenting, and Remarriage* (pp. 65–90). Mahwah, NJ: Erlbaum.

Babbie, E. 2002. *The Basics of Social Research* (2nd Ed.). Belmont, CA: Wadsworth.

Baca-Zinn, M. 1998. "Adaptation and continuity in Mexican-origin families." In R. L. Taylor (ed.), *Minority Families in the United States* (2nd Ed.), (pp. 77–94). New Jersey: Prentice-Hall.

Baca-Zinn, M., and Wells, B. 2000. "Diversity within Latino families: New lessons for family social science." In D. H. Demo, K. R. Allen, and M. A. Fine (eds.), *Handbook of Family Diversity* (pp. 252–273). New York: Oxford University Press.

Bachman, J. C. and Schulenberg, J. 1993. "How part-time work intensity relates to drug use, problem behavior, time use, and satisfaction among high school seniors: Are these consequences or merely correlates?" *Developmental Psychology* 29:220–235.

Bachrach, C., Hindin, M. J., and Thomson, E. 2000. "The changing shape of ties that bind: An overview and synthesis." In L. J. Waite (ed.), *The Ties That Bind: Perspectives on Marriage and Cohabitation* (pp. 3–16). New York: Aldine de Gruyter.

Bailey, B. L. 1988. *From Front Porch to Backseat: Courtship in Twentieth Century America*. Baltimore: Johns Hopkins University Press.

Bakan, D. 1966. *The Duality of Human Existence*. Boston: Beacon.

Baldwin, A., Baldwin, C., and Cole, R. E. 1990. "Stress-resistant families and stress-resistant children." In J. E. Rolf, A. S. Masten, D. Cicchetti, K. N. Wechterlein, and S. Weintraub (eds.), *Risk and Protective Factors in the Development of Psychopathology* (pp. 257–280). New York: Cambridge University Press.

Barber, B. 1994. "Cultural, family, and personal contexts of parent-adolescent conflict." *Journal of Marriage and the Family* 56:375–386.

Barnett, R. C. 1994. "Home-to-work spillover revisited: A study of full-time employed women in dual-earner couples." *Journal of Marriage and the Family* 56:647–656.

Barnett, R. C., and Shen, Y. 1997. "Gender, high- and low-schedule-control housework tasks,and psychological distress: A study of dual-earner couples." *Journal of Family Issues* 18:403–428.

Bart, P. B. 1972. "Depression in middle-age women." In V. Gornick and B. K. Moran (eds.), *Women in a Sexist Society* (pp. 163–168). New York: The New American Library.

Bartholet, E. 2001. "Blood knots: Adoption, reproduction, and the politics of family." In A. Cherlin (ed.), *Public and Private Families: A Reader* (2nd ed.), (pp. 354–362). Boston: McGraw-Hill.

Baucom, D., and Epstein, N. 1990. *Cognitive Behavioral Marital Therapy*. New York: Brunner/Mazel.

Baumrind, D. 1967. "Child care practices anteceding three patterns of preschool behavior." *Genetic Psychology Monographs* 75:43–88.

——. 1971. "Current patterns of parental authority." *Psychology Monograph* 4(2)(1):1–103.

——. 1972. "An exploratory study of socialization effects on black children: Some black-white comparisons." *Child Development* 43:261–267.

Becker, G. 1981. *A Treatise on the Family*. Cambridge, MA: Harvard University Press.

Becker, G., Landis, E. M., and Michael, R. T. 1977. "An economic analysis of marital instability." *Journal of Political Economy* 85:1141–1187.

Becker, H. S. 1960. "Notes on the concept of commitment." *American Journal of Sociology* 6:32–40.

Becker, W. C. 1964. "Consequences of different kinds of parental discipline." In M. L. Hoffman, and L. W. Hoffman (eds.), *Review of Child Development Research* 1:169–208. New York: Russell Sage Foundation.

Beers, J. R. 1996. *The Desire to Parent in Gay Men*. Unpublished doctoral dissertation. Columbia University, New York, NY.

Bell, A. P., and Weinberg, M. S. 1978. *Homosexualities: A Study of Diversity Among Men and Women*. New York: Simon & Schuster.

Bell, C., and Jenkins, E. (1991). Traumatic stress and children. *Journal of Health Care for the Poor and Underserved* 2:175–188.

Bellah, R. N., Madsen, R., Sullivan, W. M., Swidler, A., and Tipton, S. M. 1985. *Habits of the Heart: Individualism and Commitment in American Life*. Berkeley: University of California Press.

Belsky, J. 1981. Early human experience: A family perspective. *Developmental Psychology* 17:3–23.

——. 1984. "The determinants of parenting: A process model." *Child Development* 55:83–96.

Belsky, J., and Kelly, J. 1994. *The Transition to Parenthood*. New York: Delacorte.

Belsky, J., and Pensky, E. 1988. "Marital change across the transition to parenthood." *Marriage and Family Review* 12:133–156.

Belsky, J., Ward, H., and Rovine, M. 1986. "Prenatal expectations, postnatal experiences and the transition to parenthood." In R. Ashmore, and D. Brodzinsky (eds.), *Perspectives on the Family* (pp. 119–146). Hillsdale, NJ: Erlbaum.

Bengtson, V. L. 1993. "Is the 'contract across generations' changing? Effects of population aging on obligations and expectations across age groups." In V. L. Bengtson, and W. A. Achenbaum (eds.), *The Changing Contract Across Generations* (pp. 3–23). New York: Walter de Gruyter.

——, 2001. "Beyond the nuclear family: The increasing importance of multigenerational bonds." *Journal of Marriage and the Family* 63:1–16.

Bengtson, V. L., and Kuypers, J. A. 1971. "Generational differences and the developmental stake." *International Journal of Aging and Human Development* 2:249–260.

Bengtson, V. L., and Schrader, S. S. 1982. "Parent-child relations." In D. J. Mangen, and W. A. Peterson (eds.), *Handbook of Research Instruments in Social Gerontology* 2:115–185. Minneapolis: University of Minnesota Press.

Benokraitis, N. V. 1999. *Marriages and Families: Changes, Choices, and Constraints* (3rd ed.). Upper Saddle River, NJ: Prentice Hall.

Bergen, R. K. 1998. *Issues in Intimate Violence*. Thousand Oaks, CA: Sage.

Berger, P., and Kellner, H. 1964. "Marriage and the construction of reality: An exercise in the microsociology of knowledge." *Diogenes* 46:1–25.

Bergeron, L. R. 2001. "An elder abuse case study: Caregiver stress or domestic violence? You decide." *Journal of Gerontological Social Work* 34:47–63,

Bergman, L. 1992. "Dating violence among high school students." *Social Work* 37:21–27.

Berk, S. F. 1985. *The Gender Factory: The Apportionment of Work in American Households*. New York: Plenum Press.

Berman, S., Kurtines, W., Silverman, W., and Serafini, L. (1996). "The impact of crime and violence on urban youth." *American Journal of Orthopsychiatry, 66*:329–336.

Bernard, J. 1972. *The Future of Marriage*. New York: Bantam.

——. 1981. "The Good Provider Role: Its Rise and Fall." *American Psychologist* 36:1–12.

Berry, G. L. 1998. "Black family life on television and the socialization of the African American child: Images of marginality." *Journal of Comparative Family Studies* 29:233–242.

Berry, H. 2002. *Entertainment Weekly*, January 18, p. 24.

Berscheid, E., and Reis, H. T. 1998. "Attraction and close relationships." In D. T. Gilbert, S. T. Fiske, and G. Lindzey (eds.), *The Handbook of Social Psychology* (4th ed.), (pp. 193–281). New York: McGraw-Hill.

Biblarz, T. J., and Gottainer, G. 2000. "Family structure and children's success: A comparison of widowed and divorced single-mother families." *Journal of Marriage and the Family* 62:533–548.

Biglan, A., Lewin, L., and Hops, H. 1990. "A contextual approach to the problem of aversive practices in families." In G. R. Patterson (ed.), *Depression and Aggression in Family Interaction* (pp. 103–129). Hillsdale, NJ: Erlbaum.

Bigner, J. J., 1998. *Parent-Child Relations: An Introduction to Parenting* (5th ed.). Upper Saddle River, NJ: Prentice-Hall.

Bigner, J. J., and Jacobsen R. B. 1989a. "The value of children to gay and heterosexual fathers." In F. W. Bozett (ed.), *Homosexuality and the Family* (pp. 163–172). New York: Harrington Park.

——. 1989b. "Parenting behaviors of homosexual and heterosexual fathers." In F. W. Bozett (ed.), *Homosexuality and the Family* (pp. 173–186). New York: Harrington Park.

Billy, J. O. G. 2001. "Better ways to do contextual analysis: Lessons from Duncan and Raudenbush." In A. Booth, and A. C. Crouter (eds.), *Does It Take a Village? Community Effects on Children, Adolescents, and Families* (pp. 137–147). Mahwah, NJ: Erlbaum.

Binstock, G., and Thornton, A. 2003. "Separations, reconciliations, and living apart in cohabiting and marital unions." *Journal of Marriage and Family* 65:432–443.

Black, C. 1981. *It Will Never Happen to Me*. New York: Ballantine Books.

Black, D., Gates, G., Sanders, S., and Taylor, L. 2000. "Demographics of the gay and lesbian population in the United States: Evidence from available systematic data sources." *Demography, 37*:139–154.

Blair, S. L. 1992. "The sex-typing of children's household labor: Parental influence on daughters' and sons' housework." *Youth and Society* 24:178–203.

Blank, R. M. 1995. "Outlook for the U.S. labor market and prospects for low-wage entry jobs." In G. Nightingale, and R. Haveman (eds.), *The Work Alternative* (pp. 33–69). Washington, DC: The Urban Institute.

——. 1997. *It Takes a Nation*. Princeton, NJ: Princeton University Press.

Blankenship, J. 2003. *War's Toll on Marriage: Veterans of Foreign Wars of the United States*. Washington, DC: Gale Group.

Blood, R. O., and Wolfe, D. M. 1960. *Husbands and Wives: The Dynamics of Marital Living*. Glencoe, IL: The Free Press.

Bloom, B. L., Hodges, W. F., Caldwell, R. A., Systra, L., and Cedrone, A. R. 1977. "Marital separation: A community survey." *Journal of Divorce* 1:7–19.

Bluestone, C., and Tamis-LeMonda, C. S. 1999. "Correlates of parenting styles in predominantly working- and middle-class African American mothers." *Journal of Marriage and the Family* 61:881–893.

Blumstein, P., and Schwartz, P. 1983. *American Couples: Money, Work, and Sex.* New York: Morrow.

Bogenschneider, K. 2000. "Has family policy come of age? A decade review of the state of U.S. family policy in the 1990s." *Journal of Marriage and the Family* 62:1136–1159.

———. 2002. *Family Policy Matters: How Policymaking Affects Families and What Professionals Can Do.* Mahwah, NJ: Erlbaum.

Bogenschneider, K., and Corbett, T. 2004. "Building enduring family policies in the 21st century." In M. Coleman, and L. Ganong (eds.), *Handbook of Contemporary Families: Considering the Past, Contemplating the Future* (pp. 451–468). Thousand Oaks, CA: Sage.

Boland, J. P., and Follingstad, D. R. 1987. "The relationship between communication and marital satisfaction: A review." *Journal of Sex and Marital Therapy* 13:286–313.

Bolea, P. S. 2000. "Talking about identity: Individual, family, and intergenerational issues." In R. D. Harold (ed.), *Becoming a Family* (pp. 39–73). Mahwah, NJ: Erlbaum.

Bologna, M. J., Waterman, C. K., and Dawson, L. J. 1987. "Violence in gay male and lesbian relationships: Implications for practitioners and policy makers." Paper presented at the Third National Conference of Family Violence Researchers, Durham, NH.

Bond, J. T., Galinsky, E., and Swanberg, J. E. 1998. *The 1997 National Study of the Changing Workforce.* New York: Families and Work Institute.

Booth, A., and Amato, P. 1991. "Divorce and psychological stress." *Journal of Health and Social Behavior* 32:396–407.

Booth, A., and Edwards, J. N. 1985. "Age at marriage and marital instability." *Journal of Marriage and the Family* 47:67–75.

———. 1992. "Starting over: Why remarriages are more unstable." *Journal of Family Issues* 13:179–194.

Booth, A., and Johnson, E. 1988. "Premarital cohabitation and marital success." *Journal of Family Issues* 9:387–394.

Booth, C. L., Clark-Steward, K. A., Vandell, D. L., McCartney, K. and Owen, M. T. 2002. "Child-care usage and mother-infant 'quality time.'" *Journal of Marriage and Family* 64:16–26.

Bornstein, M. H. 1995. "Parenting infants." In M. H. Bornstein (ed.), *Handbook of Parenting, I: Children and Parents* (pp. 3–39). Hillsdale, NJ: Erlbaum.

Bossard, N. H. , and Boll, E. S. 1956. *The Large Family System.* Philadelphia: University of Pennsylvania Press.

Boudreau, F. A. 1993. "Elder abuse." In R. L. Hampton, T. P. Gullota, G. R. Adams, E. H. Potter, III, and R. P. Weissberg, (ed.), *Family Violence: Prevention and Treatment* (pp. 142–158). Newbury Park, CA: Sage.

Bowen, G. L., Richman, J. M., and Bowen, N. K. 2000. "Families in the context of community across time." In S. Price, P. McKenry, and M. Murphy, (eds.), *Families Across Time* (pp. 117–128). Los Angeles: Roxbury.

Bowman, P. J., and Sanders, R. 1998. "Unmarried African American fathers: A comparative life span analysis." *Journal of Comparative Family Studies* 29:39–56.

Bradbury, T. N., and Karney, B. R. 1993. "Longitudinal study of marital interaction and dysfunction: Review and analysis." *Clinical Psychology Review* 13:15–28.

Brandl, B., and Horan, D. L. 2002. "Domestic violence in later life: An overview for health care providers." *Women and Health* 35:41–54.

Braver, S. L., Ellman, I. M., and Fabricius, W. V. 2003. "Relocation of children after divorce and children's best interest: New evidence and legal considerations." *Journal of Family Psychology* 17:206–219.

Braver, S. L., Fitzpatrick, P. J., and Bay, R. C. 1991. "Noncustodial parent's report of child support payments." *Family Relations* 40:180–185.

Braver, S. L., Whitley, M., and Ng, C. 1993. "Who divorced whom? Methodological and theoretical issues." *Journal of Divorce and Remarriage* 20:1–19.

Bray, J. H. 1999. "From marriage to remarriage and beyond: Findings from the developmental issues in stepfamilies research project." In E. M. Hetherington (ed.), *Coping with Divorce, Single Parenting, and Remarriage* (pp. 253–271). Mahway, NJ: Erlbaum.

Brecher, E. M. 1990–1991. *Love, Sex and Aging.* Annual Editions. Consumers Union Report.

Briar-Lawson, K., Lawson, H. A., Hennon, C. B., and Jones, A. R. 2001. *Family-centered Policies and Practices: International Implications.* New York: Columbia University Press.

Briere, J. N., and Elliot, D. M. 1994. "Immediate and long-term impacts of child sexual abuse." *The Future of Children* 4:54–69.

Brodsky, A. E. 1996. "Resilient single mothers in risky neighborhoods: Negative psychological sense of community." *Journal of Community Psychology* 24:347–363.

Brody, E. M. 1990. *Women in the Middle: Their Parent-Care Years.* New York: Springer.

Brody, G. H., and Flor, D. L. 1998. "Maternal resources, parenting practices, and child competence in rural, single-parent African American families." *Child Development* 69:803–816.

Brody, G. H., Dorsey, S., Forehand, R., and Armistead, L. 2002. "Unique and protective contributions of parenting and classroom processes to the adjustment of African American children living in single-parent families." *Child Development* 73 :274–286.

Brody, G. H., Stoneman, Z., McCoy, J. K., and Forehand, R. 1992. "Contemporaneous and longitudinal associations of sibling conflict with family relationship assessments and family discussions about sibling problems." *Child Development* 63:391–400.

Bronfenbrenner, U. 1979. *The Ecology of Human Development.* Cambridge, MA: Harvard University Press.

Bronfenbrenner, U. 1989. "Ecological systems theory." *Annals of Child Development* 6:187–249.

Bronfenbrenner, U., Moen, P., and Garbarino, J. 1984. "Child, family, and community." In R. Parke (ed.), *Review of Child Development Research* (pp. 283–328). Chicago: University of Chicago Press.

Brooks, J. B. 1999. *The Process of Parenting* (5th ed.). Mountain View, CA: Mayfield.

Brooks, J. L., Hair, E. C., and Zaslow, M. J. 2001. "Welfare reform's impact on adolescents: Early warning signs." *Child Trends Research Brief.* Washington, DC, July.

Brown, J., and Dunn, J. 1992. "Talk with your mother or your sibling? Developmental changes in early family conversations about feelings." *Child Development* 63:336–349.

Brubaker, T. 1985. *Later Life Families.* Beverly Hills, CA: Sage.

Bryson, K., and Casper, L. M. 1999. "Co-resident grandparents and grandchildren." *Current Population Reports: Special Reports* P23–P198. Washington DC: U.S. Bureau of the Census.

Buchalter, G. 2001. "You just have to keep going." *Parade Magazine,* March 4, p. 5.

Buchanan, C. M., Maccoby, E. E., and Dornbusch, S. M. 1996. *Adolescents After Divorce.* Cambridge, MA: Harvard University Press.

Buehler, C. 1995. "Divorce law in the United States." In L. J. McIntyre, and M. B. Sussman (eds.), *Families and Law* (pp. 99–120). New York: The Haworth Press.

Bulcroft, R., and Bulcroft, K. 1993. "Race differences in attitudinal and motivational factors in the decision to marry." *Journal of Marriage and the Family* 55:338–355.

Bulcroft, R. A., Carmody, D. C., and Bulcroft, K. A. 1998. "Family structure and patterns of independence giving to adolescents." *Journal of Family Issues* 19:404–435.

Bumpass, L. L., and Lu, H. H. 2000. "Trends in cohabitation and implications for children's family contexts in the United States." *Population Studies* 54:29–41.

Bumpass, L. L., Martin, T. C., and Sweet, J. A. 1991. "The impact of family background and early marital factors on marital disruption." *Journal of Family Issues* 12:22–42.

Bumpass, L. L, Raley, K., and Sweet, J. 1994. "The changing character of stepfamilies: Implications of cohabitation and nonmarital childbearing." *Demography* 32:425–436.

Bumpass, L. L., and Sweet, J. A. 1989. "National estimates of cohabitation." *Demography* 26:615–625.

Bumpass, L. L., Sweet, J. A., and Cherlin, A. 1991. "The role of cohabitation in declining rates of marriage." *Journal of Marriage and the Family* 53:913–927.

Burke, P. J., and Reitzes, D.C. 1991. "An identity theory approach to commitment." *Social Psychology Quarterly* 54:239–251.

Burton, D., Foy, D., Bwanausa, C., Johnson, J., and Moore, L. 1994. "The relationship between traumatic exposure to family dysfunctions and posttraumatic stress symptoms in male juvenile offenders." *Journal of Traumatic Stress* 7:83–93.

Burton, L., Tubbs, C., Odoms, A. M., Oh, H. J., Mello, Z., and Cherlin, A. 2002. "Health and low-income families." *Poverty Research News* 6:6–8.

Buss, D., Shackelford, T. K., Kirkpatrick, L. A., and Larsen, R. J. 2001. "A half century of mate preferences: The cultural evolution of values." *Journal of Marriage and the Family* 63:491–503.

Cahn, D. D. (1992). *Conflict in Intimate Relationships.* New York, NY: Guilford.

Cain, R. L., Pedersen, F. A., Zaslow, M. J., and Kramer, E. 1984. "Effects of the father's presence or absence during a Cesarean delivery." *Birth and the Family Journal* 11:10–15.

Calhoun, A. W. 1945. *A Social History of the American Family, Vol. 1: Colonial Period.* New York: Barnes and Noble.

Call, V., Sprecher, S., and Schwartz, S. 1995. "The incidence and frequency of marital sex in a national sample." *Journal of Marriage and the Family* 57:639–652.

Campbell, C., and Schwartz, D. (1996). "Prevalence and impact of exposure to interpersonal violence among suburban and urban middle school students." *Pediatrics* 98: 396–402.

Campbell, L. D., Connidis, I. A., and Davies, L. 1999. "Sibling ties in later life: A social network analysis." *Journal of Family Issues* 20:114–148.

Canary, D. J., Stafford, L., and Semic, B. A. 2002. "A panel study of the associations between maintenance strategies and relational characteristics." *Journal of Marriage and Family* 64:395–406.

Cancian, F. M. 1994. "Marital conflict over intimacy." In G. Handel and Whitchurch, G. G. (eds.), *The Psychosocial Interior of the Family* (4th ed.), (pp. 401–417). New York: Aldine.

——. 1986. "The feminization of love." *Signs: Journal of Women in Culture and Society 11*:692–709.

Capizzano, J., and Adams, G. 2004. "Children in low-income families are less likely to be in center-based child care." No. 16 in Series, *Snapshots of American Families III*. Urban Institute. Accessed at <http://www.urban.org/urlprint.cfm?ID=8701>.

Caplow, T., Hicks, L., and Wattenberg, B. J. 2001. *The First Measured Century*. Washington, DC: AEI Press.

Carlson, M. J., and Corcoran, M. E. 2001. "Family structure and children's behavioral and cognitive outcomes." *Journal of Marriage and Family 63*:779–792.

Carpenter, B. D. 2001. "Attachment bonds between adult daughters and their older mothers: Associations with contemporary caregiving." *Journal of Gerontology: Psychological Sciences 56B*:P257–P266.

Carr, D., House, J. S., Wortman, C., Nesse, R., and Kessler, R. C. 2001. "Psychological adjustment to sudden and anticipated spousal loss among older widowed persons." *Journal of Gerontology: Social Sciences 56B*:S237–S248.

Carr, D., House, J. S., Kessler, R. C., Nesse, R. M., Sonnega, J., and Wortman, C. 2000. "Marital quality and psychological adjustment to widowhood among older adults: A longitudinal analysis." *Journal of Gerontology: Social Sciences 55B*:S197–S207.

Carstensen, L. L. 1992. "Social and emotional patterns in adulthood: Support for the socioemotional selectivity theory." *Psychology and Aging 7*:331–338.

Carstensen, L. L., Gottman, J. M., and Levenson, R. W. 1995. "Emotional behavior in long-term marriage." *Psychology of Aging 10*:140–149.

Casper, L. M., and Bianchi, S. M. 2002. *Continuity and Change in the American Family*. Thousand Oaks, CA: Sage.

Casper, L. M., and Sayer, L. 2000. "Cohabitation transitions: Different attitudes and purposes, different paths." Paper presented at the annual meeting of the Population Association of America, March, Los Angeles.

Cavanaugh, J., and Kinney, J. M. 1994. *Marital Satisfaction as an Important Contextual Factor in Spousal Caregiving*. Seventh International Conference on Personal Relationships, Groningen, The Netherlands.

Cazenave, N. A., and Straus, M. A. 1990. "Race, class, network embeddedness, and family violence: A search for potent support systems." In M. Straus, and R. Gelles (ed.), *Physical Violence in American Families: Risk Factors and Adaptations to Violence in 8,145 Families* (pp. 321–339). New Brunswick, NJ: Transaction Publishers.

CBC News. 2001. "Oldest boy may help resolve Idaho standoff." From <http://cbc.ca>, June 1.

Center on Budget and Policy Priorities. 2000. Press release, September 4, 2000.

Chadwick, B. A., and Heaton, T. B. 1999. *Statistical Handbook on the American Family* (2nd ed.). Phoenix, AZ: The Oryx Press.

Chamberlain, R. 2003. *Shattered Love: A Memoir*. New York: HarperCollins.

Chao, R. 2001. "Extending research on the consequences of parenting style for Chinese Americans and European Americans." *Child Development 72*:1832–1843.

Charles, A. V. 1986. "Physically abused parents." *Journal of Family Violence 4*:343–355.

Chatters, L. M., and Taylor, R. J. 1993. "Intergenerational support: The provision of assistance to parents by adult children." In J. S. Jackson, L. M. Chatters, and R. J. Taylor (eds.), *Aging in Black America* (pp. 69–83). Newbury Park. CA: Sage.

Cherlin, A. J. 1978. "Remarriage as an incomplete institution." *American Journal of Sociology 84*:634–650.

——. 1992. *Marriage, Divorce, Remarriage* (2nd ed.). Cambridge, MA: Harvard University Press.

——. 1996. *Public and Private Families*. New York: McGraw-Hill, Inc.

——. 2002. *Public and Private Families: An Introduction* (3rd ed.). Boston: McGraw-Hill.

Cherlin, A. J., Chase-Lansdale, P. L., and McRae, C. 1998. "Effects of parental divorce on mental health throughout the life course." *American Sociological Review 63*:239–249.

Cherlin, A. J., and Furstenberg, F. F., Jr. 1986. *The New American Grandparent: A Place in the Family, a Life Apart*. New York: Basic Books.

——. 1994. "Stepfamilies in the United States: A reconsideration." In J. Blake, and J. Hagen (eds.), *Annual Review of Sociology 20*:359–381. Palo Alto, CA: Annual Reviews.

Cheung, F. K., and Snowden, L. R. 1990. "Community mental health and ethnic minority populations." *Community Mental Health Journal 26*:277–291.

Chow, E., and Berheide, C. 1988. "The interdependence of family and work: A framework for family life education, policy, and practice." *Family Relations 37*:23–28.

Christensen, A., and Heavey, C. L. 1990. "Gender and social structure in the demand/withdraw pattern of marital interaction." *Journal of Personality and Social Psychology 59*:73–81.

Christiansen, S. L., and Palkovitz, R. 2001. "Why the 'good provider' role still matters: Providing as a form of paternal involvement." *Journal of Family Issues 22(1)*:84–106.

Church, E. 1999. "Who are the people in your family? Stepmothers' diverse notions of kinship." *Journal of Divorce and Remarrige 31*:83–105.

Cicirelli, V. G. 1989. "Feelings of attachment to siblings and well-being in later life." *Psychology and Aging 4*:211–216.

Clark, R. 1983. *Family Life and School Achievement: Why Poor Black Children Succeed or Fail.* Chicago: The University of Chicago Press.

Clarke, L. H. 2003. "Later life families." In J. J. Ponzetti, Jr. (ed.), *International Encyclopedia of Marriage and Family,* Vol. 3, (2nd ed.), (pp. 1019–1026). New York: Macmillan Reference USA.

Clarke, S. C. 1995. *Advance Report of Final Divorce Statistics 1989 and 1990* [Monthly Vital Statistics Report, 43(9):Supplement]. Hyattsville, MD: National Center for Health Statistics.

Clark-Nicolas, P., and Gray-Little, B. 1991. "Effect of economic resources on marital quality in black married couples." *Journal of Marriage and the Family 53*:645–655.

Clausen, J. A., and Clausen, S. R. 1973. "The effects of family size on parents and children." In J. T. Fawcett (ed.), *Psychological Perspectives on Population* (pp. 185–208). New York: Basic Books.

Cleek, M. G., and Pearson, T. A. 1985. "Perceived causes of divorce: An analysis of interrelationships." *Journal of Marriage and the Family 47*:179–183.

CNN.com. 2004. Law Center: Comparing marriage and civil unions. Found at <http://www.cnn.com/2004/LAW/02/26/bush.civil.unions/>.

Cochran, M., and Brassard, J. 1979. "Child development and personal social networks." *Child Development 50*:601–616.

Colarossi, L. G., and Lynch, S. A. 2000. "Tales of social support throughout family development." In R. D. Harold (ed.), *Becoming a Family* (pp. 115–153). Mahwah, NJ: Erlbaum.

Coleman, J. 1988. "Social capital in the creation of human capital." *American Journal of Sociology 94*:S95–S120.

Coleman, M., Ganong, L., and Fine, M. 2000. "Reinvestigating remarriage: Another decade of progress." *Journal of Marriage and the Family 62*:1288–1307.

Coleman, V. E., 1996. "Lesbian battering: The relationship between personality and the perpetration of violence." In L. K. Hamberger, and C. Renzetti (eds.), *Domestic Partner Abuse* (pp. 77–101). New York: Springer Publishing Company.

Coll, C. G. T., Hoffman, J., and Oh, W. 1987. "The social ecology and early parenting of Caucasian adolescent mothers." *Child Development 58*:955–963.

Collins, C., Leondan-Wright, B., and Skalar, H. 1999. *Shifting Fortunes: The Perils of the Growing American Wealth Gap.* Boston: United for a Fair Economy.

Collins, W. A., Harris, M. L., and Susman, A. 1995. "Parenting during middle childhood." In M. H. Bornstein (ed.), *Handbook of Parenting. Volume I: Children and Parenting* (pp. 65–89). Mahwah, NJ: Erlbaum.

Coltrane, S. 1996. *Family Man: Fatherhood, Housework, and Gender Equity.* New York: Oxford University Press.

———. 2000. "Research on household labor: Modeling and measuring the social embeddedness of routine family work." *Journal of Marriage and the Family 62*:1208–1233.

Coltrane, S., and Messineo, M. 2000. "The perpetuation of subtle prejudice: Race and gender imagery in 1990s television advertising." *Sex Roles 42*:363–389.

Columbia Daily Tribune. (2001). "Children hold off police from rural Idaho house." May 31. <http://www.showmenews.com>.

Compliance Guide to the Family and Medical Leave Act. 2002. <http://www.dol.gov/dol/esa/public/regs/compliance/whd/1421.htm>.

Conger, K. J., Conger, R. D., and Elder, G. H., Jr. 1994. "Sibling relations during hard times. In R. D. Conger, and G. H. Elder, Jr. (eds.), *Families in Troubled Times: Adapting to Change in Rural America* (pp. 235–151). New York: Aldine de Gruyter.

Conger, R. D., and Conger, K. J. 2002. "Resilience in midwestern families: Selected findings from the first decade of a prospective, longitudinal study." *Journal of Marriage and Family 64*:361–373.

Conger, R. D., Elder, G. H., Jr., Lorenz, F. O., Conger, K. J., Simons, R. L., Whitbeck, L. B., Huck, S., and Melby, J. N. 1990. "Linking economic hardship to marital quality and instability." *Journal of Marriage and the Family 52*:643–656.

Connidis, I. A. 1992. "Life transitions and the adult sibling tie: A qualitative study." *Journal of Marriage and the Family 54*:972–982.

Connolly, J., Furman, W., and Konarski, R. 1995, March. "The role of social networks in the emergence of romantic relationships in adolescence. Paper presented at the biennial meetings of the Society for Research in Adolescence, Boston.

Connolly, J., and Goldberg, A. 1999. "Romantic relationships in adolescence: The role of friends and peers in their emergence and development." In W. Furman, B. B. Brown, and C. Feiring (eds.), *The Development of Romantic Relationships in Adolescence* (pp. 266–290). Cambridge: Cambridge University Press.

Cook, P. W. 1997. *Abused Men: The Hidden Side of Domestic Violence.* Westport, CT: Praeger.

Cooley, C. 1902. *Human Nature and the Social Order.* New York: Scribner's.

Cooney, T. M. 1994. "Young adults' relations with parents: The influence of recent parental divorce." *Journal of Marriage and the Family* 56:45–56.

Cooney, T. M., and Dunne, K. 2001. "Intimate relationships in later life." *Journal of Family Issues* 22:838–858.

Cooney, T. M., and Gable, S. 2001. "Chores." In J. Lerner and R. Lerner (eds.), *Adolescence in America,* Vol. 1, (pp. 115–118). Denver: ABC-CLIO.

Cooney, T. M., Smyer, M. A., Hagestad, G. O., and Klock, R. 1986. "Parental divorce in young adulthood: Some preliminary findings." *American Journal of Orthopsychiatry* 56:470–477.

Cooney, T. M., and Uhlenberg, P. 1989. "Family-building patterns of professional women: A comparison of lawyers, physicians, and postsecondary teachers." *Journal of Marriage and the Family* 51:749–758.

——. 1990. "The role of divorce in men's relations with their adult children after mid-life." *Journal of Marriage and the Family* 52:677–688.

——. 1992. "Support from parents over the life course: The adult child's perspective." *Social Forces* 71:63–84.

Coontz, S. 1992. *The Way We Never Were: American Families and the Nostalgia Trap.* New York: Basic Books.

Cooperman, A., and Finer, J. (2004). "Massachusetts makes history: A first in the Union." TwinCites.com, Pioneer Press. Retrieved May 18, 2004 from <http://www.twincities.com>.

Costa, P. T., Herbst, J. H., McCrae, R. R., and Siegler, I. C. 2000. "Personality at midlife: Stability, intrinsic maturation, and response to life events." *Assessment* 7:365–378.

Cowan, C. P., and Cowan, P. A. 2000. *When Partners Become Parents: The Big Life Change for Couples.* Mahwah, NJ: Erlbaum.

Cowan, P. A., and Cowan, C. P. 1988. "Who does what when partners become parents: Implications for men, women, and marriage." *Marriage and Family Review* 12:105–131.

Cox, M. J., Paley, B., Burchinal, M., and Payne, C. C. 1999. "Marital perceptions and interactions across the transition to parenthood." *Journal of Marriage and the Family* 61:611–625.

Crnic, K. A., and Greenberg, M. T. 1990. "Minor parenting stresses with young children." *Child Development* 61:1628–1637.

Crohan, S. E. 1996. "Marital quality and conflict across the transition to parenthood in African American and white couples." *Journal of Marriage and the Family* 58:933–944.

Cromwell, R. E., and Olson, D. H. 1975. *Power in Families.* Newbury Park, CA: Sage.

Crosnoe, R. 2004. "Social capital and the interplay of families and schools." *Journal of Marriage and Family* 66:267–280.

Crouter, A. C., Manke, B. A., and McHale, S. M. 1995. "The family context of gender intensification in early adolescence." *Child Development* 66:317–329.

Crouter, S. C., and Maguire, M. C. 1998. "Seasonal and weekly rhythms: Windows into variability in family socialization experiences in early adolescence." *New Directions for Child and Adolescent Development* 82:69–82.

Crowder, K. D., and Tolnay, S. E. 2000. "A new marriage squeeze for black women: The role of racial intermarriage by black men." *Journal of Marriage and the Family* 62:792–807.

Cuber, J., and Harroff, P. 1965. *The Significant Americans.* New York: Random House.

Cummings, E. M., and Davies, P. T. 1996. "Emotional security as a regulatory process in normal development of psychopathology." *Development and Psychopathology* 8:123–139.

Cunningham, M. 2001. "Parental influences on the gendered division of housework." *American Sociological Review* 66:184–203.

Curry, L. C., and Stone, J. G. 1995. "Understanding elder abuse: The social problem of the 1990s." *Journal of Clinical Geropsychology* 1:147–156.

Dail, P. W., and Way, W. L. 1985. "What do parents observe about parenting from prime time television?" *Family Relations* 34:491–499.

Dainton, M., and Stafford, L. 1993. "Routine maintenance behaviors: A comparison of relationship type, partner similarity, and sex differences." *Journal of Social and Personal Relationships* 10:255–272.

Dallas, C., Wilson, T., and Salgado, V. 2000. "Gender differences in teen parents' perceptions of parental responsibilities." *Public Health Nursing* 17:423–433.

Daniel, J. 2001. "Looking after: A son's memoir." In A. J. Walker, M. Manoogian-O'Dell, L. A. McGraw, and D. L. G. White (eds.), *Families in Later Life: Connections and Transitions* (pp. 107–109). Thousand Oaks, CA: Pine Forge Press.

Daniels, A. K. 1988. *Invisible Careers.* Chicago: University of Chicago Press.

Daniels, D., and Plomin, R. 1985. "Differential experience of siblings in the same family." *Developmental Psychology* 21:747–760.

Darabi, K. F., Graham, E. H., Namerow, P. B., Philliber, S. G., and Varga, P. 1984. "The effect of maternal age on the well-being of children." *Journal of Marriage and the Family* 46:933–936.

Datzman, J., and Gardner, C. B. 2000. "In my mind, we are all humans": Notes on the public management of black-white interracial romantic relationships." *Marriage and Family Review* 30:5–24.

Davey, A., and Szinovacz, M. E. 2004. "Dimensions of marital quality and retirement." *Journal of Family Issues* 25:431–464.

Davies, L., Avison, W. R., and McAlpine, D. D. 1997. "Significant life experiences and depression among single and married mothers." *Journal of Marriage and the Family* 59:294–308.

Deater-Deckard, K., Dodge, K. A., Bates, J. E., and Pettit, G. S. 1996. "Physical discipline among African American and European American mothers: Links to children's externalizing behavior." *Developmental Psychology* 32:1065–1072.

Decalmer, P. 1993. "Clinical presentation." In P. Decalmer, and F. Glendenning (eds.), *The Mistreatment of Elderly People* (pp. 5–61). Newbury Park, CA: Sage.

DeGenova, M. K. 1997. *Families in Multicultural Context.* Mountain View, CA: Mayfield.

Delgado-Gaitan, C. 1987. "Tradition and transitions in the learning process of Mexican children: An ethnographic view." In G. Spindler, and L. Spindler (eds.), *Interpretive Ethnography of Education: At Home and Abroad* (pp. 333–359). Hillsdale, NJ: Erlbaum.

DeMaris, A. 2000. "Till discord do us part: The role of physical and verbal conflict in union disruption." *Journal of Marriage and Family* 62:683–692.

DeMaris, A., Benson, M. L., Fox, G. L., Hill, T., and Wyk, J. V. 2003. "Distal and proximal factors in domestic violence: A test of an integrated model." *Journal of Marriage and Family* 65:652–667.

Demo, D. H., and Acock, A. 1988. "The impact of divorce on children." *Journal of Marriage and the Family* 50:619–648.

———. 1993. "Family diversity and the division of domestic labor." *Family Relations* 42:323–331.

Demo, D. H., Small, S. A., and Savin-Williams, R. C. 1987. "Family relations and the self-esteem of adolescents and their parents." *Journal of Marriage and the Family* 49:705–715.

Demos, J. 1973. *A Little Commonwealth: Family Life in Plymouth Colony.* London: Oxford University Press.

DeVault, M. 1991. *Feeding the Family: The Social Organization of Caring and Gendered Work.* Chicago: University of Chicago Press.

Diebold, F. X., Neumark, D., and Polsky, D. 1997. "Job stability in the United States." *Journal of Labor Economics* 15:206–223.

Dietz, T. L. 1995. "Patterns of intergenerational assistance within the Mexican-American family: Is the family taking care of the older generation's needs?" *Journal of Family Issues* 16:344–356.

Dillon, P., and Emery, R. E. 1996. "Divorce mediation and resolution of child custody disputes: Long-term effects." *American Journal of Orthopsychiatry* 66:131–151.

Dilworth, J. E. L. 2004. "Predictors of negative spillover from family to work." *Journal of Family Issues* 25:241–261.

Dilworth-Anderson, P., Williams, I. C., and Gibson, B. E. 2002. "Issues of race, ethnicity, and culture in caregiving research: A 20-year review (1980–2000)." *Gerontologist* 42:237–272.

Dilworth-Anderson, P., Williams, S. W., and Cooper, T. 1999. "Family caregiving to elderly African Americans: Caregiver types and structures." *Journal of Gerontology: Social Sciences* 54B:S237–S241.

Dodson, L., and Dickert, J. 2004. "Girls' family labor in low-income households: A decade of qualitative research." *Journal of Marriage and Family* 66:318–332.

Doka, K. J., and Mertz, M. E. 1988. "The meaning and significance of great-grandparenthood." *Gerontologist* 28:192–197.

Donn, J., and Sherman, R. C. 2002. "Attitudes and practices regarding the formation of romantic relationships on the Internet." *Cyberpsychology and Behavior* 5:107–123.

Dore, M. M., Kauffman, E., Nelson-Zlupko, L., and Granfort, E. 1996. "Psychological functioning and treatment needs of latency-age children from drug-involved families." *Families in Society* 77:595–604.

Dornbusch, S. M., Carlsmith, J. M., Bushwall, S. J., Ritter, P. L., Leiderman, H., Hastorf, A. H., and Gross, R. T. 1985. "Single parents, extended households, and the control of adolescents." *Child Development* 56:326–341.

Dorr, A., Kovaric, P., and Doubleday, C. 1990. "Age and content influences on children's perceptions of the realism of television families." *Journal of Broadcasting and Electronic Media* 34:377–397.

Dorr, A., and Rabin, B. E. 1995. "Parents, children, and television." In M. H. Bornstein (ed.), *Handbook of Parenting. Volume 4: Applied and Practical Parenting* (pp. 323–351). Mahwah, NJ: Erlbaum.

Downey, D. B., and Powell, B. 1993. "Do children in single-parent households fare better living with same-sex parents?" *Journal of Marriage and the Family* 55:55–71.

Drobnic, S., Blossfeld, H., and Rohwer, G. 1999. "Dynamics of women's employment patterns over the family life course: A comparison of the United States and Germany." *Journal of Marriage and the Family 61*:133–146.

Drotar, D. 1992. "Prevention of neglect and nonorganic failure to thrive." In D. J. Willis, E. W. Holden, and M. Rosenberg (eds.), *Prevention of Child Maltreatment: Developmental and Ecological Perspectives* (pp. 115–149). New York: John Wiley.

Dubrow, N., and Garbarino, J. (1989). Living in the war zone: Mothers and young children in a public housing development. *Child Welfare 89*:3–18.

Duggan, A. K., McFarlane, E. C., Windham, A. M., Rohde, C. A., Salkever, D. S., Fuddy, L., Rosenberg, L. A., Buchbinder, S. B., and Sla, C. C. J. 1999. "Evaluation of Hawaii's healthy start program." *The Future of Children 9*:66–90.

Duncan, G. J., and Hoffman, S. D. 1985. "A reconsideration of the economic consequences of divorce." *Demography 22*:485–497.

Dunn, J. 1996. "Siblings: The first society." In N. Vanzetti, and S. Duck (eds.), *A Lifetime of Relationships* (pp. 105–124). Pacific Grove, CA: Brooks/Cole.

Dunn, J., and Kendrick, C. 1981. "Interaction between young siblings: Association with the interaction between mother and firstborn." *Developmental Psychology 17*:336–343.

Dunn, J., and Munn, P. 1987. "Development of justifications in disputes with mothers and sibling." *Developmental Psychology 23*:791–798.

Dura, J. R., and Kiecolt-Glaser, J. K. 1991. "Family transitions, stress, and health." In P. A. Cowan, and M. A. Hetherington (eds.), *Family Transitions* (pp. 59–76). Hillsdale, NJ: Erlbaum.

DuRant, R., Cadenhead, C., Pendergrast, R., Slavens, G., and Linder, C. (1994). "Factors associated with the use of violence among black adolescents." *American Journal of Public Health 84*:612–617.

Dutton, D. 1996. "Patriarchy and wife assault." In L. K. Hamberger, and C. Renzetti, (eds.), *Domestic Partner Abuse* (pp. 125–151). New York: Springer Publishing Company.

Eccles, J., and Harold, A. 1993. "Parent-school involvement during the early adolescent years." *Teachers College Record 94*:568–587.

Edwards, T. M. 2000. "Flying solo." *Time 28*:47–53.

Eggebeen, D. J., and Hogan, D. P. 1990. "Giving between generations in American families." *Human Nature 1*:211–232.

Eggebeen, D. J., Snyder, A. R., and Manning, W. D. 1996. "Children in single-father families in demographic perspective." *Journal of Family Issues 17*:441–465.

Ekerdt, D. J., and DeViney, S. 1990. "On defining persons as retired." *Journal of Aging Studies 4*:211–229.

Ekerdt, D. J., and Vinick, B. H. 1991. "Marital complaints in husband-working and husband-retired couples." *Research on Aging, 13*:364–382.

Elder, G. H. 1998. "The life course as developmental theory." *Child Development 69*:1–12.

Elder, G. H., and Clipp, E. 1988. "Wartime losses and social bonding: Influences over 40 years of men's lives." *Psychiatry 51*:177–198.

Elder, G. H., Jr. 1968. *Adolescent Socialization and Personality Development*. Chicago: Rand McNally.

Elder, G. H., Jr. 1974. *Children of the Great Depression*. Chicago: University of Chicago Press.

Elliot, D. M., and Briere, J. 1995. "Posttraumatic stress associated with delayed recall of sexual abuse: A general population study." *Journal of Traumatic Stress 8*:629–647.

Ellison, C. G., and Bartkowski, J. P. 2002. "Conservative Protestantism and the division of household labor among married couples." *Journal of Family Issues 23*:950–985.

Ellison, C. G., Bartkowski, J. P., and Anderson, K. L. 1999. "Are there religious variations in domestic violence?" *Journal of Family Issues 20*:87–113.

Ellison, C. G., and Sherkat, D. E. 1993. "Obedience and autonomy: Religion and parental values reconsidered." *Journal for the Scientific Study of Religion 32*:313–329.

Emery, R. E. 1988. *Marriage, Divorce, and Children's Adjustment*. Newbury Park, CA: Sage.

——. 1995. "Divorce mediation: Negotiating agreements and renegotiating relationships." *Family Relations 44*:377–383.

Emery, R. E., Kitzmann, K. M., and Waldron, M. 1999. "Psychological interventions for separated and divorced families." In M. A. Hetherington (ed.), *Coping with Divorce, Single Parenting, and Remarriage: A Risk and Resiliency Perspective* (pp. 323–344). Mahway, NJ: Erlbaum.

Emery, R. E., Matthews, S., and Kitzmann, K. 1994. "Child custody mediation and litigation: Parents' satisfaction and functioning a year after settlement." *Journal of Consulting and Clinical Psychology 62*:124–129.

Epstein, J. L., 1990. "School and family connection: Theory, research and implications for integrating sociologies of education and family." In D. G. Unger and M. B. Sussman (eds.), *Families in Community Settings: Interdisciplinary Perspectives* (pp. 99–126). New York: Hayworth Press.

Epstein, J. L. 1994. "Theory to practice: School and family partnerships lead to school improvement and student success." In C. L. Fagnano, and B. Z. Werber (eds.), *School, Family and Community Interaction: A View From the Firing Lines* (pp. 39–52). Boulder, CO: Westview Press.

Epstein, M. A., and Bottoms, B. L. 1998. "Memories of childhood sexual abuse: A survey of young adults. *Child Abuse and Neglect 22*:1217–1238.

Epstein, N., and Eidelson, R. J. 1981. "Unrealistic beliefs of clinical couples: Their relationship to expectations, goals, and satisfaction." *American Journal of Family Therapy 9*:13–22.

Erikson, E. H. 1968. *Identity: Youth and Crisis.* New York: Norton.

Fagot, B. I. 1995. "Parenting boys and girls." In M. H. Bornstein (ed.), *Handbook of Parenting 1*:163–183. Mahwah, NJ: Erlbaum.

Farber, B. 1964. *Family: Organization and Interaction.* San Francisco: Chandler Press.

——. 1987. "The future of the American family: A dialectical account." *Journal of Family Issues 8*:431–433.

Farley, R. 1996. *The New American Reality.* New York: Russel Sage Foundation.

Farran, C. J., Miller, B. H., Kaufman, J. E., and Davis, L. 1997. "Race, finding meaning, and caregiver distress." *Journal of Aging and Health 9*:316–333.

Farrell, M. P., and Rosenberg, S. D. 1981. "Parent-child relations at middle age." In C. Betty, and W. Humphreys (eds.), *Understanding the Family: Stress and Change in American Family Life* (pp. 57–76). New York: Appleton Century Crofts.

Fauber, R., Forehand, R., Thomas, A. M., and Wierson, M. 1990. "A mediational model of the impact of marital conflict on adolescent adjustment in intact and divorced families: The role of disrupted parenting." *Child Development 61*:1112–1123.

Fawcett, J. T. 1988. "The value of children and the transition to parenthood." *Marriage and Family Review 12(3/4)*:11–34.

Federal Register. 2003. *Federal Register 68(26)*:6456–6458.

Feigelman, W. C. 2000. "Adjustments of transracially and intraracially adjusted young adults." *Child and Adolescent Social Work Journal 17*:165–183.

Felmlee, D., and Sprecher, S. 2000. "Close relationships and social psychology: Intersections and future paths." *Social Psychology Quarterly 63*:365–376.

Felson, R. B. 1983. "Aggression and violence between siblings." *Social Psychology Quarterly 46*:271–285.

Fernandez-Kelly, M. P., and Garcia, A. M. 1998. "Hispanic women and homework: Women in the informal economy of Miami and Los Angeles." In A. S. Wharton (ed.), *Working in America: Continuity, Conflict, and Change* (pp. 391–401). Mountain View, CA: Mayfield.

Fincham, F. D., Grych, J. H., and Osborne, L. N. 1994. "Does marital conflict cause child maladjustment? Directions and challenges for longitudinal research." *Journal of Family Psychology 8*:128–140.

Fine, M. A. 2000. "Divorce and single parenting." In C. Hendrick, and S. S. Hendrick (eds.), *Close Relationships: A Sourcebook* (pp. 139–168). Thousand Oaks, CA: Sage.

Fine, M. A., Coleman, M., Gable, S., Ganong L., Ispa, J., Morrison, J., and Thornburg, K. R. 1999. "Research-based parenting education for divorcing parents: A university-community collaboration." In *Serving Children and Families Through Community-University Partnerships: Success Stories* (pp. 249–256). Norwel, MA: Kluwer.

Fine, M. A., McKenry, P. C., Donnelly, B. W., and Voydanoff, P. 1992. "Perceived adjustment of parents and children: Variations by family structure, race, and gender." *Journal of Marriage and the Family 54*:118–127.

Fingerman, K. L. 1996. "Sources of tension in the aging mother and adult daughter relationship." *Psychology and Aging 11*:591–606.

Finkelhor, D., and Yllo, K. 1985. *License to Rape: Sexual Abuse of Wives.* New York: Holt, Rinehart and Winston.

Finz, S. 2002. "Stayner's parents fear losing another son." *San Francisco Chronicle,* October 4, p. A19, 23.

Fisher, H. 2004. *Why We Love: The Nature and Chemistry of Romantic Love.* New York: Holt.

Fitch, C. A., and Ruggles, S. 2000. "Historical trends in marriage formation: The United States 1850–1990." In L. J. Waite (ed.), *The Ties That Bind: Perspectives on Marriage and Cohabitation* (pp. 59–88). New York: Aldine.

Fitzpatrick, M. A., and Richie, L. D. 1992. "Communication theory and the family." In P. G. Boss, W. J. Doherty, R. LaRossa, W. R. Schumm, and S. K. Steinmetz (eds.), *Sourcebook of Family Theories and Methods: A Contextual Approach* (pp. 565–585). New York: Plenum.

Florsheim, P., Moore, D., Zollinger, L., MacDonald, J., and Sumida, E. 1999. "The transition to parenthood among adolescent fathers and their partners: Does antisocial behavior predict problems in parenting?" *Applied Developmental Science 3*:178–191.

Flory, J. 2001. "Students ask lawmakers to keep parents in the dark." *Columbia Daily Tribune,* February 22.

Ford, D. 2002. "Faces of adoption: Forming and finding families." *San Francisco Chronicle*, February 17, p. E5.

Forman, T. A., Williams, D. R., and Jackson, J. S. 1997. "Race, place and discrimination." *Perspectives on Social Problems 9*:231–261.

Forthofer, M. S., Markmann, H. J., Cox, M., Stanley, S., and Kessler, R. C. 1996. "Associations between marital distress and work loss in a national sample." *Journal of Marriage and the Family 58*:597 605.

Fowlkes, M. R. 1994. "Single worlds and homosexual lifestyles: Patterns of sexuality and intimacy." In A. S. Rossi (ed.), *Sexuality Across the Life Course* (pp. 151–184). Chicago: University of Chicago Press.

Fox, G. L., Benson, M. L., DeMarie, A. A., and Van Wyk, J. 2002. "Economic distress and intimate violence: Testing family stress and resources theories." *Journal of Marriage and Family 64*:793–807.

Fox, G. L., and Kelly, R. F. 1995. "Determinants of child custody arrangements at divorce." *Journal of Marriage and the Family 57*:693–708.

Fox, S., Rainie, L., Larson, E., Horrigan, J., Lenhart, A., and Spooner, T. 2001. *Wired Seniors: A Fervent Few, Inspired by Family Ties*. Washington, DC: Pew Internet and American Life Project.

Franklin, S., Ames, B., and King, S. 1994. "Acquiring the family eldercare role: Influences on female employment and adaptation." *Research on Aging 16*:27–42.

Frone, M. R., Yardley, J. K., and Markel, K. S. 1997. "Developing and testing an integrative model of the work-family interface." *Journal of Vocational Behavior 50*:145–167.

Fuller, B., and Kagan, S. L. 2000. "Remember the children: Mothers balance work and child care under welfare reform." Executive Summary. *The Growing up in Poverty Project*, Wave 1 Report, 3–6, February.

Fulmer, T. T. 1989. "Mistreatment of elders: Assessment, diagnosis, and intervention." *Nursing Clinics of North America 23*:707–716.

Furman, W. 1995. "Parenting siblings." In M. H. Bornstein (ed.), *Handbook of Parenting, I: Children and Parents* (pp. 143–162). Hillsdale, NJ: Erlbaum.

Furstenberg, F. F. 2001. "Managing to make it: Afterthoughts." *Journal of Family Issues 22*:150–162.

Furstenberg, F. F., Cook, T. D., Eccles, J., Elder, G. H. Jr., and Sameroff, A. 1999. *Managing to Make It: Urban Families and Adolescent Success*. Chicago: University of Chicago Press.

Furstenberg, F. F., Jr. 1987. "The new extended family: The experience of parents and children after remarriage." In K. Pasley, and M. Ihinger-Tallman (eds.), *Remarriage and Stepparenting: Current Research and Theory* (pp. 42–61). New York: Guilford.

——. 1995. "Dealing with dads: The changing role of fathers." In P. L. Chase-Lansdale, and J. Brooks-Gunn (eds.), *Escape from Poverty: What Makes a Difference for Children?* (pp. 189–210). Cambridge, England: Cambridge University Press.

——. 2001. "Managing to make it: Afterthoughts." *Journal of Family Issues 22*:150–162.

Furstenberg, F. F., Jr., and Cherlin, A. J. 1991. *Divided Families: What Happens to Children When Parents Part*. Cambridge, MA: Harvard University Press.

Furstenberg, F. F., Jr., and Spanier, G. B. 1984. *Recycling the Family: Remarriage After Divorce*. Beverly Hills: Sage.

Gable, S., Belsky, J., and Crnic, K. 1995. "Coparenting during the child's second year: A descriptive account." *Journal of Marriage and the Family 57*:609–616.

Gager, C. T., Cooney, T. M., and Call, K. T. 1999. "The effects of family characteristics and time use on teenagers' household labor." *Journal of Marriage and the Family 61*:982–994.

Gagnon, J. H. 1990. "Gender preferences in erotic relations: The Kinsey Scale in sexual scripts." In D. McWhirter, S. A. Sanders, and J. Reinisch (eds.), *Homosexuality/Heterosexuality: Concepts of Sexual Orientation* (pp. 177–07). Oxford: Oxford University Press.

Galinsky, E. 1981. *Between Generations: The Six Stages of Parenthood*. New York: Times Books.

Galinsky, E., Bond, J. T., and Friedman, D. E. 1993. *The Changing Workforce: Highlights of the National Study*. New York: Families and Work Institute.

Gallagher, S. K., and Gerstel, N. 2001. "Connections and constraints: The effects of children on caregiving." *Journal of Marriage and the Family 63*:265–275.

Galvin, K. M., and Brommel B. J. 1986. *Family Communication: Cohesion and Change* (2nd Ed.). Glenview, IL: Scott Foresman.

Ganong, L. H., and Coleman, M. 1994. "Adolescent stepchild-stepparent relationships: Changes over time." In K. Pasley and M. Ihinger-Tallman (eds.), *Stepparenting: Issues in Theory, Research, and Practice* (pp. 87–104). Westport, CT: Greenwood Press.

——. 1997. "How society views stepfamilies." In I. Levin, and M. B. Sussman (eds.), *Stepfamilies: History, Research, and Policy* (pp. 85–106). New York: The Haworth Press.

Gara, M. A., Rosenberg, S., and Herzog, E. P. 1996. "The abused child as parent." *Child Abuse and Neglect 20*:797–807.

Garasky, S., and Meyer, D. R. 1996. "Reconsidering the increase in father-only families." *Demography* 33:385–394.

Garbarino, J. 1983. "Social support networks: Rx for the helping professionals." In J. K. Whittaker, and J. Garbarino (eds.), *Social Support Networks: Informal Helping in the Human Services* (pp. 3–28). New York: Aldine.

———. 1995. *Raising Children in a Socially Toxic Environment*. San Francisco: Jossey-Bass.

Garbarino, J., and Benn, J. L. 1992. "The ecology of childbearing and child rearing." In J. Garbarino (ed.), *Children and Families in the Social Environment* (2nd ed.), (pp. 133–177). New York: Aldine de Gruyter.

Garbarino, J., and Ebata, A. 1983. "On the significance of ethnic and cultural differences in child maltreatment." *Journal of Marriage and the Family* 45:773–783.

Garbarino, J., Gaboury, M. T., and Plantz, M. C. 1992." Social policy, children, and their families." In J. Garbarino (ed.), *Children and Families in the Social Environment* (2nd ed.), (pp. 271–302). New York: Aldine.

Garbarino, J., Galambos, N. L., Plantz, M. C., and Kostelny, K. 1992. "The territory of childhood." In J. Garbarino (ed.), *Children and Families in the Social Environment* (2nd ed.), (pp. 201–229). New York: Aldine.

Garbarino, J. and Kostelny, K. 1995. "Parenting and public policy." In M. H. Bornstein (ed.), *Handbook of Parenting. Volume 3: Status and Social Conditions of Parenting*. Mahwah, NJ: Erlbaum.

Garbarino, J., and Long, F. N. 1992. "Developmental issues in the human services." In J. Garbarino (ed.), *Children and Families in the Social Environment* (2nd ed.), (pp. 231–270). New York: Aldine.

Garbarino, J., Schellenbach, C. J., and Sebes, J. 1986. *Troubled Youth, Troubled Families*. Hawthorne, New York: Aldine Publishing Company.

Garbarino, J., and Sherman, D. 1980. "High-risk neighborhoods and high-risk families: The human ecology of child maltreatment." *Child Development* 51:188–198.

Garfinkel, I., McLanahan, S. S., and Hanson, T. L. 1998. "A patchwork portrait of nonresident fathers." In I. Garfinkel, S. S. McLanahan, D. R. Meyer, and J. A. Seltzer (eds.), *Fathers Under Fire: The Revolution in Child Support Enforcement* (pp. 31–60). New York: Russell Sage Foundation.

Gecas, V. 1980. "Identity as a basis for a theory of commitment." Unpublished paper.

Gecas, V., and Burke, P. 1995. "Self and identity." In K. S. Cook, G. A. Fine, and J. S. House (eds.), *Sociological Perspectives on Social Psychology* (pp. 41–67). Boston: Allyn & Bacon.

Geiss, S., K., and O'Leary, K. D. 1981. "Therapist ratings of frequency and severity of marital problems: Implications for research." *Journal of Marital and Family Therapy* 7:515–520.

Gelles, R. J. 1993. "Alcohol and other drugs are associated with violence—they are not its cause." In R. J. Gelles, and D. R. Loseke (eds.), *Current Controversies on Family Violence* (pp. 182–196). Newbury Park, CA: Sage.

———. 1997. *Intimate Violence in Families* (3rd Ed.). Thousand Oaks, CA: Sage.

———. 1999. Family violence. In R. L. Hampton (ed.), *Family Violence: Prevention and Treatment* (pp. 1–31). Thousand Oaks, CA: Sage Publications.

Gelles, R. J., and Cornell, C. P. 1990. *Intimate Violence in Families* (2nd Ed.). Newbury Park, CA: Sage.

Gelles, R. J., and Loseke, D. R. (eds.), 1993. *Current Controversies on Family Violence* Newbury Park, CA: Sage.

Gerris, J. R. M., Dekovic, M., and Janssens, J. M. A. M. 1997. "The relationship between social class and childrearing behaviors: Parents' perspective taking and value orientations." *Journal of Marriage and the Family* 59:834–847.

Gershoff, E. T., Miller, P. C., and Holden, G. W. 1999. " Parenting influences from the pulpit: Religious affiliation as a determinant of parental corporal punishment." *Journal of Family Psychology* 13:307–320.

Gerson, K. 1985. *Hard Choices: How Women Decide About Work, Career, and Motherhood*. Berkeley: University of California Press.

Gerstel, N., and Gross, H. 1984. *Commuter Marriage*. New York: The Gilford Press.

Giancola, P., and Parker, A. 2001. "A six-year prospective study of pathways toward drug use in adolescent boys with and without a family history of a substance use disorder." *Journal of Studies on Alcohol* 62:166–178.

Gibbs, N. 2001. "What kids (really) need." *Time*, April 30, pp. 48–49.

Gibson, R. C. 1989. "Minority aging research: Opportunity and challenge." *Journal of Gerontology* 44:S2–S3.

Gilliland, T., Hawkins, A. J., Christiaens, G., and Carroll, J. S. 2002. *Marriage Moments: An Activity Guidebook*. Provo, UT: Family Studies Center, Brigham Young University.

Ginsberg, L. H. 1998. *Social Work in Rural Communities* (3rd Ed.). Washington, DC: Council of Social Work Education.

Glass, G., Bengtson, V. L., and Chorn Dunham, C. 1986. "Attitude similarity in three-generation families: Socialization, status inheritance, or reciprocal influence?" *American Sociological Review* 51:685–698.

Glenn, N. D. 1991. "The recent trend of marital success in the United States." *Journal of Marriage and the Family* 53:261–270.

Gold, D. T. 1989. "Sibling relationships in old age: A typology." *International Journal of Aging and Human Development* 28:37–51.

——. 1990. "Later-life sibling relationships: Does race affect typological distribution?" *Gerontologist* 30:741–748.

——. 1996. "Continuities and discontinuities in sibling relationships across the life span." In V. L. Bengtson (ed.), *Adulthood and Aging: Research on Continuities and Discontinuities* (pp. 228–243). New York: Springer.

Goldberg, W. A., and Easterbrooks, M. A. 1984. "Role of marital quality in toddler development." *Developmental Psychology* 20:504–514.

Goldscheider, F. K., and DaVanzo, J. 1985. "Living arrangements and the transition to adulthood." *Demography* 22:545–563.

Goldscheider, F. K., and Goldscheider, C. 1994. "Leaving and returning home in 20th-century America." *Population Bulletin* 49:1–34.

Goldscheider, F., and Waite, L. 1991. *New Families, No Families? The Transformation of the American Home.* Berkeley: University of California Press.

Gondolf, E. W., Fisher, E., and McFerron, J. R. 1991. "Racial differences among shelter residents: A comparison of Anglo, Black and Hispanic battered women." In R. L. Hampton (ed.), *Black Family Violence.* Lexington, MA: Lexington Books.

Goode, W. J. 1959. The theoretical importance of love. *American Sociological Review* 24:38–47.

——. 1971. "Force and violence in the family." *Journal of Marriage and the Family* 33:624–636.

Goodwin, M. P., and Roscoe, B. 1990. "Sibling violence and agonistic interactions among middle adolescents." *Adolescence* 25:451–467.

Gordon, C. 1968. "Self-conceptions: Configurations of content." In C. Gordon and K. J. Gergen (eds.), *The Self in Social Interaction* (pp. 115–136). New York: Wiley.

Gorey, K. M., Rice, R. W., and Brice, G. C. 1992. "The prevalence of elder care responsibilities among the work force population: Response bias among a group of cross-sectional surveys." *Research on Aging* 14:399–418.

Gormly, A. V., Gormly, J. B., and Weiss, H. 1987. "Motivations for parenthood among young adult college students." *Sex Roles* 16:31–39.

Gottlieb, B. 1980. "The role of individual and social support in preventing child maltreatment." In J. Garbarino, S. H. Stocking, and Associates, (eds.), *Protecting Children From Abuse and Neglect* (pp. 37–60). San Francisco: Jossey-Bass.

Gottman, J. M. 1994. *Why Marriages Succeed or Fail.* New York: Simon and Schuster.

——. 1999. *The Seven Principles for Making Marriage Work.* New York: Crown.

Gottman, J. M., Coan, J., Carrere, S., and Swanson, C. 1998. "Predicting marital happiness and stability from newlywed interactions." *Journal of Marriage and the Family* 60:5–22.

Gottman, J. M., Katz, L. F., and Hooven, C. 1996. "Parental meta-emotion philosophy and the emotional life of families: Theoretical models and preliminary data." *Journal of Family Psychology* 10:243–268.

Gottman, J., and Levenson, R. 1988. "The social psychophysiology of marriage." In P. Noller, and M. A. Fitzpatrick (eds.), *Perspectives on Marital Interaction* (pp. 75–102). Hillsdale, NJ: Erlbaum.

Greene, A. L., and Boxer, A. M. 1986. "Daughters and sons as young adults: Restructuring the ties that bind." In N. Datan, A. L. Greene, and H. W. Reese (eds.), *Life-Span Developmental Psychology: Intergenerational Relations* (pp. 125–149). Hillsdale, NJ: Erlbaum.

Greer, S. 1960. "The social structure and political process of suburbia." *American Sociological Review* 25:514–526.

Greven, P. J., Jr. 1983. "Family structure in seventeenth-century Andover, Massachusetts." In M. Gordon (ed.), *The American Family in Social-historical Perspective* (3rd Ed.), (pp. 77–99). New York: St. Martins Press.

Grief, G. L., and DeMaris, A. 1995. "Single fathers with custody." In W. Marsiglio (ed.), *Fatherhood: Contemporary Theory, Research, and Social Policy* (pp. 193–210). Thousand Oaks, CA: Sage.

Griffin, L. W. 1993. "Adult day care and adult protective services." *Journal of Gerontological Social Work* 20:115–133.

——. 1999. "Understanding elder abuse." In R. L. Hampton (ed.), *Family Violence* (2nd Ed.), (pp. 260–287). Thousand Oaks, CA: Sage.

Griffin, L. W., Williams, O. J., and Reed, J. G. 1998. "Abuse of African American elders." In R. K. Bergen (ed.), *Issues in Intimate Violence* (pp. 267–284). Thousand Oaks, CA: Sage.

Grote, N. K., and Frieze, I. H. 1998. "Remembrance of things past: Perceptions of marital love from its beginnings to the present." *Journal of Social and Personal Relationships* 15:91–109.

Grotevant, H. D., and Cooper, C. R. 1982. "Identity formation and role-taking skill in adolescence: An investigation of family structure and family process antecedents." Final Report prepared for the National Institute of Child Health and Human Development, University of Texas at Austin.

Grotevant, H. D., McRoy, R. G., Elde, C. L., and Fravel, D. L. 1994. "Adoptive family system dynamics: Variations by level of openness in the adoption." *Family Process* 33:125–146.

Grzywacz, J. G., and Marks, N. F. 2000. "Family, work, work-family spillover, and problem drinking during midlife." *Journal of Marriage and the Family* 62:336–348.

Guisinger, S., Cowan, P. A., and Schuldberg, D. 1989. "Changing parent and spouse relations in the first years of remarriage of divorced fathers." *Journal of Marriage and the Family* 51:445–456.

Gupta, S. 1999. "The effects of transitions in marital status on men's performance of housework." *Journal of Marriage and the Family* 61:700–711.

Gurin, G., Veroff, J., and Feld, S. 1960. *Americans View Their Mental Health: A Nationwide Interview Survey.* New York: Basic Books.

Gusfield, J. 1975. *Community: A Critical Response.* Oxford: Blackwell.

Guthrie, D. M., and Noller, P. 1988. "Spouses' perceptions of one another in emotional situations." In P. Noller and J. A. Fitzpatrick (eds.), *Perspectives on Marital Interaction* (pp. 153–181). Clevedon, England: Multilingual Matters.

Haas, S. M., and Stafford, L. 1998. "An initial examination of maintenance behaviors in gay and lesbian relationships." *Journal of Social and Personal Relationships* 15:846–855.

Hackstaff, K. B. 1999. *Marriage in a Culture of Divorce.* Philadelphia: Temple University Press.

Hagestad, G. O. 1979. "Patterns of communication and influence between grandparents and grandchildren in a changing society." Paper presented at the World Congress of Sociology, Uppsala, Sweden.

Hagestad, G. O., and Burton, L. M. 1986. "Grandparenthood: Life context and family development." *American Behavioral Scientist* 29:471–484.

Hagestad, G. O., and Neugarten, B. L. 1985. "Age and the life course." In E. Shanas and R. Binstock (eds.), *Handbook of Aging and the Social Sciences* (2nd ed.), (pp. 36–61). New York: Van Nostrand and Reinhold.

Hahlweg, K., Revenstorf, D., and Schindler, L. (1984). Effects of behavioral marital therapy on couples' communication and problem-solving skills. *Journal of Consulting & Clinical Psychology* 52:553–566.

Haine, R. A., Sandler, I. N., Wolchik, S. A., Tein, J., and Dawson-McClure, S. R. 2003. "Changing the legacy of divorce: Evidence from prevention programs and future directions." *Family Relations* 52:397–405.

Halle, D. 1984. *America's Working Man: Work, Home, and Politics Among Blue-collar Property Owners.* Chicago: The University of Chicago Press.

Hamby, S. L., and Sugarman, D. B. 1999. "Acts of psychological aggression against a partner and their relation to physical assault and gender." *Journal of Marriage and the Family* 61:959–970.

Hamer, J., and Marchioro, K. 2002. "Becoming custodial dads: Exploring parenting among low-income and working-class African American fathers." *Journal of Marriage and Family* 64:116–129.

Hampton, R. L., Gelles, R. J., and Harrop, J. 1991. "Is violence in black families increasing? A comparison of 1975 and 1985 national survey rates." In R. L. Hampton (ed.), *Black Family Violence* (pp. 1–18). Lexington, MA: Lexington Books.

Hand, S. I. 1991. "The lesbian parenting couple." Unpublished doctoral dissertation, Professional School of Psychology, San Francisco.

Hanson, B., and Maroney, T. 1999. "HIV and same-sex domestic violence." In B. Leventhall, and S. E. Lundy (eds.), *Same-Sex Domestic Violence* (pp. 97–110). Thousand Oaks, CA: Sage.

Hanson, T. L., McLanahan, S. S., and Thomson, E. 1998. "Windows on divorce: Before and after." *Social Science Research* 27:329–349.

Hardin, B. J. and Koblinsky, S. A. 1999. Double exposure: Children affected by family and community violence. In R. L. Hampton, (ed.), *Family Violence* (2nd Ed.), (pp. 66–102). Thousand Oaks, CA: Sage.

Hardy, M. A., and Shuey, K. 2000. "Retirement." In E. F. Borgatta and R. J. V. Montgomery (eds.), *Encyclopedia of Sociology* (2nd Ed.), (pp. 2401–2410). New York: Macmillan References USA.

Harkins, E. B. 1978. "Effects of empty nest transition on self-report of psychological and physical well-being." *Journal of Marriage and the Family* 40:549–556.

Harrington , D., and Dubowitz, H. 1999. "Preventing child maltreatment." In R. L. Hampton (ed.), *Family Violence: Prevention and Treatment* (2nd Ed.), (pp. 122–147). Thousand Oaks, CA: Sage.

Harrison, A. O., Wilson, M. N., Pine, C. J., Chan, S. Q., and Buriel, R. 1990. "Family ecologies of ethnic minority children." *Child Development* 61:347–362.

Hatch, L. R., and Bulcroft, K. 1992. "Contact with friends in later life: Disentangling the effects of gender and marital status." *Journal of Marriage & the Family* 54:222–232.

Hatfield, E. 1988. "Passionate and companionate love." In R. J. Sternberg and M. L. Barnes (eds.), *The Psychology of Love* (pp. 191–217). New Haven, CT: Yale University Press.

Hatfield, E., and Sprecher, S. 1986. *Mirror, Mirror: The Importance of Looks in Everyday Life.* New York: State University of New York.

Hatfield, E., and Walster, G. W. 1978. *A New Look at Love.* Lantham, MA: University Press of America.

Hausman, A., Spivak, H., and Prothrow-Stith, D. (1992). "Patterns of teen exposure to a community-based violence prevention project." *Journal of Adolescent Health 13*:668–675.

Hayes, H. R., and Emshoff, J. G. 1993. "Substance abuse and family violence." In R. L. Hampton, T. P. Gullota, G. R. Adams, E. H. Potter III, and R. P. Weissberg (eds.), *Family Violence: Prevention and Treatment* (pp. 281–310). Newbury Park, CA: Sage.

Hays, J. C., Landerman, L. R., George, L. K., Flint, E. P., Koenig, H. G., Land, K. C., and Blazer, D. G. 1998. "Social correlates of the dimensions of depression in the elderly." *Journal of Gerontology: Psychological Sciences 53B*:32–39.

Hays, S. 2003. *Flat Broke With Children: Women in the Age of Welfare Reform.* New York: Oxford University Press.

Hayward, M. D., Hardy, M. A., and Grady, W. 1989. "Labor force withdrawal patterns among older men in the United States." *Social Science Quarterly 70*:425–448.

Heaton, T. B. 1991. "Time-related determinants of marital dissolution." *Journal of Marriage and the Family 53*:285–295.

Henderson, D. A., Tickamyer, A. R., White, J. A., and Tadlock, B. L. 2002. "Welfare recipients' views of the success of welfare reform in rural Appalachia." *Poverty Research News 6*:9–11.

Henderson, S. H., Hetherington, E. M., Mekos, D., and Riess, D. 1996. "Stress, parenting, and adolescent psychopathology in nondivorced and stepfamilies: A within-family perspective." In E. M. Hetherington, and E. A. Blechman (eds.), *Stress, Coping, and Resiliency in Children and Families* (pp. 39–66). Mahwah, NJ: Erlbaum.

Hendrick, S. S., and Hendrick, C. 1993. "Lovers as friends." *Journal of Social and Personal Relationships 10*:459–466.

Hendrick, S. S., Hendrick, C., and Adler, N. L. 1988. "Romantic relationships: Love, satisfaction, and staying together." *Journal of Personality and Social Psychology 54*:980–988.

Henk, J. K. 2003. *Family Leave: Can Public and Private Policies Be Supportive of America's Families?* Columbia, MO: Center for Family Policy and Research.

Henry, C. S., and Ceglian, C. P. 1989. *Stepgrandmothers and Grandmothers of Stepfamilies: Role Behaviors, Role Meanings and Grandmothering Styles* (ERIC Document Reproduction Service No. ED 311 383).

Hetherington, E. M. 1988. "Parents, children, and siblings: Six years after divorce." In R. A. Hinde, and J. Stevenson-Hinde (eds.), *Relationships within Families: Mutual Influences* (pp. 311–331). New York: Oxford University Press.

——. 2003. "Intimate pathways: Changing patterns in close personal relationships across time." *Family Relations 52*:318–331.

Hetherington, E. M., and Jodl, K. M. 1994. "Stepfamilies as settings for child development." In A. Booth and J. Dunns (eds.), *Stepfathers: Who Benefits? Who Does Not?* Hillsdale, NJ: Lawrence Erlbaum Associates.

Hetherington, E. M., and Kelly, J. 2002. *For Better or Worse: Divorce Reconsidered.* New York: W. W. Norton.

Hetherington, E. M., and Stanley-Hagan, M. M. 1999. "The adjustment of children with divorced parents: A risk and resiliency perspective." *Journal of Child Psychology and Psychiatry 40*:129–140.

——. 2000. "Diversity among stepfamilies." In D. H. Demo, K. R. Allen, and M. A. Fine (eds.), *Handbook of Family Diversity* (pp. 173–196). New York: Oxford University Press.

Hiedemann, B., Suhomlinova, O., and O'Rand, A. M. 1998. "Economic independence, economic status, and empty nest in midlife marital disruption." *Journal of Marriage and the Family 60*:219–231.

Hill, C. R., and Stafford, F. P. 1980. "Parental care of children: Time diary estimates of quantity, predictability, and variety." *Journal of Human Resources 15*:219–239.

Hill, C. T., Rubin, Z., and Peplau, L. A. 1976. "Breakups before marriage: The end of 103 affairs." *Journal of Social Issues 32*:147–168.

Hill, E. J., Hawkins, A. J., Ferris, M., and Weitzman, M. 2001. "Finding an extra day a week: The positive influence of perceived job flexibility of work and family life balance." *Family Relations 50*:49–58.

Hill, E. J., Hawkins, A. J., and Miller, B. C. 1996. "Work and family in the virtual office: Perceived influences of mobile telework." *Family Relations 45*:293–301.

Hill, M. S., and Yeung, W. J. 1997. "How has the changing structure of opportunities affected transitions to adulthood?" Paper presented at the Penn State Symposium, "Transitions to Adulthood in a Changing Economy." October, University Park, PA.

Himes, C. L. 1994. "Parental caregiving by adult women: A demographic perspective." *Research on Aging 16*:191–211.

Hines, A. M. 1997. "Divorce-related transitions, adolescent development, and the role of the parent-child relationship: A review of the literature." *Journal of Marriage and the Family 59*:375–388.

Hochschild, A. 1989. *The Second Shift*. New York: Avon Press.

——. 1997. *Time Bind*. New York: Henry Holt.

Hodson, R., and Sullivan, T. A. 1990. *The Social Organization of Work*. Belmont, CA: Wadsworth.

Hofferth, S. 2003. "Race/ethnic differences in father involvement in two-parent families: Culture, context, or economy?" *Journal of Family Issues* 24:185–216.

Hogan, D. P., and Astone, N. M. 1986. "The transition to adulthood." *Annual Review of Sociology* 12:109–130.

Hogan, D. P., Eggebeen, D. J., and Clogg, C. C. 1993. "The structure of intergenerational exchanges in American families." *American Journal of Sociology* 98:1428–1458.

Holahan, C. J., Valentiner, D. P., and Moos, R. H. 1994. "Parental support and psychological adjustment during the transition to young adulthood in a college sample." *Journal of Family Psychology* 8:215–223.

Holman, T. 1981. "The influence of community involvement on marital quality." *Journal of Marriage and the Family* 43:143–149.

Holmbeck, G. N., Paikoff, R. L., and Brooks-Gunn, J. 1995. "Parenting adolescents." In H. Bornstein (ed.), *Handbook of Parenting. Volume I: Children and Parenting* (pp. 91–118). Mahwah, NJ: Erlbaum.

Holtzworth-Munroe, A., and Stuart, G. L. 1994. "Typologies of male batterers: Three subtypes and the differences among them." *Psychological Bulletin* 116:476–497.

Homes for the Homeless. 1998. *Ten Cities 1997–1998: A Snapshot of Family Homelessness Across America*. Available from Homes for the Homeless and the Institute for Children and Poverty, 36 Cooper Square, 6th Floor, New York, NY 10003.

Hong, L. K., and Duff, R. W. 1994. "Widows in retirement communities: The social context of subjective well-being." *Gerontologist* 34:347–352.

Hops, H., Sherman, L., and Biglan, A. 1990. "Maternal depression, marital discord and children's behavior: A developmental perspective." In G. R. Patterson (ed.), *Depression and Aggression in Family Interaction* (pp. 185–208). Hillsdale, NJ: Erlbaum.

Horowitz, K. Weine, S., and Jekel, J. 1995. "PTSD symptoms in urban adolescent girls: Compounded community trauma." *Journal of the American Academy of Child and Adolescent Psychiatry* 34:1353–1361.

Houseknecht, S. K., Vaughan, S., and Macke, A. S. 1984. "Marital disruption among professional women: Timing of career and family events." *Social Problems* 31:273–284.

Howard, J. A., Blumstein, P., and Schwartz, P. 1986. "Sex, power, and influence tactics in intimate relationships." *Journal of Personality and Social Psychology* 51:102–109.

Howard, J., and Hollander, J. 1996. *Gendered Situations, Gendered Selves*. Thousand Oaks, CA: Sage.

Howard, P. E. N., Raine, L., and Jones, S. 2001. "Days and nights on the Internet: The impact of a diffusing technology." *American Behavioral Scientist* 45:383–404.

Howes, P., and Markman, H. J. 1989. "Marital quality and child functioning: A longitudinal investigation." *Child Development*, 60:1044–1051.

Hu, Y., and Goldman, N. 1990. "Mortality differentials by marital status: An international comparison." *Demography* 27:233–250.

Hubbard, A. S. E. 2001. "Conflict between relationally uncertain romantic partners: The influence of relational responsiveness and empathy." *Communication Monographs* 68:400–414.

Hughes, P., and Lieberman, S. 1990. "Troubled parents: Vulnerability and stress in childhood cancer." *British Journal of Medical Psychology* 63:53–64.

Hunter, A. G., and Ensminger, M. E. 1992. "Diversity and fluidity in children's living arrangements: Family transitions in an urban Afro-American community." *Journal of Marriage and the Family* 54:418–426.

Hunter, M. 1999. "Work, work, work!: It's taking over our lives," *Modern Maturity*, May-June, pp. 36–41.

Hurd, E. P., Moore, C., and Rogers, R. 1995. "Quiet success: Parenting strengths among African Americans." *Families in Society: The Journal of Contemporary Human Services* 76:434–443.

Hurwitz, S. 1994. *Working Together Against Homelessness*. New York: The Rosen Publishing Group.

Huston, T. L. 1983. "Power." In H. H. Kelley, E. Berscheid, A. Christenson, J. H. Harvey, T. L. Huston, G. Levinger, E. McClintock, L. A. Peplau, and D. R. Peterson (eds.), *Relationships* (pp. 169–219). New York: Freeman.

——. 2000. "The social ecology of marriage and other intimate unions." *Journal of Marriage and the Family* 62:298–320.

Huston, T. L., and Houts, R. M. 1998. "The psychological infrastructure of courtship and marriage: The role of personality and compatibility in romantic relationships." In T. N. Bradbury (ed.), *The Developmental Course of Marital Dysfunction* (pp. 114–151). Cambridge: Cambridge University Press.

Huston, T. L., McHale, S. M., and Crouter, A. C. 1986. "When the honeymoon's over: Changes in the marriage relationship over the first year." In R. Gilmore, and S. Duck (eds.), *The Emerging Field of Personal Relationships* (pp. 109–132). Hillsdale, NJ: Erlbaum.

Ihinger-Tallman, M. 1986. "Stepsibling relationships." Unpublished paper.

Ihinger-Tallman, M., and Pasley, B. K. 1987. *Remarriage*. Newbury Park, CA: Sage.

Independent Sector National Survey. 1999. Giving and volunteering in the United States: Findings from a national survey. <http://www.indepsec.org/GandV/s_demo.htm>.

Inman-Amos, J., Hendrick, S. S., and Hendrick, C. 1994. "Love attitudes: Similarities between parents and between parents and children." *Family Relations* 43:456–461.

International Labor Organization. 2003. *Key Indicators of the Labor Market* (3rd Ed.).

Ishii-Kuntz, M., and Coltrane, S. 1992. "Remarriage, stepparenting, and household labor." *Journal of Family Issues* 13:215–233.

James, W. 1892/1968. "The self." In C. Gorden and K. J. Gergen (eds.), *The Self in Social Interaction* (pp. 41–49). New York: John Wiley and Sons.

Janus, M. D., McCormack, A., Burgess, A., and Hartman, C. 1987. *Adolescent Runaways*. Lexington, MA: Lexington Books.

Jarrett, R. L. 1994. "Living poor: Family life among single parent, African American women." *Social Problems* 41:30–49.

Jarrett, R. L. 1995. "Growing up poor: The family experience of socially mobile youth in low income African-American neighborhoods." *Journal of Adolescent Research* 10:111–135.

Jencks, C., and Mayer, S. E. 1990. "The social consequences of growing up in a poor neighborhood." In E. L. Lynn, Jr., and G. H. M. McGeary (eds.), *Inner-City Poverty in the United States* (pp. 111–186). Washington, DC: National Academy Press.

Jendrek, M. P. 1994. "Grandparents who parent their grandchildren: Circumstances and decisions." *Gerontologist* 34:206–216.

Jenkins, J. 1992. "Sibling relationships in disharmonious homes: Potential difficulties and protective effects." In F. Boer, and J. Dunn (eds.), *Children's Sibling Relationships* (pp. 125–138). Hillsdale, NJ: Erlbaum.

Johnson, C. J. 1985. "The impact of illness on late-life marriages." *Journal of Marriage and the Family* 47:165–172.

Johnson, C. L. 1989. "In-law relationships in the American kinship system: The impact of divorce and remarriage." *American Ethnologist* 16:87–99.

Johnson, D. R., and Wu, J. 2002. "An empirical test of crisis, social selection, and role explanations of the relationship between marital disruption and psychological distress: A pooled time-series analysis of four-wave panel data." *Journal of Marriage and Family* 64:211–224.

Johnson, M. P. 1991. "Commitment to personal relationships." In W. H. Jones and D. W. Perlman (eds.), *Advances in Personal Relationships* 3:117–143. London: Jessica Kingsley.

——. 1995. "Patriarchal terrorism and common couple violence: Two forms of violence against women." *Journal of Marriage and the Family* 57:283–294.

——. 1999. "Personal, moral, and structural commitment to relationships." In J. M. Adams, and W. H. Jones (eds.), *Handbook of Interpersonal Commitment and Relationship Stability*. New York: Kluwer Academin/Plenum Publishers.

Johnson, M. P., and Ferarro, K. J. 2000. "Research on domestic violence in the 1990s: Making distinctions." *Journal of Marriage and the Family* 62:948–963.

Johnson, M. P., Caughlin, J. P., and Huston, T. L. 1999. "The tripartite nature of marital commitment: Personal, moral, and structural reasons to stay married." *Journal of Marriage and the Family* 61:160–177.

Jones Hardin, B., and Koblinsky, S. A. 1999. "Double exposure: Children affected by family and community violence." In R. L. Hampton (ed.), *Family Violence: Prevention and Treatment* (2nd Ed.), (pp. 66–102). Thousand Oaks, CA: Sage.

Jones, D. J., Forehand, R., Brody, G., and Armistead, L. 2002. "Psychosocial adjustment of African American children in single-mother families: A test of three risk factors." *Journal of Marriage and Family* 64:105–115.

Josselson, R. 1988. "The embedded self: I and thou revisited." In D. K. Lapsley and F. C. Power (ed.), *Self, Ego, and Identity: Integrative Approaches* (pp. 91–106). New York: Springer-Verlag.

Joung, I. M. A., Stronks, K., Van De Mheen, H., Van Poppel, F. W. A., van Der Meer, J. B. W., and Machenback, J. P. 1997. "The contribution of intermediate factors to marital status differences in self-reported health." *Journal of Marriage and the Family* 59:476–490.

Kach, J. A., and McGhee, P. E. 1982. "Adjustment in early parenthood: The role of accuracy of preparenthood experiences." *Journal of Family Issues* 3:375–388.

Kahana, E., and Kahana, B. 1971. "Theoretical and research perspectives on grandparenthood." *Aging and Human Development* 10:229–310.

Kahn, A. J. 1979. *Social Policy and Social Services* (2nd Ed.). New York: Random House.

Kamerman, S. B., and Kahn, A. J. 1995. *Starting Right: How America Neglects Its Youngest Children and What We Can Do About It*. New York: Oxford University Press.

——. 2001. "Child and family policies in an era of social policy retrenchment and restructuring." In T. Smeeding, and K. Vleminckx (eds.), *Child Well-Being, Child Poverty and Child Policy in Modern Nations* (pp. 501–525). Bristol, UK: Policy Press.

Karney, B. R., and Bradbury, T. N. 1995. "The longitudinal course of marital quality and stability: A review of theory, method, and research." *Psychological Bulletin 118*:3–34.

——. 1997. "Neuroticism, marital interaction, and the trajectory of marital satisfaction." *Journal of Personality and Social Psychology 72*:1075–1092.

Kaufman, G. 1999. "The portrayal of men's family roles in television commercials." *Sex Roles 41*:439–458.

Kaufman, L. 2003. "Millions have left welfare, but are they better off? Yes, no, and maybe." *New York Times*, p. A16, October 20.

Kaufman-Kantor, G., Jasinski, J., and Aldarondod, E. 1994. "Sociocultural status and incidence of marital violence in Hispanic families." *Violence and Victims 9*:207–222.

Kayser, K. 1993. *When Love Dies: The Process of Marital Disaffection.* New York: Guilford Press.

Kee, A. M. 2000. "The force of work. *Statistical Abstract of the United States*, 2000 (120th Ed.). Washington, DC: U.S. Bureau of the Census. Accessed at <http://www.poppolitics.com/articles/2000-10-12-laborstats.shtml>.

Kellner, D. 1990. *Television and the Crisis of Democracy.* Boulder, CO: Westview.

Kelly, J. B. 1996. "A decade of divorce mediation research: Some answers and questions." *Family and Conciliation Courts Review 34*:373–385.

Kelly, J. B., and Emery, R. E. 2003. "Children's adjustment following divorce: Risk and resilience perspectives." *Family Relations 52*:352–362.

Kendall-Tackett, K. A. 2003. "Sexual abuse." In J. J. Ponzetti, Jr. (ed.), *International Encyclopedia of Marriage and Family* (2nd Ed.), (pp. 227–230). New York: Macmillan Reference, USA.

Kendall-Tackett, K. A., and Marshall, R. 1998. "Sexual victimization of children: Incest and child sexual abuse." In R. K. Bergen (ed.), *Issues in Intimate Violence* (pp. 47–63). Newbury Park, CA: Sage.

Kendall-Tackett, K. A., Williams, L. M., and Finkelhor, D. 1993. "The effects of sexual abuse on children: A review and synthesis of recent empirical studies." *Psychological Bulletin 113*:164–180.

Kenney, M. E. 1987. "The extent and function of parental attachment among first-year college students." *Journal of Youth and Adolescence 16*:17–29.

Kerckhoff, A. C., and Davis, K. E. 1962. "Value consensus and need complementarity in mate selection." *American Sociological Review 27*:295–303.

Kerig, P. K., Cowan, P. A., and Cowan, C. P. 1993. "Marital quality and gender differences in parent-child interaction." *Developmental Psychology 29*:931–939.

Kiernan, K. E. 1992. "The impact of family disruption in childhood on transitions made in young adult life." *Population Studies 46*:213–224.

King, V., and Heard, H. E. 1999. "Nonresident father visitation, parental conflict, and mother's satisfaction: What's best for child well-being." *Journal of Marriage and the Family 61*:385–396.

Kinney, J. M., and Stephens, M. A. 1989. "Hassles and uplifts of giving care to a family member with dementia." *Gerontologist 29*:402–408.

Kinsella, K. 1995. "Aging and the family: Present and future demographic issues." In R. Blieszner and V. H. Bedford (eds.), *Handbook of Aging and the Family* (pp. 32–56). Westport, CT: Greenwood.

Kinsey, A. C., Pomeroy, W. B., and Martin, C. E. 1948. *Sexual Behavior in the Human Male.* Philadelphia: W. B. Saunders.

Kirkwood, C. 1993. *Leaving Abusive Partners.* Newbury Park, CA: Sage.

Kitson, G. C. 1992. *Portrait of Divorce: Adjustment to Marital Breakdown.* New York: Guilford Press.

Kitson, G. C., and Langlie, J. K. 1984. "Couples who file for divorce but change their minds." *American Journal of Orthopsychiatry 54*:469–489.

Kleban, M. H., Brody, E. M., Schoonover, C. B., and Hoffman, C. 1989. "Family help to the elderly: Perceptions of sons-in-law regarding parent care." *Journal of Marriage and the Family 51*:303–312.

Klein, M. 1995. *The American Street Gang.* New York: Oxford University Press.

Klinetob, N. A., and Smith, D. A. 1996. "Demand-withdraw communication in marital interaction: Tests of interspousal contingency and gender role hypothesis." *Journal of Marriage and the Family 58*:945–957.

Knitzer, J., and Page, S. 1998. *Map and Track: State Initiatives for Young Children and Families* (1998 Ed.). New York: Columbia University School of Public Health, National Center for Children in Poverty.

Knox, D., and Schach, C. 2002. *Choices in Relationships: An Introduction to Marriage and the Family* (7th Ed.). Belmont, CA: Wadsworth.

Knox, D., Gibson, L., Zusman, M. E., and Gallmeier, C. 1997. "Why college students end relationships." *College Student Journal 31*:449–452.

Knudson-Martin, C., and Mahoney, A. R. 1998. "Language and processes in the construction of equality in new marriages." *Family Relations 47*:81–91.

Kohl, J. 1993. "School-based child sexual abuse prevention program." *Journal of Family Violence* 8:137–150.

Kohn, M. L. 1969. *Class and Conformity: A Study in Values*. Homewood, IL: Dorsey.

——. 1976. "Social class and parental values: Another confirmation of the relationship." *American Sociological Review* 41:538–545.

——. 1977. *Class and Conformity: A Study in Values* (2nd Ed.). Chicago: The University of Chicago Press.

Kohn, M. L., and Schooler, C. 1983. *Work and Personality: An Inquiry into the Impact of Social Stratification*. Norwood, NJ: Ablex.

Kohn, M. L., Slomczynski, K. M. and Schoenbach, C. 1986. "Social stratification and the transmission of values in the family: A cross-national assessment." *Sociological Forum I*:73–102.

Kollock, P., Blumstein, P., and Schwartz, P. 1985. "Sex and power in interaction: Conversational privileges and duties." *American Sociological Review* 50:34–46.

Komarovsky, M. 1940. *The Unemployed Man and His Family*. New York: Dryden.

——. 1962. *Blue-Collar Marriage*. New York: Random House.

Kowal, A., and Kramer, L. 1997. "Children's understanding of parental differential treatment." *Child Development* 68:113–126.

Kozuch, P., and Cooney, T. M. 1995. "Young adults' attitudes toward marriage and divorce: The effects of recent parental divorce, and family and parental conflict." *Journal of Divorce and Remarriage* 23:45–62.

Kranichfeld, M. 1987. "Rethinking family power." *Journal of Family Issues* 8:42–56.

Kraut, R., Patterson, M., Lundmark, V., Kiesler, S., Mukophadhyay, T., and Scherlis, W. 1998. "Internet paradox: A social technology that reduces social involvement and psychological well-being?" *American Psychologist* 53:1017–1031.

Kurdek, L. A. 1993a. "Predicting marital dissolution: A 5-year prospective longitudinal study of newlywed couples." *Journal of Personality and Social Psychology* 64:221–242.

——. 1993b. "The allocation of household labor in gay, lesbian, and heterosexual married couples." *Journal of Social Issues* 49:127–139.

——. 1994a. "Areas of conflict for gay, lesbian, and heterosexual couples: What couples argue about influences relationship satisfaction." *Journal of Marriage and the Family* 56:923–934.

——. 1994b. "Conflict resolution styles in gay, lesbian, heterosexual nonparent and heterosexual parent couples." *Journal of Marriage and the Family* 56: 705–722.

——. 1998a. "Developmental changes in marital satisfaction: A 6-year prospective longitudinal study of newlywed couples." In T. N. Bradbury (ed.), *The Developmental Course of Marital Dysfunction* (pp. 180–204). Cambridge: Cambridge University Press.

——. 1998b. "Relationship outcomes and their predictors: Longitudinal evidence from heterosexual married, gay cohabiting, and lesbian cohabiting couples." *Journal of Marriage and the Family* 60:553–568.

Kurdek, L. A., and Fine, M. A. 1993. "The relation between family structure and young adolescents' appraisals of family climate and parenting behavior." *Journal of Family Issues* 14:279–290.

Lackey, C. 2003. "Violent family heritage, the transition to adulthood, and later partner violence." *Journal of Family Issues* 24:74–98.

Larson, R., and Gillman, S. 1999. "Transmission of emotions in the daily interactions of single-mother families." *Journal of Marriage and the Family* 61:21–37.

Larson, R., and Richards, M. H. 1991. "Daily companionship in late childhood and early adolescence: Changing developmental contexts." *Child Development* 62:284–300.

——. 1994. *Divergent Realities: The Emotional Lives of Mothers, Fathers and Adolescents*. New York: Basic Books.

Lauer, R. H., and Lauer, J. C. 1986. "Factors in long-term marriages." *Journal of Family Issues* 7:382–390.

Lawton, L., Silverstein, M., and Bengtson, V. 1994. "Affection, social contact, and geographic distance between adult children and their parents." *Journal of Marriage & the Family* 56:57–68.

Lawton, M. P., Rajagopal, D., Brody, E., and Kleban, M. H. 1992. "The dynamics of caregiving for a demented elder among black and white families." *Journal of Gerontology: Social Sciences* 47:S156–S164.

Lee, B. A. 2001. "Taking neighborhoods seriously." In A. Booth and A. C. Crouter (eds.), *Does It Take a Village: Community Effects on Children, Adolescents, and Families* (pp. 31–40). Mahwah, NJ: Erlbaum.

Lee, B. A., and Campbell, K. E. 1998. "Neighborhood networks of black and white Americans." In B. Wellman (ed.), *Networks in the Global Village*. Boulder, CO: Westview.

Lee, G. R., DeMaris, A., Bavin, S., and Sullivan, R. 2001. "Gender differences in the depressive effect of widowhood in later life." *Journal of Gerontology: Social Sciences* 56B:S56–S61.

Lee, G. R., and Shehan, C. L. 1989. "Retirement and marital satisfaction." *Journal of Gerontology* 44:S226–S230.

Lee, G. R., Willetts, M. C., and Seccombe, K. 1998. "Widowhood and depression." *Research on Aging* 20(5):611–630.

Lee, J. A. 1973. *The Colors of Love: An Exploration of the Ways of Loving*. Don Mills, Ontario: New Press.

Lee, T. R., Mancini, J. A., and Maxwell, J. W. 1990. "Sibling relationships in adulthood: Contact patterns and motivations." *Journal of Marriage and the Family* 52:431–440.

Lenzner, R., and McCormack, S. 1998. "Obtaining immortality via the family office." *Forbes 400*, October 12, 62–64.

Lerner, J. V. 1993. "The influence of child temperamental characteristics on parent behaviors." In T. Luster, and L. Okagaki (eds.), *Parenting: An Ecological Perspective* (pp. 101–120). Hillsdale, NJ: Erlbaum.

Levenson, R. W., Carstensen, L. L., and Gottman, J. M. 1998. "Long-term marriage: Age, gender, and satisfaction." *Psychology and Aging* 8:301–313.

Leventhal, B., and Lundy, S. E. 1999. *Same-Sex Domestic Violence: Strategies for Change.* Thousand Oaks, CA: Sage.

Levinger, G. 1965. "Marital cohesiveness and dissolution: An integrative review." *Journal of Marriage and the Family* 27:19–28.

———. 1976. "A social psychological perspective on marital dissolution." *Journal of Social Issues* 32:21–47.

Levitt, M. J., Guacci-Franco, N., and Levitt, J. L. 1993. "Convoys of social support in childhood and early adolescence: Structure and function." *Developmental Psychology* 29:811–818.

Lewin, K. 1948. "The background of conflict in marriage." In G. W. Lewin (ed.), *Resolving Social Conflicts: Selected Papers on Group Dynamics* (pp. 84–102). New York: Harper.

Lewin, T. 2000. "Study finds welfare changes lead a million into child care." *New York Times* on the Web, February 4.

Lewis, R. A. 1973. "Social reaction and the formation of dyads: An interactionist approach to mate selection." *Sociometry* 36:409–418.

———. 1981. "Patterns of strength of American Indian families." In J. Redhorse, A. Shattuck, and F. Hoffman, (eds.), *The American Indian Family: Strengths and Stresses* (pp. 101–106). Isleta, NM: American Indian Social Research and Development Associates.

Lichter, D. T., McLaughlin, D. K., Kephart, G., and Landry, D. J. 1992. "Race and the retreat from marriage: A shortage of marriageable men?" *American Sociological Review* 57:781–799.

Lillard, L. A., and Waite, L. J. 1995. "Til death do us part: Marital disruption and mortality." *American Journal of Sociology* 100:1131–1156.

Lindsey, E. W. 1998. "The impact of homelessness and shelter life on family relationships." *Family Relations* 47:243–252.

Lindsey, L. L. 1990. *Gender Roles: A Sociological Perspective.* Englewood Cliffs, NJ: Prentice-Hall.

Liss, L. 1987. "Families and the law." In M. B. Sussman and S. Steinmetz (eds.), *Handbook of Marriage and the Family* (pp. 767–793). New York: Plenum.

Livingstone, S. 2002. *Young People and the New Media.* Thousand Oaks, CA: Sage.

Lloyd, S. A., and Emery, B. C. 2000. *The Dark Side of Courtship.* Thousand Oaks, CA: Sage.

Locke, D. 1992. *Increasing Multicultural Understanding.* Newbury Park, CA: Sage.

Lockheart, L. L. 1991. "Spousal violence: A cross-racial perspective." In R. L. Hampton (ed.), *Black Family Violence* (pp. 85–101). Lexington, MA: Lexington Books.

Lofland, J., and Lofland, L. H. 1984. *Analyzing Social Settings: A Guide to Qualitative Observation and Analysis* (2nd Ed.). Belmont, CA: Wadsworth.

Long, F. 1983. "Social support networks in day care and early child development." In J. K. Whittaker, and J. Garbarino (eds.), *Social Support Networks: Informal Helping in the Human Services* (pp. 189–217). New York: Aldine.

Loprest, P. J. 2002. "The next welfare reform: Counter boomerang effect." *Christian Science Monitor* (electronic edition). <http://www.urban.org/url.cfm?ID=900557>. Retrieved May 13, 2004.

Lovell, V. and Hill, C. 2001. *Today's Women Workers.* Publication # A127. Washington, DC: Institute for Women's Policy Research.

Lozoff, B., Jordan, B., and Malone, S. 1988. "Childbirth in cross-cultural perspective." *Marriage and Family Review* 12:35–60.

Lubben, J. E., and Becerra, R. M. 1987. "Social support among Black, Mexican, and Chinese elderly." In D. E. Gelfand and C. M. Barresi (eds.), *Ethnic Dimensions of Aging* (pp. 130–144).

Luster, T., Rhoades, K., and Haas, B. 1989. "The relation between parental beliefs and parenting behaviors: A test of the Kohn hypothesis." *Journal of Marriage and the Family* 51:139–147.

Lye, D. N. 1996. "Adult child-parent relations." *Annual Review of Sociology* 22:79–102.

Lye, D. N., and Klepinger, D. 1995. "Race, Hispanic ethnicity, childhood living arrangements and adult child-parent relations." Paper presented at the annual meetings of the Population Association of America, San Francisco.

Lynd, R., and Lynd, H. 1929. *Middletown: A Study in Contemporary American Culture.* New York: Harcourt.

Lytton, H., and Romney, D. M. 1991. "Parents' sex-related differential socialization of boys and girls: A meta-analysis." *Psychological Bulletin* 109:267–296.

Maccoby, E. 1990. "Gender and relationships: A reprise." *American Psychologist 46*:538–539.

Maccoby, E. E., and Jacklin, C. N. 1974. *The Psychology of Sex Differences*. Stanford CA: Stanford University Press.

Maccoby, E. E., and Martin, J. A. 1983. "Socialization in the context of the family: Parent-child interaction." In P. H. Mussen (ed.), *Handbook of Child Psychology* 4:1–101. New York: Wiley.

MacDonald, W. L., and DeMaris, A. 1995. "Remarriage, stepchildren, and marital conflict: Challenges to the incomplete institutionalization hypothesis." *Journal of Marriage and the Family* 57:387–398.

———. 1996. "Parenting stepchildren and biological children." *Journal of Family Issues* 17:5–25.

Mace, D. R. 1983. "What this book is about." In D. R. Mace (ed.), *Prevention in Family Services: Approaches to Family Wellness* (pp. 15–25). Beverly Hills, CA: Sage.

Mahoney, A., Pargament, K. I., Tarakeshwar, N., and Swank, A. B. 2001. "Religion in the home in the 1980s and 1990s: A Meta-analytic review and conceptual analysis of inks between religion, marriage, and parenting." *Journal of Family Psychology* 15:559–596.

Mahoney, P., and Williams, L. M. 1998. "Sexual assault in marriage." In J. L. Jasinski, and L. M. Williams (eds.), *Partner Violence: A Comprehensive Review of 20 Years of Research* (pp. 113–157). Thousand Oaks, CA: Sage.

Manning, W. D. 1990. "Parenting employed teenagers." *Youth and Society* 22:184–200.

Manning, W. D., Steward, S. D., and Smock, P. J. 2003. "The complexity of fathers' parenting responsibilities and involvement with nonresident children." *Journal of Family Issues* 24:645–667.

Marans, S., and Cohen, D. 1993. "Children and inner-city violence: Strategies for intervention." In L. Leavitt and N. Fox (eds.), *The Psychological Effects of War and Violence on Children*. Hillsdale, NJ: Lawrence Eribaum.

Margolin, L., and Craft, J. L. 1989. "Child sexual abuse by caretakers." *Family Relations* 38:450–455.

Markman, H. J., Duncan, S. W., Storaasli, R. D., and Howes, P. W. 1987. "The prediction and prevention of marital distress: A longitudinal investigation." In K. Hahlweg and M. J. Goldstein (eds.), *Understanding Major Mental Disorder: The Contribution of Family Interaction Research* (pp. 266–289). New York: Family Process Press.

Marks, S. 2002. "New face of hunger in U.S." *Christian Science Monitor*, September 6, pp. 2–3.

Marsiglio, W., and Donnelly, D. 1991. "Sexual relations in later life: A national study of married persons." *Journal of Gerontology: Social Sciences*, 46:S338–S344.

Martin, C. D. 2000. "More than work: Race and gender differences in caregiving burden." *Journal of Family Issues*, 21:986–1005.

Marx, K. 1977. *Capital*, Vol. 1. New York: Vintage Books.

Masheter, C. 1997. "Healthy and unhealthy friendship and hostility between ex-spouses." *Journal of Marriage and the Family*, 59:463–475.

Matthews, L. S., Conger, R. D., and Wickrama, K. A. S. 1996. "Work-family conflict and marital quality: Mediating processes." *Social Psychology Quarterly* 59:62–79.

Matthews, S. H., and Rosner, T. T. 1988. "Shared filial responsibility: The family as the primary caregiver." *Journal of Marriage and the Family* 50:185–195.

Matthias, R. E., Lubben, J. E., Atchison, K. A., and Schweitzer, S. O. 1997. "Sexual activity and satisfaction among very old adults: Results from a community-dwelling Medicare population survey." *Gerontologist* 37:6–14.

Maynard, S. 1997. "Growing up in an alcoholic family system: The effects on anxiety and differentiation of self." *Journal of Substance Abuse* 9:161–170.

McAdoo, H. P. 1992. "Reaffirming African-American families and our identities." *Psychology Discourse, 23(3)*. Excerpted from the Distinguished Psychologist Address, Aug. 17, 1991, New Orleans.

McCall, G. J., and Simmons, J. L. 1966. *Identities and Interactions*. New York: The Free Press.

McCandlish, B. 1987. "Against all odds: Lesbian mother family dynamics." In F. W. Bozett (ed.), *Gay and Lesbian Parents* (pp. 23–38). New York: Praeger.

McCauley, M., Schwartz-Kenney, B. M., Epstein, M. A., and Tucker, E. J. 2001. "United States." In B. M. Schwartz-Kenney, M. McCauley, and M. A. Epstein, (eds.), *Child Abuse: A Global View* (pp. 241–255). Westport, CT: Greenwood Press.

McCubbin, H. I., McCubbin, M. A., Thompson, A. I., Han, S.-Y., and Allen, C. T. 1997. *Families Under Stress*. AAFCS Commemorative Lecture, Washington, DC.

McCullough, D. 1992. *Truman*. New York: Simon and Schuster.

McCurdy, K., and Daro, D. 1993. "Current trends in child abuse reporting and fatalities: The results of the 1992 Annual Fifty State Survey." Working paper 808. April. Chicago, IL: National Committee for the Prevention of Child Abuse.

McDonough, P., Duncan, G., Williams, D., and House, J. 1997. "Income dynamics and adult mortality in the United States, 1972 through 1989." *American Journal of Public Health* 87:1476–1483.

McHale, J. P., and Rasmussen, J. L. 1998. "Coparental and family group-level dynamics during infancy: Early family precursors of child and family functioning during preschool." *Development and Psychopathology* 10:39–50.

McHale, S., and Huston, T. 1985. "The effect of the transition to parenthood on the marriage relationship." *Journal of Family Issues* 6:409–433.

McKenna, K. Y. A., Green, A. S., and Gleason, M. E. J. 2002. "Relationship formation on the Internet: What's the big attraction?" *Journal of Social Issues* 58:9–31.

McLanahan, S. S. 1999. "Father absence and the welfare of children." In E. M. Hetherington (ed.), *Coping with Divorce, Single Parenting, and Remarriage: A Risk and Resiliency Perspective* (pp. 117–146). Mahwah, NJ: Erlbaum.

———. 2002. "Life without father: What happens to the children." *Contexts* 1:35–44.

McLanahan, S., and Sandefur, G. 1994. *Growing Up With a Single Parent: What Hurts, What Helps.* Cambridge, MA: Harvard University Press.

McLaughlin, K. 1998. "Teachers go afield to connect with parents." *Columbia Daily Tribune,* November 2.

McLoyd, V. C., Cauce, A. M., Takeuchi, D., and Wilson, L. 2000. "Marital processes and parental socialization in families of color: A decade review of research." *Journal of Marriage and the Family* 62:1070–1093.

McManus, P. A., and DiPrete, T. A. 2001. "Losers and winners: The financial consequences of separation and divorce for men." *American Sociological Review* 66:246–268.

McPherson, D. 1993. "Gay parenting and couples: Parenting arrangements, arrangement satisfaction, and relationship satisfaction." Unpublished doctoral dissertation, Pacific Graduate School of Psychology.

McRoy, R. G. Grotevant, H. D. and Zurcher, C. A. 1988. *The Development of Emotional Disturbances in Adopted Adolescents.* NY: Praeger.

Mead, G. H. 1934. *Mind, Self, and Society.* Chicago: University of Chicago Press.

Meese, J. L. 1997. "Personal, social, and moral development." In J. L. Meese (ed.), *Child and Adolescent Development for Educators* (pp. 320–387). New York: McGraw-Hill.

Merrill, D. M. 1997. *Caring for Elderly Parents: Juggling Work, Family, and Caregiving in Middle and Working Class Families.* Westport, CT: Auburn House.

Merriwether-de Vries, C., Burton, L. M., and Eggeletion, L. 1996. "Early parenting and intergenerational family relationships within African American families." In J. A. Graber, J. Brooks-Gunn, and A. C. Petersen (eds.), *Transitions Through Adolescence: Interpersonal Domains and Context* (pp. 233–248). Mahwah, NJ: Erlbaum.

Meyer, D. 1997. *Views From Our Shoes: Growing Up With a Brother or Sister With Special Needs.* Bethesda, MD: Woodbine House.

Meyer, D. R., and Garasky, S. 1993. "Custodial fathers: Myths, realities, and child support policy." *Journal of Marriage and the Family* 55:73–89.

Meyers, T. J. 2003. "Anabaptists (Amish, Mennonite)." In J. J. Ponzetti, Jr. (ed.), *International Encyclopedia of Marriage and Family* (pp. 65–69). New York: Macmillan Reference USA.

Michael, R., H., Gagnon, J. H., Laumann, E. O., and Kolata, G. B. 1994. *Sex in America: A Definitive Survey.* Boston: Little, Brown.

Migliaccio, T. A. 2002. "Abused husbands." *Journal of Family Issues* 23:26–52.

Milardo, R, M. 2000. "The decade in review." *Journal of Marriage and the Family* 62:873–875.

Milardo, R. M., and Allan, G. 2000. "Social networks and marital relationships." In R. M. Milardo and S. Duck (eds.), *Families As Relationships* (pp. 117–133). London: John Wiley and Sons.

Milkie, M. A., Simon, R. W., and Powell, B. 1997. "Through the eyes of children: Youths' perceptions and evaluations of maternal and paternal roles." *Social Psychology Quarterly* 60:218–237.

Miller, J. G. 1978. *Living Systems.* New York: McGraw-Hill.

Miller, S. L. 1996. "Expanding the boundaries: Toward a more inclusive and integrated study of intimate violence." In L. K. Hamberger, and C Renzetti, (eds.), *Domestic Partner Abuse* (pp. 191–212). New York: Springer Publishing Company.

Minkler, M. 1999. "Intergenerational households headed by grandparents: Contexts, realities, and implications for policy." *Journal of Aging Studies* 13:199–218.

Mitchell, V. 1996. "Two moms: Contribution of the planned lesbian family to the deconstruction of gendered parenting." In J. Laird, and R. J. Green (eds.), *Lesbians and Gays in Couples and Families: A Handbook for Therapists* (pp. 343–357). San Francisco: Jossey-Bass.

Moen, P., Kim, J. E., and Hofmeister, H. 2001. "Couples' work/retirement transitions, gender, and marital quality." *Social Psychology Quarterly* 64:55–71.

Moffitt, R. A. 2002. "From welfare to work: What the evidence shows." *Policy Brief* No. 13, Washington, DC: The Brookings Institute.

Money, J. 1980. *Love and Love Sickness: The Science of Sex, Gender Difference, and Pair-Bonding.* Baltimore: Johns Hopkins University Press.

Monroe, P. A. 1995. "Family policy advocacy: Putting knowledge to work." *Family Relations* 44:425–437.

Montgomery, M. J., and Sorell, G. T. 1997. "Differences in love attitudes across family life stages." *Family Relations* 46:55–61.

Mooradian, A. D., and Greiff, V. 1990. "Sexuality in older women." *Archives of Internal Medicine 150*:1033–1038.

Moore, K. A. 2001. "How do state policymakers think about family processes and child development in low-income families?" In G. J. Duncan, and P. L. Chase-Lansdale (eds.), *For Better or for Worse: Welfare Reform and the Well-Being of Children and Families* (pp. 53–62). New York: Russell Sage Foundation.

Moore, V. L., and Schwebel, A. I. 1993. "Factors contributing to divorce: A study of race differences." *Journal of Divorce and Remarriage 20*:123–135.

Morgan, L. A. 1991. *After Marriage Ends: Economic Consequences for Midlife Women.* Newbury Park, CA: Sage.

Morgan, M., Leggett, S., and Shanahan, J. 1999. "Television and family values: Was Dan Quayle right?" *Mass Communication and Society 2*:47–63.

Morrow, K. B., and Sorell, G. T. 1989. "Factors affecting self-esteem, depression, and negative behaviors in sexually abused female adolescents." *Journal of Marriage and the Family 51*:677–686.

Mortimer, J. T. 2003. *Working and Growing Up in America.* Cambridge, MA: Harvard University Press.

——. 2004. Personal Communication, March.

Moser, R. P., and Jacob, T. 1997. "Parent-child interactions and child outcomes as related to gender of alcoholic parent." *Journal of Substance Abuse 9*:189–208.

Moss, M. S., and Moss, S. Z. 1995. "Death and bereavement." In R. Blieszner, and V. Bedford (eds.), *Handbook of Aging and the Family* (pp. 422–439). Westport, CT: Greenwood Press.

Moss, M. S., Resch, N., and Moss, S. Z. 1997. "The role of gender in middle-aged children's responses to parent death." *Omega 35*:43–65.

Muller, C., Dixler, B., and Mascia, J. L. 1993. "Parent involvement and academic achievement: An analysis of family resources available to the child." In B. Schneider, and J. S. Coleman (eds.), *Parents, Their Children, and Schools* (pp. 77–113). Boulder: Westview Press.

Muller, C., and Kerbow, D. 1993. "Parent involvement in the home, school, and community." In B. Schneider, and J. S. Coleman (eds.), *Parents, Their Children, and Schools* (pp. 13–42). Boulder: Westview Press.

Mutschler, P. H. 1994. "From executive suite to production line: How employees in different occupations manage elder care responsiblities." *Research on Aging 16*:7–26.

Myers, S. M. and Booth, A. 1996. "Men's retirement and marital quality." *Journal of Family Issues 17*:336–57.

Nadel, M. V. 1997. "Welfare reform: Implications of increased work participation. GAO/HEHS-97-75 *Welfare Reform and Child Care Supply.* Retrieved from the web 5/5/2004 from <http://wwwchildcareresearch.org>.

Naifeh, M. 1998. *Trap Door? Revolving Door? Or Both?* U.S. Bureau of the Census, Current Population Reports, P70-63. Washington, DC: U.S. Government Printing Office.

National Center for Health Statistics. 1999. New CDC Report Shows Teen Birth Rate Hits Record Low. Found at <www.cdc.gov/nchs/pressroom/01news/newbirth>.

——. 2002. *Cohabitation, Marriage, Divorce, and Remarriage in the United States.* 23(22):103. (PHS) 98-1998. Washington, DC: U.S. Government Printing Office.

National Coalition for the Homeless. 2001. "Homeless families with children." NCH Fact Sheet #7 (<http://www.Nationalhomeless.org/families.html>).

National Elder Abuse Incidence Study. 1998. Retrieved July 23, 1999, from <http://www.gwjapan.com/NCEA/basic/index.html>.

National Institute on Alcohol Abuse and Alcoholism. 2000. "Fetal alcohol exposure and the brain." Alcohol Alert, series #50.

National Research Council. 1993. *Understanding Child Abuse and Neglect.* Washington, DC: National Academy Press.

National Runaway Switchboard Statistics. 2003. <http://www.nrscrisisline.org/2003stat.asp>.

National Telecommunications and Information Administration. 2002. A nation online: How Americans are expanding their use of the Internet. (<http://www.ntia.doc.gov/ntiahome/dn>).

Neal, M. B., Chapman, N. J., Ingersoll-Dayton, B., and Emlen, A. 1993. *Balancing Work and Caregiving for Children, Adults, and Elders.* Newbury Park, CA: Sage.

Neugarten, B. L. 1979. "Time, age, and the life cycle." *American Journal of Psychiatry 136*:887–894.

Neugarten, B. L., and Weinstein, K. K. 1964. "The changing American grandparent." *Journal of Marriage and the Family 26*:199–204.

Newman, K. S. 1988. *Falling From Grace: The Experience of Downward Mobility in the American Middle Class.* New York: Free Press.

——. 1996. "Working poor: Low-wage employment in the lives of Harlem youth." In J. A. Graber, J. Brooks-Gunn, and A. C. Petersen (eds.), *Transitions Through Adolescence: Interpersonal Domains and Contex* (pp. 323–343). Mahwah, NJ: Erlbaum.

Newsweek. 2001. "Motherhood and murder." *Newsweek 138*:20–25, July 2.

Nock, S. L. 1998. *Marriage in Men's Lives*. New York: Oxford University Press.

Noller, P. 1984. *Nonverbal Communication and Marital Interaction*. Oxford: Pergamon.

Noller, P., Feeney, J. A., Bonnell, D., and Callan, V. J. 1994. "A longitudinal study of conflict in early marriage." *Journal of Social and Personal Relationships 11*:233–252.

Noonan, M. C. 2001. "The impact of domestic work on men's and women's wages." *Journal of Marriage and Family 63*:1134–1145.

Norris, K. 2001. "Waiting for Dakota." *Modern Maturity*, (pp. 36–37), March/April.

Nydegger, C. 1991. "The development of paternal and filial maturity." In K. Pillemer and K. McCartney (eds.), *Parent-child Relations Throughout Life* (pp. 93–112). Hillsdale, NJ: Erlbaum.

Nye, F. I., Carlson, J., and Garrett, G. 1970. "Family size, interaction, affect and stress." *Journal of Marriage and the Family 32*:216–226.

O'Connell, P. L. 2003. "Love Clicks." *New York Times*, February 13.

O'Keefe, N. K., Brockopp, K., and Chew, E. 1986. "Teen dating violence." *Social Work 31*:465–468.

O'Leary, K. D., Barling, J., Arias, I., Rosenbaum, A., Malone, J., and Tyree, A. 1989. "Prevalence and stability of physical aggression between spouses: A longitudinal analysis." *Journal of Counseling and Clinical Psychology 57*:263–268.

O'Leary, K. D., and Cascardi, M. 1998. "Physical aggression in marriage: A developmental analysis." In T. N. Bradbury (ed.), *The Developmental Course of Marital Dysfunction* (pp. 343–374). Cambridge, UK: Cambridge University Press.

Oakley, A. 1974. *Woman's Work: The Housewife, Past and Present*. New York: Pantheon Books.

Oates, R. K. 1984. "Similarities and differences between nonorganic failure to thrive and deprivation dwarfism." *Child Abuse and Neglect 8*:439–445.

Ogburn, W. F., and Thomas, D. S. 1922. "The influence of the business cycle on certain social conditions." *Journal of the American Statistical Association 18*:324–340.

Oggins, J., Veroff, J., and Leber, D. (1993). Perceptions of marital interaction among Black and White newlyweds. *Journal of Personality & Social Psychology 65*:494–511.

Oh, H. J. 2001. "An exploration of the influence of household poverty spells on mortality risk." *Journal of Marriage and Family 63*:224–234.

Olasky, M. 1997. "Charitable aid should replace government welfare." In C. P. Cozie and P. A. Winters (eds.), *Welfare: Opposing Viewpoints* (pp. 56–64). San Diego: Greenhaven Press.

Olds, D. L., Henderson, C. R., Chamberlin, R., and Tatelbaum, R. 1986. "Preventing child abuse and neglect: A randomized trial of nurse home visitation." *Pediatrics 78*:65–78.

Olson, B., and Douglas, W. 1997. "The family on television: Evaluation of gender roles in situation comedy." *Sex Roles 36*:409–427.

Olson, D. H. 1977. "Insiders' and outsiders' views of relationships: Research and strategies." In G. Levinger, and H. Rausch (eds.), *Close Relationships* (pp. 115–136). Amherst: University of Massachusetts Press.

Olson, D. H., and DeFrain, J. 2000. *Marriages and Families: Intimacy, Diversity, and Strengths* (4th Ed.). Boston: McGraw-Hill.

Olson, D. H., and Olson, A. K. 2000. *Empowering Couples: Building on Your Strengths*. Minneapolis: Life Innovations.

Ono, H. 1998. "Husbands' and wives' resources and marital dissolution." *Journal of Marriage and the Family 60*:674–689.

Orbuch, T. L., House, J. S., Mero, R. P., and Webster, P. S. 1996. "Marital quality over the life course." *Social Psychology Quarterly 59*:162–171.

Orleans, M., and Laney, M. C. 2000. "Children's computer use in the home: Isolation or sociation?" *Social Science Computer Review 18*:56–72.

Ortega, S., Whitt, H., and William, J., Jr. 1988. "Religious homogamy and marital happiness." *Journal of Family Issues 9*:224–239.

Osofsky, J. D., Wewers, S., Hann, D. M., and Fick, A. C. "Chronic community violence: What is happening to our children?" *Psychiatry 56*:36–45.

Osterweil, D. A. 1991. "Correlates of relationship satisfaction in lesbian couples who are parenting their first child together." Unpublished doctoral dissertation, California School of Professional Psychology, Berkeley/Alameda.

Ostrander, S. A. 1984. *Women of the Upper Class*. Philadelphia, PA: Temple University Press.

Pagelow, M. D. 1984. *Family Violence*. New York: Praeger.

——. 1985. "The 'battered husband syndrome': Social problem or much ado about nothing?" In N. Johnson (ed.), *Marital Violence* (pp. 172–195). Boston: Routledge Kegan Paul.

Pan, H. S., Neidig, P. H., and O'Leary, K. D. 1994. "Predicting mild and severe husband to wife physical aggression." *Journal of Consulting and Clinical Psychology 62*:975–981.

Parental Resonsibility Laws. (February 15, 2003). Found on the World Wide Web at: <ojjdp.ncjrs.org> under *Juvenile Justice Reform Initiatives in the States, 1994–1996.*

Parke, R. D., and Tinsley, B. J. 1987. "Family interaction in infancy." In J. Osofsky (ed.), *Handbook of Infant Development* (2nd Ed.), (pp. 579–641). New York: Wiley.

Parks, M. R. 1997. "Communication networks and relationship life cycles." In S. Duck (ed.), *Handbook of Personal Relationships* (2nd Ed.), (pp. 351–372). Chichester, England: John Wiley and Sons.

Patterson, C. 1995a. "Families of the lesbian baby boom: Parents' division of labor and children's adjustment." *Developmental Psychology 31*:115–123.

——. 1995b. "Lesbian mothers, gay fathers, and their children." In A. R. D'Augelli, and C. J. Patterson (eds.), *Lesbian, Gay, and Bisexual Identities Over the Lifespan: Psychological Perspectives* (pp. 262–290). New York: Oxford University Press.

——. 1996. "Lesbian mothers and their children: Findings from the Bay Area Families Study." In J. Laird, and R. J. Green (eds.), *Lesbians and Gays in Couples and Families: A Handbook for Therapists* (pp. 420–438). San Francisco: Jossey-Bass.

——. 2000. "Family relationships of lesbians and gay men." *Journal of Marriage and the Family 62*:1052–1069.

Patterson, G. 1986. "The contribution of siblings to training for fighting: A microsocial analysis." In D. Olweus, J. Block, and M. R. Radke-Yarrow (eds.), *Development of Antisocial and Prosocial Behavior: Research, Theories, and Issues* (pp. 235–261). New York: Academic Press.

Peacock, P. 1998. "Marital rape." In R. K. Bergen (ed.), *Issues in Intimate Violence* (pp. 225–235). Thousand Oaks, CA: Sage.

Pearson, J., and Thoennes, N. 1998. "Programs to increase fathers' access to their children." In I. Garfinkel, S. S. McLanahan, D. R. Meyer, and J. A. Seltzer (eds.), *Fathers Under Fire: The Revolution in Child Support Enforcement* (pp. 220–252). New York: Russell Sage Foundation.

Peek, C W., Fischer, J. L., and Kidwell, J. S. 1985. "Teenage violence toward parents: A neglected dimension of family violence." *Journal of Marriage and the Family 47*:1051–1058.

Penrod, J. D., Kane, R. A., Kane, R. L., and Finch, M. M. 1995. "Who cares: The size, scope, and composition of the caregivers support system." *Gerontologist 35*:489–497.

Peplau, L. A. and Cochran, S. D. 1990. "A relational perspective on homosexuality." In D. McWhirter, S. A. Sanders., and J. Reinisch (eds.), *Homosexuality/Heterosexuality: Concepts of Sexual Orientation* (pp. 321–349). Oxford: Oxford University Press.

Peplau, L. A., Hill, C. T., and Rubin, Z. 1993. "Sex role attitudes in dating and marriage: A 15-year follow-up of the Boston Couples Study." *Journal of Social Issues 49*:31–52.

Perez, C. M., and Widom, C. S. 1994. "Childhood victimization and long-term intellectual and academic outcomes." *Child Abuse and Neglect 18*:617–633.

Perry-Jenkins, M. 2000. Paper presented at the National Council on Family Relations conference, November.

Perry-Jenkins, M., Repetti, R. L., and Crouter, A. C. 2000. "Work and family in the 1990s." *Journal of Marriage and the Family 62*:981–998.

Peters, M. F., and Massey, G. 1983. "Mundane extreme environmental stress in family stress theories. The case of black families in white America." *Marriage and Family Review 6*:193–218.

Peterson, G. W., Bodman, D. A., Bush, K. R., and Madden-Derdich, D. 2000. "Gender and parent-child relationships." In D. H. Demo, K. R. Allen, and M. A. Fine (eds.), *Handbook of Family Diversity* (pp. 82–104). New York: Oxford University Press.

Peterson, G. W., Madden-Derdich, D., and Leonard, S. A. 2000. "Parent-child relations across the life course: Autonomy within the context of connectedness." In S. J. Price, P. C. McKenry, and M. J. Murphy (eds.), *Families Across Time* (pp. 187–203). Los Angeles: Roxbury.

Peterson, G. W., and Rollins, B. C. 1987. "Parent-child socialization." In M. B. Sussman and S. K. Steinmetz (eds.), *Handbook of Marriage and the Family* (pp. 471–507). New York: Plenum.

Peterson, K. S. 1997. "For today's teens, race is not an issue anymore." *USA TODAY*, November, 3, pp. 1–2.

Peth-Pierce, R. 1997. *The NICHD Study of Early Child Care*. Bethesda, MD: National Institute of Child Health and Human Development. <http://www.nih.gov/news/pr/apr97/nichd-03.htmi>.

Petronio, S. 1994. "Privacy binds in family interactions: The case of parental privacy invasion." In W. R. Cupach and B. H. Spitzberg (eds.), *The Dark Side of Interpersonal Communication* (pp. 241–257). Hillsdale, NJ: Erlbaum.

Pettit, G. S., Bates, J. E., and Dodge, K. A. 1998. "Supportive parenting, ecological context, and children's adjustment: A seven-year longitudinal study." *Child Development 68*:908–923.

Phillips, K. 2002. *Wealth and Democracy: A Political History of the American Rich*. New York: Broadway Books.

Pineo, P. C. 1961. "Disenchantment in the later years of marriage." *Marriage and Family Living 23*:3–11.

Piotrkowski, C. S., Hughes, D., Pleck, J. H., Kessler-Sklar, S., and Staines, G. L. 1993. *The Experience of Childbearing Women in the Workplace: The Impact of Family-Friendly Policies and Practices*. Washington, DC: Women's Bureau, United States Department of Labor.

Pirog, M., and Magee, C. 1997. "High school completion: The influence of schools, families, and adolescent parenting." *Social Science Quarterly* 78:710–724.

Polansky, N. A., Chalmers, M. A., Buttenwieser, E., and Williams, D. P. 1981. *Damaged Parents: An Anatomy of Child Neglect.* Chicago: University of Chicago Press.

Ponza, M., Duncan, G. J., Corcoran, M., and Groskind, F. 1988. "The guns of autumn? Age differences in support for income transfers to the young and old." *Public Opinion Quarterly* 52:492–512.

Popenoe, D. 1994. "The evolution of marriage and the problem of stepfamilies: A biosocial perspective." In A. Booth, and J. Dunn (eds.), *Stepfamilies: Who Benefits, Who Does Not?* (pp. 3–27). Hillsdale, NJ: Erlbaum.

Poverty and Well-Being in Rural America. 1999. *Family Economics and Nutrition Review* 12:93–95.

Presser, H. 1988. "Shift work and child care among young dual-earner American parents." *Journal of Marriage and the Family* 50:133–148.

———. 2000. "Nonstandard work schedules and marital instability." *Journal of Marriage and the Family* 62:93–110.

Presser, H., and A. Cox. 1997. "The work schedules of low-educated American women and welfare reform." *Monthly Labor Review* 120:25–35.

Preston, S. H. 1984. "Children and the elderly in the United States." *Scientific American* 251:44–49.

Price, S. J., and McKenry, P. C. 1988. *Divorce.* Newbury Park, CA: Sage.

Putnam, R. D. 2000. *Bowling Alone: The Collapse and Revival of American Community.* New York: Simon & Schuster.

Pyke, K. D. 1994. "Women's employment as a gift or burden? Marital power across marriage, divorce, and remarriage." *Gender and Society* 8:73–91.

Pyke, K., and Bengtson, V. L. 1996. "Caring more or less: Individualistic and collectivist systems of family elder care." *Journal of Marriage and the Family* 58:379–392.

Quick, D. S., McHenry, P. C., and Newman, B. M. 1995. "Stepmothers and their adolescent children: Adjustment to new family roles." In K. Pasley, and M. Ihinger-Tallman (eds.), *Stepparenting: Issues in Theory, Research, and Practice* (pp. 105–125). Westport, CT: Praeger.

Quindlen, A. 2001. "Playing God on no sleep." *Newsweek* 138:64, July 2.

Rabasca, L. 1999. "Child-abuse prevention efforts still too few." *APA Monitor* April, 30. Washington, D.C: American Psychological Association.

Raffaelli, M. 1992. "Sibling conflict in early adolescence." *Journal of Marriage and the Family* 54:652–663.

Raley, R. K. 1995. "Black-white differences in kin contact and exchange among never married adults." *Journal of Family Issues* 16:77–103.

Rank, M. R. 1982. "Determinants of conjugal influence in wives' employment decision-making." *Journal of Marriage and the Family* 44:591–604.

———. 1994. *Living on the Edge: The Realities of Welfare in America.* New York: Columbia University Press.

———. 2001. "The effect of poverty on America's families." *Journal of Family Issues* 22:882–903.

Rank, M. R., and Cheng, L. 1995. "Welfare use across generations: How important are the ties that bind?" *Journal of Marriage and the Family* 57:673–684.

Rasmussen, P. K., and Ferraro, K. J. 1979. "The divorce process." *Alternative Lifestyles* 2:443–460.

Reece, R. M. 2000. *Treatment of Child Abuse: Common Grounds for Mental Health, Medical, and Legal Practitioners.* Baltimore, MD: The Johns Hopkins University Press.

Reimann, R. 1997. "Does biology matter?: Lesbian couples' transition to parenthood and their division of labor." *Qualitative Sociology* 20(2):153–185.

Reiss, I. 1960. "Toward a sociology of the heterosexual love relationship." *Marriage and Family Living* 22:139–145.

Reitz, M., and Watson, K. W. 1992. *Adoption and the Family System.* New York: Guilford Press.

Rempel, J. K., Holmes, J. G., and Zanna, M. P. 1985. "Trust in close relationships." *Journal of Personality and Social Psychology* 49:95–112.

Renzetti, C. M. 1992. *Violent Betrayal: Partner Abuse in Lesbian Relationships.* Thousand Oaks, CA: Sage.

———. 1998. "Violence and abuse in lesbian relationships: theoretical and empirical issues." In R. K. Bergen (ed.), *Issues in Intimate Violence* (pp. 117–127). Thousand Oaks, CA: Sage.

Repetti, R. L. 1989. "Effects of daily workload on subsequent behavior during marital interaction: The roles of social withdrawal and spouse support." *Journal of Personality and Social Psychology* 57:651–659.

———. 1993. "Short-term effects of occupational stressors on daily mood and health complaints." *Health Psychology* 12:125–131.

Rice, K. G., Cole, D. A., and Lapsley, D. K. 1990. "Separation, individuation, family cohesion, and adjustment to college: Measurement validation and test of a theoretical model. *Journal of Counseling Psychology* 37:195–202.

Richters, J., and Martinez, P. 1993a. "The NIMH Community Violence Project: I. Children as victims of and witnesses to violence [Special Issue: Children and Violence]". *Psychiatry* 56:7–21.

——. 1993b. "Violent communities, family choices, and children's chances: An algorithm for improving the odds." *Development and Psychopathology* 5:609–627.

Riley, D. 1990. "Network influences on father involvement in childrearing." In M. Cochran, M. Larner, D. Riley, L. Gunnarson, and C. R. Henderson, Jr. (eds.), *Extending Families: The Social Networks of Parents and Their Children* (pp. 131–153). Cambridge, England: Cambridge University Press.

Riley, M. W., Johnson, M., and Foner, A. 1972 . *Aging and society, Vol. 3. A sociology of age stratification.* New York: Russell Sage.

Rindfuss, R. R., and VandenHeuvel, A. 1990. "Cohabitation: A precursor to marriage or an alternative to being single?" *Population and Development Review* 16:703–726.

Rivers, R. Y. 1995. "Clinical issues and intervention with ethnic minority women." In J. F. Aponte, R. Y. Rivers, and J. Wohl (eds.), *Psychological Interventions and Cultural Diversity* (pp. 181–198). Boston: Allyn and Bacon.

Roach, M., Orsmond, G. I., and Barratt, M. S. 1999. "Mothers and fathers of children with Down syndrome." *American Journal of Mental Retardation* 104:422–436.

Roberts, S. R. 1981. *Runaways and Nonrunaways in an American Suburb.* New York: The John Jay Press.

Robertson, E. B., Elder, G. H., Jr., Skinner, M. L., and Conger, R. D. 1991. "The costs and benefits of social support in families." *Journal of Marriage and the Family* 53:403–416.

Robinson, J. P. 1993. *The Demographics of Time Use.* Ithaca, NY: American Demographics.

Robinson, J. P., and Milkie, M. 1998. "Back to basics: Trends in the role determinants of women's attitudes toward housework." *Journal of Marriage and the Family* 60:205–218.

Rogers, S. J. 1999. "Wives' income and marital quality: Are there reciprocal effects?" *Journal of Marriage and the Family* 61:123–132.

——. 2004. "Dollars, dependency, and divorce: Four perspectives on the role of wives' income." *Journal of Marriage and the Family* 66:59–74.

Rogers, S. J., and Amato, P. R. 1997. "Is marital quality declining? Evidence from two generations." *Social Forces* 75:1089–1100.

Rogers, S. J., and May, D. C. 2003. "Spillover between marital quality and job satisfaction: Long-term patterns and gender differences." *Journal of Marriage and the Family,* 65:482–495.

Rohner, R. P., and Pettengill, S. M. 1985. "Perceived parental acceptance-rejection and parental control among Korean adolescents." *Child Development,* 56:524–528.

Rokeach, M. 1970. *Beliefs, Attitudes, and Values: A Theory of Organization and Change.* San Francisco, CA: Jossey-Bass.

Romans, S., Martin, J. L., and Mullen, P. E. 1997. "Childhood sexual abuse and later psychological problems: Neither necessary, sufficient nor acting alone." *Criminal Behavior and Mental Health,* 7:327–338.

Roosa, M. W., Gensheimer, L. K., Short, J. L., Ayers, T. S., and Shell, R. 1989. "A preventive intervention for children in alcoholic families: Results of a pilot study." *Family Relations,* 38:295–300.

Roscoe, B., Diana, M. S., and Brooks, R. H. II. 1987. "Early, middle and late adolescents' views on dating and factors influencing partner selection." *Adolescence* 22:59–68.

Rose, P. 1983. *Parallel Lives: Five Victorian Marriages.* New York: Vintage Books.

Rosenbaum, E., and Harris, L. E. 2001. "Low-income families in their new neighborhoods: The short-term effects of moving from Chicago's public housing." *Journal of Family Issues* 22:183–210.

Rosenthal, C. J., Martin-Matthews, A., and Matthews, S. H. 1996. "Caught in the middle? Occupancy in multiple roles and help to parents in a national probability sample of Canadian adults." *Journal of Gerontology: Social Sciences* 51B:S274–S283.

Ross, C. E., Mirowsky, J., and Huber, J. 1983. "Dividing work, sharing work, and in between: Marriage patterns and depression." *American Sociological Review* 48:809–823.

Ross, C., and Mirowsky, J. 1999. "Parental divorce, life-course disruption, and adult depression." *Journal of Marriage and the Family* 61:1034–1045.

Ross, E. 2002. "Marriage good for women, too, study finds." *San Francisco Chronicle,* p. A2. October 5.

Rossman, B. B. R. 2003. "Interparental violence-effects on children." In J. J. Ponzetti, Jr. (ed.), *International Encyclopedia of Marriage and Family* (pp. 932–937). New York: Macmillan Reference USA.

Rothman, E. K. 1984. *Hands and Hearts: A History of Courtship in America.* Cambridge, MA: Harvard University Press.

Rotter, J. B. 1980. "Interpersonal trust, trustworthiness, and gullibility." *American Psychologist* 35:1–7.

Rubin, H. J., and Rubin, I. S. 1995. *Qualitative Interviewing: The Art of Hearing Data.* Thousand Oaks, CA: Sage.

Rubin, L. B. 1976. *Worlds of Pain: Life in the Working-class Family.* New York: Basic Books.

——. 1985. *Just Friends: The Role of Friendship in Our Lives.* New York: Harper & Row.

——. 1994. *Families on the Faultline: America's Working Class Speaks About the Family, the Economy, Race, and Ethnicity.* New York: HarperCollins.

Russel, C. S. 1974. "Transition to parenthood: Problems and gratifications." *Journal of Marriage and the Family 36*:294–302.

Russell, D. E. H. 1984. "The prevalence and seriousness of incestuous abuse: Stepfathers vs. biological fathers." *Child Abuse and Neglect 8*:15–22.

———. 1990. *Rape in Marriage*. Indianapolis: Indiana University Press.

Rutter, V., and Schwartz, P. 2000. "Gender, marriage, and diverse possibilities for cross-sex and same-sex pairs." In D. H. Demo, K. R. Allen, and M. A. Fine (eds.), *Handbook of Family Diversity* (pp. 59–81). New York: Oxford University Press.

Salari, S. M., and Baldwin, B. M. 2002. "Verbal, physical, and injurious aggression among intimate couples over time." *Journal of Family Issues 23*:523–550.

Saltzman. W. (1992). "The effect of children's exposure to community violence." Unpublished master's thesis, University of Maryland, College Park.

Sampson, R. J. 2001. "How do communities undergird or undermine human development? Relevant contexts and social mechanisms." In A. Booth and A. C. Crouter (eds.), *Does It Take a Village? Community Effects on Children, Adolescents, and Families* (pp. 3–33). Mahwah, NJ: Erlbaum.

Sampson, R. J., Raudenbush, S., and Earls, F. 1997. "Neighborhoods and violent crime: A multilevel study of collective efficacy." *Science 277*:918–924.

San Francisco Chronicle. 2000. March 2, pp. A1, 8.

Sanchez, Y. M. 1997. "Families of Mexican origin." In M. K. DeGenova (ed.), *Families in Cultural Context: Strengths and Challenges in Diversity* (pp. 61–83). Mountain View, CA: Mayfield.

Sanders, G. F., and Trygstad, D. W. 1989. "Stepgrandparents and grandparents: The view from young adults." *Family Relations 38*:71–75.

Scanlon, W. J. 1988. "A perspective on long-term care for the elderly." *Health Care Financing Review, Annual Supplement*:7–15.

Schaap, C., Bruunk, B., and Kerkstra, A. 1988. "Marital conflict resolution." In P. Noller and M. A. Fitzpatrick (eds.), *Perspectives on Marital Interaction*. Clevedon, England: Multilingual Matters.

Scharlach, A. E., and Fredriksen, K. I. 1993. "Reactions to the death of a parent during midlife." *Omega 27*:307–319.

Scharlach, A. E., Sobel, E. L., and Roberts, R. E. L. 1991. "Employment and caregiving strain: An integrative model." *Gerontologist 31*:778–787.

Scheibe, C. L., and Grossman, S. 1993. "Parenting styles on prime-time television (1983–1991)." Paper presented at the biennial meeting of the Society for Research in Child Development, New Orleans, March.

Schiamberg, L. B., and Gans, D. 2000. "Elder abuse by adult children: An applied ecological framework for understanding contextual risk factors and the intergenerational character of quality of life." *International Journal of Aging and Human Development 50*:329–359.

Schinke, S. P., Barth, R. P., Gilchrist, L. D., and Maxwell, J. S. 1986. "Adolescent mothers, stress, and prevention." *Journal of Human Stress 4*:162–167.

Schoen, R., Young, J. K., Nathanson, C. A., Fields, J., and Astone, N. M. 1997. "Why do Americans want children?" *Population and Development Review 23*:333–358.

Schorr, L. 1988. *Within Our Reach: Breaking the Cycle of Disadvantage*. Garden City, NJ: Anchor Press/Doubleday.

Schrader, L. 2004. "What does it cost to raise a child?" (<http://www.missourifamilies.org/features/finance articles/raisechild.htm>).

Schulenberg, J., Bachman, J. G., Johnston, L. D., and O'Malley, P. M. 1995. "American adolescents' views of family and work: Historical trends from 1976–1992. In. P. Noack, M. Hofer, and J. Youniss (eds.), *Psychological Responses to Social Change: Human Development in Changing Environments* (pp. 37–64). New York: Walter de Gruyter.

Schwab-Stone, M. Ayers, T., and Weissberg, R. (1995). "No safe haven: A study of violence exposure in an urban community." *Journal of the American Academy of Children and Adolescents 34*:1343.

Schwartz, P. 1994. *Peer Marriage: How Love Between Equals Really Works*. New York: Free Press.

Scott-Jones, D., and Nelson-LeGall, S. 1986. "Defining black families: Past and present." In E. Seidman and J. Rappaport (eds.), *Redefining Social Problems* (pp. 83–100). New York: Plenum.

Seabrook, J. 2002. *Class, Caste, and Hierarchies*. Oxford: New Internationalist Publications.

Seccombe, K. 2000. "Families in poverty in the 1990s: Trends, causes, consequences, and lessons learned." *Journal of Marriage and the Family 62*:1094–1113.

———. 2002. "'Beating the odds' versus 'changing the odds': Poverty, resilience, and family policy." *Journal of Marriage and Family 64*:384–394.

Sedlak, A., and Broadhurst, D. D. 1996. "Third national incidence study of child abuse and neglect." Final Report. Washington, DC: U.S. Department of Health and Human Services.

Seltzer, J. A. 1991. "Relationships between fathers and children who live apart: The father's role after separation." *Journal of Marriage and the Family 53*:79–101.

——. 1994. "Consequences of marital dissolution for children." In J. Hagan, and K. S. Cook (eds.), *Annual Review of Sociology 20*:235–266. Palo Alto, CA: Annual Reviews Inc.

Seltzer, J. A., and Brandreth, Y. 1994. "What fathers say about involvement with children after separation." *Journal of Family Issues 15*:49–77.

Shahinfar, A. (1997). "Preschool children's exposure to community violence: Prevalence, correlates, and moderating factors." Unpublished doctoral dissertation, University of Maryland, College Park.

Shakoor, B., and Chalmers, D. 1991. "Co-victimization of African-American children who witness violence: Effects on cognitive, emotional, and behavioral development." *Journal of the National Medical Association 83*:233–238.

Shapiro, A., and Lambert, J. D. 1999. "Longitudinal effects of divorce on the quality of the father-child relationship and on fathers' psychological well-being." *Journal of Marriage and the Family 61*:397–408.

Sharp, E. A., and Ispa, J. M. forthcoming. "Matters of the heart: Romantic relationships." In J. M. Ispa, K. R. Thornburg, and M. A. Fine (eds.), *Keepin' On, Keepin' On: Nine Young Mothers in Poverty*. Baltimore: Brookes Publishing.

Shelton, B. A., and John, D. 1993. "Does marital status make a difference? Housework among married and cohabiting men and women." *Journal of Family Issues 14*:401–420.

Shelton, S. K. 2001. "One week until college." In A. J. Walker, M. Manoogian-O'Dell, L. A. McGraw, and D. L. G. White (eds.), *Families in Later Life: Connections and Transitions* (pp. 36–38). Thousand Oaks, CA: Pine Forge Press.

Shinn, M., Knickman, J. R., and Weitzman, B. C. 1991. "Social relationships and vulnerability to becoming homeless among poor families." *American Psychologist 46*:1180–1187.

Shumow, L., and Miller, J. D. 2001. "Parents' at-home and at-school academic involvement with young adolescents." *Journal of Early Adolescence 21*:68–91.

Showmenews.com. 2001. "Children hold off police from rural Idaho house." May 31.

Signorielli, N. 1991. "Adolescents and ambivalence towards marriage." *Youth and Society 23*:121–149.

Silverberg, S. B. 1996. "Parents' well-being at their children's transition to adolescence." In C. Ryff (ed.), *Parental Experience in Midlife* (pp. 215–254). Chicago: University of Chicago Press.

Silverberg, S. B., Jacobs, S. L., and Raymond, M. 1998. "When mothers turn to their adolescent daughters: Predicting daughters' vulnerability to negative adjustment outcomes." Paper presented at the meetings of the Society for Research on Adolescence, San Diego.

Silverstein, M., and Bengtson, V. L. 1997. "Intergenerational solidarity and the structure of adult child-parent relationships in American families." *American Journal of Sociology 103*:429–460.

Simmel, G. 1964. *The Sociology of Georg Simmel*. K. H. Wolff (Translator). New York: The Free Press.

Simons, R. L., Whitbeck, L. B., Beaman, J., and Conger, R. D. 1994. "The impact of mothers' parenting, involvement by nonresidential fathers, and parental conflict on the adjustment of adolescent children." *Journal of Marriage and the Family 56*:356–374.

Simons, R. L., Whitbeck, L. S., Conger, R. D., and Chyi-In, W. 1991. "Intergenerational transmission of harsh parenting." *Developmental Psychology 27*:159–171.

Sirignano, S. W., and Lachman, M. E. 1985. "Personality change during the transition to parenthood: The role of perceived infant temperament." *Developmental Psychology 21*:558–567.

Sloan, E. 1985. *Biology of Women*. (2nd Ed.). New York: John Crieley.

Small, S., and Supple, A. 2001. "Communities as systems: Is a community more than the sum of its parts?" In A. Booth and A. C. Crouter (eds.), *Does It Take a Village? Community Effects on Children, Adolescents, and Families* (pp. 161–174). Mahwah, NJ: Erlbaum.

Smith, D. B., and Moen, P. 2004. "Retirement satisfaction for retirees and their spouses: Do gender and the retirement decision-making process matter?" *Journal of Family Issues 25*:262–285.

Smith, J. 1991. "Attitudes of prospective parents towards agency adoption practices, particularly open adoption." Paper presented at the meeting of the National Committee for Adoption, Washington, DC, April.

Smith, J. P., Williams, J. 1992. "From abusive household to dating violence." *Journal of Family Violence 7*:153–165.

Smith, K. R., Zick, C. D., and Duncan, G. J. 1991. "Remarriage patterns among recent widows and widowers." *Demography 28*:361–374.

Smith, T. W. 1994. "Attitudes toward sexual permissiveness: Trends, correlates, and behavioral connections." In A. S. Rossi (ed.), *Sexuality Across the Life Course* (pp. 63–97). Chicago: University of Chicago Press.

Smock, P. J., Manning, W. D., and Gupta, S. 1999. "The effects of marriage and divorce on women's economic well-being." *American Sociological Review 64*:794–812.

Snider, J. 2001. "Foreign adoptions on the rise." *USA Today,* July 12.

Soldo, B. J. 1996. "Cross pressures on middle-aged adults: A broader view." *Journal of Gerontology: Social Sciences 51B*:S271–S273.

Sorensen, A. 1994. "Women, family and class." In J. Hagan and J. K. Cook (eds.), *Annual Review of Sociology 20*:27–47. Palo Alto, CA: Annual Reviews Inc.

Sorensen, A., and McLanahan, S. 1987. "Married women's economic dependency, 1940–1980." *American Journal of Sociology 93*:659–687.

Sorensen, E. 1997. "A national profile of nonresident fathers and their ability to pay child support." *Journal of Marriage and the Family 59*:785–797.

Sorenson, P., and Tableman, B. 2002. "Impact of welfare reform." *Best Practice Briefs* No. 26. East Lansing: Michigan State University.

Sorenson, S. B., and Telles, C. A. 1991. "Self-reports of spousal violence in a Mexican-American and non-Hispanic white population." *Violence and Victims 6*:3–16.

South, S. J. 1985. "Economic conditions and the divorce rate: A time-series analysis of the postwar United States." *Journal of Marriage and the Family 47*:31–41.

——. 1995. "Do you need to shop around? Age at marriage, spousal alternatives, and marital dissolution." *Journal of Family Issues 16*:432–449.

——. 2001. "The geographic context of divorce: Do neighborhoods matter?" *Journal of Marriage and the Family 63*:755–766.

South, S. J., and Lloyd, K. M. 1995. "Spousal alternatives and marital dissolution." *American Sociological Review 60*:21–35.

South, S. J., Trent, K., and Shen, Y. 2001. "Changing partners: Toward a macrostructural-opportunity theory of marital dissolution." *Journal of Marriage and the Family 63*:743–754.

Spain, D., and Bianchi, S. M. 1996. *Balancing Act: Motherhood, Marriage, and Employment Among American Women.* New York: Russel Sage Foundation.

Spanier, G. B. 1976. "Measuring dyadic adjustment: New scales for assessing the quality of marriage and similar dyads." *Journal of Marriage and the Family 38*:15–28.

Spencer, M. B. 2001. "Resiliency and fragility factors associated with the contextual experiences of low resource urban African American male youth and families." In A. Booth and A. C. Crouter (eds.), *Does It Take a Village? Community Effects on Children, Adolescents, and Families* (pp. 51–77). Mahwah, NJ: Erlbaum.

Spitze, G., and Logan, J. R. 1990. "More evidence on women (and men) in the middle." *Research on Aging 12*:182–198.

——. 1992. "Helping as a component of parent-adult child relations." *Research on Aging 14*:291–312.

Sprecher, S., and Felmlee, D. 1992. "The influence of parents and friends on the quality and stability of romantic relationships: A three-wave longitudinal investigation." *Journal of Marriage and the Family 54*:888–900.

Sprecher, S., and Metts, S. 1989. "Development of the 'romantic beliefs scale' and examination of the effects of gender and gender role orientation." *Journal of Social and Personal Relationships 6*:387–411.

Sprecher, S., and Regan, P. C. 1998. "Passionate and companionate love in courting and young married couples." *Sociological Inquiry 68*:163–185.

Sroufe, L. A., Cooper, R. G., and DeHart, G. B. 1996. *Child Development: Its Nature and Course* (3rd Ed.). New York: McGraw-Hill.

Stack, C. 1974. *All Our Kin: Strategies for Survival in a Black Community.* New York: Harper and Row.

Stacy, J. 1991. *Brave New Families: Stories of Domestic Upheaval in Late Twentieth Century America.* New York: Basic Books.

Stafford, L., and Canary, D. J., 1991. "Maintenance strategies and romantic relationship type, gender, and relational characteristics." *Journal of Social and Personal Relationships 8*:217–242.

Staines, G. 1980. "Spillover versus compensation: A review of the literature on the relationship between work and nonwork." *Human Relations 33*:111–129.

Stanley, S. M., and Markman, H. J. 1997. *Marriage in the 90s: A Nationwide Random Phone Survey.* Denver: Prep, Inc.

Starrels, M. E., Ingersoll-Dayton, B., Dowler, D. W., and Neal, M. B. 1997. "The stress of caregiving for a parent: Effects of the elder's impairment on an employed adult child." *Journal of Marriage and the Family 59*:860–872.

Steil, J. M., and Weltman, K. 1992. "Influence strategies at home and work: A study of sixty dual career couples." *Journal of Social and Personal Relationships 9*:65–88.

Steinberg, L. 1990. "Interdependence in the family: Autonomy, conflict, and harmony in the parent-adolescent relationship." In S. S. Feldman, and G. L. Elliott (eds.), *At the Threshold: The Developing Adolescent* (pp. 255–276). Cambridge, MA: Harvard University Press.

Steinberg, L., Mounts, N. S., Lamborn, S. D., and Dornbusch, S. M. 1991. "Authoritative parenting and adolescent adjustment across varied ecological niches." *Journal of Research on Adolescence* I:19–36.

Steinmetz, S. K. 1978. "Violence between family members." *Marriage and Family Review* 1:1–16.

Stemmler, M., Bingham, C. R., Crockett, L. J., Petersen, A. C., and Meyer, A. 1991. Normative expectations in different developmental contexts. Paper presented at the meeting of the International Society for the Study of Behavioral Development, Minneapolis, MN., July.

Stephens, L. S. 1996. "Will Johnny see daddy this week? An empirical test of three theoretical perspectives of postdivorce contact." *Journal of Family Issues* 17:466–494.

Sternberg, R. J. 1986. "A triangular theory of love." *Psychological Review* 93:119–135.

——. 1998. *Cupid's Arrow: The Course of Love Through Time.* Cambridge: Cambridge University Press.

Sternberg, R. J., and Grajek, S. 1984. "The nature of love." *Journal of Personality and Social Psychology* 47:312–329.

Stets, J. E., and Hammons, S. A. 2002. "Gender, control, and marital commitment." *Journal of Family Issues* 23:3–25.

Stets, J. E., and Straus, M. A. 1990. "Gender differences in reporting marital violence and its medical and psychological consequences." In M. A. Straus, and R. J. Gelles (eds.), *Physical Violence in American Families* (pp. 151–165). New Brunswick, NJ: Transaction Publishers.

Stevens, A. H. 1994. "Persistence in poverty and welfare: The dynamics of poverty spells: Updating Bane and Ellwood." *American Economic Review, 84*:34–37.

Stewart, A., and Rubin, Z. 1976. "The power motive in the dating couple." *Journal of Personality and Social Psychology, 34*:305–309.

Stewart, S. D. 1999. "Nonresident mothers' and fathers' social contact with children." *Journal of Marriage and the Family, 61*:894–907.

——. 2003. "Nonresident parenting and adolescent adjustment: The quality of nonresident father-child interaction." *Journal of Family Issues, 24*:217–244.

Stocker, C. M., and Youngblade, L. 1999. "Marital conflict and parental hostility: Links with children's sibling and peer relationships." *Journal of Family Psychology* 13:598–609.

Stone, L. 1993. *Broken Lives: Separation and Divorce in England 1660–1857.* New York: Oxford University Press.

Stone, R., Cafferata, G. L., and Sangle, J. 1987. "Caregivers of the frail elderly: A national profile." *Gerontologist* 27:616–626.

Straus, M. A. 1999. "The controversy over domestic violence by women: A methodological, theoretical, and sociology of science analysis." In X. B. Arriaga and S. Oskamp, (eds.), *Violence in Intimate Relationships* (pp. 17–44). Thousand Oaks, CA: Sage.

Straus, M. A., and Gelles, R. J. 1990. *Physical Violence in American Families.* New Brunswick, NJ: Transaction Publishers.

Straus, M. A., and Kantor, G. K. 1994. "Corporal punishment of adolescents by parents: A risk factor in the epidemiology of depression, suicide, alcohol abuse, child abuse, and wife beating." *Adolescence, 29*:543–561.

Straus, M. A., and Smith, C. 1990. "Violence in Hispanic families in the United States: Incidence rates and structural interpretations." In M. A. Straus, and R. J. Gelles (eds.), *Physical Violence in American Families* (pp. 341–367). New Brunswick, NJ: Transaction Publishers.

Stryker, S., and Serpe, R. T. 1982. "Commitment, identity salience, and role behavior: Theory and research example." In W. Ickes, and E. Knowles (eds), *Personality, Roles, and Social Behavior* (pp. 199–218). New York: Springer-Verlag.

Substance Abuse and Mental Health Service Administration. 2003. "Overview of findings from the 2002 national survey on drug use and health." Office of Applied Statistics, NHSDA Series H-21, DHHS Publication No. SMA 03-3774. Rockville, MD.

Suitor, J. 1991. "Marital quality and satisfaction with division of household labor." *Journal of Marriage and the Family* 53:221–230.

Suitor, J. J., and Pillemer, K. 1994. "Family caregiving and marital satisfaction: Findings from a 1-year panel study of women caring for parents with dementia." *Journal of Marriage and the Family, 56*:681–690.

Suitor, J. J., Pillemer, K., Keeton, S., and Robison, J. 1995. "Aged parents and aging children: Determinants of relationship quality." In R. Blieszner and V. H. Bedford (eds.), *Handbook of Aging and the Family* (pp. 223–242). Westport, CT: Greenwood.

Sullaway, M., and Christensen, A. 1983. "Assessment of dysfunctional interaction patterns in couples." *Journal of Marriage and the Family* 45:653–660.

Sullivan, O. 1997. "The division of housework among 'remarried' couples." *Journal of Family Issues 18*:205–223.

Sun, Y., and Li, Y. 2002. "Children's well-being during parents' marital disruption process: A pooled time-series analysis." *Journal of Marriage and Family 64*:472–488.

Surra, C. A. 1988. "The influence of the interactive network on developing relationships." In R. M. Milardo (ed.), *Families and Social Networks* (pp. 48–82). Newbury Park, CA: Sage.

Swann, W. B., Jr., 1990. "To be adored or to be known?: The interplay of self-enhancement and self-verification." In E. T. Higgins, and R. M. Sorrentino (eds.), *Handbook of Motivation and Cognition* 2:408–450. New York: Guilford.

Swann, W. B., Jr., Hixon, G., and De La Ronde, C. 1992. "Embracing the bitter 'truth': Negative self-concepts and marital commitment." *Psychological Science 3*:118–121.

Sweeney, M. M. 2002. "Remarriage and the nature of divorce: Does it matter which spouse chose to leave?" *Journal of Family Issues 23*:410–440.

Swinford, S. P., DeMaris, A., Cernkovich, S. A., and Giordino, P. C. 2000. "Harsh physical discipline in childhood and violence in later romantic involvements: The mediating role of problem behaviors." *Journal of Marriage and the Family 62*:508–519.

Szinovacz, M. 1995. "Retirement." In D. Levinson (ed.), *Encyclopedia of Marriage and the Family*, Vol. 2 (pp. 596–600). New York: Simon and Schuster.

——. 1998. "Grandparents today: A demographic profile." *Gerontologist 38*:37–52.

——. 2000. "Retirement." In D. Levinson (ed.), *International Encyclopedia of Marriage and the Family*, Vol. 3 (2nd Ed.), (pp. 1349–1358). New York: Macmillan Reference USA.

Szinovacz, M., and Davey, A. 2001. "Retirement effects on parent-adult child contacts." *Gerontologist 41*:191–200.

Tallman, I. 1976. *Passion, Action, and Politics: A Perspective on Social Problems and Social-problem Solving.* San Francisco: W. H. Freeman.

——. 1995. *Work and Children: A Modern Dilemma.* Pullman, WA: Washington State University.

——. 2003. "Parental identification, couple commitment and problem solving among newlyweds." In J. T. Mortimer and M. Shanahan (eds.), *Handbook of the Life Course* (pp. 103–121). New York: Plenum.

Tallman, I., Burke, P. J., and Gecas, V. 1998. "Socialization into marital roles: Testing a contextual, developmental model of marital functioning." In T. N. Bradbury (ed.), *The Developmental Course of Marital Dysfunction* (pp. 312–342). New York: Cambridge University Press.

Tallman, I., Gray, L., and Leik, R. 1991. "Decisions, dependency and commitment: An exchange based theory of group commitment." In J. E. Lawler, B. Markovsky, C. Ridgeway, and H. A. Walker (eds.), *Advances in Group Processes 8*:227–257. Greenwich, CT: JAI Press.

Taylor, L., Zuckerman, B., Harik, V., and McAlister Groves, B. 1994. "Witnessing violence by young children and their mothers." *Developmental and Behavioral Pediatrics 15*:120–123. (References are from pp. 24, 56).

Taylor, R. 2000. "Diversity within African American families." In D. D. Demo, K. R. Allen, and M. A. Fine (eds.), *Handbook of Family Diversity* (pp. 232–251). New York: Oxford University Press.

Teachman, J. D., Paasch, K., and Carver, K. 1996. "Social capital and dropping out of school early." *Journal of Marriage and the Family 58*:773–783.

Teachman, J. D., Polonko, K. A., and Scanzoni, J. 1987. "Demography of the family." In M. B. Sussman and S. K. Steinmetz (eds.), *Handbook of Marriage and the Family* (pp. 3–36). New York: Plenum Press.

Teachman, J. D., Tedrow, L. M., and Crowder, K. D. 2000. "The changing demography of America's families." *Journal of Marriage and the Family 62*:1234–1246.

Thoits, P. A. 1992. "Identity structures and psychological well-being: Gender and marital status comparisons." *Social Psychology Quarterly 55*:236–256.

Thomas, V. G. 1990. "Determinants of global life happiness and marital happiness in dual-career black couples." *Family Relations 39*:174–178.

Thomas, W. I., and Thomas, Q. S. 1928. *The Child in America.* New York: Knopf.

Thompson, K. 2002. "Battered men." *Pacific Sun*, July 31–August 6, 2002, (pp. 13–17).

Thompson, M. S. 1986. "The influence of supportive relations on the psychological well-being of teenage mothers." *Social Forces 64*:1006–1024.

Thomson, E., McLanahan, S. S., and Braun Curtin, R. 1992. "Family structure, gender, and parental socialization." *Journal of Marriage and the Family 54*:368–378.

Thornburg, K. R., and Brookes, S. J. 2003. "The state of children and families: 2003–2004." Report of the Center for Family Policy and Research, University of Missouri-Columbia.

Thorndike, J. J., Jr. 1976. *The Very Rich: A History of Wealth.* New York: American Heritage/Bonanza Books.

Ting-Toomey, S. 1983. "An analysis of verbal communication patterns in high and low marital adjustment groups." *Human Communication Research 9*:306–319.

Title IX: 25 Years of Progress. 1997. Archived Information, part 3, part 5, <http://www.ed.gov/pubs/TitleIX/title.html>.

Tjaden, P., and Thoennes, N. 2000. *Extent, Nature, and Consequences of Intimate Partner Violence: Findings from the National Violence Against Women Survey.* Washington, DC: U.S. Department of Justice.

Tomb, D. 1991. "The runaway adolescent." In M. Lewis (ed.), *Child and Adolescent Psychiatry* (pp. 171–184). Baltimore, MD: Williams and Wilkins.

Tomita, S. T. 1990. "The denial of elder mistreatment by victims and abusers: The application of neutralization theory." *Violence and Victims* 5:171–184.

Tronner, M. 2000. "A day in the life of Twin Cities media." *Minnesota Law and Politics* 116:13.

Tucker, M. B. 2000. "Marital values and expectations in context: Results from a 21-city survey." In L. J. Waite (ed.), *The Ties That Bind: Perspectives on Marriage and Cohabitation* (pp. 166–187). New York: Aldine de Gruyter.

Twenge, J. M. 1997. " 'Mrs. his name': Women's preferences for married names." *Psychology of Women Quarterly* 21:417–430.

Twiggs, J., McQuillan, J., and Ferree, M. 1999. "Meaning and measurement: Reconceptualizing measure of the division of labor." *Journal of Marriage and the Family* 61:712–724.

Uchitelle, L. 1994. "Moonlighting plus: 3-job families on the rise." *New York Times,* August 16:D1, D18.

Uhlenberg, P. 1980. "Death and the family." *Journal of Family History* 5:313–320.

Uhlenberg, P., and Cooney, T. M. 1990. "Family size and mother-child relations in later life." *Gerontologist* 30:618–625.

Uhlenberg, P., Cooney, T., and Boyd, R. 1990. "Divorce for women after mid-life." *Journal of Gerontology* 45:S3–S11.

Umana-Taylor, A. J., and Fine, M. A. 2003. "Predicting commitment to wed among Hispanic and Anglo partners." *Journal of Marriage and the Family* 65:117–139.

Umberson, D. 1992. "Gender, marital status and the social control of health behavior." *Social Science and Medicine* 34:907–917.

Umberson, D., and Chen, M. D. 1994. "Effects of a parent's death on adult children: Relationship salience and reaction to loss." *American Sociological Review* 59:152–168.

Umberson, D., and Slaten, E. 2000. "Gender and intergenerational relationships." In D. H. Demo, K. R. Allen, and M. A. Fine (eds.), *Handbook of Family Diversity* (pp. 105–127). New York: Oxford University Press.

Umberson, D., Wortman, C. B., and Kessler, R. C. 1992. "Widowhood and depression: Explaining long-term gender differences in vulnerability." *Journal of Health and Social Behavior* 33:10–24.

Unger, D. G., and Wandersman, L. P. 1988. "The relations of family and partner support to the adjustment of adolescent mothers." *Child Development* 59:1056–1060.

U.S. Bureau of the Census. 1996. *Household and Family Characteristics.* March 1995 (Current Population Reports, Series P-20, No 488). Washington, DC: U.S. Government Printing Office.

——. 1998. *Current Population Survey.* Washington, DC: U.S. Government Printing Office.

——. 1999a. "Current population report." *Black Population in the United States,* March. Washington, DC: U.S. Government Printing Office.

——. 1999b. "Population profiles of the U.S: America at the close of the 20th century." *Current Population Reports: Special Studies.* Washington DC: U.S. Government Printing Office.

——. 2000a. Who's minding the kids? Child care arrangements. *Current Population Reports,* Series P70–70. Washington, DC: U.S. Government Printing Office.

——. 2000b. *Statistical Abstract of the United States* (120th Ed.). Table 145. Washington DC: U.S. Government Printing Office.

——. 2000c. "Teen marriages on the rise." Accessed through <http://www.dailyillini.com/nov02/nov14/news/stories/news_story03.shtml>.

——. 2001a. *Poverty in the United States.* Washington, DC: U.S. Government Printing Office.

——. 2001b. *America's Families and Living Arrangements 2000.* Washington, DC: U.S. Government Printing Office.

——. 2001c. *Statistical Abstract of the United States: 2001* (121st Ed.). Table 118, 88. Washington, DC: U.S. Government Printing Office.

——. 2001d. *Current Population Reports Series P60-210.* Washington, DC: U.S. Government Printing Office.

——. 2001e. *Statistical Abstract of the United States: 2001* (121st Ed.). Table 547 355. Washington, DC: U.S. Government Printing Office.

——. 2002a. "Living arrangements of children." *Current Population Reports,* P70-74, March, Washington DC: U.S. Government Printing Office.

——. 2002b. "Mother's Day, 2002: May 12: How many mothers—how many children." (<http://www.census.gov/Press-release/www/2002/cb02ff08.html>).

——. 2003. *African Americans by the Numbers.* <http://www.infoplease.com/spot/bhmcensus1.html>.

——. 2004a. "Women by the numbers." <http://www.infoplease.com/spot/womencensus1.html>.

——. 2004b. *Percent of People in Poverty, by Definition of Income and Selected Characteristics: 2002,* Table 5. April 9. Washington DC: U.S. Government Printing Office.

U.S. Bureau of Labor Statistics. 2000a. *Current Population Survey.* Washington, DC: U.S. Government Printing Office.

——. 2000b. "Trends in Youth Employment: Data from the current population survey." In *The Report on the Youth Labor Force,* Chapter 4 (pp. 30–39). Washington, DC: U.S. Government Printing Office.

——. 2001. *Bulletin 2307.* Washington, DC: U.S. Government Printing Office.

——. 2003. *Employment Situation Summary.* <http://www.bls.gov/news.release/empsit.nr0.htm>.

U.S. Centers for Disease Control. 2000. "U.S. HIV and AIDS cases reported through December 1999 year-end edition." *HIV/AIDS Surveillance Report, 11(2):* PAGE #S??.

U.S. Conference of Mayors. 2000. *A Status Report on Hunger and Homelessness in America's Cities: 1998.* Washington, DC.

U.S. Department of Agriculture. 1997. Expenditures on children by families: 1997 annual report. Washington, DC: Department of Agriculture.

U.S. Department of Health and Human Services. 2002. *National Center for Health Statistics.* <http://www.cdc.gov/nchs>.

U.S. Department of Housing and Urban Development. 2003. *Estimated Median Family Income,* PDR-2003-01, February 20. Washington, DC: U.S. Government Printing Office.

U.S. Department of Justice. 2000a. *1998 Statistical Yearbook of the Immigration and Naturalization Service.* Washington, DC: U.S. Government Printing Office.

——. 2000b. *Intimate Partner Violence,* NCJ 178247.

U.S. Department of Labor. 2002. "A profile of the working poor, 2000." *Bureau of Labor Statistics, Current Population Survey, Report 957.* Washington, DC: U.S. Government Printing Office.

U.S. House of Representatives. 1998. *Green Book: Overview of Entitlement Programs.* Committee on Ways and Means. Washington, DC: U.S. Government Printing Office.

USA Today. 2004. "High court grills pledge plaintiff." March 25, p. 3A.

USA Weekend. 2000. *Parents vs. Nonparents @ Work. USA Weekend,* March 10–12, (pp. 6–7).

Vaillant, C. O., and Vaillant, G. E. 1993. "Is the U-curve of marital satisfaction an illusion? A 40-year study of marriage." *Journal of Marriage and the Family 55:*230–239.

Van Lear, C. A. 1998. "Dialectic empiricism: Science and relationship metaphors." In B. M. Montgomery, and L. A. Baxter (eds.), *Dialectical Approaches to Studying Personal Relationships* (pp. 109–136). Mahwah, NJ: Erlbaum.

Vandell, D. L., McCartney, K., Owen, M. T., Booth, C., and Clarke-Stewart, A. 2003. "Variations in child care by grandparents during the first three years." *Journal of Marriage and the Family 65:*375–381.

VanLaningham, J., Johnson, D. R., and Amato, P. 2001. "Marital happiness, marital duration, and the U-shaped curve: Evidence from a five-wave panel study." *Social Forces 78:*1313–1341.

Vogel, E. F. and Bell, N. W. 1985. "The emotionally disturbed child as the family scapegoat." In G. Handel (ed.), *The Psychological Interior of the Family* (3rd Ed.), (pp. 401–419). New York: Aldine.

von Salisch, M. 2000. "The emotional side of sharing, social support, and conflict negotiation between siblings and between friends." In R. S. L. Mills, and S. Duck (eds.), *The Developmental Psychology of Personal Relationships* (pp. 49–69). Chichester, England: Wiley and Sons.

Voydanoff, P. 1983. "Unemployment: Strategies for family adaptation." In C. R. Figley and H. I. McCubbin (eds.), *Stress and the Family: Catastrophic Stressors,* Vol. II (pp. 90–102). New York: Bruner Mazel.

Voydanoff, P., and Donnelly, B. 1999. "The intersection of time in activities and perceived unfairness in relation to psychological distress and marital quality." *Journal of Marriage and the Family 61:*739–751.

Vuchinich, S., Emery, R., and Cassidy, J. 1988. "Family members as third parties in dyadic family conflict: Strategies, alliances, and outcomes." *Child Development 59:*1293–1302.

Waite, L. J. 2000. "Trends in men's and women's well-being in marriage." In L. J. Waite (ed.), *The Ties That Bind: Perspectives on Marriage and Cohabitation* (pp. 368–392). New York: Aldine.

Waldfogel, J. 1999. "Family leave coverage in the 1990s." *Monthly Labor Review 122:*12–21.

——. 2001. "Family and medical leave: Evidence from the 2000 surveys." *Monthly Labor Review 124:*17–23.

Walker, J. 2003. "Radiating messages: An international perspective." *Family Relations 52:*406–417.

Walker, J. P., and Lee, R. E. 1998. "Uncovering strengths of children of alcoholic parents." *Contemporary Family Therapy 20:*521–538.

Waller, W. 1951. *The Family: A Dynamic Interpretation.* New York: Dryden.

Wallerstein, J., and Blakeslee, S. 1989. *Second Chances.* New York: Ticknor and Fields.

Wallerstein, J. S., and Kelly, J. B. 1980. *Surviving the Breakup: How Children and Parents Cope With Divorce.* London: Grant McIntyre.

Wallerstein, J. S., Lewis, J. M., and Blakeslee. 2000. *The Unexpected Legacy of Divorce: A 25 Year Landmark Study*. New York: Hyperion.

Ward, R. A. 1993. "Marital happiness and household equity in later life." *Journal of Marriage and the Family* 55:427–438.

Waring, E. M. 1988. *Enhancing Marital Intimacy Through Facilitating Cognitive Self-Disclosure*. New York: Brunner/Mazel.

Warner, W. L., and Lund, P. S. 1941. *The Social Life of a Modern Community*. New Haven, CT: Yale University Press.

Warshak, R. A. 2003. "Payoffs and pitfalls of listening to children." *Family Relations* 52:373–384.

Watkins, S. C., Menken, J. A., and Bongaarts, J. 1987. "Demographic foundations of family change." *American Sociological Review* 52:346–358.

Watkins, S. C., Menken, J. A., and Vaughan, B. 1981. *The Fertility of the Formerly Married*. Paper presented at the annual P.A.A. meetings, Washington, DC.

Watt, T. T. 2002. "Marital and cohabiting relationships of adult children of alcoholics: Evidence from the National Survey of Families and Households." *Journal of Family Issues* 23:256–265.

Webster, P. S., and Herzog, A. R. 1995. "Effects of parental divorce and memories of family problems on relationships between adult children and their parents." *Journal of Gerontology: Social Sciences* 50:S24–S34.

Weigel, D. J., and Ballard-Reisch, D. S. 1999. "How couples maintain marriages: A closer look at self and spouse influences upon the use of maintenance behaviors in marriages." *Family Relations* 48:263–269.

Wellman, B., Haase, A. Q., Witte, J., and Hampton, K. 2001. "Does the Internet increase, decrease, or supplement social capital?" *American Behavioral Scientist* 45:436–455.

West, C. 1998. "Lifting the 'political gag order': Breaking the silence around partner violence in ethnic minority families." In J. L. Jasinski, and L. M. Williams (eds.), *Partner Violence: A Comprehensive Review of 20 Years of Research* (pp. 184–209). Thousand Oaks, CA: Sage.

What mothers honestly think about motherhood. Wednesday, April 16, 2003. <http://www.oprah.com>.

Wheaton, B. 1990. "Life transitions, role histories, and mental health." *American Sociological Review* 55:209–223.

Whitbeck, L. B., and Hoyt, D. R. 1999. *Nowhere to Grow: Homeless and Runaway Adolescents and Their Families*. New York: Aldine de Gruyter.

Whitbeck, L. B., Hoyt, D. R., and Huck, S. M. 1994. "Early family relationships, intergenerational solidarity, and support provided to parents by their adult children." *Journal of Gerontology: Social Sciences* 49:S85–S94.

White, L. K. 1990. "Determinants of divorce: A review of research in the eighties." *Journal of Marriage and the Family* 52:904–912.

——. 2001. "Sibling relationships over the life course: A panel analysis." *Journal of Marriage and the Family* 63:555–568.

White, L. K., and Booth, A. V. 1985. "The transition to parenthood and marital quality." *Journal of Family Issues* 6:435–449.

White, L. K., Booth, A., and Edwards, J. N. 1986. "Children and marital happiness: Why the negative correlation?" *Journal of Family Issues* 7:131–147.

White, L. K., and Edwards, J. N. 1990. "Emptying the nest and parental well-being: An analysis of national panel data." *American Sociological Review* 55:235–242.

White, L. K., and Gilbreth, J. G. 2001. "When children have two fathers: Effects of relationships with stepfathers and noncustodial fathers on adolescent outcomes." *Journal of Marriage and the Family* 63:155–167.

White, L. K., and Keith, B. 1990. "The effect of shift work on the quality and stability of marital relations." *Journal of Marriage and the Family* 52:453–462.

White, L. K., and Riedmann, A. 1992a. "When the Brady Bunch grows up: Step-/half- and full sibling relationships in adulthood." *Journal of Marriage and the Family* 54:197–208.

——. 1992b. "Ties Among Adult Siblings." *Social Forces* 71:85–102.

Whitehead, B. D. 1996. *The Divorce Culture*. New York: Knopf.

White-Means, S. I., and Thornton, M. C. 1990. "Ethnic differences in the production of informal home health care." *Gerontologist* 30:758–768.

Widom, C. S. 1989. "The cycle of violence." *Science* 244:160–166.

Wilber, K. H., and McNeilly, D. P. 2001. "Elder abuse and victimization." In J. E. Birren, and K. W. Schaie (eds.), *Handbook of the Psychology of Aging* (pp. 569–591). San Diego: Academic Press.

Wilcox, B. L., and O'Keeffe, J. E. 1991. "Families, policy, and family support policies." In D. Unger, and D. R. Powell (eds.), *Families as Nurturing Systems* (pp. 109–126). New York: Haworth.

Wilcox, W. B. 2002. "Religion, convention, and paternal involvement." *Journal of Marriage and the Family* 64:780–792.

Wiles, C. P. 1995. "Runaway children." In D. Levinson (ed.), *Encyclopedia of Marriage and the Family* 2:600–603. New York: Simon and Schuster Macmillan.

Williams, C. W. 1991. *Black Teenage Mothers: Pregnancy and Child Rearing From Their Perspective.* Lexington, MA: DC Heath, Lexington Books.

Williamson, G. M., and Schulz, R. 1990. "Relationship orientation, quality of prior relationship, and distress among caregivers of Alzheimer's patients." *Psychology and Aging* 5:502–509.

Wilson, B. F., and Clarke, S. C. 1992. "Remarriages: A demographic profile." *Journal of Family Issues* 13:123–141.

Wilson, K. J. 1997. *When Violence Begins at Home: A Comprehensive Guide to Understanding and Ending Domestic Abuse.* Alameda, CA: Hunter House Publications.

Wilson, W. J. 1987. *The Truly Disadvantaged: The Inner City, the Underclass, and Public Policy.* Chicago: University of Chicago Press.

——. 1996. *When Work Disappears: The World of the New Urban Poor.* New York: Knopf.

——. 1998. "When work disappears: The world of the new urban poor." In A. S. Wharton, (ed.), *Working in America* (pp. 167–177). Mountain View, CA: Mayfield.

Wineberg, H., and McCarthy, J. 1993. "Separation and reconciliation in American marriages." *Journal of Divorce and Remarriage* 20:21–42.

Winsborough, H. H., Bumpass, L. L., and Aquilino, W. S. 1991. "The death of parents and the transition to old age." National Survey of Families and Households, Working Paper 39. Madison: Center for Demography and Ecology, University of Wisconsin-Madison.

Wisensale, S. K. 1997. "The White House and Congress on child care and family leave policy: From Carter to Clinton." *Policy Studies Journal* 25:75–86.

Wolf, D. A. 1999. "The family as provider of long-term care: Efficiency, equity, and externalities." *Journal of Aging and Health* 11:360–382.

Wolf, R. S. 2003. "Elder abuse." In J. J. Ponzetti, Jr. (ed.), *International Encyclopedia of Marriage and Family* (2nd Ed.), (pp. 511–513). New York: Macmillan Reference USA.

Wolf, R. S., and Pillemer, K. 1989. *Helping Elderly Victims: The Reality of Elder Abuse.* New York: Columbia University Press.

Wood, D., Valdez, B., Hayaski, T., and Shew, A. 1990. "Homeless and housed families in Los Angeles: A study comparing demographic, economic, and family function characteristics." *American Journal of Public Health* 80:1049–1052.

Working Mother. 2003. "Top 100 companies." *26*:9, 40–62.

Wright, J. W. 2002a. "The number of homeless." *New York Times Almanac: 2002* (p. 294). New York: Penguin Reference Books.

——. 2002b. "Households and families." *New York Times Almanac, 2002* (p. 286–289). New York: Penguin Reference.

——. 2003a. *New York Times 2004 Almanac.* New York: Penguin Reference.

——. 2003b. "Households and families: Growth and change, 1960–2000." *New York Times 2004 Almanac*, p. 287. New York: Penguin Reference.

——. 2003c. "Median age at first marriage, by sex, 1890–2000." *New York Times Almanac, 2004*, p. 283. New York: Penguin Reference.

——. 2003d. "Resident population of the U.S. by race and Hispanic origin, 1990–2000." *New York Times 2004 Almanac*, p. 268. New York: Penguin Reference.

Wright, L. K. 1991. "The impact of Alzheimer's disease on the marital relationship." *Gerontologist* 31:224–237.

Yllo, K. 1993. "Through a feminist lens: Gender, power, and violence." In R. J. Gelles, and D. Loseke (eds.), *Current Controversies on Family Violence* (pp. 47–62). Newbury Park, CA: Sage.

Youniss, J., and Smollar, J. 1985. *Adolescent Relations With Mothers, Fathers, and Friends.* Chicago: University of Chicago Press.

Zedeck, S. 1992. *Work, Families, and Organization.* San Francisco: Jossey-Bass.

Zedlewski, S. R. 2002. "Many families turn to food pantries for help." *Snapshots 3(17)*:17. Retrieved from <http://www.urban.org>, July 22, 2003.

Zillmann, D., Bryant, J., and Huston, A. C. 1994. *Media, Children, and the Family: Social Scientific, Psychodynamic, and Clinical Perspectives.* Hillsdale, NJ: Erlbaum.

Zimmerman, S. L. 1995. *Understanding Family Policy: Theories and Applications* (2nd Ed.). Thousand Oaks, CA: Sage. ✦

Author Index

A, B, C

Abel, E. K. 186
Acitelli, L. K. 123
Acock, A. 230, 273, 275
Adams, G. 212
Adams, J. M. 47, 53, 61, 62, 72
Adler, N. L. 77
Ahrons, C. A. 262, 263, 265, 268, 282
Akiyama, H. 153
Aldarondod, E. 304, 333
Alford-Cooper, F. 193
Allan, G. 86
Allen, C. T. 68, 328
Allen, K. R. 205
Allen, M. P. 24, 25
Alwin, D. F. 166, 167
Amato, P. R. 35, 61, 64, 124, 125,
    192, 253, 254, 257, 258, 259,
    261, 262, 264, 266, 268, 269,
    270, 271, 272, 273, 279
Ames, B. 190
Anda, R. F. 281, 293
Anderson, E. R. 282, 305
Anderson, K. L. 279, 282, 303, 306,
    307,
Anderson, S. A. 117
Angel, J. L. 185, 186
Angel, R. J. 185, 186
Antonucci, T. C. 153
Aquilino, W. S. 175, 177, 181, 286
Archer, M. 25
Arditti, J. A. 265
Arendell, T. 240
Arias, I. 308
Armistead, L. 149
Arnold, C. 281
Arond, M. 119
Asbury, J. 305
Aseltine, R. H. 261, 273
Astone, N. M. 103, 273
Atchison, K. A. 115
Auger, D. G. 86
Avenevoli, S. 264, 274
Avison, W. R. 257
Ayers, T. S. 330, 347
Babbie, E. 34, 35
Baca-Zinn, M. 224, 305
Bachman, J. C. 232

Bachman, J. G. 202
Bachrach, C. 92
Bailey, B. L. 84
Bakan, D. 118
Baldwin, A. 274
Baldwin, B. M. 305–308
Baldwin, C. 274
Barber, B. 160, 231
Barling, J. 308
Barnett, R. C. 217, 222, 223–224, 248
Barratt, M. S. 142
Bart, P. B. 180
Barth, R. P. 151
Bartholet, E. 145
Bartkowski, J. P. 16, 305
Bates, J. E. 149
Baucom, D. 79
Baumrind, D. 148, 149
Bavin, S. 199
Beaman, J. 236
Becerra, R. M. 186
Becker, G. 258
Becker, H. S. 48
Becker, W. C. 148
Beers, J. R. 133
Bell, A. P. 89
Bell, C. 329
Bell, N. W. 12
Bellah, R. N. 96, 293, 294
Belsky, J. 136, 137, 139, 140, 149,
    150, 151, 153, 155, 173
Bengtson, V. L. 151, 177, 181, 182,
    183, 184, 191, 283
Benn, J. L. 143
Benokraitis, N. V. 82
Benson, M. L. 304
Bergen, R. K. 309, 333
Berger, P. 60
Bergeron, L. R. 319
Bergman, L. 308
Berheide, C. 217
Berk, S. F. 56, 230, 231
Berman, S. 329
Berry, G. L. 168
Berry, H. 45
Berscheid, E. 82
Bianchi, S. M. 91, 99, 131
Biblarz, T. J. 165, 286

Biglan, A. 151, 327
Bigner, J. J. 132, 152, 159
Billy, J. O. G. 335, 340
Bingham, C. R. 338
Binstock, G. 255
Black, C. 322
Black, D. 88, 100
Blair, S. L. 226
Blank, R. M. 202, 246
Blankenship, J. 113, 288
Blau, J. R. 25
Blazer, D. G. 239
Blood, R. O. 111
Bloom, B. L. 254
Blossfeld, H. 207
Bluestone, C. 150, 151
Blumstein, P. 31, 110–116
Bodman, D. A. 55
Bogenschneider, K. 244, 347, 348,
    349, 353
Boland, J. P. 147
Bolea, P. S. 59, 60, 132
Boll, E. S. 167
Bologna, M. J. 311
Bond, J. T. 210
Bonnell, D. 119
Booth, A. 33, 64, 72, 109, 125, 139,
    192, 237, 239, 261, 270, 272,
    276, 293
Booth, C. L. 212
Bornstein, M. H. 156, 157, 173
Bossard, N. H. 167
Bottoms, B. L. 314
Boudreau, F. A. 318
Bowen, G. L. 62
Bowen, N. K. 62
Bradbury, T. N. 109, 123
Brandl, B. 318
Brandreth, Y. 266
Brassard, J. 153, 154
Braun Curtin, R. 273, 281
Braver, S. L. 254, 269, 274
Bray, J. H. 277
Brecher, E. M. 115, 116
Brice, G. C. 190
Briere, J. 314, 315
Broadhurst, D. D. 314
Brockopp, K. 308

Brodsky, A. E. 64
Brody, E. M. 187, 189, 191, 205
Brody, G. H. 149, 164, 165
Brommel B. J. 117
Bronfenbrenner, U. 18, 20
Brooks, J. B. 158
Brooks, J. L. 355
Brooks, R. H. II. 82
Brooks-Gunn, J. 161
Brown, J. 162
Brubaker, T. 194, 237
Bruunk, B. 119
Bryson, K. 197, 283
Buchalter, G. 60
Buchanan, C. M. 273
Buchbinder, S. B. 345, 346
Buehler, C. 290
Bulcroft, K. 102, 200, 273
Bulcroft, R. A. 102, 273
Bumpass, L. L. 90, 91, 92, 175, 268, 275, 287
Burchinal, M. 141
Burgess, A. 324
Buriel, R. 151
Burke, P. J. 48, 49, 105
Burton, D. 329
Burton, L. M. 29, 131, 197
Bush, K. R. 55
Bushwall, S. J. 273
Buss, D. 82, 94, 95
Buttenwieser, E. 313, 328
Bwanausa, C. 329
Cadenhead, C. 329
Cafferata, G. L. 186
Cahn, D. D. 119
Cain, R. L. 143
Caldwell, R. A. 254
Calhoun, A. W. 287
Call, K. T. 152, 230
Call, V. 195
Callan, V. J. 119
Campbell, C. 329
Campbell, K. E. 64
Campbell, L. D. 194
Canary, D. J. 122, 123
Cancian, F. M. 118
Capizzano, J. 212
Caplow, T. 271
Carlsmith, J. M. 273
Carlson, M. J. 166, 272
Carmody, D. C. 273
Carpenter, B. D. 191
Carr, D. 200
Carrere, S. 128
Carroll, J. S. 141
Carstensen, L. L. 185, 193
Carver, K. 340
Cascardi, M. 300, 303, 308
Casper, L. M. 197, 283
Cauce, A. M. 224
Caughlin, J. P. 61
Cavanaugh, J. 192
Cazenave, N. A. 315, 317
Cedrone, A. R. 254
Ceglian, C. P. 284
Cernkovich, S. A. 300, 301, 308, 314
Chadwick, B. A. 129, 131, 133

Chalmers, D. 329
Chalmers, M. A. 313, 328
Chamberlain, R. 89
Chamberlin, R. 144
Chan, S. Q. 151
Chao, R. 149
Chapman, D. 322
Chapman, N. J. 190
Charles, A. V. 317
Chase-Lansdale, P. L. 273
Chatters, L. M. 183
Chen, M. D. 198
Cheng, L. 28
Cherlin, A. J. 89, 91, 210, 240, 268, 273, 276, 277, 281, 282, 283, 284, 293, 295, 329
Cheung, F. K. 344
Chew, E. 308
Chorn Dunham, C. 55
Chow, E. 217
Christensen, A. 119, 120, 156
Christiansen, S. L. 138
Church, E. 281
Chyi-In, W. 150
Cicirelli, V. G. 195
Clark-Nicolas, P. 110
Clark-Steward, K. A. 212, 213
Clarke, L. H. 237
Clarke, S. C. 253, 275
Clausen, J. A. 166
Clausen, S. R. 166
Cleek, M. G. 61
Clingempeel, W. G. 282, 305
Clogg, C. C. 182
Cochran, M. 153, 154, 173
Cohen, D. 329
Colarossi, L. G. 137
Cole, D. A. 180
Cole, R. E. 274
Coleman, J. 67, 340, 360
Coleman, M. 59, 275, 281, 282, 283, 284, 293, 296
Coleman, V. E. 311
Coll, C. G. T. 150
Collins, C. 209
Collins, W. A. 159, 160
Coltrane, S. 169, 210, 224, 225
Conger, K. J. 236
Conger, R. D. 10, 150, 218, 236, 250
Conley, C. 86
Connidis, I. A. 194, 199
Connolly, J. 84, 97
Cook, P. W. 309
Cook, T. D. 66
Cooley, C. 51, 53, 68, 70
Cooney, T. M. 92, 98, 131, 152, 165, 175, 184, 185, 202, 205, 230, 231, 238, 253, 256, 272
Coontz, S. 169
Cooper, C. R. 176, 177
Cooper, R. G. 158
Cooperman, A. 357
Corbett, T. 348
Corcoran, M. E. 272, 340
Cornell, C. P. 306, 317
Costa, P. T. 262

Cowan, C. P. 105, 122, 134, 135, 138, 139, 140, 141, 155
Cowan, P. A. 105, 122, 134, 135, 138, 139, 140, 141, 155, 281
Cox, A. 212
Cox, M. J. 141, 212
Craft, J. L. 314, 316, 385
Crnic, K. 154, 155, 157
Crockett, L. J. 338
Crohan, S. E. 121, 139
Cromwell, R. E. 111
Crosnoe, R. 341, 342
Crouter, A. C. 55, 72, 123, 218, 250
Crouter, S. C. 231
Crowder, K. D. 102, 129
Cuber, J. 11
Cummings, E. M. 314
Cunningham, M. 224
Curry, L. C. 318

D, E, F

DaVanzo, J. 202
Dail, P. W. 169
Dainton, M. 123
Dallas, C. 156
Daniel, J. 190–191
Daniels, A. K. 25
Daniels, D. 163
Darabi, K. F. 150
Daro, D. 313
Datzman, J. 86
Davey, A. 237, 239
Davies, L. 194, 257
Davies, P. T. 314
Davis, K. E. 81
Dawson, L. J. 311
Dawson-McClure, S. R. 275
De La Ronde, C. 53
DeFrain, J. 32, 118
DeGenova, M. K. 154
DeHart, G. B. 158
DeMarie, A. A. 304
DeMaris, A. 199, 266, 276, 277, 279, 304, 308
DeVault, M. 230
DeViney, S. 239
Deater-Deckard, K. 274
Decalmer, P. 318, 319
Dekovic, M. 152
Delgado-Gaitan, C. 151
Demo, D. H. 43, 55, 230, 273, 275
Demos, J. 16, 287
Diana, M. S. 82
Dickert, J. 212
Diebold, F. X. 202
Dietz, T. L. 183, 186
Dillon, P. 290
Dilworth, J. E. L. 217, 218
Dilworth-Anderson, P. 186, 187, 189, 191
DiPrete, T. A. 260, 269
Dixler, B. 342
Dodge, K. A. 149
Dodson, L. 212
Doka, K. J. 284
Donn, J. 82
Donnelly, B. W. 226, 279, 290

Donnelly, D. 116
Dore, M. M. 321
Dornbusch, S. M. 273
Dorr, A. 29, 167, 169
Dorsey, S. 149
Doubleday, C. 169
Douglas, W. 169
Dowler, D. W. 190
Downey, D. B. 263
Drobnic, S. 207, 208
Drotar, D. 313
DuRant, R. 329
Dube, S. R. 281, 293
Dubowitz, H. 316
Dubrow, N. 329
Duff, R. W. 239
Duggan, A. K. 345, 346
Duncan, G. J. 28, 260, 285, 340
Duncan, S. W. 118
Dunn, J. 129, 162, 163, 164, 173
Dunne, K. 98, 205, 238
Dura, J. R. 261
Dutton, D. 311, 312, 326
Earls, F. 63
Easterbrooks, M. A. 155
Ebata, A. 306
Eccles, J. 342
Edwards, J. N. 109, 180, 192
Edwards, T. M. 73
Edwards, V. J. 281, 293
Eggebeen, D. J. 175, 182, 185, 267
Eggeletion, L. 131
Eidelson, R. J. 79
Ekerdt, D. J. 237, 239
Elde, C. L. 145
Elder, G. H. 262, 288
Elder, G. H., Jr. 10, 54, 236, 250
Elliot, D. M. 314, 315
Ellison, C. G. 16
Ellman, I. M. 274
Emery, B. C. 300, 303
Emery, R. E. 36, 265, 272, 289, 290, 291
Emlen, A. 190
Emshoff, J. G. 322
Ensminger, M. E. 265
Epstein, J. L. 64, 79, 340
Epstein, M. A. 314, 333
Epstein, N. 79
Erikson, E. H. 58, 177
Fabricius,W. V. 274
Fagot, B. I. 56
Farber, B. 292, 293, 295, 296
Farley, R. 183
Farran, C. J. 191
Farrell, M. P. 177
Fauber, R. 155
Fawcett, J. T. 132
Feeney, J. A. 119
Feigelman,W. C. 146
Feld, S. 107
Felitti, V. J. 281, 293
Felmlee, D. 86, 87, 88
Felson, R. B. 163
Ferarro, K. J. 257, 297, 301, 302
Fernandez-Kelly, M. P. 210
Ferree, M. 223

Ferris, M. 220
Fick, A. C. 329
Fields, J. 131, 132, 133
Finch, M. M. 189
Fincham, F. D. 155
Fine, M. A. 48, 87, 264, 273, 275, 279, 280, 281, 290
Finer, J. 357
Fingerman, K. L. 177, 184, 185
Finkelhor, D. 310, 315
Finz, S. 299
Fischer, J. L. 317
Fisher, E. 306
Fisher, H. 76
Fitch, C. A. 101, 201
Fitzpatrick, M. A. 117, 269
Flint, E. P. 239
Flor, D. L. 149
Florsheim, P. 139, 140, 151
Flory, J. 178
Follingstad, D. R. 117
Foner, A. 38
Ford, D. 31
Forehand, R. 149, 155
Forman, T. A. 83
Forney, R. 27
Forthofer, M. S. 217
Fowlkes, M. R. 89, 90, 100, 304
Fox, G. L. 266
Fox, S. 168, 306
Foy, D. 329
Franklin, S. 43, 190
Fravel, D. L. 145
Fredriksen, K. I. 199
Friedman, D. E. 209
Frieze, I. H. 78
Frone, M. R. 217
Fuddy, L. 345, 346
Fuller, B. 354
Fulmer, T. T. 330
Furman, W. 84, 164
Furstenberg, F. F. 66, 68, 265, 276, 277, 280, 282, 284, 293, 340
Furstenberg, F. F., Jr. 66

G, H, I

Gable, S. 155, 231
Gaboury, M. T. 338, 348, 349
Gager, C. T. 152, 167, 230, 231
Gagnon, J. H. 81, 90
Galambos, N. L. 339, 340
Galinsky, E. 134, 147, 157, 171, 172, 209
Gallagher, S. K. 55
Gallmeier, C. 73
Galvin, K. M. 117
Ganong, L. H. 59, 282, 283, 284, 293, 296
Gans, D. 318, 330
Gara, M. A. 150
Garasky, S. 267
Garbarino, J. 63, 143, 306, 315, 317, 329, 337–340, 343, 345, 346, 348, 349, 350
Garcia, A. M. 211
Gardner, C. B. 86
Garfinkel, I. 269

Garrett, G. 166
Gates, G. 88, 100
Gecas, V. 48, 49, 105
Geiss, S. K. 117
Gelles, R. J. 298, 300, 303–306, 308, 313, 314, 316, 317, 320, 326, 327
Gensheimer, L. K. 330, 347
George, L. K. 239
Gerris, J. R. M. 152
Gershoff, E. T. 152
Gerson, K. 125
Gerstel, N. 55, 216
Giancola, P. 321
Gibbs, N. 213
Gibson, B. E. 191
Gibson, L. 73
Gibson, R. C. 320
Gilbreth, J. G. 268, 269, 280
Gilchrist, L. D. 151
Gilliland, T. 141
Gillman, S. 219
Ginsberg, L. H. 29
Giordino, P. C. 300, 301, 308, 314
Glass, G. 55
Gleason, M. E. J. 82
Glenn, N. D. 79, 125
Gold, D. T. 195, 99
Goldberg, A. 97
Goldberg, W. A. 155
Goldman, N. 99
Goldscheider, C. 202
Goldscheider, F. K. 202, 213, 231
Gondolf, E. W. 306
Goode, W. J. 83, 306
Goodwin, M. P. 163
Gordon, C. 50
Gorey, K. M. 190
Gormly, A. V. 131, 133
Gormly, J. B. 131, 133
Gottainer, G. 286
Gottlieb, B. 344
Gottman, J. M. 76, 117, 119, 120, 128, 158, 193, 209, 258
Grady, W. 238
Graham, E. H. 150
Grajek, S. 96
Granfort, E. 321
Gray, L. 48–50
Gray-Little, B. 110
Green, A. S. 82
Greenberg, M. T. 154, 157
Greene, A. L. 178, 179
Greene, S. M. 282, 305
Greer, S. 65
Greiff, V. 115
Greven, P. J., Jr. 16
Grief, G. L. 266
Griffin, L. W. 318–320
Groskind, F. 340
Gross, H. 216
Gross, R. T. 273
Grossman, S. 169
Grote, N. K. 78
Grotevant, H. D. 145, 146, 176, 177
Grych, J. H. 155
Grzywacz, J. G. 218
Guacci-Franco, N. 159

Guisinger, S. 281
Gupta, S. 223, 225, 260
Gurin, G. 107
Gusfield, J. 63
Guthrie, D. M. 117
Haas, B. 152
Haas, S. M. 123
Hackstaff, K. B. 105, 108, 293
Hagestad, G. O. 57, 165, 179, 197
Hahlweg, K. 120
Haine, R. A. 275
Hair, E. C. 355
Halle, D. 20, 27
Hamby, S. L. 302
Hamer, J. 267
Hammons, S. A. 303
Hampton, R. L. 313, 314
Han, S.-Y. 68
Hand, S. I. 136
Hann, D. M. 329
Hanson, B. 311
Hanson, T. L. 260
Hardin, B. J. 311
Hardy, M. A. 238
Harik, V. 329
Harkins, E. B. 180
Harold, A. 343
Harrington, D. 316
Harris, L. E. 65
Harris, M. L. 159
Harrison, A. O. 149, 151
Harroff, P. 11
Harrop, J. 313, 314
Hartman, C. 341
Hastorf, A. H. 273
Hatch, L. R. 200
Hatfield, E. 77, 78, 82
Hausman, A. 329
Hawkins, A. J. 220
Hayaski, T. 30
Hayes, H. R. 322
Hays, J. C. 239
Hays, S. 357, 360
Hayward, M. D. 238
Heard, H. E. 265, 267, 268, 270
Heaton, T. B. 33, 129, 131, 133
Heavey, C. L. 120, 156
Henderson, C. R. 277
Henderson, D. A. 29, 243
Hendrick, C. 78
Hendrick, S. S. 78
Henry, C. S. 284
Herbst, J. H. 262
Herzog, A. R. 184
Herzog, E. P. 150
Hetherington, E. M. 251, 254, 261,
    262, 269, 273, 276, 282, 283, 296
Hicks, L. 271
Hiedemann, B. 256
Hill, C. R. 157, 211
Hill, C. T. 85, 112, 211
Hill, E. J. 219, 220
Hill, M. S. 202
Hill, T. 304
Himes, C. L. 175, 202
Hindin, M. J. 92
Hines, A. M. 273, 275, 279, 280

Hixon, G. 53
Hochschild, A. 36, 112, 219, 220, 221,
    223
Hodges, W. F. 254
Hodson, R. 207
Hofferth, S. 150
Hoffman, C. 189
Hoffman, J. 150
Hoffman, S. D. 28, 260
Hofmeister, H. 237
Hogan, D. P. 103, 175, 182, 183, 185
Holahan, C. J. 177
Holden, G. W. 152
Hollander, J. 309
Holman, T. 64
Holmbeck, G. N. 161
Holmes, J. G. 75
Holtzworth-Munroe, A. 303
Hong, L. K. 239
Hooven, C. 158
Hops, H. 151
Horan, D. L. 318
Horowitz, K. 329
Horrigan, J. 168, 306
House, J. S. 28, 192, 200
Houseknecht, S. K. 122
Houts, R. M. 192
Howard, J. A. 113, 309
Howard, P. E. N. 168
Howes, P. W. 155
Hoyt, D. R. 184, 322, 324, 325, 328
Hu, Y. 99
Hubbard, A. S. E. 76
Huber, J. 209
Huck, S. 184
Hughes, D. 241
Hughes, P. 142
Hunter, A. G. 265
Hunter, M. 209, 211
Hurd, E. P. 147
Hurwitz, S. 29
Huston, T. L. 61, 123, 136, 137, 139,
    192, 259, 303
Ihinger-Tallman, M. 59, 277. 278
Ingersoll-Dayton, B. 190
Inman-Amos, J. 78
Ishii-Kuntz, M. 225
Ispa, J. M. 102

J, K, L

Jacklin, C. N. 55
Jackson, J. S. 83
Jacob, T. 321
Jacobs, S. L. 179
Jacobsen R. B. 132, 152
James, W. 50
Janssens, J. M. A. M. 152
Janus, M. D. 324
Jarrett, R. L. 66, 138
Jasinski, J. 304, 333
Jekel, J. 329
Jencks, C. 337, 340
Jendrek, M. P. 197
Jenkins, E. 329
Jenkins, J. 165
Jodl, K. M. 269
John, D. 225

Johnson, C. J. 192
Johnson, C. L. 284
Johnson, D. R. 125, 192
Johnson, E. 33
Johnson, J. 329
Johnson, M. P. 38, 61, 259, 297, 301–
    307, 314, 326
Johnston, L. D. 202
Jones, A. R. 347
Jones, D. J. 266
Jones, S. 168
Jones, W. H. 61, 72
Jones Hardin, B. 328
Jordan, B. 144
Josselson, R. 176
Joung, I. M. A. 108, 274
Kach, J. A. 141
Kagan, S. L. 354
Kahana, B. 196
Kahana, E. 196
Kahn, A. J. 63, 339, 345, 350, 351,
    352
Kamerman, S. B. 339, 350, 351, 352
Kane, R. A. 189
Kane, R. L. 189
Kantor, G. K. 314
Karney, B. R. 109, 123
Katz, L. F. 158
Kauffman, E. 321
Kaufman, G. 169
Kaufman, J. E. 191
Kaufman, L. 355, 356
Kaufman-Kantor, G. 304
Kayser, K. 253
Kee, A. M. 220
Keeton, S. 181
Keith, B. 214, 218, 272
Kellner, D. 167
Kellner, H. 60
Kelly, J. B. 137, 173, 265, 272, 273,
    286, 289, 296
Kelly, R. F. 266
Kendall-Tackett, K. A. 315
Kendrick, C. 164
Kenney, M. E. 180
Kephart, G. 102
Kerbow, D. 341
Kerckhoff, A. C. 81
Kerig, P. K. 155
Kerkstra, A. 119
Kessler, R. C. 200, 261
Kessler-Sklar, S. 241
Kidwell, J. S. 317
Kiecolt-Glaser, J. K. 261
Kiernan, K. E. 272
Kiesler, S. 168
Kim, J. E. 237
King, S. 190
King, V. 265, 267, 268, 270
Kinney, J. M. 190, 192
Kinsella, K. 203
Kinsey, A. C. 88, 89
Kirkpatrick, L. A. 82
Kirkwood, C. 303
Kitson, G. C. 254, 255, 258
Kitzmann, K. M. 289, 290
Kleban, M. H. 189

Klein, M. 304
Klepinger, D. 183
Klinetob, N. A.
Klock, R. 165
Knickman, J. R. 30
Knitzer, J. 339
Knox, D. 73, 103, 104, 358
Knudson-Martin, C. 230
Koblinsky, S. A. 315, 328, 329
Koenig, H. G. 239
Kohl, J. 330
Kohn, M. L. 26, 27, 151
Kolata, G. B. 81
Kollock, P. 113
Komarovsky, M. 107, 118
Konarski, R. 84
Kostelny, K. 339, 340, 348, 360
Kovaric, P. 169
Kowal, A. 163
Kozuch, P. 92
Kramer, E. 143
Kramer, L. 163
Kranichfeld, M. 112, 113
Kraut, R. 168
Kurdek, L. A. 109, 112, 113, 121, 139, 192, 225, 259, 260, 273, 279, 281
Kurtines, W. 329
Kuypers, J. A. 177
Lachman, M. E. 134, 142
Lackey, C. 297, 314
Lambert, J. D. 266, 272
Lamborn, S. D. 274
Land, K. C. 239
Landerman, L. R. 239
Landis, E. M. 258
Landry, D. J. 102
Laney, M. C. 168
Langlie, J. K. 255
Lansford, J. 153
Lapsley, D. K. 180
Larsen, R. J. 82, 94, 95
Larson, E. 168, 306
Larson, R. 160, 219, 221, 222
Lauer, J. C. 259
Lauer, R. H. 259
Laumann, J. H. 81
Lawton, L. 183
Lawton, M. P. 191
Leber, D. 110
Lee, B. A. 64, 65
Lee, G. R. 192, 193, 194, 199, 200
Lee, J. A. 77
Lee, T. R. 195
Leggett, S. 169
Leiderman, H. 273
Leik, R. 48
Lenhart, A. 168, 306
Lenzner, R. 24
Leonard, S. A. 104
Leondan-Wright, B. 209
Lerner, J. V. 142
Levenson, R. W. 120, 193
Leventhal, B. 311, 328
Levinger, G. 159, 258, 259, 288
Levitt, J. L. 159
Levitt, M. J. 159
Lewin, C. 151, 327

Lewin, K. 59
Lewin, T. 353, 354
Lewis, R. A. 87, 305
Li, Y. 253
Lichter, D. T. 102
Lieberman, S. 142
Lillard, L. A. 274
Linder, C. 329
Lindsey, E. W. 29, 30
Lindsey, L. L. 32
Liss, L. 106
Livingstone, S. 168
Lloyd, K. M. 257, 288
Lloyd, S. A. 300, 303
Locke, D. 153
Lockheart, L. L. 304, 306
Lofland, J. 37
Lofland, L. H. 37
Logan, J. R. 175, 185, 188
Long, F. N. 339, 343, 345
Loprest, P. J. 355, 356
Lorenz, F. O. 184
Loseke, D. R. 303
Lovell, V. 211
Lozoff, B. 144
Lu, H. H. 90–92
Lubben, J. E. 115, 186
Lundmark, V. 168
Lundy, S. E. 311
Luster, T. 152, 173
Lynch, S. A. 137
Lynd, H. 166
Lynd, R. 166
Lytton, H. 152

M, N, O

MacDonald, J. 51, 139, 140,
MacDonald, W. L. 276, 277, 297
Maccoby, E. E. 55, 118, 148, 273
Mace, D. R. 346
Machenback, J. P. 108, 274
Macke, A. S. 122
Madden-Derdich, D. 104
Madsen, R. 96
Magee, C. 150
Maguire, M. C. 231
Mahoney, A. R. 152
Mahoney, P. 230, 309, 310
Malone, J. 308
Malone, S. 144
Mancini, J. A. 194
Manke, B. A. 55
Manning, W. D. 260, 267, 268
Marans, S. 329
Marchioro, K. 267
Margolin, L. 314, 316
Markel, K. S. 217
Markman, H. J. 99, 118, 155
Marks, N. F. 218
Marks, S. 28
Maroney, T. 311
Marshall, R. 315
Marsiglio, W. 116
Martin, C. D. 119
Martin, C. E. 88, 89
Martin, J. A. 148
Martin, J. L. 313

Martin, T. C. 287
Martin-Matthews, A. 188
Martinez, P. 329
Marx, K. 25
Mascia, J. L. 342
Masheter, C. 261, 262
Massey, G. 149
Matthews, L. S. 188, 218
Matthews, S. H. 186, 187, 289, 290
Matthias, R. E. 115
Maxwell, J. S. 151
Maxwell, J. W. 194
May, D. C. 218
Mayer, S. E. 337, 340
Maynard, S. 321
McAdoo, H. P. 147
McAlister Groves, B. 329
McAlpine, D. D. 257
McCall, G. J. 50
McCandlish, B. 140
McCarthy, J. 254
McCartney, K. 212, 213
McCauley, M. 300, 312, 313, 330, 333
McCormack, A. 324
McCormack, S. 24
McCoy, J. K. 149, 164, 165
McCrae, R. R. 262
McCubbin, H. I. 68, 328
McCubbin, M. A. 68, 328
McCullough, D. 233
McCurdy, K. 313
McDonough, P. 28
McFarlane, E. C. 345, 346
McFerron, J. R. 306
McGhee, P. E. 141
McHale, J. P. 155
McHale, S. M. 55, 123, 136, 137, 139, 250
McHenry, P. C. 263, 265, 287, 290, 360
McKenna, K. Y. A. 82
McLanahan, S. S. 124, 260, 271, 272, 273
McLaughlin, D. K. 102
McLaughlin, K. 342
McLoyd, V. C. 224
McManus, P. A. 260, 269
McNeilly, D. P. 318, 330
McPherson, D. 140
McQuillan, J. 223
McRae, C. 273
McRoy, R. G. 145, 146
Mead, G. H. 51, 52, 53, 70, 72
Meese, J. L. 53
Melby, J. N. 184
Menken, J. A. 181
Mero, R. P. 28, 192, 200
Merrill, D. M. 187–189
Merriwether-de Vries, C. 131, 140
Mertz, M. E. 284
Messineo, M. 169, 210, 224, 225
Metts, S. 79
Meyer, A. 338
Meyer, D. R. 163, 267
Meyers, T. J. 16
Michael, R. H. 88, 93, 114, 115, 116
Michael, R. T. 256

Migliaccio, T. A. 309
Milardo, R, M. 38, 86
Milkie, M. A. 37, 226, 229
Miller, B. C. 219, 220
Miller, J. D. 342
Miller, J. G. 4, 13
Miller, M. 98
Miller, P. C. 152
Miller, S. L. 312, 326
Minkler, M. 197
Mirowsky, J. 209, 261, 272, 273
Mitchell, V. 135–137
Moen, P. 237, 238, 239, 337
Moffitt, R. A. 355
Money, J. 78
Monroe, P. A. 348, 349
Montgomery, M. J. 78
Mooradian, A. D. 115
Moore, C. 147
Moore, D. 139, 140, 151
Moore, K. A. 354
Moore, L. 329
Moore, V. L. 259
Moos, R. H. 177
Morgan, L. A. 285
Morgan, M. 169
Morrison, J. 102
Morrow, K. B. 315
Mortimer, J. T. 231–233
Moser, R. P. 321
Moss, M. S. 198, 199, 201
Moss, S. Z. 198, 199, 201
Mounts, N. S. 273
Mukophadhyay, T. 168
Mullen, P. E. 313
Muller, C. 341, 342
Munn, P. 163
Mutschler, P. H. 190
Myers, S. M. 237, 239
Nadel, M. V. 354
Naifeh, M. 28
Namerow, P. B. 150
Nathanson, C. A. 103, 273
Neal, M. B. 190
Neidig, P. H. 307
Nelson-LeGall, S. 224
Nelson-Zlupko, L. 321
Nesse, R. M. 200
Neugarten, B. L. 57, 196, 199
Neumark, D. 202
Newman, B. M. 280
Newman, K. S. 23, 178, 234, 235
Ng, C. 254
Nock, S. L. 106–108
Noller, P. 117, 119, 121
Noonan, M. C. 222
Norris, K. 58
Nydegger, C. 176, 180, 205
Nye, F. I. 166
Oakley, A. 134
Oates, R. K. 313
Ogburn, W. F. 291
Oggins, J. 110
Oh, H. J. 28, 29
Oh, W. 150
Olasky, M. 63, 345
Olds, D. L. 144

Olson, A. K. 117
Olson, B. 169
Olson, D. H. 32, 34, 35, 111, 169
Ono, H. 256
Orbuch, T. L. 192
Orleans, M. 168
Orsmond, G. I. 142
Ortega, S. 83
Osborne, L. N. 155
Osofsky, J. D. 329
Osterweil, D. A. 137, 140
Ostrander, S. A. 24
Owen, M. T. 212, 213
O'Connell, P. L. 73
O'Keefe, N. K. 308
O'Keeffe, J. E. 203
O'Leary, K. D. 117, 300, 303, 307
O'Malley, P. M. 202
O'Rand, A. M. 256

P, Q, R

Paasch, K. 340
Page, S. 339
Pagelow, M. D. 309, 310
Paikoff, R. L. 161
Paley, B. 141
Palkovitz, R. 138
Pan, H. S. 307
Pargament, K. I. 152
Parke, R. D. 155
Parker, A. 321
Parks, M. R. 117
Pasley, B. K. 59, 277, 278
Patterson, C. 31, 137, 140
Patterson, G. 164
Patterson, M. 168
Pauker, S. L. 119
Payne, C. C. 141
Peacock, P. 309, 310
Pearson, J. 289
Pearson, T. A. 61
Pedersen, F. A. 143
Peek, C. W. 317
Pendergrast, R. 329
Penrod, J. D. 189
Pensky, E. 136, 137, 139, 141
Peplau, L. A. 85,
Perez, C. M. 313
Perry-Jenkins, M. 215, 216, 218
Peters, M. F. 149
Petersen, A. C. 338
Peterson, G. W. 55, 104
Peterson, K. S. 73
Peth-Pierce, R. 211, 213
Petronio, S. 177
Pettengill, S. M. 149
Pettit, G. S. 149
Philliber, S. G. 150
Phillips, K. 24, 244
Pillemer, K. 181, 189, 319, 330
Pine, C. J. 151
Pineo, P. C. 192
Piotrkowski, C. S. 241
Pirog, M. 150
Plantz, M. C. 338, 339, 340, 348, 349
Pleck, J. H. 72, 241
Plomin, R. 163

Polansky, N. A. 313, 328
Polonko, K. A. 9
Polsky, D. 202
Pomeroy, W. B. 88, 89
Ponza, M. 340
Popenoe, D. 98, 125
Powell, B. 37, 263
Presser, H. 212, 214, 215, 218
Preston, S. H. 202
Previti, D. 61, 254, 258, 259, 262
Price, S. J. 263, 266, 289, 290, 360
Prothrow-Stith, D. 329
Putnam, R. D. 65
Pyke, K. D. 112, 151
Quick, D. S. 280, 282
Quindlen, A. 145
Rabasca, L. 328
Rabin, B. E. 167
Raffaelli, M. 163, 164
Raine, L. 168
Rajagopal, D. 189, 205
Raley, K. 275
Raley, R. K. 183
Rank, M. R. 28, 112, 245, 246
Rasmussen, J. L. 155
Rasmussen, P. K. 257
Raudenbush, S. 63, 64
Raymond, M. 179
Reece, R. M. 297
Reed, J. G. 320
Regan, P. C. 78
Reimann, R. 137
Reis, H. T. 82
Reiss, I. 62
Reitz, M. 145
Reitzes, D. C. 48, 49
Rempel, J. K. 75, 76
Renzetti, C. M. 311
Repetti, R. L. 218, 219
Resch, N. 198
Revenstorf, D. 120
Rezac, S. J. 270
Rhoades, K. 152
Rice, A. M. 282
Rice, K. G. 180
Rice, R. W. 190
Richards, M. H. 142, 160, 167, 219, 220, 222
Richie, L. D. 171
Richman, J. M. 62
Richters, J. 329
Riedmann, A. 194, 282
Riley, D. 153
Riley, M. W. 38
Rindfuss, R. R. 91
Ritter, P. L. 273
Rivera, F. 279
Rivers, R. Y. 344
Roach, M. 142
Roberts, R. E. L. 190
Roberts, S. R. 322–340
Robertson, E. B. 10
Robinson, J. P. 223, 226, 229
Robison, J. 181
Rogers, R. 125, 147, 256, 257, 258
Rogers, S. J. 125, 217, 218
Rohde, C. A. 345, 346

Rohner, R. P. 149
Rohwer, G. 207
Rokeach, M. 8
Rollins, B. C. 55
Romans, S. 313
Romney, D. M. 152
Roosa, M. W. 330
Roscoe, B. 82, 163
Rose, P. 59
Rosenbaum, A. 308
Rosenbaum, E. 65
Rosenberg, L. A. 345, 346
Rosenberg, S. 150
Rosenberg, S. D. 157
Rosenthal, C. J. 188, 190
Rosner, T. T. 186, 187
Ross, C. E. 209, 261, 272, 273
Ross, E. 108
Rossman, B. B. R. 314
Rothman, E. K. 184
Rotter, J. B. 75
Rovine, M. 141
Rubin, H. J. 34
Rubin, I. S. 34
Rubin, L. B. 27, 43, 74, 85, 113, 118, 138, 234, 235, 244
Rubin, Z. 85, 112, 211
Ruggles, S. 101
Russel, C. S. 142
Russell, D. E. H. 310, 314
Rutter, V. 121

S, T, U, V

Sabatelli, R. M. 117
Salari, S. M. 305, 306, 307, 308
Salgado, V. 156
Salkever, D. S. 345, 346
Saltzman. W. 329
Sameroff, A. 342
Sampson, R. J. 28, 63, 67
Sanchez, Y. M. 152
Sandefur, G. 272
Sanders, S. 88. 100, 138, 284
Sandler, I. N. 275
Sangle, J. 186
Savin-Williams, R. C. 55
Sayer, L. 91, 92
Scanlon, W. J. 186
Scanzoni, J. 9
Schaap, C. 119
Schach, C. 103, 104, 358
Scharlach, A. E. 190, 199
Scheibe, C. L. 169
Schellenbach, C. J. 317
Scherlis, W. 168
Schiamberg, L. B. 318, 330
Schindler, L. 120
Schinke, S. P. 151
Schoen, R. 131
Schoenbach, C. 26
Schoonover, C. B. 189, 205
Schorr, L. 103, 273, 350
Schrader, L. 129
Schrader, S. S. 81
Schuldberg, D. 281
Schulenberg, J. 202, 232
Schulz, R. 192

Schwab-Stone, M. 329
Schwartz, D. 329
Schwartz, P. 31, 110–116, 121, 128, 225, 309
Schwartz, S. 195
Schwartz-Kenney, B. M. 314, 333
Schwebel, A. I. 259
Schweitzer, S. O. 115
Scott-Jones, D. 224
Seabrook, J. 21
Sebes, J. 317
Seccombe, K. 68, 199, 246, 250
Sedlak, A. 314
Seltzer, J. A. 266, 267, 268, 289
Semic, B. A. 122, 123
Serafini, L. 329
Serpe, R. T. 48
Sessa, F. M. 264, 274
Shackelford, T. K. 82, 94, 95
Shahinfar, A. 329
Shakoor, B. 329
Shanahan, J. 169
Shapiro, A. 266
Sharp, E. A. 102
Shehan, C. L. 192, 193
Shell, R. 330
Shelton, B. A. 225
Shelton, S. K. 176
Shen, Y. 222, 224, 248, 292, 294
Sherkat, D. E. 152
Sherman, D. 315
Sherman, L. 151, 327
Sherman, R. C. 82
Shew, A. 30
Shinn, M. 30
Short, J. L. 30
Shuey, K. 238
Shumow, L. 342
Siegler, I. C. 262
Signorielli, N. 169
Silverberg, S. B. 179, 180, 209
Silverman, W. 329
Silverstein, M. 181, 182, 183, 184
Simmel, G. 288
Simmons, J. L. 50
Simon, R. W. 37
Simons, R. L. 150, 152, 236
Sirignano, S. W. 134, 142
Skalar, H. 209
Skinner, M. L. 10
Sla, C. C. J. 345, 346
Slaten, E. 286
Slavens, G. 329
Sloan, E. 209
Slomczynski, K. M. 26
Small, S. 62, 63, 67
Small, S. A. 55
Smith, C. 306
Smith, D. A. 120
Smith, D. B. 238
Smith, J. P. 145, 308
Smith, K. R. 285
Smith, T. W. 88, 89
Smock, P. J. 260
Smollar, J. 160
Smyer, M. A. 165
Snowden, L. R. 344

Snyder, A. R. 175, 182, 185, 267
Sobel, E. L. 190
Soldo, B. J. 188
Sonnega, J. 200
Sorell, G. T. 78, 315
Sorensen, A. 22, 124
Sorensen, E. 268
Sorenson, P. 353
Sorenson, S. B. 311
South, S. J. 33, 256, 257, 288, 291, 292, 294
Spain, D. 131, 165
Spanier, G. B. 109, 276, 280, 284
Spencer, M. B. 64, 65
Spitze, G. 175, 185, 188
Spivak, H. 329
Spooner, T. 168, 306
Sprecher, S. 78, 79, 82, 86, 87, 88, 98, 192
Sroufe, L. A. 158
Stack, C. 155
Stacy, J. 37
Stafford, F. P. 157
Stafford, L. 122, 123
Staines, G. L. 216
Stanley, S. M. 99
Stanley-Hagan, M. M. 251, 276
Starrels, M. E. 190
Steil, J. M. 113
Steinberg, L. 160, 264, 274
Steinmetz, S. K. 315
Stemmler, M. 338
Stephens, L. S. 289
Stephens, M. A. 190, 192
Sternberg, R. J. 76, 78, 79, 96
Stets, J. E. 301, 303
Stevens, A. H. 28
Steward, S. D. 260, 267, 268
Stewart, A. 113
Stewart, S. D. 265, 269, 270
Stocker, C. M. 165
Stone, J. G. 318
Stone, L. 37
Stone, R. 186, 202
Stoneman, Z. 149, 155
Storaasli, R. D. 155
Straus, M. A. 298, 300, 301, 304, 306, 308, 314, 315, 316, 317
Stronks, K. 108, 274
Stryker, S. 48
Stuart, G. L. 303
Sugarman, D. B. 302
Suhomlinova, O. 256
Suitor, J. J. 181, 189, 226
Sullaway, M. 119, 120, 156
Sullivan, O. 225
Sullivan, R. 199
Sullivan, T. A. 207
Sullivan, W. M. 96, 293, 294
Sumida, E. 139, 140, 151
Sun, Y. 253
Supple, A. J. 62, 63, 67, 177, 180
Surra, C. A. 6
Susman, A. 159
Swanberg, J. E. 210
Swank, A. B. 152
Swann, W. B., Jr. 53

Swanson, C. 128
Sweet, J. A. 90, 91, 268, 275, 287
Swidler, A. 96
Swinford, S. P. 300, 301, 308, 314
Systra, L. 254
Szinovacz, M. E. 237, 238, 239
Tableman, B. 353
Tadlock, B. L. 29, 243
Takeuchi, D. 224
Tallman, I. 48, 49–50, 54, 105, 209, 226
Tamis-LeMonda, C. S. 150, 151
Tanner, J. L. 262, 265, 268, 282
Tarakeshwar, N. 152
Tatelbaum, R. 144
Taylor, L. 88, 100, 329
Taylor, R. 224
Taylor, R. J. 183
Teachman, J. D. 9, 129, 244, 240
Tedrow, L. M. 129
Tein, J. 275
Telles, C. A. 311
Thoennes, N. 289, 300, 301, 305, 307, 308, 314
Thoits, P. A. 50, 216
Thomas, A. M. 149, 155
Thomas, D. S. 291
Thomas, Q. S. 248
Thomas, V. G. 110, 117, 118
Thomas, W. I. 248
Thompson, A. I. 68, 328
Thompson, K. 303, 308
Thompson, M. S. 151
Thomson, E. 273, 281
Thornburg, K. R. 102, 343
Thornton, A. 255
Thornton, M. C. 185, 186
Tickamyer, A. R. 29, 243
Ting-Toomey, S. 119
Tinsley, B. J. 155
Tipton, S. M. 96, 293, 294
Tjaden, P. 300, 301, 305, 307, 308, 314
Tolnay, S. E. 102, 129
Tomb, D. 322
Tomita, S. T. 319
Trent, K. 292, 294
Tronner, M. 221
Tucker, E. J. 314, 333
Tucker, M. B. 101
Twenge, J. M. 105
Twiggs, J. 223, 224
Tyree, A. 308
Uchitelle, L. 211
Uhlenberg, P. 131, 175, 185, 196, 198, 202, 253, 256, 272
Umana-Taylor, A. J. 87
Umberson, D. 108, 198, 200, 286

V, X, Y, Z

Vaillant, C. O. 192

Vaillant, G. E. 192
Valdez, B. 30
Valentiner, D. P. 177
Van De Mheen, H. 108, 274
van Der Meer, J. B. W. 108, 274
Van Lear, C. A. 122
Van Poppel, F. W. A. 108, 274
Van Wyk, J. 304
VanLaningham, J. 192
Vandell, D. L. 212
VandenHeuvel, A. 91
Varga, P. 150
Vaughan, S. 122, 255
Veroff, J. 107, 110
Vinick, B. H. 237
Vogel, E. F. 12
von Salisch, M. 164
Voydanoff, P. 226, 234
Vuchinich, S. 36
Waite, L. J. 108, 231, 274
Waldfogel, J. 350, 351, 352, 353
Waldron, M. 289
Walker, J. P. 205, 262, 291, 321
Waller, W. 85
Wallerstein, J. S. 59, 286, 291
Walster, G. W. 77–78
Ward, H. 141
Ward, R. A. 239
Waring, E. M. 75
Warner, W. L. 26
Warshak, R. A. 291
Waterman, C. K. 311
Watkins, S. C. 181, 255
Watson, K. W. 145, 299, 321
Watt, T. T. 299, 321
Wattenberg, B. J. 271
Way, W. L. 169
Webster, P. S. 28, 184, 192, 200
Weigel, D. J. 123
Weinberg, M. S. 89
Weine, S. 329
Weinstein, K. K. 196
Weiss, H. 131, 133
Weissberg, R. 329
Weitzman, B. C. 30
Weitzman, M. 220
Wellman, B. 168
Wells, B. 224
Weltman, K. 113
West, C. 305
Wewers, S. 329
Wheaton, B. 180
Whitbeck, L. B. 150, 184, 322, 324, 325, 328
White, J. A. 29, 343
White, L. K. 139, 175, 180, 192, 194, 195, 214, 218, 252, 257, 280
White-Means, S. I. 185, 186
Whitehead, B. D. 98, 348
Whitfield, C. L. 281, 293
Whitley, M. 254

Whitt, H. 83
Wickrama, K. A. S. 218
Widom, C. S. 313, 314
Wierson, M. 155
Wilber, K. H. 318, 330
Wilcox, B. L. 203
Wilcox, W. B. 294
Wiles, C. P. 323, 324
Willetts, M. C. 199
William, J., Jr. 83
Williams, C. W. 132, 133
Williams, D. 28
Williams, D. P. 313, 328
Williams, D. R. 83
Williams, I. C. 191
Williams, J. 308
Williams, L. M. 315, 333
Williams, O. J. 309, 310, 320
Williams, S. W. 186
Williamson, D. F. 281, 293
Williamson, G. M. 182
Wilson, B. F. 275
Wilson, K. J. 300, 305, 320, 321, 333
Wilson, L. 224
Wilson, M. N. 151
Wilson, T. 156
Wilson, W. J. 65, 233, 236, 245, 248
Windham, A. M. 345, 346
Wineberg, H. 254
Winsborough, H. H. 175, 198
Wisensale, S. K. 350
Witte, J. 168
Wolchik, S. A. 275
Wolf, D. A. 203, 242
Wolf, R. S. 318, 319, 330
Wolfe, D. M. 111
Wood, D. 30
Wortman, C. B. 200
Wright, J. W. 1, 16, 21, 29, 30, 38, 208, 252
Wright, L. K. 192
Wu, J. 257
Wyk, J. V. 304
Yardley, J. K. 217
Yeung, W. J. 202
Yllo, K. 303, 310
Young, J. K. 103, 273
Youngblade, L. 165
Youniss, J. 160
Zanna, M. P. 75
Zaslow, M. J. 355
Zedeck, S. 221
Zedlewski, S. R. 335
Zick, C. D. 285
Zillmann, D. 17
Zimmerman, S. L. 347, 348, 349
Zollinger, L. 139, 140, 151
Zuckerman, B. 329
Zurcher, C. A. 146
Zusman, M. E. 73 ✦

Subject Index

A, B, C

Adaptability, 12, 39, 40
Adolescent/adolescence, 50, 54–55, 212, 265, 267, 279–282, 313–314, 317, 323–325, 335, 342, 354–355
  employment, 232–233, 235–236, 247
  individuation, 58, 176, 180, 205, 231, 264, 269–270, 272–274
  parents, 139, 150–151
  sex and dating, 84, 97, 269
Adoption, 131, 145–146
  children's adjustment to, 146
  parenting issues, 145
  types of, 146
AFDC (Aid to Families with Dependent Children), 29–30, 353
Alcoholism/addictions, 29, 37, 232, 236, 245–246, 256, 261, 269, 272, 274, 282, 298–300, 310–311, 314–316, 319–320, 322, 324, 326, 328, 330
  effects on children, 69, 197–198, 321, 330–331
Anticipatory socialization, 147, 171
Asian Americans, 21, 149, 151, 245–246, 271, 274, 305, 314, 320, 341, 349
Attraction
  commitment, 61, 69
  filter, 81–82
Authoritative parenting, 148–152, 169–171, 180, 269, 274
Authoritarian parenting, 148–149, 169–171, 273–274
Autonomy, 112, 262
  adolescent, 58, 177–178, 233, 355
  couples and, 6, 31, 104–106, 122, 194, 293, 307
  parents' valuing of, 26, 166–167
Blacks, 21, 23, 29, 31, 64, 89, 93, 149, 208, 232, 245, 260, 271, 285, 306
  childbearing, 131
  cohabitation/marriage/divorce, 90, 101–103, 254–256, 259, 275, 279, 281, 285
  employment issues, 101–102

family relationships, 110, 121, 150–151, 155, 159, 183, 185, 187, 191, 195–196, 218, 224, 274, 305, 314, 317, 319–320, 324, 342
nonmarital childbearing, 101–102, 132, 138–140, 267
Boundaries, 9, 10, 12–13, 27, 31, 39, 40, 43, 57–59, 62–64, 104, 148, 159, 178–179, 204–205, 247, 277, 282, 292, 322–333
Boundary
  recognition, 179, 204
  task, 223, 248
Break-ups (ending relationships), 85, 112, 141, 202, 252, 254, 260, 271, 337
Businesses
  effects on families/communities, 15, 26, 70, 100, 210, 240–243, 245, 248, 335, 337–340, 347, 351
Caregiving, 204
  employment and, 188–190
  formal services for the elderly, 203, 320, 347, 349
  for aged parents, 186, 199, 202, 318–320
  for infants, 156, 172
  grandparents, 197
  marriage and, 188–189, 192
  types of shared caregiving, 186–188
  uplifts of, 190–191
Child abuse and neglect, 69, 148–149, 170, 172, 197, 297, 299–300, 312–313, 316–318, 323–324, 328, 331,
  causes, 316, 326–328
  physical abuse, 61, 313–314
  sexual abuse, 61, 282, 297–300, 304, 310, 314–317, 322, 330–332
  siblings, 163, 316–317
  social impoverishment theory, 315, 332
Child support, 138, 260, 266, 268–269, 277, 289–290, 294, 345, 353
Childbearing
  likelihood, 131

motivations for, 132–133
nonmarital, 129
Childcare, 17–19, 29, 41, 56, 58, 62–63, 65, 69, 137–138, 141, 143, 156, 170, 175, 181, 211–213, 215, 220–225, 231, 235, 247, 267, 281, 315, 338, 353–356, 358
  community effects on, 240–242, 337–340, 343
  consequences for children, 211–214
  quality, 29, 212–213, 240, 339, 350, 354
Childlessness, 131, 292
Childrearing, 151, 259, 289,
  cost, 129
Children's Health Insurance Program (CHIP), 29
Chronosystem, 18, 20, 32, 39–40, 97, 126, 201, 287
Civil rights movement, 74, 92–94, 124
Cohabitation, 33, 40, 83, 90. 92, 97, 268, 292, 293, 309
  characteristics associated with, 90
  children in household, 90–91
  comparisons of cohabiting and married couples, 91, 107
  comparisons with single non-cohabiting persons, 91
  gender roles, 225
  step in the marriage process, 83
Cohesion, 11, 14, 40, 66–68, 109, 236, 277, 295
Collective efficacy, 66–67, 69
Collective socialization, 340, 358
Commitment, 14, 39, 40, 42, 45–47, 69
  attraction commitment, 61, 69
  constraint commitment, 61, 69
  moral commitment, 61, 69
  to children, 58, 268, 292
  to community, 62–68
  to family, 57, 59
  to marriage/intimate relationships, 6, 24, 31, 40, 46, 60, 62, 77–80, 86–87, 92, 97, 103–104, 108, 125, 258–259, 277, 292–293
  to self, 47–49

Communication, 117–118
    agency and, 118
    code abbreviation, 117
    code substitution, 117
    communion and, 118
    gender differences, 118
    marital distress, 120–121
Community, 62–68, 335, 337–346
    geographic, 62
    services, 3, 320, 343–346
Commuter marriages, 216
Compadrazgo, 154, 171
Compatibility filter, 81, 83
Concepts, 3–5, 18
Conflict
    avoidance of, 119–120, 321
    gender differences in approach to
        resolution, 118–121
Conjugal unit, 25, 40
Connection vs. autonomy in relation-
        ships, 6, 26, 31, 58, 104–106,
        118, 122, 307
Consensus, 63, 69, 109, 204
Constructive/functional conflict reso-
        lution strategies, 119
Cottage industry, 210, 248
Couple-to-state commitment, 104
Covenant Marriage, 45, 61
Coverture, 106, 127
Cross-sectional data/research, 38–39,
        40
Custodial
    fathers, 251, 265–267
    mothers, 251, 260, 263–265
Custody
    income differences for parents,
        260, 267
    visitation by the non-resident par-
        ent, 268–270
    types of, 263

D, E, F

Daily hassles of parenting, 154, 157,
        171
Dating, 47, 73, 82, 84, 86, 88, 92,
        113, 123, 192
    breaking-up, 85
    historical changes in, 84
    network influences on, 85–87
    violence and, 300–303, 308
Death
    adult child, 200–201
    parental, 175, 198–199
    sibling, 201
    spousal (*see* Widowhood)
Defense of Marriage Act, 349, 350,
        357–358
Demand-withdraw behavior, 119,
        121, 127
Demilitarized zones, 179, 204
Descriptive studies/research, 33
Destructive conflict strategies, 119
Developmental schisms, 177, 184,
        204
Developmental stages, 54, 69
Direct power tactics, 113, 127

Division of labor , 4, 9, 137, 139,
        222–223, 303
    for cohabitors, 225
    fairness of, 226
    in late life, 193
    in Latino families, 224
    in remarried couples, 225
    in same-sex couples, 137, 225
    parenting and, 136–137
    race differences, 224
Divorce, 27, 90, 92, 210, 252–253,
        331
    attributions of fault, 254, 258
    child outcomes, 92, 179, 281–284,
        324
    child support, 290
    custody (*see* Custody)
    economic adjustment, 28, 260, 285
    effects of the economy, 287, 291
    family support and, 202, 204
    feelings leading up to, 109
    health outcomes, 108, 261
    historical changes, 125–126
    individualism and, 125–126
    late-life, 184
    legal system, 106, 287–289, 348
    mediation, 289–290, 294–295
    neighborhood effects on, 288
    no-fault divorce, 61, 289, 348
    parenting and, 262–273
    post-divorce attachment, 261–262
    predictors of, 33, 120, 122, 124,
        141, 214–216, 255–256
    psychological adjustment, 261–262
    rates, 251, 276, 287, 291
    reasons for, 79, 116–117, 157–159,
    reconciliation, 254–255
    remarriage and divorce, 252, 257,
        275–279
    same-sex couples and break-ups,
        259–260
    services, 346
    sex ratios and, 292
    siblings, 165
    stereotypes, 293
    stress, 274
    visitation, 268–271
    who initiates, 253–254
Domestic partnership laws, 358
Dyadic
    adjustment, 109
    cohesion, 109
    consensus, 109
    satisfaction, 109
Ecological systems, 20, 39, 62, 142,
        237, 259, 327, 330, 337
    theory, 17–19
Economy, 201–202, 208, 210, 241–
        243, 245, 247, 287, 291, 294,
        327, 338
Education Amendments Act Title IX,
        57
Efficacy, 66–67, 69, 180, 232
Elder
    abuse, 308, 317–320, 330
    care, 186, 199, 202, 318–320
Empathy, 74, 76, 96–97

Employment
    adolescent, 232–233, 247, 355
    child care arrangements and (*see*
        Child care)
    dual-earner couples, 36, 110, 215,
        217, 224, 260
    hours worked, 25, 91, 124, 137,
        209, 211, 214, 218, 220–222,
        225–226, 232–233, 235, 237,
        243, 351, 355
    part-time, 29, 58, 208, 211–212
    retirement, 193–194, 204, 237–240,
        242, 247–249
    shift work and split-shifts, 214–
        216, 240, 339
    unemployment, 5, 26, 65, 102, 138,
        202, 208, 233–237, 241–242,
        244, 256, 304–305, 315–316,
        323, 327–328, 343
    (*see also* Women's labor force
        participation)
Empty nest stage, 179–180, 192, 204
Endogamy (endogamous), 25, 40
Equilibrium, 39, 41, 69, 280
Ethnicity, 8, 20–21, 83, 86, 102, 146,
        183, 185, 248, 271, 274, 305–
        306, 321
Exchange of help/support in families,
        154, 172, 175, 181, 194–195,
        205, 272,
Exosystem, 18–20, 28–30, 41, 47, 62,
        81, 89, 100, 143–144, 154, 190,
        201, 203, 213, 237, 241–242,
        248, 263, 286, 288–289, 290,
        294, 315–316, 319, 328, 330,
        345–347
Explanatory studies/research, 33
Extended family, 4, 11, 24, 41, 105,
        121, 131, 144, 283–284, 305, 320
Family
    as a small group, 2–3,
    as a social institution, 3–4, 15–17
    extended, 4, 11, 24, 41, 121, 131,
        144, 283, 305, 320
    identity, 6, 9, 59–60, 69
    income, 1, 22–30, 42, 63, 91, 103,
        107, 110, 112, 124, 213, 217,
        224, 230, 233–234, 238, 244,
        255–256, 259–260, 267–269, 272,
        274, 285, 304–305, 307, 327,
        344, 353, 355
    macro perspective, 3, 5, 7, 18–20,
        41, 81, 87, 89, 92–96, 124–126,
        144–145, 165–170, 201–203, 237,
        240–243, 245–246, 259–260,
        286–287, 292–293, 303–304, 311,
        316, 327–328, 330, 346–349
    myths, 59, 70
    nuclear, 5, 10, 37, 41, 198, 264,
        283
    of orientation, 5, 41, 58, 246, 328
    of procreation, 5, 41
    rituals, 11, 59–60, 69, 104, 155
    rules, 10, 12, 159
    scripts, 60, 70
    size, 1, 4, 166, 202
    solidarity, 181, 204–205

structure, 195–196, 197, 225, 274–281, 283, 317, 327
Family and Medical Leave Act, 203, 240, 247, 337
experience of leave takers, 352–353
firm size minimums, 351
history of legislation, 351
outcomes of, 351–352
policies in other countries, 352
requirements, 241, 350–351
Family policy, 38, 68, 81, 89, 130, 143–144, 170, 180, 203, 240, 252, 287–288, 296, 335, 337, 343, 347, 350–358
agenda setting, 347–348
explicit, 347
focus of, 349–350
implicit, 348
role of values in, 348–349
Family systems, 4–5, 13–14, 17, 20, 39, 59, 161, 176, 343
theory, xv, 4, 189
Family violence
age of couples, 307–308
alcohol and, 320–322
child abuse/neglect, 300, 312–316
couple status incongruence and, 307
ecological influences on, 64–65
explanations for, 302–304, 315–316, 325
marital rape, 301, 309–310
marital status, 308
neighborhood influences on, 327–330
partner violence, 113, 127, 298, 300–302
prevention programs, 328–330
psychiatric approach to, 312, 325
race and ethnic variations, 305–307
same-sex couples, 310–311
sex of perpetrator, 301–302, 308–309
shelters, 29
siblings, 316–317
social class and, 304, 306
social-psychological approach to, 325–327
sociocultural approach to, 304–305, 311–312, 327–330
transmission of, 297
types of, 300, 302
Feedback, 13, 17, 20, 39, 41, 259
Fertility levels, 16, 131, 165–167, 202–203
Filter theory of mate selection, 81–85
Food pantry use, 335
Formal institutions, 337, 359
Fundamentalist religious beliefs, 16, 152

G, H, I

Game stage, 52, 70
Gay men, 5, 8–9, 31, 86, 88–90, 100, 103, 111–116, 120–121, 123, 225, 269–260, 288–289, 311, 312
as parents, 31, 132–133, 137, 152

Gay rights movement, 92
Gender roles, 16, 56, 91, 94–96, 118, 137, 187, 226, 235–236, 257, 285
socialization for, 55–57, 303
Generalized other, 52, 70
Geographic community, 62–63, 70
Good provider role, 107, 137
Grandparents, 212
surrogate parents,197
styles of grandparenting, 196–197
High-risk
environments/neighborhoods, 63, 68, 236, 274
His and her marriage, 106–107
HIV/Aids, 92–93, 95, 324
Homeless, 21, 23, 27, 29–30, 63, 269, 324, 345
Homeostasis, 11, 39, 41, 58, 277, 280
Homogamy, 81–83, 85, 97
Homosexuality (*see also* same-sex relationships, gay men, lesbians)
Kinsey's studies of, 88–89
legal issues, 89, 93, 103, 288–289, 357–358
parenting and, 31, 90, 132, 135–137, 140
relationship dynamics, 100, 110–115, 117, 120–121, 123, 225, 259–260, 310–312, 325,
racial differences in, 89
Housework (*see also* Division of labor), 16, 119, 124, 137, 142, 186, 207, 218, 222, 230
children's contributions, 230–232
Human capital, 246, 249
Human/personal social services, 13, 15, 17, 32, 38, 63, 66, 203, 313, 319–320, 324, 329–330, 336, 339–340, 343–346, 350
faithbased, 63, 345, 359
prevention services, 346–347, 359
remediation/intervention services, 346–347, 359
scope of, 345–346, 359
Hypotheses, 4
Identity(ies), 48–50, 55, 58, 67, 133, 146, 176–177, 235, 239, 262, 283, 309
changes with parenthood, 134–135, 140, 147, 201
couple, 86, 105, 123
family, 6, 9, 59–60, 69
salience, 50, 70
Income disparity, 244
Indirect power tactics113, 127
Individualism, 25–26, 96–97, 124–126, 293, 349
Individuation, 161, 176, 205
Indulgent-permissive parenting, 148–149, 172, 269
Interdependence, 5–6, 20, 31, 39, 41, 51, 58–59, 78, 117, 130, 136, 151, 156, 164, 170–171, 176, 199
Internet, 35, 62, 73, 82, 165, 167–168, 209
contact with family and, 168
dating, 73, 82

Interrelatedness, 5, 6, 17, 20, 39, 41, 59, 176, 259, 265,
Internalization, 69
Interpersonal communication, 51, 273
Inter-racial relationships, 73, 92–93
Interview methods, 34–35, 37, 216, 239, 350

J, K, L

Kinkeeping (kinkeepers), 113, 184, 199–200, 205
Latinos, 21, 31, 249, 320, 324
childbearing, 133
family relationships, 183, 185–186, 271, 282, 304–306, 311, 314
homeless, 29
labor force issues, 208, 232
marriage, 87, 101–102, 275
nonmarital childbearing, 129
poverty, 245–246
roles, 218, 224
Lesbians, 5, 9, 86, 88–90, 100, 103, 111–114, 121, 123, 225, 259–260, 288–289, 311–312, 328
parents, 31, 135–136, 140
Longitudinal data/research, 38–39, 41
Looking glass self, 51, 71
Love, 76–80
companionate, 78–79, 97
consummate, 79
empty, 78
infatuated, 78
passionate, 78
styles of, 77

M, N, O

Macrosystem, 18–20, 41, 81, 89, 100, 125–126, 144, 165–170, 233, 237, 240, 245, 259–260, 288–293, 316, 327–330, 346–349
Maintenance behaviors, 122–123, 127
as predictors of relationship outcomes, 123–124
gender differences, 123
in same-sex relationships, 123
Marital
commitments, 61, 103–104, 125
happiness/experiences over recent decades, 125–126
rape, 309–310
roles, 107, 145, 188–189, 193, 224–229
satisfaction/dissatisfaction, 10, 64, 78–80, 101, 108–111, 113–114, 117–118, 121–125, 127, 135, 139–141, 155–156, 180, 189, 192–193, 214–217, 237–239, 247
separation/disruption, 13, 33, 37, 76, 251–260
stability, 101, 109–111, 114, 127
subsystem, 9, 136, 142, 150, 155–156, 164–165, 171, 200, 204
Marriage
age at (marital timing), 16–17, 25–26, 33, 101, 103, 201, 251, 257, 292

community involvement and, 107
economic achievement and, 107–108
economy and, 201–202, 242
endogamous, 24, 40
expectations for, 73, 101
health status and, 99, 108
historical changes in age at marriage, 101
historical changes in meaning of marriage, 125–126
historical changes in preferred characteristics for a mate, 93–94
late life/long-term, 78, 115–116, 191–194
legislation, 45, 61, 89, 349, 350, 357–358
likelihood, 99
market, 102
mortality rates and, 99
preferences for, 101, 202
role of economic security in marriage decisions, 101–102
social class, 103
Media influences on family life, 21, 79, 100, 160, 163, 166–170, 304, 316, 327–328
Mental images, 51
Mesosystem, 18–19, 41, 62, 143–144, 170, 216, 218, 237, 259, 290, 322, 330, 340–341, 342, 345–346, 349–350
Meta-analysis, 269, 295
Microsystem, 18–20, 41, 294, 349
Middle class/white collar, 23, 25–26, 131, 157, 209, 222, 224, 246, 274
National Survey of Families and Households (NSFH), 38–39
Neighborhood
    high-risk, 63, 68, 236, 274
    infrastructure, 64, 70
Network influences
    on parenting, 150, 153–155, 170–171
    on relationship formation/dating, 6, 85
    on relationship stability, 123
Nomos-building, 60, 70
Non-marital cohabitation (see Cohabitation)
Norms, 8, 15–17, 19, 52, 54, 63, 67, 81, 258, 260, 281, 288, 292–293, 327, 337, 346
Novelty vs. predictability in relationships, 122, 192
Nuclear family, 4–5, 10, 37, 41, 198, 264, 283
Objectivity, 34, 41
Observation, 35–36
    laboratory, 36
    naturalistic, 36–37, 41
    participant, 37
    unobtrusive, 35, 42

P, Q, R

Parental control, 149
    of offspring's dating and marital behavior, 24–25, 84, 87
Parental maturity, 180, 205
Parenthood
    changes in self, 134–136
    couple/marriage relations and, 139–141, 155
    decision-making about, 131–134
    effects on division of labor, 136–138
    expectations for, 141
    gay men and, 132–133
    lesbians and, 135–136
    planning for, 133–134, 140, 141
    teenage, 150–151
    transition to, 59, 121, 130, 142–145
    visiting nurse programs and, 144
Parenting
    adolescents, 147–148, 160–161
    child characteristics and, 142, 152
    co-parenting, 155, 171
    determinants of, 149
    educational attainment and, 150
    facilitation, 155
    functions, 148
    infants/toddlers, 147, 156–157
    parental differential treatment, 163, 172
    postdivorce 260–261
    social class variations in values, 26–27
    stages, 147
    styles, 148–149
    time spent with children, 129, 168
    values and historical change, 166–167
    young adults, 176–180, 201–202
    young children, 147, 157–160
Parents and adult offspring, 184–185, 198–199, 200–201
    caregiving for parents, 186–191, 202–203
    contact, 181
    exchange of support, 181–182, 185
    gender differences in relationships, 183
    living together, 189, 202
    racial differences, 183, 185–186
    types of relationships, 181–182
Passion, 76–80. 97
Permissive, 148–149, 169–170, 172, 269, 273–274, 279
Play stage, 52, 70
Poor, 21, 23, 26–30, 178, 243–246, 264, 267, 269, 288, 306, 353–357
Positions, 3, 7, 9, 15, 17, 20
Positivism, 34–35, 37, 42
Post-positivism, 34–35, 37, 42
Poverty, 1, 27–30, 42, 65, 68, 245–246, 248, 264, 285, 294, 304–306, 316, 327–328, 348, 355
    food pantry use, 335
    line, 27–28, 42
    rates, 1, 245–246
    spell, 28, 42, 246

Power, 22, 111–113, 118, 127, 147, 162, 172, 218, 303, 306, 327, 332
    couple conflict over, 113, 127
    family, 14–15, 112–113, 293, 304
    hierarchy, 8–9
    interpersonal power theory, 302, 326–327, 332
    marital, 2–3, 111–112, 124, 224, 230, 256, 310, 313–314
    sex and, 116–117
Prediction, 4, 33, 49
Primary data, 34–35, 37, 42
Primary groups, 46, 68–69
Principle of least interest, 85, 98
Propinquity, 24, 42
    filter, 81
Propositions, 4
Race, 21
    racism, 246
Rejecting-neglectful parenting, 148–149, 172
Relationship centeredness, 111
Remarriage, 59, 225
    after widowhood, 285
    children's outcomes, 272–273, 281–283
    economic adjustment in, 28, 260
    extended families and, 283–284
    prevalence, 31, 251, 275
    sex differences in likelihood of, 275
    sibling relationships and, 282–283
    stereotypes, 293
    subsequent divorce, 252, 276
    timing, 275
    types of, 277–281
Resiliency, 65, 68, 262, 280, 283, 326–327
Resource theory of power, 111–112, 127
Respect, 74, 76, 98
Retirement, 242
    labor force involvement, 239–240
    patterns for spouses, 237–238
    quality of marriage, 237–239
    reasons for, 238
    roles, 193–194
    satisfaction with, 238
Roles, 7, 15, 17, 42, 50–54
    overload, 215, 249
Romantic beliefs/ideal
Runaways, 322–325
    family problems, 322–323
    risks on the street, 324–325

S, T, U, V

Same-sex partners (*see also* Gay men; Lesbians), 31, 88–90, 93, 110–111, 120, 123, 137, 225, 259–260, 310–311, 357–358
    likelihood of marriage-like relationships, 110
Sampling methods, 35
Schools, 20, 64, 147, 149–150, 242, 246, 335, 340
    barriers to parent involvement, 342–343

community effects on, 338, 340
parents' involvement in, 340–342
Scientific method, 34
Secondary data/analysis, 34, 37–38, 42
Self
changes with parenthood, 134–135
concept, 51, 53, 70
disclosure, 74–75, 98, 118
esteem, 49, 53, 70, 134–135, 138, 146, 232–234, 345
meanings, 48, 50–51
reports, 34
verification theory, 53
Serial monogamy, 276, 295
Sex
frequency in relationships, 115–116
health and, 116
initiation point in relationship, 114
monogamy, 116, 276, 295
ratios and divorce, 292
ratios and marriage, 82, 102
which partner initiates, 116–117
Sexual
abuse (*see* Abuse)
experimentation, 90
revolution, 74, 92–94
scripts, 117
Shared experiences, 59, 74, 75, 96
Siblings, 9, 56, 74, 96, 212, 230–231, 322, 355
adult, 175, 186–188, 194–196, 199, 201
birth of, 161
conflict, 162–164,
effects on parents' marriage, 164–165
family structure differences in relationships, 195–196
influences on development, 162
prevalence, 129
race differences in adult relationships, 195
remarried families, 278, 280
step-siblings, 10, 278, 282–283
violence, 303, 314, 31–317
Sibling subsystem, 9, 42, 130, 161, 164–165, 236–237
Single-parent households, 167, 245
characteristics, 264
child outcomes, 272–273, 275, 281, 286–287
parenting in, 251, 273–273
prevalence, 29–30, 271
racial comparisons, 271, 279
Social capital, 67, 71, 340–341, 359
Social class, 8, 21–30, 42, 83
marriage patterns, 103

parenting, 151–152,
school involvement, 342–343
work-family connections, 243–245
Social institution, 3, 5, 15, 19, 42, 62
Social network, 71
engagement, 123
personal, 153–155, 172
Social placement, 49
Social system, 5–7, 42, 153
Socialization 53–57, 71, 90, 148, 166–170, 273–274, 281, 328
agents, 54, 71
anticipatory, 147, 171
collective, 340–341, 358
gender, 55–57, 65, 107, 303, 312
Socioeconomic status (*see* Social class)
Skipped-generation household, 31, 197, 205
Status hierarchies, 7, 15
Stepfamilies, 9, 598, 276–278, 293
stepchildren, 231?, 281–283
stepparents, 273, 279–281
Stimulus input exchange, 12–13, 42
Stimulus output exchange, 12–13, 42
Structure
family, 7, 9, 13, 24, 30, 39, 42, 195–197, 225, 274–275, 277–279, 281, 283, 317
Subsystems, 9, 17, 42
Support
informal, 64–65, 87, 113–114, 150–151, 153–155, 159–160, 175, 181–186, 194–195, 202, 219, 264, 267, 283, 286, 305, 315, 320–321, 326, 332, 343–344
formal, 66, 170, 202–203, 241, 287, 316, 319, 328, 337–339, 343–344, 346
Survey research, 35, 42
Systems
closed, 12, 41
open, 12, 41
semi-open, 12
TANF (Temporary Assistance to Needy Families), 29–30, 353
Taking the role of the other, 51, 71
Teenagers (*see* Adolescent)
Telecommuting, 210, 219–220
Tender years doctrine, 296
Theory, 4
Triangular theory of love, 78
Trust, 9, 61, 63, 66–70, 74–76, 80, 96, 98, 258, 261, 273, 309, 322, 324, 331
Unemployment, 6, 26, 138, 202, 210, 241–242, 244, 248, 305,327
behavioral reactions, 102, 235–237, 256, 304, 315–316, 323, 328
during The Great Depression, 236

inner city, 65, 236
personal meaning of, 233–235
Upper class/elite/wealthy, 21, 23–25, 244, 246
Validation, 53, 119–120
Variables, 4
Volunteer work, 25, 45, 58, 65, 292, 337, 341, 343

W, X, Y, Z

Wedding ceremonies, 60, 103–104
Wedding costs, 100
Welfare reform (*see also* TANF), 353–357
childcare consequences, 353–354
economic self-sufficiency, 355–357
features of the law, 353
impact on adolescents, 354–355
impact on pre-school age children, 353–354
reactions of participants, 357
We-ness, 60
Wheel theory of love, 80
White-collar (*see* Middle-class)
Wholeness, 6, 39, 43
Widowhood, 199–200, 239, 266–267, 276, 285
kin support, 184, 184, 286
labor force participation, 285–286
remarriage, 275, 285, 294
Women's economic dependence on men, 110, 125
Women's labor force participation, 3, 19
Women's name choices in marriage, 105
appeal for women, 219, 221–222
effects on home, 6, 210, 218, 222–225
effects on marriage, 110, 124
rates, 208–209, 247
"second shift," 193, 222, 249
telecommuting, 210, 219–220
Work-family
spillover, 216–218
stress, 218–219
Workplace policies, 17, 190, 203, 240–243, 247, 337–338
retirement, 242
Working class/blue collar/lower class, 23, 25–27, 84, 110, 138, 178, 197, 209, 215, 242–244, 248, 274, 342
Young adults
college adjustment, 177, 202, 297
parents and, 176–180, 201–202
poor families, 178
work and, 178, 201–202 ✦